BARRON'S

HOW TO PREPARE FOR THE

CPA

CERTIFIED PUBLIC ACCOUNTANT EXAMINATION

6TH EDITION

Nick Dauber, MS, CPA
Person/Wolinsky CPA Review Courses®

BARRON'S

The authors are indebted to the American Institute of Certified Public Accountants, Inc., for permission to use the following copyright © materials:

1. *Information for CPA Candidates,* Thirteenth Edition, 1996. An abridged version of the Content Specification Outline, copyright © 1996 by the American Institute of Certified Public Accountants, Inc., is reprinted with permission.

2. *Uniform CPA Examinations*
   a. For the November 1995 Examination, questions from the Uniform CPA Examination, copyright © 1995 by the American Institute of Certified Public Accountants, Inc., are reprinted with permission.
   b. For the May 1995 CPA Examination, questions from the Uniform CPA Examination, copyright © 1995 by the American Institute of Certified Public Accountants, Inc., are reprinted with permission.
   c. For the preliminary readiness tests, selected past four-option multiple-choice questions were used.

All inquiries should be addressed to:
Barron's Educational Series, Inc.
250 Wireless Boulevard
Hauppauge, New York 11788
http://www.barronseduc.com

Library of Congress Catalog Card No. 97-44962
International Standard Book No. 0-7641-0185-4

Library of Congress Cataloging in Publication Data

Dauber, Nick.
    How to prepare for the CPA certified public accountant examination
/ by Person/Wolinsky CPA Review Courses, Nicky Dauber.—6th ed.
        p.   cm.
    Rev. ed. of: How to prepare for the CPA certified public
accountant examination / by Person/Wolinsky CPA Review Courses,
Samuel Person, Andrew N. Gusman.
    Includes bibliographical references.
    ISBN 0-7641-0185-4
    1. Accounting—Examinations, questions, etc.   I. Dauber, Nick A.
II. Person, Samuel.   How to prepare for the CPA certified public-
accountant examination.   III. Person/Wolinsky CPA Review Courses
(Firm)   IV. Title.
HF5661.P48 1998
657'.076—dc21   97-44962
                                                 CIP

PRINTED IN THE UNITED STATES OF AMERICA

98765

Contents

Abbreviations

Term	Meaning
Aa	Designation used by *Moody's* and *Standard & Poor's* to indicate bond quality. "Aa" is considered high quality, having very strong capacity to pay interest and repay principal.
ACRS	Accelerated Cost Recovery System
AICPA	American Institute of Certified Public Accountants
APB	Accounting Principles Board
CPI	Consumer Price Index
CS	Consulting Services
DSE	Development-Stage Enterprise
EDP	Electronic Data Processing
EOQ	Economic Order Quantity
EPS	Earnings Per Share
EU	Equivalent Units (of production)
FAC	Financial Accounting Concept
FAS	Financial Accounting Standard
FASB	Financial Accounting Standards Board
FIFO	First-In, First-Out (inventory method)
FOB	Free On Board
GAAP	Generally Accepted Accounting Principle
GAAS	Generally Accepted Auditing Standard
GASB	Governmental Accounting Standards Board
LIFO	Last-In, First-Out (inventory method)
NASBA	National Association of State Boards of Accountancy
R & D	Research and Development
SAS	Statement on Auditing Standards
SEC	Securities and Exchange Commission
SSAE	Statement on Standards for Attestation Engagements
SSARS	Statement on Standards for Accounting and Review Services
SYD	Sum-of-the-Years' Digits (inventory method)
UCC	Uniform Commercial Code

Preface

Objectives of This Book

This book has three goals:

1. To provide CPA candidates with an overall study plan, time-saving techniques, and skills necessary for success on the CPA exam.
2. To acquaint future CPA candidates with the form and content of the CPA examination.
3. To provide CPA candidates with the information they need in order to make an informed choice about review program alternatives.

This book is not intended as a comprehensive review of subject matter tested on the CPA exam; rather, it is a guide to the preparation process that must precede the examination. That process is one that extends over a period of months, and that requires of the candidate a level of insight and discipline experienced in few other situations in life. How a candidate goes about preparing for the exam is the primary determinant of his or her success on it. This book provides the candidate with the basis for feeling confident about passing the CPA exam. It contains information about the form and content of the exam, a detailed discussion of how to prepare for the exam, and two CPA exams with answers fully explained.

In instances where the pronouns *he* and *him* appear, they have been used to conform with standard business prose. It should be understood that, in every case except where specifically stated, these references apply to both men and women.

About Person/Wolinsky

PERSON/WOLINSKY CPA Review Courses® has been preparing candidates for the CPA exam since 1967. Over the years it has grown to be one of the largest review courses in the country with over 200,000 alumni and many locations nationwide.

The firm's founders, Sam Person and Dan Wolinsky, are both CPAs with many years of experience in business, academic, and professional circles. Mr. Person is a former Professor of Accounting (now Professor Emeritus), School of Professional Accountancy, C.W. Post Campus, Long Island University. He has been a member of the AICPA Council, the Board of Directors of the New York State Society for CPAs, and a trustee of the Society's Foundation for Accounting Education. Mr. Wolinsky is a charter holder of the CMA, awarded by the Institute of Management Accountants. He is also Professor Emeritus, School of Professional Accountancy, C.W. Post Campus, Long Island University.

The firm's president, Nick Dauber, is a CPA with over 20 years experience in public accounting. He is the firm's lead instructor in auditing and taxation. Mr. Dauber received his MS in taxation degree from the School of Professional Accountancy, C.W. Post Campus, Long Island University. He lectured for the Foundation for Accounting Education of the New York State Society of CPAs. Teaching awards were bestowed upon Mr. Dauber by both the Foundation for Accounting Education and the AICPA. Mr. Dauber is also a lecturer in auditing at Queens College of the City University of New York, where he was the 1992 recipient of the Golden Apple Award for being the professor of the year. He is coauthor of four books and many professional journal articles.

The Person/Wolinsky course is presented in a variety of formats in an effort to meet the differing needs of individual candidates. Options include classroom courses, self-study courses, and in-house training courses for CPA firms. Computer software is also available. The ideas presented in this book reflect the wisdom achieved during Person/Wolinsky's many years of training CPA candidates.

The author would like to thank Joan Fitzgerald for her singular efforts in the coordination of this publication. Her dedication, attention to detail, and high sense of order are deeply appreciated.

How to Use This Guide

This book contains three types of informational material. The background chapters (Chapters 1, 2, 10) describe the form and content of the CPA examination. The test-efficiency technique chapters (Chapters 3 through 6) develop an overall study plan and provide test strategies for the various question types. The practice examination chapters (Chapters 7 through 9) include two examinations with explained answers and readiness tests.

Success on the CPA examination depends, in part, on familiarity with past test questions and, in part, on test-taking efficiency (since all questions must be answered in order to do well). This book will help you gain familiarity and efficiency on the exam. The overall study plan will help you determine your weaknesses and decide on the best course of action. The test tactics will help you make the best use of your allotted time. The test questions included will provide you with an opportunity to become familiar with actual CPA examination questions. Nothing should faze you when you get to the examination.

The best way to use this book is as follows:

STEP 1: GET AN OVERVIEW OF THE EXAM

Read Chapters 1 and 2. These will provide you with information on content, conditioning requirements, and where to seek information and application forms. They will also provide you with an *abridged AICPA Content Specification Outline*, which you should read carefully in order to get an overview of the material covered on the exam.

STEP 2: ORGANIZE YOUR STRATEGY

In order to plan your course of action, you should read Chapters 3 through 6 very carefully.

Chapter 3 provides you with an insight into the kind of commitment that is necessary in order to pass this examination. *Your 7-Stage Study Program* is outlined, along with guidelines as to whether you should plan a self-study program or seek help in a review course.

Chapter 4 provides you with a detailed summary of the subject matter covered on the exam and bibliographies by exam section.

Chapter 5 provides you with test tactics for each type of question found on the examination: four-option multiple-choice, other objective formats, computational, and essay. Sample questions and solutions are also included in order to show you how to apply your knowledge.

Chapter 6 shows you *how to chart your progress and plan your course of action*. Once you have taken any of the preliminary readiness tests and the sample examinations, you will score your work and analyze your weak areas.

STEP 3: BEGIN YOUR REVIEW

Now, begin your practice. Take each section of the preliminary readiness tests (a typical sampling of AICPA questions) according to the instructions given in Chapter 7. Be sure to practice the test tactics outlined in Chapter 5. When you have completed these tests, turn to Chapter 6 to plan your course of action.

STEP 4: TWO SAMPLE EXAMINATIONS— PRACTICE YOUR STRATEGY

Chapters 8 and 9 provide you with two practice examinations: (1) the May 1995 CPA Examination and (2) the November 1995 CPA Examination. Both exams contain questions from LPR, AUDIT, ARE, and FARE.

First, take the May CPA Examination. Analyze your weaknesses and look at the Content Specification Outline to determine the relative importance of a topic area, and then review using one of the recommended methods described in Chapter 3. Chapter 6 will guide your study plan.

Then, take the November 1995 Examination, following the guidelines outlined in the previous paragraph.

STEP 5: A FINAL WORD

Don't forget to read Chapter 10 just before taking the examination. The two days of test-taking during the CPA examination are an extremely pressured time, so you should thoroughly prepare yourself for it. This chapter will help you do this. And be sure to read carefully the *Instructions for the Uniform Certified Public Accountant Examination*. Not following instructions can cause you to fail.

The use of this book along with the guidelines outlined will provide you with a clear understanding of what you must do in order to prepare effectively for the CPA examination.

Best of luck!

1. An Introduction to the CPA Examination

GENERAL PURPOSE AND CHARACTER

One function, historically, of the CPA exam has been to identify persons able to demonstrate a certain level of accounting competence. That level, as established by the exam, becomes the standard by which all accountants are judged. One either is a CPA or is not a CPA and, rightly or wrongly, is subject to a variety of value judgments regarding one's professional credentials. For someone planning a career in accounting, it is not a question of *whether* to take the CPA exam, but of *when* to take it, and of *how to prepare* for it.

Passing the CPA exam is, for the aspiring accountant, the achievement of professional stature. As an occupational standard, the exam provides a means of ensuring that those who offer their services to the public as professional accountants possess the degree of competence called for in such engagements. To succeed on the exam, one must know not only the subject matter tested but also the nature of the test itself: how it is constructed, how it is graded, what is likely to appear, and so on.

The CPA exam does not presuppose extensive work experience in public accounting. Having a general familiarity with business situations is certainly an advantage when dealing with question situations, but it is not essential. The CPA exam is textbook oriented. It presents questions having a difficulty level suitable for an entry-level accountant recently graduated from college. Ideally, the candidate should sit for the examination during the semester before graduation (if allowed by state law), or as soon as possible after completing college.

The exam is prepared by the Board of Examiners of the American Institute of Certified Public Accountants (AICPA), a private, professional organization made up of CPAs and CPA firms across the country. The test is administered by individual state boards of accountancy and the National Association of State Boards of Accountancy (NASBA). Each state, through its board of accountancy, establishes its own licensing requirements for CPAs. Each state, however, has adopted the Uniform CPA Examination as its measure of academic preparation. Further licensing requirements regarding work experience and educational background differ slightly from state to state. Grading of the exam is done by the AICPA's Advisory Grading Service. This ensures uniformity of evaluation without regard to where the exam was taken. After grading, papers are returned to the body that administered the exam for reporting results to candidates.

STRUCTURE AND GENERAL CONTENT

The Uniform CPA Examination is divided into four sections: Business Law & Professional Responsibilities (LPR), Auditing (AUDIT), Accounting & Reporting—Taxation, Managerial, and Governmental and Not-for-Profit Organizations (ARE), and Financial Accounting & Reporting—Business Enterprises (FARE). The following schedule indicates the length of each section and when it is administered:

Section	Hours	Day	Time
LPR	3.0	Wed.	9:00–12:00 Noon
AUDIT	4.5	Wed.	1:30–6:00 P.M.
ARE	3.5	Thurs.	8:30–12:00 Noon
FARE	4.5	Thurs.	1:30–6:00 P.M.
Total	15.5		

The exam is given twice yearly in early May and November. Fifty to 60 percent of each section is made up of four-option multiple-choice questions; 20 to 30 percent is in the form of essay or computational questions (none in the case of ARE), and 20 to 30 percent is in the form of other objective formats questions (40 to 50 percent in the case of ARE).

It should be noted that approximately 10 percent of the four-option multiple-choice questions on each section are for pretesting purposes only and are not included in a candidate's grade. Do not attempt to guess which are the items involved. This is not designed to hurt you in any way; pretesting ensures the quality of future examinations.

In 1996, the exam became nondisclosed. Accordingly, candidates will no longer be permitted to keep or receive their question booklets after the exam. In keeping with this policy, questions and unofficial answers will no longer be published routinely by the AICPA after each examination.

The *LPR* section deals with legal concepts rather than with the practice of law. The examiners presume that a CPA should be able to recognize the legal implications of situations that arise in the practice of accounting or auditing. Essay and objective questions present hypothetical situations in which the candidate must decide how a legal dispute should be resolved and, in essay questions, support conclusions with reasons. The focus is on federal or widely adopted laws such as the Uniform Commercial Code, Model Business Corporation Act, and Uniform Partnership Act. The LPR section also focuses on professional ethics. In particular, candidates must be familiar with the AICPA *Code of Professional Conduct.*

The *AUDIT* section tests candidates' knowledge of generally accepted auditing standards and procedures. In answering the essay and objective questions presented, the candidate must demonstrate an ability to apply auditing concepts and procedures to specific fact situations.

Candidates are expected to have a general knowledge of EDP and statistical sampling. As with ARE and FARE, candidates are generally not expected to be familiar with auditing pronouncements issued within the six months preceding the examination.

The focus of the *ARE* section is on federal taxation, managerial accounting, and accounting for governmental and not-for-profit organizations. The underlying computations are not difficult

since testing computational dexterity is not the aim of the ARE section. Rather, its aim is to test underlying theory and the reasoning involved in its application.

The concern of the *FARE* section is with the conceptual underpinnings and applications of generally accepted accounting principles for business enterprises. The candidate's grasp of accounting concepts is tested in essay, computational, and objective questions that ask him to define, explain, evaluate, or discuss accounting procedures appropriate for particular situations. In both the ARE and FARE sections, the candidate is generally *not* expected to be familiar with technical pronouncements (or tax law changes, in the case of the ARE section) issued within the six months preceding the examination.

ABRIDGED AICPA CONTENT SPECIFICATION OUTLINE

The AICPA has promulgated its "Content Specification Outlines" to formally and officially communicate to exam preparers, accounting educators, and candidates what can be tested on the CPA exam. Obviously, such a document is helpful for anyone seeking to organize his study effort. The body of knowledge encompassed by the exam is so enormous that a candidate needs to be able to select for study not only the right topics, but those aspects of a topic that are likely to be tested.

Following is an abridged version of the AICPA's "Content Specification Outlines" for each exam section. The relative emphasis each topical area receives on the exam is indicated in parentheses next to each item with a Roman numeral:

Business Law & Professional Responsibilities (LPR)

The Business Law & Professional Responsibilities (LPR) section tests candidates' knowledge of the CPA's professional responsibilities and of the legal implications of business transactions, particularly as they relate to accounting and auditing. Content covered in this section includes a CPA's professional responsibilities, business organizations, contracts, debtor-creditor relationships, government regulation of business, the

Uniform Commercial Code, and property. Candidates will be required to
- Recognize relevant legal issues.
- Recognize the legal implications of certain business situations.
- Apply the underlying principles of law to accounting and auditing situations.

This section deals with federal and widely adopted uniform laws. If there is no federal or uniform law on a topic, the questions are intended to test knowledge of the law of the majority of jurisdictions. Professional ethics questions are based on the AICPA *Code of Professional Conduct* because it is national in its application, whereas codes of other organizations and jurisdictions may be limited in their application. In preparing for this section, candidates should study the following publications:
- AICPA *Code of Professional Conduct*
- AICPA Statements on Auditing Standards dealing explicitly with proficiency, independence, and due care
- AICPA Statement on Standards for Consulting Services
- AICPA Statements on Responsibilities in Personal Financial Planning Practice
- Books covering business law, auditing, and accounting

LPR Section

I. Professional and Legal Responsibilities (15 percent)

A. Code of Professional Conduct
B. Proficiency, independence, and due care
C. Responsibilities in other professional services
D. Disciplinary systems within the profession
E. Common law liability to clients and third parties
F. Federal statutory liability
G. Privileged communications and confidentiality

II. Business Organizations (20 percent)

A. Agency
  1. Formation and termination
  2. Duties of agents and principals
  3. Liabilities and authority of agents and principals

B. Partnership and Joint Ventures
  1. Formation, operation, and termination
  2. Liabilities and authority of partners and joint owners
C. Corporations
  1. Formation and operation
  2. Stockholders, directors, and officers
  3. Financial structure, capital, and distributions
  4. Reorganization and dissolution
D. Estates and Trusts
  1. Formation, operation, and termination
  2. Allocation between principal and income
  3. Fiduciary responsibilities
  4. Distributions

III. Contracts (10 percent)

A. Formation
B. Performance
C. Third-party assignments
D. Discharge, breach, and remedies

IV. Debtor-Creditor Relationships (10 percent)

A. Rights, duties, and liabilities of debtors and creditors
B. Rights, duties, and liabilities of guarantors
C. Bankruptcy

V. Government Regulation of Business (15 percent)

A. Federal securities acts
B. Employment regulation
C. Environmental regulation

VI. Uniform Commercial Code (20 percent)

A. Negotiable instruments
B. Sales
C. Secured transactions
D. Bailments and documents of title

VII. Property (10 percent)

A. Real property
B. Personal property
C. Fire insurance

Auditing (AUDIT)

The Auditing (AUDIT) section covers knowledge of generally accepted auditing standards and procedures and the skills needed to apply them in auditing and other attestation engagements. This section tests that knowledge and those skills, as appropriate, in the context of the four broad engagement tasks that follow. In preparing for this section, candidates should study publications such as the following:

- AICPA Statements on Auditing Standards
- AICPA Statements on Standards for Accounting and Review Services
- AICPA Statements on Quality Control Standards
- AICPA Statements on Standards for Attestation Engagements
- U.S. General Accounting Office *Government Auditing Standards*
- AICPA Audit and Accounting Guides:
  -Audit Sampling
  -Audits of State and Local Governmental Units
  -Consideration of Internal Control in a Financial Statement Audit
- Books and articles on auditing
- Committee of Sponsoring Organizations of the Treadway Commission: *Internal Control—Integrated Framework*

AUDIT Section

I. Evaluate the prospective client and engagement, decide whether to accept or continue the client and the engagement, enter into an agreement with the client, and plan the engagement (40 percent).

   A. Determine nature and scope of engagement.
      1. Generally accepted auditing standards
      2. Standards for accounting and review services
      3. Standards for attestation engagements
      4. Compliance auditing applicable to governmental entities and other recipients of governmental financial assistance
      5. Filings under federal securities statutes
      6. Letters for underwriters and certain other requesting parties
   B. Assess engagement risk and the CPA firm's ability to perform the engagement.
      1. Engagement responsibilities
      2. Staffing and supervision requirements

      3. Quality control considerations
      4. Management integrity
   C. Communicate with the predecessor accountant/auditor.
   D. Decide whether to accept or continue the client and engagement.
   E. Enter into an agreement with the client as to the terms of the engagement.
   F. Obtain an understanding of the client's operations, business, and industry.
   G. Perform analytical procedures.
   H. Determine preliminary engagement materiality.
   I. Assess inherent risk and risk of misstatements.
      1. Errors (inadvertent misstatements)
      2. Fraud (intentional misstatements)
      3. Illegal acts by clients
   J. Consider the internal controls.
      1. Obtain and document an understanding of the internal controls.
      2. Assess control risk.
      3. Assess override and collusion risk.
   K. Consider other planning matters.
      1. Using the work of other independent auditors
      2. Using the work of a specialist
      3. Internal audit function
      4. Related parties and related party transactions
      5. Segment information
      6. Interim financial information
   L. Identify financial statement assertions and formulate audit objectives.
      1. Accounting estimates
      2. Routine financial statement balances, classes of transactions, and disclosures
      3. Unusual financial statement balances, classes of transactions, and disclosures
   M. Determine and prepare the work program defining the nature, timing, and extent of the auditor's procedures.
      1. Tests of controls
      2. Analytical procedures
      3. Confirmation of balances and/or transactions with third parties
      4. Physical examination of inventories and other assets
      5. Other tests of details
      6. Substantive tests prior to the balance sheet date

II. Obtain and document information to form a basis for conclusions (35 percent).

    A. Perform planned procedures including planned applications of audit sampling.
       1. Tests of controls
       2. Analytical procedures
       3. Confirmation of balances and/or transactions with third parties
       4. Physical examination of inventories and other assets
       5. Other tests of details
       6. Substantive tests prior to the balance sheet date

    B. Evaluate contingencies and obtain and evaluate lawyers' letters.
    C. Review subsequent events.
    D. Obtain representations from management.
    E. Identify reportable conditions and other control deficiencies.
    F. Identify matters for communication with audit committees.
    G. Review unusual year-end transactions.

III. Review the engagement to provide reasonable assurance that objectives are achieved and evaluate information obtained to reach and to document engagement conclusions (5 percent).

    A. Perform analytical procedures.
    B. Evaluate the sufficiency and competence of audit evidence and document engagement conclusions.
       1. Consider substantial doubt about an entity's ability to continue as a going concern.
       2. Evaluate whether financial statements are free of material misstatements, either inadvertent or intentional, and in conformity with generally accepted accounting principles or another comprehensive basis of accounting.
       3. Consider other information in documents containing audited financial statements.
    C. Review the work performed to provide reasonable assurance that objectives are achieved.

IV. Prepare communications to satisfy engagement objectives (20 percent).

    A. Prepare reports.
       1. Reports on audited financial statements
       2. Reports on reviewed and compiled financial statements
       3. Reports required by *Government Auditing Standards*
       4. Reports on compliance with laws and regulations
       5. Reports on internal control
       6. Reports on prospective financial information
       7. Reports on other attestation engagements
       8. Reports on the processing of transactions by service organizations
       9. Reports on elements of financial statements
      10. Reports on supplementary financial information
      11. Reissuance of auditors' reports

    B. Prepare letters and other required communications.
       1. Errors and fraud
       2. Illegal acts
       3. Special reports
       4. Communication with audit committees
       5. Other reporting considerations covered by statements on auditing standards and statements on standards for attestation engagements

    C. Other matters
       1. Subsequent discovery of facts existing at the date of the auditor's report
       2. Consideration of omitted procedures after the report date

Accounting & Reporting—Taxation, Managerial, and Governmental and Not-for-Profit Organizations (ARE)

The Accounting & Reporting—Taxation, Managerial, and Governmental and Not-for-Profit Organizations (ARE) section tests candidates' knowledge of principles and procedures for federal taxation, managerial accounting, and accounting for governmental and not-for-profit organizations, and the skills needed to apply them in a public accounting engagement. In preparing for this section, candidates should study publications such as the following:

- Internal Revenue Code and Income Tax Regulations
- Internal Revenue Service Circular 230
- AICPA Statements on Responsibilities in Tax Practice
- Income tax textbooks
- Governmental Accounting Standards Board (GASB) Statements, Interpretations, and Technical Bulletins
- Financial Accounting Standards Board (FASB) Statements of Financial Accounting Standards and Interpretations, Accounting Principles Board Opinions, AICPA Accounting Research Bulletins, and FASB Technical Bulletins
- FASB Statement of Financial Accounting Concepts No. 4 "Objectives of Financial Reporting by Nonbusiness Organizations," and FASB Statement of Financial Concepts No. 6, "Elements of Financial Statements"
- AICPA Statement on Auditing Standards No. 69, "The Meaning of *Present Fairly in Conformity With Generally Accepted Accounting Principles* in the Independent Auditor's Report"
- AICPA Audit and Accounting Guides and Statements of Position relating to governmental and not-for-profit organizations
- Governmental and not-for-profit accounting textbooks and other accounting textbooks containing pertinent chapters
- Managerial accounting textbooks and other accounting textbooks containing pertinent chapters
- Accounting periodicals

ARE Section

Federal Taxation—this portion covers knowledge applicable to federal taxation and its application in practice. Candidates will

- analyze information and identify data relevant for tax purposes;
- identify issues, elections, and alternative tax treatments;
- perform required calculations;
- formulate conclusions.

I. Federal Taxation—Individuals (20 percent)

A. Inclusions in gross income
B. Exclusions and adjustments to arrive at adjusted gross income
C. Deductions from adjusted gross income
D. Filing status and exemptions
E. Tax accounting methods
F. Tax computations, credits, and penalties
G. Alternative minimum tax
H. Tax procedures

II. Federal Taxation—Corporations (20 percent)

A. Determination of taxable income or loss
B. Tax accounting methods
C. S corporations
D. Personal holding companies
E. Consolidated returns
F. Tax computations, credits, and penalties
G. Alternative minimum tax
H. Other
   1. Distributions
   2. Incorporation, reorganization, liquidation, and dissolution
   3. Tax procedures

III. Federal Taxation—Partnerships (10 percent)

A. Basis of partner's interest and bases of assets contributed to the partnership
B. Determination of partner's share of income, credits, and deductions
C. Partnership and partner elections
D. Partner dealing with own partnership
E. Treatment of partnership liabilities
F. Distribution of partnership assets
G. Termination of partnership

IV. Federal Taxation—Estates and Trusts, Exempt Organizations, and Preparers' Responsibilities (10 percent)

A. Estates and trusts
   1. Income taxation
   2. Determination of beneficiary's share of taxable income
   3. Estate and gift taxation
B. Exempt organizations
   1. Types of organization
   2. Requirements for exemption
   3. Unrelated business income tax
C. Preparers' responsibilities

Governmental and Not-for-Profit Organizations—this portion covers knowledge applicable to accounting for governmental and not-for-profit organizations and its application in practice. Candidates will
- analyze and identify information relevant to governmental and not-for-profit accounting and reporting;
- identify alternative accounting and reporting policies and select those appropriate in specific situations;
- distinguish the relative weight of authority of differing sources of generally accepted accounting principles;
- perform procedures, formulate conclusions, and present results.

V. Accounting for Governmental and Not-for-Profit Organizations (30 percent)

   A. Governmental organizations
      1. Measurement focus and basis of accounting
      2. Objectives of financial reporting
      3. Use of fund accounting
      4. Budgetary process
      5. Financial reporting entity
      6. Elements of financial statements
      7. Conceptual reporting issues
   B. Not-for-profit organizations
      1. Objectives of financial reporting
      2. Elements of financial statements
      3. Formats of financial statements
   C. Accounting and financial reporting for governmental organizations
      1. Governmental-type funds and account groups
      2. Proprietary-type funds
      3. Fiduciary-type funds
   D. Accounting and financial reporting for not-for-profit organizations
      1. Revenues and contributions
      2. Restrictions on resources
      3. Expenses, including depreciation

Managerial Accounting—this portion covers knowledge applicable to managerial accounting and its application in accounting practice. Candidates will
- analyze and interpret information as a basis for decision making;
- determine product and service costs;
- prepare and interpret information for planning and control.

VI. Managerial Accounting (10 percent)

   A. Cost estimation, cost determination, and cost drivers
   B. Job costing, process costing, and activity based costing
   C. Standard costing and flexible budgeting
   D. Inventory planning, inventory control, and just-in-time purchasing
   E. Budgeting and responsibility accounting
   F. Variable and absorption costing
   G. Cost-volume-profit analysis
   H. Cost allocation and transfer pricing
   I. Joint and by-product costing
   J. Capital budgeting
   K. Special analyses for decision making
   L. Product and service pricing

Financial Accounting & Reporting—Business Enterprises (FARE)

The Financial Accounting & Reporting—Business Enterprises (FARE) section tests candidates' knowledge of generally accepted accounting principles for business enterprises and the skills needed to apply them in a public accounting engagement. Content covered in this section includes financial accounting concepts and standards as well as their application in a public accounting engagement. Candidates will
- obtain and document entity information for use in financial statement presentations;
- evaluate, analyze, and process entity information for reporting in financial statements;
- communicate entity information and conclusions;
- analyze information and identify data relevant to financial accounting and reporting;
- identify financial accounting and reporting methods and select those that are suitable;
- perform calculations and formulate conclusions;
- present results in writing in a financial statement format or other appropriate format.

In preparing for this section, candidates should study publications such as the following:

- Financial Accounting Standards Board (FASB) Statements of Financial Accounting Standards and Interpretations, Accounting Principles Board Opinions, and AICPA Accounting Research Bulletins
- FASB Technical Bulletins
- AICPA Statement on Auditing Standards No. 69, "The Meaning of *Present Fairly in Conformity With Generally Accepted Accounting Principles* in the Independent Auditor's Report," and Statement on Auditing Standards No. 62, "Special Reports"
- AICPA Personal Financial Statements Guide
- FASB Statements of Financial Accounting Concepts
- AICPA Statements of Position
- Books and articles on accounting

FARE Section

I. Concepts and Standards for Financial Statements (20 percent)

    A. Financial accounting concepts

    B. Financial accounting standards for presentation and disclosures in general purpose financial statements

        1. Consolidated and combined financial statements

        2. Balance sheet

        3. Statement of income and changes in equity accounts

        4. Statement of cash flows

        5. Accounting policies and other notes to financial statements

    C. Other presentations of financial data

        1. Financial statements prepared in conformity with comprehensive basis of accounting other than generally accepted accounting principles

        2. Personal financial statements

II. Recognition, Measurement, Valuation, and Presentation of Typical Items in Financial Statements in Conformity with Generally Accepted Accounting Principles (40 percent)

    A. Cash, cash equivalents, and marketable securities

    B. Receivables

    C. Inventories

    D. Property, plant, and equipment

    E. Investments

    F. Intangible and other assets

    G. Payables and accruals

    H. Deferred revenues

    I. Notes and bonds payable

    J. Other liabilities

    K. Contingent liabilities and commitments

    L. Equity accounts

        1. Corporations

        2. Partnerships

        3. Proprietorships

    M. Revenue, cost, and expense accounts

    N. Financing, investing, and operating components of cash flows

III. Recognition, Measurement, Valuation, and Presentation of Specific Types of Transactions and Events in Financial Statements in Conformity with Generally Accepted Accounting Principles (40 percent)

    A. Accounting changes and corrections of errors

    B. Business combinations

    C. Discontinued operations

    D. Employee benefits

        1. Deferred compensation agreements

        2. Paid absences

        3. Pension plans

        4. Postemployment benefits other than pensions

        5. Stock purchase and stock option plans

    E. Extinguishment and restructuring of debt

    F. Extraordinary items

    G. Financial instruments requiring recognition or disclosure in financial statements

        1. Futures contracts

        2. Concentration of credit risk

        3. Disclosure of fair values

        4. Other contractual obligations

    H. Foreign currency transactions and translation

    I. Income taxes

    J. Interest costs

    K. Interim financial reporting

    L. Leases

    M. Lending activities

    N. Nonmonetary transactions

    O. Public companies

        1. Earnings per share

        2. Segment reporting

P. Quasi-reorganizations, reorganizations, and changes in entity
Q. Real estate transactions
R. Related parties
S. Research and development costs

GRADING

As noted previously, grading the CPA exam is the responsibility of the AICPA Advisory Grading Service. Actual grading of essay and computational answers is performed mainly by CPAs and attorneys who serve as graders on a per-diem basis during the grading period.

Graders work from "grading guides" that contain the AICPA "unofficial answers." Also listed in the guides are key words, concepts, or check figures, along with point values assigned to each.

The grading guides for some questions may contain more points of available credit than are actually necessary to get a perfect score. A grading guide for a ten-point essay question, for example, may contain as many as fourteen or fifteen one-point gradable concepts for which credit will be given until the maximum of ten is reached. A "perfect" answer would include every gradable concept, but obviously a perfect answer is not necessary in order to receive a perfect score. Indeed, the examiners are well aware that it would be unreasonable to expect perfection under the time-pressured situation of the CPA exam. For most questions, however, candidates need to correctly identify all concepts in the grading guide to receive the maximum number of technical points.

Answers to selected essay responses on the LPR, AUDIT, and FARE sections are used to assess candidates' writing skills. Five (5) percent of the total points available on these sections will be allocated to writing skills. The characteristics of writing skills include (1) coherent organization, (2) conciseness, (3) clarity, (4) use of standard English, (5) responsiveness to the requirements of the question, and (6) appropriateness for the reader.

It should be noted that the assignment of credit for writing skills will be positive credit, and not a penalty deducted from the candidate's grade. Further, the grading of writing skills will be performed by the same individuals who grade for substance; there will *not* be a separate grading.

The candidate should keep in mind that the AICPA is looking for "comprehensiveness and control" of the English language. Accordingly, if the candidate's paper meets these criteria on the first reading by the grader, maximum writing skills credit will probably be awarded.

The minimum passing score for the CPA exam is 75. As you might expect, no grades between 69 and 75 are given. Those that fall within that range are adjusted either up or down. Further adjustment may be made to grades of all candidates on a particular section. If the overall passing percentage for a particular section is unacceptably low, the Board of Examiners will curve the results by awarding bonus points to the final grade a candidate receives. Individual questions are neither curved nor thrown out.

Each section is graded horizontally, which is to say, each grader sees only one question. Each section, therefore, is graded by multiple graders (including an optical scanner for objective-type questions), none of whom knows how the candidate is performing on other questions. When all questions on a section have been graded, they are reassembled and a total score is computed.

Objectivity is further enhanced by the anonymity given to each candidate's answer papers. The only identifying information is a preassigned candidate number and the state in which the exam is being given. Thus, the grader knows nothing about the candidate's name, age, race, sex, or number of times sitting for the exam.

An elaborate system of pretest and post-test analysis and review has been established by the AICPA. During "initial production grading," obvious passes and obvious failures are identified.

The first review, performed by highly experienced graders, is applicable to papers receiving adjusted scores in the 58–74 range. This review serves as a quality control mechanism over the consistency of the grading process because a reviewer can compare the work of different graders. Inconsistencies in the application of essay and problem answer grading guides, if any, will result in adjustment to candidate scores.

The second review is applicable to papers with grades between 68 and 74. This review involves (1) manual verification of the accuracy of the objective answer grade, and (2) independent verification of the accuracy of the essay and problem grading by a reviewer who did not perform the first review. Papers meeting the passing requirements are awarded an advisory grade of 75;

otherwise, a maximum advisory grade of 69 is assigned. Minimum grade requirements for certain jurisdictions are also considered at this point.

Grades are released approximately 90 days after the exam. In general, grades will be accompanied by a "Candidate Diagnostic Report." This report is tied to the Content Specification Outline and may be useful to candidates who must retake one or more sections of the exam. A sample "Candidate Diagnostic Report" appears on page 11.

Indeed, the AICPA does everything that fairness and reasonableness will allow to help candidates pass the CPA exam.

UNIFORM CPA EXAMINATION— CANDIDATE DIAGNOSTIC REPORT

CPA candidates must pass the Uniform CPA Examination to be licensed as certified public accountants in the 50 states, the District of Columbia, Puerto Rico, the U.S. Virgin Islands, and Guam. The Uniform CPA Examination comprises four sections: Auditing (AUDIT); Financial Account & Reporting (FARE); Accounting & Reporting—Taxation, Managerial, and Governmental and Not-for-Profit Organizations (ARE); and Business Law & Professional Responsibilities (LPR).

The passing grade for each section is 75. Your **grades** on all **sections** taken during the last examination session are reported on the reverse side of this page. In addition, there is a summary of your examination performance for the content areas included on each examination section. This summary gives an estimate of how well you did in each of the content areas. For each content area, the summary gives the relative weight (**percent coverage**) assigned to each and the approximate

percentage of area earned. Candidates should refer to *Information for Uniform CPA Examination Candidates* or *Uniform CPA Examination Candidate Brochure*, each of which gives a complete description of the content areas covered in each section.

How to Use This Report

The content area percentages earned can be valuable to candidates who have passed the various examination sections, as well as to those who have failed. By considering the content area percentages earned for each section, candidates can get an indication of their relative strengths and weaknesses. This information can be helpful to candidates preparing to retake any sections of the Uniform CPA Examination, or in planning their near-term continuing professional education needs. However, caution should be used in interpreting these percentages because they are based on answers to relatively few questions.

Section grades are based on larger numbers of questions than the individual content area percentages. Because of this, total grades provide better representations of a candidates's overall knowledge and skills than the individual content area percentages. If candidates were to take a comparable Uniform CPA Examination *without gaining any new knowledge or skills*, most of their examination grades would fall within five points (up or down) of those earned on this examination. For example, most candidates who received grades of 55 would likely receive grades between 50 and 60 if they took that section again under similar conditions. Additional preparation increases candidates' chances of improving their grades.

UNIFORM CPA EXAMINATION—CANDIDATE DIAGNOSTIC REPORT

JURISDICTION		CANDIDATE NUMBER		EXAMINATION DATE					
				PERCENTAGE OF AREA EARNED					
SECTION	GRADE	CONTENT AREAS AND PERCENT COVERAGE		<50	51–60	61–70	71–80	81–90	>90
AUDIT		I Evaluate Client and Plan Engagement	40%						
		II Obtain and Document Information	35%						
		III Review Engagement	5%						
		IV Prepare Communications	20%						
			100%						
LPR		I Professional and Legal Responsibilities	15%						
		II Business Organizations	20%						
		III Contracts	10%						
		IV Debtor-Creditor Relationships	10%						
		V Government Regulation of Business	15%						
		VI Uniform Commercial Code	20%						
		VII Property	10%						
			100%						
FARE		I Concepts and Standards for Financial Statements	20%						
		II Typical Items in Financial Statements	40%						
		III Specific Transactions and Events in Financial Statements	40%						
			100%						
ARE		I Federal Taxation—Individuals	20%						
		II Federal Taxation—Corporations	20%						
		III Federal Taxation—Partnerships	10%						
		IV Federal Taxation—Other	10%						
		V Government and Not-for-Profit Organizations	30%						
		VI Managerial Accounting	10%						
			100%						

2.   Apply for the CPA Examination

HOW TO APPLY FOR THE CPA EXAMINATION

After an accounting student has decided to become a CPA, one of the first things to do is to ascertain the application deadline to sit for the exam. The deadline varies from state to state. Usually it falls around the first of April or September, but in some states it can be as many as ninety days or as few as thirty before the date of the exam. Also, the deadline can differ depending upon whether the candidate is sitting for the first time or applying for reexamination. Incredibly, many candidates are lax about attending to such mundane details, and end up taking the CPA exam six months later than they should have only because they didn't apply on time.

When applying for the exam, an application fee and/or an examination fee must be paid to the board administering the exam. For the first sitting, fees range from $35 to $220. This out-of-pocket cost represents one more reason why the CPA exam should be approached with every intention of passing it the first time through.

CONDITIONING REQUIREMENTS

State accountancy boards also establish what are called "conditioning requirements." That is, conditions that must be met in order for a candidate to receive credit for individual CPA exam sections passed, even though all four sections have not been passed. Typically, credit will be granted when a candidate first succeeds in passing at least two sections.

In general, the conditioning requirement pertains to the number of sections to be passed initially. Once a candidate is "conditioned," she may thereafter be credited for sections passed individually. For example: candidate Andrews sits for all four sections, passes ARE and FARE, but fails AUDIT and LPR. If Andrews is conditioned (see additional considerations following), and at the next exam she passes only one of the two remaining sections, she will nevertheless receive credit for it because she has been "conditioned" at her first sitting.

Many states impose a time limit on the conditional credit given by stipulating an upper limit stated in either years or examinations beyond which conditional credit earned will be lost unless the entire exam is passed. The next five or six exams is the most common limit imposed.

Further variations from state to state are found in other conditions established. Some states set minimum failing scores on sections not passed in order for a candidate to receive credit for the section(s) she did pass. Some states require candidates for reexamination to continue to sit for all sections for which conditional credit has not been granted. Some states require candidates who fail the entire exam to wait one full year before sitting again. As noted in Chapter 1, the CPA examination is designed and graded by the AICPA, but it is the state boards of accountancy that determine how exam results will be evaluated and used as part of the licensing process.

STATE REQUIREMENTS

The CPA examination requirements vary from state to state. The candidate should check with his particular state board at the time of his decision to become a CPA. A listing of state board addresses follows later in this chapter.

WHERE TO SEEK INFORMATION AND APPLICATION FORMS

As noted previously, entry into the accountancy profession is controlled by the individual state boards of accountancy. Accordingly, one of the first things a prospective CPA candidate should do is to ascertain the various requirements for becoming a CPA by contacting the state board of accountancy. Following is a list of the addresses and phone numbers for each of the boards within the United States and its territories.

The State Boards of Accountancy of the United States

ALABAMA STATE BOARD OF PUBLIC
ACCOUNTANCY
RSA Plaza
770 Washington Avenue
Montgomery, AL 36130
Tel: (334) 242-5700
Fax: (334) 242-2711

ALASKA STATE BOARD OF PUBLIC
ACCOUNTANCY
Department of Commerce and Economic
Development
Div. of Occupational Licensing
Box 110806
Juneau, AK 99811-0806
Tel: (907) 465-2580
Fax: (907) 465-2974
http://www.state.ak.us/local/akpages/
COMMERCE/occlic.htm

ARIZONA STATE BOARD OF ACCOUNTANCY
3877 North 7th Street, Suite 106
Phoenix, AZ 85014
Tel: (602) 255-3648
Fax: (602) 255-1283

ARKANSAS STATE BOARD OF
ACCOUNTANCY
101 East Capitol, Suite 430
Little Rock, AR 72201
Tel: (501) 682-1520
Fax: (501) 682-5538

CALIFORNIA STATE BOARD OF
ACCOUNTANCY
2000 Evergreen Street, Suite 250
Sacramento, CA 95815-3832
Tel: (916) 263-3680
Fax: (916) 263-3674

COLORADO STATE BOARD OF
ACCOUNTANCY
1560 Broadway, Suite 1370
Denver, CO 80202
Tel: (303) 894-7800
Fax: (303) 894-7790
http:/www.state.co.us
e-mail: Mary.Burgess@STATE.CO.US

CONNECTICUT STATE BOARD OF
ACCOUNTANCY
Secretary of the State
30 Trinity Street
PO Box 150470
Hartford, CT 06106
Tel: (860) 566-7835
Fax: (860) 566-5757

DELAWARE STATE BOARD OF
ACCOUNTANCY
Cannon Building, Suite 203
PO Box 1401
Dover, DE 19903
Tel: (302) 739-4522
Fax: (302) 739-2711
e-mail: Sheila.Wolfe@BOARD@PROF#REG

DISTRICT OF COLUMBIA BOARD OF
ACCOUNTANCY
Dept. of Consumer and Regulatory Affairs
Room 923
614 H Street, NW, c/o PO Box 37200
Washington, DC 20013-7200
Tel: (202) 727-7468
Fax: (202) 727-8030

FLORIDA BOARD OF ACCOUNTANCY
2610 NW 43rd Street, Suite 1A
Gainesville, FL 32606-4599
Tel: (352) 955-2165
Fax: (352) 955-2164

GEORGIA STATE BOARD OF ACCOUNTANCY
166 Pryor Street, SW
Atlanta, GA 30303
Tel: (404) 656-2281
Fax: (404) 651-9532

GUAM BOARD OF ACCOUNTANCY
PO Box 5753
Agana, GU 96932
Tel: (671) 646-5044
Fax: (671) 646-5045

HAWAII BOARD OF PUBLIC ACCOUNTANCY
Department of Commerce and Consumer
Affairs
PO Box 3469
Honolulu, HI 96801-3469
Tel: (808) 586-2694
Fax: (808) 586-2689

IDAHO STATE BOARD OF ACCOUNTANCY
PO Box 83720
Boise, ID 83720-0002
Tel: (208) 334-2490
Fax: (208) 334-2615

ILLINOIS BOARD OF EXAMINERS
University of Illinois
505 E. Green Street, Suite 216
Champaign, IL 61820
Tel: (217) 333-4213
Fax: (217) 333-3126
e-mail: jvician@ux1.cso.ulus.edu

ILLINOIS PUBLIC ACCOUNTANTS
REGISTRATION COMMITTEE
Public Accountancy Section
320 W. Washington Street, 3rd Floor
Springfield, IL 62786-0001
Tel: (217) 785-0800
Fax: (217) 782-7645

INDIANA BOARD OF ACCOUNTANCY
Professional Licensing Agency
Indiana Government Center S.
302 West Washington Street, Room E034
Indianapolis, IN 46204-2246
Tel: (317) 232-5987
Fax: (317) 232-2312

IOWA ACCOUNTANCY EXAMINING BOARD
1918 SE Hulsizer Avenue
Ankeny, IA 50021-3941
Tel: (515) 281-4126
Fax: (515) 281-7411
http://www/state.ia.us/government/com/prof/
acct
e-mail: bschroe@max.state.ia.us

KANSAS BOARD OF ACCOUNTANCY
Landon State Office Building
900 SW Jackson, Suite 556
Topeka, KS 66612-1239
Tel: (913) 296-2162

KENTUCKY STATE BOARD OF ACCOUNTANCY
332 West Broadway, Suite 310
Louisville, KY 40202-2115
Tel: (502) 595-3037
Fax: (502) 595-4281

STATE BOARD OF CPAS OF LOUISIANA
Pan-American Life Center
601 Poydras Street, Suite 1770
New Orleans, LA 70130
Tel: (504) 566-1244
Fax: (504) 566-1252

MAINE STATE BOARD OF ACCOUNTANCY
Department of Professional & Financial
Regulation
Division of Licensing & Enforcement
State House Station 35
Augusta, ME 04333
Tel: (207) 624-8603
Fax: (207) 624-8637
e-mail: sandra.a.leach@state.me.us

MARYLAND STATE BOARD OF PUBLIC
ACCOUNTANCY
501 St. Paul Place, 9th Floor
Baltimore, MD 21202-2272
Tel: (410) 333-6322
Fax: (410) 333-6314
http://sailor.lib.md.us/dllr/account.htm

MASSACHUSETTS BOARD OF PUBLIC
ACCOUNTANCY
Saltonstall Building, Government Center
100 Cambridge Street, Room 1315
Boston, MA 02202-0001
Tel: (617) 727-1806
Fax: (617) 727-0139

MICHIGAN BOARD OF ACCOUNTANCY
Department of Commerce—BOPR
PO Box 30018
Lansing, MI 48909-7518
Tel: (517) 373-0682
Fax: (517) 373-2795
e-mail: Suzanne.U.Jolicoeur
@COMMERCE.STATE.MI.US

MINNESOTA STATE BOARD OF
ACCOUNTANCY
85 East 7th Place, Suite 125
St. Paul, MN 55101
Tel: (612) 296-7937
Fax: (612) 282-2644

MISSISSIPPI STATE BOARD OF PUBLIC
ACCOUNTANCY
653 N. State Street
Jackson, MS 39202
Tel: (601) 354-7320
Fax: (601) 354-7290

MISSOURI STATE BOARD OF ACCOUNTANCY
PO Box 613
Jefferson City, MO 65102-0613
Tel: (573) 751-0012
Fax: (573) 751-0890
e-mail: bboston@mail.state.mo.us

MONTANA STATE BOARD OF PUBLIC
ACCOUNTANTS
Arcade Building, Lower Level
111 North Jackson, PO Box 200513
Helena, MT 59620-0513
Tel: (406) 444-3739
Fax: (406) 444-1667

NEBRASKA STATE BOARD OF PUBLIC
ACCOUNTANCY
PO Box 94725
Lincoln, NE 68509-4725
Tel: (402) 471-3595
Fax: (402) 471-4484

NEVADA STATE BOARD OF ACCOUNTANCY
200 South Virginia Street, Suite 670
Reno, NV 89501-2408
Tel: (702) 786-0231
Fax: (702) 786-0234

NEW HAMPSHIRE BOARD OF ACCOUNTANCY
57 Regional Drive
Concord, NH 03301
Tel: (603) 271-3286
Fax: (603) 271-2856

NEW JERSEY STATE BOARD OF
ACCOUNTANCY
PO Box 45000
Newark, NJ 07101
Tel: (201) 504-6380
Fax: (201) 648-3355

NEW MEXICO STATE BOARD OF PUBLIC
ACCOUNTANCY
1650 University NE, Suite 400-A
Albuquerque, NM 87102
Tel: (505) 841-9108
Fax: (505) 841-9113

NEW YORK STATE BOARD FOR PUBLIC
ACCOUNTANCY
State Education Department
Cultural Education Center, Room 3013
Albany, NY 12230
Tel: (518) 474-3836
Fax: (518) 473-6995
e-mail: dstubbs2@nysed.mail.gov

NORTH CAROLINA STATE BOARD OF CPA
EXAMINERS
1101 Oberlin Road, Suite 104
PO Box 12827
Raleigh, NC 27605-2827
Tel: (919) 733-4222
Fax: (919) 733-4209

NORTH DAKOTA STATE BOARD OF
ACCOUNTANCY
2701 S. Columbia Road
Grand Forks, ND 58201
Tel: (701) 775-7100
Fax: (701) 775-7430

ACCOUNTANCY BOARD OF OHIO
77 South High Street, 18th Floor
Columbus, OH 43266-0301
Tel: (614) 466-4135
Fax: (614) 466-2628

OKLAHOMA ACCOUNTANCY BOARD
4545 Lincoln Boulevard, Suite 165
Oklahoma City, OK 73105-3413
Tel: (405) 521-2397
Fax: (405) 521-3118

OREGON STATE BOARD OF ACCOUNTANCY
3218 Pringle Road, SE
Salem, OR 97302-6307
Tel: (503) 378-4181
Fax: (503) 378-3575
http://www.boa.state.or.us/boa.html
e-mail: Karen.J.Delorenzo@state.or.us

PENNSYLVANIA STATE BOARD OF
ACCOUNTANCY
116 Pine Street
Harrisburg, PA 17101
Tel: (717) 783-1404
Fax: (717) 787-7769

PUERTO RICO BOARD OF ACCOUNTANCY
Box 3271
Old San Juan Station
San Juan, PR 00902-3271
Tel: (787) 722-2122
Fax: (787) 721-8399

RHODE ISLAND BOARD OF
ACCOUNTANCY
Department of Business Regulation
233 Richmond Street, Suite 236
Providence, RI 02903-4236
Tel: (401) 277-3185
Fax: (401) 277-6654

SOUTH CAROLINA BOARD OF
ACCOUNTANCY
Board of Accountancy, Suite 101
PO Box 11329
Columbia, SC 29211-1329
Tel: (803) 734-4228
Fax: (803) 734-9571
http://www.llr.sc.edu/good.htm
e-mail: WilesR@zieur.sc.edu

SOUTH DAKOTA BOARD OF
ACCOUNTANCY
301 East 14th Street, Suite 200
Sioux Falls, SD 57104
Tel: (605) 367-5770
Fax: (605) 367-5773

TENNESSEE STATE BOARD OF
ACCOUNTANCY
500 James Robertson Parkway, 2nd Floor
Nashville, TN 37243-1141
Tel: (615) 741-2550
Fax: (615) 532-8800

TEXAS STATE BOARD OF PUBLIC
ACCOUNTANCY
333 Guadalupe Tower III, Suite 900
Austin, TX 78701-3900
Tel: (512) 505-5500
Fax: (512) 505-5575

UTAH BOARD OF ACCOUNTANCY
160 East 300 South
PO Box 45805
Salt Lake City, UT 84145-0805
Tel: (801) 530-6720
Fax: (801) 530-6511
e-mail: brcmrc.brdopl.dsjones
@email.state.ut.us

VERMONT BOARD OF PUBLIC ACCOUNTANCY
Redstone Building
26 Terrace Street
Montpelier, VT 05609
Tel: (802) 828-2837
Fax: (802) 828-2496
e-mail: Irollins@sec.state.vt.us

VIRGINIA BOARD FOR ACCOUNTANCY
3600 West Broad Street
Richmond, VA 23230-4917
Tel: (804) 367-8590
Fax: (804) 367-2474

VIRGIN ISLANDS BOARD OF PUBLIC
ACCOUNTANCY
PO Box 3016
No. 1A Gallows Bay Market Plaza
Christiansted
St. Croix, VI 00822
Tel: (809) 773-4305
Fax: (809) 773-9850

WASHINGTON STATE BOARD OF
ACCOUNTANCY
210 East Union, Suite H
PO Box 9131
Olympia, WA 98507-9131
Tel: (360) 753-2585
Fax: (360) 664-9190

WEST VIRGINIA BOARD OF ACCOUNTANCY
200 L & S Building
812 Quarrier Street
Charleston, WV 25301-2695
Tel: (304) 558-3557
Fax: (304) 558-1325

WISCONSIN ACCOUNTING EXAMINING BOARD
1400 E. Washington Avenue
PO Box 8935
Madison, WI 53708-8935
Tel: (608) 266-1397
Fax: (608) 267-0644

WYOMING BOARD OF CERTIFIED PUBLIC
ACCOUNTANTS
First Bank Building
2020 Carey Avenue
Cheyenne, WY 82002-0610
Tel: (307) 777-7551
Fax: (307) 777-3796
e-mail: PMORGA@MISSC.STATE.WY.US

Prospective candidates wishing information
from the American Institute of Certified Public
Accountants may contact them at 1211 Avenue of
the Americas, New York, NY 10036-8775; (212)
596-6200. Or visit their websites:

AICPA Online—http://www.aicpa.org

Examinations Division—http://www.aicpa.
org/members/div/examiner/index.htm

Of particular interest is their booklet entitled,
"Information for CPA Candidates."
Candidates will also find organizations sponsoring CPA review courses to be helpful in providing information concerning necessary steps to
follow in becoming a CPA.

3. Develop Your Study Program

Each year well over 100,000 candidates sit for the CPA examination. Most don't make it. The passing statistics are well known: only about 20 percent of first-time candidates sitting for all four sections pass; only about 30 percent of the papers in each of the four sections are rated as passing. Typically, many of the candidates are sitting for fewer than all four sections, usually because they failed to pass every section at an earlier sitting.

Leaving aside anxiety that causes some people to freeze up in test situations, there are generally *two reasons for poor performance on the CPA exam:* (1) *inadequate preparation,* and (2) *lack of "examsmanship" skills.* Learning examsmanship skills is ultimately part of a sound preparation program, but it is useful to speak of the two separately.

The more a candidate knows about the ingredients for success on the CPA exam, the better able he will be to do what he must to assure success. One of the first things he must do is to approach the exam with a positive attitude about his prospects for passing. From the first day of preparation to the days of the exam, confidence is crucial. Similarly, he must approach the task of studying for the exam with enthusiasm and with a willingness to work harder than he has ever worked before. Attitude and motivation are ultimately as important as subject mastery.

The CPA exam is a very passable exam. The overall difficulty level of questions is seldom more than that experienced in Intermediate Accounting (or a comparable level for nonaccounting topics on the exam). The average student who works hard *can* pass the CPA exam. It is the *approach* to passing the exam that is more important than a candidate's academic record. This is borne out by the fact that ultimately 80 to 90 percent of *serious* candidates do pass the CPA exam within three years of their first sitting. Some people, it appears, have to fall on their faces once or twice before they are ready to make a commitment to becoming a serious candidate.

MAKE A COMMITMENT

Like most things of value in life, becoming a professional by passing a rigorous licensing examination is a matter of wanting it badly enough—badly enough to undergo a review program that must extend over a period of months and that will require all of the self-discipline, maturity, and commitment that the candidate can muster. It is far from impossible to pass the CPA exam, but it cannot be accomplished without a systematic, efficient, on-target review program.

Young candidates, fresh out of undergraduate accounting programs, often do not realize this. Having never experienced a situation like the CPA examination, they assume that study habits that got them through college will transfer effectively to the CPA exam. Their approach is understandable but potentially self-defeating. As seen in Chapter 1, the scope of the CPA exam is far greater than anything experienced in college. The CPA exam is drawing from an entire accounting curriculum, not just topics studied within the previous 15 weeks. The CPA exam is 15 and one-half hours over two days, not three or four final exams spread over a week. The first-time candidate who fails to appreciate the special demands of the CPA exam will almost surely become a second- or a third-time candidate.

The successful candidate's success is directly proportional to the extent to which his review program has been an organized, systematic effort. That requires hard work and commitment. Space must be created in an already busy life to accomplish a successful review. Certain obligations, such as job and family responsibilities, cannot be ignored, but optional social activities must often be suspended for the duration of the review period. It is a matter of setting priorities. Passing the CPA exam must be the paramount objective, fixed in the mind's eye, during the months preceding the examination.

The ability to set such priorities and to stick with decisions made is a mark of a candidate's maturity. While it may be disagreeable to forego the pleasures of a weekend off, it must be done if you are to accomplish the sustained, coherent study necessary. Such pleasures will still be there after you become a CPA, and in any event, the review period, in the long run, is a brief interlude in a larger continuum. Whatever sacrifices must be made will be only temporary and will be ultimately offset by the benefits of becoming a CPA.

At least that is the frame of mind with which you should approach the review period: with firm resolve and established goals. Very likely you *will* take a weekend off or "waste" an evening watching television, but the resulting pangs of conscience will probably send you back to the books with renewed fervor. The resolutions you make at the start of review serve as ideals that ultimately may be beyond your reach, but nevertheless they will continue to motivate you during the long hours of drudgery that the effort entails.

YOUR 7-STAGE STUDY PROGRAM

Stage 1—Apply to sit for the exam. Secure necessary forms, and so on, from your state board of accountancy and/or NASBA. Complete and return as instructed.

Stage 2—Self-appraisal. Take stock of yourself, your academic preparation, as well as your work habits and other strengths and weaknesses. Use the abridged AICPA Content Specification Outlines in Chapter 1 as a checklist of subject mastery. Working through the outlines, determine how familiar you are with each topic listed, keeping in mind the percentage indicator of relative emphasis given to each topical area. As you might expect, your familiarity will range from "knowledgeable" to "no prior learning." That variability will have implications for how you review. (After you take the Preliminary Readiness Tests in Chapter 7, you will have a rough indicator of your readiness for the CPA exam.)

Stage 3—Decide what kind of review program to undertake. Your options range from self-designed self-study to a formal review course. Selecting the right option is a matter of making an honest self-appraisal and deciding which approach is most likely to produce the desired result. You must consider how up-to-date your knowledge is, how much new learning will be necessary, how much you know about the CPA exam itself, how much time you have to devote to review, how inclined you are to procrastinate, and how well you can study on your own. The chief concern at this stage is to decide on the best possible game plan *for you.* Success will depend on the choice you make and how well you stick to it.

Stage 4—Arrange your life to accommodate the necessities of review. You must plan on setting aside a minimum of two to three hours per day for either classroom attendance or self-study. This represents a sizeable chunk of time that will force dislocations in other areas of your life. That in turn may adversely affect friends and family. Since their cooperation and support can make your task much more manageable, and since your ties to them should endure long after you become a CPA, you should seek their understanding and share with them the sense of purpose you feel. If they are made to feel a part of your hopes and plans, they will forgive your irritability and unsociability during the review period.

At the office, your supervisors and coworkers are not likely to be as sympathetic. Your efforts to become a CPA are viewed as a worthy endeavor by your employer, but not one that should affect your availability for overtime, business travel, or other job requirements. In other words, there will be little opportunity for you to find much flexibility in your job responsibilities to accommodate your review program. You are expected to show that you can become a CPA even while you are giving your full effort to job performance. The arrangements necessary to allow for the hours that must be set aside are usually made by forgoing participation in all nonessential personal and social activities during the review period.

In many ways, your life off the job during the two to three months of review may come to resemble that of a recluse. If, however, you keep your focus on the long-term benefits of whatever temporary sacrifices you have to endure, the inevitable tedium will seem more bearable. The worst part of failing the CPA exam is having to gear up for and go through the review process all over again. It should be done right the first time.

Stage 5—Take the plunge. After the necessary decisions have been made about your strengths and weaknesses, after you have decided what kind of review program to undertake, and after you have arranged your life to allow for review time, go to it! Procrastination is the thief of time, and time is the candidate's scarcest resource.

Usually, the hardest part of any large undertaking is getting started. Some people procrastinate by busying themselves with preparatory details, telling themselves that everything must be arranged and in place before they can start. Other people simply postpone: "First thing Monday morning," they'll say, or "As soon as I clear up a few things at work . . . , " and so on.

The point to remember is that things in your life will never be exactly as you would like them to be; once a decision is made, action should follow. Natural inertia must be overcome.

Stage 6—Maintain momentum. As you might expect, it is not easy to sustain an intense and tedious effort over a long period of time. As one encounters setbacks or obstacles, it is easy to become discouraged. Self-doubt is a natural human reaction. Expect it and deal with it. But recognize it as nothing more than a passing mood. If you have the self-discipline and motivation that characterizes successful candidates, you will not lose the momentum of effort that you have established.

There are certain things a candidate can do during the review period that will help maintain momentum:

1. *Set daily goals.* Decide which topics will be studied, which set of questions will be answered, which deficiencies will be corrected, and so forth. Specific goals give purpose and direction to a review session.
2. *Maintain a progress record of your study.* Since the mass of information that must be assimilated is so vast, and the review period so long, a perpetual record of work done and work to be done helps the candidate control his time and effort better.
3. *Monitor performance of questions answered.* This is really part of #2, preceding, but deserves special mention, nevertheless. Since your ability to answer questions is ultimately what counts, your performance with practice questions from past exams

should be noted carefully. Maintain answer sheets that highlight incorrect responses. You will want to review those items in the final days before the exam.

4. *Keep fit—both physically and mentally.* Believe it or not, sitting for the CPA exam is almost as grueling physically as it is mentally. Imagine sitting hunched over a writing surface that may or may not be at a comfortable height for periods of three to four and one-half hours at a stretch, four times in two days! It will help if, during the review period, you can prepare for that eventuality by maintaining a modest regimen of daily exercise.

Actually, you will need such exercise during the review period as well, since some physical counterbalance will be necessary for the periods during which you must remain relatively immobile while in class or studying at home. Beyond that, it is well established that physical fitness and mental alertness are connected.

To reduce mental fatigue, it helps to "walk away from it" periodically when you feel, during study sessions, that your brain has become overloaded with information. A brief respite will usually help to clear the neurological circuitry.

Stage 7—Final readiness review. Ideally, the entire review program should be completed at least four or five days before the exam begins. If that is accomplished, there will be no last-minute panic because of material not covered. At that point a relatively leisurely final readiness review can be undertaken that will round out the overall effort. You will want to review study aids for those topics about which you still feel unsure or which you are almost certain will appear on your exam. Also review any past questions that were answered incorrectly, because they indicate potential gaps in your understanding.

Refresh your memory of key formulas, definitions, concepts, and acronyms, one last time. Likewise, you should mentally rehearse your handling of the test situation itself (i.e., exam-day reminders and the question-answering techniques discussed in Chapter 5). Finally, on the eve of the examination, relax. You will be too apprehensive to study, anyway, but your apprehensiveness will be allayed by the knowledge that you have done all that you could to get ready and that you stand as good a chance of passing as anybody else.

SELECT THE RIGHT PREPARATION APPROACH

How you review is something you will have to decide based upon an honest appraisal of your strengths and weaknesses. No one knows better than you the quality of your academic preparation, the extent of your familiarity with the CPA exam, or the capacity you have for establishing a regimen and sticking to it. One of the most discouraging feelings you can have is knowing that you failed because you didn't do the job you could have done and should have done in reviewing the material tested.

Of course, preparation really begins with the first accounting course you take. *Preparation is a two-stage process. Stage one* consists of building a solid academic foundation during your college years; *stage two* is the formal review program undergone immediately prior to the examination. A review program should be precisely that: a review of things previously learned, not an initial learning experience. Invariably there will be topics on the CPA exam that were not studied in college. Those gaps will have to be filled, and a well-designed review program will anticipate that necessity, but the primary activity should be review.

The candidate who, as an accounting major, had his sights aimed toward passing the CPA exam is in a position to be confident about his prospects for passing. The candidate who only lately has arrived at a decision to become a CPA, and who therefore may not have an exam-directed accounting background, will have to work extra hard during his review program.

A solid, exam-directed academic background (STAGE ONE) implies that a candidate as an accounting major was involved in genuine learning, as opposed to the intellectual chicanery that often allows one to pass courses but come away with little real understanding. At one time or another we all do what we must to get through a required course just to get it over with and get a respectable grade. Obviously, if CPA exam-related courses are handled this way, a candidate is ill-prepared to take the CPA exam despite his nominal status as a graduate accountant. He may have retained some of the information crammed in during "all-nighters." He may be fairly proficient at parroting textbook solutions—even without the help of his friends—but he will probably lack the overall grasp of the body of knowledge that, in its coherent entirety, comprises his accounting curriculum and the CPA exam. The successful CPA candidate must be adept at problem solving in a pressure situation. The exam tests reasoning ability, which is predicated on genuine understanding rather than temporary familiarity.

One point to note regarding adequacy of undergraduate preparation: the most successful candidates are not necessarily those with the highest grade-point averages. Super achievers in terms of grades are often overly thorough perfectionists. Such an inclination is more of a hindrance than an advantage. Perfect answers to questions are not needed. And the candidate who gets hung up trying to write perfect answers will often fail to budget time wisely and end up turning in a paper with some perfect answers and some incomplete answers. The idea is to get the job done within the constraints of the CPA exam format, not self-imposed constraints that demand perfection. Satisfying the graders is a matter of giving the graders what they are looking for—no more, no less. The average student whose knowledge and test-taking skills are sound, and whose attitude is pragmatic, will often outperform a colleague with a higher academic standing.

Your Review Program

STAGE TWO of the preparation process is the formal review program undertaken in the final months before the examination. It should be a formal review in terms of having a well-thought-out sequence of study that takes into account the relative coverage each topic receives on the CPA exam. It follows that such a program, given the scope of the CPA exam, can only be carried out over a period of months.

That necessity can be a stumbling block for many candidates, particularly first-timers. Never before (and probably never again) has the typical first-time candidate been required to sustain a months-long study effort aimed toward passing a single exam. The challenge is formidable but certainly not unreasonable. As a gateway to professional status, the CPA exam should be a test of character as well as intellect.

One of the first decisions a candidate faces after deciding to sit for the exam is what type of review program to follow. There are basically two ways to go: (1) self-designed self-study, and (2) a commercial review or "coach" course. Often, a candidate right out of college will have had some sort of exam-directed course work during her final semester that may or may not have been adequate preparation. Often, such courses concentrate on certain segments of the exam, such as accounting problems or business law, but, because of time constraints, cannot provide coverage comprehensive enough to ensure success. Commercial courses include both private, proprietary types, and university-operated, noncredit courses offered to the public.

THE COMMERCIAL REVIEW COURSE

A high-quality commercial review course makes use of the talents and backgrounds of its staff in developing a professionally designed, experience-tested program of study. Like college, a good review course should be viewed as an investment for the future: by enabling one to pass sooner than later, it pays for itself. What is purchased is the knowledge and skill of CPAs who have not only been through the exam but who have made a special study of its form and content. Through study aids, lectures, and demonstration, they pass their wisdom along to others. The ability of a professional review course to increase a candidate's chances for success has been attested to by several independent studies.

Such courses are presented in a variety of modes: (1) live classroom, (2) audio classroom, and (3) home-study. A *live classroom format* is the conventional arrangement in which an instructor presents to students, in lecture fashion, selected topics for that particular session. The length of a session is usually three hours. An *audio classroom mode* involves the use of audio-cassette recordings of previously presented live lectures. In a well-run audio classroom, an instructor uses the tapes as a teaching aid. If it is well-run, an audio classroom format can be just as effective as a completely live arrangement. In fact, it can be even better if the instructor on tape is superior to the one in the classroom. A *home-study review course* usually contains a combination of cassette lectures and printed materials. Such courses may or may not be classroom-based. Those that are have the benefit of containing classroom-tested materials and instructional techniques.

There are many ways to achieve the same end, of course, and this is nowhere better illustrated than in the descriptive brochures distributed by commercial review courses. The greatest variable seems to be course length: some courses run five or six months; some less than one month. Usually those of five or six months spend a lot of time reviewing elementary material. Often, they will devote a portion of class time to in-class problem solving. Those of less than a month usually are presented as intensive, "live-in" crash courses designed to provide a candidate with a final refresher before exam day.

Selecting a particular review course is not easy. To a large extent, you are entrusting your immediate professional future to the organization involved. Your tuition becomes a sound investment only if it achieves its expected return. As with any investment decision, you should choose the option that best meets your needs and objectives. In CPA review, you have to consider which arrangement will be most effective for you. You must take into account the quality of your academic preparation, your present knowledge, and your psychological strengths and weaknesses.

Certain features distinguish a superior review course. It should have an established track record of turning out successful candidates. Its faculty should consist of experienced, dynamic instructors who not only impart knowledge effectively, but also instill the confidence crucial to success. The course must be flexible enough to accommodate the individual needs of its students. Students typically are forced to miss an occasional lecture because of job or personal requirements. Provision for convenient make-up opportunities should be available. Instructional materials should be streamlined yet comprehensive. They should contain cogent summaries that illuminate core information and maximize memory retention. They should contain past question-and-answer material that trains candidates to write passing answers to future questions. They should not require the use of supplemental textbooks or pronouncements, nor should they require extensive supplemental note taking. A questionnaire for selecting a good review course follows.

CPA REVIEW COURSE QUESTIONNAIRE

1. **Reputation**
   Does the course have the recommendation of people whose opinions you respect?

2. **Faculty**

   Are faculty members experienced CPA *review* instructors?

3. **Materials**

   Are materials comprehensive? They must strike the proper balance between giving a candidate more than is necessary and giving the candidate too little.

   Are materials up-to-date?

   Are materials organized for maximum usability?

   Are materials complete, or must they be supplemented by textbooks, pronouncements, etc.? Are materials well-written?

   Is computer software available for supplemental study?

4. **Convenience**

   In terms of geographic location and class meeting times, is the course compatible with your work schedule?

5. **Class size**

   Is class size so large as to be an impediment to effective learning?

6. **Make-up and review**

   What provisions does the course make for reviewing a lecture already presented? What provisions are made for make-up of lectures missed because of absence?

7. **Course structure**

   Is the course organized into four subcourses directed at individual examination sections (i.e., LPR, AUDIT, ARE, and FARE)? Can you enroll in individual subcourses or must you enroll in some combination?

8. **Course schedules**

   Are the sessions for individual courses (i.e., LPR, AUDIT, ARE, and FARE) evenly distributed over the length of the review period so as to enhance learning effectiveness and memory retention?

9. **Organizational strength**

   Is the sponsoring organization a solid, well-established entity? What is its reputation in the business and academic community?

10. **Cost**

    Is the course fairly and competitively priced? Is the price all-inclusive? What discounts are available? What payment terms are available?

In order to ensure an organized, successful review effort, most candidates should enroll in a professional review course. A recent survey of candidates by NASBA disclosed that more than half of the candidates sitting for the exam had taken some type of coaching course that had contributed to examination success. Additional hours of independent study were also cited as factors accounting for success.

THE SELF-DESIGNED STUDY PROGRAM

The biggest advantage of a self-designed, self-study program is that it is inexpensive, at least in terms of initial out-of-pocket costs. In such a program, the individual candidate performs his own research into the requirements of the CPA exam and then designs for himself a program of study that takes into account his relative strengths and weaknesses. Such a program usually would be built around relevant textbooks, FASB and AICPA pronouncements, AICPA Unofficial Questions and Answers, and so on. It might also include one of the numerous review manuals that attempt to capture all of the necessary information a candidate needs within the confines of 2,000 or so pages.

The biggest disadvantage of a self-designed self-study program is that the candidate may unwittingly become his own worst enemy. He may fail to get an accurate picture of examination form and content. He may fail to be objective about his strengths and weaknesses. Operating on his own, he may fail to structure his activity in the most efficient way. In the end, what looked to be the cheapest, easiest way turns out to be the most costly. The exam will have to be repeated, salary increases that follow exam success will have to be forgone, and additional review costs will have to be incurred. Psychologically, the candidate must deal with the knowledge of having wasted a significant block of valuable time. Even worse, he must face the depressing prospect of having to repeat the review process all over again. A self-designed, self-study review program *can* work, but it requires an uncommon degree of insight, confidence, and self-discipline.

Review Manuals

There are several CPA review manuals that provide assistance to candidates in the form of study outlines and past exam questions and answers. Some of them, in an effort to be comprehensive, overwhelm the reader with more than 2,000 pages of material that the candidate is expected to assimilate. Someone working on her own can easily feel intimidated by the task ahead if she has not yet worked out an organized plan of study. Such manuals are most useful when they are supplemental to, or part of, a classroom CPA review course. Printed materials generally need an instructor to illuminate them and to guide the candidate through.

GUIDELINES FOR SELECTING A CPA REVIEW MANUAL

1. **Comprehensiveness.** This is difficult for the inexperienced candidate to judge since a clear understanding of the nature of exam coverage is not usually possible until *after* the review program has begun. Nevertheless, comprehensive coverage is a must.

    Many authors err on the side of including *too* much, of giving the reader more than he actually needs for efficient exam preparation. That approach clutters the candidate's mind with nonessential information. A good manual must demonstrate the exercise of editorial selectivity. The authors should provide the candidate with only what he needs to know to pass the exam.

2. **Convenience.** A two-volume, 2,000 page, 8-1/2 x 11 manual weighs about 9-1/2 pounds. Carrying such a mass can be a nuisance. Portability is a consideration since a candidate will often want to study on the run (i.e., on the way to work, during lunch hour, or while away on business). A multivolume work can help overcome the problem of bulky materials.

3. **Coherence.** Coherence is a matter of parts relating smoothly to one another. In order to be coherent, a manual must be user-friendly. The internal structure of parts and chapters must be logically sequenced. Layout and typeface should enhance readability. Internal cross-references should be clear. The overall impression should be one of a unified whole rather than a fragmented assemblage of parts.

4. **Currency.** It is essential to use only up-to-date materials when preparing for the CPA exam. The AICPA Board of Examiners expects candidates to have a knowledge of ac-

counting and auditing pronouncements six months after a pronouncement's effective date unless early application is permitted, in which case candidates are responsible for knowledge of the new pronouncement six months after the date of issue. With respect to federal taxation, candidates are expected to be familiar with the Internal Revenue Code and Federal Tax Regulations in effect six months prior to the exam.

5. **Completeness.** A determination must be made of the extent to which the manual can stand alone as a self-sustaining review vehicle. Will additional books or tutoring be necessary? Obviously, a manual that purports to provide a complete review must contain more than outlines of pronouncements and past exam questions. It must also meet the candidate's need for developing examsmanship skills. It must help the candidate set up a carefully planned, intensive review program. It must provide the candidate with the confidence to pass.

Computer Software

Those who enjoy working with computers may find this type of study tool useful—particularly as a supplemental study aid.

Original Source Material

Another way to prepare for the CPA exam, of course, is to use neither a professional review course nor a review manual but, rather, to go directly to the source publications embodying the knowledge tested by the exam. Such an approach presupposes that the candidate (1) has unhampered access to those publications, and (2) has the necessary knowledge to select the right information for review.

If one were to assemble the published body of information tested by the AICPA, the following would be included:

1. Current textbooks for intermediate accounting, advanced accounting, auditing, cost accounting, managerial accounting, governmental and not-for-profit accounting, federal income taxes, and business law.
2. FASB and GASB pronouncements.
3. AICPA Statements on Auditing Standards.
4. AICPA publications such as *Code of Professional Conduct, Statements on Standards*

for Accounting and Review Services, Statements on Quality Control Standards, Statements on Standards for Attestation Engagements, Statements on Standards for Accountants' Services on Prospective Financial Statements, Standards for Consulting Services, Statements on Responsibilities in Tax Practice, Statements on Responsibilities in Personal Financial Planning Practice, and Industry Audit Guides.

5. A standard tax service.
6. U.S. General Accounting Office Government Auditing Standards
7. Federal statutes and uniform acts: Securities Act of 1933, Securities Exchange Act of 1934, Federal Bankruptcy Act, Uniform Commercial Code, Uniform Partnership Act, Uniform Limited Partnership Act, and Model Business Corporation Act.
8. AICPA *Questions and Unofficial Answers for the Uniform CPA Examination* for the most recently disclosed exams.

The sheer mass of paper represented by such a list is enough to frighten all but the most masochistic of candidates. After considering the cost of such publications and the long hours of solitary review ahead, the average, sensible candidate is likely to opt for a more efficient, less burdensome approach.

DEVELOP "EXAMSMANSHIP"

One of the things a quality review course does best is to teach examsmanship. "Examsmanship" can be defined as skillful test taking (i.e., the ability to deal effectively with a test situation and the demands of a particular test). Certain examsmanship skills are almost universal while others relate only to particular examinations. On the CPA exam, examsmanship consists of five elements:

1. Familiarity with exam format.
2. Anticipating exam content.
3. Dealing with the unexpected.
4. Budgeting time.
5. Working efficiently.

To become a successful candidate, it is not enough just to know accounting, auditing, taxes, or business law. You must also know how that material will be tested. You must be familiar with the format of the exam so that there are no surprises when you open your test booklet and survey the task in front of you. The questions that appear—at least in terms of format—should look like old friends that you have seen many times before during your review program.

The best way of developing a comfortable familiarity with exam format is through practice with past questions. After weeks of working through recent objective, essay, and computational questions, you develop a feel for their idiosyncrasies. Patterns of structure and style emerge. Narratives unfold in certain ways; requirements are set up in familiar patterns. As a candidate, although you're anxious about answering specific points of content, you're not distracted by format. You know what to expect.

The same type of assurance should exist when you contemplate the general content of the exam. Of course, the AICPA Content Specification Outlines go a long way toward telling you what to expect. It is your responsibility to familiarize yourself with the contents of these outlines, and to see to it that your final review program focuses on them—both in terms of overall content and of relative emphasis allotted to individual areas. As is the case with exam format, an ability to anticipate exam content distinguishes the successful candidates from the unsuccessful.

So much of examination success is dependent on psychological factors. The first thing a candidate usually does when he receives his examination booklet is to leaf through it quickly to see what his task will be—which topics appear, what the essay, computational, and other objective formats questions deal with, and so forth. The fewer surprises there are, the more confident the candidate will be. Obviously, the sort of familiarity and resulting confidence necessary for success is something that can be achieved by thorough preparation. There are enough obstacles to overcome in formulating answers to questions without the testing instrument itself being an impediment.

As with many situations in life, however, there will usually be one or two surprises in each of the examination sections: a topic appearing for the first time, a topic reappearing after an absence that suggested it was to be honored more in the breach than the observance, or an aspect of a topic heretofore not tested. The successful candidate will be able to deal with such surprises without falling to pieces. He may be taken aback momentarily. He may feel an unaccustomed twinge of anxiety, but it will pass and he will be able to get on with answering the question. Even if the question at hand deals with a topic unfamiliar to the candidate, he knows certain things:

1. If the topic is appearing for the first time on the CPA exam, the question is probably very easy. Closer analysis will reveal this.
2. If he is experiencing difficulty handling it, so are all of his fellow candidates.
3. His own instincts as a well-prepared candidate are probably his truest guide. He should resist the urge to second-guess himself.

The successful candidate under such circumstances remains cool and does not allow his concentration to be interrupted or his confidence shaken. Indeed, that is the *essence of examsmanship—the ability to deal with the pressures of the examination experience.*

TIME-SAVING TECHNIQUES ARE ESSENTIAL

A CPA candidate's biggest challenge, both before and during the CPA exam, is to use her time well. During the review period, procrastination will be a candidate's undoing. During the exam, an inability to establish a time budget for each question and stick to it at all costs will almost guarantee a return trip to next May or November's exam. An inability to work within the time constraints created by the exam ranks with poor reading ability, poor communication skills, and careless work habits as one of the primary reasons for failure.

The CPA exam is a very passable exam—but only for those who have done their homework. The candidate walking into the test site must know her information cold. She must be able to recall and apply it almost automatically. She must be like a highly complex, fine-tuned mechanism that can work through the exam with a minimum of wasted time or motion. A candidate who is well-prepared—both in terms of content review and examsmanship skills—should have no difficulty working within the time parameters of each question. The candidate who is not will find that even 15 and one-half hours for the entire exam is inadequate.

One of the best ways of developing time management skills is through practice with past questions. During the review program, the candidate should devote about half of her study effort to answering past questions. Such questions should be answered under simulated exam conditions. At the least, this means spending no more time with the question than would be available on the exam itself. The candidate will find, in the beginning at least, that budgeted time has expired before she has finished her answer. With practice, and by learning the test tactics in Chapter 5, she will be able to compose a point-winning answer within the time allotted.

Efficient use of time is a cornerstone of overall efficient work habits. The candidate must consciously learn systematic question answering techniques that, when combined with her knowledge of content, enable her to get the job done. Such talents will be a necessary part of her success as a CPA, so it is not inappropriate that they be requirements of the certification process.

Becoming a CPA *is* within the grasp of the average accounting graduate. As noted at the beginning of this chapter, most candidates do make it eventually. It's mainly a matter of making up their minds that they want it badly enough. The discouraging passing rates are more a function of poor preparation than they are of inherent difficulty. And therein lies the crucial point for candidates. The CPA exam requires study skills, test taking skills, and attributes of character that they have never had to practice before. If they are not up to it, they will fail until they are. Successful candidates are prepared, confident, self-disciplined, and motivated.

4. Review Examination Content

WHAT YOU SHOULD STUDY: A SUMMARY

The subject areas reviewed herein are those categorized in the AICPA *Content Specification Outlines for the Uniform Certified Public Accountant Examination*, which are presented in abridged form in Chapter 1. An indication of the relative weight given to each subject may be determined by examining the outline for each section.

Following is a review of the subject areas that are unique to each section. Note that the nature of the examination is such that the subject matter covered might appear in four-option multiple-choice questions, other objective formats questions, and essay or computational questions (none in the case of the ARE exam). In many instances, objective-type questions that require computations are smaller versions of computational-type questions, in that isolated computations are required.

Business Law and Professional Responsibilities (LPR): Subject Matter Covered

The LPR section tests an overview level of knowledge about selected areas of professional responsibilities and of law encountered in business situations. The emphasis is on testing a candidate's grasp of general concepts, legal principles, and ethical considerations. Candidates are not expected to be familiar with the practice of law, but rather with textbook information. They must demonstrate an ability to recall and apply such information to hypothetical situations contained in examination questions. Following are the areas tested. The candidate's background for these topics will usually come from a college-level course in business law. Certain topics, however, are not covered in a college course, or are covered too superficially, and therefore require extracurricular study.

RULES OF CONDUCT (SUMMARY OF AICPA CODE OF PROFESSIONAL CONDUCT)

Independence

Specific relationships prohibited:

Direct and certain indirect financial relationships with clients, officers, directors, or principal stockholders.

Relationships in which the CPA can be considered part of management.

Integrity and Objectivity

A member should not knowingly misrepresent facts or subordinate his judgment to others.

General Standards

The CPA should not undertake any engagement that he cannot reasonably expect to complete with professional competence. The CPA shall adequately plan, supervise, and exercise due professional care in the performance of professional services. He must obtain sufficient relevant data to afford a basis for conclusions or recommendations in relation to any services performed.

Compliance with Standards

A member who performs professional services must comply with the appropriate standards (GAAS, GAAP, etc.).

Confidential Client Information

A CPA should not disclose any confidential client information without the consent of the client, unless required to do so by law, or AICPA regulations.

Contingent Fees

A member in public practice should not, except for certain tax-related matters, perform professional services for a contingent fee.

Acts Discreditable

A CPA should not commit an act that is discreditable to the profession.

Advertising

A CPA may advertise as long as it is not done in a false, misleading, or deceptive manner.

Commissions and Referral Fees

A CPA may accept a commission for recommending or referring to a client a product or service if the CPA does not also perform certain attest services. In situations where commissions are permitted, disclosure to certain parties is required.

Form of Practice and Name

Public accounting may be practiced in a form of organization permitted by a state law or regulation (e.g., proprietorship, partnership, professional corporation, and, in most states, limited liability partnerships). Misleading names should not be used.

STANDARDS FOR CONSULTING SERVICES

Consulting services provided by CPAs have evolved from advice on accounting-related matters to a wide range of services involving technical disciplines, industry knowledge, and consulting skills.

Consulting services include consultations, advisory services, implementation services, transaction services, staff and other supporting services, and product services.

The practice standards to be followed consist of general standards (appropriate competence, due care, adequate planning and supervision, and gathering sufficient relevant data as a basis for conclusions or recommendations) and compliance standards (such as integrity and objectivity, and arriving at an understanding with the client about the engagement).

RESPONSIBILITIES IN TAX PRACTICE

The CPA should apply the same standards of professional conduct in performing tax work for a client as are applied in an audit and other professional activities. The CPA should not knowingly perform any act or prepare any return or related document that she has reason to believe is false or misleading or for which she does not have sufficient competence to handle.

RESPONSIBILITIES IN PERSONAL FINANCIAL PLANNING PRACTICE

Personal financial planning engagements involve developing strategies and making recommendations to assist a client in defining and achieving personal financial goals. In performing a personal financial planning engagement, the CPA should adhere to the AICPA Code of Professional Conduct (as it relates to integrity and objectivity), general standards, confidential client information, and contingent fees.

THE CPA AND THE LAW

The liability of the CPA to clients and third parties for breach of contract, negligence, and fraud is the basis for questions on this topic. The CPA is liable under both common law and statutory law. The candidate is expected to be familiar with relevant court decisions as well as with liability under federal securities statutes and the Internal Revenue Code. Also tested are concepts concerning work papers and accountant/client privilege.

AGENCY

Agency law deals with the rights and obligations that principals and agents have toward each other and toward third parties. Candidates are expected to know the nature of agency authority as well as the responsibilities of parties when an agency relationship is terminated. Particular attention is given to distinction between actual and apparent authority.

PARTNERSHIPS AND JOINT VENTURES

CPA exam questions test the major provisions of the Uniform Partnership Act and Uniform Limited Partnership Act. Candidates should be familiar with the rights, duties, and liabilities of partners during partnership operation, as well as allocation of profit or loss during partnership dissolution.

CORPORATIONS

The Model Business Corporation Act is the basis for CPA exam questions on this subject. Questions focus on the legal aspects of corporate stock, the fiduciary responsibility of corporate officers and directors, rights of shareholders, and federal income tax implications of the corporate form of business. The candidate must also be familiar with the legal implications of merger, consolidation, and dissolution.

ESTATES AND TRUSTS

Questions deal with the creation and administration of estates and trusts. This involves knowing the elements of valid trusts and the rules for allocation of trust principal and income. Further considerations involve fiduciary responsibilities as well as distributions and termination.

CONTRACTS

The primary focus of this fundamental topic is the enforceability of a contract as determined by the presence of certain requisite legal elements. In analyzing a question situation, the candidate must determine whether offer and acceptance have taken place; whether consent is mutual; whether subject matter is legal; whether the parties have capacity to contract, have given consideration, and have complied with the Statute of Frauds. Candidates must also be familiar with the rights of third parties, standards of performance, discharge of obligation, and remedies for breach.

SURETYSHIP AND CREDITOR'S RIGHTS

Suretyship and guarantee are based on common law and deal with promises of one party to be responsible for the debt of another. The candidate must know the rights of a surety upon default by the debtor and payment by the surety, including the computation of pro-rata share in a co-surety situation. He must also be familiar with the defenses a surety has against a creditor and certain exceptions to those defenses.

BANKRUPTCY

Questions are based on the Bankruptcy Reform Act of 1994. Candidates must be familiar with voluntary and involuntary petitions, management of a debtor's estate, voidable preferences, priority of claims, and discharge of debts. Also tested is an awareness of the general provisions governing corporate reorganizations. Questions often focus on the powers of trustees and priorities of claims in bankruptcy proceedings.

EMPLOYMENT REGULATIONS

Mastery of this subject is a matter of having a passing familiarity with the broad provisions of the Federal Insurance Contributions Act (social security), the Federal Unemployment Tax Act, employee safety laws including the various workers' compensation laws and the Federal Occupational and Safety Health Act (OSHA), wage and hour laws, and relevant employment discrimination laws. Question situations typically reflect the impact of these statutes on the employer/employee relationship.

FEDERAL SECURITIES ACTS

The Securities Act of 1933 and the Securities Exchange Act of 1934 are the two sources of questions on this topic. Candidates must know the 1933 Act provisions regarding registration, exemptions to registration, and parties' bases for liability. For the 1934 Act, they must know the periodic reporting and registration requirements. The 1934 Act's antifraud provisions are tested chiefly through their impact on CPAs associated with reports filed with the SEC.

COMMERCIAL PAPER

The candidate is tested on the major provisions of Articles 3 and 4 of the Uniform Commercial Code (UCC). Article 3 deals with the various types of commercial paper, the concept and requisites of negotiability, transfer of commercial paper, holders in due course, and liabilities of parties to commercial paper. Article 4 pertains to banking. The candidate is expected to be familiar with concepts relating to the bank/depositor and bank/third-party relationships.

The candidate is also expected to be somewhat familiar with two other types of negotiable instruments: documents of title and investment securities. Documents of title are governed by Article 7 of the UCC, and investment securities by Article 8. Both are similar in form and function to commercial paper instruments. An understanding of Article 3 will enable candidates to grasp concepts contained in Articles 7 and 8 very quickly.

SALES

This topic is concerned with Article 2 of the Uniform Commercial Code. Questions deal with modifications of common law contract rules governing contracts for the sale of goods. Additional Article 2 provisions concerning warranties, product liability rights of parties upon breach and passage of title, and risk of loss are also tested. A solid understanding of contract fundamentals will be most helpful here.

SECURED TRANSACTIONS

Secured transactions are governed by Article 9 of the Uniform Commercial Code. The candidate must be familiar with the characteristics of a secured credit sale and a secured loan transaction. Also required is knowledge of the mechanics and implications of attachment and perfection of security interest. Questions often deal with conflicting security interests and the rights of parties upon disposition of collateral.

PROPERTY

The primary focus of questions for this topic is on real property: types of ownership, transfer of real property, tenancies and leases, and mortgages. The candidate is expected to distinguish between realty and personalty, joint tenancy and tenancy in common, and reversionary and remainder interests. The liabilities associated with assuming a mortgage as opposed to purchasing subject to a mortgage, and the recording of deeds and mortgages are also tested. Questions also focus on bailments and types of ownership relating to personal property, as well as environmental liability.

INSURANCE

Fundamentals of fire and casualty insurance as they relate to business situations are tested for this topic. Familiarity with terminology is important as well as with concepts of insurable interest, multiple insurance coverage, and co-insurance. Frequent questions require the candidate to compute recovery in a partial loss situation using the co-insurance formula.

Auditing (AUDIT): Subject Matter Covered

Pronouncements issued by the American Institute of CPAs are tested extensively on the CPA examination. As such, this section has been prepared and organized to acquaint CPA candidates with those pronouncements that have particular applicability to the CPA exam.

The pronouncement summaries reflect the impact of any subsequent amendments and interpretations likely to be of significance to the CPA candidate. Pronouncements that have been omitted are either obsolete or not relevant for the CPA exam.

The abbreviated references to the pronouncements relevant to the Auditing exam are as follows:

FAS —Financial Accounting Standards Board Statement
SAS —Statement on Auditing Standards
SSAE —Statement on Standards for Attestation Engagements
SSARS —Statement on Standards for Accounting and Review Services

AUDITING PRONOUNCEMENTS

Generally Accepted Auditing Standards— Extracted from SAS #1

General Standards
1. Adequate technical training and proficiency.
2. Independence in mental attitude.
3. Due professional care in performance.

Fieldwork Standards
1. Adequately planned work and a properly supervised staff.
2. Sufficient understanding of internal control.
3. Gathering of sufficient competent evidential matter to form a basis for an opinion.

Reporting Standards

1. Use of generally accepted accounting principles.
2. Identify inconsistent application of such principles.
3. Informative disclosures.
4. Expression of an opinion on financial statements taken as a whole or an explanation as to why one cannot be given.

Audit Planning

1. **SAS #7—Communications Between Predecessor and Successor Auditors**

   This pronouncement provides guidance in obtaining information from the predecessor that will assist in determining whether to accept the engagement. The prospective client should be requested to authorize the predecessor to respond fully. Inquiries should be specific, and reasonable response should be prompt and full, subject to specific reasons for limiting the reply.

   This pronouncement is utilized after acceptance to facilitate the successor's procedures about matters that he believes may affect the audit. The client should be requested to authorize the predecessor to allow the review of working papers. If the successor comes to believe that financial statements prepared by the predecessor may require revisions, he should request that the client arrange a meeting among the three parties to discuss and attempt to resolve the matter.

2. **SAS #22—Planning and Supervision**

   The auditor should learn enough about the client's business to permit the planning and performance of the audit in accordance with GAAS. Planning should consider such things as business and industry background, accounting policies and procedures, and assessed level of control risk.

   Planning procedures should involve the auditor in such items as review of her work papers, discussions with other personnel of her firm, and discussions with client personnel. Efforts should culminate with the preparation of a written audit program.

   Supervision should include such matters as instructing assistants, keeping informed of significant problems in progress, and reviewing work performed.

3. **SAS #41—Working Papers**

   Working papers provide the main documentation supporting the auditor's report. They are the property of the auditor. They may take many different forms including written documents, tapes, and films.

4. **SAS #47—Audit Risk and Materiality in Conducting an Audit**

   Audit risk is the risk that the auditor may unknowingly fail to modify an opinion on financial statements that are materially misstated. The constituent parts of audit risk are inherent, control, and detection risks. Materiality, which relates to the financial importance of an item, is a matter of the auditor's professional judgment.

5. **SAS #56—Analytical Procedures**

   Analytical procedures involve the study and comparison of relationships among financial and nonfinancial data. These include such procedures as comparison of financial information with prior periods, budgets, and industry patterns. Analytical procedures should be used in the planning and overall review stages of the audit and may be used in substantive testing.

6. **SAS #65—The Auditor's Consideration of the Internal Audit Function in an Audit of Financial Statements**

   When an internal audit staff exists, the independent auditor must obtain an understanding of the internal audit function and decide if its activities are relevant to the audit. If the auditor decides that they are, and it is efficient to consider their work, then their competence and objectivity must be assessed. If the auditor concludes that they are competent and objective, then the effect and extent of their work on the audit must be considered, as well as evaluating and testing its effectiveness. The auditor may also use internal auditors to provide direct assistance during the audit.

7. **SAS #73—Using the Work of a Specialist**

   The work done by an outside specialist and the auditor's understanding of that work should be documented. The auditor should be able to understand the methods and assumptions used and should know whether the findings support the representations of the client.

Internal Control

1. **SAS #48—The Effects of Computer Processing on the Audit of Financial Statements**

   Classifying controls into general and application controls has no effect on the objectives of internal control, since assets still need to be safeguarded and financial records must be reliable for the preparation of financial statements.

   Computer processing characteristics that may be distinguished from manual processing relate to transactions trails, uniform processing of transactions, segregation of functions, potential for errors and fraud, potential for increased management supervision, and initiation or subsequent authorization of transactions.

2. **SAS #55—Consideration of Internal Control in a Financial Statement Audit**

   To properly plan an audit, the auditor should obtain sufficient knowledge of the entity's internal control. Internal control consists of five interrelated components: control environment, risk assessment, control activities, information and communication, and monitoring.

   a. *Control environment*—Sets the tone of the organization, influencing the control consciousness of its people. It is the foundation for all other components of internal control, providing discipline and structure.

   b. *Risk assessment*—The entity's risk assessment for financial reporting purposes is its identification, analysis, and management of risks relevant to the preparation of financial statements that are fairly presented.

   c. *Control activities*—The policies and procedures that help ensure that management directives are carried out. They help ensure that necessary actions are taken to address risks to the achievement of the entity's objectives. Control activities include: performance reviews, information processing, physical controls, and segregation of duties.

   d. *Information and communication*—Includes the information system relevant to financial reporting objectives. Communication involves providing an understanding of individual roles and responsibilities pertaining to internal control over financial reporting.

   e. *Monitoring*—Represents the process that assesses the quality of internal control performance over time.

The auditor will first obtain an understanding of internal control. Next, the auditor will assess control risk. If the auditor desires to seek a reduction in the assessed level of control risk below the maximum level, he will perform tests of controls. The auditor will use the knowledge obtained in the above steps to determine the nature, timing, and extent of substantive tests to be performed.

3. **SAS #60—Communication of Internal Control Related Matters Noted in an Audit**

   The independent auditor must communicate to the audit committee or the board of directors any reportable conditions in internal control the auditor discovers while performing an audit under GAAS. While a written report is preferable, an oral report documented in the audit work papers is also acceptable.

4. **SAS #61—Communication with Audit Committees**

   Requires the auditor to determine that certain significant items related to the conduct of the audit are communicated to the audit committee. The communication can be made orally or in writing.

5. **SAS #70—Reports on the Processing of Transactions by Service Organizations**

   If an entity uses services of other organizations to process significant transactions (e.g., EDP service centers) or to handle significant assets or liabilities (e.g., bank trust departments), the internal control of the service organization may be considered part of the user organization's internal control and thus be subject to audit planning and control risk assessment considerations by the user organization auditor.

   The user organization auditor should consider obtaining, from the service organization auditor, a report on controls placed in operation at the service organization and related tests of operating effectiveness.

6. **SSAE #2—Reporting on an Entity's Internal Control Over Financial Reporting**
   The purpose and scope of an engagement to examine and report on management's written assertion about the effectiveness of an entity's internal control over financial reporting are different from the purpose and scope of the auditor's consideration of internal control during an audit of financial statements. The content of the report would include an appropriate title, identification of the assertion in an introductory paragraph, a scope paragraph, a paragraph referring to inherent limitations and, in a final paragraph, an opinion as to whether management's assertion is fairly stated in all material respects, based upon stated or established criteria.

Audit Evidence and Procedures

1. **SAS #12—Inquiry of a Client's Lawyer Concerning Litigation, Claims, and Assessments**
   Matters that should be covered in an audit inquiry letter include a description and evaluation of pending or threatened litigation, unasserted claims, and so on, for which the lawyer has been engaged and a request submitted for the lawyer's comment on those matters with which the auditor differs with management.
   The lawyer's response may be limited to matters to which he has given substantial attention and/or matters that he considered material. The lawyer's refusal to furnish the information requested is a limitation of the scope of the audit precluding an unqualified opinion.

2. **SAS #19—Client Representations**
   The auditor must obtain certain written representations from management as part of an audit under GAAS. These representations include such matters as management's responsibility for fair presentation of financial statements, availability and completeness of records, and subsequent events.

3. **SAS #31—Evidential Matter**
   Evidence gathered should form an internally consistent pattern. It should be competent and sufficient. Competence is determined by validity and relevance, with the greatest assurance coming from evidence obtained in an environment with good internal control and from independent external sources. Regarding sufficiency, the auditor must judge the relative risk and the relationship between the cost of obtaining evidence and its usefulness.

4. **SAS #39—Audit Sampling**
   Sampling may be performed either through the use of nonstatistical or statistical methodology. Statistical sampling involves the sampling risk that the sample chosen may not be representative of the population. It also requires the establishment of a tolerable misstatement and rate under which deviation may exist without causing material misstatement of financial statements. In general, statistical sampling allows for (a) design of an efficient sample, (b) measurement of the sufficiency of evidential matter, and (c) objective evaluation of sample results.
   Sampling may be used for both tests of controls and substantive testing. However, in the former, it should not be used for procedures that depend primarily on segregation of duties for effectiveness. In the latter, the more reliable the internal control, the smaller the sample required, but critical items should be examined in full (100 percent) and not sampled.

5. **Extracted from SAS #45 and FAS #57—Related-Party Transactions**
   A related party is any one with which the reporting entity may deal when one party directly or indirectly has the ability to significantly influence the management or operating policies of the other, to the extent that one of the parties might be prevented from fully pursuing its own separate interest. Examples that may indicate related-party matters are such things as interest-free or low-rate loans, real estate sold well below appraised value, and so on.
   The auditor should review for the presence of an environment that might motivate related-party transactions (e.g., insuf-

ficient working capital or credit). He should evaluate the client's procedures for identifying and accounting for related-party transactions.

6. **SAS #54—Illegal Acts by Clients**
Illegal acts refer to violations of laws or governmental regulations. The auditor's responsibility to detect and report misstatements resulting from illegal acts having a direct and material effect on the financial statements is the same as that for material errors and fraud, as described in SAS #82. The auditor should also be aware of the possibility of illegal acts having an indirect financial statement effect.

When the auditor becomes aware of information about a possible illegal act, the auditor should inquire of management at a level above those involved. If the auditor concludes that an illegal act has or is likely to have occurred, the audit committee should be informed.

The auditor should express a qualified or adverse opinion if an illegal act having a material effect on the financial statements has not been accounted for or disclosed, and disclaim an opinion if he is precluded by the client from obtaining the evidential matter needed to determine whether such an act has occurred. If the client refuses to accept the modified report, the auditor should withdraw from the engagement.

7. **SAS #57—Auditing Accounting Estimates**
The auditor is responsible for evaluating the reasonableness of accounting estimates. When evaluating such estimates, the auditor should obtain sufficient evidential matter to provide reasonable assurance that all estimates that could be material have been developed, are reasonable, are presented in conformity with GAAP, and are properly disclosed.

8. **SAS #59—The Auditor's Consideration of an Entity's Ability to Continue as a Going Concern (as amended)**
The auditor must consider if there is substantial doubt about an entity's ability to continue as a going concern for a reasonable period of time. In making the evaluation, the auditor considers certain nega-

tive conditions and events, and the mitigating plans of management. If the auditor concludes that substantial doubt remains, the unqualified auditor's report will include an explanatory paragraph.

9. **SAS #67—The Confirmation Process**
Confirmation of accounts receivable is considered to be a generally accepted auditing procedure. The auditor should consider whether the positive or negative form of confirmations should be utilized. Throughout the confirmation process, the auditor should adopt an attitude of professional skepticism.

10. **SAS #81—Auditing Investments**
The procedures the auditor performs vary depending on the type of investments involved and the auditor's assessment of audit risk. However, in gaining audit satisfaction about the existence, ownership, and completeness of investments, the procedures should include one or more of the following: physical inspection, confirmation with the issuer, confirmation with the custodian, confirmation of unsettled transactions with the broker-dealer, confirmation with the counterparty, and reading executed partnership and other similar agreements. Further, the auditor should ascertain whether the entity's accounting policies for investments are in conformity with GAAP.

11. **SAS #82—Consideration of Fraud in a Financial Statement Audit**
This statement requires the auditor to obtain reasonable assurance that material misstatements in the financial statements, including those arising from fraud, are detected.

The primary factor that distinguishes fraud from error is whether the underlying action that results in the misstatement in financial statements is intentional or unintentional. Errors refer to unintentional misstatements or omissions of amounts or disclosures in financial statements, including mistakes, incorrect accounting estimates, and misinterpretations.

Two types of misstatements are relevant to an auditor's consideration of fraud in a financial statement audit: misstatements arising from fraudulent financial reporting and misstatements arising from misappropriation of assets.

The statement also identifies factors to be considered in assessing the risk of material misstatement arising from the two types of fraud. The auditor's response to the assessment of the risk of material misstatement due to fraud may involve an overall response, a specific response, or both.

If an auditor determines that there is evidence of fraud, that matter (even if considered inconsequential) should be brought to the attention of an appropriate level of management. Fraud involving senior management, and fraud (whether caused by senior management or other employees) that causes the financial statements to be materially misstated, should be reported directly to the audit committee.

Reporting Standards and Types of Reports

1. **SAS #32—Adequacy of Disclosure in Financial Statements**

   The auditor should express a qualified or adverse opinion if management omits information from financial statements that is required by GAAP. If practicable, the information should be provided in the auditor's report.

2. **SAS #58—Reports on Audited Financial Statements (as amended)**

   The standard report consists of an introductory paragraph, a scope paragraph, and an opinion paragraph. These may be modified, depending upon the nature of the opinion.

   The following opinions may be rendered:

   a. *Unqualified*—Financial statements are presented fairly, in conformity with GAAP. May under certain circumstances include an explanatory paragraph.

   b. *Qualified*—Adds an explanatory paragraph and, in the opinion paragraph, states "except for [insufficient evidence, scope restrictions, departure from GAAP], the financial statements are presented fairly."

   c. *Adverse*—The financial statements are not presented fairly, in conformity with GAAP; a separate paragraph discloses reasons and principal effects.

   d. *Disclaimer*—No opinion expressed; a separate paragraph states why.

   A continuing auditor should update her report on prior periods presented on a comparative basis with the current period.

   The auditor should disclose all the substantive reasons for a changed opinion, using a separate explanatory paragraph. She may modify or disclaim an opinion for one period while expressing an unqualified opinion on financial statements of another period presented.

   A predecessor auditor may reissue her report for a prior period at the client's request if she performs certain additional procedures, such as obtaining a letter from the successor auditor stating whether the successor's audit revealed any matters that might affect the predecessor auditor's report. If the successor's audit did, the predecessor must perform other needed procedures. The reissued report bears the date of the previous report; if the report is revised, she should dual-date it.

   A successor auditor, when not presenting the predecessor's audit report, should include in the introductory paragraph the fact that another auditor audited that period, giving the type of opinion and reasons if other than an unqualified opinion.

   For unaudited reports, pages must be clearly marked "unaudited" and be accompanied by a disclaimer of opinion.

3. **SAS #62—Special Reports**

   a. *Financial statements not using GAAP*

   Such statements must offer a comprehensive basis of accounting other than GAAP such as that used to comply with requirements of a government agency, or cash, or modified cash basis. The auditor's report should contain a title that includes the word *independent* and the following paragraphs: (1) financial statements were audited and are the responsibility of management, (2) audit was conducted in accordance with GAAS, (3) the basis of presentation, and (4) either an expression or disclaimer of an opinion on the presentation in conformity with the accounting basis described.

b. *Reports expressing an opinion on elements of financial statements*
GAAP does not have to apply. The auditor's report should contain a title that includes the word *independent* and the following paragraphs: (1) the specific elements were audited and are the responsibility of management; (2) the audit was conducted in accordance with GAAS; (3) the basis on which the items are presented; and (4) either an expression or disclaimer of opinion in conformity with the basis of accounting described.

c. *Reports on compliance with agreements/regulations*
The auditor can provide negative assurance relating to applicable covenants of an agreement, provided the auditor has audited the financial statements to which they relate. The assurance can be given in the auditor's report accompanying the financial statements or given separately.

d. *Reports in prescribed form*
When a printed form requires an auditor's assertion the auditor believes is not justified, he should reword it or attach a separate report.

4. **SAS #74—Compliance Auditing Considerations in Audits of Governmental Entities and Recipients of Governmental Financial Assistance**
The SAS applies when the auditor is engaged to audit governmental entities under GAAS and engaged to test and report on compliance with laws and regulations under "Government Auditing Standards" (referred to as the "Yellow Book"). The auditor should be concerned with the effects of laws and regulations that have a direct and material effect on the entity's financial statements. As part of an audit of a governmental entity, an auditor is required to issue a report on the consideration of internal control. Further, the auditor is required to determine and report on whether the federal financial assistance has been administered in accordance with applicable laws and regulations.

5. **SAS #69—The Meaning of "Present Fairly in Conformity with Generally Accepted Accounting Principles" in the Independent Auditor's Report**
Fairness requires presentation under GAAP; conformity with GAAP requires general acceptance of principles applied that reflect the substance of transactions and offer informative, classified financial statements within limits that are reasonable.

6. **SAS #71—Interim Financial Information**
The objective of a review of interim financial information is to provide the accountant, through inquiries and analytical procedures, with a basis for reporting whether material modifications should be made for such information to conform to GAAP. Procedures include inquiries, analyses, reviews, and obtaining written representations from management. To perform a review of interim financial information, sufficient knowledge of the client's internal control as it relates to both annual and interim financial information is also needed.

If the accountant believes that financial information is misstated as a result of a GAAP departure, and certain conditions are met, the matter should be discussed with the appropriate level of management and, if management does not appropriately respond, with the audit committee. If the audit committee does not respond within a reasonable time, the accountant may consider withdrawing.

The accountant's report, among other things, indicates that a review is not an audit; gives any material modifications required under GAAP; and states that, subject to exceptions noted, the reviewer is not aware of any modifications to make the statements conform to GAAP. Each page of information must bear the "unaudited" label.

7. **SSARS #1—Compilation and Review of Financial Statements (as amended)**
This pronouncement relates to unaudited statements of nonpublic entities. A "compilation" pertains to preparation of financial statements from management-supplied data, without the expression of

any assurance concerning them. A "review" involves inquiry and analytical procedures to provide a basis for expressing limited assurance that the financial statements conform to GAAP or another comprehensive accounting basis.

The report accompanying a compilation, among other matters, identifies the performance of a compilation in accordance with Statements on Standards for Accounting and Review Services issued by the AICPA, and is limited to statement preparation, with no audit or review involved. Each page of the compiled financial statements should be marked "See Accountant's Compilation Report."

The report accompanying a review, among other matters, identifies the performance of a review in accordance with Statements on Standards for Accounting and Review Services issued by the AICPA and what it is and is not, and states that subject to exceptions noted, the accountant is not aware of any material modifications to make the financial statements conform to GAAP. Each page of the financial statements should be marked "See Accountant's Review Report." An accountant who is not independent cannot issue a review report.

8. **SSARS #2—Reporting on Comparative Financial Statements**
If the same level of service (e.g., compilation in both periods) is used for each period, utilize the SSARS #1 type of accountant's report. If the level of service is stepped up or down, then the report must be modified following specific guidelines.

In the case of a predecessor's report, the predecessor is not required to reissue her report but may do so at the client's request. When reissuing, the previous report date is used unless a revision is made. Then, a dual-dated report for the revised aspect is used.

9. **SSARS #3—Compilation Reports on Financial Statements Included in Certain Prescribed Forms**
The compilation report, among other things, should identify the statements and that they have been compiled. No audit or review was performed and no opinion or

other form of assurance is expressed. The presentation differs from GAAP but conforms to the prescribed form.

10. **SSARS #4—Communication Between Predecessor and Successor Accountants**
A successor may, but is not required to, communicate with a predecessor about acceptance of a compilation or review engagement. The client should be requested to permit the successor to inquire and to authorize the predecessor to respond. The predecessor should respond promptly and fully unless, because of circumstances, he must place limits on such response.

11. **SSARS #6—Reporting on Personal Financial Statements Included in Written Personal Financial Plans**
This statement provides that under certain conditions, the accountant may submit a written personal financial plan containing unaudited personal financial statements without complying with the requirements of SSARS #1.

Other Reporting Considerations

1. **Extracted from SAS #1—Subsequent Events**
Subsequent events are those that have a material effect and occur after the balance sheet date but before the issuance of financial statements and the auditor's report. One type provides additional information about conditions that actually existed at the balance sheet date; this type requires adjustment of the financial statements. A second type provides information about conditions that did not exist at the balance sheet date but arose thereafter; here, financial statements should not be adjusted but disclosure may be required.

2. **Extracted from SAS #1—Subsequent Discovery of Facts**
Subsequent discovery of facts arises when the auditor becomes aware of facts that may have existed at the date of the report that might have affected it had she been aware of them. The auditor must undertake to determine reliability of the facts and their existence at the date of the auditor's report. Action must be taken if the audit report would have been affected had

the auditor known of the facts at the date of the report and if it is believed persons in possession of the financial statements would attach importance to the facts.

3. **SAS #8—Other Information in Documents Containing Audited Financial Statements**
The auditor has no obligation to corroborate other information contained in the document. However, the auditor should read it and judge whether it is materially inconsistent with the financial statements. If it is inconsistent, revision must take place.

4. **SAS #21—Segment Information**
The auditor is not required to apply special audit procedures or express a separate opinion on segment information. The auditor should, however, evaluate and test the methods of determining segment information. If the segment information is not disclosed, the auditor is not required to provide it, but he should comment on its absence.

5. **SAS #26—Association with Financial Statements**
The accountant's association arises when (a) he consents to the use of his name in a written communication containing audited or unaudited financial statements, or (b) the auditor has prepared or assisted in the preparation of such statements even though his name does not appear.
A disclaimer on unaudited statements should be issued indicating that no audit has been made and no opinion is expressed. Each page of the financial statements should be marked "unaudited."
If the information is presented in a document containing financial statements of a public entity that have not been audited or reviewed, the accountant's name should be excluded or the statements marked "unaudited," and a notation included that the accountant expressed no opinion on them.

6. **SAS #29—Reporting on Information Accompanying the Basic Financial Statements in Auditor-Submitted Documents**
When the auditor submits to a client a document containing financial statements

and other information, she must report on all of the client representations in that document (e.g., schedules, summaries, etc.).

7. **SAS #37—Filings Under the Federal Securities Statutes**
The accountant's responsibility is that of an expert when his report is included in a registration statement and his standard of reasonableness therefor is "that required of a prudent person in the management of his or her own property."
In connection with a prospectus, the accountant should not allow his name to be used in any way to indicate greater responsibility than he intends to undertake.

8. **SAS #42—Reporting on Condensed Financial Statements and Selected Financial Data**
Condensed financial statements should be so marked but do not constitute fair presentation under GAAP. The auditor's report, among other things, should state whether they are fairly stated in relation to the complete statements. The naming of the auditor in a client-prepared document does not, in itself, require the auditor to report on condensed statements, provided these statements are included with audited statements or are incorporated by reference.
Entity management determines the specific selected financial data to be presented. The auditor, in reporting, should limit the report to data derived from audited statements.

9. **SAS #46—Consideration of Omitted Procedures After the Report Date**
If the auditor concludes, subsequent to the audit report date, that she omitted one or more audit procedures, the auditor must determine if the omission impairs the present ability to support the original opinion. If necessary, the CPA should arrange either to apply the omitted procedures or to apply alternate ones.

10. **SAS #50—Reports on the Application of Accounting Principles**
When an accountant (i.e., reporting accountant) is asked to evaluate accounting principles or is requested to render an opinion on the application of accounting

principles by an entity that is audited by another CPA (i.e., continuing accountant), the reporting accountant, after accepting the engagement, should consult with the continuing accountant to ascertain all the available facts relevant to forming a professional judgment.

11. **SAS #52—Required Supplementary Information**

If supplementary information is required by the FASB or the GASB, it is not a required part of the basic financial statements and is not audited. The auditor need not refer in the report to the supplementary information or the limited procedures unless (a) the information is omitted, (b) it departs from guidelines, or (c) prescribed audit procedures cannot be accomplished. If supplementary information is omitted, the auditor need not present it.

12. **SAS #72—Letters for Underwriters and Other Requesting Parties**

The types of services that CPAs perform include examination of financial statements and schedules included in registration statements filed with the SEC. As such, CPAs confer with various parties with respect to certain aspects of the Securities Act of 1933, and of the SEC, as well as perform other services. Issuance of letters for underwriters (comfort letters) is one of them.

A typical letter includes, among other things, (a) a statement regarding the independence of the accountants; (b) an opinion regarding the audited financial statements and schedules included in the registration statement, and whether they are in compliance in all material respects with the applicable requirements of the 1933 Act and related published rules and regulations; (c) negative assurance with respect to unaudited condensed interim financial statements, and changes in certain account balances during a specified period.

13. **SAS #75—Engagements to Apply Agreed-Upon Procedures to Specified Elements, Accounts, or Items of a Financial Statement**

An accountant may accept an engagement to apply agreed-upon procedures to specified elements, accounts, or items of a financial statement. In this engagement, the accountant does not express an opinion or negative assurance; rather, the report should be in the form of procedures or findings.

14. **Statement on Standards for Accountants' Services on Prospective Financial Information**

A CPA may compile, examine, or apply agreed-upon procedures to prospective financial statements (i.e., financial forecasts and financial projections).

A financial forecast is an entity's expected financial position, results of operations, and changes in cash flows, based on assumptions reflecting conditions expected to exist and the course of action expected to be taken. A financial projection, however, is based on one or more hypothetical assumptions that are not necessarily expected to occur.

15. **SSAE #1—Statement on Standards for Attestation Engagements**

Attestation engagements involve the issuance of a written communication containing the expression of a conclusion as to the reliability of a written assertion (e.g., the investment performance of a mutual fund) that is the responsibility of another party. A CPA may examine, review, or apply agreed-upon procedures to an assertion.

16. **SSAE #3—Compliance Attestation**

A practitioner may accept an engagement to examine or apply agreed-upon procedures to management's assertion about (a) compliance with requirements of specified laws, regulations, rules, contracts, or grants (referred to as compliance with specified requirements) and (b) the effectiveness of an entity's internal control over compliance with specified requirements (referred to as internal control over compliance).

An examination engagement leads to the expression of an opinion about whether management's assertion is fairly stated in all material respects based on established or agreed-upon criteria.

The objective of an agreed-upon procedures engagement is to present specific findings about an entity's compliance with specified requirements or about the effectiveness of an entity's internal control over compliance based on procedures agreed upon by the users of the report; no opinion or negative assurance is provided about whether the assertion is presented fairly.

17. **SSAE #4—Agreed-Upon Procedures Engagements**

    A practitioner may accept an agreed-upon procedures attestation engagement. The report issued in connection with such an engagement may not include negative assurance; rather, the report should be in the form of procedures and findings. The report should clearly indicate that its use is restricted to the specified users.

U.S. GENERAL ACCOUNTING OFFICE GOVERNMENT AUDITING STANDARDS

General Standards

1. *Qualifications*—Adequate professional proficiency for the tasks required.
2. *Independence*—Free from personal and external impairments to independence, organizationally independent, and maintain an independent attitude and appearance.
3. *Due professional care* should be exercised in conducting the audit and in preparing related reports.
4. *Quality control*—Have an internal quality control system and an external quality control review program.

Fieldwork Standards for Financial Audits

1. Generally Accepted Government Auditing Standards (GAGAS) incorporate GAAS standards of fieldwork for financial audits and prescribe additional standards for the unique needs of governmental financial audits.
2. Additional fieldwork standards
   a. Follow up on known material findings and recommendations from previous audits.
   b. Design the audit to provide reasonable assurance of detecting material misstatements resulting from noncompli-

ance with provisions of contracts or grant agreements that have a direct and material effect on the determination of financial statement amounts.
   c. Working papers should contain sufficient information to support the auditor's significant conclusions and judgments, including:
      (1) The objectives, scope, and methodology, including any sampling criteria used.
      (2) Documentation of the work performed to support significant conclusions and judgments, including descriptions of transactions and records examined that would enable an experienced auditor to examine the same transactions and records.
      (3) Evidence of supervisory reviews of the work performed.

Reporting Standards for Financial Audits

1. GAGAS incorporates the GAAS standards of reporting for financial statement audits and the related statements on auditing standards that interpret the reporting standards.
2. GAGAS prescribes additional standards of reporting needed to satisfy the unique needs of governmental financial audits.
3. Additional reporting standards
   a. Communicate the following information to the audit committee or to the individuals with whom they contracted for the audit.
      (1) The auditor's responsibilities in a financial statement audit, including responsibilities for testing and reporting on internal controls and compliance with laws and regulations.
      (2) The nature of any additional testing of internal controls and compliance required by laws and regulations.
   b. State that the audit was made in accordance with generally accepted government auditing standards.
   c. Either (1) describe the scope of the auditor's testing of compliance with laws and regulations and internal controls,

and present the results of those tests, or (2) refer to separate reports containing that information.

d. If certain information is prohibited from general disclosure, the audit report should state the nature of the information omitted and the requirement that makes the omission necessary.

e. Submit written audit reports to the appropriate officials both inside and outside the audited organization. Unless restricted by law or regulation, copies should be made available for public inspection.

Accounting & Reporting— Taxation, Managerial, and Governmental and Not-for-Profit Organizations (ARE): Subject Matter Covered

FEDERAL INCOME TAXATION

Material dealing with federal income taxation does not require extensive arithmetic computations.

There are many specific areas relative to federal taxation that appear on the examination. An overview of these may be seen in the "Content Specification Outline" (pages 2–9).

In general terms, exam coverage focuses on the taxation of individuals, corporations, partnerships, estates and trusts, and exempt organizations. The material tested has not significantly emphasized the calculation of tax liability and/or tax credits.

For the past several years, there has been great frequency of change in the Internal Revenue Code. Candidates are responsible for knowledge of the Internal Revenue Code and Tax Regulations in effect six months before the examination date.

The major considerations in this area are:

1. An awareness of basic gross income inclusions for individual taxpayers, including business income, interest, rents and royalties, dividends, and capital gains and losses.
2. An awareness of exclusions and adjustments in arriving at adjusted gross income of individuals.
3. An awareness of the determination of capital gains and losses, including the recognition of gains and losses and holding period.
4. An awareness of itemized deductions for individuals, including interest, taxes, contributions, medical expenses, casualty losses, and miscellaneous deductions.
5. An awareness of filing status and exemptions for individuals.
6. An awareness of tax accounting methods, tax computations, penalties, and other administrative tax procedures applicable to individuals.
7. An awareness of the determination of taxable income or loss for corporations.
8. An awareness of special considerations for corporations, including background on incorporation, S corporations, personal holding companies, consolidated returns, distributions to stockholders, and the area of reorganization and liquidation.
9. An awareness of tax accounting methods, tax computations, penalties, and other administrative tax procedures applicable to corporations.
10. An awareness of the background of partnership taxation, including the formation of a partnership, the basis of a partner's interest and how it is determined, the basis of property contributed to a partnership, the determination of a partner's taxable income, transactions between a partner and the partnership, the distribution of partnership assets, and the termination of a partnership.
11. An awareness of relevant tax credits with respect to all types of taxpayers.
12. An awareness of the broad aspects of exempt organizations, including types of organizations, requirements for exemption, and the tax on unrelated business income.
13. An awareness of the broad aspects relative to the taxation of estates and trusts, including gift taxation.
14. An awareness of preparers' responsibilities applicable to tax returns of individuals and corporations.

Note: The candidate should realize that due to the very nature of the subject, examination questions in this area can occasionally be very specific and narrow. It is the authors' belief that a more meaningful method of testing candidates in this area must evolve; indeed, open-book examinations would be appropriate. The type of material appearing on examination questions over the past several years does not seem to mesh with the profile of the CPA candidate as an entry-level accountant. However, it is probable that all candidates taking the examination face the same problem, and it must be assumed that this is taken into consideration during the grading process.

Managerial Accounting

As indicated in the "Content Specification Outline" (pages 2–9), this is a rather broad subject area that encompasses a number of subtopics.

The subject area includes material on *quantitative techniques*, which are highly mathematically oriented. However, on balance, exam coverage of such material over the past decade has not been extremely deep in concept, difficult in application, or regular in appearance.

The major considerations in this area are:

1. An awareness of the various elements that enter into the components of a product (i.e., material, labor, and overhead—both actual and applied).
2. An awareness of the various cost accounting methods and systems, with particular emphasis on job order costing, process costing, standard costing, joint and by-product costing.
3. An awareness of the various techniques for planning and control, including budgeting, breakeven and cost-volume-profit analysis, capital budgeting techniques, and other quantitative techniques.
4. An awareness of analytical methods and procedures including, but not limited to, regression and correlation analysis, probability analysis, and ratio analysis.
5. The ability to make the calculations and computations that are essential to this subject area. Included in this category are items such as the determination of equivalent units of production in process costing, variance analysis in standard costing, and the allocation of costs in joint costing.

The background for this area is provided by a college-level course in cost accounting or its equivalent.

Accounting for Governmental and Not-for-Profit Organizations

This subject area requires familiarity with *fund accounting, types of funds and account groups, types of not-for-profit and governmental organizations, and the presentation of financial statements for various not-for-profit and governmental organizations.*

The major considerations in this area are:

1. Knowledge of the essentials of fund accounting and the nuances that make it unique, as well as such conceptual reporting issues as the budgetary process and differing bases of accounting.
2. Knowledge of the types of funds and the rationale for establishing each fund.
3. An awareness of the various types of not-for-profit and governmental organizations.
4. While the ARE exam does not require the preparation of journal entries and financial statements for various types of government and not-for-profit entities, it is essential to have an understanding of the underlying logic and terminology.

The background for this area is provided in either a special college-level course or in a course in advanced accounting that includes these topics.

OFFICIAL ACCOUNTING PRONOUNCEMENTS

While professional pronouncements issued by the Financial Accounting Standards Board are tested extensively on the FARE section of the exam, the following Financial Accounting Standards Board Statements are relevant to the topic of accounting for not-for-profit organizations (other than governmental units) tested on the ARE exam:

1. **FAS #93—Recognition of Depreciation by Not-for-Profit Organizations**
   Depreciation must be recognized as an expense by all not-for-profit organizations other than governmental units. (It should also be noted that proprietary funds and nonexpendable trust funds of governmental units will recognize depreciation as an expense.)
   Collections (works of art and similar items) are likely to have estimated useful lives that are extraordinarily long. Accordingly, depreciation of these items is generally not recognized.

2. **FAS #116—Accounting for Contributions Received and Contributions Made**

In general, all unconditional contributions of assets, services, or liability reductions should be recorded at fair market value on the date of receipt. Further, revenue, gain, or support received should be recorded.

3. **FAS #117—Financial Statements of Not-for-Profit Organizations**

This statement establishes standards for general-purpose external financial statements. All not-for-profit organizations are required to present a statement of financial position, a statement of activities, and a statement of cash flows:

a. The statement of financial position requires reporting of total amounts for assets (which are presented in the order of relative liquidity, or by classifying them as current or noncurrent), liabilities (which are presented according to their nearness to maturity or use of cash, or by classifying them as current or noncurrent), and net assets or equity (classified as unrestricted, temporarily restricted, or permanently restricted). Display of funds is not required.

b. The statement of activities is required to report the totals, and the amounts of changes in, the permanently, temporarily restricted, and unrestricted net assets for the period. In general, reporting of gross revenues and expenses is required.

c. The statement of cash flows will generally be prepared in accordance with FAS #95, "Statement of Cash Flows." It should be noted that changes in terminology may be necessary. For example, "changes in net assets" and "statement of activities" are used in place of "net income" and "income statement," respectively.

4. **FAS #24—Accounting for Certain Investments Held by Not-for-Profit Organizations**

This statement establishes standards for accounting for certain investments held by not-for-profit organizations. It requires that investments in equity securities with readily determinable fair values and all investments in debt securities be reported at fair value with gains and losses included in a statement of activities.

Note: While the Governmental Accounting Standards Board issues pronouncements relative to governmental accounting, no summaries are contained herein since none to date have had any significant impact on the CPA examination.

Financial Accounting & Reporting—Business Enterprises (FARE): Subject Matter Covered

Concepts, Standards, and Financial Statements

Questions in this subject area include:

1. Definitions of accounting terms and objectives of financial statement presentation and disclosure.
2. Review of environmental factors behind generally accepted accounting concepts.
3. Explanation of drawbacks and/or seeming contradictions between or among two or more concepts, principles, or methods.
4. Defending or explaining theoretical positions that are and are not generally accepted.
5. Problem situations presented in which the proper concepts, principles, or methods must be applied and defended.

The background for this area is provided by college-level courses in intermediate and advanced financial accounting.

Recognition, Measurement, Valuation, and Presentation of Assets in Conformity with Generally Accepted Accounting Principles

In this subject area, the candidate must be familiar with *cash, accounts and notes receivable, marketable securities and investments, accruals, inventories, property, plant and equipment, capitalized lease assets, intangibles,* and *prepaid expenses and deferred charges.*

The major considerations in this area include:

1. An awareness of professional pronouncements relative to such matters as investments in debt and equity securities, lease transactions, capitalization of interest, property, plant and equipment, depreciation and intangible assets.

2. The ability to prepare appropriate schedules and computations relative to the assets involved, including schedules of inventories, presentation of investments in the balance sheet, and so forth.
3. The ability to determine allowance items for such assets as accounts receivable, property, plant and equipment, and intangible assets, along with the related expense charges.
4. An awareness of inventory methods of all types, including the retail inventory method and dollar-value LIFO techniques.
5. An awareness of the application of lower-of-cost-or-market techniques.

The candidate's background for this area will come from college-level courses in elementary and intermediate accounting or their equivalents.

Recognition, Measurement, Valuation, and Presentation of Liabilities in Conformity with Generally Accepted Accounting Principles

This subject area requires familiarity with *payables and accruals, deferred revenue, deferred income tax liabilities, capitalized lease liability, bonds payable, long-term notes payable*, and *contingent liabilities and commitments*.

The major considerations in this area are

1. An awareness of professional pronouncements relative to such matters as accounting for income taxes (but not federal income taxes *per se*), lease transactions, accounting for transactions in bonds, contingent liabilities, and accounting for pension costs.
2. The ability to prepare appropriate schedules and computations, including determination of capitalized leases, guarantees and warranties, and the book (carrying) value of bonds outstanding.
3. The ability to determine expense charges associated with these liabilities.
4. An awareness of the types of temporary and permanent differences with respect to accounting for income taxes.
5. An awareness of different methods for amortizing bond discount or premium, with particular emphasis on the "effective interest" method.

A candidate's preparation in intermediate accounting or its equivalent will provide the necessary background.

Recognition, Measurement, Valuation, and Presentation of Equity Accounts in Conformity with Generally Accepted Accounting Principles

Subjects that will be tested in this area include *preferred and common stock, additional paid-in capital, retained earnings and dividends, treasury stock and other contra accounts, stock options, warrants and rights, change in entity,* as well as *partnerships and proprietorships.*

The major considerations in this area are

1. An awareness of the appropriate accounting treatment of various classes of capital stock, including the issuance and retirement of stock and the determination of book value per share.
2. An awareness of the various elements of additional paid-in capital.
3. An awareness of retained earnings, including prior-period adjustments and dividend payments of various types.
4. An awareness of accounting for treasury stock based on the par value and cost methods.
5. An awareness of the treatment of stock options, warrants, and rights.
6. An awareness of quasi-reorganization and changes in entity.
7. An awareness of accounting for partnerships, including admission of partners, withdrawal of partners, dissolution, and liquidation.

This particular subject area is one in which the ability to make computations is not an overwhelming concern.

The background for this area is provided in college-level courses in intermediate accounting and advanced accounting or their equivalents.

Recognition, Measurement, and Presentation of Revenues and Expenses in Conformity with Generally Accepted Accounting Principles

This area includes coverage of *revenues and gains, cost of goods sold, expenses, provision for income tax, recurring vs. nonrecurring transactions and events, accounting changes,* and *earnings per share.*

Obviously, in many instances, the measurement of revenue and expense items is directly associated with the valuation of assets and liabilities. To this extent, there is an overlap between the material in this subject area and that in subject areas previously reviewed. By the same token, there is necessary duplication of coverage. For example, a knowledge of the equity method of accounting for investments in common stock is categorized both with respect to valuation of the asset and recognition of income.

The major considerations in this area are:

1. An awareness of professional pronouncements relative to such matters as investments in common stock, accounting for intangible assets, foreign currency transactions, reporting the results of operations, accounting for income taxes, accounting changes, and reporting earnings per share.
2. An awareness of various revenue recognition methods, including the installment sales method, the cost recovery method, the percentage of completion method, the equity method of accounting for investments in common stock, and revenue recognition for sales of real estate.
3. An awareness of the components and nature of the cost of goods sold.
4. An awareness of expenses of all types, including general and administrative expenses and selling expenses.
5. An awareness of the determination and components of the provision for income tax.
6. An awareness of the treatment of discontinued operations, extraordinary items, and accounting changes.
7. The ability to make computations relative to the various income and expense items that form part of an income statement, including earnings-per-share computations.

The background for this area is generally provided in college-level courses in intermediate accounting and advanced accounting or their equivalents.

Other Financial Accounting and Reporting Issues

For this area also, it should be noted that there are overlaps and/or duplications. *For an indication of the items included in this subject area, see the details in the "Content Specification Outline"* (pages 2–9).

The major considerations in this area are

1. An awareness of professional pronouncements relative to such matters as the

statement of cash flows, consolidated and combined financial statements, business combinations, accounting policies, nonmonetary transactions, interim financial statements, financial instruments, segment reporting, development stage enterprises, personal financial statements, and loss contingencies.
2. The ability to make appropriate determinations relative to the subject matter involved.

The background for the various areas involved is provided in college-level courses in intermediate accounting and advanced accounting or their equivalents.

OFFICIAL ACCOUNTING PRONOUNCEMENTS

Professional pronouncements issued by the Financial Accounting Standards Board and the American Institute of CPAs are tested extensively on the CPA examination. As such, this section has been prepared and organized to acquaint CPA candidates with those pronouncements that have particular applicability to the FARE section of the exam. Its organization reflects the "Content Specification Outline" in Chapter 1.

The pronouncement summaries reflect the impact of any subsequent amendments and interpretations likely to be of significance to the CPA candidate. Pronouncements that have been omitted are either obsolete or not relevant for the CPA examination.

The abbreviated references to the accounting pronouncements below are for the following:

FAC —Statement of Financial Accounting Concepts

APB —Accounting Principles Board Opinion (The Accounting Principles Board was a predecessor to the Financial Accounting Standards Board.)

FAS —Financial Accounting Standards Board Statement

General Concepts and Standards

1. **FAC #1—Objectives of Financial Statements**
   Objectives include the providing of information that is useful in making economic decisions, particularly those related to investment and credit granting. However,

financial accounting alone is not meant to measure directly the value of an enterprise.

2. **FAC #2—Qualitative Characteristics Making Accounting Information Useful**
   Primary qualities are relevance (timeliness, predictive value, and feedback value) and reliability (verifiability, representational faithfulness, and neutrality). Other qualities include comparability, understandability, and favorable cost/benefit relationship.

3. **FAC #5—Recognition and Measurement in Financial Statements of Business Enterprises**
   Recognition involves incorporating an item into the financial statements as an asset, liability, revenue, expense, and so on. The item should be expressed in both words and dollars, with the amount included in the totals of the financial statements. Recognition of an asset or liability not only involves recognizing it initially, but also recognizing later changes such as disposition and liquidation.
   Recognition of an item should satisfy the following four criteria subject to materiality and cost/benefit:
   a. *Definition*—The item conforms to the definition of a financial statement element.
   b. *Measurability*—Reliable measurement exists.
   c. *Relevance*—It affects a user's decision.
   d. *Reliability*—Information is verifiable and neutral.

4. **FAC #6—Elements of Financial Statements**
   The statement replaces FAC #3 ("Elements of Financial Statements of Business Enterprises") and amends FAC #2 to apply to not-for-profit as well as to for-profit entities.
   Financial statements reflect in numbers and words resources, claims to resources, and transactional effects and other events causing a change in resources and claims.
   There are ten interrelated elements in measuring entity financial position and performance:
   1. *Assets*—Possible future economic benefits occurring because of past events.

(A valuation account is part of the related asset.)
   2. *Liabilities*—Possible future sacrifices of economic benefits as a result of past transactions. (A valuation account is part of the related liability.)
   3. *Equity (net assets)*—Represents residual interest; the excess of assets over liability.
   4. *Investments by owners*—May be the form of assets or represent services or conversion of liabilities of the entity.
   5. *Distributions to owners*—Decreases in equity resulting from transferring assets, performing services, or incurring debt to owners.
   6. *Comprehensive income*—The equity change arising from transactions and other events with nonowners. (Over an entity's life, comprehensive income equals the excess of cash receipts over cash outlays, excluding cash invested or disinvested by owners.)
   Comprehensive income consists not only of its basic components—revenues, expenses, gains and losses, but all intermediate components that result from combining the basic components (i.e., gross margin).
   7. *Revenues*—Increases in assets or reductions in liabilities from delivering goods or performing services related to major operational activities.
   8. *Expenses*—Reductions in assets or increases in liabilities from delivering goods or performing services related to major operational activities.
   9. *Gains*—Increases in equity arising from incidental transactions.
   10. *Losses*—Decreases in equity arising from incidental transactions.

5. **APB #22—Disclosure of Accounting Policies**
   Accounting policies are the specific policies determined for use by the entity's management. Every financial statement, whether presented singly or in combination, should present a description of all such material policies used (e.g., depreciation methods, inventory pricing, etc.) in a separate section preceding footnotes or as the first such note.

6. **APB #29—Accounting for Nonmonetary Transactions**
   a. *Dissimilar assets*—Utilize fair value of the asset given up or asset received if the latter is not ascertainable, recognizing gain or loss.
   b. *Similar assets*—For transactions not resulting in a culmination of the earning process, utilize net book value of the asset given up. Gain is generally not recognized, but a loss is recognized if the asset received has a lower fair value than the book value of the asset given up.

7. **FAS #130—Reporting Comprehensive Income**
   Entities must report comprehensive income (defined in FAC #6) with the same prominence as other financial statements. The statement does not prescribe a format for presentation; thus, comprehensive income may be presented in a separate statement or in a combined statement of income and comprehensive income.

Assets

1. **APB #17—Intangible Assets**
   A purchased intangible, whether of limited life or indeterminable useful life, shall be amortized over the period of benefit using the straight-line method unless some other method is more appropriate. Such period should be the lesser of legal life, useful life, or forty years.

2. **APB #18—The Equity Method of Accounting for Investments in Common Stock (as amended)**
   The equity method should be used to account for investments in common stock on consolidated and parent company financial statements, and financial statements of companies owning at least 20 percent but not more than 50 percent of the common stock, and/or where the investor is able to exercise significant influence over the operations of the investee.

   The equity method adds to the initial cost of the investment, the investor's share of the investee's post acquisition net income/loss on an accrual basis; dividends reduce the investment's carrying value.

3. **FAS #13—Accounting for Leases (as amended)**
   Leases that transfer substantially all the economic benefits and risks of ownership should be accounted for by:
   a. Lessee as the present value of an asset acquired and liability incurred.
   b. Lessor as a sale or transfer.
   All other leases are considered operating leases.
   Criteria for lessee capitalization require the presence of any one of the following:
   a. Ownership transfer at end of lease.
   b. Bargain price option to buy at end of lease.
   c. Lease term of 75 percent or more of property economic life.
   d. Present value of minimum lease payments is 90 percent or more of the fair value of leased property.
   Criteria for lessor capitalization require existence of criteria for lessee capitalization and that both of the following conditions exist:
   a. Reasonable predictability as to collection of minimum lease payments.
   b. Absence of uncertainties regarding the amount of reimbursable costs not yet incurred by the lessor.

4. **FAS #34—Capitalization of Interest Cost (as amended)**
   Interest incurred during the construction period of the following must be capitalized as part of their cost:
   a. Assets built for the entity's own use.
   b. Assets built as identifiable projects for sale or lease (e.g., ships, real estate developments).

5. **FAS #115—Accounting for Certain Investments in Debt and Equity Securities**
   This statement establishes standards of financial accounting and reporting for investments in equity securities that have readily determinable fair (market) values, and for all investments in debt securities.

   At acquisition, an enterprise shall classify debt and equity securities into one of three categories; namely, trading securities, held-to-maturity securities, and available-for-sale securities.

   The statement provides that trading securities be presented at fair value on the statement date, with unrealized gains and losses included in earnings. Held-to-maturity securities are to be presented at amortized cost on the statement date, with unrealized gains and losses not recognized. Available-for-sale securities should be presented at fair value on the statement date, with unrealized gains and losses reported as a separate component of stockholders' equity.

Further, in a classified statement of financial position, trading securities are classified as current assets, and securities in the other categories are classified as either current or noncurrent under the normal one-year or operating cycle rule.

6. **FAS #121—Accounting for the Impairment of Long-Lived Assets and for Long-Lived Assets to Be Disposed of**
Management should review its long-lived assets in use for recoverability and write them down to fair value whenever the undiscounted expected cash flow from the asset is less than its carrying amount. Assets to be disposed of should be stated at the lower of carrying amount or fair value less cost to sell.

Liabilities

1. **APB #14—Accounting for Convertible Debt and Debt Issued with Stock Purchase Warrants**
When the warrants are detachable from the bonds, the portion of the proceeds allocable to the warrants should be accounted for as paid-in capital. When the warrants are not detachable, no allocation of proceeds to the conversion feature is needed.

2. **APB #21—Interest on Receivables and Payables**
The difference between the present value, using an imputed interest rate, and the face amount of a note should be treated as premium or discount, and amortized, using the interest method, as interest expense or income so as to produce a constant rate of interest. Presentation of discount/premium on the balance sheet should be as additions/deductions to/from the items with which they are associated.

This pronouncement does not relate to trade receivables/payables.

3. **APB #26 and FAS #4—Early Extinguishment of Debt**
All extinguishments before maturity are basically the same. A gain or a loss resulting therefrom is treated as extraordinary, whether resulting from early extinguishment, at scheduled maturity, or later.

4. **FAS #5—Accounting for Contingencies**
Accrue a loss from a contingency by a charge to income if:
a. Information prior to issuance of financial statements indicates that it is probable that an asset has been impaired or a liability incurred at the statement date.
b. The amount of loss can be reasonably estimated.
Gain contingencies should not be recognized until realized.

5. **FAS #6—Classification of Short-Term Obligations Expected to Be Refinanced**
Short-term obligations (other than trade payables) should be excluded from current liabilities only if the entity intends to refinance them on a long-term basis and if such intent is supported by documented ability to refinance.

6. **FAS #15—Accounting by Debtors and Creditors for Troubled Debt Restructuring**
Restructuring takes place if the creditor grants a concession to the debtor for economic or legal reasons related to the latter's financial difficulties. A debtor may recognize a gain on restructuring of the payable. A creditor may recognize a loss for the difference between the fair value of assets received and the book value of the receivable in a transfer-in-full settlement. (See FAS #114.)

7. **FAS #43—Accounting for Compensated Absences**
Accrue a liability for employees' compensation for future absences if all the following conditions exist:
a. Employees' rights to such compensation are attributable to services already rendered.
b. Such rights are not contingent upon continued employment.

c. Payment is probable.

d. The amount can be reasonably estimated.

8. FAS #47—Disclosure of Long-Term Obligations

All unconditional purchase obligations not otherwise recognized should be disclosed on the balance sheet, provided they:

a. Are noncancellable in form or in substance.

b. Were negotiated as part of arranging financing for facilities that will provide the contracted goods/services.

c. Have a remaining term in excess of one year.

9. FAS #49—Accounting for Product Financing Arrangements

In a product financing arrangement, one party "sells" an asset to a second party and simultaneously agrees to "buy" the asset, or its equivalent, back at a price equal to the original selling price plus holding costs and interest costs. In substance, this is a financing transaction. Accordingly, the selling party should keep the assets on its books and record a note payable for the amount of the "sale."

10. FAS #109—Accounting for Income Taxes

The objectives of accounting for income taxes are to (a) recognize the amount of taxes payable or refundable for the current year, and (b) recognize deferred tax assets and liabilities for the future consequences of events that have been recognized in the financial statements or tax returns.

The statement requires comprehensive allocation of income taxes among financial periods in accounting for temporary differences. A temporary difference is the difference between the tax basis of an asset or liability and its basis as reported in the financial statements (i.e., book basis).

The year-end deferred item is determined by applying tax rates expected to be in effect in future years (based on existing tax laws) to reversals of temporary differences expected to occur in such future years.

The provision for income taxes is the sum of the current income tax payable for the year and the net change in the deferred tax assets and liabilities.

11. FAS #112—Employers' Accounting for Postemployment Benefits

An employer who provides benefits to former or inactive employees after employment, but before retirement, should account for such benefits following the conditions of FAS #43 (reviewed above), or FAS #5 (also reviewed in the above section) if FAS #43 conditions cannot be met, but a liability nevertheless exists (i.e., the event is probable and can be reasonably estimated).

12. FAS #114—Accounting by Creditors for Impairment of a Loan

A loan is impaired when a debtor is unlikely to fulfill the original terms of the loan agreement. When the terms of the loan are modified, the creditor should write the receivable down to fair value or the present value of the new contractual cash flows discounted at the loan's original effective interest rate. If the loan is collateral-dependent, the fair value of the collateral should be considered.

Ownership

1. APB #16—Business Combinations

The purchase method of accounting for a business combination should be used when cash and other assets are distributed or liabilities incurred to effect a combination. Recording should be at fair market value of net assets acquired, recognizing goodwill for any difference between these net assets and the purchase price.

The pooling method applies only if voting stock (at least 90 percent) is issued to effect the combination of common stock interests, and certain other conditions are fulfilled. Recording is made at the book value of net assets acquired. No goodwill results.

2. FAS #16—Prior-Period Adjustments

All items of profit and loss from a period are to be included in arriving at net income, except for items specified as prior-period adjustments. Only corrections of errors in previously issued financial statements are prior-period adjustments. Prior-period adjustments are reflected as adjustments to opening retained earnings for the year in which determined or realized.

3. **FAS #52—Foreign Currency Translation**
   Translation gains/losses from translated financial statements from the functional currency into reporting currency should *not* be included in period net income. The accumulated sum should be disclosed as a separate component of equity until sale/liquidation of the investment in the foreign entity.

   Transaction gains/losses (arising from specific transactions) *are* considered part of period net income for the period in which exchange rates change.

4. **FAS #94—Consolidation of All Majority-Owned Subsidiaries**
   Consolidated financial statements must be prepared whenever one company owns more than 50 percent of the outstanding voting common stock of another company unless control is temporary or does not rest with the majority owner.

5. **FAS #123—Accounting for Stock-Based Compensation**
   A corporation offering a stock-based compensation (i.e., stock option) plan may account for compensatory plans under either the intrinsic value method or the fair value method. Under the intrinsic value method, compensation is recognized for the excess of the fair value of the stock at the date of grant over the option price. Under the fair value method, compensation is recognized based upon the fair value of the option as estimated through an option pricing model.

Income and Expense

1. **APB #30—Reporting the Results of Operations**
   Net income should reflect all items of profit/loss with the single exception of prior-period adjustments. In determination of net income, separate discontinued operations of a segment of a business (net of tax effect), extraordinary gains/losses (net of tax effect), and the cumulative effect of accounting changes (net of tax) from and following income from continuing operations.

The income statement will include two elements of gain or loss on disposal of a segment in a year that includes a measurement date. First, the operating profit or loss (net of tax) up to the measurement date. Second, the gain or loss (net of tax) on the sale of the segment, including the estimated operating losses during the phase-out period.

Extraordinary items to be so categorized for the entity must be material, unusual in nature, and occur infrequently. Generally these involve events caused by major catastrophes, governmental expropriation, and/or prohibition.

2. **FAS #2—Accounting for Research and Development Costs**
   R & D costs are charged to expense when incurred. For materials, equipment, and facilities applicable to R & D projects, but with no alternative uses, cost capitalization and depreciation to R & D is the appropriate accounting.

3. **FAS #45—Accounting for Franchise Fee Revenue**
   The franchisor recognizes franchise fee revenue from the initial sale of a franchise only when he has substantially performed all material services/conditions. Start of operations by a franchisee sets the earliest date at which substantial performance takes place unless an earlier date can be justified.

4. **FAS #48—Revenue Recognition When Right of Return Exists**
   If the buyer has the right of return, revenue should be recognized at the time of sale only if certain conditions exist. These include: (a) sales price is determinable; (b) obligation to pay is not contingent on merchandise resale; (c) loss/damage does not change the obligation; (d) seller is not required to make additional performance; and (e) returns can be reasonably estimated.

5. **FAS #128—Earnings Per Share**
   Publicly held corporations must disclose both primary and diluted earnings per share (EPS) for each year that an income statement is presented. Basic EPS is earnings available to common stockholders (income less preferred dividends) divided

by the weighted average number of common shares outstanding. Diluted EPS is basic EPS adjusted for the assumed conversion of convertible securities (if-converted method) and the assumed exercise of stock options and similar items (treasury-stock method).

6. **FAS #129—Disclosure of Information About Capital Structure**

An entity must disclose information about the rights and privileges of the holders of the various securities outstanding. Examples of required disclosures include information about dividend and liquidation preferences, participation rights, and conversion of exercise prices and dates.

Other Financial Topics

1. **APB #20—Accounting Changes**
   a. *Accounting principle change*—Use of a generally accepted accounting method different from one used previously in financial statements. The cumulative effect of the change, net of taxes, must be presented on the income statement between extraordinary items and net income. Disclosure should include the nature and justification for change, explaining why the new method is preferred.
   b. *Accounting estimate change*—Estimates change as new information becomes available. This affects only current and future periods, and its impact is included in arriving at income from continuing operations. Footnote disclosure should be employed for material changes.
   c. *Reporting entity change*—Occurs when components of the accounting entity change (e.g., consolidated statements instead of individual statements). Financial statements of all prior periods presented must be restated as to income only from continuing operations, extraordinary items, net income, and EPS. Disclosure of the reason for change must also be made.

2. **APB #28—Interim Financial Reporting**

An interim period should be viewed as an integral part of an annual period. Its objective is to achieve a fair measure of both the annual operating results and the ending balance sheet. Reporting should be for current quarter, current year-to-date, or the past 12-months-to-date, along with comparable data for the preceding year.

3. **FAS #7—Accounting and Reporting by Development Stage Enterprises**

A development stage enterprise (D.S.E.) is one devoting substantially all of its efforts to establishing a new business, and either of the following conditions exist:
   a. Planned principal operations have not started.
   b. Principal operations have started, but there has been no significant revenue therefrom.

Financial statements of such enterprises must disclose cumulative deficit on the balance sheet, cumulative revenue, expense from inception on the operating statement, and cumulative sources and uses on the changes statement. The first year in which a D.S.E. is no longer considered as such, it must disclose that in prior years it had been a D.S.E.

4. **FAS #57—Related-Party Disclosures**

An entity must disclose transactions with affiliates, principal owners, and other related parties. The nature of the relationship, the amount of the transaction, and the amount due to or from the party at the balance sheet date must be disclosed.

5. **FAS #87—Employers' Accounting for Pensions**

This statement establishes standards for pension plans. The two broad types of pension plans are
   a. *Defined-contribution*—A pension plan that specifies an amount to be contributed annually by an employer, rather than the benefits to be paid. (This type of plan operates simply.)
   b. *Defined-benefit*—A pension plan that specifies a determinable pension benefit, usually based on factors such as age, years of service, and salary.

For defined benefit plans, the components of pension expense are
   a. *Service (normal) cost*—Based on the actuarial present value of benefits at-

tributed by the pension plan formula to employee service during the current period.

b. *Prior service cost* —The cost of retroactive benefits allocated to future years of service.

c. *Expected return on plan assets*—A reduction of the pension expense based on investment income.

d. *Interest cost*—The increase in the projected benefit obligation due to the passage of time.

e. *Actuarial gains and losses*—Changes resulting from experience that differs from assumptions that have been made.

6. **FAS #88—Employers' Accounting for Settlements and Curtailments of Defined Benefit Pension Plans and for Termination of Benefits**
This statement requires the immediate recognition of gain or loss from a settlement upon plan termination. A settlement occurs when there is a discharge of all or a portion of an employer's pension benefit obligation. Immediate recognition of gain or loss is also required upon curtailment, which is an event materially reducing future expected years of service of current employees or eliminating (for a substantial number of employees) the accrual of defined benefits for future services. Under certain circumstances, termination of benefits may result in the recognition of a liability and a loss.

7. **FAS #95—Statement of Cash Flows**
This requires a statement of cash flows as part of a full set of financial statements. The statement provides that cash receipts and cash payments be classified according to whether they stem from operating, investing, or financing activities. Operating activities include the cash effects of all transactions and other events that generally involve producing and delivering goods and providing services. Investing activities include: making and collecting loans; acquiring and disposing of debt or equity instruments and property; plant and equipment, and other productive assets (other than inventories). Financing activities include: (a) obtaining resources

from owners and providing them with a return on, and a return of, their investment; (b) borrowing money and repaying amounts involved, or otherwise settling the obligation; and (c) obtaining and paying for other resources obtained from creditors on long-term credit.

The statement encourages use of the direct method, but permits use of the indirect method.

8. **FAS #106—Employers' Accounting for Postretirement Benefits Other than Pension Costs**
This statement establishes standards for employers' accounting for postretirement benefits other than pensions. Specifically, it applies to postretirement life insurance plans, health care plans, and/or welfare benefits plans.

It significantly changes the current practice of accounting for such benefits on a pay-as-you-go basis by requiring accrual, during the years the employee renders the necessary service, of the expected cost of providing those benefits to the employee, his or her dependents, and/or designated beneficiaries.

9. **FAS #131—Disclosures About Segments of an Enterprise and Related Information**
Public business enterprises must report financial and descriptive information about reportable operating segments. Financial information to be disclosed includes a measure of profit or loss, certain specific revenue and expense items, and segment assets. A reconciliation of segment measure with similar measures for the entire entity must also be presented. Geographic information and information about major customers must also be disclosed.

BIBLIOGRAPHIES BY EXAM SECTIONS

The CPA examination is largely a test of the information contained in the following publications. Additionally, however, candidates are expected to be familiar with provisions of the Internal Revenue Code, federal securities regulations, and professional pronouncements of the FASB, AICPA, and GASB not covered by textbooks.

Business Law and Professional Responsibilities (LPR)

AICPA, Professional Standards; Code of Professional Conduct; U.S. Auditing Standards; Tax Practice; Consulting Services.

Clarkson, Miller, Jentz, & Cross, *West's Business Law,* 5th ed. (West, 1991).

Federal Bankruptcy Code.

Mann & Roberts, *Smith & Roberson's Business Law,* 8th ed. (West, 1991).

Metzger, Mallor, Barnes, Bowers, & Phillips, *Business Law and the Regulatory Environment,* 8th ed. (Irwin, 1992).

Schantz & Jackson, *Business Law,* 2d ed. (West, 1987).

Uniform Commercial Code—Commercial Paper Article; Sales Article; Secured Transactions Article.

Auditing (AUDIT)

AICPA, *Audit and Accounting Guide, Audit Sampling* (AICPA, 1983).

AICPA, *Audit and Accounting Manual, Nonauthoritative Practice Aids* (Commerce Clearing House, 1992).

AICPA, *Audit Guide, Consideration of the Internal Control Structure in a Financial Statement Audit* (AICPA, 1990).

AICPA, Auditing Procedure Study, *Auditors' Use of Microcomputers* (AICPA, 1986).

AICPA, Auditing Procedure Study, *Audit of Inventories* (AICPA, 1986).

AICPA, Auditing Procedure Study, *Confirmation of Accounts Receivable* (AICPA, 1984).

AICPA, Auditing Procedure Study, *The Independent Auditor's Consideration of the Work of Internal Auditors* (AICPA, 1989).

AICPA, *Codification of Statements on Auditing Standards,* nos. 1 to 73 (Commerce Clearing House, 1994).

AICPA, Codification of Statements on Standards for Accounting and Review Services, nos. 1 to 7 (Commerce Clearing House, 1993).

AICPA, *Codification of Statements on Standards for Attestation Engagements* (Commerce Clearing House, 1993).

AICPA, *Professional Standards,* vols. 1 & 2 (Commerce Clearing House, 1994).

Arens and Loebbecke, *Auditing: An Integrated Approach,* 6th ed. (Prentice-Hall, 1994).

Cushing and Romney, *Accounting Information Systems,* 5th ed. (Addison Wesley, 1990).

Dauber, Siegel, and Shim, *The Vest Pocket CPA* (Prentice-Hall, 1988).

Defliese, Jaenicke, O'Reilly, and Hirsch, *Montgomery's Auditing,* 11th ed. College Version (Wiley, 1990).

General Accounting Office, *Government Auditing Standards* (U.S. Government Printing Office, 1994).

Guy, Alderman, and Winters, *Auditing,* 3d ed. (Harcourt Brace Jovanovich, 1993).

Guy and Carmichael, *Audit Sampling,* 2d ed. (Wiley, 1986).

Hermanson, Strawser, and Strawser, *Auditing Theory and Practice,* 5th ed. (Irwin, 1989).

Kell and Boynton, *Modern Auditing,* 5th ed. (Wiley, 1992).

Robertson, *Auditing,* 6th ed. (Irwin, 1990).

Taylor and Glezen, *Auditing: Integrated Concepts and Procedures,* 6th ed. (Wiley, 1993).

Wallace, *Auditing,* 2d ed. (PWS-Kent, 1991).

Watne and Turney, *Auditing,* EDP Systems, 2d ed. (Prentice-Hall, 1990).

Weber, EDP *Auditing,* 2d ed. (McGraw-Hill, 1988).

Whittington, Pany, Meigs, and Meigs, *Principles of Auditing,* 10th ed. (Irwin, 1992).

Accounting & Reporting—Taxation, Managerial, and Governmental and Not-for-Profit Organizations (ARE)

Afterman and Jones, Governmental Accounting and Auditing Disclosure Manual (Warren, Gorham, and Lamont, 1992).

AICPA, Audit and Accounting Guide, *Audits of State and Local Government Units* (AICPA, 1992).

AICPA, Industry Audit Guide, *Audits of Colleges and Universities* (AICPA, 1992).

AICPA, Audit and Accounting Guide, *Audits of Providers of Health Care Services* (AICPA, 1992).

Anderson, Needles, and Caldwell, *Managerial Accounting* (Houghton Mifflin, 1989).

Dauber, Siegel, and Shim, *The Vest Pocket CPA* (Prentice-Hall, 1988).

Federal Tax Course (Commerce Clearing House, 1997).

Fischer, Taylor, and Leer, *Advanced Accounting,* 7th ed. (South-Western, 1997).

GASB, *Codification of Governmental Accounting and Financial Reporting Standards* (GASB).

Hay and Wilson, *Accounting for Governmental and Nonprofit Entities,* 10th ed. (Richard D. Irwin, Inc., 1994).

Horngren, Foster, and Datar, *Cost Accounting: A Managerial Emphasis,* 9th ed. (Prentice-Hall, 1997).

Larsen, *Modern Advanced Accounting,* 7th ed. (McGraw-Hill, 1996).

Pahler and Mori, *Advanced Accounting: Concepts and Practices,* 5th ed. (Dryden Press, 1994).

Polimeni, Fabozzi, and Adelberg, *Cost Accounting: Concepts and Applications for Managerial Decision Making,* 3d ed. (McGraw-Hill, 1991).

U.S. Master Tax Guide (Commerce Clearing House).

Usry and Hammer, *Cost Accounting: Planning and Control,* 11th ed. (South-Western, 1994).

A standard tax service, the Internal Revenue Code, and Income Tax Regulations.

Financial Accounting & Reporting—Business Enterprises (FARE)

AICPA, *Personal Financial Statements Guide* (AICPA, 1991).

AICPA, *Technical Practice Aids* (AICPA, 1991).

Beams, *Advanced Accounting,* 6th ed. (Prentice-Hall, 1995).

Chasteen, Flaherty, O'Connor, *Intermediate Accounting,* 4th ed. (Random House, 1992).

Dauber, Siegel, and Shim, *The Vest Pocket CPA* (Prentice-Hall, 1988).

FASB, *Current Text, Accounting Standards* (FASB).

FASB, *Original Pronouncements, Accounting Standards* (FASB).

Kieso & Weygandt, *Intermediate Accounting,* 8th ed. (Wiley, 1995).

Nikolai & Bazley, *Intermediate Accounting,* 6th ed. (PWS-Kent, 1994).

Pahler, Mori, *Advanced Accounting: Concepts and Practice,* 4th ed. (Harcourt Brace Jovanovich, 1991).

Smith, Skousen, *Intermediate Accounting,* 12th ed. (South-Western, 1995).

Welsch, Zlatkovich, *Intermediate Accounting,* 8th ed. (Irwin, 1989).

Williams, Stanga, Holder, *Intermediate Accounting,* 4th ed. (Harcourt Brace Jovanovich, 1992).

5. How to Approach CPA Examination Questions

One of the first things a successful CPA candidate learns is that questions on the CPA exam cannot be approached as if they were college homework or quiz questions. They are significantly different and require the learning of new skills in order to answer them successfully under examination conditions.

The first difference is that they must be answered within a specified time period. The examiners do not tell candidates when to start and stop answering individual questions. They merely recommend time estimates within which questions should be answered. It is up to you to establish a time budget and stick to it. Resist the temptation to spend more than the allotted time on a question despite the fact that an answer can be developed further. Stealing time allotted for a question yet to be answered increases the risk that the test will be over with questions still unanswered.

Ultimately, the absence of an answer will fail you more surely than a poor answer to a question. As noted in Chapter 1, you don't need a perfect answer to receive maximum credit. Candidates who were perfectionists as accounting students must resist the impulse to try to write perfect answers to CPA exam questions. It is more important to get the whole job done than to get it partly perfect.

Another important difference, particularly with the essay and computational questions, is that the solution requirements are often more precise and more rigidly graded than, say, a college midterm or final exam. Graders work from highly structured grading guides that are keyed to the set of requirements given in each question. One grader sees only one question's solutions. The hundreds, perhaps thousands, of solutions that he compares to his grading guide are totally anonymous. Unlike the classroom instructor, he is not influenced by subjective factors such as good looks, friendliness, conscientious attendance, or participation in class discussion.

Candidates who were sometimes able to bluff their way through college exam questions will find no opportunity for that on the CPA exam. Question requirements must be read, analyzed, and answered in full. An essay or computational solution that evades or ignores some of these requirements, or that tries to work around them, will not contain the key computations or concepts that the grader is looking for. The candidate only receives credit for items that appear both in the answer and on the grading guide.

A further difference between CPA exam questions and college exam questions is that the former are often broader in scope than the latter. A computational question on financial accounting on the FARE exam may, for example, require the candidate to synthesize his knowledge of fixed asset accounting, interim reporting, income tax deferral, earnings per share, and income recognition all in a single question. Questions encountered in college assignments generally deal with a much narrower body of information. The CPA exam is intended to be a comprehensive test of a candidate's overall mastery. The same breadth of topical coverage appears in essay questions for AUDIT and LPR.

The objective questions are probably the most familiar type of question for the candidate. Currently 50 to 60 percent of the exam consists of four-option multiple-choice questions. Candidates have been encountering such questions since their grammar school days. Here again, however, CPA exam items have been subject to a rigorous pre-exam analysis and testing. There are very few poorly made or "giveaway"-type objective questions.

In answering CPA exam questions, you must work systematically and efficiently. *Time is your scarcest resource.* You must know what to expect in the way of question format, and you must have learned and practiced question-answering skills long before you sit down to take the exam. Indeed, on examination day the last thing that should be on your mind is *how* to answer a CPA exam question. The time for developing question-answering techniques is *before* the exam. At the exam, the only thing you should be uncertain of is what specific points of substance will be tested.

QUESTION TYPES AND SPECIFIC TEST TACTICS

Four-Option Multiple-Choice Questions

In format, objective questions on the CPA exam are the familiar four-option multiple-choice variety found on most standardized tests. The advantages—from the AICPA's viewpoint—of using multiple-choice items are two: (1) they can be quickly and uniformly machine-scored; and (2) they enable the examiners to cover a wider range of topics than would be possible with a few long essay or computational questions.

Objective questions, despite their simplicity of construction and ease of grading, can be quite sophisticated in terms of cognitive skills tested. Some questions ask little more than simple recall of rote learning, while most require higher-level reasoning abilities in which the candidate must synthesize and evaluate information, make a decision regarding an answer choice, and move on quickly to the next question.

TYPICAL FARE QUESTION

How would the retained earnings of a subsidiary acquired in a business combination usually be treated in a consolidated balance sheet prepared immediately after the acquisition?

A. Excluded for both a purchase and a pooling of interests.
B. Excluded for a pooling of interests but included for a purchase.
C. Included for both a purchase and a pooling of interests.
D. Included for a pooling of interests but excluded for a purchase.

The correct answer, "D," would be entered on a machine-scored answer sheet by blackening in a circle containing the letter "D."

TYPICAL ARE QUESTION

The following information pertains to Spruce City's liability for claims and judgments:

Current liability at January 1, 1997	$100,000
Claims paid during 1997	800,000
Current liability at December 31, 1997	140,000
Noncurrent liability at December 31, 1997	200,000

What amount should Spruce report for 1997 claims and judgments expenditures?
A. $1,040,000
B. $ 940,000
C. $ 840,000
D. $ 800,000

The correct answer choice is "C." The other answer choices represent feasible alternatives resulting from a mishandling of the data given. The candidate who is not completely sure of how to account for information presented is deluded into thinking her computation is correct because it corresponds to one of the answer choices given.

Be careful to note the answer sheet structure before you start blackening circles. The answer spaces will be arrayed horizontally on some sheets and vertically on others—for the same test! This is done purposely so that candidates in neighboring rows will have differently structured answer sheets and therefore will not be able to copy from one another.

TEST TACTICS

Don't Be Confused by the Phrasing of Questions—Read Carefully!

One point that cannot be overemphasized is the necessity for *careful reading of the questions*. While there are never any deliberate verbal or numerical tricks in the questions, certain techniques of phrasing questions can be confusing.

In particular, the use of qualifying words such as *most, least,* or *best,* or of negative terms such as *not, incorrect,* or *inappropriate* can cause the candidate to misinterpret his task. Such words are generally printed in **boldface** type on the exam but even that may not prevent their being overlooked by a careless reading. The mind must remain alert to the shifts in thought patterns that such expressions require.

Throughout the exam, you must *work quickly yet read carefully.* That ability can be developed through practice with past questions.

Move Along Briskly

Decisions regarding answer choices must be made. You cannot afford to get hung up on any particular question. Move along briskly and concentrate on the question at hand—don't agonize over past uncertainties or future obstacles. If you find yourself "spinning wheels" on a particular question and unable to attempt an educated guess, place a large question mark in the margin and return to it after the others have been completed. A fresh perspective may prove helpful.

Account for All Key Facts

In approaching four-option multiple-choice questions, *make certain that key facts have been noted and accounted for.* When two or more questions relate to a single set of facts, all questions should be scanned and solved as a group. Key words or phrases should be highlighted by underlining or circling.

Remember that wrong answer choices represent feasible alternatives likely to be selected by candidates with only a partial understanding. A combination of knowledge and careful analysis will minimize the chance of selecting wrong answer choices. Generally, concentration is enhanced by ignoring answer choices until the question narrative has been studied and a tentative answer attempted.

Avoid Answer Transcription Errors

Answer choices selected should be *entered directly on the machine-scored answer sheet.* This reduces the possibility of transcription errors that occur when answers are noted in the test booklet and later transferred en masse to the official answer sheet.

Guess Correctly

When logic or memory fails, and an answer must be *guessed* at, certain techniques increase the probability of selecting the right answer. For example, when more than one answer choice

seems correct, the one that should be selected is the one that does not require any qualifications in order to make it correct. Often, all but two of the choices can be eliminated. This at least creates a 50 percent probability of being right.

This technique is illustrated by the following example from LPR:

Which of the following employees are exempt from the minimum and maximum hour provisions of the Fair Labor Standards Act?
A. Children.
B. Railroad and airline employees.
C. Members of a union recognized as the bargaining agent by the National Labor Relations Board.
D. Office workers.

This is a question requiring recall of particular facts that usually are either there or not there in a candidate's memory. Nevertheless, common-sense logic should enable the candidate to narrow the choices to "B" or "D." Choice "D" would be correct if one views office workers as including administrative employees. But that would necessitate qualifying the answer in order to make it correct. (Administrative employees *are* exempt from the minimum and maximum hour provisions of the Fair Labor Standards Act.) The *best* choice, therefore, arrived at by elimination, is "B."

Inasmuch as no penalties for incorrect answers have been associated with objective questions, *no question should be left blank.* Even a wild guess has a 25 percent probability of being right.

"Other Objective Formats" Questions

These questions, like the four-option multiple-choice questions, are machine-scored, but the questions and answers will be in different formats.

These formats consist of matching questions to answers, questions requiring yes or no responses, and/or numerical answers to questions (FARE and ARE exams, only).

About twenty to thirty of the available points on the FARE, AUDIT, and LPR sections and forty to fifty of the available points on the ARE section will be allocated to these types of questions.

Recording Answers

All answers are recorded using a blacken-the-oval answer sheet, as used for four-option multiple-choice questions.

Answer sheets may vary from examination to examination. It is important to pay strict attention to the manner in which the answer sheet is structured. As you proceed, be absolutely certain that the space in which you have indicated your answer corresponds directly in number with the item in your question booklet.

Note that a matching question may have many answers from which to choose (perhaps ten or more). Furthermore, an answer may or may not be allowed to be used more than once. As such, when an answer may be used only once, it is wise to check it off directly on the exam to prevent it from being used a second time.

SAMPLE QUESTIONS AND ANSWERS

The purpose of this illustration is to provide examples of "other objective formats" questions that appear on the examination, and to illustrate how you would record the answers to them on your answer sheets.

Example 1 is an AUDIT question, and the portion of the Objective Answer Sheet related to this question is presented on page 61. The correct answers have been filled in.

Example 2 is applicable to the ARE exam, and the portion of the Objective Answer Sheet related to this question is shown on page 63. The correct answers have been filled in.

Example 1

Number 4

Instructions

Question Number 4 consists of 13 items. Select the **best** answer for each item. Use a No. 2 pencil to blacken the appropriate ovals on the *Objective Answer Sheet* to indicate your answers. **Answer all items.** Your grade will be based on the total number of correct answers.

Required:

The flowchart on page 60 depicts part of a client's revenue cycle. Some of the flowchart symbols are labeled to indicate control procedures and records. For each symbol numbered **61 through 73,** select one response from the answer lists below and blacken the corresponding oval on the *Objective Answer Sheet*. Each response in the lists may be selected once, more than once, or not at all.

Operations and Control Procedures

(A) Enter shipping data.
(B) Verify agreement of sales order and shipping document.
(C) Write off accounts receivable.
(D) To warehouse and shipping department.
(E) Authorize account receivable writeoff.
(F) Prepare aged trial balance.
(G) To sales department.
(H) Release goods for shipment.
(I) To accounts receivable department.
(J) Enter price data.
(K) Determine that customer exists.
(L) Match customer purchase order with sales order.
(M) Perform customer credit check.
(N) Prepare sales journal.
(O) Prepare sales invoice.

Documents, Journals, Ledgers, and Files

(P) Shipping document.
(Q) General ledger master file.
(R) General journal.
(S) Master price file.
(T) Sales journal.
(U) Sales invoice.
(V) Cash receipts journal.
(W) Uncollectable accounts file.
(X) Shipping file.
(Y) Aged trial balance.
(Z) Open order file.

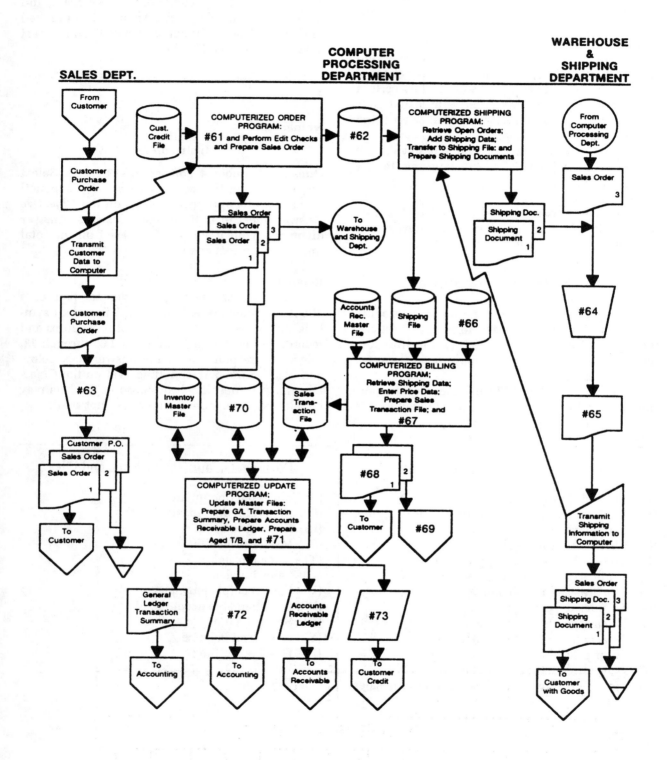

(10 points)

Select one

Item	Select one
61	Ⓐ Ⓑ Ⓒ Ⓓ Ⓔ Ⓕ Ⓖ Ⓗ Ⓘ Ⓙ Ⓚ ● Ⓜ Ⓝ Ⓞ Ⓟ Ⓠ Ⓡ Ⓢ Ⓣ Ⓤ Ⓥ Ⓦ Ⓧ Ⓨ Ⓩ
62	Ⓐ Ⓑ Ⓒ Ⓓ Ⓔ Ⓕ Ⓖ Ⓗ Ⓘ Ⓙ Ⓚ Ⓛ Ⓜ Ⓝ Ⓞ Ⓟ Ⓠ Ⓡ Ⓢ Ⓣ Ⓤ Ⓥ Ⓦ Ⓧ ● Ⓩ
63	Ⓐ Ⓑ Ⓒ Ⓓ Ⓔ Ⓕ Ⓖ Ⓗ Ⓘ Ⓙ ● Ⓛ Ⓜ Ⓝ Ⓞ Ⓟ Ⓠ Ⓡ Ⓢ Ⓣ Ⓤ Ⓥ Ⓦ Ⓧ Ⓨ Ⓩ
64	Ⓐ ● Ⓒ Ⓓ Ⓔ Ⓕ Ⓖ Ⓗ Ⓘ Ⓙ Ⓚ Ⓛ Ⓜ Ⓝ Ⓞ Ⓟ Ⓠ Ⓡ Ⓢ Ⓣ Ⓤ Ⓥ Ⓦ Ⓧ Ⓨ Ⓩ
65	Ⓐ Ⓑ Ⓒ Ⓓ Ⓔ Ⓕ Ⓖ Ⓗ Ⓘ Ⓙ Ⓚ Ⓛ Ⓜ Ⓝ Ⓞ Ⓟ Ⓠ Ⓡ Ⓢ Ⓣ Ⓤ Ⓥ Ⓦ Ⓧ Ⓨ Ⓩ
66	Ⓐ Ⓑ Ⓒ Ⓓ Ⓔ Ⓕ Ⓖ ● Ⓘ Ⓙ Ⓚ Ⓛ Ⓜ Ⓝ Ⓞ Ⓟ Ⓠ ● Ⓢ Ⓣ Ⓤ Ⓥ Ⓦ Ⓧ Ⓨ Ⓩ
67	Ⓐ Ⓑ Ⓒ Ⓓ Ⓔ Ⓕ Ⓖ Ⓗ Ⓘ Ⓙ Ⓚ Ⓛ Ⓜ ● ● Ⓟ Ⓠ Ⓡ Ⓢ Ⓣ Ⓤ Ⓥ Ⓦ Ⓧ Ⓨ Ⓩ
68	Ⓐ Ⓑ Ⓒ Ⓓ Ⓔ Ⓕ Ⓖ Ⓗ Ⓘ Ⓙ Ⓚ Ⓛ Ⓜ Ⓝ Ⓞ Ⓟ Ⓠ Ⓡ Ⓢ Ⓣ ● Ⓥ Ⓦ Ⓧ Ⓨ Ⓩ
69	Ⓐ Ⓑ Ⓒ Ⓓ Ⓔ Ⓕ Ⓖ Ⓗ ● Ⓙ Ⓚ Ⓛ Ⓜ Ⓝ Ⓞ Ⓟ ● Ⓡ Ⓢ Ⓣ Ⓤ Ⓥ Ⓦ Ⓧ Ⓨ Ⓩ
70	Ⓐ Ⓑ Ⓒ Ⓓ Ⓔ Ⓕ Ⓖ Ⓗ Ⓘ Ⓙ Ⓚ Ⓛ Ⓜ Ⓝ Ⓞ Ⓟ Ⓠ Ⓡ Ⓢ Ⓣ Ⓤ Ⓥ Ⓦ Ⓧ Ⓨ Ⓩ
71	Ⓐ Ⓑ Ⓒ Ⓓ Ⓔ Ⓕ Ⓖ Ⓗ Ⓘ Ⓙ Ⓚ Ⓛ Ⓜ ● Ⓞ ● Ⓠ Ⓡ Ⓢ Ⓣ Ⓤ Ⓥ Ⓦ Ⓧ Ⓨ Ⓩ
72	Ⓐ Ⓑ Ⓒ Ⓓ Ⓔ Ⓕ Ⓖ Ⓗ Ⓘ Ⓙ Ⓚ Ⓛ Ⓜ Ⓝ Ⓞ Ⓟ Ⓠ Ⓡ Ⓢ ● Ⓤ Ⓥ Ⓦ Ⓧ Ⓨ Ⓩ
73	Ⓐ Ⓑ Ⓒ Ⓓ Ⓔ Ⓕ Ⓖ Ⓗ Ⓘ Ⓙ Ⓚ Ⓛ Ⓜ Ⓝ Ⓞ Ⓟ Ⓠ Ⓡ Ⓢ Ⓣ Ⓤ Ⓥ Ⓦ Ⓧ ● Ⓩ

ANSWER 4

Example 2

Number 2

Instructions

Question Number 2 consists of 20 items. Select the **best** answer for each item. Use a No. 2 pencil to blacken the appropriate ovals on the *Objective Answer Sheet* to indicate your answers. **Answer all items.** Your grade will be based on the total number of correct answers.

Cole, a newly-licensed CPA, opened an office in 1997 as a sole practitioner engaged in the practice of public accountancy. Cole reports on the cash basis for income tax purposes. Listed on the following page are Cole's 1997 business and nonbusiness transactions, as well as possible tax treatments.

Required:

For each of Cole's transactions **(Items 61 through 80),** select the appropriate tax treatment and blacken the corresponding oval on the *Objective Answer Sheet*. A tax treatment may be selected once, more than once, or not at all.

Transactions

61. Fees received for jury duty.
62. Interest income on mortgage loan receivable.
63. Penalty paid to bank on early withdrawal of savings.
64. Writeoffs of uncollectible accounts receivable from accounting practice.
65. Cost of attending review course in preparation for the Uniform CPA Examination.
66. Fee for the biennial permit to practice as a CPA.
67. Cost of attending CPE courses in fulfillment of state board requirements.
68. Contribution to a qualified Keogh retirement plan.
69. Loss sustained from nonbusiness bad debt.
70. Loss sustained on sale of "Small Business Corporation" (Section 1244) stock.
71. Taxes paid on land owned by Cole and rented out as a parking lot.
72. Interest paid on installment purchases of household furniture.
73. Alimony paid to former spouse who reports the alimony as taxable income.
74. Personal medical expenses charged on credit card in December 1997 but not paid until January 1998.
75. Personal casualty loss sustained.
76. State inheritance tax paid on bequest received.
77. Foreign income tax withheld at source on dividend received.
78. Computation of self-employment tax.
79. One-half of self-employment tax paid with 1997 return filed in April 1998.
80. Insurance premiums paid on Cole's life.

Tax Treatments

(A) Taxable as interest income in Schedule B—Interest and Dividend Income.
(B) Taxable as other income on page 1 of Form 1040.
(C) Not taxable.
(D) Deductible on page 1 of Form 1040 to arrive at adjusted gross income.
(E) Deductible in Schedule A—Itemized Deductions, subject to threshold of 7.5% of adjusted gross income.
(F) Deductible in Schedule A—Itemized Deductions, subject to threshold of 10% of adjusted gross income and additional threshold of $100.
(G) Deductible in full Schedule A—Itemized Deductions (cannot be claimed as a credit).
(H) Deductible in Schedule B—Interest and Dividend Income.
(I) Deductible in Schedule C—Profit or Loss from Business.
(J) Deductible in Schedule D—Capital Gains or Losses.
(K) Deductible in Schedule E—Supplemental Income and Loss.
(L) Deductible in Form 4797—Sales of Business Property.
(M) Claimed in Form 1116—Foreign Tax Credit, or in Schedule A—Itemized Deductions, at taxpayer's option.
(N) Based on gross self-employment income.
(O) Based on net earnings from self-employment.
(P) Not deductible.

ARE
VERSION 1

(30 points)

	Item	Tax Treatments (Select one)
—	61	Ⓐ ● Ⓒ Ⓓ Ⓔ Ⓕ Ⓖ Ⓗ Ⓘ Ⓙ Ⓚ Ⓛ Ⓜ Ⓝ Ⓞ Ⓟ
—	62	● Ⓑ Ⓒ Ⓓ Ⓔ Ⓕ Ⓖ Ⓗ Ⓘ Ⓙ Ⓚ Ⓛ Ⓜ Ⓝ Ⓞ Ⓟ
—	63	Ⓐ Ⓑ Ⓒ ● Ⓔ Ⓕ Ⓖ Ⓗ Ⓘ Ⓙ Ⓚ Ⓛ Ⓜ Ⓝ Ⓞ Ⓟ
—	64	Ⓐ Ⓑ Ⓒ Ⓓ Ⓔ Ⓕ Ⓖ Ⓗ Ⓘ Ⓙ Ⓚ Ⓛ Ⓜ Ⓝ Ⓞ ●
—	65	Ⓐ Ⓑ Ⓒ Ⓓ Ⓔ Ⓕ Ⓖ Ⓗ Ⓘ Ⓙ Ⓚ Ⓛ Ⓜ Ⓝ Ⓞ ●
—	66	Ⓐ Ⓑ Ⓒ Ⓓ Ⓔ Ⓕ Ⓖ Ⓗ ● Ⓙ Ⓚ Ⓛ Ⓜ Ⓝ Ⓞ Ⓟ
—	67	Ⓐ Ⓑ Ⓒ Ⓓ Ⓔ Ⓕ Ⓖ Ⓗ ● Ⓙ Ⓚ Ⓛ Ⓜ Ⓝ Ⓞ Ⓟ
—	68	Ⓐ Ⓑ Ⓒ ● Ⓔ Ⓕ Ⓖ Ⓗ Ⓘ Ⓙ Ⓚ Ⓛ Ⓜ Ⓝ Ⓞ Ⓟ
—	69	Ⓐ Ⓑ Ⓒ Ⓓ Ⓔ Ⓕ Ⓖ Ⓗ Ⓘ ● Ⓚ Ⓛ Ⓜ Ⓝ Ⓞ Ⓟ
—	70	Ⓐ Ⓑ Ⓒ Ⓓ Ⓔ Ⓕ Ⓖ Ⓗ Ⓘ Ⓙ Ⓚ ● Ⓜ Ⓝ Ⓞ Ⓟ
—	71	Ⓐ Ⓑ Ⓒ Ⓓ Ⓔ Ⓕ Ⓖ Ⓗ Ⓘ Ⓙ ● Ⓛ Ⓜ Ⓝ Ⓞ Ⓟ
—	72	Ⓐ Ⓑ Ⓒ Ⓓ Ⓔ Ⓕ Ⓖ Ⓗ Ⓘ Ⓙ Ⓚ Ⓛ Ⓜ Ⓝ Ⓞ ●
—	73	Ⓐ Ⓑ Ⓒ ● Ⓔ Ⓕ Ⓖ Ⓗ Ⓘ Ⓙ Ⓚ Ⓛ Ⓜ Ⓝ Ⓞ Ⓟ
—	74	Ⓐ Ⓑ Ⓒ Ⓓ ● Ⓕ Ⓖ Ⓗ Ⓘ Ⓙ Ⓚ Ⓛ Ⓜ Ⓝ Ⓞ Ⓟ
—	75	Ⓐ Ⓑ Ⓒ Ⓓ Ⓔ ● Ⓖ Ⓗ Ⓘ Ⓙ Ⓚ Ⓛ Ⓜ Ⓝ Ⓞ Ⓟ
—	76	Ⓐ Ⓑ Ⓒ Ⓓ Ⓔ Ⓕ Ⓖ Ⓗ Ⓘ Ⓙ Ⓚ Ⓛ Ⓜ Ⓝ Ⓞ ●
—	77	Ⓐ Ⓑ Ⓒ Ⓓ Ⓔ Ⓕ Ⓖ Ⓗ Ⓘ Ⓙ Ⓚ Ⓛ ● Ⓝ Ⓞ Ⓟ
—	78	Ⓐ Ⓑ Ⓒ Ⓓ Ⓔ Ⓕ Ⓖ Ⓗ Ⓘ Ⓙ Ⓚ Ⓛ Ⓜ Ⓝ ● Ⓟ
—	79	Ⓐ Ⓑ Ⓒ ● Ⓔ Ⓕ Ⓖ Ⓗ Ⓘ Ⓙ Ⓚ Ⓛ Ⓜ Ⓝ Ⓞ Ⓟ
—	80	Ⓐ Ⓑ Ⓒ Ⓓ Ⓔ Ⓕ Ⓖ Ⓗ Ⓘ Ⓙ Ⓚ Ⓛ Ⓜ Ⓝ Ⓞ ●

ANSWER 2

Computational Questions

FARE computational questions must be struggled with and mastered to be truly appreciated. Every accounting student, upon completing a textbook "AICPA-adapted" homework question, has probably despaired of ever being able to answer a similar question under CPA exam conditions within the time frame allowed. There he sits, after having just spent an hour solving a CPA exam problem for homework that should have been answered by a CPA candidate within thirty minutes. Chances of ever passing the CPA exam seem remote.

Fortunately, it's a long road from Intermediate Accounting to the FARE exam, and the accounting student/CPA candidate can learn the examsmanship techniques necessary for solving computational problems more efficiently.

Computational problems are intended to simulate real-world accounting situations. Ultimately, they are much too neat and simple to realistically portray real-world situations, but their requirement that candidates analyze and account for a series of sometimes related, sometimes unrelated facts within a question narrative is a valid analogue to real-world accounting situations. In both situations the accountant needs to be able to synthesize data and decide how to best handle it.

On the FARE exam, the approach you take to solve a computational question is all important. You must work methodically and efficiently. Resist the urge to rush into beginning a solution before the entire narrative is digested. Otherwise, you're likely to waste time with false starts and poorly presented solutions.

The following section presents an approach to answering computational questions.

TEST TACTICS

Read Questions Twice—for Understanding, for Analysis

Computational questions, like essay questions, must be read very carefully. As with essay questions, *two readings are necessary—once for a general understanding and once for a careful analysis*. Techniques of highlighting key facts through underlining, marginal notes, or circling should be used. The requirements section should be studied very carefully, both to ensure that a complete solution is presented and to provide guidance on organizing the solution. Information presented should be interpreted straightforwardly without looking for hidden meanings or tricks.

Use of Calculators

Calculators will be provided at the exam site for the ARE and FARE exams. The purpose is to save time, and should not be taken to mean an increase in the difficulty level of the exams.

A calculator can be ordered through the AICPA Order Department (1-800-862-4272); cost is $6.30 for students and $9 for all others.

Before the start of the ARE and FARE exams, candidates are instructed to perform certain test calculations so that they can learn how to operate the calculator and to ensure that it is functioning properly. A replacement calculator will be available in the event of a malfunction. Each candidate must sign, date, and submit the "calculator sign-off record," which is included on page 1 of the Examination Answer Booklet.

Candidates need to use the calculators for only four primary functions: addition, subtraction, multiplication, and division. However, calculators also have function keys for square root, percentage, and memory.

Use Standard Abbreviations

To save time, use abbreviations whenever appropriate. Use only those that have general currency.

Keep Computations Brief for Obvious Answers

It is not essential that answers to exam questions contain laborious computations in support of obvious answers, as unofficial AICPA answers are inclined to do.

Explain Journal Entries

Journal entries should always contain brief explanations unless the requirements state otherwise.

Basic Problem-Solving Techniques

The following problem-solving techniques are useful for ensuring a systematic approach that will produce an organized, coherent answer:

A. Getting Ready for the Answer

1. *Always read the requirements first.*
2. After the first reading for "feel," which should take a minute or so, read the question again slowly and begin to solve.

In this connection, time devoted to a careful analysis of the facts will be well spent. While reading, underline key points in the statement of fact and cross out information that has no meaning (or seems to have no meaning).

3. If a question has two or more unrelated subparts, answer the easier part(s) first; the order of answering parts of a question is not important.

4. *Do not read into questions.*

   In the *rare case* that an assumption must be made, state the nature of the assumption clearly on the answer, giving reasons, if any.

5. Draw a mental image of the solution format before proceeding.

   In this connection, very often the requirements will specifically indicate the desired format. If this is not the case, there are only two possibilities:

   a. The format will be specific (e.g., an income statement, a balance sheet).

   b. If the format is not indicated or specific, adhere to real-world rules for working-paper construction; express the answer logically, using good schedule technique.

6. In short, this implies that one should solve for the efficient solution.

B. Developing the Answer

1. The depth of writing is not essential; getting the key points is.

2. *Organizing the answer.*

   a. Do not copy any more of the question than is essential to the solution; do not prepare unnecessary worksheets or journal entries.

   b. It is perfectly acceptable to abbreviate. For example, "accounts receivable" can be written as "A/R," etc. (The graders are experienced accountants who will understand the abbreviations.)

   c. *With respect to journal entries:* (1) it does not matter how many are made to handle a particular situation; and (2) brief, obvious, abbreviated explanations should be given unless a require-

ment specially states that explanations are to be omitted.

   If in doubt, remember that there is no penalty for too many entries, only for not expressing the facts required. However, journal entries that contradict each other should be avoided.

   d. Always include an appropriate heading with the solution. This can best be accomplished by paraphrasing the requirements.

   e. Do not waste time on minor arithmetic matters. For the most part, arithmetic is simple and reasonable. Therefore, evaluate the reasonableness of computations.

   f. *Don't plug answers.* If an error is discovered, rather than redo the solution, indicate where the correct number should appear with a marginal note.

3. *Handling the facts in a question.*

   In working through a question, as a specific piece of information is handled, it should be "ticked off." In this manner, each question "falls apart" and information to be dealt with is eliminated.

   Thus, where an item is not used in proceeding through a question, it will be handled later or has no bearing, in which event it will disappear.

   It should also be kept in mind that for exam purposes, all facts, unless indicated otherwise, must be assumed to be material.

4. *"Massaging" the facts.*

   On recent exams, questions have appeared that have two or more unrelated parts based on the same facts.

   These questions do not present difficulty with respect to the concepts; indeed, the more difficult part of the question deals with placing the facts in the appropriate portions of the solution. For example, the current portion of a long-term debt would appear in one part, the long-term portion in another, and related expenses in the third.

   With respect to such questions, care should be taken to handle the information appropriately.

SAMPLE QUESTION AND SOLUTION

The preceding advice is illustrated by the following problem and solution:

Question (AICPA Adapted)

The following information pertains to Woodbine Circle Corporation:

Adjusted Trial Balance
December 31, 1997

	Debit	Credit
Cash	$ 500,000	
Accounts receivable, net	1,500,000	
Inventory	2,500,000	
Property, plant, and equipment	15,100,000	
Accumulated depreciation		$ 4,900,000
Accounts payable		1,400,000
Income taxes payable		100,000
Notes payable		1,000,000
Common stock ($1 par value)		1,100,000
Additional paid-in capital		6,100,000
Retained earnings, 1/1/97		3,000,000
Sales—regular		10,000,000
Sales—AL Division		2,000,000
Interest on municipal bonds		100,000
Cost of sales—regular	6,200,000	
Cost of sales—AL Division	900,000	
Administrative expenses—regular	2,000,000	
Administrative expenses—AL Division	300,000	
Interest expense—regular	210,000	
Interest expense—AL Division	140,000	
Loss on disposal of AL Division	250,000	
Gain on repurchase of bonds payable		300,000
Income tax expense	400,000*	
	$30,000,000	$30,000,000

Other financial data for the year ended December 31, 1997:

Federal income taxes

Paid on Federal Tax Deposit Forms	$300,000
Accrued	100,000
Total charged to income tax expense (estimated)	$400,000*

*Does not properly reflect current or deferred income tax expense or intraperiod income tax allocation for income statement purposes.

Income per tax return	$2,150,000
Tax rate on all types of taxable income	40%

Temporary difference

Depreciation, per financial statements	$ 600,000
Depreciation, per tax return	750,000

Income not taxable

Interest on municipal bonds	100,000

Discontinued operations

On September 30, 1997, Woodbine sold its Auto Leasing (AL) Division for $4,000,000. Book value of this business segment was $4,250,000 at that date. For financial statement purposes, this sale was considered as discontinued operations of a segment of a business. There was no phase-out period. The measurement date was September 30, 1997.

Liabilities

On June 30, 1997, Woodbine repurchased $1,000,000 carrying value of its long-term bonds for $700,000. All other liabilities mature in 1997.

Capital Structure

Common stock, par value $1 per share, traded on the New York Stock Exchange:

Number of shares outstanding at 1/1/97	900,000
Number of shares sold for $8 per share on 6/30/97	200,000
Number of shares outstanding at 12/31/97	1,100,000

Required:

Using the multiple-step format, prepare a formal income statement for Woodbine for the year ended December 31, 1997, together with the appropriate supporting schedules. Recurring and nonrecurring items in the income statement should be properly separated. All income taxes should be appropriately shown.

Approach

1. Estimate the time to spend answering the question based on its point value.
2. Scan information presented, developing a sense of how it fits together and how it will be used to respond to the requirements. A first reading indicates the following:
   — The trial balance contains items that are explained in the "other financial data."
   — The balance sheet items on the trial balance are not relevant, since the question concerns an income statement. They should be ignored.
   — The results of the "AL Division" are segregated because they are related to discontinued operations.
   — The gain on repurchase of bonds (i.e., extinguishment of debt), further explained under "liabilities" in the "other financial data," is an extraordinary item.
   — Any income from discontinued items (net of taxes) and extraordinary items (net of taxes) must be presented separately.
   — The $400,000 income tax expense on the trial balance, as per the "other financial data," represents an estimated amount that is *not* allocated to the various income statement sections and may therefore be ignored.
   — Income taxes must be appropriately allocated to income from continuing operations, discontinued operations, and extraordinary items.
   — Basic earnings per share must be disclosed on the face of the income statement.
   — The "income per tax return" is of no consequence, since an income statement must be prepared.

3. As a matter of technique, prior to preparing the statement, the candidate should use initials or some other means to indicate the presentation of the various items (e.g., continuing operations, discontinued operations). This is done by making notations on the question sheet.
4. On the answer sheet, lay out the solution format (e.g., a multiple-step income statement).
   — Remember the heading.
   — Leave enough space between line items to insert financial data as it is developed.

Woodbine Circle Corporation
Income Statement
For the Year Ended 12/31/97

Sales	$
Cost of goods sold	
Gross profit on sales	
Operating expenses	
Operating income	
Other revenue and expense items:	
Income from continuing operations before income tax	
Provision for income taxes:	
Net income from continuing operations	
Discontinued operations, net of income taxes	
Extraordinary gain, net of tax	
Net Income to retained earnings	$
Earnings per common share	$

5. The first computational step is determination of *income from continuing operations.*
   a. *To arrive at operating income*, the operating items referred to as "regular" are listed (ignoring those items related to the discontinued AL Division). This includes sales of $10,000,000 less cost of sales of $6,200,000. Gross profit is $3,800,000, from which is subtracted the operating (administrative) expenses of $2,000,000, to arrive at *operating income of $1,800,000*. These amounts should be entered directly on the pro forma statement created in step #4 above.
   b. Next, examination of the trial balance indicates, consistent with the "multi-

ple-step format," that there are other revenue and expense items consisting of interest on municipal bonds of $100,000 and interest expense of $210,000, or a reduction of *$110,000*. Income from continuing operations is therefore $1,690,000, which, of course, is subject to a provision for income taxes. Working down the statement being created, these items are entered as line items. (See completed solution following.)

6. There are two portions of the income tax provision related to income from continuing operations—*the taxes currently payable and the deferred portion on temporary differences.*

   a. As to temporary differences, there is a depreciation temporary difference of $750,000 less $600,000, or *$150,000*. The interest on municipal bonds will never be taxed. It is a so-called "permanent" difference. Therefore it is not a factor in the income tax provision.

   b. Since depreciation is higher for tax purposes, taxable income will be lower. Taxable income from continuing operations is therefore $1,690,000 less the $150,000 temporary difference and the $100,000 municipal bond interest, or *$1,440,000*, which requires a tax currently payable at 40 percent, or *$576,000*, as noted on the completed solution following.

   c. The *deferred portion* of the tax provision, which is an expense debit (and a balance sheet credit, since taxable income is lower), is 40 percent of the $150,000 temporary difference, or *$60,000*, as noted. The total tax is *$636,000* and *net income from continuing operations* is *$1,054,000*, as noted.

7. The next item to consider is the results of discontinued operations, the details of which appear in *supporting schedule #1*, which should be set up at this time. Here, also, a pro forma skeleton may be created, with computations inserted step by step. The two components of discontinued operations relate to (a) the results of operations, and (b) the gain or loss on disposal, both of which are presented net of taxes.

   a. As to the *results of operations*, the figures flow from the trial balance reference to "AL Division." Sales less costs and expenses results in income before taxes of *$660,000*, against which a 40-percent tax provision, or *$264,000*, is made. The net income from discontinued operations is therefore *$396,000*, as noted in schedule #1 of the completed solution following.

   b. As to the *loss on disposal*, the amount before taxes, which appears on the trial balance, and which agrees with the "other financial data" of $4,250,000 less $4,000,000, is *$250,000*. Against this loss, there is a "negative" provision for taxes, since the loss reduces the tax by $250,000 $\times$ 40 percent, or *$100,000*. The net loss from disposal is *$150,000*. The total results of discontinued operations, net of tax effect, *transferred to the income statement*, are *$246,000*.

8. The next income item appearing on the trial balance is the "gain on repurchase of bonds payable" of *$300,000*, which is substantiated by the "other financial data," indicating a repurchase at $700,000 of $1,000,000 worth of bonds. Gains or losses on the early retirement of bonds are classified as extraordinary items, net of tax effect. This is indicated on the income statement wherein the gain, reduced by the 40 percent tax, is *$180,000*.

9. At this point, net income transferred to retained earnings, in the amount of *$1,480,000*, is computed.

10. The last piece of "other financial data" to be handled concerns the capital structure. It serves as a clue that *earnings-per-share data must be disclosed* on the face of the income statement.

    a. Set up *supporting schedule #2*. First, since shares were issued during the year, a weighting is required. From January 1 through June 30, 900,000 shares were outstanding. For six months, this results in a weight of *450,000* shares. Next, there were 1,100,000 shares outstanding from July 1 through December 31, which results in a weight of *550,000*. Accordingly, the weighted-average shares outstanding are *1,000,000* shares.

b. The earnings-per-share computations, based on 1,000,000 weighted-average shares, are presented for continuing operations, $1.05; discontinued operations, $.40; loss on disposal of a segment ($.15); the total before extraordinary items, $1.30; extraordinary items, $.18, and the total earnings per share, *$1.48*. Note also that the numbers are rounded to two decimal places and the total agrees with the income statement bottom line. The total of *schedule #2* is transferred to the income statement.

11. At this point, the solution—a multiple-step income statement with supporting schedules—is complete. A quick review of the question narrative should indicate that all information has been accounted for in one way or another. Irrelevant information has been ignored and relevant information has been used to generate the required solution.

Completed Solution

Woodbine Circle Corporation
Income Statement
For the Year Ended December 31, 1997

Sales		$10,000,000
Cost of goods sold		6,200,000
Gross profit on sales		3,800,000
Operating expenses—		2,000,000
Administrative expenses		
Operating income		1,800,000
Other revenue and expense items:		
Interest on municipal bonds	$ 100,000	
Interest expense	(210,000)	(110,000)
Income from continuing operations before income tax		1,690,000
Provision for income taxes:		
Taxes currently payable	576,000	
Deferred portion on temporary difference	60,000	636,000
Net income from continuing operations		1,054,000
Discontinued operations, net of income taxes (Sch. #1)		246,000
Extraordinary gain (net of $120,000 provision for income taxes)		180,000
Net income to retained earnings		$ 1,480,000
Earnings per common share (Sch. #2)		$1.48

Schedule #1
Discontinued Operations

Income from operations of discontinued AL Division:

Sales		$2,000,000
Less: Cost of sales	$900,000	
Administrative expenses	300,000	
Interest expense	140,000	1,340,000
Income before taxes		660,000
Less income taxes		264,000 $ 396,000
Loss on disposal of division:		
Loss on sale		250,000
Less income tax effect		100,000 (150,000)
Discontinued operations, net of income taxes		$ 246,000

Schedule #2

Part 1—Weighted-Average Shares Outstanding

	Shares	Period	Weighted-Average Shares Outstanding
1/1/97 to 6/30/97	900,000	6/12	450,000
Issuance of common stock on 7/1/97	200,000		
7/1/97 to 12/31/97	1,100,000	6/12	550,000
Weighted-average shares for computing basic EPS			1,000,000

Part 2—Basic EPS Computation

EPS before discontinued division operations and extraordinary item	$1.05	<1>
EPS from operations of discontinued division	.40	<2>
EPS on disposal of discontinued division	(.15)	<3>
EPS before extraordinary item	1.30	
EPS—extraordinary item	.18	<4>
Net income per share	$1.48	

Note that there is no diluted EPS

Calculations:
<1> $1,054,000 ÷ 1,000,000 shares
<2> $ 396,000 ÷ 1,000,000 shares
<3> $ 150,000 ÷ 1,000,000 shares
<4> $ 180,000 ÷ 1,000,000 shares

Essay Questions

Essay questions on LPR, AUDIT, and FARE test your ability to verbalize your conceptual understanding of topics covered in each section. An accomplished writing style is not as important as an ability to package and communicate the key words and phrases looked for by the graders.

Skill in communication, of course, is no mean achievement. It requires organization, clarity, and a sense of the audience. The main objective is to convey to the grader as effectively as possible your response to the question requirements. In so doing, you are expected to observe the conventions of standard written English and generally to write with the competence of a learned professional.

A "learned professional" does not mean sounding like a university scholar or the author of an accounting pronouncement. You should write in your most natural, business-like English. It will save you time and it will please the grader.

On the **LPR** section, you can expect to encounter three types of essay questions:

1. *Argumentative*—Here, you are placed in the role of judge. You must analyze facts, draw conclusions, and support your conclusions with references to facts in the narrative and appropriate legal principles.
2. *Identification of legal principles or requirements.* Your ability to recall rote learning is being tested in these types of questions.
3. *Discussion of legal implications or consequences.* Here, you are more of a counselor than a magistrate. You are to discuss rather than render judgment, theorize rather than decide.

Three types of questions also appear on the **FARE** section:

1. *Classification and definition.* For the most part, these require you to recall rote learning and to write in clear, precise language. Remember not to give examples in place of definitions.
2. *Description of accounting procedures.* These are "how to" type questions in which you write what amounts to a set of directions on how to account for a transaction or situation.
3. *General discussion.* These usually contain the most open-ended type requirements and burden you with structuring an adequately developed response.

Similar type questions appear on the **AUDIT** section. Additionally, certain auditing questions require you to analyze a particular business situation and to present findings or make recommendations.

Two conclusions can be drawn from the above:

1. Several types of questions fall under the heading "essay": straight definitional, directions on "how to" or "what to," presentations of checklist findings, analysis, discussion, argument, and persuasion.
2. A broad range of cognitive and technical skills is tested: simple recall of rote learning, systematic analysis of facts and presentation of conclusions, and the ability to organize and present thoughts.

As with computational problems, you must resist the impulse to plunge right into a written solution. Too often candidates simply write down thoughts as they occur, regardless of sequence or relative importance. The result is often a disconnected, disorganized series of thoughts that needlessly loses points because the grader cannot follow a logical pattern of idea development.

Candidates must not forget the humanity of the grader. Graders work under less than ideal conditions, often after having worked a full day somewhere else. They work on what is essentially a piecework basis. If, in the midst of all this, a grader comes face to face with an essay of run-on sentences, without paragraphs, written illegibly in red ink, it is safe to conclude that he will not be disposed to give the candidate any benefit of doubt or charitable consideration.

TEST TACTICS

Communicate Clearly, Using Effective Writing Skills

CPAs are expected to communicate recommendations and conclusions in clear, unequivocal language. The ability of the candidate, therefore, to organize and present what he knows in acceptable written English is considered by the examiners. As previously noted, answers to selected essay responses are used to assess candidates' writing skills. Five percent of the total points available on all exam sections other than ARE will be allocated to writing skills.

Six qualities of good writing are expected in responses to essay questions:

1. *Coherent organization.* Ideas, in order to be communicated effectively, need to be

structured in a natural, logical way. A well-organized essay requires a certain amount of prior planning. Responses should be organized so that each principal idea is placed in the first sentence of the paragraph, followed by supporting concepts and examples.

2. *Conciseness.* Important points should be conveyed in as few words as possible (i.e., short sentences and simple wording).

3. *Clarity.* Use precise words linked together in well-formed coherent sentences. Coherence is a matter of words, sentences, and paragraphs fitting together smoothly. Prevent uncertainty; choose words that relay the intended meaning.

4. *Use of standard English.* Include proper punctuation, capitalization, and accurate spelling. While CPAs are not expected to be masters of the essay form, they are expected to have competence in standard written English.

5. *Responsiveness to the requirements of the question.* Answers should address the requirements of the question and not be a broad explanation of the general subject area.

6. *Appropriateness for the reader.* Unless otherwise instructed, candidates should assume that the intended reader is a knowledgeable CPA.

Address Your Answer to the Question

The first and most important stage in developing a good answer to any essay question is to *closely read* the question requirements. The organization of the answer should follow logically from the specified requirements. If the requirements consist of three subparts, organize your answer into three subparts; if they suggest a chart-like answer, make a chart. If the requirements tell you to "set forth reasons for conclusions stated," make sure that you do. Interpret the requirements in a straightforward, common-sense fashion, circling or underlining the key words or phrases and making sure that your answer addresses those items.

Focus on Key Facts

In addition to a careful analysis of the question requirements, *an equally careful reading of the question narrative must be made.* To ensure that key facts are noted as points to address in your answer, highlight those facts by underlining, circling, making marginal notes, tick marks, or checks. Careful reading usually means reading the narrative *twice*—once for general comprehension and once for specific focus on relevant facts.

Outline to Ensure Completeness and Coherence

One of the things that must be guarded against is incompleteness. This happens when *all* of the requirements have not been dealt with. As previously noted, prior planning is necessary to prevent this. The impulse to launch into paragraph one and to develop the essay as you go along must be resisted. Too much time and too many words are wasted that way. Rather, *a brief thumbnail outline of the answer-to-be should be used to collect and organize ideas.* The resulting answer will be concise and complete.

A "thumbnail outline," as the term implies, is a rough, brief sketch of the proposed answer. It need not take more than one or two minutes to write. Its value lies in forcing one to think before writing, in crystallizing key thoughts, and in establishing a framework for essay development. Since it is generally not feasible to write a rough draft *plus* a finished draft of each essay answer, a thumbnail outline also serves as the equivalent of a rough draft. It helps to prevent false starts, poor coherence, or writing oneself into a corner.

Be Concise

After the narrative has been digested, and after the appropriate answer has been thought through and mapped out, the writing itself should be done. Prior analysis and organization have ensured completeness and coherence so that at this point the task becomes primarily one of expressing thoughts in a readable style—not literary or scintillating, perhaps, but readable. Sentences should be short and precise. Paragraphs should be brief and limited to one principal idea.

Use Examples to Support Your Arguments

All good expository writing alternates between the abstract and the concrete, the general and the specific. Your essay answers should do likewise. For exam purposes, a paragraph should start with the statement of a general idea and be followed by supporting facts or arguments. This leads to a formula-like approach to paragraph development that, when combined with the analysis and organization techniques described above, produces a systematic approach to answering essay questions.

Practice to Increase Your Efficiency

The time constraints of the exam make it imperative to have an efficient, effective, systematic approach. The time to develop such an approach is *before* the exam by practicing with past exam questions. You should practice developing answers through at least an outline stage. Such practice will enable you to walk into the exam with no doubt in your mind about how to approach and develop a response to an essay question.

SAMPLE QUESTION AND SOLUTION

The preceding advice is illustrated by the following question and solution:

Question (AICPA Adapted)

(Note that while this question is applicable to the FARE section, the techniques have equal applicability to LPR and AUDIT.)

Deskin Company purchased a new machine to be used in its operations. The new machine was delivered by the supplier, installed by Deskin, and placed into operation. It was purchased under a long-term payment plan for which the interest charges approximated the prevailing market rates. The estimated useful life of the new machine is ten years, and its estimated residual (salvage) value is significant. Normal maintenance was performed to keep the new machine in usable condition.

Deskin also added a wing to the manufacturing building that it owns. The addition is an integral part of the building. Furthermore, Deskin made significant leasehold improvements to office space used as corporate headquarters.

Required:

a. What costs should Deskin capitalize for the new machine? How should the machine be depreciated? **Do not discuss specific methods of depreciation.**
b. How should Deskin account for the normal maintenance performed on the new machine? Why?
c. How should Deskin account for the wing added to the manufacturing building? Where should the added wing be reported on Deskin's financial statements?
d. How should Deskin account for the leasehold improvements made to its office space? Where should the leasehold improvements be reported on Deskin's financial statements?

Approach

1. Estimate the amount of time to allocate to the question based on its point value.
2. Study requirements:
   a. Read requirements first to develop a sense of what is required overall and in each part.
   b. Understand the requirements. Read carefully. Follow directions—do not discuss specific methods of depreciation.
   c. Jot down your thoughts relative to the requirements. These notes may be written on a piece of scrap paper or in the margin of the question.
   The following are sample thoughts:
   (1) *Part a*—What is the general rule for capitalizing? Describe in general terms how the amount of depreciation is determined.
   (2) *Part b*—"Account for" can be answered with a journal entry. "Why" requires explanation of the theoretical rationale.
   (3) *Parts c and d*—"Where reported" refers to the balance sheet and/or income statement effect.
   d. Visualize the answer.
   Mentally outline short sentences and paragraphs to respond to *each* part. Remember to label the part you are answering before starting. Following are relevant thoughts.
   Part a—What gets capitalized? Why? Reason. How is a machine depreciated?
   Part b—Accounting treatment for normal maintenance? Why? Reason.
   Part c—Accounting treatment—wing. On balance sheet; on income statement.
   Part d—Accounting treatment—leasehold improvements. On balance sheet; on income statement.

3. Read and analyze the narrative.
   a. Be careful and thorough.
   b. Highlight key facts.
   c. As you read, jot down pertinent thoughts on a piece of scrap paper or in the margin of the question.
   d. A mental review of concepts, principles, key phrases and/or acronyms should be made at this time; jot these down.
   e. Interpret straightforwardly; do not read into the questions what is not there.
4. Refocus on requirements. Organize key phrases and/or acronyms into a solution outline.

Solution outline

a. *Part a*
   Delivered; freight S/B capitalized.
   Installation S/B capitalized.
   Interest is expensed.
   Concept; capital expenditure vs. revenue expenditure.
   Key phrases; related to a future period, period of benefit, matching.
   Depreciable cost; cost—est. salvage.
   Depreciation; depreciable cost/est. useful life.
b. *Part b*
   Normal maintenance S/B expensed.
c. *Part c*
   Capitalize.
   Depreciate over shorter of remaining life or useful life of addition.
   Balance sheet—cost less accumulated depreciation.
d. *Part d*
   Capitalize and amortize.
   Balance sheet—cost less amortization.
   Income statement—amortization expense based on shorter of remaining lease term or useful life.
5. Write essay
   Note that the question has been thought through and visualized. Write essay answers using the preceding as a guide to development.

Completed Solution

Part a

Generally, the capitalizable costs of an asset include all costs necessary to bring an asset to its state of intended end use and to the location of such use.

Specifically, when fixed (plant) assets are purchased under a deferred (long-term) payment plan, they are recorded at the current cash price; interest is not capitalized. In addition, Deskin would capitalize delivery and installation costs.

Depreciation represents the systematic and rational allocation of the capitalizable cost of an asset over its estimated useful life. Depreciable cost is the capitalizable cost less any salvage (residual) value.

Part b

Normal maintenance costs should be expensed as incurred. Such costs do not prolong the life of an asset or make it more useful. Hence, they benefit only the period in which they are incurred.

Part c

The wing added to the building should be capitalized as a building addition. It should be depreciated over the remaining useful life of the building or the useful life of the addition, whichever is shorter.

The wing should be reported on the balance sheet under property, plant, and equipment.

Part d

Leasehold improvements are amortized over the life of the improvement, or the life of the lease, whichever is shorter.

In the balance sheet, the unamortized cost of leasehold improvements may be presented (separately) under either property, plant, and equipment, or intangible assets. The periodic amortization expense is reported in the income statement.

Comments

1. Note how essay and paragraph structure parallel the requirement structure.
2. Note how the question requirements are kept in focus. They provide the stimuli; the essay answer provides the response.
3. Note that the writing style is systematic and precise. Vagueness, ambiguity, and wordiness are successfully avoided.
4. The grader, in evaluating an answer, would work from a grading guide that outlines an ideal answer and that lists key

words or thoughts to look for in a candidate's answer. A good answer will have most of those words or thoughts listed in the thumbnail outline. The essay itself serves mainly as a vehicle for relating ideas and for communicating them effectively.

GENERAL REMINDERS FOR ESSAY AND COMPUTATIONAL QUESTIONS

Be Prepared

Bring adequate writing supplies. Writing essays or preparing schedules in pencil is permitted. An answer written with a sharp pencil looks better than one in ink with numerous cross-outs.

Budget Your Time

1. For each question, *allocate the total examination time* in proportion to the question's point value. Do not exceed the allotted time.
2. If time is running out, *outline*, in sentence form, the remainder of the answer or state how it should be completed. You may return to it after all of the questions have been answered but not before.

Plan Your Answers

1. Spend the first few minutes *scanning* the exam and *planning* the order of question attack.
2. Keep in mind that graders work from *grading guides* that outline specific items to be looked for in evaluating your answer. Your answer must contain a majority of items enumerated in order to earn sufficient credit.
3. *Support conclusions with reasons.* Demonstration of reasoning ability is just as important as arriving at correct conclusions.
4. In essay questions, use phraseology employed by the question but *do not recopy the requirements verbatim.* Such copying is a waste of time and will be construed as unnecessary padding.
5. *Concentrate on the question at hand.* Do not worry about questions already answered or questions to come.
6. *Respond directly to the requirements.* Do not present extraneous material.
7. *Say what you mean and mean what you say.* Don't equivocate or contradict yourself.

Be Legible

1. *Leave plenty of space between answers to subparts.* (Sometimes separate sheets of paper will be appropriate.) This also allows for later additions as necessary.
2. If your penmanship is so poor that legibility is a real problem, skip lines when writing answers.
3. Try to make your answer pages as *visually presentable* as possible under the circumstances. That is, observe adequate margins, use appropriate headings, use a straight-edge for charts or lines, skip a line between paragraphs and so on.
4. *Identify and turn in all answer papers.* Question number and part should be clearly indicated at the top of the page.

6. Chart Your Progress and Plan Your Course of Action

HOW TO USE THIS CHAPTER

This chapter is aimed at analyzing your test material in order to help you pinpoint your weak areas, and then providing you with a course of action.

If you have not already done so, you should now read Chapter 3—Develop Your Study Program. This chapter provides you with insight into the kind of commitment that is necessary in order to pass this examination. *Your 7-Stage Study Program* is outlined, along with guidelines as to whether you should plan a self-study program or seek help in a review course.

In order to plan your course of action, you will be taking tests in the following order:
- *Preliminary Readiness Tests* (Chapter 7)
- *May 1995 CPA Examination* (Chapter 8)
- *November 1995 CPA Examination* (Chapter 9)

Please note that certain multiple-choice questions that originally appeared on the May 1995 and November 1995 exams have been omitted due to the fact that they are no longer valid in light of recent promulgations. Also, selected questions in the area of professional responsibilities, previously contained on the LPR exam, have been moved (where appropriate) to the ARE exams.

In view of the above, the approximate point value of each question has been modified for your self-grading purposes.

Be sure to take each test, using the directions provided at the beginning of each chapter. When you have completed each test, you will use the following procedure:

Pinpoint Your Weak Areas for Each Test Section

I. *CHECK YOUR ANSWERS*
In order to do this, you should refer to the Answer Key—Four-Option Multiple-Choice Questions section of the examination chapter to check your answers. For "other objective formats," essay, and computational questions, you should compare your answers with the model answers provided.

II. *SCORE YOURSELF*
You must figure out the percentage of questions that you answer correctly. For "other objective formats," essay, and computational questions, you must compare your answer to the model answer provided and, based on correspondences between the two, estimate the percentage of credit you would be likely to achieve under exam conditions. With respect to writing skills points, the average candidate is likely to receive three to five points.

III. *EVALUATE YOUR SCORE*
If you did not get at least 75 percent of the credit available, you should prepare for intensive work.

In any event, review the section Solutions and Explained Answers for *all* questions you answered incorrectly. (This section pertains to the May 1995 CPA Examination and the November 1995 CPA Examination.)

IV. *ANALYZE YOUR ERRORS*
The charts in this chapter will help you determine your specific *Topical Area* weaknesses. You should list the number of correct answers you had (or points you achieved) under each category listed and, based on the percentage answered correctly, determine your strength or weakness in that area.

Determine Your Overall Priorities

I. *ANALYZE YOUR OVERALL SCORE*
Align your scores for each of the four sections of the test and determine which sections need the most attention. (Place your

scores in A Summary of Your Test Scores on this page.) Consider any section in which you did not get at least 75 percent of the credit available to need a great deal of work.

Now, taking those sections that need the most attention, determine which Topical Areas need the most work.

II. *REVIEW OF TEST TACTICS*

Review the test tactics in Chapter 5 for each question type. Your time-saving approach in answering questions must become automatic in order for you to do well on the examination.

Begin Your Study Program

Now that you have analyzed your overall score and determined those areas that should be worked on most diligently, you are ready to begin your actual review. Refer to Chapter 3 for guid-ance in selecting a review program that is best suited to your needs.

Test What You've Learned

When you feel you are stronger in your weak areas, take another test. This procedure should be used for the Preliminary Readiness Tests, as well as for the May 1995 CPA Examination and the November 1995 CPA Examination.

Between each test:
- Pinpoint your weak areas.
- Determine your overall priorities.
- Begin your study program.
- Test what you've learned.

To compare your test scores, fill in the spaces below. If you have not improved, you should spend more time reviewing those Topical Areas in which you have performed poorly and reviewing the test tactics in Chapter 5.

A SUMMARY OF YOUR TEST SCORES

In the space provided, place the percentage of the items that you answered correctly. Be sure that you add the scores for *four-option multiple-choice* questions, *"other objective formats"* questions, and *essay/computational* questions on both the May 1995 and November 1995 examinations.

	PRELIMINARY READINESS TESTS	MAY 1995 CPA EXAM	NOVEMBER 1995 CPA EXAM
Business Law & Professional Responsibilities (LPR)	50%		
Auditing (AUDIT)	35%		
Accounting & Reporting—Taxation, Managerial, and Governmental and Not-for-Profit Organizations (ARE)			
Financial Accounting & Reporting—Business Enterprises (FARE)			

(Minimum Percent Needed = 75 percent)

A RECORD OF YOUR TEST SCORES

Preliminary Readiness Tests

BUSINESS LAW & PROFESSIONAL RESPONSIBILITIES (LPR) TEST

I. CHECK YOUR ANSWERS using the Answer Key—Four-Option Multiple-Choice Questions on this page.

II. SCORE YOURSELF:

    Total Items ___30___

    Number Correct ___15___

    Percent Correct ___50%___

    (Minimum Percent Needed = 75 percent)

Record your score in A Summary of Your Test Scores on page 76.

III. EVALUATE YOUR SCORE: If you did not get at least 75 percent of the questions correct, you should prepare for intensive work.

IV. ANALYZE YOUR ERRORS: To determine your specific weaknesses, list the number of correct answers you had under each of the following categories and, based on the percentage answered correctly, determine your strength or weakness in that area.

FOUR-OPTION MULTIPLE-CHOICE QUESTIONS

TOPICAL AREA	QUESTIONS	NUMBER OF QUESTIONS	NUMBER CORRECT
Accountants' Legal Responsibility	1, 2	2	1
Agency	3	1	1
Bankruptcy	4, 5	2	1
Commercial Paper	6, 7	2	0
Contracts	8, 9	2	2
Corporations	10, 11	2	1
Documents of Title	12	1	1
Employment Regulations	13	1	1
Estates & Trusts	14, 15	2	2
Federal Securities Regulations	16, 17	2	1
Insurance	18	1	1
Investment Securities	19	1	0
Partnerships	20, 21	2	0
Professional Responsibilities	22	1	0
Property	23, 24	2	0
Sales	25, 26	2	1
Secured Transactions	27, 28	2	1
Suretyship and Creditor's Rights	29, 30	2	1

Total: ___15___

AUDITING (AUDIT) TEST

I. CHECK YOUR ANSWERS using the Answer Key—Four-Option Multiple-Choice Questions on this page.

II. SCORE YOURSELF:

Total Items ___30___

Number Correct ___12___

Percent Correct ___25%___

(Minimum Percent Needed = 75 percent)

Record your score in A Summary of Your Test Scores on page 76.

III. EVALUATE YOUR SCORE: If you did not get at least 75 percent of the questions correct, you should prepare for intensive work.

IV. ANALYZE YOUR ERRORS: To determine your specific weaknesses, list the number of correct answers you had under each of the following categories and, based on the percentage answered correctly, determine your strength or weakness in that area.

FOUR-OPTION MULTIPLE-CHOICE QUESTIONS

Topical Area	Questions	Number of Questions	Number Correct
Audit Evidence	1–6	6	2
Audit Planning	7–10	4	1
Audit Reporting Standards	11–15	5	3
Auditing Concepts and Standards	16–18	3	0
Electronic Data Processing (EDP)	19, 20	2	2
Internal Control	21–25	5	2
Other Reporting Areas	26–28	3	1
Statistical Sampling	29, 30	2	1

Total: ___12___

ACCOUNTING & REPORTING—TAXATION, MANAGERIAL, AND GOVERNMENTAL AND NOT-FOR-PROFIT ORGANIZATIONS (ARE) TEST

I. CHECK YOUR ANSWERS using the Answer Key—Four-Option Multiple-Choice Questions on this page.

II. SCORE YOURSELF:

    Total Items   __30__

    Number Correct   __17__

    Percent Correct _____

    (Minimum Percent Needed = 75 percent)

Record your score in A Summary of Your Test Scores on page 76.

III. EVALUATE YOUR SCORE: If you did not get at least 75 percent of the questions correct, you should prepare for intensive work.

IV. ANALYZE YOUR ERRORS: To determine your specific weaknesses, list the number of correct answers you had under each of the following categories and, based on the percentage answered correctly, determine your strength or weakness in that area.

FOUR-OPTION MULTIPLE-CHOICE QUESTIONS

TOPICAL AREA	QUESTIONS	NUMBER OF QUESTIONS	NUMBER CORRECT
Cost Accounting	1–5	5	2
Federal Income Taxes—Capital Gains & Losses	6	1	0
Federal Income Taxes—Corporations	7–9	3	2
Federal Income Taxes—Estates & Trusts	10	1	1
Federal Income Taxes—Exempt Organizations	11	1	1
Federal Income Taxes—Individuals	12–14	3	3
Federal Income Taxes—Partnerships	15	1	1
Managerial Accounting & Quantitative Methods	16–20	5	4
Not-for-Profit Accounting—Governmental Units	21–25	5	1
Not-for-Profit Accounting—Other than Governmental Units	26–30	5	2

Total: __17__

FINANCIAL ACCOUNTING & REPORTING— BUSINESS ENTERPRISES (FARE) TEST

I. CHECK YOUR ANSWERS using the Answer Key—Four-Option Multiple-Choice Questions on this page.

II. SCORE YOURSELF:
    Total Items ___30___
    Number Correct ___18___
    Percent Correct _____
    (Minimum Percent Needed = 75 percent)
    Record your score in A Summary of Your Test Scores on page 76.

III. EVALUATE YOUR SCORE: If you did not get at least 75 percent of the questions correct, you should prepare for intensive work.

IV. ANALYZE YOUR ERRORS: To determine your specific weaknesses, list the number of correct answers you had under each of the following categories and, based on the percentage answered correctly, determine your strength or weakness in that area.

FOUR-OPTION MULTIPLE-CHOICE QUESTIONS

TOPICAL AREA	QUESTIONS	NUMBER OF QUESTIONS	NUMBER CORRECT
Accounting Concepts	1	1	1
Accounting Fundamentals	2, 3	2	1
Bonds, Accounting for	4	1	0
Cash Flows	5, 6	2	0
Consolidation and Business Combination	7, 8	2	2
Financial Statements	9, 10	2	2
Fixed Assets	11, 12	2	1
Foreign Currency Translation	13	1	0
Income Taxes, Accounting for	14	1	1
Installment Sales	15	1	1
Intangibles	16	1	0
Inventories	17	1	1
Investments	18, 19	2	1
Leases	20, 21	2	1
Liabilities	22, 23	2	1
Long-Term Contracts	24	1	0
Partnerships	25	1	1
Pension Costs	26	1	0
Receivables	27, 28	2	2
Stockholders' Equity	29, 30	2	2

Total: ___18___

Turn to How to Use This Chapter (page 75) for guidance in planning your course of action.

May 1995 CPA Examination

BUSINESS LAW & PROFESSIONAL RESPONSIBILITIES (LPR) SECTION

I. CHECK YOUR ANSWERS using the Answer Key—Four-Option Multiple-Choice Questions on page 179 and the Solutions and Explained Answers section on page 183.

II. SCORE YOURSELF: To estimate points earned on *"other objective formats" and essay questions*, compare your answers to the model answers provided in the section Solutions and Explained Answers (see page 183). Based on correspondences between your answers and the model answers, you should be able to get a rough idea of how many points your answers would earn under exam conditions.

	Four-Option Multiple-Choice	Other Objective Formats	Essay
Total Items	59*	2†	2†
Points Earned	_____	_____	_____

Total Points Earned = ____

* 1.02 point each
† 10 points each

Record your score in A Summary of Your Test Scores on page 76.

III. EVALUATE YOUR SCORE: If you did not get at least 75 percent of the questions correct, you should prepare for intensive work.

In any event, you should begin your study program by reviewing the section Solutions and Explained Answers (see page 183) for *all* questions you answered incorrectly.

IV. ANALYZE YOUR ERRORS: To determine your specific weaknesses, list the number of correct answers you had under each of the following categories and, based on the percentage answered correctly, determine your strength or weakness in that area.

FOUR-OPTION MULTIPLE-CHOICE QUESTIONS

TOPICAL AREA	QUESTIONS	NUMBER OF QUESTIONS	NUMBER CORRECT
Agency	6–9	4	
Bankruptcy	28–35	8	
Commercial Paper	41–50	10	
Contracts	16–25	10	
Employment Regulations	36–40	5	
Estates and Trusts	10–15	6	
Insurance	59, 60	2	
Professional Responsibilities	1–3, 5	4	
Property	51–58	8	
Suretyship and Creditor's Rights	26, 27	2	

Total: _____

"OTHER OBJECTIVE FORMATS" QUESTIONS

TOPICAL AREA	QUESTIONS	POINTS AVAILABLE	POINTS EARNED
Corporations	2b	5	
Partnerships	2a	5	
Sales	3a	5	
Secured Transactions	3b	5	

Total: _____

ESSAY QUESTIONS

TOPICAL AREA	QUESTIONS	POINTS AVAILABLE	POINTS EARNED
Accountants' Legal Responsibility	4	10	
Federal Securities Regulations	5	10	

Total: _____

AUDITING (AUDIT) SECTION

I. CHECK YOUR ANSWERS using the Answer Key—Four-Option Multiple-Choice Questions on page 179 and the Solutions and Explained Answers section on page 203.

II. SCORE YOURSELF: To estimate points earned on *"other objective formats" and essay questions*, compare your answers to the model answers provided in the section Solutions and Explained Answers (see page 203). Based on correspondences between your answers and the model answers, you should be able to get a rough idea of how many points your answers would earn under exam conditions.

	Four-Option Multiple-Choice	Other Objective Formats	Essay
Total Items	88*	2†	2†
Points Earned	_____	_____	_____

Total Points Earned = _____

* .68 point each
† 10 points each

Record your score in A Summary of Your Test Scores on page 76.

III. EVALUATE YOUR SCORE: If you did not get at least 75 percent of the questions correct, you should prepare for intensive work.

In any event, begin your study program by reviewing the section Solutions and Explained Answers (see page 203) for *all* questions you answered incorrectly.

IV. ANALYZE YOUR ERRORS: To determine your specific weaknesses, list the number of correct answers you had under each of the following categories and, based on the percentage answered correctly, determine your strength or weakness in that area.

FOUR-OPTION MULTIPLE-CHOICE QUESTIONS

Topical Area	Questions	Number of Questions	Number Correct
Audit Evidence	9, 13–15, 32, 34, 37, 39–46, 52–57, 63, 66–69, 73	27	
Audit Planning	1–4, 7, 8, 10–12, 16, 18, 47, 48, 59–62, 70, 71, 74	20	
Audit Reporting Standards	65, 77, 85, 87	4	
Auditing Concepts and Standards	5, 6, 23	3	
Electronic Data Processing (EDP)	72	1	
Internal Control	17, 19, 24, 26, 27, 29–31, 33, 38, 84, 88	12	
Other Reporting Areas	20–22, 58, 75, 76, 78–83, 86, 89, 90	15	
Statistical Sampling	28, 35, 36, 49–51	6	

Total: _____

"OTHER OBJECTIVE FORMATS" QUESTIONS

Topical Area	Questions	Points Available	Points Earned
Audit Reporting	2	10	
Internal Control	3	10	

Total: _____

ESSAY QUESTIONS

Topical Area	Questions	Points Available	Points Earned
Audit Evidence	5	10	
Internal Control	4	10	

Total: _____

ACCOUNTING & REPORTING—TAXATION, MANAGERIAL, AND GOVERNMENTAL AND NOT-FOR-PROFIT ORGANIZATIONS (ARE) SECTION

I. CHECK YOUR ANSWERS using the Answer Key—Four-Option Multiple-Choice Questions on page 180 and the Solutions and Explained Answers section on page 241.

II. SCORE YOURSELF: To estimate points earned on *"other objective formats"* questions, compare your answers to the model answers provided in the section Solutions and Explained Answers (see page 241). Based on correspondences between your answers and the model answers, you should be able to get a rough idea of how many points your answers would earn under exam conditions.

	Four-Option Multiple-Choice	Other Objective Formats
Total Items	_____61*_____	_2†_
Points Earned	_____	_____
	Total Points Earned = ____	

* .98 point each
† 20 points each

Record your score in A Summary of Your Test Scores on page 76.

III. EVALUATE YOUR SCORE: If you did not get at least 75 percent of the questions correct, you should prepare for intensive work.

In any event, begin your study program by reviewing the section Solutions and Explained Answers (see page 241) for all questions you answered incorrectly.

IV. ANALYZE YOUR ERRORS: To determine your specific weaknesses, list the number of correct answers you had under each of the following categories and, based on the percentage answered correctly, determine your strength or weakness in that area.

FOUR-OPTION MULTIPLE-CHOICE QUESTIONS

TOPICAL AREA	QUESTIONS	NUMBER OF QUESTIONS	NUMBER CORRECT
Cost Accounting	40–43	4	
Federal Income Taxes— Capital Gains & Losses	3, 4	2	
Federal Income Taxes— Corporations	21–25	5	
Federal Income Taxes— Depreciation & Depreciation Recapture	2, 5	2	
Federal Income Taxes— Estates & Trusts	31–33	3	
Federal Income Taxes— Exempt Organizations	34, 35	2	
Federal Income Taxes— Individuals	1, 6–14, 17, 18	12	
Federal Income Taxes— Partnerships	26–30	5	
Federal Income Taxes— Tax Accounting Methods	15	1	
Federal Income Taxes— Tax Preparers' Responsibilities	LPR#4	1	
Federal Income Taxes— Tax Procedures & Administration	16, 19, 20	3	
Managerial Accounting & Quantitative Methods	36–39, 44–50	11	
Not-for-Profit Accounting— Governmental Units	51–53, 55, 56	5	
Not-for-Profit Accounting— Other than Governmental Units	54, 57–60	5	

Total: _____

"OTHER OBJECTIVE FORMATS" QUESTIONS

TOPICAL AREA	QUESTIONS	POINTS AVAILABLE	POINTS EARNED
Federal Incomes Taxes— Corporations	3	20	
Not-for-Profit Accounting— Governmental Units	2	20	

Total: _____

FINANCIAL ACCOUNTING & REPORTING—BUSINESS ENTERPRISES (FARE) SECTION

I. CHECK YOUR ANSWERS using the Answer Key—Four-Option Multiple-Choice Questions on page 182 and the Solutions and Explained Answers section on page 271.

II. SCORE YOURSELF: To estimate points earned on *"other objective formats" and essay/computational questions*, compare your answers to the model answers provided in the section Solutions and Explained Answers (see page 271). Based on correspondences between your answers and the model answers, you should be able to get a rough idea of how many points your answers would earn under exam conditions.

Record your score in A Summary of Your Test Scores on page 76.

III. EVALUATE YOUR SCORE: If you did not get at least 75 percent of the questions correct, you should prepare for intensive work.

In any event, begin your study program by reviewing the section Solutions and Explained Answers (see page 271) for *all* questions you answered incorrectly.

IV. ANALYZE YOUR ERRORS: To determine your specific weaknesses, list the number of correct answers you had under each of the following categories and, based on the percentage answered correctly, determine your strength or weakness in that area.

	Four-Option Multiple-Choice	Other Objective Formats	Essay/Computational
Total Items	56*	2†	2†
Points Earned	_____	_____	_____

Total Points Earned = _____

* 1.07 point each
† 10 points each

FOUR-OPTION MULTIPLE-CHOICE QUESTIONS

TOPICAL AREA	QUESTIONS	NUMBER OF QUESTIONS	NUMBER CORRECT
Accounting Concepts	1, 38	2	
Accounting Fundamentals	14, 25	2	
Bonds, Accounting for	19, 20	2	
Cash Flows	47–49	3	
Consolidation and Business Combination	50–54	5	
Financial Statements	2, 34, 40, 44–46, 55, 56	8	
Fixed Assets	12, 30, 36, 37	4	
Foreign Currency Translation	31, 32	2	
Income Taxes, Accounting for	16, 17, 41–43	5	
Installment Sales	27	1	
Intangibles	13	1	
Inventories	10, 11, 33	3	
Investments	6, 29	2	
Leases	28	1	
Liabilities	4, 5, 15, 21, 22	5	
Long-Term Contracts	26	1	
Partnerships	23, 24	2	
Pension Costs	18, 39, 57	3	
Receivables	7–9, 35	4	

Total: _____

"OTHER OBJECTIVE FORMATS" QUESTIONS

TOPICAL AREA	QUESTIONS	POINTS AVAILABLE	POINTS EARNED
Financial Accounting	3	10	
Stockholders' Equity	2	10	

Total: _____

ESSAY/COMPUTATIONAL QUESTIONS

TOPICAL AREA	QUESTIONS	POINTS AVAILABLE	POINTS EARNED
Investments	4	10	
Leases	5	10	

Total: _____

November 1995 CPA Examination

BUSINESS LAW & PROFESSIONAL RESPONSIBILITIES (LPR) SECTION

I. CHECK YOUR ANSWERS using the Answer Key—Four-Option Multiple-Choice Questions on page 304 and the Solutions and Explained Answers section on page 374.

II. SCORE YOURSELF: To estimate points earned on *"other objective formats" and essay questions*, compare your answers to the model answers provided in the section Solutions and Explained Answers (see page 374). Based on correspondences between your answers and the model answers, you should be able to get a rough idea of how many points your answers would earn under exam conditions.

Record your score in A Summary of Your Test Scores on page 76.

III. EVALUATE YOUR SCORE: If you did not get at least 75 percent of the questions correct, you should prepare for intensive work.

In any event, begin your study program by reviewing the section Solutions and Explained Answers (see page 374) for *all* questions you answered incorrectly.

IV. ANALYZE YOUR ERRORS: To determine your specific weaknesses, list the number of correct answers you had under each of the following categories and, based on the percentage answered correctly, determine your strength or weakness in that area.

	Four-Option Multiple-Choice	Other Objective Formats	Essay
Total Items	58*	2†	2†
Points Earned	_____	_____	_____

Total Points Earned = _____

* 1.03 point each
† 10 points each

FOUR-OPTION MULTIPLE-CHOICE QUESTIONS

Topical Area	Questions	Number of Questions	Number Correct
Accountants' Legal Responsibility	8–15	8	
Corporations	21–25	5	
Employment Regulations	31–40	10	
Insurance	60	1	
Partnerships	16–20	5	
Professional Responsibilities	1–5	5	
Property	51–59	9	
Sales	41–50	10	
Suretyship and Creditor's Rights	26–30	5	

Total: _____

"OTHER OBJECTIVE FORMATS" QUESTIONS

TOPICAL AREA	QUESTIONS	POINTS AVAILABLE	POINTS EARNED
Agency	2a	5	
Bankruptcy	3a	5	
Estates and Trusts	2b	5	
Federal Securities Regulations	3b	5	

Total: _____

ESSAY QUESTIONS

TOPICAL AREA	QUESTIONS	POINTS AVAILABLE	POINTS EARNED
Contracts	4	10	
Secured Transactions/ Commercial Paper	5	10	

Total: _____

AUDITING (AUDIT) SECTION

I. CHECK YOUR ANSWERS using the Answer Key—Four-Option Multiple-Choice Questions on page 369 and the Solutions and Explained Answers section on page 394.

II. SCORE YOURSELF: To estimate points earned on *"other objective formats" and essay questions,* compare your answers to the model answers provided in the section Solutions and Explained Answers (see page 394). Based on correspondences between your answers and the model answers, you should be able to get a rough idea of how many points your answers would earn under exam conditions.

	Four-Option Multiple-Choice	Other Objective Formats	Essay
Total Items	87*	2†	2†
Points Earned	_____	_____	_____

Total Points Earned = _____

* .68 point each
† 10 points each

Record your score in A Summary of Your Test Scores on page 76.

III. EVALUATE YOUR SCORE: If you did not get at least 75 percent of the questions correct, you should prepare for intensive work.

In any event, begin your study program by reviewing the section Solutions and Explained Answers (see page 394) for *all* questions you answered incorrectly.

IV. ANALYZE YOUR ERRORS: To determine your specific weaknesses, list the number of correct answers you had under each of the following categories and, based on the percentage answered correctly, determine your strength or weakness in that area.

FOUR-OPTION MULTIPLE-CHOICE QUESTIONS

TOPICAL AREA	QUESTIONS	NUMBER OF QUESTIONS	NUMBER CORRECT
Audit Evidence	28, 38–40, 45–51, 55, 57–59, 72	16	
Audit Planning	1, 2, 4, 41, 53, 54, 60	7	
Audit Reporting Standards	56, 61–63, 65–67, 69, 71, 73–78, 85, 87	17	
Auditing Concepts and Standards	68	1	
Electronic Data Processing (EDP)	3, 10, 14, 52	4	
Internal Control	5–9, 11–13, 15, 16, 18, 20–24, 26, 27, 29–32, 34–37, 84	27	
Other Reporting Areas	79–83, 86, 88–90	9	
Statistical Sampling	17, 19, 25, 33, 43, 44	6	

Total: _____

"OTHER OBJECTIVE FORMATS" QUESTIONS

TOPICAL AREA	QUESTIONS	POINTS AVAILABLE	POINTS EARNED
Audit Evidence	2	10	
Other Reporting Areas	3	10	

Total: _____

ESSAY QUESTIONS

TOPICAL AREA	QUESTIONS	POINTS AVAILABLE	POINTS EARNED
Audit Evidence	4	10	
Audit Evidence	5	10	

Total: _____

ACCOUNTING & REPORTING—TAXATION, MANAGERIAL, AND GOVERNMENTAL AND NOT-FOR-PROFIT ORGANIZATIONS (ARE) SECTION

I. CHECK YOUR ANSWERS using the Answer Key—Four-Option Multiple-Choice Questions on page 370 and the Solutions and Explained Answers section on page 430.

II. SCORE YOURSELF: To estimate points earned on *"other objective formats" questions*, compare your answers to the model answers provided in the section Solutions and Explained Answers (see page 430). Based on correspondences between your answers and the model answers, you should be able to get a rough idea of how many points your answers would earn under exam conditions.

	Four-Option Multiple-Choice	Other Objective Formats
Total Items	77*	4†
Points Earned		

Total Points Earned = ____

* .78 point each
† 10 points each

III. EVALUATE YOUR SCORE: If you did not get at least 75 percent of the questions correct, you should prepare for intensive work.

In any event, begin your study program by reviewing the section Solutions and Explained Answers (see page 430) for *all* questions you answered incorrectly.

IV. ANALYZE YOUR ERRORS: To determine your specific weaknesses, list the number of correct answers you had under each of the following categories and, based on the per-

FOUR-OPTION MULTIPLE-CHOICE QUESTIONS

TOPICAL AREA	QUESTIONS	NUMBER OF QUESTIONS	NUMBER CORRECT
Cost Accounting	40, 46–49, 56	6	
Federal Income Taxes— Capital Gains & Losses	6	1	
Federal Income Taxes— Corporations	1, 3, 4, 7–9, 12–15, 17–22	16	
Federal Income Taxes— Depreciation & Depreciation Recapture	5	1	
Federal Income Taxes— Estates & Trusts	35, 36	2	
Federal Income Taxes— Exempt Organizations	37, 38	2	
Federal Income Taxes— Partnerships	27–34	8	
Federal Income Taxes— Tax Accounting Methods	2, 11	2	
Federal Income Taxes— Tax Preparers' Responsibilities	LPR#6, LPR#7, 26	3	
Federal Income Taxes— Tax Procedures & Administration	10, 16, 23–25	5	
Managerial Accounting & Quantitative Methods	39, 41–45, 50–55	12	
Not-for-Profit Accounting— Governmental Units	57–73	17	
Not-for-Profit Accounting— Other than Governmental Units	74, 75	2	

Total: _____

"OTHER OBJECTIVE FORMATS" QUESTIONS

TOPICAL AREA	QUESTIONS	NUMBER OF QUESTIONS	NUMBER CORRECT
Federal Income Taxes— Corporations, Special Organizational Considerations	2	10	
Federal Income Taxes— Individuals	3	10	
Not-for-Profit Accounting, Governmental Units	5	10	
Not-for-Profit Accounting, Other than Governmental Units	4	10	

Total: _____

centage answered correctly, determine your strength or weakness in that area.

FINANCIAL ACCOUNTING & REPORTING— BUSINESS ENTERPRISES (FARE) SECTION

I. CHECK YOUR ANSWERS using the Answer Key—Four-Option Multiple-Choice Questions on page 372 and the Solutions and Explained Answers section on page 469.

II. SCORE YOURSELF: To estimate points earned on *"other objective formats" and essay/computational* questions, compare your answers to the model answers provided in the section Solutions and Explained Answers (see page 469). Based on correspondences between your answers and the model answers, you should be able to get a rough idea of how many points your answers would earn under exam conditions.

	Four-Option Multiple-Choice	Other Objective Formats	Essay/ Compu-tational
Total Items	60*	2†	2†
Points Earned	_____	_____	_____

Total Points Earned = ____

* 1 point each
† 10 points each

Record your score in A Summary of Your Test Scores on page 76.

III. EVALUATE YOUR SCORE: If you did not get at least 75 percent of the questions correct, you should prepare for intensive work.

In any event, begin your study program by reviewing the section Solutions and Explained Answers (see page 469) for *all* questions you answered incorrectly.

IV. ANALYZE YOUR ERRORS: To determine your specific weaknesses, list the number of correct answers you had under each of the following categories and, based on the percentage answered correctly, determine your strength or weakness in that area.

FOUR-OPTION MULTIPLE-CHOICE QUESTIONS

Topical Area	Questions	Number of Questions	Number Correct
Accounting Concepts	1–3, 5, 6	5	
Accounting Fundamentals	24, 30	2	
Cash Flows	47, 48	2	
Consolidation and Business Combination	49–53	5	
Financial Statement Analysis	58, 60	2	
Financial Statements	4, 7, 8, 39–44, 54–56	12	
Foreign Currency Translation	32	1	
Income Taxes, Accounting for	36–38	3	
Inflation Accounting	57	1	
Installment Sales	10, 31	2	
Intangibles	33	1	
Inventories	9	1	
Investments	26–28, 35	4	
Leases	11, 12, 29, 34	4	
Liabilities	13, 16, 17, 59	4	
Partnerships	23	1	
Pension Costs	14, 15	2	
Stockholders' Equity	18–22, 25, 45, 46	8	

Total: _____

"OTHER OBJECTIVE FORMATS" QUESTIONS

Topical Area	Questions	Number of Questions	Number Correct
Corporation Bonds & Liabilities	3	10	
Investments	2	10	

Total: _____

ESSAY/COMPUTATIONAL QUESTIONS

Topical Area	Questions	Number of Questions	Number Correct
Accounting Fundamentals	4	10	
Intangible Assets	5	10	

Total: _____

Answer Sheet

PRELIMINARY READINESS TESTS

LPR	AUDIT	ARE	FARE
1. Ⓐ Ⓑ Ⓒ Ⓓ	1. Ⓐ Ⓑ Ⓒ Ⓓ	1. Ⓐ Ⓑ Ⓒ Ⓓ	1. Ⓐ Ⓑ Ⓒ Ⓓ
2. Ⓐ Ⓑ Ⓒ Ⓓ	2. Ⓐ Ⓑ Ⓒ Ⓓ	2. Ⓐ Ⓑ Ⓒ Ⓓ	2. Ⓐ Ⓑ Ⓒ Ⓓ
3. Ⓐ Ⓑ Ⓒ Ⓓ	3. Ⓐ Ⓑ Ⓒ Ⓓ	3. Ⓐ Ⓑ Ⓒ Ⓓ	3. Ⓐ Ⓑ Ⓒ Ⓓ
4. Ⓐ Ⓑ Ⓒ Ⓓ	4. Ⓐ Ⓑ Ⓒ Ⓓ	4. Ⓐ Ⓑ Ⓒ Ⓓ	4. Ⓐ Ⓑ Ⓒ Ⓓ
5. Ⓐ Ⓑ Ⓒ Ⓓ	5. Ⓐ Ⓑ Ⓒ Ⓓ	5. Ⓐ Ⓑ Ⓒ Ⓓ	5. Ⓐ Ⓑ Ⓒ Ⓓ
6. Ⓐ Ⓑ Ⓒ Ⓓ	6. Ⓐ Ⓑ Ⓒ Ⓓ	6. Ⓐ Ⓑ Ⓒ Ⓓ	6. Ⓐ Ⓑ Ⓒ Ⓓ
7. Ⓐ Ⓑ Ⓒ Ⓓ	7. Ⓐ Ⓑ Ⓒ Ⓓ	7. Ⓐ Ⓑ Ⓒ Ⓓ	7. Ⓐ Ⓑ Ⓒ Ⓓ
8. Ⓐ Ⓑ Ⓒ Ⓓ	8. Ⓐ Ⓑ Ⓒ Ⓓ	8. Ⓐ Ⓑ Ⓒ Ⓓ	8. Ⓐ Ⓑ Ⓒ Ⓓ
9. Ⓐ Ⓑ Ⓒ Ⓓ	9. Ⓐ Ⓑ Ⓒ Ⓓ	9. Ⓐ Ⓑ Ⓒ Ⓓ	9. Ⓐ Ⓑ Ⓒ Ⓓ
10. Ⓐ Ⓑ Ⓒ Ⓓ	10. Ⓐ Ⓑ Ⓒ Ⓓ	10. Ⓐ Ⓑ Ⓒ Ⓓ	10. Ⓐ Ⓑ Ⓒ Ⓓ
11. Ⓐ Ⓑ Ⓒ Ⓓ	11. Ⓐ Ⓑ Ⓒ Ⓓ	11. Ⓐ Ⓑ Ⓒ Ⓓ	11. Ⓐ Ⓑ Ⓒ Ⓓ
12. Ⓐ Ⓑ Ⓒ Ⓓ	12. Ⓐ Ⓑ Ⓒ Ⓓ	12. Ⓐ Ⓑ Ⓒ Ⓓ	12. Ⓐ Ⓑ Ⓒ Ⓓ
13. Ⓐ Ⓑ Ⓒ Ⓓ	13. Ⓐ Ⓑ Ⓒ Ⓓ	13. Ⓐ Ⓑ Ⓒ Ⓓ	13. Ⓐ Ⓑ Ⓒ Ⓓ
14. Ⓐ Ⓑ Ⓒ Ⓓ	14. Ⓐ Ⓑ Ⓒ Ⓓ	14. Ⓐ Ⓑ Ⓒ Ⓓ	14. Ⓐ Ⓑ Ⓒ Ⓓ
15. Ⓐ Ⓑ Ⓒ Ⓓ	15. Ⓐ Ⓑ Ⓒ Ⓓ	15. Ⓐ Ⓑ Ⓒ Ⓓ	15. Ⓐ Ⓑ Ⓒ Ⓓ
16. Ⓐ Ⓑ Ⓒ Ⓓ	16. Ⓐ Ⓑ Ⓒ Ⓓ	16. Ⓐ Ⓑ Ⓒ Ⓓ	16. Ⓐ Ⓑ Ⓒ Ⓓ
17. Ⓐ Ⓑ Ⓒ Ⓓ	17. Ⓐ Ⓑ Ⓒ Ⓓ	17. Ⓐ Ⓑ Ⓒ Ⓓ	17. Ⓐ Ⓑ Ⓒ Ⓓ
18. Ⓐ Ⓑ Ⓒ Ⓓ	18. Ⓐ Ⓑ Ⓒ Ⓓ	18. Ⓐ Ⓑ Ⓒ Ⓓ	18. Ⓐ Ⓑ Ⓒ Ⓓ
19. Ⓐ Ⓑ Ⓒ Ⓓ	19. Ⓐ Ⓑ Ⓒ Ⓓ	19. Ⓐ Ⓑ Ⓒ Ⓓ	19. Ⓐ Ⓑ Ⓒ Ⓓ
20. Ⓐ Ⓑ Ⓒ Ⓓ	20. Ⓐ Ⓑ Ⓒ Ⓓ	20. Ⓐ Ⓑ Ⓒ Ⓓ	20. Ⓐ Ⓑ Ⓒ Ⓓ
21. Ⓐ Ⓑ Ⓒ Ⓓ	21. Ⓐ Ⓑ Ⓒ Ⓓ	21. Ⓐ Ⓑ Ⓒ Ⓓ	21. Ⓐ Ⓑ Ⓒ Ⓓ
22. Ⓐ Ⓑ Ⓒ Ⓓ	22. Ⓐ Ⓑ Ⓒ Ⓓ	22. Ⓐ Ⓑ Ⓒ Ⓓ	22. Ⓐ Ⓑ Ⓒ Ⓓ
23. Ⓐ Ⓑ Ⓒ Ⓓ	23. Ⓐ Ⓑ Ⓒ Ⓓ	23. Ⓐ Ⓑ Ⓒ Ⓓ	23. Ⓐ Ⓑ Ⓒ Ⓓ
24. Ⓐ Ⓑ Ⓒ Ⓓ	24. Ⓐ Ⓑ Ⓒ Ⓓ	24. Ⓐ Ⓑ Ⓒ Ⓓ	24. Ⓐ Ⓑ Ⓒ Ⓓ
25. Ⓐ Ⓑ Ⓒ Ⓓ	25. Ⓐ Ⓑ Ⓒ Ⓓ	25. Ⓐ Ⓑ Ⓒ Ⓓ	25. Ⓐ Ⓑ Ⓒ Ⓓ
26. Ⓐ Ⓑ Ⓒ Ⓓ	26. Ⓐ Ⓑ Ⓒ Ⓓ	26. Ⓐ Ⓑ Ⓒ Ⓓ	26. Ⓐ Ⓑ Ⓒ Ⓓ
27. Ⓐ Ⓑ Ⓒ Ⓓ	27. Ⓐ Ⓑ Ⓒ Ⓓ	27. Ⓐ Ⓑ Ⓒ Ⓓ	27. Ⓐ Ⓑ Ⓒ Ⓓ
28. Ⓐ Ⓑ Ⓒ Ⓓ	28. Ⓐ Ⓑ Ⓒ Ⓓ	28. Ⓐ Ⓑ Ⓒ Ⓓ	28. Ⓐ Ⓑ Ⓒ Ⓓ
29. Ⓐ Ⓑ Ⓒ Ⓓ	29. Ⓐ Ⓑ Ⓒ Ⓓ	29. Ⓐ Ⓑ Ⓒ Ⓓ	29. Ⓐ Ⓑ Ⓒ Ⓓ
30. Ⓐ Ⓑ Ⓒ Ⓓ	30. Ⓐ Ⓑ Ⓒ Ⓓ	30. Ⓐ Ⓑ Ⓒ Ⓓ	30. Ⓐ Ⓑ Ⓒ Ⓓ

7. Preliminary Readiness Tests

Honest self-appraisal is one of the first steps to take in deciding what sort of review program will work best for you. As noted in Chapter 3, self-appraisal involves an honest assessment of academic preparation as well as individual work habits. Regarding the latter, it is obvious that different people require differing degrees of outside direction. Some candidates function best in a review course that makes no assumptions about their ability to learn independently of the course activities. Others require the structure of a well-designed course but have the ability to guide their own efforts within the course framework.

Assessment of academic preparation is best begun by looking at the AICPA's *Content Specification Outlines* (see Chapter 1). They should be used as checklists for you to evaluate the range and depth of your subject mastery. After this procedure is performed, the need for an organized review program becomes apparent. A second procedure is the use of diagnostic readiness tests that present you with representative CPA exam questions. Such tests give you a rough idea of how, given your current state of knowledge, you could expect to do on the CPA exam were you to sit for it immediately.

The following tests comprise a total of 120 four-option multiple-choice questions. These questions have been selected from past questions on actual CPA examinations. They are of average difficulty and were selected to represent the range of topics tested by four-option multiple-choice questions on each examination section. Though no essay, computational, or other objective formats questions have been included, your score on these tests will provide you with a good idea as to your overall preparedness for the CPA examination.

Allow no more than 45 to 55 minutes for the Business Law and Professional Responsibilities (LPR) and Auditing (AUDIT) sections, no more

than 60 to 70 minutes for Accounting and Reporting—Taxation, Managerial, and Governmental and Not-for-Profit Organizations (ARE), and no more than 65 to 75 minutes for Financial Accounting and Reporting—Business Enterprises (FARE). Take each section in one sitting.

Before beginning these readiness tests, be sure to review the test tactics outlined in Chapter 5—How to Approach CPA Examination Questions. After completing the readiness tests, check your answers against the Answer Key on page 116. Then turn to Chapter 6—Chart Your Progress and Plan Your Course of Action for guidance in analyzing your score and planning your review program.

Remember: Read directions carefully!

TESTS

Business Law & Professional Responsibilities (LPR)

(Estimated time: 45 to 55 minutes)

Directions: Select the **best** answer for each of the following items. Select only one answer for each item. Answer all items.

1. A CPA firm issues an unqualified opinion on financial statements not prepared in accordance with GAAP. The CPA firm will have acted with scienter in all the following circumstances **except** where the firm
   A. Intentionally disregards the truth.
   B. Has actual knowledge of fraud.
   C. Negligently performs auditing procedures.
   D. Intends to gain monetarily by concealing fraud.

2. A CPA partnership may, without being lawfully subpoenaed or without the client's consent, make client workpapers available to
   A. An individual purchasing the entire partnership.
   B. The IRS.
   C. The SEC.
   D. Any surviving partner(s) on the death of a partner.

3. Generally, an agency relationship is terminated by operation of law in all of the following situations **except** the
   A. Principal's death.
   B. Principal's incapacity.
   C. Agent's renunciation of the agency.
   D. Agent's failure to acquire a necessary business license.

4. On June 5, 1996, Gold rented equipment under a four-year lease. On March 8, 1997, Gold was petitioned involuntarily into bankruptcy under the Federal Bankruptcy Code's liquidation provisions. A trustee was appointed. The fair market value of the equipment exceeds the balance of the lease payments due. The trustee
   A. May **not** reject the equipment lease because the fair market value of the equipment exceeds the balance of the lease payments due.
   B. May elect **not** to assume the equipment lease.
   C. Must assume the equipment lease because its term exceeds one year.
   D. Must assume and subsequently assign the equipment lease.

5. A claim will **not** be discharged in a bankruptcy proceeding if it
   A. Is brought by a secured creditor and remains unsatisfied after receipt of the proceeds from the disposition of the collateral.
   B. Is for unintentional torts that resulted in bodily injury to the claimant.
   C. Arises from an extension of credit based upon false representations.
   D. Arises out of the breach of a contract by the debtor.

6. Which of the following negotiable instruments is subject to the provisions of the UCC Commercial Paper Article?
   A. Installment note payable on the first day of each month.
   B. Warehouse receipt.
   C. Bill of lading payable to order.
   D. Corporate bearer bond with a maturity date of January 1, 1999.

7. Bond fraudulently induced Teal to make a note payable to Wilk, to whom Bond was indebted. Bond delivered the note to Wilk. Wilk negotiated the instrument to Monk, who purchased it with knowledge of the fraud and after it was overdue. If Wilk qualifies as a holder in due course, which of the following statements is correct?
   A. Monk has the standing of a holder in due course through Wilk.
   B. Teal can successfully assert the defense of fraud in the inducement against Monk.
   C. Monk personally qualifies as a holder in due course.
   D. Teal can successfully assert the defense of fraud in the inducement against Wilk.

8. To satisfy the consideration requirement for a valid contract, the consideration exchanged by the parties must be
   A. Legally sufficient.
   B. Payable in legal tender.
   C. Simultaneously paid and received.
   D. Of the same economic value.

9. Payne entered into a written agreement to sell a parcel of land to Stevens. At the time the agreement was executed, Payne had consumed alcoholic beverages. Payne's ability to understand the nature and terms of the contract was not impaired. Stevens did not believe that Payne was intoxicated. The contract is
   A. Void as a matter of law.
   B. Legally binding on both parties.
   C. Voidable at Payne's option.
   D. Voidable at Steven's option.

10. In general, which of the following must be contained in articles of incorporation?
    A. Names of the initial officers and their terms of office.
    B. Classes of stock authorized for issuance.
    C. Names of states in which the corporation will be doing business.
    D. Name of the state in which the corporation will maintain its principal place of business.

11. Which of the following statements is correct concerning the similarities between a limited partnership and a corporation?
    A. Each is created under a statute and must file a copy of its certificate with the proper state authorities.
    B. All corporate stockholders and all partners in a limited partnership have limited liability.
    C. Both are recognized for federal income tax purposes as taxable entities.
    D. Both are allowed statutorily to have perpetual existence.

12. Under a nonnegotiable bill of lading, a carrier who accepts goods for shipment must deliver the goods to
    A. Any holder of the bill of lading.
    B. Any party subsequently named by the seller.
    C. The seller who was issued the bill of lading.
    D. The consignee of the bill of lading.

13. Workers' Compensation Acts require an employer to
    A. Provide coverage for all eligible employees.
    B. Withhold employee contributions from the wages of eligible employees.
    C. Pay an employee the difference between disability payments and full salary.
    D. Contribute to a federal insurance fund.

14. Jay properly created an inter vivos trust naming Kroll as trustee. The trust's sole asset is a fully rented office building. Rental receipts exceed expenditures. The trust instrument is silent about the allocation of items between principal and income. Among the items to be allocated by Kroll during the year are insurance proceeds received as a result of fire damage to the building and the mortgage interest payments made during the year. Which of the following items is(are) properly allocable to principal?

	Insurance proceeds on building	Current mortgage interest payments
A.	No	No
B.	No	Yes
C.	Yes	No
D.	Yes	Yes

15. A trustee's fiduciary duty will probably be violated if the trustee
    A. Invests trust property in government bonds.
    B. Performs accounting services for the trust.
    C. Sells unproductive trust property.
    D. Borrows money from the trust.

16. Under the Securities Act of 1933, the registration of an interstate securities offering is
    A. Required only in transactions involving more than $500,000.
    B. Mandatory, unless the cost to the issuer is prohibitive.
    C. Required, unless there is an applicable exemption.
    D. Intended to prevent the marketing of securities that pose serious financial risks.

17. Corporations that are exempt from registration under the Securities Exchange Act of 1934 are subject to the Act's
    A. Provisions dealing with the filing of annual reports.
    B. Provisions imposing periodic audits.
    C. Antifraud provisions.
    D. Proxy solicitation provisions.

18. Daly tried to collect on a property insurance policy covering a house that was damaged by fire. The insurer denied recovery, alleging that Daly had no insurable interest in the house. In which of the following situations will the insurer prevail?

A. The house belongs to a corporation of which Daly is a 50 percent stockholder.

B. Daly is **not** the owner of the house but a long-term lessee.

C. The house is held in trust for Daly's mother and, on her death, will pass to Daly.

D. Daly gave an unsecured loan to the owner of the house to improve the house.

19. A person who loses a stock certificate is entitled to a new certificate to replace the lost one, provided certain requirements are satisfied. Which of the following is **not** such a requirement?

A. The request for a new certificate is made before the issuer has notice that the lost certificate has been acquired by a bona fide purchaser.

B. The owner files a sufficient indemnity bond with the issuer.

C. The owner satisfies any reasonable requirements of the issuer.

D. The fair market value of the security is placed in escrow with the issuer for six months.

20. Eller, Fort, and Owens do business as Venture Associates, a general partnership. Trent Corp. brought a breach of contract suit against Venture and Eller individually. Trent won the suit and filed a judgment against both Venture and Eller. Trent will generally be able to collect the judgment from

A. Partnership assets only.

B. The personal assets of Eller, Fort, and Owens only.

C. Eller's personal assets only after partnership assets are exhausted.

D. Eller's personal assets only.

21. Lewis, Clark, and Beal entered into a written agreement to form a partnership. The agreement required that the partners make the following capital contributions: Lewis, $40,000; Clark, $30,000; and Beal, $10,000. It was also agreed that in the event the partnership experienced losses in excess of available capital, Beal would contribute additional capital to the extent of the losses. The partnership agreement was otherwise silent about division of profits and losses. Which of the following statements is correct?

A. Profits are to be divided among the partners in proportion to their relative capital contributions.

B. Profits are to be divided equally among the partners.

C. Losses will be allocated in a manner different from the allocation of profits because the partners contributed different amounts of capital.

D. Beal's obligation to contribute additional capital would have an effect on the allocation of profit or loss to Beal.

22. A violation of the profession's ethical standards most likely would have occurred when a CPA

A. Compiled the financial statements of a client that employed the CPA's spouse as a bookkeeper.

B. Received a fee for referring audit clients to a company that sells limited partnership interests.

C. Purchased the portion of an insurance company that performs actuarial services for employee benefit plans.

D. Arranged with a financial institution to collect notes issued by a client in payment of fees due.

23. Ivor, Queen, and Lear own a building as joint tenants with the right of survivorship. Ivor donated his interest in the building to Day Charity by executing and delivering a deed to Day. Both Queen and Lear refused to consent to Ivor's transfer to Day. Subsequently, Queen and Lear died. After their deaths, Day's interest in the building consisted of

A. Total ownership due to the deaths of Queen and Lear.

B. No interest because Queen and Lear refused to consent to the transfer.

C. A 1/3 interest as a joint tenant.

D. A 1/3 interest as a tenant in common.

24. On April 6, Ford purchased a warehouse from Atwood for $150,000. Atwood had executed two mortgages on the property: a purchase money mortgage given to Lang on March 2, which was not recorded; and a mortgage given to Young on March 9,

which was recorded the same day. Ford was unaware of the mortgage to Lang. Under the circumstances,

A. Ford will take title to the warehouse subject only to Lang's mortgage.
B. Ford will take title to the warehouse free of Lang's mortgage.
C. Lang's mortgage is superior to Young's mortgage because Lang's mortgage is a purchase money mortgage.
D. Lang's mortgage is superior to Young's mortgage because Lang's mortgage was given first in time.

25. An important factor in determining if an express warranty has been created is whether the

A. Statements made by the seller became part of the basis of the bargain.
B. Sale was made by a merchant in the regular course of business.
C. Statements made by the seller were in writing.
D. Seller intended to create a warranty.

26. Under the UCC Sales Article, which of the following statements is correct concerning a contract involving a merchant seller and a nonmerchant buyer?

A. Only the seller is obligated to perform the contract in good faith.
B. The contract will be either a sale or return or sale on approval contract.
C. The contract may **not** involve the sale of personal property with a price of more than $500.
D. Whether the UCC Sales Article is applicable does **not** depend on the price of the goods involved.

27. Sun, Inc., manufactures and sells household appliances on credit directly to wholesalers, retailers, and consumers. Sun can perfect its security interest in the appliances without having to file a financing statement or take possession of the appliances if the sale is made by Sun to

A. Consumers.
B. Wholesalers that sell to buyers in the ordinary course of business.
C. Retailers.
D. Wholesalers that sell to distributors for resale.

28. Under the UCC Transactions Article, if a debtor is in default under a payment obligation secured by goods, the secured party has the right to

	Peacefully repossess goods without judicial process	Reduce the claim to a judgment	Sell the goods and apply the proceeds toward the debt
A.	Yes	Yes	Yes
B.	No	Yes	Yes
C.	Yes	Yes	No
D.	Yes	No	Yes

29. Mane Bank lent Eller $120,000 and received securities valued at $30,000 as collateral. At Mane's request, Salem and Rey agreed to act as uncompensated co-sureties on the loan. The agreement provided that Salem's and Rey's maximum liability would be $120,000 each. Mane released Rey without Salem's consent. Eller later defaulted when the collateral held by Mane was worthless and the loan balance was $90,000. Salem's maximum liability is

A. $30,000
B. $45,000
C. $60,000
D. $90,000

30. A distinction between a surety and a co-surety is that only a co-surety is entitled to

A. Reimbursement (Indemnification).
B. Subrogation.
C. Contribution.
D. Exoneration.

Auditing (AUDIT)

(Estimated time: 45 to 55 minutes)

Directions: Select the **best** answer for each of the following items. Select only one answer for each item. Answer all items.

1. Tracing bills of lading to sales invoices provides evidence that

A. Shipments to customers were invoiced.
B. Shipments to customers were recorded as sales.
C. Recorded sales were shipped.
D. Invoiced sales were shipped.

2. Which of the following procedures is **least** likely to be performed before the balance sheet date?
A. Testing of internal control over cash.
B. Confirmation of receivables.
C. Search for unrecorded liabilities.
D. Observation of inventory.

3. Which of the following statements concerning evidential matter is correct?
A. Competent evidence supporting management's assertions should be convincing rather than merely persuasive.
B. Effective internal control contributes little to the reliability of the evidence created within the entity.
C. The cost of obtaining evidence is **not** an important consideration to an auditor in deciding what evidence should be obtained.
D. A client's accounting data **cannot** be considered sufficient audit evidence to support the financial statements.

4. The negative request form of accounts receivable confirmation is useful particularly when the

Assessed level of control risk relating to receivables is	Number of small balances is	Consideration by the recipient is
A. Low	Many	Likely
B. Low	Few	Unlikely
C. High	Few	Likely
D. High	Many	Likely

5. To satisfy the valuation assertion when auditing an investment accounted for by the equity method, an auditor most likely would
A. Inspect the stock certificates evidencing the investment.
B. Examine the audited financial statements of the investee company.
C. Review the broker's advice or canceled check for the investment's acquisition.
D. Obtain market quotations from financial newspapers or periodicals.

6. Which of the following is **not** an audit procedure that the independent auditor would perform concerning litigation, claims, and assessments?
A. Obtain assurance from management that it has disclosed all unasserted claims that the lawyer has advised are probable of assertion and must be disclosed.
B. Confirm directly with the client's lawyer that all claims have been recorded in the financial statements.
C. Inquire of and discuss with management the policies and procedures adopted for identifying, evaluating, and accounting for litigation, claims, and assessments.
D. Obtain from management a description and evaluation of litigation, claims, and assessments existing at the balance sheet date.

7. As the acceptable level of detection risk decreases, an auditor may change the
A. Timing of substantive tests by performing them at an interim date rather than at year end.
B. Nature of substantive tests from a less effective to a more effective procedure.
C. Timing of tests of controls by performing them at several dates rather than at one time.
D. Assessed level of inherent risk to a higher amount.

8. Analytical procedures used in planning an audit should focus on identifying
A. Material weaknesses in the internal control.
B. The predictability of financial data from individual transactions.
C. The various assertions that are embodied in the financial statements.
D. Areas that may represent specific risks relevant to the audit.

9. When considering the objectivity of internal auditors, an independent auditor should
A. Test a sample of the transactions and balances that the internal auditors examined.
B. Determine the organizational level to which the internal auditors report.
C. Evaluate the quality control program in effect for the internal auditors.
D. Examine documentary evidence of the work performed by the internal auditors.

10. Which of the following procedures would an auditor **least** likely perform in planning a financial statement audit?
    A. Coordinating the assistance of entity personnel in data preparation.
    B. Discussing matters that may affect the audit with firm personnel responsible for non-audit services to the entity.
    C. Selecting a sample of vendors' invoices for comparison to receiving reports.
    D. Reading the current year's interim financial statements.

11. In which of the following circumstances would an auditor be most likely to express an adverse opinion?
    A. The chief executive officer refuses the auditor access to minutes of board of directors' meetings.
    B. Tests of controls show that the entity's internal control is so poor that it **cannot** be relied upon.
    C. The financial statements are **not** in conformity with the FASB Statements regarding the capitalization of leases.
    D. Information comes to the auditor's attention that raises substantial doubt about the entity's ability to continue as a going concern.

12. If a publicly held company issues financial statements that purport to present its financial position and results of operations but omits the statement of cash flows, the auditor ordinarily will express a(an)
    A. Unqualified opinion with a separate explanatory paragraph.
    B. Disclaimer of opinion.
    C. Adverse opinion.
    D. Qualified opinion.

13. An auditor has previously expressed a qualified opinion on the financial statements of a prior period because of a departure from generally accepted accounting principles. The prior-period financial statements are restated in the current period to conform with generally accepted accounting principles. The auditor's updated report on the prior-period financial statements should

A. Express an unqualified opinion concerning the restated financial statements.
B. Be accompanied by the original auditor's report on the prior period.
C. Bear the same date as the original auditor's report on the prior period.
D. Qualify the opinion concerning the restated financial statements because of a change in accounting principle.

14. King, CPA, was engaged to audit the financial statements of Newton Company after its fiscal year had ended. King neither observed the inventory count nor confirmed the receivables by direct communication with debtors, but was satisfied concerning both after applying alternative procedures. King's auditor's report most likely contained a(an)
    A. Qualified opinion.
    B. Disclaimer of opinion.
    C. Unqualified opinion.
    D. Unqualified opinion with an explanatory paragraph.

15. How does an auditor make the following representations when issuing the standard auditor's report on comparative financial statements?

	Examination of evidence on a test basis	Consistent application of accounting principles
A.	Explicitly	Explicitly
B.	Implicitly	Implicitly
C.	Implicitly	Explicitly
D.	Explicitly	Implicitly

16. A CPA firm evaluates its personnel advancement experience to ascertain whether individuals meeting stated criteria are assigned increased degrees of responsibility. This is evidence of the firm's adherence to which of the following prescribed standards?
    A. Quality control.
    B. Human resources.
    C. Supervision and review.
    D. Professional development.

17. Which of the following statements is correct concerning an auditor's responsibilities regarding financial statements?

A. Making suggestions that are adopted about the form and content of an entity's financial statements impairs an auditor's independence.

B. An auditor may draft an entity's financial statements based on information from management's information system.

C. The fair presentation of audited financial statements in conformity with GAAP is an implicit part of the auditor's responsibilities.

D. An auditor's responsibilities for audited financial statements are **not** confined to the expression of the auditor's opinion.

18. For an entity's financial statements to be presented fairly in conformity with generally accepted accounting principles, the principles selected should

A. Be applied on a basis consistent with those followed in the prior year.

B. Be approved by the Auditing Standards Board or the appropriate industry subcommittee.

C. Reflect transactions in a manner that presents the financial statements within a range of acceptable limits.

D. Match the principles used by most other entities within the entity's particular industry.

19. When an auditor tests a computerized accounting system, which of the following is true of the test data approach?

A. Test data must consist of all possible valid and invalid conditions.

B. The program tested is different from the program used throughout the year by the client.

C. Several transactions of each type must be tested.

D. Test data are processed by the client's computer program under the auditor's control.

20. An auditor would **least** likely use computer software to

A. Access client data files.

B. Prepare spreadsheets.

C. Assess EDP control risk.

D. Construct parallel simulations.

21. Which of the following statements about internal control is correct?

A. Properly maintained internal control reasonably ensures that collusion among employees cannot occur.

B. The establishment and maintenance of the internal control is an important responsibility of the internal auditor.

C. Exceptionally strong internal control is enough for the auditor to eliminate substantive tests on a significant account balance.

D. The cost-benefit relationship is a primary criterion that should be considered in designing internal control.

22. After obtaining an understanding of an entity's internal control, an auditor may assess control risk at the maximum level for some assertions because the auditor

A. Believes the internal controls are unlikely to be effective.

B. Determines that the pertinent internal control components are **not** well documented.

C. Performs tests of controls to restrict detection risk to an acceptable level.

D. Identifies internal controls that are likely to prevent material misstatements.

23. To obtain evidential matter about control risk, an auditor ordinarily selects tests from a variety of techniques, including

A. Analysis.

B. Confirmation.

C. Reperformance.

D. Comparison.

24. When control risk is assessed at the maximum level for all financial statement assertions, an auditor should document the auditor's

	Understanding of the entity's internal control components elements	Conclusion that control risk is at the maximum level	Basis for concluding that control risk is at the maximum level
A.	Yes	No	No
B.	Yes	Yes	No
C.	No	Yes	Yes
D.	Yes	Yes	Yes

25. Which of the following controls would be most effective in assuring that the proper custody of assets in the investing cycle is maintained?
    A. Direct access to securities in the safety deposit box is limited to only one corporate officer.
    B. Personnel who post investment transactions to the general ledger are **not** permitted to update the investment subsidiary ledger.
    C. The purchase and sale of investments are executed on the specific authorization of the board of directors.
    D. The recorded balances in the investment subsidiary ledger are periodically compared with the contents of the safety deposit box by independent personnel.

26. An auditor's report would be designated a special report when it is issued in connection with
    A. Interim financial information of a publicly held company that is subject to a limited review.
    B. Compliance with aspects of regulatory requirements related to audited financial statements.
    C. Application of accounting principles to specified transactions.
    D. Limited use prospective financial statements such as a financial projection.

27. Before issuing a report on the compilation of financial statements of a nonpublic entity, the accountant should
    A. Apply analytical procedures to selected financial data to discover any material misstatements.
    B. Corroborate at least a sample of the assertions management has embodied in the financial statements.
    C. Inquire of the client's personnel whether the financial statements omit substantially all disclosures.
    D. Read the financial statements to consider whether the financial statements are free from obvious material errors.

28. Which of the following statements concerning prospective financial statements is correct?

A. Only a financial forecast would normally be appropriate for limited use.
B. Only a financial projection would normally be appropriate for general use.
C. Any type of prospective financial statements would normally be appropriate for limited use.
D. Any type of prospective financial statements would normally be appropriate for general use.

29. An auditor is testing internal controls that are evidenced on an entity's vouchers by matching random numbers with voucher numbers. If a random number matches the number of a voided voucher, that voucher ordinarily should be replaced by another voucher in the random sample if the voucher
    A. Constitutes a deviation.
    B. Has been properly voided.
    C. Cannot be located.
    D. Represents an immaterial dollar amount.

30. The risk of incorrect acceptance and the likelihood of assessing control risk too low relate to the
    A. Effectiveness of the audit.
    B. Efficiency of the audit.
    C. Preliminary estimates of materiality levels.
    D. Allowable risk of tolerable error.

Accounting & Reporting— Taxation, Managerial, and Governmental and Not-for-Profit Organizations (ARE)

(Estimated time: 60 to 70 minutes)

Directions: Select the **best** answer for each of the following items. Select only one answer for each item. Answer all items.

1. At the end of Killo Co.'s first year of operations, 1,000 units of inventory remained on hand. Variable and fixed manufacturing costs per unit were $90 and $20, respectively. If Killo uses absorption costing rather than direct (variable) costing, the result would be a higher pretax income of

A. $0
B. $20,000
C. $70,000
D. $90,000

2. Jones, a department manager, exercises control over the department's costs. Following is selected information relating to the department for July:

Variable factory overhead

Budgeted based on standard hours allowed	$80,000
Actual	85,000

Fixed factory overhead

Budgeted	25,000
Actual	27,000

The department's unfavorable spending variance for July was
A. $7,000
B. $5,000
C. $2,000
D. $0

3. Cay Co.'s 1997 fixed manufacturing overhead costs totaled $100,000, and variable selling costs totaled $80,000. Under direct costing, how should these costs be classified?

	Period costs	Product costs
A.	$0	$180,000
B.	$ 80,000	$100,000
C.	$100,000	$ 80,000
D.	$180,000	$0

4. In a traditional job order cost system, the issue of indirect materials to a production department increases
A. Stores control.
B. Work in process control.
C. Factory overhead control.
D. Factory overhead applied.

5. A manufacturing company prepares income statements using both absorption and variable costing methods. At the end of a period actual sales revenues, total gross profit, and total contribution margin approximated budgeted figures; whereas net income was substantially greater than the budgeted amount. There were no beginning or ending inventories. The most likely explanation of the net income increase is that, compared to budget, actual

A. Manufacturing fixed costs had increased.
B. Selling and administrative fixed expenses had decreased.
C. Sales prices and variable costs had increased proportionately.
D. Sales prices had declined proportionately less than variable costs.

6. On June 1, 1997, Ben Rork sold 500 shares of Kul Corp. stock. Rork had received this stock on May 1, 1997, as a bequest from the estate of his uncle, who died on March 1, 1997. Rork's basis was determined by reference to the stock's fair market value on March 1, 1997. Rork's holding period for this stock was
A. Short-term.
B. Long-term.
C. Short-term if sold at a gain; long-term if sold at a loss.
D. Long-term if sold at a gain; short-term if sold at a loss.

7. With regard to consolidated returns, which one of the following statements is correct?
A. The common parent must directly own 51 percent or more of the total voting power of all corporations included in the consolidated return.
B. Of all intercompany dividends paid by the subsidiaries to the parent, 70 percent are excludible from taxable income on the consolidated return.
C. Only corporations that issue their audited financial statements on a consolidated basis may file consolidated tax returns.
D. Operating losses of one group member may be used to offset operating profits of the other members included in the consolidated return.

8. Ati Corp. has two common stockholders. Ati derives all of its income from investments in stocks and securities, and it regularly distributes 51 percent of its taxable income as dividends to its stockholders. Ati is a
A. Personal holding company.
B. Regulated investment company.
C. Corporation subject to the accumulated earnings tax.
D. Corporation subject to tax only on income **not** distributed to stockholders.

9. An S corporation may deduct
   A. Charitable contributions within the percentage of income limitation applicable to corporations.
   B. Net operating loss carryovers.
   C. Foreign income taxes.
   D. Compensation of officers.

10. In 1997, Sayers, who is single, gave an outright gift of $50,000 to a friend, Johnson, who needed the money to pay medical expenses. In filing the 1997 gift tax return, Sayers was entitled to a maximum exclusion of
    A. $0
    B. $ 3,000
    C. $10,000
    D. $20,000

11. To qualify as an exempt organization other than an employees' qualified pension or profit-sharing trust, the applicant
    A. Is barred from incorporating and issuing capital stock.
    B. Must file a written application with the Internal Revenue Service.
    C. Cannot operate under the "lodge system" under which payments are made to its members for sick benefits.
    D. Need **not** be specifically identified as one of the classes on which exemption is conferred by the Internal Revenue Code, provided that the organization's purposes and activities are of a nonprofit nature.

12. Ed and Ann Ross were divorced in January 1997. In accordance with the divorce decree, Ed transferred the title in their home to Ann in 1997. The home, which had a fair market value of $150,000, was subject to a $50,000 mortgage that had 20 more years to run. Monthly mortgage payments amount to $1,000. Under the terms of settlement, Ed is obligated to make the mortgage payments on the home for the full remaining 20-year term of the indebtedness, regardless of how long Ann lives. Ed made 12 mortgage payments in 1997. What amount is taxable as alimony in Ann's 1997 return?
    A. $0
    B. $ 12,000
    C. $100,000
    D. $112,000

13. In 1997, Smith paid $6,000 to the tax collector of Wek City for realty taxes on a two-family house owned by Smith's mother. Of this amount, $2,800 covered back taxes for 1996, and $3,200 covered 1997 taxes. Smith resides on the second floor of the house, and his mother resides on the first floor. In Smith's itemized deductions on his 1997 return, what amount was Smith entitled to claim for realty taxes?
    A. $6,000
    B. $3,200
    C. $3,000
    D. $0

14. Which one of the following expenditures qualifies as a deductible medical expense for tax purposes?
    A. Vitamins for general health **not** prescribed by a physician.
    B. Health club dues.
    C. Transportation to physician's office for required medical care.
    D. Mandatory employment taxes for basic coverage under Medicare A.

15. The basis of property (other than money) distributed by a partnership to a partner, in complete liquidation of the partner's interest, shall be an amount equal to the
    A. Fair market value of the property.
    B. Book value of the property.
    C. Adjusted basis of such partner's interest in the partnership, reduced by any money distributed in the same transaction.
    D. Adjusted basis of such partner's interest in the partnership, increased by any money distributed in the same transaction.

16. Kim Co.'s profit center Zee had 1997 operating income of $200,000 before a $50,000 imputed interest charge for using Kim's assets. Kim's aggregate net income from all of its profit centers was $2,000,000. During 1997, Kim declared and paid dividends of $30,000 and $70,000 on its preferred and common stock, respectively. Zee's 1997 residual income was
    A. $140,000
    B. $143,000
    C. $147,000
    D. $150,000

17. The following information pertains to Syl Co.:

Sales	$800,000
Variable costs	160,000
Fixed costs	40,000

What is Syl's breakeven point in sales dollars?
A. $200,000
B. $160,000
C. $ 50,000
D. $ 40,000

18. Lin Co. is buying machinery it expects will increase average annual operating income by $40,000. The initial increase in the required investment is $60,000, and the average increase in required investment is $30,000. To compute the accrual accounting rate of return, what amount should be used as the numerator in the ratio?
A. $20,000
B. $30,000
C. $40,000
D. $60,000

19. Controllable revenue would be included in a performance report for a

	Profit center	Cost center
A.	No	No
B.	No	Yes
C.	Yes	No
D.	Yes	Yes

20. Vince Inc. has developed and patented a new laser disc reading device that will be marketed internationally. Which of the following factors should Vince consider in pricing the device?

I. Quality of the new device.
II. Life of the new device.
III. Customers' relative preference for quality compared to price.

A. I and II only.
B. I and III only.
C. II and III only.
D. I, II, and III.

21. The following information for the year ended June 30, 1997, pertains to a proprietary fund established by Burwood Village in connection with Burwood's public parking facilities:

Receipts from users of parking facilities	$400,000
Expenditures	
Parking meters	210,000
Salaries and other cash expenses	90,000
Depreciation of parking meters	70,000

For the year ended June 30, 1997, this proprietary fund should report net income of
A. $0
B. $ 30,000
C. $100,000
D. $240,000

22. During its fiscal year ended June 30, 1997, Lake County financed the following projects by special assessments:

Capital improvements	$2,000,000
Service-type projects	800,000

For financial reporting purposes, what amount should appear in special assessment funds?
A. $2,800,000
B. $2,000,000
C. $ 800,000
D. $0

23. Ridge City issued the following bonds during the year ended July 31, 1997:

General obligation bonds issued for the Ridge water and sewer enterprise fund that will service the debt	$700,000
Revenue bonds to be repaid from admission fees collected by the Ridge municipal swimming pool enterprise fund	290,000

The amount of these bonds that should be accounted for in Ridge's general long-term debt account group is
A. $990,000
B. $700,000
C. $290,000
D. $0

24. The fund balance reserved for encumbrances account of a governmental unit is decreased when

A. Supplies previously ordered are received.
B. A purchase order is approved.
C. The vouchers are paid.
D. Appropriations are recorded.

25. The revenues control account of a governmental unit is increased when
A. The budget is recorded.
B. Property taxes are recorded.
C. Appropriations are recorded.
D. The budgetary accounts are closed.

26. In April 1997, Alice Reed donated $100,000 cash to her church, with the stipulation that the income generated from this gift is to be paid to Alice during her lifetime. The conditions of this donation are that, after Alice dies, the principal can be used by the church for any purpose voted on by the church elders. The church received interest of $8,000 on the $100,000 for the year ended March 31, 1998, and the interest was remitted to Alice. In the church's March 31, 1998, financial statements
A. $8,000 should be reported under support and revenue in the activity statement.
B. $92,000 should be reported under support and revenue in the activity statement.
C. $100,000 should be reported as support in the activity statement.
D. The gift and its terms should be disclosed only in notes to the financial statements.

27. The following information was available from Forest College's accounting records for its current funds for the year ended March 31, 1998:

Restricted gifts received
  Expended $100,000
  Temporarily restricted   300,000
Unrestricted gifts received
  Expended   600,000
  Not expended   75,000

What amount should be included in unrestricted current funds revenues for the year ended March 31, 1998?

A. $ 600,000
B. $ 700,000
C. $ 775,000
D. $1,000,000

28. The following expenditures were among those incurred by Alma University during 1997:

Administrative data processing $50,000
Scholarships and fellowships   100,000
Operation and maintenance of
physical plant   200,000

The amount to be included in the functional classification "Institutional Support" expenditures account is
A. $ 50,000
B. $150,000
C. $250,000
D. $350,000

29. Which of the following funds are usually encountered in a not-for-profit private university?

	Current funds	Plant funds
A.	No	Yes
B.	No	No
C.	Yes	No
D.	Yes	Yes

30. Revenue of a hospital from grants specified by the grantor for research would normally be included in
A. Nonoperating gains.
B. Other operating revenue.
C. Patient service revenue.
D. Ancillary service revenue.

Financial Accounting and Reporting—Business Enterprises (FARE)

(Estimated time: 65 to 75 minutes)

Directions: Select the **best** answer for each of the following items. Select only one answer for each item. Answer all items.

1. At December 31, 1997, Date Co. awaits judgment on a lawsuit for a competitor's infringement of Date's patent. Legal counsel believes it is probable that Date will

win the suit and indicated the most likely award together with a range of possible awards. How should the lawsuit be reported in Date's 1997 financial statements?

A. In note disclosure only.
B. By accrual for the most likely award.
C. By accrual for the lowest amount of the range of possible awards.
D. Neither in note disclosure **nor** by accrual.

2. On February 12, 1997, VIP Publishing, Inc. purchased the copyright to a book for $15,000 and agreed to pay royalties equal to 10 percent of book sales, with a guaranteed minimum royalty of $60,000. VIP had book sales of $800,000 in 1997. In its 1997 income statement, what amount should VIP report as royalty expense?

A. $60,000
B. $75,000
C. $80,000
D. $95,000

3. Dunne Co. sells equipment service contracts that cover a two-year period. The sales price of each contract is $600. Dunne's past experience is that, of the total dollars spent for repairs on service contracts, 40 percent is incurred evenly during the first contract year and 60 percent evenly during the second contract year. Dunne sold 1,000 contracts evenly throughout 1997. In its December 31, 1997, balance sheet, what amount should Dunne report as deferred service contract revenue?

A. $540,000
B. $480,000
C. $360,000
D. $300,000

4. On July 1, 1997, York Co. purchased as a long-term investment $1,000,000 of Park, Inc.'s 8 percent bonds for $946,000, including accrued interest of $40,000. The bonds were purchased to yield 10 percent interest. The bonds mature on January 1, 2004, and pay interest annually on January 1. York uses the effective interest method of amortization. In its December 31, 1997, balance sheet, what amount should York report as investment in bonds?

A. $911,300
B. $916,600
C. $953,300
D. $960,600

5. Lance Corp.'s statement of cash flows for the year ended September 30, 1997, was prepared using the indirect method and included the following:

Net income	$60,000
Noncash adjustments:	
Depreciation expense	9,000
Increase in accounts receivable	(5,000)
Decrease in inventory	40,000
Decrease in accounts payable	(12,000)
Net cash flows from operating activities	$92,000

Lance reported revenues from customers of $75,000 in its 1997 income statement. What amount of cash did Lance receive from its customers during the year ended September 30, 1997?

A. $80,000
B. $70,000
C. $65,000
D. $55,000

6. On September 1, 1997, Canary Co. sold used equipment for a cash amount equaling its carrying amount for both book and tax purposes. On September 15, 1997, Canary replaced the equipment by paying cash and signing a note payable for new equipment. The cash paid for the new equipment exceeded the cash received for the old equipment. How should these equipment transactions be reported in Canary's 1997 statement of cash flows?

A. Cash outflow equal to the cash paid less the cash received.
B. Cash outflow equal to the cash paid and note payable less the cash received.
C. Cash inflow equal to the cash received and a cash outflow equal to the cash paid and note payable.
D. Cash inflow equal to the cash received and a cash outflow equal to the cash paid.

7. Parker Corp. owns 80 percent of Smith Inc.'s common stock. During 1997, Parker sold Smith $250,000 of inventory on the

same terms as sales made to third parties. Smith sold all of the inventory purchased from Parker in 1997. The following information pertains to Smith and Parker's sales for 1997:

	Parker	Smith
Sales	$1,000,000	$700,000
Cost of sales	400,000	350,000
	$ 600,000	$350,000

What amount should Parker report as cost of sales in its 1997 consolidated income statement?
  A. $750,000
  B. $680,000
  C. $500,000
  D. $430,000

8. Penn, Inc., a manufacturing company, owns 75 percent of the common stock of Sell, Inc., an investment company. Sell owns 60 percent of the common stock of Vane, Inc., an insurance company. In Penn's consolidated financial statements, should consolidation accounting or equity method accounting be used for Sell and Vane?
  A. Consolidation used for Sell and equity method used for Vane.
  B. Consolidation used for both Sell and Vane.
  C. Equity method used for Sell and consolidation used for Vane.
  D. Equity method used for both Sell and Vane.

9. What is the purpose of information presented in notes to the financial statements?
  A. To provide disclosures required by generally accepted accounting principles.
  B. To correct improper presentation in the financial statements.
  C. To provide recognition of amounts **not** included in the totals of the financial statements.
  D. To present management's responses to auditor comments.

10. On January 2, 1997, Air, Inc. agreed to pay its former president $300,000 under a deferred compensation arrangement. Air should have recorded this expense in 1996 but did not do so. Air's reported income tax expense would have been $70,000 lower in 1996 had it properly accrued this deferred compensation. In its December 31, 1997, financial statements, Air should adjust the beginning balance of its retained earnings by a
  A. $230,000 credit.
  B. $230,000 debit.
  C. $300,000 credit.
  D. $370,000 debit.

11. South Co. purchased a machine that was installed and placed in service on January 1, 1996, at a cost of $240,000. Salvage value was estimated at $40,000. The machine is being depreciated over 10 years by the double-declining-balance method. For the year ended December 31, 1997, what amount should South report as depreciation expense?
  A. $48,000
  B. $38,400
  C. $32,000
  D. $21,600

12. Bensol Co. and Sable Co. exchanged similar trucks with fair values in excess of carrying amounts. In addition, Bensol paid Sable to compensate for the difference in truck values. As a consequence of the exchange, Sable recognizes
  A. A gain equal to the difference between the fair value and carrying amount of the truck given up.
  B. A gain determined by the proportion of cash received to the total consideration.
  C. A loss determined by the proportion of cash received to the total consideration.
  D. Neither a gain **nor** a loss.

13. On September 22, 1994, Yumi Corp. purchased merchandise from an unaffiliated foreign company for 10,000 units of the foreign company's local currency. On that date, the spot rate was $.55. Yumi paid the bill in full on March 20, 1995, when the spot rate was $.65. The spot rate was $.70 on December 31, 1994. What amount should Yumi report as a foreign currency transaction loss in its income statement for the year ended December 31, 1994?

A. $0
B. $ 500
C. $1,000
D. $1,500

14. West Corp. leased a building and received the $36,000 annual rental payment on June 15, 1997. The beginning of the lease was July 1, 1997. Rental income is taxable when received. West's tax rates are 30 percent for 1997 and 40 percent thereafter. West had no other permanent or temporary differences. West determined that no valuation allowance was needed. What amount of deferred tax asset should West report in its December 31, 1997, balance sheet?
A. $ 5,400
B. $ 7,200
C. $10,800
D. $14,400

15. Dolce Co., which began operations on January 1, 1996, appropriately uses the installment method of accounting to record revenues. The following information is available for the years ended December 31, 1996 and 1997:

	1996	1997
Sales	$1,000,000	$2,000,000
Gross profit realized on sales made in:		
1996	150,000	90,000
1997	—	200,000
Gross profit percentages	30%	40%

What amount of installment accounts receivable should Dolce report in its December 31, 1997, balance sheet?
A. $1,225,000
B. $1,300,000
C. $1,700,000
D. $1,775,000

16. Malden, Inc., has two patents that have allegedly been infringed by competitors. After investigation, legal counsel informed Malden that it had a weak case on patent A34 and a strong case in regard to patent B19. Malden incurred additional legal fees to stop infringement on B19. Both patents have a remaining legal life of 8 years. How should Malden account for these legal costs incurred relating to the two patents?

A. Expense costs for A34 and capitalize costs for B19.
B. Expense costs for both A34 and B19.
C. Capitalize costs for both A34 and B19.
D. Capitalize costs for A34 and expense costs for B19.

17. Jel Co., a consignee, paid the freight costs for goods shipped from Dale Co., a consignor. These freight costs are to be deducted from Jel's payment to Dale when the consignment goods are sold. Until Jel sells the goods, the freight costs should be included in Jel's
A. Cost of goods sold.
B. Freight-out costs.
C. Selling expenses.
D. Accounts receivable.

18. The following information pertains to Lark Corp.'s available-for-sale securities portfolio:

	December 1997	1996
Cost	$200,000	$200,000
Market value	240,000	180,000

Differences between cost and market values are considered to be temporary. The decline in market value was properly accounted for at December 31, 1996 under the provisions of FASB Statement #115, "Accounting for Certain Investments in Debt and Equity Securities." By what amount should the unrealized holding gain or loss account on available-for-sale securities be credited from December 31, 1996, to December 31, 1997?
A. $60,000
B. $40,000
C. $20,000
D. $0

19. Pal Corp.'s 1997 dividend income included only part of the dividend received from its Ima Corp. investment. Ima Corp.'s common stock is not publicly-traded. The balance of the dividend reduced Pal's carrying amount for its Ima investment. This reflects that Pal accounts for its Ima investment by the

A. Cost method, and only a portion of Ima's 1997 dividends represent earnings after Pal's acquisition.

B. Cost method, and its carrying amount exceeded the proportionate share of Ima's market value.

C. Equity method, and Ima incurred a loss in 1997.

D. Equity method, and its carrying amount exceeded the proportionate share of Ima's market value.

20. On December 31, 1997, Day Co. leased a new machine from Parr with the following pertinent information:

Lease term	6 years
Annual rental payable at beginning of each year	$50,000
Useful life of machine	8 years
Day's incremental borrowing rate	15%
Implicit interest rate in lease (known by Day)	12%
Present value of an annuity of 1 in advance for 6 periods at	
12%	4.61
15%	4.35

The lease is not renewable, and the machine reverts to Parr at the termination of the lease. The cost of the machine on Parr's accounting records is $375,500. At the beginning of the lease term, Day should record a lease liability of

A. $375,500
B. $230,500
C. $217,500
D. $0

21. Jay's lease payments are made at the end of each period. Jay's liability for a capital lease would be reduced periodically by the

A. Minimum lease payment less the portion of the minimum lease payment allocable to interest.

B. Minimum lease payment plus the amortization of the related asset.

C. Minimum lease payment less the amortization of the related asset.

D. Minimum lease payment.

22. Case Cereal Co. frequently distributes coupons to promote new products. On October 1, 1997, Case mailed 1,000,000 coupons for $.45 off each box of cereal purchased. Case expects 120,000 of these coupons to be redeemed before the December 31, 1997, expiration date. It takes 30 days from the redemption date for Case to receive the coupons from the retailers. Case reimburses the retailers an additional $.05 for each coupon redeemed. As of December 31, 1997, Case had paid retailers $25,000 related to these coupons and had 50,000 coupons on hand that had not been processed for payments. What amount should Case report as a liability for coupons in its December 31, 1997, balance sheet?

A. $35,000
B. $29,000
C. $25,000
D. $22,500

23. In 1996, a contract dispute between Dollis Co. and Brooks Co. was submitted to binding arbitration. In 1996, each party's attorney indicated privately that the probable award in Dollis' favor could be reasonably estimated. In 1997, the arbitrator decided in favor of Dollis. When should Dollis and Brooks recognize their respective gain and loss?

	Dollis' gain	Brooks' loss
A.	1996	1996
B.	1996	1997
C.	1997	1996
D.	1997	1997

24. A company uses the completed-contract method to account for a long-term construction contract. Revenue is recognized when recorded progress billings

	Are collected	Exceed recorded costs
A.	Yes	Yes
B.	No	No
C.	Yes	No
D.	No	Yes

25. Roberts and Smith drafted a partnership agreement that lists the following assets contributed at the partnership's formation:

| | Contributed by | |
	Roberts	Smith
Cash	$20,000	$30,000
Inventory	—	15,000
Building	—	40,000
Furniture &		
Equipment	15,000	—

The building is subject to a mortgage of $10,000, which the partnership has assumed. The partnership agreement also specifies that profits and losses are to be distributed evenly. What amounts should be recorded as capital for Roberts and Smith at the formation of the partnership?

	Roberts	Smith
A.	$35,000	$85,000
B.	$35,000	$75,000
C.	$55,000	$55,000
D.	$60,000	$60,000

26. Nome Co. sponsors a defined benefit plan covering all employees. Benefits are based on years of service and compensation levels at the time of retirement. Nome determined that, as of September 30, 1997, its accumulated benefit obligation was $380,000, and its plan assets had a $290,000 fair value. Nome's September 30, 1997, trial balance showed prepaid pension cost of $20,000. In its September 30, 1997, balance sheet, what amount should Nome report as additional pension liability?
    A. $110,000
    B. $360,000
    C. $380,000
    D. $400,000

27. The following information pertains to Tara Co.'s accounts receivable at December 31, 1997:

Days outstanding	Amount	Estimated percent uncollectible
0–60	$120,000	1%
61–120	90,000	2%
Over 120	100,000	6%
	$310,000	

During 1997, Tara wrote off $7,000 in receivables and recovered $4,000 that had been written off in prior years. Tara's December 31, 1996, allowance for uncollectible accounts was $22,000. Under the aging method, what amount of allowance for uncollectible accounts should Tara report at December 31, 1997?
    A. $ 9,000
    B. $10,000
    C. $13,000
    D. $19,000

28. On Merf's April 30, 1996, balance sheet a note receivable was reported as a noncurrent asset and its accrued interest for eight months was reported as a current asset. Which of the following terms would fit Merf's note receivable?
    A. Both principal and interest amounts are payable on August 31, 1996, and August 31, 1997.
    B. Principal and interest are due December 31, 1996.
    C. Both principal and interest amounts are payable on December 31, 1996, and December 31, 1997.
    D. Principal is due August 31, 1997, and interest is due August 31, 1996, and August 31, 1997.

29. Rudd Corp. had 700,000 shares of common stock authorized and 300,000 shares outstanding at December 31, 1996. The following events occurred during 1997:

January 31	Declared 10 percent stock dividend
June 30	Purchased 100,000 shares
August 1	Reissued 50,000 shares
November 30	Declared 2-for-1 stock split

At December 31, 1997, how many shares of common stock did Rudd have outstanding?
    A. 560,000
    B. 600,000
    C. 630,000
    D. 660,000

30. Quoit, Inc. issued preferred stock with detachable common stock warrants. The issue price exceeded the sum of the warrants' fair value and the preferred stocks' par value. The preferred stocks' fair value was not determinable. What amount should be assigned to the warrants outstanding?

A. Total proceeds.
B. Excess of proceeds over the par value of the preferred stock.
C. The proportion of the proceeds that the warrants' fair value bears to the preferred stocks' par value.
D. The fair value of the warrants.

ANSWER KEY—FOUR-OPTION MULTIPLE-CHOICE QUESTIONS

Be sure to read Chapter 6—Chart Your Progress and Plan Your Course of Action. It will help you analyze your test and plan your study program.

Business Law & Professional Responsibilities (LPR)

QUESTION #	ANSWER	TOPICAL AREA
1	C	Accountants' Legal Responsibility
2	D	Accountants' Legal Responsibility
3	C	Agency
4	B	Bankruptcy
5	C	Bankruptcy
6	A	Commercial Paper
7	A	Commercial Paper
8	A	Contracts
9	B	Contracts
10	B	Corporations
11	A	Corporations
12	D	Documents of Title
13	A	Employment Regulations
14	C	Estates and Trusts
15	D	Estates and Trusts
16	C	Federal Securities Regulations
17	C	Federal Securities Regulations
18	D	Insurance
19	D	Investment Securities
20	C	Partnerships
21	B	Partnerships
22	B	Professional Responsibilities
23	D	Property

QUESTION #	ANSWER	TOPICAL AREA
24	B	Property
25	A	Sales
26	D	Sales
27	A	Secured Transactions
28	A	Secured Transactions
29	B	Suretyship and Creditor's Rights
30	C	Suretyship and Creditor's Rights

Auditing (AUDIT)

QUESTION #	ANSWER	TOPICAL AREA
1	A	Audit Evidence
2	C	Audit Evidence
3	D	Audit Evidence
4	A	Audit Evidence
5	B	Audit Evidence
6	B	Audit Evidence
7	B	Audit Planning
8	D	Audit Planning
9	B	Audit Planning
10	C	Audit Planning
11	C	Audit Reporting Standards
12	D	Audit Reporting Standards
13	A	Audit Reporting Standards
14	C	Audit Reporting Standards
15	D	Audit Reporting Standards
16	A	Auditing Concepts and Standards
17	B	Auditing Concepts and Standards
18	C	Auditing Concepts and Standards
19	D	Electronic Data Processing
20	C	Electronic Data Processing
21	D	Internal Control
22	A	Internal Control
23	C	Internal Control
24	B	Internal Control
25	D	Internal Control
26	B	Other Reporting Areas

QUESTION #	ANSWER	TOPICAL AREA
27	D	Other Reporting Areas
28	C	Other Reporting Areas
29	B	Statistical Sampling
30	A	Statistical Sampling

Accounting & Reporting—Taxation, Managerial, and Governmental and Not-for-Profit Organizations (ARE)

QUESTION #	ANSWER	TOPICAL AREA
1	B	Cost Accounting
2	A	Cost Accounting
3	D	Cost Accounting
4	C	Cost Accounting
5	B	Cost Accounting
6	B	Federal Income Taxes—Capital Gains & Losses
7	D	Federal Income Taxes—Corporations
8	A	Federal Income Taxes—Corporations
9	D	Federal Income Taxes—Corporations
10	C	Federal Income Taxes—Estates & Trusts
11	B	Federal Income Taxes—Exempt Organizations
12	A	Federal Income Taxes—Individuals
13	D	Federal Income Taxes—Individuals
14	C	Federal Income Taxes—Individuals
15	C	Federal Income Taxes—Partnerships
16	D	Managerial Accounting & Quantitative Methods
17	C	Managerial Accounting & Quantitative Methods
18	C	Managerial Accounting & Quantitative Methods
19	C	Managerial Accounting & Quantitative Methods

QUESTION #	ANSWER	TOPICAL AREA
20	D	Managerial Accounting & Quantitative Methods
21	D	Not-for-Profit Accounting—Governmental Units
22	D	Not-for-Profit Accounting—Governmental Units
23	D	Not-for-Profit Accounting—Governmental Units
24	A	Not-for-Profit Accounting—Governmental Units
25	B	Not-for-Profit Accounting—Governmental Units
26	C	Not-for-Profit Accounting—Other than Governmental Units
27	C	Not-for-Profit Accounting—Other than Governmental Units
28	A	Not-for-Profit Accounting—Other than Governmental Units
29	D	Not-for-Profit Accounting—Other than Governmental Units
30	B	Not-for-Profit Accounting—Other than Governmental Units

Financial Accounting and Reporting—Business Enterprises (FARE)

QUESTION #	ANSWER	TOPICAL AREA
1	A	Accounting Concepts
2	C	Accounting Fundamentals
3	B	Accounting Fundamentals

Question #	Answer	Topical Area	Question #	Answer	Topical Area
4	A	Bonds, Accounting for	16	A	Intangibles
5	B	Cash Flows	17	D	Inventories
6	D	Cash Flows	18	A	Investments
7	C	Consolidation and	19	A	Investments
		Business Combination	20	B	Leases
8	B	Consolidation and	21	A	Leases
		Business Combination	22	A	Liabilities
9	A	Financial Statements	23	C	Liabilities
10	B	Financial Statements	24	B	Long-Term Contracts
11	B	Fixed Assets	25	B	Partnerships
12	B	Fixed Assets	26	A	Pension Costs
13	D	Foreign Currency	27	A	Receivables
		Translation	28	D	Receivables
14	B	Income Taxes,	29	A	Stockholders' Equity
		Accounting for	30	D	Stockholders'
15	C	Installment Sales	Equity**LPR**		

Answer Sheet

May 1995 CPA Examination

LPR

1. Ⓐ Ⓑ Ⓒ Ⓓ	31. Ⓐ Ⓑ Ⓒ Ⓓ	
2. Ⓐ Ⓑ Ⓒ Ⓓ	32. Ⓐ Ⓑ Ⓒ Ⓓ	
3. Ⓐ Ⓑ Ⓒ Ⓓ	33. Ⓐ Ⓑ Ⓒ Ⓓ	
4. obsolete	34. Ⓐ Ⓑ Ⓒ Ⓓ	
5. Ⓐ Ⓑ Ⓒ Ⓓ	35. Ⓐ Ⓑ Ⓒ Ⓓ	
6. Ⓐ Ⓑ Ⓒ Ⓓ	36. Ⓐ Ⓑ Ⓒ Ⓓ	
7. Ⓐ Ⓑ Ⓒ Ⓓ	37. Ⓐ Ⓑ Ⓒ Ⓓ	
8. Ⓐ Ⓑ Ⓒ Ⓓ	38. Ⓐ Ⓑ Ⓒ Ⓓ	
9. Ⓐ Ⓑ Ⓒ Ⓓ	39. Ⓐ Ⓑ Ⓒ Ⓓ	
10. Ⓐ Ⓑ Ⓒ Ⓓ	40. Ⓐ Ⓑ Ⓒ Ⓓ	
11. Ⓐ Ⓑ Ⓒ Ⓓ	41. Ⓐ Ⓑ Ⓒ Ⓓ	
12. Ⓐ Ⓑ Ⓒ Ⓓ	42. Ⓐ Ⓑ Ⓒ Ⓓ	
13. Ⓐ Ⓑ Ⓒ Ⓓ	43. Ⓐ Ⓑ Ⓒ Ⓓ	
14. Ⓐ Ⓑ Ⓒ Ⓓ	44. Ⓐ Ⓑ Ⓒ Ⓓ	
15. Ⓐ Ⓑ Ⓒ Ⓓ	45. Ⓐ Ⓑ Ⓒ Ⓓ	
16. Ⓐ Ⓑ Ⓒ Ⓓ	46. Ⓐ Ⓑ Ⓒ Ⓓ	
17. Ⓐ Ⓑ Ⓒ Ⓓ	47. Ⓐ Ⓑ Ⓒ Ⓓ	
18. Ⓐ Ⓑ Ⓒ Ⓓ	48. Ⓐ Ⓑ Ⓒ Ⓓ	
19. Ⓐ Ⓑ Ⓒ Ⓓ	49. Ⓐ Ⓑ Ⓒ Ⓓ	
20. Ⓐ Ⓑ Ⓒ Ⓓ	50. Ⓐ Ⓑ Ⓒ Ⓓ	
21. Ⓐ Ⓑ Ⓒ Ⓓ	51. Ⓐ Ⓑ Ⓒ Ⓓ	
22. Ⓐ Ⓑ Ⓒ Ⓓ	52. Ⓐ Ⓑ Ⓒ Ⓓ	
23. Ⓐ Ⓑ Ⓒ Ⓓ	53. Ⓐ Ⓑ Ⓒ Ⓓ	
24. Ⓐ Ⓑ Ⓒ Ⓓ	54. Ⓐ Ⓑ Ⓒ Ⓓ	
25. Ⓐ Ⓑ Ⓒ Ⓓ	55. Ⓐ Ⓑ Ⓒ Ⓓ	
26. Ⓐ Ⓑ Ⓒ Ⓓ	56. Ⓐ Ⓑ Ⓒ Ⓓ	
27. Ⓐ Ⓑ Ⓒ Ⓓ	57. Ⓐ Ⓑ Ⓒ Ⓓ	
28. Ⓐ Ⓑ Ⓒ Ⓓ	58. Ⓐ Ⓑ Ⓒ Ⓓ	
29. Ⓐ Ⓑ Ⓒ Ⓓ	59. Ⓐ Ⓑ Ⓒ Ⓓ	
30. Ⓐ Ⓑ Ⓒ Ⓓ	60. Ⓐ Ⓑ Ⓒ Ⓓ	

AUDIT

1. Ⓐ Ⓑ Ⓒ Ⓓ	31. Ⓐ Ⓑ Ⓒ Ⓓ	61. Ⓐ Ⓑ Ⓒ Ⓓ
2. Ⓐ Ⓑ Ⓒ Ⓓ	32. Ⓐ Ⓑ Ⓒ Ⓓ	62. Ⓐ Ⓑ Ⓒ Ⓓ
3. Ⓐ Ⓑ Ⓒ Ⓓ	33. Ⓐ Ⓑ Ⓒ Ⓓ	63. Ⓐ Ⓑ Ⓒ Ⓓ
4. Ⓐ Ⓑ Ⓒ Ⓓ	34. Ⓐ Ⓑ Ⓒ Ⓓ	64. obsolete
5. Ⓐ Ⓑ Ⓒ Ⓓ	35. Ⓐ Ⓑ Ⓒ Ⓓ	65. Ⓐ Ⓑ Ⓒ Ⓓ
6. Ⓐ Ⓑ Ⓒ Ⓓ	36. Ⓐ Ⓑ Ⓒ Ⓓ	66. Ⓐ Ⓑ Ⓒ Ⓓ
7. Ⓐ Ⓑ Ⓒ Ⓓ	37. Ⓐ Ⓑ Ⓒ Ⓓ	67. Ⓐ Ⓑ Ⓒ Ⓓ
8. Ⓐ Ⓑ Ⓒ Ⓓ	38. Ⓐ Ⓑ Ⓒ Ⓓ	68. Ⓐ Ⓑ Ⓒ Ⓓ
9. Ⓐ Ⓑ Ⓒ Ⓓ	39. Ⓐ Ⓑ Ⓒ Ⓓ	69. Ⓐ Ⓑ Ⓒ Ⓓ
10. Ⓐ Ⓑ Ⓒ Ⓓ	40. Ⓐ Ⓑ Ⓒ Ⓓ	70. Ⓐ Ⓑ Ⓒ Ⓓ
11. Ⓐ Ⓑ Ⓒ Ⓓ	41. Ⓐ Ⓑ Ⓒ Ⓓ	71. Ⓐ Ⓑ Ⓒ Ⓓ
12. Ⓐ Ⓑ Ⓒ Ⓓ	42. Ⓐ Ⓑ Ⓒ Ⓓ	72. Ⓐ Ⓑ Ⓒ Ⓓ
13. Ⓐ Ⓑ Ⓒ Ⓓ	43. Ⓐ Ⓑ Ⓒ Ⓓ	73. Ⓐ Ⓑ Ⓒ Ⓓ
14. Ⓐ Ⓑ Ⓒ Ⓓ	44. Ⓐ Ⓑ Ⓒ Ⓓ	74. Ⓐ Ⓑ Ⓒ Ⓓ
15. Ⓐ Ⓑ Ⓒ Ⓓ	45. Ⓐ Ⓑ Ⓒ Ⓓ	75. Ⓐ Ⓑ Ⓒ Ⓓ
16. Ⓐ Ⓑ Ⓒ Ⓓ	46. Ⓐ Ⓑ Ⓒ Ⓓ	76. Ⓐ Ⓑ Ⓒ Ⓓ
17. Ⓐ Ⓑ Ⓒ Ⓓ	47. Ⓐ Ⓑ Ⓒ Ⓓ	77. Ⓐ Ⓑ Ⓒ Ⓓ
18. Ⓐ Ⓑ Ⓒ Ⓓ	48. Ⓐ Ⓑ Ⓒ Ⓓ	78. Ⓐ Ⓑ Ⓒ Ⓓ
19. Ⓐ Ⓑ Ⓒ Ⓓ	49. Ⓐ Ⓑ Ⓒ Ⓓ	79. Ⓐ Ⓑ Ⓒ Ⓓ
20. Ⓐ Ⓑ Ⓒ Ⓓ	50. Ⓐ Ⓑ Ⓒ Ⓓ	80. Ⓐ Ⓑ Ⓒ Ⓓ
21. Ⓐ Ⓑ Ⓒ Ⓓ	51. Ⓐ Ⓑ Ⓒ Ⓓ	81. Ⓐ Ⓑ Ⓒ Ⓓ
22. Ⓐ Ⓑ Ⓒ Ⓓ	52. Ⓐ Ⓑ Ⓒ Ⓓ	82. Ⓐ Ⓑ Ⓒ Ⓓ
23. Ⓐ Ⓑ Ⓒ Ⓓ	53. Ⓐ Ⓑ Ⓒ Ⓓ	83. Ⓐ Ⓑ Ⓒ Ⓓ
24. Ⓐ Ⓑ Ⓒ Ⓓ	54. Ⓐ Ⓑ Ⓒ Ⓓ	84. Ⓐ Ⓑ Ⓒ Ⓓ
25. obsolete	55. Ⓐ Ⓑ Ⓒ Ⓓ	85. Ⓐ Ⓑ Ⓒ Ⓓ
26. Ⓐ Ⓑ Ⓒ Ⓓ	56. Ⓐ Ⓑ Ⓒ Ⓓ	86. Ⓐ Ⓑ Ⓒ Ⓓ
27. Ⓐ Ⓑ Ⓒ Ⓓ	57. Ⓐ Ⓑ Ⓒ Ⓓ	87. Ⓐ Ⓑ Ⓒ Ⓓ
28. Ⓐ Ⓑ Ⓒ Ⓓ	58. Ⓐ Ⓑ Ⓒ Ⓓ	88. Ⓐ Ⓑ Ⓒ Ⓓ
29. Ⓐ Ⓑ Ⓒ Ⓓ	59. Ⓐ Ⓑ Ⓒ Ⓓ	89. Ⓐ Ⓑ Ⓒ Ⓓ
30. Ⓐ Ⓑ Ⓒ Ⓓ	60. Ⓐ Ⓑ Ⓒ Ⓓ	90. Ⓐ Ⓑ Ⓒ Ⓓ

Answer Sheet

ARE

1.	Ⓐ Ⓑ Ⓒ Ⓓ		31.	Ⓐ Ⓑ Ⓒ Ⓓ
2.	Ⓐ Ⓑ Ⓒ Ⓓ		32.	Ⓐ Ⓑ Ⓒ Ⓓ
3.	Ⓐ Ⓑ Ⓒ Ⓓ		33.	Ⓐ Ⓑ Ⓒ Ⓓ
4.	Ⓐ Ⓑ Ⓒ Ⓓ		34.	Ⓐ Ⓑ Ⓒ Ⓓ
LPR 4.	Ⓐ Ⓑ Ⓒ Ⓓ		35.	Ⓐ Ⓑ Ⓒ Ⓓ
5.	Ⓐ Ⓑ Ⓒ Ⓓ		36.	Ⓐ Ⓑ Ⓒ Ⓓ
6.	Ⓐ Ⓑ Ⓒ Ⓓ		37.	Ⓐ Ⓑ Ⓒ Ⓓ
7.	Ⓐ Ⓑ Ⓒ Ⓓ		38.	Ⓐ Ⓑ Ⓒ Ⓓ
8.	Ⓐ Ⓑ Ⓒ Ⓓ		39.	Ⓐ Ⓑ Ⓒ Ⓓ
9.	Ⓐ Ⓑ Ⓒ Ⓓ		40.	Ⓐ Ⓑ Ⓒ Ⓓ
10.	Ⓐ Ⓑ Ⓒ Ⓓ		41.	Ⓐ Ⓑ Ⓒ Ⓓ
11.	Ⓐ Ⓑ Ⓒ Ⓓ		42.	Ⓐ Ⓑ Ⓒ Ⓓ
12.	Ⓐ Ⓑ Ⓒ Ⓓ		43.	Ⓐ Ⓑ Ⓒ Ⓓ
13.	Ⓐ Ⓑ Ⓒ Ⓓ		44.	Ⓐ Ⓑ Ⓒ Ⓓ
14.	Ⓐ Ⓑ Ⓒ Ⓓ		45.	Ⓐ Ⓑ Ⓒ Ⓓ
15.	Ⓐ Ⓑ Ⓒ Ⓓ		46.	Ⓐ Ⓑ Ⓒ Ⓓ
16.	Ⓐ Ⓑ Ⓒ Ⓓ		47.	Ⓐ Ⓑ Ⓒ Ⓓ
17.	Ⓐ Ⓑ Ⓒ Ⓓ		48.	Ⓐ Ⓑ Ⓒ Ⓓ
18.	Ⓐ Ⓑ Ⓒ Ⓓ		49.	Ⓐ Ⓑ Ⓒ Ⓓ
19.	Ⓐ Ⓑ Ⓒ Ⓓ		50.	Ⓐ Ⓑ Ⓒ Ⓓ
20.	Ⓐ Ⓑ Ⓒ Ⓓ		51.	Ⓐ Ⓑ Ⓒ Ⓓ
21.	Ⓐ Ⓑ Ⓒ Ⓓ		52.	Ⓐ Ⓑ Ⓒ Ⓓ
22.	Ⓐ Ⓑ Ⓒ Ⓓ		53.	Ⓐ Ⓑ Ⓒ Ⓓ
23.	Ⓐ Ⓑ Ⓒ Ⓓ		54.	Ⓐ Ⓑ Ⓒ Ⓓ
24.	Ⓐ Ⓑ Ⓒ Ⓓ		55.	Ⓐ Ⓑ Ⓒ Ⓓ
25.	Ⓐ Ⓑ Ⓒ Ⓓ		56.	Ⓐ Ⓑ Ⓒ Ⓓ
26.	Ⓐ Ⓑ Ⓒ Ⓓ		57.	Ⓐ Ⓑ Ⓒ Ⓓ
27.	Ⓐ Ⓑ Ⓒ Ⓓ		58.	Ⓐ Ⓑ Ⓒ Ⓓ
28.	Ⓐ Ⓑ Ⓒ Ⓓ		59.	Ⓐ Ⓑ Ⓒ Ⓓ
29.	Ⓐ Ⓑ Ⓒ Ⓓ		60.	Ⓐ Ⓑ Ⓒ Ⓓ
30.	Ⓐ Ⓑ Ⓒ Ⓓ			

FARE

1.	Ⓐ Ⓑ Ⓒ Ⓓ		31.	Ⓐ Ⓑ Ⓒ Ⓓ
2.	Ⓐ Ⓑ Ⓒ Ⓓ		32.	Ⓐ Ⓑ Ⓒ Ⓓ
3.	obsolete		33.	Ⓐ Ⓑ Ⓒ Ⓓ
4.	Ⓐ Ⓑ Ⓒ Ⓓ		34.	Ⓐ Ⓑ Ⓒ Ⓓ
5.	Ⓐ Ⓑ Ⓒ Ⓓ		35.	Ⓐ Ⓑ Ⓒ Ⓓ
6.	Ⓐ Ⓑ Ⓒ Ⓓ		36.	Ⓐ Ⓑ Ⓒ Ⓓ
7.	Ⓐ Ⓑ Ⓒ Ⓓ		37.	Ⓐ Ⓑ Ⓒ Ⓓ
8.	Ⓐ Ⓑ Ⓒ Ⓓ		38.	Ⓐ Ⓑ Ⓒ Ⓓ
9.	Ⓐ Ⓑ Ⓒ Ⓓ		39.	Ⓐ Ⓑ Ⓒ Ⓓ
10.	Ⓐ Ⓑ Ⓒ Ⓓ		40.	Ⓐ Ⓑ Ⓒ Ⓓ
11.	Ⓐ Ⓑ Ⓒ Ⓓ		41.	Ⓐ Ⓑ Ⓒ Ⓓ
12.	Ⓐ Ⓑ Ⓒ Ⓓ		42.	Ⓐ Ⓑ Ⓒ Ⓓ
13.	Ⓐ Ⓑ Ⓒ Ⓓ		43.	Ⓐ Ⓑ Ⓒ Ⓓ
14.	Ⓐ Ⓑ Ⓒ Ⓓ		44.	Ⓐ Ⓑ Ⓒ Ⓓ
15.	Ⓐ Ⓑ Ⓒ Ⓓ		45.	Ⓐ Ⓑ Ⓒ Ⓓ
16.	Ⓐ Ⓑ Ⓒ Ⓓ		46.	Ⓐ Ⓑ Ⓒ Ⓓ
17.	Ⓐ Ⓑ Ⓒ Ⓓ		47.	Ⓐ Ⓑ Ⓒ Ⓓ
18.	Ⓐ Ⓑ Ⓒ Ⓓ		48.	Ⓐ Ⓑ Ⓒ Ⓓ
19.	Ⓐ Ⓑ Ⓒ Ⓓ		49.	Ⓐ Ⓑ Ⓒ Ⓓ
20.	Ⓐ Ⓑ Ⓒ Ⓓ		50.	Ⓐ Ⓑ Ⓒ Ⓓ
21.	Ⓐ Ⓑ Ⓒ Ⓓ		51.	Ⓐ Ⓑ Ⓒ Ⓓ
22.	Ⓐ Ⓑ Ⓒ Ⓓ		52.	Ⓐ Ⓑ Ⓒ Ⓓ
23.	Ⓐ Ⓑ Ⓒ Ⓓ		53.	Ⓐ Ⓑ Ⓒ Ⓓ
24.	Ⓐ Ⓑ Ⓒ Ⓓ		54.	Ⓐ Ⓑ Ⓒ Ⓓ
25.	Ⓐ Ⓑ Ⓒ Ⓓ		55.	Ⓐ Ⓑ Ⓒ Ⓓ
26.	Ⓐ Ⓑ Ⓒ Ⓓ		56.	Ⓐ Ⓑ Ⓒ Ⓓ
27.	Ⓐ Ⓑ Ⓒ Ⓓ		57.	Ⓐ Ⓑ Ⓒ Ⓓ
28.	Ⓐ Ⓑ Ⓒ Ⓓ		58.	obsolete
29.	Ⓐ Ⓑ Ⓒ Ⓓ		59.	obsolete
30.	Ⓐ Ⓑ Ⓒ Ⓓ		60.	obsolete

Step 4: Two Sample Examinations—
Practice Your Strategy

with • Solutions to Essay and Computational Questions
• Explanatory Answers for Objective Questions

8. May 1995 CPA Examination

This chapter includes the first of two practice examinations that you will be taking. This examination consists of questions from the actual May 1995 CPA examination.*

Be sure to take each of the four sections of this examination just as you would the actual test. *Allow no more time than each examination section indicates. Take each test in one sitting, and do no more than two sections in a day.* You will then become accustomed to concentrating for the duration of a test period and to working efficiently during this time.

Before beginning this practice examination, be sure to review the test tactics outlined in Chapter 5—How to Approach CPA Examination Questions. After completing this examination, turn to Chapter 6—Chart Your Progress and Plan Your Course of Action for guidance in analyzing your score and planning your review program.

Remember: Read directions carefully!

---

*NOTE: All answer explanations are the author's

EXAMINATION QUESTIONS

The point values for each question, and estimated time allotments based primarily on point value, are as follows:

	Point Value	Estimated Minutes Minimum	Estimated Minutes Maximum
No. 1	60	90	100
No. 2	10	10	15
No. 3	10	10	15
No. 4	10	15	25
No. 5	10	15	25
Totals	100	140	180

CANDIDATE NUMBER

Record your 7-digit candidate number in the boxes.

Q-LPR

May 3, 1995; 9:00 A.M. to 12:00 NOON

INSTRUCTIONS TO CANDIDATES   *Failure to follow these instructions may have an adverse effect on your Examination grade.*

Do not break the seal around *Examination Questions* (pages 3 through 18) until you are told to do so.

Question Numbers 1, 2, and 3 should be answered on the *Objective Answer Sheet*, which is pages 27 and 28. You should attempt to answer all objective items. There is no penalty for incorrect responses. Since the objective items are computer-graded, your comments and calculations associated with them are not considered. Be certain that you have entered your answers on the *Objective Answer Sheet* before the examination time is up. The objective portion of your examination will not be graded if you fail to record your answers on the *Objective Answer Sheet*. You will not be given additional time to record your answers.

Question Numbers 4 and 5 should be answered beginning on page 19. If you have not completed answering a question on a page, fill in the appropriate spaces in the wording on the bottom of the page "**QUESTION NUMBER ____ CONTINUES ON PAGE ____.**" If you have completed answering a question, fill in the appropriate space in the wording on the bottom of the page "**QUESTION NUMBER ____ ENDS ON THIS PAGE.**" Always begin the start of an answer to a question on the top of a new page (which may be the reverse side of a sheet of paper).

4. Although the primary purpose of the examination is to test your knowledge and application of the subject matter, selected essay responses will be graded for writing skills.

5. You are required to turn in by the end of each session:

   a. Attendance Record Form, page 1;
   b. *Examination Questions*, pages 3 through 18;
   c. *Essay Ruled Paper*, pages 19 through 26;
   d. *Objective Answer Sheet*, pages 27 and 28; and
   e. All unused examination materials.

   Your examination will not be graded unless the above listed items are handed in before leaving the examination room.

6. Unless otherwise instructed, if you want your *Examination Questions* mailed to you, write your name and address in both places indicated on page 18 and place 55 cents postage in the space provided. *Examination Questions* will be distributed no sooner than the day following the administration of this examination.

56518

BOOKLET NO.

MAY 1995 CPA EXAMINATION

Business, Law & Professional Responsibilities (LPR)

Number 1

Instructions

Select the **best** answer for each of the following items. Use a No. 2 pencil to blacken the appropriate ovals on the Objective Answer Sheet to indicate your answers. **Mark only one answer for each item. Answer all items.** Your grade will be based on the total number of correct answers.

1. According to the standards of the profession, which of the following circumstances will prevent a CPA performing audit engagements from being independent?
   A. Obtaining a collateralized automobile loan from a financial institution client.
   B. Litigation with a client relating to billing for consulting services for which the amount is immaterial.
   C. Employment of the CPA's spouse as a client's internal auditor.
   D. Acting as an honorary trustee for a not-for-profit organization client.

2. Which of the following best describes what is meant by the term generally accepted auditing standards?
   A. Rules acknowledged by the accounting profession because of their universal application.
   B. Pronouncements issued by the Auditing Standards Board.
   C. Measures of the quality of the auditor's performance.
   D. Procedures to be used to gather evidence to support financial statements.

3. According to the standards of the profession, which of the following events would require a CPA performing a consulting services engagement for a nonaudit client to withdraw from the engagement?
   I. The CPA has a conflict of interest that is disclosed to the client and the client consents to the CPA continuing the engagement.
   II. The CPA fails to obtain a written understanding from the client concerning the scope of the engagement.

   A. I only.
   B. II only.
   C. Both I and II only.
   D. Neither I nor II.

4. This question is obsolete.

5. A CPA is permitted to disclose confidential client information without the consent of the client to
   I. Another CPA firm if the information concerns suspected tax return irregularities.
   II. A state CPA society voluntary quality control review board.

   A. I only.
   B. II only.
   C. Both I and II.
   D. Neither I nor II.

6. Trent was retained, in writing, to act as Post's agent for the sale of Post's memorabilia collection. Which of the following statements is correct?
   I. To be an agent, Trent must be at least 21 years of age.
   II. Post would be liable to Trent if the collection was destroyed before Trent found a purchaser.

   A. I only.
   B. II only.
   C. Both I and II.
   D. Neither I nor II.

7. Thorp was a purchasing agent for Ogden, a sole proprietor, and had the express authority to place purchase orders with Ogden's suppliers. Thorp placed an order with Datz, Inc. on Ogden's behalf after Ogden was declared incompetent in a judicial proceeding. Thorp was aware of Ogden's incapacity. Which of the following statements is correct concerning Ogden's liability to Datz?
   A. Ogden will be liable because Datz was **not** informed of Ogden's incapacity.
   B. Ogden will be liable because Thorp acted with express authority.
   C. Ogden will **not** be liable because Thorp's agency ended when Ogden was declared incompetent.
   D. Ogden will **not** be liable because Ogden was a nondisclosed principal.

8. When a valid contract is entered into by an agent on the principal's behalf, in a nondisclosed principal situation, which of the following statements concerning the principal's liability is correct?

	The principal may be held liable once disclosed	The principal must ratify the contract to be held liable
A.	Yes	Yes
B.	Yes	No
C.	No	Yes
D.	No	No

9. Young Corp. hired Wilson as a sales representative for six months at a salary of $5,000 per month plus 6% of sales. Which of the following statements is correct?

 A. Young does **not** have the power to dismiss Wilson during the six-month period without cause.
 B. Wilson is obligated to act solely in Young's interest in matters concerning Young's business.
 C. The agreement between Young and Wilson is **not** enforceable unless it is in writing and signed by Wilson.
 D. The agreement between Young and Wilson formed an agency coupled with an interest.

10. On the death of the grantor, which of the following testamentary trusts would fail?

 A. A trust created to promote the public welfare.
 B. A trust created to provide for a spouse's health care.
 C. A trust created to benefit a charity.
 D. A trust created to benefit a childless person's grandchildren.

11. An irrevocable trust that contains **no** provision for change or termination can be changed or terminated only by the

 A. Courts.
 B. Income beneficiaries.
 C. Remaindermen.
 D. Grantor.

12. Frost's will created a testamentary trust naming Hill as life income beneficiary, with the principal to Brown when Hill dies. The trust was silent on allocation of principal and income. The trust's sole asset was a commercial office building

originally valued at $100,000 and having a current market value of $200,000. If the building was sold, which of the following statements would be correct concerning the allocation of the proceeds?

 A. The entire proceeds would be allocated to principal and retained.
 B. The entire proceeds would be allocated to income and distributed to Hill.
 C. One half of the proceeds would be allocated to principal and one half to income.
 D. One half of the proceeds would be allocated to principal and one half distributed to Brown.

13. Which of the following fiduciary duties may be violated by the trustee if the trustee, without express direction in the trust instrument, invests trust assets in unsecured loans to a co-trustee?

 I. Duty to invest prudently.
 II. Duty of loyalty to the trust.

 A. I only.
 B. II only.
 C. Both I and II.
 D. Neither I nor II.

14. Absent specific directions, which of the following parties will ordinarily receive the assets of a terminated trust?

 A. Income beneficiaries.
 B. Remaindermen.
 C. Grantor.
 D. Trustee.

15. Cord's will created a trust to take effect on Cord's death. The will named Cord's spouse as both the trustee and personal representative (executor) of the estate. The will provided that all of Cord's securities were to be transferred to the trust and named Cord's child as the beneficiary of the trust. Under the circumstances,

 A. Cord has created an inter vivos trust.
 B. Cord has created a testamentary trust.
 C. The trust is invalid because it will **not** become effective until Cord's death.
 D. Cord's spouse may **not** serve as both the trustee and personal representative because of the inherent conflict of interest.

16. Which of the following facts must be proven for a plaintiff to prevail in a common law negligent misrepresentation action?

A. The defendant made the misrepresentations with a reckless disregard for the truth.
B. The plaintiff justifiably relied on the misrepresentations.
C. The misrepresentations were in writing.
D. The misrepresentations concerned opinion.

17. A building subcontractor submitted a bid for construction of a portion of a high-rise office building. The bid contained material computational errors. The general contractor accepted the bid with knowledge of the errors. Which of the following statements best represents the subcontractor's liability?
A. Not liable because the contractor knew of the errors.
B. Not liable because the errors were a result of gross negligence.
C. Liable because the errors were unilateral.
D. Liable because the errors were material.

18. Where the parties have entered into a written contract intended as the final expression of their agreement, which of the following agreements will be admitted into evidence because they are **not** prohibited by the parol evidence rule?

	Subsequent oral agreements	Prior written agreements
A.	Yes	Yes
B.	Yes	No
C.	No	Yes
D.	No	No

19. Which of the following types of conditions affecting performance may validly be present in contracts?

	Conditions precedent	Conditions subsequent	Concurrent conditions
A.	Yes	Yes	Yes
B.	Yes	Yes	No
C.	Yes	No	Yes
D.	No	Yes	Yes

20. Grove is seeking to avoid performing a promise to pay Brook $1,500. Grove is relying on lack of consideration on Brook's part. Grove will prevail if he can establish that

A. Prior to Grove's promise, Brook had already performed the requested act.
B. Brook's only claim of consideration was the relinquishment of a legal right.
C. Brook's asserted consideration is only worth $400.
D. The consideration to be performed by Brook will be performed by a third party.

21. Generally, which of the following contract rights are assignable?

	Option contract rights	Malpractice insurance policy rights
A.	Yes	Yes
B.	Yes	No
C.	No	Yes
D.	No	No

22. One of the criteria for a valid assignment of a sales contract to a third party is that the assignment must
A. Be supported by adequate consideration from the assignee.
B. Be in writing and signed by the assignor.
C. Not materially increase the other party's risk or duty.
D. Not be revocable by the assignor.

23. Which of the following actions will result in the discharge of a party to a contract?

	Prevention of performance	Accord and satisfaction
A.	Yes	Yes
B.	Yes	No
C.	No	Yes
D.	No	No

24. Under a personal services contract, which of the following circumstances will cause the discharge of a party's duties?
A. Death of the party who is to receive the services.
B. Cost of performing the services has doubled.
C. Bankruptcy of the party who is to receive the services.
D. Illegality of the services to be performed.

25. Ordinarily, in an action for breach of a construction contract, the statute of limitations time period would be computed from the date the

A. Contract is negotiated.
B. Contract is breached.
C. Construction is begun.
D. Contract is signed.

26.   Green was unable to repay a loan from State Bank when due. State refused to renew the loan unless Green provided an acceptable surety. Green asked Royal, a friend, to act as surety on the loan. To induce Royal to agree to become a surety, Green fraudulently represented Green's financial condition and promised Royal discounts on merchandise sold at Green's store. Royal agreed to act as surety and the loan was renewed. Later, Green's obligation to State was discharged in Green's bankruptcy. State wants to hold Royal liable. Royal may avoid liability

A. If Royal can show that State was aware of the fraudulent representations.
B. If Royal was an uncompensated surety.
C. Because the discharge in bankruptcy will prevent Royal from having a right of reimbursement.
D. Because the arrangement was void at the inception.

27.   Wright cosigned King's loan from Ace Bank. Which of the following events would release Wright from the obligation to pay the loan?

A. Ace seeking payment of the loan only from Wright.
B. King is granted a discharge in bankruptcy.
C. Ace is paid in full by King's spouse.
D. King is adjudicated mentally incompetent.

Items 28 through 33 are based on the following:

Dart Inc., a closely held corporation, was petitioned involuntarily into bankruptcy under the liquidation provisions of Chapter 7 of the Federal Bankruptcy Code. Dart contested the petition.

Dart has not been paying its business debts as they became due, has defaulted on its mortgage loan payments, and owes back taxes to the IRS. The total cash value of Dart's bankruptcy estate after the sale of all assets and payment of administration expenses is $100,000.

Dart has the following creditors:

• Fracon Bank is owed $75,000 principal and accrued interest on a mortgage loan secured by Dart's real property. The property was valued at and sold, in bankruptcy, for $70,000.

• The IRS has a $12,000 recorded judgment for unpaid corporate income tax.
• JOG Office Supplies has an unsecured claim of $3,000 that was timely filed.
• Nanstar Electric Co. has an unsecured claim of $1,200 that was not timely filed.
• Decoy Publications has a claim of $14,000, of which $2,000 is secured by Dart's inventory that was valued and sold, in bankruptcy, for $2,000. The claim was timely filed.

28.   Which of the following creditors must join in the filing of the involuntary petition?

I. JOG Office Supplies
II. Nanstar Electric Co.
III. Decoy Publications

A. I, II, & III.
B. II & III.
C. I & II.
D. III only.

29.   Which of the following statements would correctly describe the result of Dart's opposing the petition?

A. Dart will win because the petition should have been filed under Chapter 11.
B. Dart will win because there are **not** more than 12 creditors.
C. Dart will lose because it is **not** paying its debts as they become due.
D. Dart will lose because of its debt to the IRS.

30.   Which of the following events will follow the filing of the Chapter 7 involuntary petition?

	A trustee will be appointed	A stay against creditor collection proceedings will go into effect
A.	Yes	Yes
B.	Yes	No
C.	No	Yes
D.	No	No

For **Items 31 through 33** assume that the bankruptcy estate was distributed.

31.   What dollar amount would Nanstar Electric Co. receive?

A. $0
B. $ 800
C. $1,000
D. $1,200

32. What total dollar amount would Fracon Bank receive on its secured and unsecured claims?
    A. $70,000
    B. $72,000
    C. $74,000
    D. $75,000

33. What dollar amount would the IRS receive?
    A. $0
    B. $ 8,000
    C. $10,000
    D. $12,000

Items 34 and 35 are based on the following:

Strong Corp. filed a voluntary petition in bankruptcy under the reorganization provisions of Chapter 11 of the Federal Bankruptcy Code. A reorganization plan was filed and agreed to by all necessary parties. The court confirmed the plan and a final decree was entered.

34. Which of the following parties ordinarily must confirm the plan?

	½ of the secured creditors	⅔ of the shareholders
A.	Yes	Yes
B.	Yes	No
C.	No	Yes
D.	No	No

35. Which of the following statements best describes the effect of the entry of the court's final decree?
    A. Strong Corp. will be discharged from all its debts and liabilities.
    B. Strong Corp. will be discharged only from the debts owed creditors who agreed to the reorganization plan.
    C. Strong Corp. will be discharged from all its debts and liabilities that arose before the date of confirmation of the plan.
    D. Strong Corp. will be discharged from all its debts and liabilities that arose before the confirmation of the plan, except as otherwise provided in the plan, the order of confirmation, or the Bankruptcy Code.

36. Which of the following payments are deducted from an employee's salary?

	Unemployment compensation insurance	Workers' compensation insurance
A.	Yes	Yes
B.	Yes	No
C.	No	Yes
D.	No	No

37. Under which of the following conditions is an on-site inspection of a workplace by an investigator from the Occupational Safety and Health Administration (OSHA) permissible?
    A. Only if OSHA obtains a search warrant after showing probable cause.
    B. Only if the inspection is conducted after working hours.
    C. At the request of employees.
    D. After OSHA provides the employer with at least 24 hours notice of the prospective inspection.

38. Under the provisions of the Americans With Disabilities Act of 1990, in which of the following areas is a disabled person protected from discrimination?

	Public transportation	Privately operated public accommodations
A.	Yes	Yes
B.	Yes	No
C.	No	Yes
D.	No	No

39. When verifying a client's compliance with statutes governing employees' wages and hours, an auditor should check the client's personnel records against relevant provisions of which of the following statutes?
    A. National Labor Relations Act.
    B. Fair Labor Standards Act.
    C. Taft-Hartley Act.
    D. Americans With Disabilities Act.

40. Under the provisions of the Employee Retirement Income Security Act of 1974 (ERISA), which of the following statements is correct?
    A. Employees are entitled to have an employer established pension plan.
    B. Employers are prevented from unduly delaying an employee's participation in a pension plan.
    C. Employers are prevented from managing retirement plans.
    D. Employees are entitled to make investment decisions.

41. Under the Commercial Paper Article of the UCC, which of the following documents would be considered an order to pay?

   I. Draft
  II. Certificate of deposit

    A. I only.
    B. II only.
    C. Both I and II.
    D. Neither I nor II.

42.

```
To: Middlesex National Bank
Nassau, NY
                          September 15, 1994
Pay to the order of Robert Silver    $4,000.00
Four Thousand and xx/100 Dollars
On October 1, 1994
                          Lynn Dexter
                          Lynn Dexter
```

The above instrument is a
    A. Draft.
    B. Postdated check.
    C. Trade acceptance.
    D. Promissory note.

43. Under the Commercial Paper Article of the UCC, for an instrument to be negotiable it must
    A. Be payable to order or to bearer.
    B. Be signed by the payee.
    C. Contain references to all agreements between the parties.
    D. Contain necessary conditions of payment.

44. Under the Commercial Paper Article of the UCC, which of the following circumstances would prevent a promissory note from being negotiable?
    A. An extension clause that allows the maker to elect to extend the time for payment to a date specified in the note.
    B. An acceleration clause that allows the holder to move up the maturity date of the note in the event of default.
    C. A person having a power of attorney signs the note on behalf of the maker.
    D. A clause that allows the maker to satisfy the note by the performance of services or the payment of money.

45. Under the Commercial Paper Article of the UCC, which of the following requirements must be met for a transferee of order paper to become a holder?

   I. Possession
  II. Endorsement of transferor

    A. I only.
    B. II only.
    C. Both I and II.
    D. Neither I nor II.

46. Under the Commercial Paper Article of the UCC, which of the following requirements must be met for a person to be a holder in due course of a promissory note?
    A. The note must be payable to bearer.
    B. The note must be negotiable.
    C. All prior holders must have been holders in due course.
    D. The holder must be the payee of the note.

47. Under the Commercial Paper Article of the UCC, which of the following circumstances would prevent a person from becoming a holder in due course of an instrument?
    A. The person was notified that payment was refused.
    B. The person was notified that one of the prior endorsers was discharged.
    C. The note was collateral for a loan.
    D. The note was purchased at a discount.

48. Under the Commercial Paper Article of the UCC, which of the following statements best describes the effect of a person endorsing a check "without recourse"?
    A. The person has **no** liability to prior endorsers.
    B. The person makes **no** promise or guarantee of payment on dishonor.
    C. The person gives **no** warranty protection to later transferees.
    D. The person converts the check into order paper.

49. Under the Commercial Paper Article of the UCC, in a nonconsumer transaction, which of the following are real defenses available against a holder in due course?

	Material alteration	Discharge in bankruptcy	Breach of contract
A.	No	Yes	Yes
B.	Yes	Yes	No
C.	No	No	Yes
D.	Yes	No	No

50.

```
Pay to Ann Tyler
    Paul Tyler
    Ann Tyler


    Mary Thomas


    Betty Ash

Pay George Green Only
    Susan Town
```

Susan Town, on receiving the above instrument, struck Betty Ash's endorsement. Under the Commercial Paper Article of the UCC, which of the endorsers of the above instrument will be completely discharged from secondary liability to later endorsers of the instrument?

A. Ann Tyler
B. Mary Thomas
C. Betty Ash
D. Susan Town

51. On August 15, 1994, Tower, Nolan, and Oak were deeded a piece of land as tenants in common. The deed provided that Tower owned ½ the property and Nolan and Oak owned ¼ each. If Oak dies, the property will be owned as follows:

A. Tower ½, Nolan ¼, Oak's heirs ¼.
B. Tower ⅓, Nolan ⅓, Oak's heirs ⅓.
C. Tower ⅝, Nolan ⅜.
D. Tower ½, Nolan ½.

52. Which of the following provisions must be included in a residential lease agreement?

A. A description of the leased premises.
B. The due date for payment of rent.
C. A requirement that the tenant have public liability insurance.
D. A requirement that the landlord will perform all structural repairs to the property.

53. For a deed to be effective between a purchaser and seller of real estate, one of the conditions is that the deed must

A. Be recorded within the permissible statutory time limits.
B. Be delivered by the seller with an intent to transfer title.
C. Contain the actual sales price.
D. Contain the signatures of the seller and purchaser.

54. Generally, which of the following federal acts regulates mortgage lenders?

	Real Estate Settlement Procedures Act (RESPA)	Federal Trade Commission Act
A.	Yes	Yes
B.	Yes	No
C.	No	Yes
D.	No	No

55. Which of the following factors help determine whether an item of personal property has become a fixture?

	Manner of affixation	Value of the item	Intent of the annexor
A.	Yes	Yes	Yes
B.	Yes	Yes	No
C.	Yes	No	Yes
D.	No	Yes	Yes

56. Under the Comprehensive Environmental Response, Compensation, and Liability Act (CERCLA), commonly known as Superfund, which of the following parties would be liable to the Environmental Protection Agency (EPA) for the expense of cleaning up a hazardous waste disposal site?

I. The current owner or operator of the site.
II. The person who transported the wastes to the site.
III. The person who owned or operated the site at the time of the disposal.

A. I and II.
B. I and III.
C. II and III.
D. I, II, and III.

57. Which of the following items is tangible personal property?

A. Share of stock.
B. Trademark.
C. Promissory note.
D. Oil painting.

58. Which of the following standards of liability best characterizes the obligation of a common carrier in a bailment relationship?
    A. Reasonable care.
    B. Gross negligence.
    C. Shared liability.
    D. Strict liability.

59. Clark Corp. owns a warehouse purchased for $150,000 in 1990. The current market value is $200,000. Clark has the warehouse insured for fire loss with Fair Insurance Corp. and Zone Insurance Co. Fair's policy is for $150,000 and Zone's policy is for $75,000. Both policies contain the standard 80 percent coinsurance clause. If a fire totally destroyed the warehouse, what total dollar amount would Clark receive from Fair and Zone?
    A. $225,000
    B. $200,000
    C. $160,000
    D. $150,000

60. Which of the following parties has an insurable interest?
    I. A corporate retailer in its inventory.
    II. A partner in the partnership property.
    A. I only.
    B. II only.
    C. Both I and II.
    D. Neither I nor II.

Number 2

Number 2 consists of two unrelated parts.

Instructions—Number 2a

Question Number 2a consists of 6 items. Select the **best** answer for each item. Use a No. 2 pencil to blacken the appropriate ovals on the Objective Answer Sheet to indicate your answers. **Answer all items.** Your grade will be based on the total number of correct answers.

a. Items 61 through 66 are based on the following:
In 1992, Anchor, Chain, and Hook created ACH Associates, a general partnership. The partners orally agreed that they would work full time for the partnership and would distribute profits based on their capital contributions. Anchor contributed $5,000; Chain $10,000; and Hook $15,000.

For the year ended December 31, 1993, ACH Associates had profits of $60,000 that were distributed to the partners. During 1994, ACH Associates was operating at a loss. In September 1994, the partnership dissolved.

In October 1994, Hook contracted in writing with Ace Automobile Co. to purchase a car for the partnership. Hook had previously purchased cars from Ace Automobile Co. for use by ACH Associates partners. ACH Associates did not honor the contract with Ace Automobile Co. and Ace Automobile Co. sued the partnership and the individual partners.

Required:

Items 61 through 66 refer to the above facts. For each item, determine whether (A) or (B) is correct. On the Objective Answer Sheet, blacken the oval that corresponds to the correct statement.

61. A. The ACH Associates oral partnership agreement was valid.
    B. The ACH Associates oral partnership agreement was invalid because the partnership lasted for more than one year.

62. A. Anchor, Chain, and Hook jointly owning and conducting a business for profit establishes a partnership relationship.
    B. Anchor, Chain, and Hook jointly owning income producing property establishes a partnership relationship.

63. A. Anchor's share of ACH Associates' 1993 profits was $20,000.
    B. Hook's share of ACH Associates' 1993 profits was $30,000.

64. A. Anchor's capital account would be reduced by ⅓ of any 1994 losses.
    B. Hooks' capital account would be reduced by ½ of any 1994 losses.

65. A. Ace Automobile Co. would lose a suit brought against ACH Associates because Hook, as a general partner, has no authority to bind the partnership.
    B. Ace Automobile Co. would win a suit brought against ACH Associates because Hook's authority continues during dissolution.

66. A. ACH Associates and Hook would be the only parties liable to pay any judgment recovered by Ace Automobile Co.
   B. Anchor, Chain, and Hook would be jointly liable to pay any judgment recovered by Ace Automobile Co.

Instructions—Number 2b

Question Number 2b consists of 6 items. Select the **best** answer for each item. Use a No. 2 pencil to blacken the appropriate ovals on the Objective Answer Sheet to indicate your answers. **Answer all items.** Your grade will be based on the total number of correct answers.

b. Items 67 through 72 are based on the following:

In 1990, Amber Corp., a closely held corporation, was formed by Adams, Frank, and Berg as incorporators and stockholders. Adams, Frank, and Berg executed a written voting agreement that provided that they would vote for each other as directors and officers. In 1994, stock in the corporation was offered to the public. This resulted in an additional 300 stockholders. After the offering, Adams holds 25 percent, Frank holds 15 percent, and Berg holds 15 percent of all issued and outstanding stock. Adams, Frank, and Berg have been directors and officers of the corporation since the corporation was formed. Regular meetings of the board of directors and annual stockholders meetings have been held.

Required:

Items 67 through 72 refer to the formation of Amber Corp. and the rights and duties of its stockholders, directors, and officers. For each item, determine whether (A), (B), or (C) is correct. On the Objective Answer Sheet, blacken the oval that corresponds to the correct statement.

67. A. Amber Corp. must be formed under a state's general corporation statute.
   B. Amber Corp.'s Articles of Incorporation must include the names of all stockholders.
   C. Amber Corp. must include its corporate bylaws in the incorporation documents filed with the state.

68. Amber Corp.'s initial bylaws ordinarily would be adopted by its

   A. Stockholders.
   B. Officers.
   C. Directors.

69. Amber Corp.'s directors are elected by its
   A. Officers.
   B. Outgoing directors.
   C. Stockholders.

70. Amber Corp.'s officers ordinarily would be elected by its
   A. Stockholders.
   B. Directors.
   C. Outgoing officers.

71. Amber Corp.'s day-to-day business ordinarily would be operated by its
   A. Directors.
   B. Stockholders.
   C. Officers.

72. A. Adams, Frank, and Berg must be elected as directors because they own 55 percent of the issued and outstanding stock.
   B. Adams, Frank, and Berg must always be elected as officers because they own 55 percent of the issued and outstanding stock.
   C. Adams, Frank, and Berg must always vote for each other as directors because they have a voting agreement.

Number 3

Number 3 consists of two unrelated parts.

Instructions—Number 3a

Question Number 3a consists of 6 items. Select the **best** answer for each item. Use a No. 2 pencil to blacken the appropriate ovals on the Objective Answer Sheet to indicate your answers. **Answer all items.** Your grade will be based on the total number of correct answers.

a. Items 73 through 78 are based on the following:

On February 1, 1995, Grand Corp., a manufacturer of custom cabinets, contracted in writing with Axle Co., a kitchen contractor, to sell Axle 100 unique, custom-designed, kitchen cabinets for $250,000. Axle had contracted to install the cabinets in a luxury condominium complex. The contract provided that the cabinets were to be ready for delivery by April 15 and were to be shipped F.O.B. sellers loading dock. On April 15,

Grand had 85 cabinets complete and delivered them, together with 15 standard cabinets, to the trucking company for delivery to Axle. Grand faxed Axle a copy of the shipping invoice, listing the 15 standard cabinets. On May 1, before reaching Axle, the truck was involved in a collision and all the cabinets were damaged beyond repair.

Required:

Items 73 through 78 refer to the above fact pattern. For each item, determine whether (A), (B), or (C) is correct. On the Objective Answer Sheet, blacken the oval that corresponds to the correct statement.

73. A. The contract between Grand and Axle was a shipment contract.
    B. The contract between Grand and Axle was a destination contract.
    C. The contract between Grand and Axle was a consignment contract.

74. A. The risk of loss for the 85 custom cabinets passed to Axle on April 15.
    B. The risk of loss for the 100 cabinets passed to Axle on April 15.
    C. The risk of loss for the 100 cabinets remained with Grand.

75. A. The contract between Grand and Axle was invalid because **no** delivery date was stated.
    B. The contract between Grand and Axle was voidable because Grand shipped only 85 custom cabinets.
    C. The contract between Grand and Axle was void because the goods were destroyed.

76. A. Grand's shipment of the standard cabinets was a breach of the contract with Axle.
    B. Grand would **not** be considered to have breached the contract until Axle rejected the standard cabinets.
    C. Grand made a counteroffer by shipping the standard cabinets.

77. A. Had the cabinets been delivered, title would **not** transfer to Axle until Axle inspected them.
    B. Had the cabinets been delivered, title would have transferred on delivery to the carrier.
    C. Had the cabinets been delivered, title would **not** have transferred because the cabinets were nonconforming goods.

78. A. Axle is entitled to specific performance from Grand because of the unique nature of the goods.
    B. Axle is required to purchase substitute goods (cover) and is entitled to the difference in cost from Grand.
    C. Axle is entitled to punitive damages because of Grand's intentional shipment of nonconforming goods.

Instructions—Number 3b

Question Number 3b consists of 6 items. Select the **best** answer for each item. Use a No. 2 pencil to blacken the appropriate ovals on the Objective Answer Sheet to indicate your answers. **Answer all items.** Your grade will be based on the total number of correct answers.

b. Items 79 through 84 are based on the following:

On January 2, 1994, Gray Interiors Corp., a retailer of sofas, contracted with Shore Furniture Co. to purchase 150 sofas for its inventory. The purchase price was $250,000. Gray paid $50,000 cash and gave Shore a note and security agreement for the balance. On March 1, 1994, the sofas were delivered. On March 10, 1994, Shore filed a financing statement.

On February 1, 1994, Gray negotiated a $1,000,000 line of credit with Float Bank, pledged its present and future inventory as security, and gave Float a security agreement. On February 20, 1994, Gray borrowed $100,000 from the line of credit. On March 5, 1994, Float filed a financing statement.

On April 1, 1994, Dove, a consumer purchaser in the ordinary course of business purchased a sofa from Gray. Dove was aware of both security interests.

Required:

Items 79 through 84 refer to the above fact pattern. For each item, determine whether (A), (B), or (C) is correct. On the Objective Answer Sheet, blacken the oval that corresponds to the correct statement.

79. Shore's security interest in the sofas attached on
    A. January 2, 1994.
    B. March 1, 1994.
    C. March 10, 1994.

80. Shore's security interest in the sofas was perfected on
    A. January 2, 1994.
    B. March 1, 1994.
    C. March 10, 1994.

81. Float's security interest in Gray's inventory attached on
    A. February 1, 1994.
    B. March 1, 1994.
    C. March 5, 1994.

82. · Float's security interest in Gray's inventory was perfected on
    A. February 1, 1994.
    B. February 20, 1994.
    C. March 5, 1994.

83. A. Shore's security interest has priority because it was a purchase money security interest.
    B. Float's security interest has priority because Float's financing statement was filed before Shore's.
    C. Float's security interest has priority because Float's interest attached before Shore's.

84. A. Dove purchased the sofa subject to Shore's security interest.
    B. Dove purchased the sofa subject to both the Shore and Float security interests.
    C. Dove purchased the sofa free of either the Shore or Float security interests.

Number 4

Verge Associates, CPAs, were retained to perform a consulting service engagement by Stone Corp. Verge contracted to advise Stone on the proper computers to purchase. Verge was also to design computer software that would allow for more efficient collection of Stone's accounts receivable. Verge prepared the software programs in a manner that allowed some of Stone's accounts receivable to be erroneously deleted from Stone's records. As a result, Stone's expense to collect these accounts was increased greatly.

During the course of the engagement, a Verge partner learned from a computer salesperson that the computers Verge was recommending to Stone would be obsolete within a year. The salesperson suggested that Verge recommend a newer, less expensive model that was more efficient. Verge intentionally recommended, and Stone purchased, the more expensive model. Verge received a commission from the computer company for inducing Stone to purchase that computer.

Stone sued Verge for negligence and common law fraud.

Required:

a. State whether Stone will be successful in its negligence suit against Verge and describe the elements of negligence shown in the above situation that Stone should argue.

b. State whether Stone will be successful in its fraud suit against Verge and describe the elements of fraud shown in the above situation that Stone should argue.

Number 5

Perry, a staff accountant with Orlean Associates, CPAs, reviewed the following transactions engaged in by Orlean's two clients: World Corp. and Unity Corp.

WORLD CORP.

During 1994, World Corp. made a $4,000,000 offering of its stock. The offering was sold to 50 nonaccredited investors and 150 accredited investors. There was a general advertising of the offering. All purchasers were provided with material information concerning World Corp. The offering was completely sold by the end of 1994. The SEC was notified 30 days after the first sale of the offering.

World did not register the offering and contends that the offering and any subsequent resale of the securities are completely exempt from registration under Regulation D, Rule 505, of the Securities Act of 1933.

UNITY CORP.

Unity Corp. has 750 equity stockholders and assets in excess of $100,000,000. Unity's stock is traded on a national stock exchange. Unity contends that it is not a covered corporation and is not required to comply with the reporting provisions of the Securities Exchange Act of 1934.

Required:

a. 1. State whether World is correct in its contention that the offering is exempt from registration under Regulation D, Rule 505, of the Securities Act of 1933. Give the reason(s) for your conclusion.

2. State whether World is correct in its contention that on subsequent resale the securities are completely exempt from registration. Give the reason(s) for your conclusion.

b. 1. State whether Unity is correct in its contention that it is not a covered corporation and is not required to comply with the reporting requirements of the Securities Exchange Act of 1934 and give the reason(s) for your conclusion.

2. Identify and describe two principal reports a covered corporation must file with the SEC.

XAMINATION QUESTIONS

he point values for each question, and estimated time lotments based primarily on point value, are as follows:

	Point Value	Estimated Minutes	
		Minimum	Maximum
No. 1	60	140	150
No. 2	10	15	25
No. 3	10	15	25
No. 4	10	25	35
No. 5	10	25	35
Totals	100	220	270

Q-AUDIT

May 3, 1995; 1:30 P.M. to 6:00 P.M.

STRUCTIONS TO CANDIDATES *Failure to follow these instructions may have an adverse effect on your Examination grade.*

Do not break the seal around *Examination Questions* (pages 3 through 22) until you are told to do so.

Question Numbers 1, 2, and 3 should be answered on the *Objective Answer Sheet*, which is pages 31 and 32. You should attempt to answer all objective items. There is no penalty for incorrect responses. Since the objective items are computer-graded, your comments and calculations associated with them are not considered. Be certain that you have entered your answers on the *Objective Answer Sheet* before the examination time is up. The objective portion of your examination will not be graded if you fail to record your answers on the *Objective Answer Sheet*. You will not be given additional time to record your answers.

Question Numbers 4 and 5 should be answered beginning on page 23. If you have not completed answering a question on a page, fill in the appropriate spaces in the wording on the bottom of the page "**QUESTION NUMBER ____ CONTINUES ON PAGE ____.**" If you have completed answering a question, fill in the appropriate space in the wording on the bottom of the page "**QUESTION NUMBER ____ ENDS ON THIS PAGE.**" Always begin the

start of an answer to a question on the top of a new page (which may be the reverse side of a sheet of paper).

4. Although the primary purpose of the examination is to test your knowledge and application of the subject matter, selected essay responses will be graded for writing skills.

5. You are required to turn in by the end of each session:
   a. Attendance Record Form, page 1;
   b. *Examination Questions*, pages 3 through 22;
   c. *Essay Ruled Paper*, pages 23 through 30;
   d. *Objective Answer Sheet*, pages 31 and 32; and
   e. All unused examination materials.

   Your examination will not be graded unless the above listed items are handed in before leaving the examination room.

6. Unless otherwise instructed, if you want your *Examination Questions* mailed to you, write your name and address in both places indicated on page 22 and place 55 cents postage in the space provided. *Examination Questions* will be distributed no sooner than the day following the administration of this examination.

pared by the Board of Examiners of the American titute of Certified Public Accountants and adopted by the mining boards of all states, the District of Columbia, am, Puerto Rico, and the Virgin Islands of the United tes.

56488

BOOKLET NO.

Auditing (AUDIT)

Number 1

Instructions

Select the **best** answer for each of the following items. Use a No. 2 pencil to blacken the appropriate ovals on the Objective Answer Sheet to indicate your answers. **Mark only one answer for each item. Answer all items.** Your grade will be based on the total number of correct answers.

1. The element of the audit planning process most likely to be agreed upon with the client before implementation of the audit strategy is the determination of the
   - A. Evidence to be gathered to provide a sufficient basis for the auditor's opinion.
   - B. Procedures to be undertaken to discover litigation, claims, and assessments.
   - C. Pending legal matters to be included in the inquiry of the client's attorney.
   - D. Timing of inventory observation procedures to be performed.

2. A successor auditor most likely would make specific inquiries of the predecessor auditor regarding
   - A. Specialized accounting principles of the client's industry.
   - B. The competency of the client's internal audit staff.
   - C. The uncertainty inherent in applying sampling procedures.
   - D. Disagreements with management as to auditing procedures.

3. Which of the following statements would **least** likely appear in an auditor's engagement letter?
   - A. Fees for our services are based on our regular per diem rates, plus travel and other out-of-pocket expenses.
   - B. During the course of our audit we may observe opportunities for economy in, or improved controls over, your operations.
   - C. Our engagement is subject to the risk that material errors and fraud may exist and will **not** be detected.
   - D. After performing our preliminary analytical procedures, we will discuss with you the other procedures we consider necessary to complete the engagement.

4. Which of the following procedures would an auditor most likely perform in planning a financial statement audit?
   - A. Inquiring of the client's legal counsel concerning pending litigation.
   - B. Comparing the financial statements to anticipated results.
   - C. Examining computer generated exception reports to verify the effectiveness of internal controls.
   - D. Searching for unauthorized transactions that may aid in detecting unrecorded liabilities.

5. The nature and extent of a CPA firm's quality controls depend on

	The CPA firm's size	The nature of the CPA firm's practice	Cost-benefit considerations
A.	Yes	Yes	Yes
B.	Yes	Yes	No
C.	Yes	No	Yes
D.	No	Yes	Yes

6. Would the following factors ordinarily be considered in planning an audit engagement's personnel requirements?

	Opportunities for on-the-job training	Continuity and periodic rotation of human resources
A.	Yes	Yes
B.	Yes	No
C.	No	Yes
D.	No	No

7. The in-charge auditor most likely would have a supervisory responsibility to explain to the staff assistants
   - A. That immaterial fraud is **not** to be reported to the client's audit committee.
   - B. How the results of various auditing procedures performed by the assistants should be evaluated.
   - C. What benefits may be attained by the assistants' adherence to established time budgets.
   - D. Why certain documents are being transferred from the current file to the permanent file.

8. Analytical procedures used in planning an audit should focus on
   A. Reducing the scope of tests of controls and substantive tests.
   B. Providing assurance that potential material misstatements will be identified.
   C. Enhancing the auditor's understanding of the client's business.
   D. Assessing the adequacy of the available evidential matter.

9. Which of the following relatively small misstatements most likely could have a material effect on an entity's financial statements?
   A. An illegal payment to a foreign official that was **not** recorded.
   B. A piece of obsolete office equipment that was **not** retired.
   C. A petty cash fund disbursement that was **not** properly authorized.
   D. An uncollectible account receivable that was **not** written off.

10. Which of the following audit risk components may be assessed in nonquantitative terms?

	Control risk	Detection risk	Inherent risk
A.	Yes	Yes	No
B.	Yes	No	Yes
C.	Yes	Yes	Yes
D.	No	Yes	Yes

11. Which of the following would an auditor most likely use in determining the auditor's preliminary judgment about materiality?
   A. The anticipated sample size of the planned substantive tests.
   B. The entity's annualized interim financial statements.
   C. The results of the internal control questionnaire.
   D. The contents of the management representation letter.

12. As the acceptable level of detection risk decreases, an auditor may
   A. Reduce substantive testing by relying on the assessments of inherent risk and control risk.
   B. Postpone the planned timing of substantive tests from interim dates to the year-end.
   C. Eliminate the assessed level of inherent risk from consideration as a planning factor.
   D. Lower the assessed level of control risk from the maximum level to below the maximum.

13. An auditor concludes that a client's illegal act, which has a material effect on the financial statements, has not been properly accounted for or disclosed. Depending on the materiality of the effect on the financial statements, the auditor should express either a(an)
   A. Adverse opinion or a disclaimer of opinion.
   B. Qualified opinion or an adverse opinion.
   C. Disclaimer of opinion or an unqualified opinion with a separate explanatory paragraph.
   D. Unqualified opinion with a separate explanatory paragraph or a qualified opinion.

14. Which of the following characteristics most likely would heighten an auditor's concern about the risk of intentional manipulation of financial statements?
   A. Turnover of senior accounting personnel is low.
   B. Insiders recently purchased additional shares of the entity's stock.
   C. Threat of imminent bankruptcy.
   D. The rate of change in the entity's industry is slow.

15. Which of the following statements reflects an auditor's responsibility for detecting errors and fraud?

   A. An auditor is responsible for detecting employee errors and simple fraud, but **not** for discovering fraud involving employee collusion or management override.

   B. An auditor should plan the audit to detect errors and fraud that are caused by departures from GAAP.

   C. An auditor is **not** responsible for detecting errors and fraud unless the application of GAAS would result in such detection.

   D. An auditor should design the audit to provide reasonable assurance of detecting errors and fraud that have a material effect on the financial statements.

16. An auditor should design the written audit program so that

   A. All material transactions will be selected for substantive testing.

   B. Substantive tests prior to the balance sheet date will be minimized.

   C. The audit procedures selected will achieve specific audit objectives.

   D. Each account balance will be tested under either tests of controls or tests of transactions.

17. The audit program usually **cannot** be finalized until the

   A. Consideration of the entity's internal control has been completed.

   B. Engagement letter has been signed by the auditor and the client.

   C. Reportable conditions have been communicated to the audit committee of the board of directors.

   D. Search for unrecorded liabilities has been performed and documented.

18. In auditing the financial statements of Star Corp., Land discovered information leading Land to believe that Star's prior year's financial statements, which were audited by Tell, require substantial revisions. Under these circumstances, Land should

   A. Notify Star's audit committee and stockholders that the prior year's financial statements **cannot** be relied on.

   B. Request Star to reissue the prior year's financial statements with the appropriate revisions.

   C. Notify Tell about the information and make inquiries about the integrity of Star's management.

   D. Request Star to arrange a meeting among the three parties to resolve the matter.

19. An auditor would **least** likely initiate a discussion with a client's audit committee concerning

   A. The methods used to account for significant unusual transactions.

   B. The maximum dollar amount of misstatements that could exist without causing the financial statements to be materially misstated.

   C. Indications of fraud and illegal acts committed by a corporate officer that were discovered by the auditor.

   D. Disagreements with management as to accounting principles that were resolved during the current year's audit.

20. If requested to perform a review engagement for a nonpublic entity in which an accountant has an immaterial direct financial interest, the accountant is

   A. Not independent and, therefore, may **not** be associated with the financial statements.

   B. Not independent and, therefore, may **not** issue a review report.

   C. Not independent and, therefore, may issue a review report, but may **not** issue an auditor's opinion.

   D. Independent because the financial interest is immaterial and, therefore, may issue a review report.

21. Kell engaged March, CPA, to submit to Kell a written personal financial plan containing unaudited personal financial statements. March anticipates omitting certain disclosures required by GAAP because the engagement's sole purpose is to assist Kell in developing a personal financial plan. For March to be exempt from complying with the requirements of SSARS 1, "Compilation and Review of Financial Statements," Kell is required to agree that the

A. Financial statements will **not** be presented in comparative form with those of the prior period.

B. Omitted disclosures required by GAAP are **not** material.

C. Financial statements will **not** be disclosed to a non-CPA financial planner.

D. Financial statements will **not** be used to obtain credit.

22. An examination of a financial forecast is a professional service that involves

A. Compiling or assembling a financial forecast that is based on management's assumptions.

B. Limiting the distribution of the accountant's report to management and the board of directors.

C. Assuming responsibility to update management on key events for one year after the report's date.

D. Evaluating the preparation of a financial forecast and the support underlying management's assumptions.

23. The third general standard states that due care is to be exercised in the performance of an audit. This standard is ordinarily interpreted to require

A. Thorough review of the existing safeguards over access to assets and records.

B. Limited review of the indications of employee fraud and illegal acts.

C. Objective review of the adequacy of the technical training and proficiency of firm personnel.

D. The exercise of professional skepticism.

24. The primary objective of procedures performed to obtain an understanding of internal control is to provide an auditor with

A. Knowledge necessary for audit planning.

B. Evidential matter to use in assessing inherent risk.

C. A basis for modifying tests of controls.

D. An evaluation of the consistency of application of management's policies.

25. This question is obsolete.

26. When considering internal control, an auditor should be aware of the concept of reasonable assurance, which recognizes that

A. Internal controls may be ineffective due to mistakes in judgment and personal carelessness.

B. Adequate safeguards over access to assets and records should permit an entity to maintain proper accountability.

C. Establishing and maintaining internal control is an important responsibility of management.

D. The cost of an entity's internal control should **not** exceed the benefits expected to be derived.

27. Control risk should be assessed in terms of
A. Specific control activities.
B. Types of potential fraud.
C. Financial statement assertions.
D. Control environment factors.

28. As a result of tests of controls, an auditor assessed control risk too low and decreased substantive testing. This assessment occurred because the true deviation rate in the population was

A. Less than the risk of assessing control risk too low, based on the auditor's sample.

B. Less than the deviation rate in the auditor's sample.

C. More than the risk of assessing control risk too low, based on the auditor's sample.

D. More than the deviation rate in the auditor's sample.

29. When an auditor assesses control risk at the maximum level, the auditor is required to document the auditor's

	Understanding of the entity's accounting system	Basis for concluding that control risk is at the maximum level
A.	No	No
B.	No	Yes
C.	Yes	No
D.	Yes	Yes

30. Sound internal control dictates that immediately upon receiving checks from customers by mail, a responsible employee should

A. Add the checks to the daily cash summary.

B. Verify that each check is supported by a prenumbered sales invoice.

C. Prepare a duplicate listing of checks received.

D. Record the checks in the cash receipts journal.

31. An auditor generally tests the segregation of duties related to inventory by
   A. Personal inquiry and observation.
   B. Test counts and cutoff procedures.
   C. Analytical procedures and invoice recomputation.
   D. Document inspection and reconciliation.

32. Tracing shipping documents to prenumbered sales invoices provides evidence that
   A. No duplicate shipments or billings occurred.
   B. Shipments to customers were properly invoiced.
   C. All goods ordered by customers were shipped.
   D. All prenumbered sales invoices were accounted for.

33. After obtaining an understanding of internal control and assessing control risk, an auditor decided to perform tests of controls. The auditor most likely decided that
   A. It would be efficient to perform tests of controls that would result in a reduction in planned substantive tests.
   B. Additional evidence to support a further reduction in control risk is **not** available.
   C. An increase in the assessed level of control risk is justified for certain financial statement assertions.
   D. There were many internal control weaknesses that could allow errors to enter the accounting system.

34. To provide assurance that each voucher is submitted and paid only once, an auditor most likely would examine a sample of paid vouchers and determine whether each voucher is
   A. Supported by a vendor's invoice.
   B. Stamped "paid" by the check signer.
   C. Prenumbered and accounted for.
   D. Approved for authorized purchases.

35. In determining the sample size for a test of controls, an auditor should consider the likely rate of deviations, the allowable risk of assessing control risk too low, and the
   A. Tolerable deviation rate.
   B. Risk of incorrect acceptance.
   C. Nature and cause of deviations.
   D. Population size.

36. An advantage of using statistical over non-statistical sampling methods in tests of controls is that the statistical methods
   A. Can more easily convert the sample into a dual-purpose test useful for substantive testing.
   B. Eliminate the need to use judgment in determining appropriate sample sizes.
   C. Afford greater assurance than a nonstatistical sample of equal size.
   D. Provide an objective basis for quantitatively evaluating sample risk.

37. An auditor vouched data for a sample of employees in a payroll register to approved clock card data to provide assurance that
   A. Payments to employees are computed at authorized rates.
   B. Employees work the number of hours for which they are paid.
   C. Segregation of duties exist between the preparation and distribution of the payroll.
   D. Internal controls relating to unclaimed payroll checks are operating effectively.

38. Which of the following statements is correct concerning reportable conditions in an audit?
   A. An auditor is required to search for reportable conditions during an audit.
   B. All reportable conditions are also considered to be material weaknesses.
   C. An auditor may communicate reportable conditions during an audit or after the audit's completion.
   D. An auditor may report that **no** reportable conditions were noted during an audit.

39. Which of the following types of audit evidence is the most persuasive?
   A. Prenumbered client purchase order forms.
   B. Client work sheets supporting cost allocations.
   C. Bank statements obtained from the client.
   D. Client representation letter.

40. An auditor most likely would inspect loan agreements under which an entity's inventories are pledged to support management's financial statement assertion of
  A. Presentation and disclosure.
  B. Valuation or allocation.
  C. Existence or occurrence.
  D. Completeness.

41. In auditing intangible assets, an auditor most likely would review or recompute amortization and determine whether the amortization period is reasonable in support of management's financial statement assertion of
  A. Valuation or allocation.
  B. Existence or occurrence.
  C. Completeness.
  D. Rights and obligations.

42. Cutoff tests designed to detect purchases made before the end of the year that have been recorded in the subsequent year most likely would provide assurance about management's assertion of
  A. Valuation or allocation.
  B. Existence or occurrence.
  C. Completeness.
  D. Presentation and disclosure.

43. An auditor most likely would make inquiries of production and sales personnel concerning possible obsolete or slow-moving inventory to support management's financial statement assertion of
  A. Valuation or allocation.
  B. Rights and obligations.
  C. Existence or occurrence.
  D. Presentation and disclosure.

44. In confirming with an outside agent, such as a financial institution, that the agent is holding investment securities in the client's name, an auditor most likely gathers evidence in support of management's financial statement assertions of existence or occurrence and
  A. Valuation or allocation.
  B. Rights and obligations.
  C. Completeness.
  D. Presentation and disclosure.

45. Which of the following statements is correct concerning the use of negative confirmation requests?
  A. Unreturned negative confirmation requests rarely provide significant explicit evidence.
  B. Negative confirmation requests are effective when detection risk is low.
  C. Unreturned negative confirmation requests indicate that alternative procedures are necessary.
  D. Negative confirmation requests are effective when understatements of account balances are suspected.

46. When an auditor does **not** receive replies to positive requests for year-end accounts receivable confirmations, the auditor most likely would
  A. Inspect the allowance account to verify whether the accounts were subsequently written off.
  B. Increase the assessed level of detection risk for the valuation and completeness assertions.
  C. Ask the client to contact the customers to request that confirmations be returned.
  D. Increase the assessed level of inherent risk for the revenue cycle.

47. Analytical procedures used in the overall review stage of an audit generally include
  A. Gathering evidence concerning account balances that have **not** changed from the prior year.
  B. Retesting controls that appeared to be ineffective during the assessment of control risk.
  C. Considering unusual or unexpected account balances that were **not** previously identified.
  D. Performing tests of transactions to corroborate management's financial statement assertions.

48. Which of the following would **not** be considered an analytical procedure?
  A. Estimating payroll expense by multiplying the number of employees by the average hourly wage rate and the total hours worked.
  B. Projecting an error rate by comparing the results of a statistical sample with the actual population characteristics.
  C. Computing accounts receivable turnover by dividing credit sales by the average net receivables.
  D. Developing the expected current-year sales based on the sales trend of the prior five years.

49. In confirming a client's accounts receivable in prior years, an auditor found that there were many differences between the recorded account balances and the confirmation replies. These differences, which were not misstatements, required substantial time to resolve. In defining the sampling unit for the current year's audit, the auditor most likely would choose
   A. Individual overdue balances.
   B. Individual invoices.
   C. Small account balances.
   D. Large account balances.

50. In statistical sampling methods used in substantive testing, an auditor most likely would stratify a population into meaningful groups if
   A. Probability proportional to size (PPS) sampling is used.
   B. The population has highly variable recorded amounts.
   C. The auditor's estimated tolerable misstatement is extremely small.
   D. The standard deviation of recorded amounts is relatively small.

51. The use of the ratio estimation sampling technique is most effective when
   A. The calculated audit amounts are approximately proportional to the client's book amounts.
   B. A relatively small number of differences exist in the population.
   C. Estimating populations whose records consist of quantities, but **not** book values.
   D. Large overstatement differences and large understatement differences exist in the population.

52. While observing a client's annual physical inventory, an auditor recorded test counts for several items and noticed that certain test counts were higher than the recorded quantities in the client's perpetual records. This situation could be the result of the client's failure to record
   A. Purchase discounts.
   B. Purchase returns.
   C. Sales.
   D. Sales returns.

53. To gain assurance that all inventory items in a client's inventory listing schedule are valid, an auditor most likely would trace

A. Inventory tags noted during the auditor's observation to items listed in the inventory listing schedule.
B. Inventory tags noted during the auditor's observation to items listed in receiving reports and vendors' invoices.
C. Items listed in the inventory listing schedule to inventory tags and the auditor's recorded count sheets.
D. Items listed in receiving reports and vendors' invoices to the inventory listing schedule.

54. When control risk is assessed as low for assertions related to payroll, substantive tests of payroll balances most likely would be limited to applying analytical procedures and
   A. Observing the distribution of paychecks.
   B. Footing and crossfooting the payroll register.
   C. Inspecting payroll tax returns.
   D. Recalculating payroll accruals.

55. In performing a search for unrecorded retirements of fixed assets, an auditor most likely would
   A. Inspect the property ledger and the insurance and tax records, and then tour the client's facilities.
   B. Tour the client's facilities, and then inspect the property ledger and the insurance and tax records.
   C. Analyze the repair and maintenance account, and then tour the client's facilities.
   D. Tour the client's facilities, and then analyze the repair and maintenance account.

56. Which of the following procedures would an auditor most likely perform in auditing the statement of cash flows?
   A. Compare the amounts included in the statement of cash flows to similar amounts in the prior year's statement of cash flows.
   B. Reconcile the cutoff bank statements to verify the accuracy of the year-end bank balances.
   C. Vouch all bank transfers for the last week of the year and first week of the subsequent year.
   D. Reconcile the amounts included in the statement of cash flows to the other financial statements' balances and amounts.

57. In determining whether transactions have been recorded, the direction of the audit testing should be from the
    A. General ledger balances.
    B. Adjusted trial balance.
    C. Original source documents.
    D. General journal entries.

58. When providing limited assurance that the financial statements of a nonpublic entity require **no** material modifications to be in accordance with generally accepted accounting principles, the accountant should
    A. Assess the risk that a material misstatement could occur in a financial statement assertion.
    B. Confirm with the entity's lawyer that material loss contingencies are disclosed.
    C. Understand the accounting principles of the industry in which the entity operates.
    D. Develop audit programs to determine whether the entity's financial statements are fairly presented.

59. An internal auditor's work would most likely affect the nature, timing, and extent of an independent CPA's auditing procedures when the internal auditor's work relates to assertions about the
    A. Existence of contingencies.
    B. Valuation of intangible assets.
    C. Existence of fixed asset additions.
    D. Valuation of related party transactions.

60. During an audit an internal auditor may provide direct assistance to an independent CPA in

	Obtaining an understanding of internal control	Performing tests of controls	Performing substantive tests
A.	No	No	No
B.	Yes	No	No
C.	Yes	Yes	No
D.	Yes	Yes	Yes

61. Which of the following statements is correct concerning an auditor's use of the work of a specialist?

A. The work of a specialist who is related to the client may be acceptable under certain circumstances.
B. If an auditor believes that the determinations made by a specialist are unreasonable, only a qualified opinion may be issued.
C. If there is a material difference between a specialist's findings and the assertions in the financial statements, only an adverse opinion may be issued.
D. An auditor may **not** use a specialist in the determination of physical characteristics relating to inventories.

62. In using the work of a specialist, an auditor may refer to the specialist in the auditor's report if, as a result of the specialist's findings, the auditor
    A. Becomes aware of conditions causing substantial doubt about the entity's ability to continue as a going concern.
    B. Desires to disclose the specialist's findings, which imply that a more thorough audit was performed.
    C. Is able to corroborate another specialist's earlier findings that were consistent with management's representations.
    D. Discovers significant deficiencies in the design of the entity's internal control that management does **not** correct.

63. The refusal of a client's attorney to provide information requested in an inquiry letter generally is considered
    A. Grounds for an adverse opinion.
    B. A limitation on the scope of the audit.
    C. Reason to withdraw from the engagement.
    D. Equivalent to a reportable condition.

64. This question is obsolete.

65. Which of the following procedures would an auditor most likely perform in obtaining evidence about subsequent events?
    A. Determine that changes in employee pay rates after year end were properly authorized.
    B. Recompute depreciation charges for plant assets sold after year end.
    C. Inquire about payroll checks that were recorded before year end but cashed after year end.
    D. Investigate changes in long-term debt occurring after year-end.

66. To which of the following matters would materiality limits **not** apply in obtaining written management representations?
   A. The availability of minutes of stockholders' and directors' meetings.
   B. Losses from purchase commitments at prices in excess of market value.
   C. The disclosure of compensating balance arrangements involving related parties.
   D. Reductions of obsolete inventory to net realizable value.

67. The date of the management representation letter should coincide with the date of the
   A. Balance sheet.
   B. Latest interim financial information.
   C. Auditor's report.
   D. Latest related party transaction.

68. When auditing related party transactions, an auditor places primary emphasis on
   A. Ascertaining the rights and obligations of the related parties.
   B. Confirming the existence of the related parties.
   C. Verifying the valuation of the related party transactions.
   D. Evaluating the disclosure of the related party transactions.

69. Which of the following procedures would an auditor ordinarily perform first in evaluating management's accounting estimates for reasonableness?
   A. Develop independent expectations of management's estimates.
   B. Consider the appropriateness of the key factors or assumptions used in preparing the estimates.
   C. Test the calculations used by management in developing the estimates.
   D. Obtain an understanding of how management developed its estimates.

70. Which of the following pairs of accounts would an auditor most likely analyze on the same working paper?
   A. Notes receivable and interest income.
   B. Accrued interest receivable and accrued interest payable.
   C. Notes payable and notes receivable.
   D. Interest income and interest expense.

71. An auditor's working papers serve mainly to
   A. Provide the principal support for the auditor's report.
   B. Satisfy the auditor's responsibilities concerning the Code of Professional Conduct.
   C. Monitor the effectiveness of the CPA firm's quality control procedures.
   D. Document the level of independence maintained by the auditor.

72. When an auditor tests a computerized accounting system, which of the following is true of the test data approach?
   A. Several transactions of each type must be tested.
   B. Test data are processed by the client's computer programs under the auditor's control.
   C. Test data must consist of all possible valid and invalid conditions.
   D. The program tested is different from the program used throughout the year by the client.

73. Which of the following procedures would an auditor **least** likely perform before the balance sheet date?
   A. Confirmation of accounts payable.
   B. Observation of merchandise inventory.
   C. Assessment of control risk.
   D. Identification of related parties.

74. What type of analytical procedure would an auditor most likely use in developing relationships among balance sheet accounts when reviewing the financial statements of a nonpublic entity?
   A. Trend analysis.
   B. Regression analysis.
   C. Ratio analysis.
   D. Risk analysis.

75. Which of the following procedures is ordinarily performed by an accountant in a compilation engagement of a nonpublic entity?

A. Reading the financial statements to consider whether they are free of obvious mistakes in the application of accounting principles.

B. Obtaining written representations from management indicating that the compiled financial statements will **not** be used to obtain credit.

C. Making inquiries of management concerning actions taken at meetings of the stockholders and the board of directors.

D. Applying analytical procedures designed to corroborate management's assertions that are embodied in the financial statement components.

76. An auditor most likely would be responsible for communicating significant deficiencies in the design of internal control

A. To the Securities and Exchange Commission when the client is a publicly held entity.

B. To specific legislative and regulatory bodies when reporting under "Government Auditing Standards."

C. To a court-appointed creditors' committee when the client is operating under Chapter 11 of the Federal Bankruptcy Code.

D. To shareholders with significant influence (more than 20 percent equity ownership) when the reportable conditions are deemed to be material weaknesses.

77. A principal auditor decides not to refer to the audit of another CPA who audited a subsidiary of the principal auditor's client. After making inquiries about the other CPA's professional reputation and independence, the principal auditor most likely would

A. Add an explanatory paragraph to the auditor's report indicating that the subsidiary's financial statements are **not** material to the consolidated financial statements.

B. Document in the engagement letter that the principal auditor assumes **no** responsibility for the other CPA's work and opinion.

C. Obtain written permission from the other CPA to omit the reference in the principal auditor's report.

D. Contact the other CPA and review the audit programs and working papers pertaining to the subsidiary.

78. Compiled financial statements should be accompanied by an accountant's report stating that

A. A compilation includes assessing the accounting principles used and significant management estimates, as well as evaluating the overall financial statement presentation.

B. The accountant compiled the financial statements in accordance with Statements on Standards for Accounting and Review Services.

C. A compilation is substantially less in scope than an audit in accordance with GAAS, the objective of which is the expression of an opinion.

D. The accountant is **not** aware of any material modifications that should be made to the financial statements to conform with GAAP.

79. Moore, CPA, has been asked to issue a review report on the balance sheet of Dover Co., a nonpublic entity. Moore will not be reporting on Dover's statements of income, retained earnings, and cash flows. Moore may issue the review report provided the

A. Balance sheet is presented in a prescribed form of an industry trade association.

B. Scope of the inquiry and analytical procedures has **not** been restricted.

C. Balance sheet is **not** to be used to obtain credit or distributed to creditors.

D. Specialized accounting principles and practices of Dover's industry are disclosed.

80. Baker, CPA, was engaged to review the financial statements of Hall Co., a nonpublic entity. During the engagement Baker uncovered a complex scheme involving client illegal acts and fraud that materially affect Hall's financial statements. If Baker believes that modification of the standard review report is **not** adequate to indicate the deficiencies in the financial statements, Baker should

A. Disclaim an opinion.

B. Issue an adverse opinion.

C. Withdraw from the engagement.

D. Issue a qualified opinion.

81. Each page of a nonpublic entity's financial statements reviewed by an accountant should include the following reference:

A. See Accompanying Accountant's Footnotes.

B. Reviewed, **No** Material Modifications Required.

C. See Accountant's Review Report.

D. Reviewed, **No** Accountant's Assurance Expressed.

82. An auditor's report on financial statements prepared on the cash receipts and disbursements basis of accounting should include all of the following **except**

A. A reference to the note to the financial statements that describes the cash receipts and disbursements basis of accounting.

B. A statement that the cash receipts and disbursements basis of accounting is **not** a comprehensive basis of accounting.

C. An opinion as to whether the financial statements are presented fairly in conformity with the cash receipts and disbursements basis of accounting.

D. A statement that the audit was conducted in accordance with generally accepted auditing standards.

83. The objective of a review of interim financial information of a public entity is to provide an accountant with a basis for reporting whether

A. Material modifications should be made to conform with generally accepted accounting principles.

B. A reasonable basis exists for expressing an updated opinion regarding the financial statements that were previously audited.

C. Condensed financial statements or pro forma financial information should be included in a registration statement.

D. The financial statements are presented fairly in accordance with generally accepted accounting principles.

84. In reporting on an entity's internal control over financial reporting, a practitioner should include a paragraph that describes the

A. Documentary evidence regarding the control environment factors.

B. Changes in the internal control since the prior report.

C. Potential benefits from the practitioner's suggested improvements.

D. Inherent limitations of internal control.

85. An auditor is considering whether the omission of a substantive procedure considered necessary at the time of an audit may impair the auditor's present ability to support the previously expressed opinion. The auditor need **not** apply the omitted procedure if the

A. Financial statements and auditor's report were **not** distributed beyond management and the board of directors.

B. Auditor's previously expressed opinion was qualified because of a departure from GAAP.

C. Results of other procedures that were applied tend to compensate for the procedure omitted.

D. Omission is due to unreasonable delays by client personnel in providing data on a timely basis.

86. Which of the following statements is correct concerning letters for underwriters, commonly referred to as comfort letters?

A. Letters for underwriters are required by the Securities Act of 1933 for the initial public sale of registered securities.

B. Letters for underwriters typically give negative assurance on unaudited interim financial information.

C. Letters for underwriters usually are included in the registration statement accompanying a prospectus.

D. Letters for underwriters ordinarily update auditors' opinions on the prior year's financial statements.

87. If information accompanying the basic financial statements in an auditor-submitted document has been subjected to auditing procedures, the auditor may include in the auditor's report on the financial statements an opinion that the accompanying information is fairly stated in

A. Accordance with generally accepted auditing standards.

B. Conformity with generally accepted accounting principles.

C. All material respects in relation to the basic financial statements taken as a whole.

D. Accordance with attestation standards expressing a conclusion about management's assertions.

88. Which of the following statements is correct concerning an auditor's required communication with an entity's audit committee?

A. This communication is required to occur before the auditor's report on the financial statements is issued.

B. This communication should include management changes in the application of significant accounting policies.

C. Any significant matter communicated to the audit committee also should be communicated to management.

D. Significant audit adjustments proposed by the auditor and recorded by management need **not** be communicated to the audit committee.

89. In reporting on compliance with laws and regulations during a financial statement audit in accordance with "Government Auditing Standards," an auditor should include in the auditor's report

A. A statement of assurance that all controls over fraud and illegal acts were tested.

B. Material instances of fraud and illegal acts that were discovered.

C. The materiality criteria used by the auditor in considering whether instances of noncompliance were significant.

D. An opinion on whether compliance with laws and regulations affected the entity's goals and objectives.

90. Which of the following statements is a standard applicable to financial statement audits in accordance with "Government Auditing Standards"?

A. An auditor should assess whether the entity has reportable measures of economy and efficiency that are valid and reliable.

B. An auditor should report on the scope of the auditor's testing of internal controls.

C. An auditor should briefly describe in the auditor's report the method of statistical sampling used in performing tests of controls and substantive tests.

D. An auditor should determine the extent to which the entity's programs achieve the desired level of results.

Number 2

Question Number 2 consists of 15 items pertaining to possible deficiencies in an auditor's report.

Select the **best** answer for each item. Use a No. 2 pencil to blacken the appropriate ovals on the Objective Answer Sheet to indicate your answers. **Answer all items.** Your grade will be based on the total number of correct answers.

Perry & Price, CPAs, audited the consolidated financial statements of Bond Company for the year ended December 31, 1993, and expressed an adverse opinion because Bond carried its plant and equipment at appraisal values, and provided for depreciation on the basis of such values.

Perry & Price also audited Bond's financial statements for the year ended December 31, 1994. These consolidated financial statements are being presented on a comparative basis with those of the prior year and an unqualified opinion is being expressed.

Smith, the engagement supervisor, instructed Adler, an assistant on the engagement, to draft the auditor's report on May 3, 1995, the date of completion of the fieldwork. In drafting the report below, Adler considered the following:

• Bond recently changed its method of accounting for plant and equipment and restated its 1993 consolidated financial statements to conform with GAAP. Consequently, the CPA firms's present opinion on those statements is different (unqualified) from the opinion expressed on May 12, 1994.

• Larkin & Lake, CPAs, audited the financial statements of BX, Inc., a consolidated subsidiary of Bond, for the year ended December 31, 1994. The subsidiary's financial statements reflected total assets and revenues of 2 percent and 3 percent, respectively, of the consolidated totals. Larkin & Lake expressed an unqualified opinion and furnished Perry & Price with a copy of the auditor's report. Perry & Price has decided to assume responsibility for the work of Larkin & Lake insofar as it relates to the expression of an opinion on the consolidated financial statements taken as a whole.

• Bond is a defendant in a lawsuit alleging patent infringement. This is adequately disclosed in the notes to Bond's financial statements, but no provision for liability has been recorded because the ultimate outcome of the litigation cannot presently be determined.

Auditor's Report

We have audited the accompanying consolidated balance sheets of Bond Company and subsidiaries as of December 31, 1994 and 1993, and the related consolidated statements of income, retained earnings, and cash flows for the years then ended. These financial statements are the responsibility of the Company's management. Our responsibility is to express an opinion on these financial statements based on our audits.

We conducted our audits in accordance with generally accepted auditing standards. Those standards require that we plan and perform the audit to obtain reasonable assurance about whether the financial statements are free of material misstatement. An audit includes examining, on a test basis, evidence supporting the amounts and disclosures in the financial statements. An audit also includes assessing the accounting principles used, as well as evaluating the overall financial statement presentation. We believe that our audits provide a reasonable basis for our opinion.

In our previous report, we expressed an opinion that the 1993 financial statements did not fairly present financial position, results of operations, and cash flows in conformity with generally accepted accounting principles because the Company carried its plant and equipment at appraisal values and provided for depreciation on the basis of such values. As described in Note 12, the Company has changed its method of accounting for these items and restated its 1993 financial statements to conform with generally accepted accounting principles. Accordingly, our present opinion on the 1993 financial statements, as presented herein, is different from that expressed in our previous report.

In our opinion, the consolidated financial statements referred to above present fairly, in all material respects, the financial position of Bond Company and subsidiaries as of December 31, 1994 and 1993, and the results of its operations and its cash flows for the years then ended in conformity with generally accepted accounting principles except for the change in accounting principles with which we concur and the uncertainty, which is discussed in the following explanatory paragraph.

The Company is a defendant in a lawsuit alleging infringement of certain patent rights. The Company has filed a counteraction, and preliminary hearings and discovery proceedings are in progress. The ultimate outcome of the litigation cannot presently be determined. Accordingly, no provision for any liability that may result upon adjudication has been made in the accompanying financial statements.

Perry & Price, CPAs
May 3, 1995

Required:

Smith reviewed Adler's draft and indicated in the "Supervisor's Review Notes" below that there were deficiencies in Adler's draft. **Items 91 through 105** represent the deficiencies noted by Smith. For each deficiency, indicate whether Smith is correct (C) or incorrect (I) in the criticism of Adler's draft and blacken the corresponding oval on the Objective Answer Sheet.

<u>Supervisor's Review Notes</u>

91. The report is improperly titled
92. All the basic financial statements are **not** properly identified in the introductory paragraph.
93. There is **no** reference to the American Institute of Certified Public Accountants in the introductory paragraph.
94. Larkin & Lake are **not** identified in the introductory and opinion paragraphs.
95. The subsidiary, BX Inc., is **not** identified and the magnitude of BX's financial statements is **not** disclosed in the introductory paragraph.
96. The report does **not** state in the scope paragraph that generally accepted auditing standards require analytical procedures to be performed in planning an audit.
97. The report does **not** state in the scope paragraph that an audit includes assessing internal control.
98. The report does **not** state in the scope paragraph that an audit includes assessing significant estimates made by management.
99. The date of the previous report (May 12, 1994) is **not** disclosed in the first explanatory paragraph.
100. It is inappropriate to disclose in the first explanatory paragraph the circumstances that caused Perry & Price to express a different opinion on the 1993 financial statements.
101. The concurrence with the accounting change is inappropriate in the opinion paragraph.

102. Reference to the (litigation) uncertainty should **not** be made in the opinion paragraph.
103. Bond's disclosure of the (litigation) uncertainty in the notes to the financial statements is **not** referred to in the second explanatory paragraph.
104. The letter of inquiry to Bond's lawyer concerning litigation, claims, and assessments is **not** referred to in the second explanatory paragraph.
105. The report is **not** dual dated, but it should be because of the change of opinion on the 1993 financial statements.

Number 3

Question Number 3 consists of 15 items. Select the **best** answer for each item. Use a No. 2 pencil to blacken the appropriate ovals on the Objective Answer Sheet to indicate your answers. **Answer all items.** Your grade will be based on the total number of correct answers.

Field, CPA, is auditing the financial statements of Miller Mailorder, Inc. (MMI) for the year ended January 31, 1995. Field has compiled a list of possible errors and fraud that may result in the misstatement of MMI's financial statements, and a corresponding list of internal controls that, if properly designed and implemented, could assist MMI in preventing or detecting the errors and fraud.

Required:

For each possible error and fraud numbered **106 through 120,** select one internal control from the answer list on page 150 that, if properly designed and implemented, most likely could assist MMI in preventing or detecting the errors and fraud. Blacken the corresponding oval on the Objective Answer Sheet. Each response in the list of internal controls may be selected once, more than once, or not at all.

Possible Errors and Fraud	Internal Controls

Possible Errors and Fraud

106. Invoices for goods sold are posted to incorrect customer accounts.
107. Goods ordered by customers are shipped, but are **not** billed to anyone.
108. Invoices are sent for shipped goods, but are **not** recorded in the sales journal.
109. Invoices are sent for shipped goods and are recorded in the sales journal, but are **not** posted to any customer account.
110. Credit sales are made to individuals with unsatisfactory credit ratings.
111. Goods are removed from inventory for unauthorized orders.
112. Goods shipped to customers do **not** agree with goods ordered by customers.
113. Invoices are sent to allies in a fraudulent scheme and sales are recorded for fictitious transactions.
114. Customers' checks are received for less than the customers' full account balances, but the customers' full account balances are credited.
115. Customers' checks are misappropriated before being forwarded to the cashier for deposit.
116. Customers' checks are credited to incorrect customer accounts.
117. Different customer accounts are each credited for the same cash receipt.
118. Customers' checks are properly credited to customer accounts and are properly deposited, but errors are made in recording receipts in the cash receipts journal.
119. Customers' checks are misappropriated after being forwarded to the cashier for deposit.
120. Invalid transactions granting credit for sales returns are recorded.

Internal Controls

A. Shipping clerks compare goods received from the warehouse with the details on the shipping documents.
B. Approved sales orders are required for goods to be released from the warehouse.
C. Monthly statements are mailed to all customers with outstanding balances.
D. Shipping clerks compare goods received from the warehouse with approved sales orders.
E. Customer orders are compared with the inventory master file to determine whether items ordered are in stock.
F. Daily sales summaries are compared with control totals of invoices.
G. Shipping documents are compared with sales invoices when goods are shipped.
H. Sales invoices are compared with the master price file.
I. Customer orders are compared with an approved customer list.
J. Sales orders are prepared for each customer order.
K. Control amounts posted to the accounts receivable ledger are compared with control totals of invoices.
L. Sales invoices are compared with shipping documents and approved customer orders before invoices are mailed.
M. Prenumbered credit memos are used for granting credit for goods returned.
N. Goods returned for credit are approved by the supervisor of the sales department.
O. Remittance advices are separated from the checks in the mailroom and forwarded to the accounting department.
P. Total amounts posted to the accounts receivable ledger from remittance advices are compared with the validated bank deposit slip.
Q. The cashier examines each check for proper endorsement.
R. Validated deposit slips are compared with the cashier's daily cash summaries.
S. An employee, other than the bookkeeper, periodically prepares a bank reconciliation.
T. Sales returns are approved by the same employee who issues receiving reports evidencing actual return of goods.

Number 4

Hart, CPA, has been approached by Unidyne Co. to accept an attest engagement to examine and report on management's written assertion about the effectiveness of Unidyne's internal control over financial reporting as of June 30, 1995, the end of its fiscal year.

Required:

a. Describe the required conditions that must be met for Hart to accept an attest engagement to examine and report on management's assertion about the effectiveness of Unidyne's internal control.

b. Describe the broad engagement activities that would be involved in Hart's performing an examination of management's assertion about the effectiveness of Unidyne's internal control.

c. Describe the other types of attest services that Hart may provide and those specifically **not** permitted in connection with Unidyne's internal control.

Number 5

On November 19, 1994, Wall, CPA, was engaged to audit the financial statements of Trendy Auto Imports, Inc. for the year ended December 31, 1994. Wall is considering Trendy's ability to continue as a going concern.

Required:

a. Describe Wall's basic responsibility in considering Trendy's ability to continue as a going concern.

b. Describe the audit procedures Wall most likely would perform to identify conditions and events that may indicate that Trendy has a going concern problem.

c. Describe the management plans that Wall should consider that could mitigate the adverse effects of Trendy's financial difficulties if Wall identified conditions and events that indicated a potential going concern problem.

XAMINATION QUESTIONS

CANDIDATE NUMBER

Record your 7-digit candidate
number in the boxes.

The point values for each question, and estimated time allotments based primarily on point value, are as follows:

	Point Value	Estimated Minutes Minimum	Estimated Minutes Maximum
No. 1	60	120	130
No. 2	20	25	40
No. 3	20	25	40
Totals	100	170	210

Q-ARE

May 4, 1995; 8:30 A.M. to 12:00 NOON

INSTRUCTIONS TO CANDIDATES *Failure to follow these instructions may have an adverse effect on your Examination grade.*

Do not break the seal around the *Examination Questions* (pages 3 through 22) until you are told to do so.

All questions should be answered on the *Objective Answer Sheet*, which is pages 23 and 24. You should attempt to answer all objective items. There is no penalty for incorrect responses. Work space to solve the objective questions is provided in the *Examination Questions* on pages 5 through 15 and pages 20 and 21. Since the objective items are computer-graded, your comments and calculations associated with them are not considered. Be certain that you have entered your answers on the *Objective Answer Sheet* before the examination time is up. Your examination will not be graded if you fail to record your answers on the *Objective Answer Sheet*. You will not be given additional time to record your answers.

3. You are required to turn in by the end of each session:

   a. Attendance Record and Calculator Sign-off Record Form, page 1;
   b. *Examination Questions*, pages 3 through 22;
   c. *Objective Answer Sheet,* pages 23 and 24;
   d. Calculator; and
   e. All unused examination materials.

   Your examination will not be graded unless the above listed items are handed in before leaving the examination room.

4. Unless otherwise instructed, if you want your *Examination Questions* mailed to you, write your name and address in both places indicated on page 22 and place 55 cents postage in the space provided. *Examination Questions* will be distributed no sooner than the day following the administration of this examination.

epared by the Board of Examiners of the American stitute of Certified Public Accountants and adopted by the amining boards of all states, the District of Columbia, am, Puerto Rico, and the Virgin Islands of the United ates.

56068

BOOKLET NO.

Accounting and Reporting (ARE)

Number 1

Instructions

Select the **best** answer for each of the following items. Use a No. 2 pencil to blacken the appropriate ovals on the Objective Answer Sheet to indicate your answers. **Mark only one answer for each item. Answer all items.** Your grade will be based on the total number of correct answers.

Items 1 through 35 are in the areas of federal taxation. The answers should be based on the Internal Revenue Code and Tax Regulations in effect for the tax period specified in the item. If <u>no</u> tax period is specified, use the <u>current</u> Internal Revenue Code and Tax Regulations.

1. Which payment(s) is(are) included in a recipient's gross income?

   I. Payment to a graduate assistant for a part-time teaching assignment at a university. Teaching is not a requirement toward obtaining the degree.
   II. A grant to a Ph.D. candidate for his participation in a university-sponsored research project for the benefit of the university.

   A. I only.
   B. II only.
   C. Both I and II.
   D. Neither I nor II.

2. Browne, a self-employed taxpayer, had 1997 business net income of $100,000 prior to any expense deduction for equipment purchases. In 1997, Browne purchased and placed into service, for business use, office machinery costing $20,000. This was Browne's only 1997 capital expenditure. Browne's business establishment was not in an economically distressed area. Browne made a proper and timely expense election to deduct the maximum amount. Browne was not a member of any pass through entity. What is Browne's deduction under the election?
   A. $ 4,000
   B. $10,000
   C. $18,000
   D. $20,000

Items 3 and 4 are based on the following:

Conner purchased 300 shares of Zinco stock for $30,000 in 1980. On May 23, 1994, Conner sold all the stock to his daughter Alice for $20,000, its then fair market value. Conner realized no other gain or loss during 1994. On July 26, 1994, Alice sold the 300 shares of Zinco for $25,000.

3. What amount of the loss from the sale of Zinco stock can Conner deduct in 1994?
   A. $0
   B. $ 3,000
   C. $ 5,000
   D. $10,000

4. What was Alice's recognized gain or loss on her sale?
   A. $0
   B. $5,000 long-term gain.
   C. $5,000 short-term loss.
   D. $5,000 long-term loss.

<u>SOURCE: LPR, MAY 1995, #4</u>

4. Kopel was engaged to prepare Raff's 1994 federal income tax return. During the tax preparation interview, Raff told Kopel that he paid $3,000 in property taxes in 1994. Actually, Raff's property taxes amounted to only $600. Based on Raff's word, Kopel deducted the $3,000 on Raff's return, resulting in an understatement of Raff's tax liability. Kopel had no reason to believe that the information was incorrect. Kopel did not request underlying documentation and was reasonably satisfied by Raff's representation that Raff had adequate records to support the deduction. Which of the following statements is correct?
   A. To avoid the preparer penalty for willful understatement of tax liability, Kopel was obligated to examine the underlying documentation for the deduction.
   B. To avoid the preparer penalty for willful understatement of tax liability, Kopel would be required to obtain Raff's representation in writing.
   C. Kopel is **not** subject to the preparer penalty for willful understatement of tax liability because the deduction that was claimed was more than 25% of the actual amount that should have been deducted.
   D. Kopel is **not** subject to the preparer penalty for willful understatement of tax liability because Kopel was justified in relying on Raff's representation.

5. On August 1, 1994, Graham purchased and placed into service an office building costing $264,000 including $30,000 for the land. What was Graham's MACRS deduction for the office building in 1994?

A. $9,600
B. $6,000
C. $3,600
D. $2,250

6. Grey, a calendar year taxpayer, was employed and resided in New York. On February 2, 1994, Grey was permanently transferred to Florida by his employer. Grey worked full-time for the entire year. In 1994, Grey incurred and paid the following unreimbursed expenses in relocating.

Lodging and travel expenses while moving	$1,000
Pre-move househunting costs	1,200
Costs of moving household furnishings and personal effects	1,800

What amount was deductible as moving expense on Grey's 1994 tax return?
A. $4,000
B. $2,800
C. $1,800
D. $1,000

7. Moore, a single taxpayer, had $50,000 in adjusted gross income for 1994. During 1994 she contributed $18,000 to her church. She had a $10,000 charitable contribution carryover from her 1993 church contribution. What was the maximum amount of properly substantiated charitable contributions that Moore could claim as an itemized deduction for 1994?
A. $10,000
B. $18,000
C. $25,000
D. $28,000

8. Matthews was a cash basis taxpayer whose records showed the following:

1994 state and local income taxes withheld	$1,500
1994 state estimated income taxes paid December 30, 1994	400
1994 federal income taxes withheld	2,500
1994 state and local income taxes paid April 17, 1995	300

What total amount was Matthews entitled to claim for taxes on her 1994 Schedule A of Form 1040?
A. $4,700
B. $2,200
C. $1,900
D. $1,500

9. Which expense, both incurred and paid in 1994, can be claimed as an itemized deduction subject to the two-percent-of-adjusted-gross-income floor?
A. Employee's unreimbursed business car expense.
B. One-half of the self-employment tax.
C. Employee's unreimbursed moving expense.
D. Self-employed health insurance.

10. In 1994, Joan Frazer's residence was totally destroyed by fire. The property had an adjusted basis and a fair market value of $130,000 before the fire. During 1994, Frazer received insurance reimbursement of $120,000 for the destruction of her home. Frazer's 1994 adjusted gross income was $70,000. Frazer had no casualty gains during the year. What amount of the fire loss was Frazer entitled to claim as an itemized deduction on her 1994 tax return?
A. $ 2,900
B. $ 8,500
C. $ 8,600
D. $10,000

11. Which items are subject to the phase out of the amount of certain itemized deductions that may be claimed by high-income individuals?
A. Charitable contributions.
B. Medical costs.
C. Nonbusiness casualty losses.
D. Investment interest deductions.

12. Tom and Sally White, married and filing joint income tax returns, derive their entire income from the operation of their retail stationery shop. Their 1994 adjusted gross income was $100,000. The Whites itemized their deductions on Schedule A for 1994. The following unreimbursed cash expenditures were among those made by the Whites during 1994:

Repair and maintenance of motorized wheelchair for physically handicapped dependent child	$ 600
Tuition, meals, and lodging at special school for physically handicapped dependent child in an institution primarily for the availability of medical care, with meals and lodging furnished as necessary incidents to that care	8,000

Without regard to the adjusted gross income percentage threshold, what amount may the Whites claim in their 1994 return as qualifying medical expenses?

A. $8,600
B. $8,000
C. $ 600
D. $0

13. Which of the following is(are) among the requirements to enable a taxpayer to be classified as a "qualifying widow(er)"?

I. A dependent has lived with the taxpayer for six months.
II. The taxpayer has maintained the cost of the principal residence for six months.

A. I only.
B. II only.
C. Both I and II.
D. Neither I nor II.

14. In 1994, Smith, a divorced person, provided over one half the support for his widowed mother, Ruth, and his son, Clay, both of whom are U.S. citizens. During 1994, Ruth did not live with Smith. She received $9,000 in social security benefits. Clay, a full-time graduate student, and his wife lived with Smith. Clay had no income but filed a joint return for 1994, owing an additional $500 in taxes on his wife's income. How many exemptions was Smith entitled to claim on his 1994 tax return?

A. 4
B. 3
C. 2
D. 1

15. A cash basis taxpayer should report gross income

A. Only for the year in which income is actually received in cash.
B. Only for the year in which income is actually received whether in cash or in property.
C. For the year in which income is either actually or constructively received in cash only.
D. For the year in which income is either actually or constructively received, whether in cash or in property.

16. An accuracy-related penalty applies to the portion of tax underpayment attributable to

I. Negligence or a disregard of the tax rules or regulations.
II. Any substantial understatement of income tax.

A. I only.
B. II only.
C. Both I and II.
D. Neither I nor II.

17. In 1996, Don Mills, a single taxpayer, had $70,000 in taxable income before personal exemptions. Mills had no tax preferences. His itemized deductions were as follows:

State and local income taxes	$5,000
Home mortgage interest on loan to acquire residence	6,000
Miscellaneous deductions that exceed 2% of adjusted gross income	2,000

What amount did Mills report as alternative minimum taxable income before the AMT exemption?

A. $72,000
B. $75,000
C. $77,000
D. $83,000

18. Alternative minimum tax preferences include

	Tax exempt interest from private activity bonds issued during 1994	Charitable contributions of appreciated capital gain property?
A.	Yes	Yes
B.	Yes	No
C.	No	Yes
D.	No	No

19. Chris Baker's adjusted gross income on her 1994 tax return was $160,000. The amount covered a 12-month period. For the 1995 tax year, Baker may avoid the penalty for the underpayment of estimated tax if the timely estimated tax payments equal the required annual amount of

I. 90% of the tax on the return for the current year, paid in four equal installments.
II. 100% of prior year's tax liability, paid in four equal installments.

A. I only.
B. II only.
C. Both I and II.
D. Neither I nor II.

20. A claim for refund of erroneously paid income taxes, filed by an individual before the statute of limitations expires, must be submitted on Form

A. 1139
B. 1045
C. 1040X
D. 843

21. Village Corp., a calendar year corporation, began business in 1990. Village made a valid S Corporation election on December 5, 1993, with the unanimous consent of its shareholders. The eligibility requirements for S status continued to be met throughout 1994. On what date did Village's S status become effective?

A. January 1, 1993.
B. January 1, 1994.
C. December 5, 1993.
D. December 5, 1994.

22. A shareholder's basis in the stock of an S corporation is increased by the shareholder's pro rata share of income from

	Tax-exempt interest	Taxable interest
A.	No	No
B.	No	Yes
C.	Yes	No
D.	Yes	Yes

23. Edge Corp. met the stock ownership requirements of a personal holding company. What sources of income must Edge consider to determine if the income requirements for a personal holding company have been met?

I. Interest earned on tax-exempt obligations.
II. Dividends received from an unrelated domestic corporation.

A. I only.
B. II only.
C. Both I and II.
D. Neither I nor II.

24. Kent Corp. is a calendar year, accrual basis C corporation. In 1994, Kent made a nonliquidating distribution of property with an adjusted basis of $150,000 and a fair market value of $200,000 to Reed, its sole shareholder. The following information pertains to Kent:

Reed's basis in Kent stock at
January 1, 1994 $500,000
Accumulated earnings and
profits at January 1, 1994   125,000
Current earnings and profits
for 1994   60,000

What was taxable as dividend income to Reed for 1994?

A. $ 60,000
B. $150,000
C. $185,000
D. $200,000

25. Jaxson Corp. has 200,000 shares of voting common stock issued and outstanding. King Corp. has decided to acquire 90% of Jaxson's voting common stock solely in exchange for 50% of its voting common stock and retain Jaxson as a subsidiary after the transaction. Which of the following statements is true?

A. King must acquire 100% of Jaxson stock for the transaction to be a tax-free reorganization.
B. The transaction will qualify as a tax-free reorganization.
C. King must issue at least 60% of its voting common stock for the transaction to qualify as a tax-free reorganization.
D. Jaxson must surrender assets for the transaction to qualify as a tax-free reorganization.

26. Dean is a 25% partner in Target Partnership. Dean's tax basis in Target on January 1, 1994, was $20,000. At the end of 1994, Dean received a nonliquidating cash distribution of $8,000 from Target. Target's 1994 accounts recorded the following items:

Municipal bond interest income $12,000
Ordinary income   40,000

What was Dean's tax basis in Target on December 31, 1994?

A. $15,000
B. $23,000
C. $25,000
D. $30,000

27. Strom acquired a 25% interest in Ace Partnership by contributing land having an adjusted basis of $16,000 and a fair market value of $50,000. The land was subject to a $24,000 mortgage, which was assumed by Ace. No other liabilities existed at the time of the contribution. What was Strom's basis in Ace?

A. $0
B. $16,000
C. $26,000
D. $32,000

28. Alt Partnership, a cash basis calendar year entity, began business on October 1, 1994. Alt incurred and paid the following in 1994:

Legal fees to prepare the partnership agreement	$12,000
Accounting fees to prepare the representations in offering materials	15,000

Alt elected to amortize costs. What was the maximum amount that Alt could deduct on the 1994 partnership return?

    A. $0
    B. $ 600
    C. $3,000
    D. $6,750

29. A guaranteed payment by a partnership to a partner for services rendered, may include an agreement to pay

    I. A salary of $5,000 monthly without regard to partnership income.
    II. A 25% interest in partnership profits.

    A. I only.
    B. II only.
    C. Both I and II.
    D. Neither I nor II.

30. Curry's adjusted basis in Vantage Partnership was $5,000 at the time he received a nonliquidating distribution of land. The land had an adjusted basis of $6,000 and a fair market value of $9,000 to Vantage. What was the amount of Curry's basis in the land?

    A. $9,000
    B. $6,000
    C. $5,000
    D. $1,000

Items 31 and 32 are based on the following:

Lyon, a cash basis taxpayer, died on January 15, 1994. In 1994, the estate executor made the required periodic distribution of $9,000 from estate income to Lyon's sole heir. The following pertains to the estate's income and disbursements in 1994:

1994 Estate Income

$20,000	Taxable interest
10,000	Net long-term capital gains allocable to corpus

1994 Estate Disbursements

$5,000	Administrative expenses attributable to taxable income

31. For the 1994 calendar year, what was the estate's distributable net income (DNI)?

    A. $15,000
    B. $20,000
    C. $25,000
    D. $30,000

32. Lyon's executor does not intend to file an extension request for the estate fiduciary income tax return. By what date must the executor file the Form 1041, U.S. Fiduciary Income Tax Return, for the estate's 1994 calendar year?

    A. Wednesday, March 15, 1995.
    B. Monday, April 17, 1995.
    C. Thursday, June 15, 1995.
    D. Friday, September 15, 1995.

33. A distribution from estate income, which was <u>currently</u> required, was made to the estate's sole beneficiary during its calendar year. The maximum amount of the distribution to be included in the beneficiary's gross income is limited to the estate's

    A. Capital gain income.
    B. Ordinary gross income.
    C. Distributable net income.
    D. Net investment income.

34. The private foundation status of an exempt organization will terminate if it

    A. Becomes a public charity.
    B. Is a foreign corporation.
    C. Does **not** distribute all of its net assets to one or more public charities.
    D. Is governed by a charter that limits the organization's exempt purposes.

35. Which of the following exempt organizations must file annual information returns?

    A. Churches.
    B. Internally supported auxiliaries of churches.
    C. Private foundations.
    D. Those with gross receipts of less than $5,000 in each taxable year.

Items 36 through 50 are in the area of managerial accounting.

36. Day Mail Order Co. applied the high-low method of cost estimation to customer order data for the first 4 months of 1995. What is the estimated variable order filling cost component per order?

Month	Orders	Cost
January	1,200	$ 3,120
February	1,300	3,185
March	1,800	4,320
April	1,700	3,895
	6,000	$14,520

A. $2.00
B. $2.42
C. $2.48
D. $2.50

37. A 1995 cash budget is being prepared for the purchase of Toyi, a merchandise item. Budgeted data are:

Cost of goods sold for 1995	$300,000
Accounts payable 1/1/95	20,000
Inventory—1/1/95	30,000
12/31/95	42,000

Purchases will be made in 12 equal monthly amounts and paid for in the following month. What is the 1995 budgeted cash payment for purchases of Toyi?
A. $295,000
B. $300,000
C. $306,000
D. $312,000

38. Pole Co. is investing in a machine with a 3-year life. The machine is expected to reduce annual cash operating costs by $30,000 in each of the first 2 years and by $20,000 in year 3. Present values of an annuity of $1 at 14% are:

Period 1	0.88
2	1.65
3	2.32

Using a 14% cost of capital, what is the present value of these future savings?
A. $59,600
B. $60,800
C. $62,900
D. $69,500

39. Del Co. has fixed costs of $100,000 and breakeven sales of $800,000. What is its projected profit at $1,200,000 sales?
A. $ 50,000
B. $150,000
C. $200,000
D. $400,000

40. Using the variable costing method, which of the following costs are assigned to inventory?

	Variable selling and administrative costs	Variable factory overhead costs
A.	Yes	Yes
B.	Yes	No
C.	No	No
D.	No	Yes

41. In its April 1995 production, Hern Corp., which does not use a standard cost system, incurred total production costs of $900,000, of which Hern attributed $60,000 to normal spoilage and $30,000 to abnormal spoilage. Hern should account for this spoilage as
A. Period cost of $90,000.
B. Inventoriable cost of $90,000.
C. Period cost of $60,000 and inventoriable cost of $30,000.
D. Inventoriable cost of $60,000 and period cost of $30,000.

42. Companies in what type of industry may use a standard cost system for cost control?

	Mass production industry	Service industry
A.	Yes	Yes
B.	Yes	No
C.	No	No
D.	No	Yes

43. Kode Co. manufactures a major product that gives rise to a by-product called May. May's only separable cost is a $1 selling cost when a unit is sold for $4. Kode accounts for May's sales by deducting the $3 net amount from the cost of goods sold of the major product. There are no inventories. If Kode were to change its method of accounting for May from a by-product to a joint product, what would be the effect on Kode's overall gross margin?
A. No effect.
B. Gross margin increases by $1 for each unit of May sold.
C. Gross margin increases by $3 for each unit of May sold.
D. Gross margin increases by $4 for each unit of May sold.

44. In an activity-based costing system, what should be used to assign a department's manufacturing overhead costs to products produced in varying lot sizes?
A. A single cause and effect relationship.
B. Multiple cause and effect relationships.
C. Relative net sales values of the products.
D. A product's ability to bear cost allocations.

45. Select Co. had the following 1994 financial statement relationships:

Asset turnover   5
Profit margin on sales   0.02

What was Select's 1994 percentage return on assets?
- A. 0.1%
- B. 0.4%
- C. 2.5%
- D. 10.0%

46. Which measures would be useful in evaluating the performance of a manufacturing system?

I. Throughput time.
II. Total setup time for machines/Total production time.
III. Number of rework units/Total number of units completed.

- A. I and II only.
- B. II and III only.
- C. I and III only.
- D. I, II, and III.

47. Which changes in costs are most conducive to switching from a traditional inventory ordering system to a just-in-time ordering system?

	Cost per purchase order	Inventory unit carrying costs
A.	Increasing	Increasing
B.	Decreasing	Increasing
C.	Decreasing	Decreasing
D.	Increasing	Decreasing

48. Dough Distributors has decided to increase its daily muffin purchases by 100 boxes. A box of muffins costs $2 and sells for $3 through regular stores. Any boxes not sold through regular stores are sold through Dough's thrift store for $1. Dough assigns the following probabilities to selling additional boxes:

Additional sales	Probability
60	.6
100	.4

What is the expected value of Dough's decision to buy 100 additional boxes of muffins?
- A. $28
- B. $40
- C. $52
- D. $68

49. Jago Co. has 2 products that use the same manufacturing facilities and cannot be subcontracted. Each product has sufficient orders to utilize the entire manufacturing capacity. For short-run profit maximization, Jago should manufacture the product with the
- A. Lower total manufacturing costs for the manufacturing capacity.
- B. Lower total variable manufacturing costs for the manufacturing capacity.
- C. Greater gross profit per hour of manufacturing capacity.
- D. Greater contribution margin per hour of manufacturing capacity.

50. Cuff Caterers quotes a price of $60 per person for a dinner party. This price includes the 6% sales tax and the 15% service charge. Sales tax is computed on the food plus the service charge. The service charge is computed on the food only. At what amount does Cuff price the food?
- A. $56.40
- B. $51.00
- C. $49.22
- D. $47.40

Items 51 through 60 are in the area of accounting for governmental and not-for-profit organizations.

51. For governmental fund types, which item is considered the primary measurement focus?
- A. Income determination.
- B. Flows and balances of financial resources.
- C. Capital maintenance.
- D. Cash flows and balances.

52. Governmental financial reporting should provide information to assist users in which situation(s)?

I. Making social and political decisions.
II. Assessing whether current-year citizens received services but shifted part of the payment burden to future-year citizens.

- A. I only.
- B. II only.
- C. Both I and II.
- D. Neither I nor II.

53. In preparing combined financial statements for a governmental entity, interfund receivables and payables should be

A. Reported as reservations of fund balance.
B. Reported as additions to or reductions from the unrestricted fund balance.
C. Reported as amounts due to and due from other funds.
D. Eliminated.

54. The expenditure element "salaries and wages" is an example of which type of classification?
    A. Object.
    B. Program.
    C. Function.
    D. Activity.

55. Cy City's Municipal Solid Waste Landfill Enterprise Fund was established when a new landfill was opened January 3, 1994. The landfill is expected to close December 31, 2015. Cy's 1994 expenses would include a portion of which of the year 2016 expected disbursements?

I. Cost of a final cover to be applied to the landfill.
II. Cost of equipment to be installed to monitor methane gas buildup.

    A. I only.
    B. II only.
    C. Both I and II.
    D. Neither I nor II.

56. Which of the following funds of a governmental unit uses the same basis of accounting as the special revenue fund?
    A. Enterprise funds.
    B. Internal service funds.
    C. Nonexpendable trust funds.
    D. Expendable trust funds.

57. On December 30, 1994, Leigh Museum, a not-for-profit organization, received a $7,000,000 donation of Day Co. shares with donor stipulated requirements as follows:

• Shares valued at $5,000,000 are to be sold with the proceeds used to erect a public viewing building.
• Shares valued at $2,000,000 are to be retained with the dividends used to support current operations.

Leigh elected early adoption of FASB Statement No. 117, "Financial Statements of Not-for-Profit Organizations." As a consequence of the receipt of the Day shares, how much should Leigh report as temporarily restricted net assets on its 1994 statement of financial position?

    A. $0
    B. $2,000,000
    C. $5,000,000
    D. $7,000,000

58. The Jones family lost its home in a fire. On December 25, 1994, a philanthropist sent money to the Amer Benevolent Society to purchase furniture for the Jones family. During January 1995, Amer purchased this furniture for the Jones family. Amer, a not-for-profit organization, elected early adoption of FASB Statement No. 116, "Accounting for Contributions Received and Contributions Made." How should Amer report the receipt of the money in its 1994 financial statements?
    A. As an unrestricted contribution.
    B. As a temporarily restricted contribution.
    C. As a permanently restricted contribution.
    D. As a liability.

59. The Pel Museum, a not-for-profit organization, elected early adoption of FASB Statement No. 116, "Accounting for Contributions Received and Contributions Made." If Pel received a contribution of historical artifacts, it need **not** recognize the contribution if the artifacts are to be sold and the proceeds used to
    A. Support general museum activities.
    B. Acquire other items for collections.
    C. Repair existing collections.
    D. Purchase buildings to house collections.

60. In April 1995, Delta Hospital purchased medicines from Field Pharmaceutical Co. at a cost of $5,000. However, Field notified Delta that the invoice was being canceled and that the medicines were being donated to Delta. Delta should record this donation of medicines as
    A. A memorandum entry only.
    B. A $5,000 credit to nonoperating expenses.
    C. A $5,000 credit to operating expenses.
    D. Other operating revenue of $5,000.

Number 2

Question Number 2 consists of 24 items. Select the **best** answer for each item. Use a No. 2 pencil to blacken the appropriate ovals on the Objective Answer Sheet to indicate your answers. **Answer all items.** Your grade will be based on the total number of correct answers.

The following information relates to Bel City, whose first fiscal year ended December 31, 1994. Assume Bel has only the long-term debt specified in the information and only the funds necessitated by the information.

1. General fund:

- The following selected information is taken from Bel's 1994 general fund financial records:

	Budget	Actual
Property taxes	$5,000,000	$4,700,000
Other revenues	1,000,000	1,050,000
Total revenues	$6,000,000	$5,750,000
Total expenditures	$5,600,000	$5,700,000

Property taxes receivable— delinquent	$420,000
Less: Allowance for estimated uncollectible taxes—delinquent	50,000
	$370,000

- There were no amendments to the budget as originally adopted.
- No property taxes receivable have been written off, and the allowance for uncollectibles balance is unchanged from the initial entry at the time of the original tax levy.
- There were no encumbrances outstanding at December 31, 1994.

2. Capital project fund:

- Finances for Bel's new civic center were provided by a combination of general fund transfers, a state grant, and an issue of general obligation bonds. Any bond premium on issuance is to be used for the repayment of the bonds at their $1,200,000 par value. At December 31, 1994, the capital project fund for the civic center had the following closing entries:

Revenues	$ 800,000	
Other financing sources —bond proceeds	1,230,000	
Other financing sources —operating transfers in	500,000	
Expenditures		$1,080,000
Other financing uses —operating transfers out		30,000
Unreserved fund balance		1,420,000

- Also, at December 31, 1994, capital project fund entries reflected Bel's intention to honor the $1,300,000 purchase orders and commitments outstanding for the center.

- During 1994, total capital project fund encumbrances exceeded the corresponding expenditures by $42,000. All expenditures were previously encumbered.
- During 1995, the capital project fund received no revenues and no other financing sources. The civic center building was completed in early 1995 and the capital project fund was closed by a transfer of $27,000 to the general fund.

3. Water utility enterprise fund:

- Bel issued $4,000,000 revenue bonds at par. These bonds, together with a $700,000 transfer from the general fund, were used to acquire a water utility. Water utility revenues are to be the sole source of funds to retire these bonds beginning in year 1999.

Required:

For **Items 61 through 76,** indicate if the answer to each item is Yes (Y) or No (N) and blacken the corresponding oval on the Objective Answer Sheet.

Items 61 through 68 relate to Bel's general fund.

61. Did recording budgetary accounts at the beginning of 1994 increase the fund balance by $50,000?
62. Should the budgetary accounts for 1994 include an entry for the expected transfer of funds from the general fund to the capital projects fund?
63. Should the $700,000 payment from the general fund, which was used to help to establish the water utility fund, be reported as an "other financing use—operating transfers out"?
64. Did the general fund receive the $30,000 bond premium from the capital projects fund?
65. Should a payment from the general fund for water received for normal civic center operations be reported as an "other financing use—operating transfers out"?
66. Does the net property taxes receivable of $370,000 include amounts expected to be collected after March 15, 1995?
67. Would closing budgetary accounts cause the fund balance to increase by $400,000?
68. Would the interaction between budgetary and actual amounts cause the fund balance to decrease by $350,000?

Items 69 through 76 relate to Bel's account groups and funds other than the general fund.

69. In the general fixed assets account group, should a credit amount be recorded for 1994 in "Investment in general fixed assets—capital projects fund"?
70. In the general fixed assets account group, could Bel elect to record depreciation in 1995 on the civic center?
71. In the general fixed assets account group, could Bel elect to record depreciation on water utility equipment?
72. Should the capital project fund be included in Bel's combined statement of revenues, expenditures, and changes in fund balances?
73. Should the water utility enterprise fund be included in Bel's combined balance sheet? In which fund should Bel report capital and related financing activities in its 1994 statement of cash flows?
74. Debt service fund.
75. Capital project fund.
76. Water utility enterprise fund.

For **Items 77 through 84,** determine the amount. To record your answer, blacken the ovals on the Objective Answer Sheet. If zeros precede your numerical answer, blacken the zeros in the ovals preceding your answer. **You cannot receive credit for your answers if you fail to blacken an oval in each column.** You may write the numbers in the boxes provided to facilitate blackening the ovals; however, the numbers written in the boxes will **not** be graded.

Items 77 and 78 relate to Bel's general fund.

77. What was the amount recorded in the opening entry for appropriations?
78. What was the total amount debited to property taxes receivable?

Items 79 through 84 relate to Bel's account groups and funds other than the general fund.

79. In the general long-term debt account group, what amount should be reported for bonds payable at December 31, 1994?
80. In the general fixed assets account group, what amount should be recorded for "Investment in general fixed assets—capital project fund" at December 31, 1994?
81. What was the completed cost of the civic center?

82. How much was the state capital grant for the civic center?
83. In the capital project fund, what was the amount of the total encumbrances recorded during 1994?
84. In the capital project fund, what was the unreserved fund balance reported at December 31, 1994?

Number 3

Question Number 3 consists of 28 items. Select the **best** answer for each item. Use a No. 2 pencil to blacken the appropriate ovals on the Objective Answer Sheet to indicate your answers. **Answer all items.** Your grade will be based on the total number of correct answers.

Reliant Corp., an accrual basis calendar-year C corporation, filed its 1994 federal income tax return on March 15, 1995.

Required:

The following **two** responses are required for each of the **Items 85 through 90.**

a. Determine the amount of Reliant's 1994 Schedule M-1 adjustment. To record your answer, blacken the ovals on the Objective Answer Sheet. If zeros precede your numerical answer, blacken the zeros in the ovals preceding your answer. **You cannot receive credit for your answers if you fail to blacken an oval in each column.** You may write the numbers in the boxes provided to facilitate blackening the ovals; however, the numbers written in the boxes will **not** be graded.

b. Indicate if the adjustment (I) increases, (D) decreases, or (N) has no effect, on Reliant's 1994 taxable income. Blacken the corresponding oval on the Objective Answer Sheet.

85. Reliant's disbursements included reimbursed employees' expenses in 1994 for travel of $100,000, and business meals of $30,000. The reimbursed expenses met the conditions of deductibility and were properly substantiated under an accountable plan. The reimbursement was not treated as employee compensation.
86. Reliant's books expensed $7,000 in 1994 for the term life insurance premiums on the corporate officers. Reliant was the policy owner and beneficiary.

87. Reliant's books indicated an $18,000 state franchise tax expense for 1994. Estimated state tax payments for 1994 were $15,000.

88. Book depreciation on computers for 1994 was $10,000. These computers, which cost $50,000, were placed in service on January 2, 1993. Tax depreciation used MACRS with the half-year convention. No election was made to expense part of the computer cost or to use a straight-line method or the alternative depreciation system.

89. For 1994, Reliant's books showed a $4,000 short-term capital gain distribution from a mutual fund corporation and a $5,000 loss on the sale of Retro stock that was purchased in 1992. The stock was an investment in an unrelated corporation. There were no other 1994 gains or losses and no loss carryovers from prior years.

90. Reliant's 1994 taxable income before the charitable contribution and the dividends received deductions was $500,000. Reliant's books expensed $15,000 in board-of-director authorized charitable contributions that were paid on January 5, 1995. Charitable contributions paid and expensed during 1994 were $35,000. All charitable contributions were properly substantiated. There were no net operating losses or charitable contributions that were carried forward.

Required:

c. For **Items 91 through 95,** indicate if the expenses are (F) fully deductible, (P) partially deductible, or (N) nondeductible for regular tax purposes on Reliant's 1994 federal income tax return. Blacken the corresponding oval on the Objective Answer Sheet.

91. Reliant purchased theater tickets for its out of town clients. The performances took place after Reliant's substantial and bona fide business negotiations with its clients.

92. Reliant accrued advertising expenses to promote a new product line. Ten percent of the new product line remained in ending inventory.

93. Reliant incurred interest expense on a loan to purchase municipal bonds.

94. Reliant paid a penalty for the underpayment of 1993 estimated taxes.

95. On December 9, 1994, Reliant's board of directors voted to pay a $500 bonus to each

non-stockholder employee for 1994. The bonuses were paid on February 3, 1995.

Required:

d. For **Items 96 through 100,** indicate if the following items are (F) fully taxable, (P) partially taxable, or (N) nontaxable for regular tax purposes on Reliant's 1994 federal income tax return. All transactions occurred during 1994. Blacken the corresponding oval on the Objective Answer Sheet.

Items 96 and 97 are based on the following:

Reliant filed an amended federal income tax return for 1992 and received a refund that included both the overpayment of the federal taxes and interest.

96. The portion of Reliant's refund that represented the overpayment of the 1992 federal taxes.

97. The portion of Reliant's refund that is attributable to the interest on the overpayment of federal taxes.

98. Reliant received dividend income from a mutual fund that solely invests in municipal bonds.

99. Reliant, the lessor, benefitted from the capital improvements made to its property by the lessee in 1994. The lease agreement is for one year ending December 31, 1994, and provides for a reduction in rental payments by the lessee in exchange for the improvements.

100. Reliant collected the proceeds on the term life insurance policy on the life of a debtor who was not a shareholder. The policy was assigned to Reliant as collateral security for the debt. The proceeds exceeded the amount of the debt.

Required:

e. For **Items 101 through 105,** indicate if the following (I) increase, (D) decrease, or (N) have no effect on Reliant's 1994 alternative minimum taxable income (AMTI) prior to the adjusted current earnings adjustment (ACE). Blacken the corresponding oval on the Objective Answer Sheet.

101. Reliant used the 70% dividends-received deduction for regular tax purposes.

102. Reliant received interest from a state's general obligation bonds.

103. Reliant used MACRS depreciation on seven-year personal property placed into service January 3, 1994, for regular tax purposes. No expense or depreciation election was made.

104. Depreciation on nonresidential real property placed into service on January 3, 1994, was under the general MACRS depreciation system for regular tax purposes.

105. Reliant had only cash charitable contributions for 1994.

Required:

f. For **Items 106 through 112**, indicate if the statement is true (T) or false (F) regarding Reliant's compliance with tax procedures, tax credits, and the alternative minimum tax. Blacken the corresponding oval on the Objective Answer Sheet.

106. Reliant's exemption for alternative minimum tax is reduced by 20% of the excess of the alternative minimum taxable income over $150,000.

107. The statute of limitations on Reliant's fraudulent 1990 federal income tax return expires six years after the filing date of the return.

108. The statute of limitations on Reliant's 1991 federal income tax return, which omitted 30% of gross receipts, expires two years after the filing date of the return.

109. The targeted job tax credit may be combined with other business credits to form part of Reliant's general business credit.

110. Reliant incurred qualifying expenditures to remove existing access barriers at the place of employment in 1994. As a small business, Reliant qualifies for the disabled access credit.

111. Reliant's tax preparer, a CPA firm, may use the 1994 corporate tax return information to prepare corporate officers' tax returns without the consent of the corporation.

112. Reliant must file an amended return for 1994 within 1 year of the filing date.

EXAMINATION QUESTIONS

The point values for each question, and estimated time allotments based primarily on point value, are as follows:

	Point Value	Estimated Minutes Minimum	Estimated Minutes Maximum
No. 1	60	130	140
No. 2	10	15	25
No. 3	10	15	25
No. 4	10	30	40
No. 5	10	30	40
Totals	100	220	270

CANDIDATE NUMBER

Record your 7-digit candidate number in the boxes.

Q-FARE

May 4, 1995; 1:30 P.M. to 6:00 P.M.

INSTRUCTIONS TO CANDIDATES *Failure to follow these instructions may have an adverse effect on your Examination grade.*

Do not break the seal around the *Examination Questions* (pages 3 through 22) until you are told to do so.

Question Numbers 1, 2, and 3 should be answered on the *Objective Answer Sheet*, which is pages 31 and 32. You should attempt to answer all objective items. There is no penalty for incorrect responses. Work space to solve the objective questions is provided in the *Examination Questions* on pages 5 through 19. Since the objective items are computer-graded, your comments and calculations associated with them are not considered. Be certain that you have entered your answers on the *Objective Answer Sheet* before the examination time is up. The objective portion of your examination will not be graded if you fail to record your answers on the *Objective Answer Sheet*. You will not be given additional time to record your answers.

Question Numbers 4 and 5 should be answered beginning on page 23. Support **all** answers with properly labeled and legible calculations that can be identified as sources of amounts used to derive your final answer. If you have not completed answering a question on a page, fill in the appropriate spaces in the wording on the bottom of the page "**QUESTION NUMBER ___ CONTINUES ON PAGE ___ .**"

If you have completed answering a question, fill in the appropriate space in the wording on the bottom of the page "**QUESTION NUMBER ___ ENDS ON THIS PAGE.**" Always begin the start of an answer to a question on the top of a new page (which may be the reverse side of a sheet of paper). Use the entire width of the page to answer requirements of a noncomputational nature. To answer requirements of a computational nature, you may wish to use the three vertical columns provided on the right side of each page.

4. Although the primary purpose of the examination is to test your knowledge and application of the subject matter, selected essay responses will be graded for writing skills.

5. You are required to turn in by the end of each session:

   a. Attendance Record and Calculator Sign-off Record Form, page 1;
   b. *Examination Questions*, pages 3 through 22;
   c. *Essay Ruled Paper*, pages 23 through 30;
   d. *Objective Answer Sheet*, pages 31 and 32;
   e. Calculator; and
   f. All unused examination materials.

Your examination will not be graded unless the above listed items are handed in before leaving the examination room.

Prepared by the Board of Examiners of the American Institute of Certified Public Accountants and adopted by the examining boards of all states, the District of Columbia, Guam, Puerto Rico, and the Virgin Islands of the United States.

Copyright © 1995 by the American Institute of Certified Public Accountants, Inc.

56128

BOOKLET NO.

FINANCIAL ACCOUNTING & REPORTING (FARE)

Number 1

Instructions

Select the **best** answer for each of the following items. Use a No. 2 pencil to blacken the appropriate ovals on the Objective Answer Sheet to indicate your answers. **Mark only one answer for each item. Answer all items.** Your grade will be based on the total number of correct answers.

1. According to the FASB conceptual framework, which of the following situations violates the concept of reliability?
   A. Data on segments having the same expected risks and growth rates are reported to analysts estimating future profits.
   B. Financial statements are issued nine months late.
   C. Management reports to stockholders regularly refer to new projects undertaken, but the financial statements never report project results.
   D. Financial statements include property with a carrying amount increased to management's estimate of market value.

2. One of the elements of a financial statement is comprehensive income. Comprehensive income excludes changes in equity resulting from which of the following?
   A. Loss from discontinued operations.
   B. Prior period error correction.
   C. Dividends paid to stockholders.
   D. Unrealized loss on investments in non-current marketable equity securities.

3. This question is obsolete.

4. Disclosure of information about significant concentrations of credit risk is required for
   A. All financial instruments.
   B. Financial instruments with off-balance-sheet credit risk only.
   C. Financial instruments with off-balance-sheet market risk only.
   D. Financial instruments with off-balance-sheet risk of accounting loss only.

5. Cali, Inc., had a $4,000,000 note payable due on March 15, 1995. On January 28, 1995, before the issuance of its 1994 financial statements, Cali issued long-term bonds in the amount of $4,500,000. Proceeds from the bonds were used to repay the note when it came due. How should Cali classify the note in its December 31, 1994, financial statements?
   A. As a current liability, with separate disclosure of the note refinancing.
   B. As a current liability, with no separate disclosure required.
   C. As a noncurrent liability, with separate disclosure of the note refinancing.
   D. As a noncurrent liability, with no separate disclosure required.

6. A company has adopted Statement of Financial Accounting Standards No. 115, "Accounting for Certain Investments in Debt and Equity Securities." It should report the marketable equity securities that it has classified as trading at
   A. Lower of cost or market, with holding gains and losses included in earnings.
   B. Lower of cost or market, with holding gains included in earnings only to the extent of previously recognized holding losses.
   C. Fair value, with holding gains included in earnings only to the extent of previously recognized holding losses.
   D. Fair value, with holding gains and losses included in earnings.

7. Gar Co. factored its receivables without recourse with Ross Bank. Gar received cash as a result of this transaction, which is best described as a
   A. Loan from Ross collateralized by Gar's accounts receivable.
   B. Loan from Ross to be repaid by the proceeds from Gar's accounts receivable.
   C. Sale of Gar's accounts receivable to Ross, with the risk of uncollectible accounts retained by Gar.
   D. Sale of Gar's accounts receivable to Ross, with the risk of uncollectible accounts transferred to Ross.

8. On December 30, 1994, Chang Co. sold a machine to Door Co. in exchange for a noninterest-bearing note requiring ten annual payments of $10,000. Door made the first payment on December 30, 1994. The market interest rate for similar notes at date of issuance was 8%. Information on present value factors is as follows:

Period	Present value of $1 at 8%	Present value of ordinary annuity of $1 at 8%
9	0.50	6.25
10	0.46	6.71

In its December 31, 1994, balance sheet, what amount should Chang report as note receivable?
   A. $45,000
   B. $46,000
   C. $62,500
   D. $67,100

9. At January 1, 1994, Jamin Co. had a credit balance of $260,000 in its allowance for uncollectible accounts. Based on past experience, 2% of Jamin's credit sales have been uncollectible. During 1994, Jamin wrote off $325,000 of uncollectible accounts. Credit sales for 1994 were $9,000,000. In its December 31, 1994, balance sheet, what amount should Jamin report as allowance for uncollectible accounts?
   A. $115,000
   B. $180,000
   C. $245,000
   D. $440,000

10. On July 1, 1994, Casa Development Co. purchased a tract of land for $1,200,000. Casa incurred additional costs of $300,000 during the remainder of 1994 in preparing the land for sale. The tract was subdivided into residential lots as follows:

Lot Class	Number of lots	Sales price per lot
A	100	$24,000
B	100	16,000
C	200	10,000

Using the relative sales value method, what amount of costs should be allocated to the Class A lots?
   A. $300,000
   B. $375,000
   C. $600,000
   D. $720,000

11. Walt Co. adopted the dollar-value LIFO inventory method as of January 1, 1994, when its inventory was valued at $500,000. Walt's entire inventory constitutes a single pool. Using a relevant price index of 1.10, Walt determined that its December 31, 1994, inventory was $577,500 at current year cost, and $525,000 at base year cost.

What was Walt's dollar-value LIFO inventory at December 31, 1994?
   A. $525,000
   B. $527,500
   C. $552,500
   D. $577,500

12. Theoretically, which of the following costs incurred in connection with a machine purchased for use in a company's manufacturing operations would be capitalized?

	Insurance on machine while in transit	Testing and preparation of machine for use
A.	Yes	Yes
B.	Yes	No
C.	No	Yes
D.	No	No

13. During 1994, Jase Co. incurred research and development costs of $136,000 in its laboratories relating to a patent that was granted on July 1, 1994. Costs of registering the patent equalled $34,000. The patent's legal life is 17 years, and its estimated economic life is 10 years. In its December 31, 1994, balance sheet, what amount should Jase report as patent, net of accumulated amortization?
   A. $ 32,300
   B. $ 33,000
   C. $161,500
   D. $165,000

14. Roro, Inc. paid $7,200 to renew its only insurance policy for three years on March 1, 1995, the effective date of the policy. At March 31, 1995, Roro's unadjusted trial balance showed a balance of $300 for prepaid insurance and $7,200 for insurance expense. What amounts should be reported for prepaid insurance and insurance expense in Roro's financial statements for the three months ended March 31, 1995?

	Prepaid insurance	Insurance expense
A.	$7,000	$300
B.	$7,000	$500
C.	$7,200	$300
D.	$7,300	$200

15. Ivy Co. operates a retail store. All items are sold subject to a 6% state sales tax, which Ivy collects and records as sales revenue. Ivy files quarterly sales tax returns when due, by the 20th day following the end of the sales quarter. However, in accordance with state requirements, Ivy remits

sales tax collected by the 20th day of the month following any month such collections exceed $500. Ivy takes these payments as credits on the quarterly sales tax return. The sales taxes paid by Ivy are charged against sales revenue.

Following is a monthly summary appearing in Ivy's first quarter 1995 sales revenue account:

	Debit	Credit
January	$ —	$10,600
February	600	7,420
March	—	8,480
	$600	$26,500

In its March 31, 1995, balance sheet, what amount should Ivy report as sales taxes payable?
- A. $ 600
- B. $ 900
- C. $1,500
- D. $1,590

16. As a result of differences between depreciation for financial reporting purposes and tax purposes, the financial reporting basis of Noor Co.'s sole depreciable asset, acquired in 1994, exceeded its tax basis by $250,000 at December 31, 1994. This difference will reverse in future years. The enacted tax rate is 30% for 1994, and 40% for future years. Noor has no other temporary differences. In its December 31, 1994, balance sheet, how should Noor report the deferred tax effect of this difference?
- A. As an asset of $75,000.
- B. As an asset of $100,000.
- C. As a liability of $75,000.
- D. As a liability of $100,000.

17. At December 31, 1994, Bren Co. had the following deferred income tax items:

- A deferred income tax liability of $15,000 related to a noncurrent asset.
- A deferred income tax asset of $3,000 related to a noncurrent liability.
- A deferred income tax asset of $8,000 related to a current liability.

Which of the following should Bren report in the noncurrent section of its December 31, 1994, balance sheet?
- A. A noncurrent asset of $3,000 and a noncurrent liability of $15,000.
- B. A noncurrent liability of $12,000.
- C. A noncurrent asset of $11,000 and a noncurrent liability of $15,000.
- D. A noncurrent liability of $4,000.

18. The following information pertains to Kane Co.'s defined benefit pension plan:

Prepaid pension cost, January 1, 1994	$ 2,000
Service cost	19,000
Interest cost	38,000
Actual return on plan assets	22,000
Amortization of unrecognized prior service cost	52,000
Employer contributions	40,000

The fair value of plan assets exceeds the accumulated benefit obligation. In its December 31, 1994, balance sheet, what amount should Kane report as unfunded accrued pension cost?
- A. $45,000
- B. $49,000
- C. $67,000
- D. $87,000

19. On July 1, 1994, Eagle Corp. issued 600 of its 10%, $1,000 bonds at 99 plus accrued interest. The bonds are dated April 1, 1994 and mature on April 1, 2004. Interest is payable semiannually on April 1 and October 1. What amount did Eagle receive from the bond issuance?
- A. $579,000
- B. $594,000
- C. $600,000
- D. $609,000

20. On January 2, 1994, Nast Co. issued 8% bonds with a face amount of $1,000,000 that mature on January 2, 2000. The bonds were issued to yield 12%, resulting in a discount of $150,000. Nast incorrectly used the straight-line method instead of the effective interest method to amortize the discount. How is the carrying amount of the bonds affected by the error?

	At December 31, 1994	At January 2, 2000
A.	Overstated	Understated
B.	Overstated	No effect
C.	Understated	Overstated
D.	Understated	No effect

21. In December 1994, Mill Co. began including one coupon in each package of candy that it sells and offering a toy in exchange for 50 cents and five coupons. The toys cost Mill 80 cents each. Eventually 60% of the coupons will be redeemed. During December, Mill sold 110,000 packages of candy and no coupons were redeemed. In its December 31, 1994, balance sheet, what amount should Mill report as estimated liability for coupons?

A. $ 3,960
B. $10,560
C. $19,800
D. $52,800

22. During 1994, Haft Co. became involved in a tax dispute with the IRS. At December 31, 1994, Haft's tax advisor believed that an unfavorable outcome was probable. A reasonable estimate of additional taxes was $200,000 but could be as much as $300,000. After the 1994 financial statements were issued, Haft received and accepted an IRS settlement offer of $275,000. What amount of accrued liability should Haft have reported in its December 31, 1994 balance sheet?

A. $200,000
B. $250,000
C. $275,000
D. $300,000

Items 23 and 24 are based on the following:

The following condensed balance sheet is presented for the partnership of Alfa and Beda, who share profits and losses in the ratio of 60:40, respectively:

Cash	$ 45,000
Other assets	625,000
Beda, loan	30,000
	$700,000
Accounts payable	$120,000
Alfa, capital	348,000
Beda, capital	232,000
	$700,000

23. The assets and liabilities are fairly valued on the balance sheet. Alfa and Beda decide to admit Capp as a new partner with a 20% interest. No goodwill or bonus is to be recorded. What amount should Capp contribute in cash or other assets?

A. $110,000
B. $116,000
C. $140,000
D. $145,000

24. Instead of admitting a new partner, Alfa and Beda decide to liquidate the partnership. If the other assets are sold for $500,000, what amount of the available cash should be distributed to Alfa?

A. $255,000
B. $273,000
C. $327,000
D. $348,000

25. Ward, a consultant, keeps her accounting records on a cash basis. During 1994, Ward collected $200,000 in fees from clients. At December 31, 1993, Ward had accounts receivable of $40,000. At December 31, 1994, Ward had accounts receivable of $60,000, and unearned fees of $5,000. On an accrual basis, what was Ward's service revenue for 1994?

A. $175,000
B. $180,000
C. $215,000
D. $225,000

26. Which of the following is used in calculating the income recognized in the fourth and final year of a contract accounted for by the percentage-of-completion method?

	Actual total costs	Income previously recognized
A.	Yes	Yes
B.	Yes	No
C.	No	Yes
D.	No	No

27. According to the installment method of accounting, gross profit on an installment sale is recognized in income

A. On the date of sale.
B. On the date the final cash collection is received.
C. In proportion to the cash collection.
D. After cash collections equal to the cost of sales have been received.

28. Farm Co. leased equipment to Union Co. on July 1, 1994, and properly recorded the sales-type lease at $135,000, the present value of the lease payments discounted at 10%. The first of eight annual lease payments of $20,000 due at the beginning of each year was received and recorded on July 3, 1994. Farm had purchased the equipment for $110,000. What amount of interest revenue from the lease should Farm report in its 1994 income statement?

A. $0
B. $5,500
C. $5,750
D. $6,750

29. Wood Co. owns 2,000 shares of Arlo, Inc.'s 20,000 shares of $100 par, 6% cumulative, nonparticipating preferred stock and 1,000 shares (2%) of Arlo's common stock. During 1994, Arlo declared and paid dividends of $240,000 on pre-

ferred stock. No dividends had been declared or paid during 1993. In addition, Wood received a 5% common stock dividend from Arlo when the quoted market price of Arlo's common stock was $10 per share. What amount should Wood report as dividend income in its 1994 income statement?

- A. $12,000
- B. $12,500
- C. $24,000
- D. $24,500

30. Slate Co. and Talse Co. exchanged similar plots of land with fair values in excess of carrying amounts. In addition, Slate received cash from Talse to compensate for the difference in land values. As a result of the exchange, Slate should recognize

- A. A gain equal to the difference between the fair value and the carrying amount of the land given up.
- B. A gain in an amount determined by the ratio of cash received to total consideration.
- C. A loss in an amount determined by the ratio of cash received to total consideration.
- D. Neither a gain nor a loss.

31. Park Co.'s wholly owned subsidiary, Schnell Corp., maintains its accounting records in German marks. Because all of Schnell's branch offices are in Switzerland, its functional currency is the Swiss franc. Remeasurement of Schnell's 1994 financial statements resulted in a $7,600 gain, and translation of its financial statements resulted in an $8,100 gain. What amount should Park report as a foreign exchange gain in its income statement for the year ended December 31, 1994?

- A. $0
- B. $ 7,600
- C. $ 8,100
- D. $15,700

32. On September 22, 1994, Yumi Corp. purchased merchandise from an unaffiliated foreign company for 10,000 units of the foreign company's local currency. On that date, the spot rate was $.55. Yumi paid the bill in full on March 20, 1995, when the spot rate was $.65. The spot rate was $.70 on December 31, 1994. What amount should Yumi report as a foreign currency transaction loss in its income statement for the year ended December 31, 1994?

- A. $0
- B. $ 500
- C. $1,000
- D. $1,500

33. During 1994, Kam Co. began offering its goods to selected retailers on a consignment basis. The following information was derived from Kam's 1994 accounting records:

Beginning inventory	$122,000
Purchases	540,000
Freight in	10,000
Transportation to consignees	5,000
Freight out	35,000
Ending inventory—held by Kam	145,000
—held by consignees	20,000

In its 1994 income statement, what amount should Kam report as cost of goods sold?

- A. $507,000
- B. $512,000
- C. $527,000
- D. $547,000

34. Which of the following should be included in general and administrative expenses?

	Interest	Advertising
A.	Yes	Yes
B.	Yes	No
C.	No	Yes
D.	No	No

35. Which method of recording uncollectible accounts expense is consistent with accrual accounting?

	Allowance	Direct write-off
A.	Yes	Yes
B.	Yes	No
C.	No	Yes
D.	No	No

36. In January 1994, Vorst Co. purchased a mineral mine for $2,640,000 with removable ore estimated at 1,200,000 tons. After it has extracted all the ore, Vorst will be required by law to restore the land to its original condition at an estimated cost of $180,000. Vorst believes it will be able to sell the property afterwards for $300,000. During 1994, Vorst incurred $360,000 of development costs preparing the mine for production and removed and sold 60,000 tons of ore. In its 1994 income statement, what amount should Vorst report as depletion?

A. $135,000
B. $144,000
C. $150,000
D. $159,000

37. Rye Co. purchased a machine with a four-year estimated useful life and an estimated 10% salvage value for $80,000 on January 1, 1992. In its income statement, what would Rye report as the depreciation expense for 1994 using the double-declining-balance method?

    A. $ 9,000
    B. $10,000
    C. $18,000
    D. $20,000

38. Under a royalty agreement with another company, Wand Co. will pay royalties for the assignment of a patent for three years. The royalties paid should be reported as expense

    A. In the period paid.
    B. In the period incurred.
    C. At the date the royalty agreement began.
    D. At the date the royalty agreement expired.

39. The following information pertains to Gali Co.'s defined benefit pension plan for 1994:

Fair value of plan assets, beginning of year	$350,000
Fair value of plan assets, end of year	525,000
Employer contributions	110,000
Benefits paid	85,000

In computing pension expense, what amount should Gali use as actual return on plan assets?

    A. $ 65,000
    B. $150,000
    C. $175,000
    D. $260,000

40. A material loss should be presented separately as a component of income from continuing operations when it is

    A. An extraordinary item.
    B. A cumulative effect type change in accounting principle.
    C. Unusual in nature and infrequent in occurrence.
    D. Not unusual in nature but infrequent in occurrence.

41. For the year ended December 31, 1994, Tyre Co. reported pretax financial statement income of $750,000. Its taxable income was $650,000. The difference is due to accelerated depreciation for income tax purposes. Tyre's effective income tax rate is 30%, and Tyre made estimated tax payments during 1994 of $90,000. What amount should Tyre report as current income tax expense for 1994?

    A. $105,000
    B. $135,000
    C. $195,000
    D. $225,000

42. Quinn Co. reported a net deferred tax asset of $9,000 in its December 31, 1993, balance sheet. For 1994, Quinn reported pretax financial statement income of $300,000. Temporary differences of $100,000 resulted in taxable income of $200,000 for 1994. At December 31, 1994, Quinn had cumulative taxable differences of $70,000. Quinn's effective income tax rate is 30%. In its December 31, 1994, income statement, what should Quinn report as deferred income tax expense?

    A. $12,000
    B. $21,000
    C. $30,000
    D. $60,000

43. Mobe Co. reported the following operating income (loss) for its first three years of operations:

1992	$ 300,000
1993	(700,000)
1994	1,200,000

For each year, there were no deferred income taxes, and Mobe's effective income tax rate was 30%. In its 1993 income tax return, Mobe elected to carry back the maximum amount of loss possible. In its 1994 income statement, what amount should Mobe report as total income tax expense?

    A. $120,000
    B. $150,000
    C. $240,000
    D. $360,000

44. On October 1, 1994, Host Co. approved a plan to dispose of a segment of its business. Host expected that the sale would occur on April 1, 1995, at an estimated gain of $350,000. The segment had actual and estimated operating losses as follows:

1/1/94 to 9/30/94	$(300,000)
10/1/94 to 12/31/94	(200,000)
1/1/95 to 3/31/95	(400,000)

In its 1994 income statement, what should Host report as a loss on disposal of the segment before income taxes?

    A. $200,000
    B. $250,000
    C. $500,000
    D. $600,000

Items 45 and 46 are based on the following:

During 1994, Orca Corp. decided to change from the FIFO method of inventory valuation to the weighted-averaged method. Inventory balances under each method were as follows:

	FIFO	Weighted-average
January 1, 1994	$71,000	$77,000
December 31, 1994	79,000	83,000

Orca's income tax rate is 30%.

45. In its 1994 financial statements, what amount should Orca report as the cumulative effect of this accounting change?

    A. $2,800
    B. $4,000
    C. $4,200
    D. $6,000

46. Orca should report the cumulative effect of this accounting change as a(an)

    A. Prior period adjustment.
    B. Component of income from continuing operations.
    C. Extraordinary item.
    D. Component of income after extraordinary items.

Items 47 and 48 are based on the following:

In preparing its cash flow statement for the year ended December 31, 1994, Reve Co. collected the following data:

Gain on sale of equipment	$ (6,000)
Proceeds from sale of equipment	10,000
Purchase of A.S., Inc. bonds (par value $200,000)	(180,000)
Amortization of bond discount	2,000
Dividends declared	(45,000)
Dividends paid	(38,000)
Proceeds from sale of treasury stock (carrying amount $65,000)	75,000

In its December 31, 1994, statement of cash flows,

47. What amount should Reve report as net cash used in investing activities?

    A. $170,000
    B. $176,000
    C. $188,000
    D. $194,000

48. What amount should Reve report as net cash provided by financing activities?

    A. $20,000
    B. $27,000
    C. $30,000
    D. $37,000

49. Which of the following information should be disclosed as supplemental information in the statement of cash flows?

	Cash flow per share	Conversion of debt to equity
A.	Yes	Yes
B.	Yes	No
C.	No	Yes
D.	No	No

Items 50 through 52 are based on the following:

Selected information from the separate and consolidated balance sheets and income statements of Pare, Inc. and its subsidiary, Shel Co., as of December 31, 1994, and for the year then ended is as follows:

	Pare	Shel	Consolidated
Balance sheet accounts			
Accounts receivable	$52,000	$38,000	$ 78,000
Inventory	60,000	50,000	104,000
Income statement accounts			
Revenues	$400,000	$280,000	$616,000
Cost of goods sold	300,000	220,000	462,000
Gross profit	100,000	60,000	154,000

Additional information:
During 1994, Pare sold goods to Shel at the same markup on cost that Pare uses for all sales.

50. What was the amount of intercompany sales from Pare to Shel during 1994?

    A. $ 6,000
    B. $12,000
    C. $58,000
    D. $64,000

51. At December 31, 1994, what was the amount of Shel's payable to Pare for intercompany sales?
    A. $ 6,000
    B. $12,000
    C. $58,000
    D. $64,000

52. In Pare's consolidating worksheet, what amount of unrealized intercompany profit was eliminated?
    A. $ 6,000
    B. $12,000
    C. $58,000
    D. $64,000

53. A business combination is accounted for properly as a purchase. Direct costs of combination, other than registration and issuance costs of equity securities, should be
    A. Capitalized as a deferred charge and amortized.
    B. Deducted directly from the retained earnings of the combined corporation.
    C. Deducted in determining the net income of the combined corporation for the period in which the costs were incurred.
    D. Included in the acquisition cost to be allocated to identifiable assets according to their fair values.

54. Poe, Inc. acquired 100% of Shaw Co. in a business combination on September 30, 1994. During 1994, Poe declared quarterly dividends of $25,000 and Shaw declared quarterly dividends of $10,000. Under each of the following methods of accounting for the business combination, what amount should be reported as dividends declared in the December 31, 1994, consolidated statement of retained earnings?

	Purchase	Pooling of interests
A.	$100,000	$130,000
B.	$100,000	$140,000
C.	$130,000	$130,000
D.	$130,000	$140,000

55. Personal financial statements usually consist of

A. A statement of net worth and a statement of changes in net worth.
B. A statement of net worth, an income statement, and a statement of changes in net worth.
C. A statement of financial condition and a statement of changes in net worth.
D. A statement of financial condition, a statement of changes in net worth, and a statement of cash flows.

56. Disclosure is required by publicly held companies if 10% or more of total revenues are derived from

	Sales to a single customer	Export sales
A.	Yes	Yes
B.	Yes	No
C.	No	Yes
D.	No	No

57. A company with a defined benefit pension plan must disclose in the notes to its financial statements a reconciliation of
    A. The vested and nonvested benefit obligation of its pension plan with the accumulated benefit obligation.
    B. The accrued or prepaid pension cost reported in its balance sheet with the pension expense reported in its income statement.
    C. The accumulated benefit obligation of its pension plan with its projected benefit obligation.
    D. The funded status of its pension plan with the accrued or prepaid pension cost reported in its balance sheet.

58. This question is obsolete.

59. This question is obsolete.

60. This question is obsolete.

Number 2

Question Number 2 consists of 10 items. Select the **best** answer for each item. Use a No. 2 pencil to blacken the appropriate ovals on the Objective Answer Sheet to indicate your answers. **Answer all items.** Your grade will be based on the total number of correct answers.

Min Co. is a publicly held company whose shares are traded in the over-the-counter market. The stockholders' equity accounts at December 31, 1993, had the following balances:

Preferred stock $100 par value, 6% cumulative; 5,000 shares authorized; 2,000 issued and outstanding	$ 200,000
Common stock, $1 par value, 150,000 shares authorized; 100,000 issued and outstanding	100,000
Additional paid-in capital	800,000
Retained earnings	1,586,000
Total stockholders' equity	$2,686,000

Transactions during 1994 and other information relating to the stockholders' equity accounts were as follows:

- February 1, 1994—Issued 13,000 shares of common stock to Ram Co. in exchange for land. On the date issued, the stock had a market price of $11 per share. The land had a carrying value on Ram's books of $135,000, and an assessed value for property taxes of $90,000.
- March 1, 1994—Purchased 5,000 shares of its own common stock to be held as treasury stock for $14 per share. Min uses the cost method to account for treasury stock. Transactions in treasury stock are legal in Min's state of incorporation.
- May 10, 1994—Declared a property dividend of marketable securities held by Min to common shareholders. The securities had a carrying value of $600,000; fair value on relevant dates were:

Date of declaration (May 10, 1994)	$720,000
Date of record (May 25, 1994)	758,000
Date of distribution (June 1, 1994)	736,000

- October 1, 1994—Reissued 2,000 shares of treasury stock for $16 per share.
- November 4, 1994—Declared a cash dividend of $1.50 per share to all common shareholders of record November 15, 1994. The dividend was paid on November 25, 1994.
- December 20, 1994—Declared the required annual cash dividend on preferred stock for 1994. The dividend was paid on January 5, 1995.
- January 16, 1995—Before closing the accounting records for 1994, Min became aware that no amortization had been recorded for 1993 for a patent purchased on July 1, 1993. The patent was properly capitalized at $320,000 and had an estimated useful life of eight years when purchased. Min's income tax rate is 30%. The appropriate correcting entry was recorded on the same day.
- Adjusted net income for 1994 was $838,000.

Required:

Items 61 through 68 represent amounts to be reported in Min's financial statements. Items 69 and 70 represent other financial information. For all items, calculate the amounts requested. To record your answer, blacken the ovals on the Objective Answer Sheet. If zeros precede your numerical answer, blacken the zeros in the ovals preceding your answer. **You cannot receive credit for your answers if you fail to blacken an oval in each column.** You may write the numbers in the boxes provided to facilitate blackening the ovals; however, the numbers written in the boxes will **not** be graded.

Items 61 through 64 represent amounts to be reported on Min's 1994 statement of retained earnings.

61. Prior period adjustment.
62. Preferred dividends.
63. Common dividends—cash.
64. Common dividends—property.

Items 65 through 68 represent amounts to be reported on Min's statement of stockholders' equity at December 31, 1994.

65. Number of common shares issued at December 31, 1994.
66. Amount of common stock issued.
67. Additional paid-in capital, including treasury stock transactions.
68. Treasury stock.

Items 69 and 70 represent other financial information for 1993 and 1994.

69. Book value per share at December 31, 1993, before prior period adjustment.
70. Numerator used in calculation of 1994 earnings per share for the year.

Number 3

Question Number 3 consists of 6 items. Select the **best** answer for each item. Use a No. 2 pencil to blacken the appropriate ovals on the Objective

Answer Sheet to indicate your answers. **Answer all items.** Your grade will be based on the total number of correct answers.

Hake Co. is in the process of preparing its financial statements for the year ended December 31, 1994.

Required:

Items 71 through 76 represent various transactions that occurred during 1994. The following **two** responses are required for each item:

- Compute the amount of gain, loss, or adjustment to be reported in Hake's 1994 financial statements. Disregard income taxes. To record your answer, blacken the ovals on the Objective Answer Sheet. If zeros precede your numerical answer, blacken the zeros in the ovals preceding your answer. **You cannot receive credit for your answers if you fail to blacken an oval in each column.** You may write the numbers in the boxes provided to facilitate blackening the ovals; however, the numbers written in the boxes will **not** be graded.
- Select from the list below the financial statement category in which the gain, loss, or adjustment should be presented, and blacken the corresponding oval on the Objective Answer Sheet. A category may be used once, more than once, or not at all.

Financial Statement Categories

A. Income from continuing operations.
B. Extraordinary item.
C. Cumulative effect of change in accounting principle.
D. Prior period adjustment to beginning retained earnings.
E. Separate component of stockholders' equity.

71. On June 30, 1994, after paying the semiannual interest due and recording amortization of bond discount, Hake redeemed its 15-year, 8% $1,000,000 par bonds at 102. The bonds, which had a carrying amount of $940,000 on January 1, 1994, had originally been issued to yield 10%. Hake uses the effective interest method of amortization, and had paid interest and recorded amortization on June 30. Compute the amount of gain or loss on redemption of the bonds and select the proper financial statement category.

72. As of January 1, 1994, Hake decided to change the method of computing depreciation on its sole piece of equipment from the sum-of-the-years'-digits method to the straight-line method. The equipment, acquired in January 1991 for $520,000, had an estimated life of five years and a salvage value of $20,000. Compute the amount of the accounting change and select the proper financial statement category.

73. In October 1994, Hake paid $375,000 to a former employee to settle a lawsuit out of court. The lawsuit had been filed in 1993, and at December 31, 1993, Hake had recorded a liability from lawsuit based on legal counsel's estimate that the loss from the lawsuit would be between $250,000 and $750,000. Compute the amount of gain or loss from settlement of the lawsuit and select the proper financial statement category.

74. In November 1994, Hake purchased two marketable equity securities, I and II, which it bought and held principally to sell in the near term, and in fact sold on February 28, 1995. Hake has adopted Statement of Financial Accounting Standards No. 115, "Accounting for Certain Investments in Debt and Equity Securities." Relevant data is as follows:

		Fair Value	
	Cost	12/31/94	2/28/95
I	$125,000	$145,000	$155,000
II	235,000	205,000	230,000

Compute the amount of holding gain or loss at December 31, 1994, and select the proper financial statement category.

75. During 1994, Hake received $1,000,000 from its insurance company to cover losses suffered during a hurricane. This was the first hurricane ever to strike in Hake's area. The hurricane destroyed a warehouse with a carrying amount of $470,000, containing equipment with a carrying amount of $250,000 and inventory with a carrying amount of $535,000 and a fair value of $600,000. Compute the amount of gain or loss from the hurricane and select the proper financial statement category.

76. At December 31, 1994, Hake prepared the following worksheet summarizing the transla-

tion of its wholly owned foreign subsidiary's financial statements into dollars. Hake had purchased the foreign subsidiary for $324,000 on January 2, 1994. On that date, the carrying amounts of the subsidiary's assets and liabilities equalled their fair values.

	Foreign currency amounts	Applicable exchange rates	Dollars
Net assets at January 2, 1994 (date of purchase)	720,000	$.45	$324,000
Net income, 1994	250,000	.42	105,000
Net assets at December 31, 1994	970,000		$429,000
Net assets at December 31, 1994	970,000	.40	$388,000

Compute the amount of the foreign currency translation adjustment and select the proper financial statement category.

Number 4

On January 2, 1994, Bing Co. purchased 39,000 shares of Latt Co.'s 200,000 shares of outstanding common stock for $585,000. On that date, the carrying amount of the acquired shares on Latt's books was $405,000. Bing attributed the excess of cost over carrying amount to goodwill. Bing's policy is to amortize intangibles over ten years.

During 1994, Bing's president gained a seat on Latt's board of directors. Latt reported earnings of $400,000 for the year ended December 31, 1994, and declared and paid dividends of $100,000 during 1994. On December 31, 1994, Latt's common stock was trading over-the-counter at $15 per share.

Required:

a. What criteria should Bing consider in determining whether to account for its investment in Latt under the equity method? Is the equity method consistent with accrual accounting? Explain.

b. Assuming Bing accounts for the investment using the equity method, prepare a schedule of the amounts related to this investment to be reported on Bing's income statement for the year ended 1994 and the amount in the investment in Latt account in the balance sheet at December 31, 1994. Show all computations.

Disregard income taxes.

Number 5

On January 2, 1994, Cody Inc. sold equipment to Griff Co. for cash of $864,000 and immediately leased it back under a capital lease for nine years. The carrying amount of the equipment was $540,000, and its estimated remaining economic life is 10 years. Annual year-end payments of $153,000, which include executory costs of $3,000, are based on an implicit interest rate of 10%, which is known to Cody. Cody's incremental borrowing rate is 13%. Cody uses the straight-line method of depreciation. The rounded present value factors of an ordinary annuity for nine years are 5.76 at 10% and 5.2 at 13%.

Required:

a. What is the theoretical basis for requiring lessees to capitalize certain long-term leases? **Do not discuss the specific criteria for classifying a lease as a capital lease.**

b. Prepare the journal entries that Cody must make to record the sale and the leaseback on January 2, 1994.

c. Prepare the journal entries, including any adjusting entries, that Cody must make at December 31, 1994.

ANSWER KEY FOUR-OPTION MULTIPLE-CHOICE QUESTIONS

Be sure to read Chapter 6—Chart Your Progress and Plan Your Course of Action. It will help you analyze your test and plan your study program.

Business Law & Professional Responsibilities (LPR)

QUESTION #	ANSWER	TOPICAL AREA
1	C	Professional Responsibilities
2	C	Professional Responsibilities
3	D	Professional Responsibilities
4	—	This question is obsolete.
5	B	Professional Responsibilities
6	D	Agency
7	C	Agency
8	B	Agency
9	B	Agency
10	D	Estates and Trusts
11	A	Estates and Trusts
12	A	Estates and Trusts
13	C	Estates and Trusts
14	B	Estates and Trusts
15	B	Estates and Trusts
16	B	Contracts
17	A	Contracts
18	B	Contracts
19	A	Contracts
20	A	Contracts
21	B	Contracts
22	C	Contracts
23	A	Contracts
24	D	Contracts
25	B	Contracts
26	A	Suretyship and Creditor's Rights
27	C	Suretyship and Creditor's Rights
28	D	Bankruptcy
29	C	Bankruptcy
30	A	Bankruptcy
31	A	Bankruptcy
32	C	Bankruptcy
33	D	Bankruptcy
34	D	Bankruptcy
35	D	Bankruptcy

QUESTION #	ANSWER	TOPICAL AREA
36	D	Employment Regulations
37	C	Employment Regulations
38	A	Employment Regulations
39	B	Employment Regulations
40	B	Employment Regulations
41	A	Commercial Paper
42	A	Commercial Paper
43	A	Commercial Paper
44	D	Commercial Paper
45	C	Commercial Paper
46	B	Commercial Paper
47	A	Commercial Paper
48	B	Commercial Paper
49	B	Commercial Paper
50	C	Commercial Paper
51	A	Property
52	A	Property
53	B	Property
54	B	Property
55	C	Property
56	D	Property
57	D	Property
58	D	Property
59	B	Insurance
60	C	Insurance

Auditing (AUDIT)

QUESTION #	ANSWER	TOPICAL AREA
1	D	Audit Planning
2	D	Audit Planning
3	D	Audit Planning
4	B	Audit Planning
5	A	Auditing Concepts and Standards
6	A	Auditing Concepts and Standards
7	B	Audit Planning
8	C	Audit Planning
9	A	Audit Evidence
10	C	Audit Planning
11	B	Audit Planning
12	B	Audit Planning
13	B	Audit Evidence
14	C	Audit Evidence
15	D	Audit Evidence
16	C	Audit Planning
17	A	Internal Control
18	D	Audit Planning

QUESTION #	ANSWER	TOPICAL AREA
19	B	Internal Control
20	B	Other Reporting Areas
21	D	Other Reporting Areas
22	D	Other Reporting Areas
23	D	Auditing Concepts and Standards
24	A	Internal Control
25	—	This question is obsolete.
26	D	Internal Control
27	C	Internal Control
28	D	Statistical Sampling
29	C	Internal Control
30	C	Internal Control
31	A	Internal Control
32	B	Audit Evidence
33	A	Internal Control
34	B	Audit Evidence
35	A	Statistical Sampling
36	D	Statistical Sampling
37	B	Audit Evidence
38	C	Internal Control
39	C	Audit Evidence
40	A	Audit Evidence
41	A	Audit Evidence
42	C	Audit Evidence
43	A	Audit Evidence
44	B	Audit Evidence
45	A	Audit Evidence
46	C	Audit Evidence
47	C	Audit Planning
48	B	Audit Planning
49	B	Statistical Sampling
50	B	Statistical Sampling
51	A	Statistical Sampling
52	D	Audit Evidence
53	C	Audit Evidence
54	D	Audit Evidence
55	A	Audit Evidence
56	D	Audit Evidence
57	C	Audit Evidence
58	C	Other Reporting Areas
59	C	Audit Planning
60	D	Audit Planning
61	A	Audit Planning
62	A	Audit Planning
63	B	Audit Evidence
64	—	This question is obsolete.
65	D	Audit Reporting Standards
66	A	Audit Evidence
67	C	Audit Evidence
68	D	Audit Evidence

QUESTION #	ANSWER	TOPICAL AREA
69	D	Audit Evidence
70	A	Audit Planning
71	A	Audit Planning
72	B	Electronic Data Processing (EDP)
73	A	Audit Evidence
74	C	Audit Planning
75	A	Other Reporting Areas
76	B	Other Reporting Areas
77	D	Audit Reporting Standards
78	B	Other Reporting Areas
79	B	Other Reporting Areas
80	C	Other Reporting Areas
81	C	Other Reporting Areas
82	B	Other Reporting Areas
83	A	Other Reporting Areas
84	D	Internal Control
85	C	Audit Reporting Standards
86	B	Other Reporting Areas
87	C	Audit Reporting Standards
88	B	Internal Control
89	B	Other Reporting Areas
90	B	Other Reporting Areas

Accounting & Reporting— Taxation, Managerial, and Governmental and Not-for-Profit Organizations (ARE)

QUESTION #	ANSWER	TOPICAL AREA
1	C	Federal Income Taxes— Individuals
2	C	Federal Income Taxes— Depreciation & Depreciation Recapture
3	A	Federal Income Taxes— Capital Gains & Losses
4	A	Federal Income Taxes— Capital Gains & Losses
LPR #4	D	Federal Income Taxes—Tax Preparers' Responsibilities
5	D	Federal Income Taxes— Depreciation & Depreciation Recapture
6	B	Federal Income Taxes— Individuals
7	C	Federal Income Taxes— Individuals

Question #	Answer	Topical Area	Question #	Answer	Topical Area
8	C	Federal Income Taxes—Individuals	32	B	Federal Income Taxes—Estates & Trusts
9	A	Federal Income Taxes—Individuals	33	C	Federal Income Taxes—Estates & Trusts
10	A	Federal Income Taxes—Individuals	34	A	Federal Income Taxes—Exempt Organizations
11	A	Federal Income Taxes—Individuals	35	C	Federal Income Taxes—Exempt Organizations
12	A	Federal Income Taxes—Individuals	36	A	Managerial Accounting and Quantitative Methods
13	D	Federal Income Taxes—Individuals	37	C	Managerial Accounting and Quantitative Methods
14	C	Federal Income Taxes—Individuals	38	C	Managerial Accounting and Quantitative Methods
15	D	Federal Income Taxes—Tax Accounting Methods	39	A	Managerial Accounting and Quantitative Methods
16	C	Federal Income Taxes—Tax Procedures & Administration	40	D	Cost Accounting
			41	D	Cost Accounting
			42	A	Cost Accounting
17	C	Federal Income Taxes—Individuals	43	B	Cost Accounting
18	B	Federal Income Taxes—Individuals	44	B	Managerial Accounting and Quantitative Methods
19	A	Federal Income Taxes—Tax Procedures & Administration	45	D	Managerial Accounting and Quantitative Methods
20	C	Federal Income Taxes—Tax Procedures & Administration	46	D	Managerial Accounting and Quantitative Methods
21	B	Federal Income Taxes—Corporations	47	B	Managerial Accounting and Quantitative Methods
22	D	Federal Income Taxes—Corporations	48	C	Managerial Accounting and Quantitative Methods
23	B	Federal Income Taxes—Corporations	49	D	Managerial Accounting and Quantitative Methods
24	C	Federal Income Taxes—Corporations	50	C	Managerial Accounting and Quantitative Methods
25	B	Federal Income Taxes—Corporations	51	B	Not-for-Profit Accounting—Governmental Units
26	C	Federal Income Taxes—Partnerships	52	C	Not-for-Profit Accounting—Governmental Units
27	A	Federal Income Taxes—Partnerships	53	C	Not-for-Profit Accounting—Governmental Units
28	B	Federal Income Taxes—Partnerships	54	A	Not-for-Profit Accounting—Other than Governmental Units
29	A	Federal Income Taxes—Partnerships	55	C	Not-for-Profit Accounting—Governmental Units
30	C	Federal Income Taxes—Partnerships	56	D	Not-for-Profit Accounting—Governmental Units
31	A	Federal Income Taxes—Estates & Trusts	57	C	Not-for-Profit Accounting—Other than Governmental Units

Question #	Answer	Topical Area
58	B	Not-for-Profit Accounting—Other than Governmental Units
59	B	Not-for-Profit Accounting—Other than Governmental Units
60	D	Not-for-Profit Accounting—Other than Governmental Units

Financial Accounting & Reporting—Business Enterprises (FARE)

Question #	Answer	Topical Area
1	D	Accounting Concepts
2	C	Financial Statements
3	—	This question is obsolete.
4	A	Liabilities
5	C	Liabilities
6	D	Investments
7	D	Receivables
8	C	Receivables
9	A	Receivables
10	C	Inventories
11	B	Inventories
12	A	Fixed Assets
13	A	Intangibles
14	B	Accounting Fundamentals
15	B	Liabilities
16	D	Income Taxes, Accounting for
17	B	Income Taxes, Accounting for
18	A	Pension Costs
19	D	Bonds, Accounting for
20	B	Bonds, Accounting for
21	A	Liabilities
22	A	Liabilities
23	D	Partnerships
24	B	Partnerships
25	C	Accounting Fundamentals

Question #	Answer	Topical Area
26	A	Long-Term Contracts
27	C	Installment Sales
28	C	Leases
29	C	Investments
30	B	Fixed Assets
31	B	Foreign Currency Translation
32	D	Foreign Currency Translation
33	B	Inventories
34	D	Financial Statements
35	B	Receivables
36	B	Fixed Assets
37	B	Fixed Assets
38	B	Accounting Concepts
39	B	Pension Costs
40	D	Financial Statements
41	C	Income Taxes, Accounting for
42	C	Income Taxes, Accounting for
43	C	Income Taxes, Accounting for
44	B	Financial Statements
45	C	Financial Statements
46	D	Financial Statements
47	A	Cash Flows
48	D	Cash Flows
49	C	Cash Flows
50	D	Consolidation & Business Combination
51	B	Consolidation & Business Combination
52	A	Consolidation & Business Combination
53	D	Consolidation & Business Combination
54	A	Consolidation & Business Combination
55	C	Financial Statements
56	A	Financial Statements
57	D	Pension Costs
58	—	This question is obsolete.
59	—	This question is obsolete.
60	—	This question is obsolete.

SOLUTIONS AND EXPLAINED ANSWERS

Business Law and Professional Responsibilities (LPR)

FOUR-OPTION MULTIPLE-CHOICE QUESTIONS

Answer 1

#1 (answer "C")

It is essential that CPAs maintain an independent attitude in fulfilling their responsibilities. It is also important that the users of financial statements have confidence in the existence of that independence. These two objectives are identified, respectively, as independence in fact and independence in appearance.

Independence in fact exists when the auditor is able to maintain an unbiased attitude throughout the audit. Independence in appearance is dependent on how others perceive this independence. Independence in appearance enhances public confidence in the profession.

Generally, independence will be considered to be impaired if the auditor, during the period of the auditor's engagement, or at the time of expressing the auditor's opinion:

1. Had any direct or material indirect financial interest in the client.
2. Was a trustee, executor, or administrator committed to acquiring a direct or material indirect interest in the client.
3. Had any joint or closely held business investment with the client.
4. Had any loan to or from the client, with the exception of "grandfathered loans" and "other permitted loans."

    "Grandfathered loans" include home mortgages, other secured loans, or loans that are not considered material to the CPA's net worth, which existed prior to January 1, 1992.

    "Other permitted loans" include automobile loans, loans on the cash surrender value under terms of an insurance policy, borrowings fully collateralized by cash deposits (e.g., passbook loans), or credit cards and cash advances on checking accounts not exceeding $5,000.

5. Acted in any capacity equivalent to that of a member of management.
6. Was a trustee for any pension or profit-sharing trust of the client.

Employment of a CPA's spouse as the internal auditor for a client of the CPA constitutes a material indirect interest for the CPA in the client. Thus, employment of the CPA's spouse as a client's internal auditor will prevent a CPA performing audit engagements from being independent.

Answer choice "A" is incorrect because automobile loans between a CPA and a client are permitted and are not considered to impair the independence of a CPA performing an audit of a financial institution client.

Answer choice "B" is incorrect because engaging in litigation for an immaterial amount and for a different type of professional service does not constitute having a direct or material indirect financial interest in the client. Thus the CPA's independence is not impaired.

Answer choice "D" is incorrect because an honorary trustee does not vote upon or actively participate in decision making. Thus, acting as an honorary trustee for a not-for-profit organization client does not impair a CPA's independence.

#2 (answer "C")

Auditing "procedures" refer to the techniques and methods used by the auditor to conduct the auditor's audit. Audit procedures may vary with the unique circumstances of the audit. In contrast, auditing "standards" rarely change and refer to measures of the quality of the performance of the procedures used by the auditor, as well as the objectives to be achieved by the use of the procedures used by the auditor. Thus, the term "generally accepted auditing standards" is best described as measures of the quality of the auditor's performance.

Answer choice "A" is incorrect because generally accepted auditing standards are not considered to have universal application.

Answer choice "B" is incorrect because generally accepted auditing standards were issued by the AICPA, rather than the Auditing Standards Board. In addition, the standards are quality measures, rather than mere pronouncements.

Answer choice "D" is incorrect because generally accepted auditing standards are used to measure the quality of the auditor's evidence gathering procedures, rather than being procedures themselves.

#3 (answer "D")

When performing consultation service engagements, the CPA should adhere to professional standards. Pursuant to the following compliance standards that address the distinctive nature of consulting services, the CPA shall:

1. Serve the client's interests, to meet stated objectives, while maintaining integrity and objectivity.
2. Obtain a written or oral understanding with the client concerning the responsibilities of the parties and the nature, scope, and limitations of services to be performed.
3. Inform the client of conflicts of interests, significant reservations of the engagement, and/or significant findings or events.

Thus, a CPA performing a consulting services engagement for a nonaudit client need not withdraw from the engagement when the CPA has a conflict of interest that is disclosed to the client and the client consents to the CPA continuing the engagement. Similarly, the CPA need not withdraw for failure to obtain a written understanding from the client concerning the scope of the engagement. The CPA may obtain an oral understanding from the client concerning the scope of the engagement.

Answer choices other than "D" are incorrect and based on incorrect interpretations of the standards of the profession.

#4 (this question is obsolete)

#5 (answer "B")

Rule 301 of the Code of Professional Conduct states that a CPA should not disclose confidential client information unless the disclosure is at the client's request, pursuant to a validly issued subpoena, or in accordance with an AICPA or a state CPA society requirement. Thus, a CPA is permitted to disclose confidential client information without the consent of the client to a state CPA society voluntary quality control review board.

However, the CPA could not disclose such information to another CPA firm if the information concerns suspected tax return irregularities.

Answer choices other than "B" are based on incorrect assumptions and/or interpretations of the law.

#6 (answer "D")

An agency relationship permits one person, the agent, to act for and stand in the place of another, the principal. Because the acts of an agent are considered the acts of the principal, almost any person has the capacity to be an agent.

Where an agent's authority relates to a specific thing that is lost or destroyed before execution of the agency, the agent's authority to act for the principal is terminated by operation of law.

Thus, Trent need not be at least 21 years of age to be an agent and Post would not be liable to Trent if the collection was destroyed before Trent found a purchaser.

Answer choices other than "D" are based on incorrect assumptions and/or interpretations of the law.

#7 (answer "C")

An agency relationship may be terminated automatically, by operation of law, by the occurrence of events that either make it impossible for the agent to continue the relationship or make it unlikely that the principal would desire the agent to continue acting on the principal's behalf. Events that terminate an agency relationship by operation of law include:

1. Death or incapacity of either agent or principal.
2. Impossibility or illegality.
3. Bankruptcy of either principal or agent.
4. Loss or destruction of subject matter.
5. Loss of qualification of principal or agent (e.g., the agent is hired to operate a business requiring a license and the agent subsequently loses the license).
6. Subsequent illegality.
7. Material change in business conditions (e.g., a change such that the agent should reasonably infer that the principal would not consent to an exercise of the agency).

Notice to third parties is not necessary where an agency relationship is terminated by operation of law.

Thus, where Thorp, Ogden's purchasing agent, placed an order on Ogden's behalf after Ogden, the principal, was declared incompetent in a judicial proceeding, <u>Ogden</u> <u>will</u> <u>not</u> <u>be</u> <u>liable</u> <u>because</u> <u>Thorp's</u> <u>agency</u> <u>ended</u> <u>when</u> <u>Ogden</u> <u>was</u> <u>declared</u> <u>incompetent</u>.

Answer choice "A" is incorrect because the incompetency of the principal terminates the agent's authority by operation of the law. Third parties need not be notified of such events. Thus, Datz is not required to be informed of Ogden's incapacity in order for Thorp's authority to purchase on Ogden's behalf to be terminated.

Answer choice "B" is incorrect because all of Thorp's authority (i.e., express, incidental, and apparent) was terminated when Ogden was declared incompetent in a judicial proceeding. This declaration occurred before Thorp's order was placed with Datz; therefore, Thorp was acting without any type of authority when the order was placed, and the transaction was void.

Answer choice "D" is incorrect because Ogden was not a nondisclosed principal. When Thorp placed the order with Datz on Ogden's behalf, Datz knew, or should have known, that Thorp was acting for a principal and knew, or should have known, the identity of the principal.

#8 (answer "B")

An undisclosed principal is liable to a third party for the actions of the principal's agent that were within the agent's actual authority. After the third party discovers the existence and identity of the undisclosed principal, then the third party may elect to enforce the contract against either the principal or the agent. Thus, when a valid contract is entered into by an agent on behalf of a nondisclosed principal, <u>the</u> <u>principal</u> <u>may</u> <u>be</u> <u>held</u> <u>liable</u> <u>once</u> <u>disclosed</u>. However, an <u>undisclosed</u> <u>principal</u> <u>cannot</u> <u>ratify</u> <u>a</u> <u>contract</u> because one requisite for ratification is that the principal be referred to when the agent contracted with the third party. Such a disclosure conflicts with the nature of the relationship between a nondisclosed principal and the principal's agent.

Answer choices other than "B" are based on incorrect assumptions and/or interpretations of the law.

#9 (answer "B")

While an agent's duties to the principal are primarily determined by the employment agreement, it is a fiduciary relationship wherein certain duties are imposed upon the agent by operation of law. These duties include the:

1. Duty of obedience.
2. Duty of diligence.
3. Duty to provide relevant, material information.
4. Duty to account.
5. Duty of loyalty.

The duty of loyalty is quite broad and includes the duty of the agent to avoid conflicts of interest. The agent must act solely in the interests of the principal and may not represent the interests of others or the agent's unless the principal consents to such dual representation, with full knowledge of all the material facts. Thus, <u>Wilson</u> <u>is</u> <u>obligated</u> <u>to</u> <u>act</u> <u>solely</u> <u>in</u> <u>Young's</u> <u>interest</u> <u>in</u> <u>matters</u> <u>concerning</u> <u>Young's</u> <u>business</u>.

Answer choice "A" is incorrect because Young does have the power (albeit not the legal right) to dismiss Wilson during the six-month period without cause. If Young exercises this power, Wilson may bring suit for damages for breach of contract.

Answer choice "C" is incorrect because the agreement between Young and Wilson is enforceable without being manifested by a writing, signed by Wilson. In general, no formality is necessary to create a valid agency relationship. Only those agency agreements that cannot possibly be fully performed in one year or less must be written. Young's agreement with Wilson was for six months and thus does not fall within the rule requiring a written agency agreement.

Answer choice "D" is incorrect because the agreement between Young and Wilson did not form an agency coupled with an interest. An agency coupled with an interest is created where an agent has given consideration in return for the right to exercise the agency authority given to the agent. Wilson did not give consideration in return for the authority to enter sales contracts for Young Corp. and therefore no agency coupled with an interest was formed.

#10 (answer "D")

A trust is a legal, taxable entity established for the purpose of holding property for the present or future benefit of some named beneficiary. A trust may be "inter vivos" (i.e., its provisions take effect during the lifetime of the creator) or "testamentary" (i.e., its provisions take effect upon the creator's death).

The elements of a valid trust are:

1. Three parties (i.e, creator, trustee, and beneficiary).
2. Corpus
3. Capacity and intent (by creator) to create a trust
4. Lawful purpose.

The beneficiary of a private trust must be ascertainable so that the trust can be enforced.

A testamentary trust created to benefit a childless person's grandchildren would fail because the beneficiaries of the trust would not be ascertainable.

Answer choice "A" is incorrect because a trust created to promote the public welfare would be treated as a charitable trust. The "cy pres" doctrine would prevent such a trust from failing. The "cy pres" doctrine results in the preservation of charitable trusts by permitting courts to change the provisions that affect the disposition of the charitable trust to prevent it from failing and to accomplish, as closely as possible, the general charitable intent of the creator.

Answer choice "B" is incorrect because a testamentary trust created to provide for a spouse's health care would not fail.

Answer choice "C" is incorrect because a testamentary trust created to benefit a charity would not fail. Charitable trusts are prevented from failing where necessary by application of the "cy pres" doctrine.

#11 (answer "A")

Unless a power of revocation is reserved in the trust instrument by the creator of the trust, the general rule is that a trust, once validly created, is irrevocable. However, courts sometimes have the power to change or terminate an otherwise irrevocable trust. Interested parties, such as the creator, trustee, and/or beneficiary of an irrevocable trust may petition a court to exercise this power.

Answer choices other than "A" are based on incorrect assumptions and/or interpretations of the law.

#12 (answer "A")

In the absence of contrary directions in the trust instrument, a trustee of a trust must allocate changes in the form of the trust property and extraordinary expenses to principal and must allocate proceeds from the use of the trust corpus and ordinary expenses to income. The trust was silent on allocation of principal and income, and the trust's sole asset was a commercial office building. Thus, if the building were sold, the entire proceeds would be allocated to principal and retained.

Answer choices other than "A" are based on incorrect assumptions and/or interpretations of the law.

#13 (answer "C")

A trustee is a fiduciary who owes the duty of loyalty, duty to account, duty to inform, and duty to exercise due care in administering the trust and in managing its assets for the trust beneficiaries and creditors. A trustee who, without express direction in the trust instrument, invests trust assets in unsecured loans to a co-trustee may have violated the fiduciary duty to invest prudently and the duty of loyalty to the trust.

Answer choices other than "C" are based on incorrect assumptions and/or interpretations of the law.

#14 (answer "B")

The assets of a terminated trust are considered principal and, absent specific directions in the trust instrument, would ordinarily be distributed to the remaindermen.

Answer choices other than "B" are based on incorrect assumptions and/or interpretations of the law.

#15 (answer "B")

A testamentary trust is provided for in the creator's will and comes into existence upon the death of the trust's creator. Cord's will created a trust to take effect on Cord's death. Thus, under the circumstances, Cord has created a testamentary trust.

Answer choice "A" is incorrect because the trust that Cord created was to take effect on Cord's death, while an inter vivos trust must take effect during the creator's lifetime.

Answer choice "C" is incorrect because the trust that Cord created is not invalid. A trust may validly be created in a will and take effect upon the death of the creator of the trust.

Answer choice "D" is incorrect because the naming of Cord's spouse as both the trustee of the trust and the personal representative of the estate does not create an inherent conflict of interest. Cord's spouse may validly serve in both capacities.

#16 (answer "B")

Negligent misrepresentation is a representation of a material fact made without the intent to deceive and without the exercise of due care to ascertain the truthfulness of the representation. While the plaintiff need not prove scienter, the plaintiff must prove all the other elements of fraud, including that the plaintiff justifiably relied on the misrepresentations.

Answer choice "A" is incorrect because a plaintiff may prevail in a common law action for negligent misrepresentation without proving that the defendant made the misrepresentations with a reckless disregard for the truth. The plaintiff need only prove that the defendant failed to exercise due care in ascertaining the truthfulness of the misrepresentations.

Answer choice "C" is incorrect because written representations are not a requirement for a common law negligent misrepresentation action. The representations may be verbal, rather than written.

Answer choice "D" is incorrect because the misrepresentations that must be proven to support a common law action for negligent misrepresentation must concern fact, as opposed to opinion.

#17 (answer "A")

While generally no relief is granted to a party who makes a unilateral mistake, relief will be granted where the nonmistaken party knew or reasonably should have known that a mistake was made. Thus, the subcontractor is not liable because the contractor knew of the errors made by the subcontractor while computing the bid for construction of a portion of the high-rise office building.

Answer choice "B" is incorrect because the general contractor possessed knowledge of the errors when the bid was accepted. The general contrac-

tor is not permitted to knowingly accept and benefit from a bid that contains errors by the subcontractor.

Answer choices "C" and "D" are incorrect because the subcontractor will not be liable for the computational errors in the subcontractor's bid.

#18 (answer "B")

Parol evidence refers to any evidence, whether oral or written, that is not contained in the written contract (i.e., the final agreement of the parties). The rule applies when there exists a contract in which the parties have assented to a certain writing or writings as the full statement of agreement between them. The rule states that no parol evidence of any prior or contemporaneous agreement will be permitted to vary, change, alter, or modify any of the terms or provisions of the written agreement.

The rule does not apply:

1. If the contract is partly written and partly oral.
2. To a clerical or typographical error that is obvious.
3. In order to prove a condition precedent.
4. To a later oral agreement to modify or rescind.
5. To prove fraud, innocent misrepresentation, duress, undue influence, mistake, illegality, or unconscionability.
6. To prove lack of contractual capacity by one party to the contract.
7. To explain ambiguous terms in the contract.

Thus, where the parties have entered into a written contract intended as the final expression of their agreement, subsequent oral agreements will be admitted into evidence because they are not prohibited by the parol evidence rule.

Answer choices other than "B" are based on incorrect assumptions and/or interpretations of the law.

#19 (answer "A")

A condition is an event whose occurrence or nonoccurrence impacts the duty to perform under a contract. Conditions may be classified according to when they affect a duty of performance as follows:

1. Conditions precedent are events that must occur before the other contracting party has a duty to perform under the contract.
2. Conditions subsequent are events whose happening terminates the other contracting party's duty to perform.
3. Concurrent conditions exist where all parties to contract have mutual duties to perform simultaneously; absent a contrary agreement, conditions are assumed to be concurrent.

Thus, <u>conditions precedent, conditions subsequent,</u> and <u>concurrent conditions</u> may validly be present in contracts.

Answer choices other than "A" are based on incorrect assumptions and/or interpretations of the law.

#20 (answer "A")

An agreement is not a contract unless each of the parties is providing consideration. Consideration exists where there is (1) legal sufficiency (i.e., something of value) and (2) a bargained-for exchange. Generally, the adequacy (i.e., equivalency of value) of the consideration given is not a factor. The law permits parties to make their own agreements as long as either of the following exists:

1. <u>Legal benefit</u>—The obtaining by the promisor of that which the promisor had no prior legal right to obtain.
2. <u>Legal detriment</u>—The doing by the promisee of that which there was no prior obligation to do, or refraining from doing that which one was previously under no obligation to refrain from doing. No tangible detriment may have been suffered, but if there is legal detriment present, it will constitute consideration.

No bargained-for exchange occurs and thus consideration is lacking where one party provides consideration in return for an act that was performed in the past (i.e., past consideration). Thus, Grove will prevail if Grove can establish that <u>prior to Grove's promise, Brook had already performed the requested act.</u>

Answer choice "B" is incorrect because Grove would not prevail on a claim of lack of consideration if Brook relinquished a legal right in return for Grove's promise to pay Brook $1,500. If Brook relinquished a legal right, then Brook has provided consideration to Grove in the form of legal detriment, and Brook could enforce Grove's promise.

Answer choice "C" is incorrect because the courts do not weigh the adequacy (i.e., equivalency) of the consideration bargained-for and exchanged by the parties to a contract. Thus, Grove would not prevail against Brook by establishing that Brook's asserted consideration is only worth $400.

Answer choice "D" is incorrect because it does not matter that the consideration bargained-for and exchanged with Grove by Brook will be performed by a third party instead of Brook. The courts do not question who will provide the consideration agreed to by the parties but only that each party is providing consideration for the other's promise.

#21 (answer "B")

Most contract rights and obligations are assignable, even where the other party to the contract fails to consent to, or objects to, the assignment. The nonassignable contract rights and duties include those that:

1. Materially increase the risk or burden on the obligor.
2. Involve highly personal contract rights.
3. Are prohibited by the contract itself, or by statute.

Since the assignment of <u>malpractice insurance policy rights</u> would materially change the risk assumed by the insurer, and because the decision to issue malpractice insurance involves an assessment that the insured is an acceptable risk (i.e., this is a highly personal contract right because the insurer does not agree to accept any risk but only those deemed acceptable after careful scrutiny), such contract rights <u>are not assignable</u>. However, <u>option contract rights are assignable</u> because they do not involve nonassignable rights or duties.

Answer choices other than "B" are based on incorrect assumptions and/or interpretations of the law.

#22 (answer "C")

Most contract rights and obligations are assignable, even where the other party to the contract fails to consent to, or objects to, the assignment. The nonassignable contract rights and duties include those that:

1. Materially increase the risk or burden on the obligor.
2. Involve highly personal contract rights.
3. Are prohibited by the contract itself, or by statute.

Thus, one of the criteria for a valid assignment of a sales contract to a third party is that the assignment must not materially increase the other party's risk or duty.

Answer choice "A" is incorrect because a gratuitous assignment of a sales contract to a third party is valid.

Answer choice "B" is incorrect because a valid assignment of a sales contract to a third party may be either oral or in writing.

Answer choice "D" is incorrect because a valid assignment of a sales contract to a third party may be either revocable or irrevocable by the assignor.

#23 (answer "A")

A party to a contract is discharged from that contract whenever the party's duty to perform under the contract has terminated. Where one party prevents the other from performing his/her duties under a contract, a material breach of contract has occurred that discharges the other party's duty to perform under the contract. Likewise, performance (i.e., satisfaction) of an accord (i.e., a contract accepting a stated performance in satisfaction of an existing obligation) discharges the original duty. Thus, both prevention of performance and an accord and satisfaction will result in the discharge of a party to a contract.

Answer choices other than "A" are based on incorrect assumptions and/or interpretations of the law.

#24 (answer "D")

A party to a contract is discharged from that contract whenever the party's duty to perform under the contract has terminated. Where performance under a personal services contract, which was legal when formed, becomes illegal as a result of a subsequent change in the law, the obligations of both parties are discharged by operation of law.

Thus, illegality of the services to be performed will cause the discharge of a party's duties under a personal services contract.

Answer choice "A" is incorrect because under a personal services contract, the death of the party who is to receive the services does not cause a discharge of the other party's duty to render performance. If the party obligated to perform dies, then that party's obligation is discharged due to impossibility.

Answer choice "B" is incorrect because a party's duties under a personal services contract will not be discharged because the cost of performing the services has doubled. A personal services contract is governed by the common law, which does not recognize the doctrine of commercial impracticability. Accordingly, discharge will not be granted.

Answer choice "C" is incorrect because the bankruptcy of the party who is to receive the services under a personal services contract will not cause a discharge of the obligations to perform for either party under the contract.

#25 (answer "B")

Ordinarily, in an action for breach of a construction contract, the statute of limitations time period would be computed from the date the contract is breached.

Answer choices other than "B" are based on incorrect assumptions and/or interpretations of the law.

#26 (answer "A")

A surety may generally raise any defense that a party to an ordinary contract may raise. Further, some defenses are available only to the debtor, including the incapacity of the debtor, death or insolvency of the debtor, and fraud by the debtor perpetrated against the surety. However, if the creditor knew or should have known that the debtor was perpetrating fraud upon the surety, then the creditor has a duty to disclose such to the surety. If the creditor does not make this disclosure, then the surety may use the debtor's fraud as a defense against a suit by the creditor to force the surety to pay the debt of the debtor. Thus, Royal may avoid liability if Royal can show that State was aware of the fraudulent representations by Green to Royal.

Answer choice "B" is incorrect because whether Royal was a compensated or an uncompensated surety will not be a determining factor in Royal's effort to avoid liability to State. In most situations, compensated and uncompensated sureties have the same rights and duties.

Answer choice "C" is incorrect because bankruptcy of the debtor is a personal defense that does not inure to the benefit of the surety. Thus, Green's bankruptcy will not create a valid defense for Royal to avoid liability to State.

Answer choice "D" is incorrect because the suretyship arrangement between Green and Royal was not void at the inception, merely voidable.

#27 (answer "C")

Performance of the debtor's obligation acts to discharge the obligations of both the debtor and the surety. Thus, if <u>Ace is paid in full by King's spouse</u>, Wright would be released from the obligation to pay the loan.

Answer choice "A" is incorrect because the liability of a surety for the debt of the surety's debtor is joint and several. Thus, upon default by the debtor, the creditor may sue the surety individually, the debtor individually, or both the surety and debtor in one suit.

Answer choice "B" is incorrect because a discharge in bankruptcy by the debtor is a personal defense for the debtor and does not inure to the benefit of the surety.

Answer choice "D" is incorrect because the incompetency or incapacity of the debtor is a personal defense for the debtor and does not inure to the benefit of the surety.

#28 (answer "D")

An involuntary petition in bankruptcy is filed by creditors under either Chapter 7 or Chapter 11. If the debtor has 12 or more creditors, then the involuntary petition must be filed by at least three creditors with aggregate unsecured claims of $10,000 or more. If the debtor has less than 12 creditors, then the petition may be filed by one or more creditors with aggregate unsecured claims of $10,000 or more.

<u>Decoy Publications</u> must join in the filing of the involuntary petition because it has an unsecured claim against Dart of $12,000 (i.e., $14,000 total

claim less $2,000 secured claim equals $12,000 in unsecured claims). The aggregate unsecured claims of JOG Office Supplies (i.e., $3,000) and Nanstar Electric Co. (i.e, $1,200) are insufficient to support the filing of an involuntary petition against Dart.

Answer choices other than "D" are based on incorrect assumptions and/or interpretations of the law.

#29 (answer "C")

The primary basis for approving a petition (voluntary or involuntary) for bankruptcy is the debtor's inability to pay debts as they become due (i.e., "insolvency in the equity sense"). Dart has not been paying its business debts as they become due, has defaulted on its mortgage loan payments, and owes back taxes to the IRS. Thus, if Dart opposes the petition for involuntary bankruptcy, <u>Dart will lose because it is not paying its debts as they become due</u>.

Answer choice "A" is incorrect because Dart will lose if it opposes the involuntary petition since Dart is insolvent in the equity sense. In addition, an involuntary petition may be filed under either Chapter 11 or Chapter 7.

Answer choice "B" is incorrect because Dart will lose if it opposes the involuntary petition since Dart is insolvent in the equity sense. In addition, a successful petition for involuntary bankruptcy may be filed where the debtor has less than 12 creditors as long as at least one of the debtor's creditors signs the involuntary petition and has $10,000 or more in unsecured claims against the debtor.

Answer choice "D" is incorrect because Dart will lose its effort to contest the involuntary bankruptcy petition since Dart is unable to pay its debts as they become due. The fact that Dart owes back taxes to the IRS is not determinative of whether or not Dart will lose in its effort to contest the involuntary petition.

#30 (answer "A")

Once an involuntary petition in bankruptcy is filed under Chapter 7, <u>a stay against creditor collection proceedings will go into effect</u> automatically <u>and a trustee will be appointed</u>. A trustee is appointed in every Chapter 7 case.

Answer choices other than "A" are based on incorrect assumptions and/or interpretations of the law.

#31 (answer "A")

Nanstar Electric Co. has an unsecured claim of $1,200 that was not filed in a timely manner. Where no proof of claim is filed by a creditor, or where it is not filed in a timely manner, no distribution is made to that creditor. However, the claim of that creditor is not discharged by the bankruptcy decree. Thus, Nanstar Electric Co. would receive $0.

Answer choices other than "A" are based on incorrect assumptions and/or interpretations of the law.

#32 (answer "C")

A creditor with a perfected, secured claim against specific property of the debtor has first priority of claim to the proceeds from the sale of that secured asset. The creditor is treated as unsecured to the extent the proceeds from the sale of the secured asset are insufficient to fully satisfy the secured party's claim.

Obviously, Fracon Bank will receive the entire $70,000 from the sale of Dart's real property.

By the same token, Fracon is entitled to a pro-rata share of its unsecured claim of $5,000 (i.e., $75,000 − $70,000). The total unsecured claims are $20,000 (i.e., Fracon's $5,000 + $3,000 due to Jog + $12,000 [i.e., $14,000 − $2,000] due to Decoy). Total assets available for unsecured creditors are $16,000 (i.e., $100,000 less $84,000 of secured claims [i.e., $12,000 due to the IRS + $70,000 due to Fracon + $2,000 due to Decoy]).

Thus, Fracon bank will receive $70,000 on its secured claim, plus $4,000 of the assets available for unsecured claims (i.e., [$5,000/$20,000] × $16,000), or a total of $74,000 on its secured and unsecured claims.

Answer choices other than "C" are based on incorrect assumptions and/or interpretations of the law.

#33 (answer "D")

Certain unsecured claims, including claims for taxes, are given priority over other unsecured claims. The unsecured claims that are given priority over other unsecured claims, and the order of their priority, are

1. Administrative expenses.
2. Debts incurred after the commencement of an involuntary bankruptcy case, but before the order for relief or appointment of a trustee—the so-called "involuntary gap."
3. Unsecured claims for wages earned within 90 days before filing of petition or cessation of business, whichever is first, limited to $4,000 for each employee.
4. Claims for contributions to employee benefit plans arising from services rendered within 180 days before petition filing; such claims are limited to $4,000 per employee.
5. Monies to the extent of $1,800 per individual deposited with debtor for purchase, rental, or lease of real property or personal services, for family or household use.
6. Claims for alimony, maintenance, and/or child support arising from a separation or divorce.
7. Taxes.

Thus, the IRS claim of $12,000, based upon a recorded judgment for unpaid corporate income taxes, will be given priority over the claims of Dart's other unsecured creditors and will be paid in full.

Answer choices other than "D" are based on incorrect assumptions and/or interpretations of the law.

#34 (answer "D")

Chapter 11 of the Federal Bankruptcy Code provides for reorganization by business debtors. The objective of Chapter 11 is to keep the financially troubled business in operation in the absence of fraud, incompetence, or gross mismanagement. Chapter 11 is available to any debtor who is eligible for Chapter 7 relief and to railroads, but does not include stock and commodity brokers. Municipalities are eligible if state law specifically authorizes such.

A Chapter 11 petition may be voluntary or involuntary, and insolvency is not a condition precedent. Once a petition has been filed by an eligible debtor, the petition operates as an order for relief and thus no formal hearing is required.

As soon as practical after the order for relief, a committee of unsecured creditors is appointed.

The committee normally consists of those parties holding the seven largest unsecured claims against the debtor.

The debtor remains in possession and control of the business unless the court appoints a trustee who may operate the business. A trustee will only be appointed for cause, such as debtor fraud or incompetence, or if the appointment is deemed in the best interests of creditors or equity security holders.

Unless a trustee has been appointed, the debtor has the exclusive right to file a reorganization plan during the first 120 days following the order for relief. If the debtor does file a plan within the 120-day period, and the plan has not been accepted by the creditors, then no others may file a reorganization plan during the first 180 days following the order for relief. Thereafter, any interested party may file a reorganization plan and more than one plan may be filed. The bankruptcy court may extend or shorten the exclusive period at the request of the debtor. A creditor can appeal such an order immediately to the appropriate federal district court.

A proposed plan must be accepted by each class of creditors and then confirmed by the court. A class of creditors accepts a proposed plan when it is approved by creditors holding at least two-thirds of the debt owed to that class of creditors and holding more than one-half of the allowed claims for that class.

Once the proposed plan is confirmed and a final decree entered, the business debtor is discharged from most debts that arose before confirmation of the plan.

Thus, ordinarily neither the secured creditors nor the shareholders confirm a reorganization plan. Instead, a reorganization plan is confirmed by the court.

Answer choices other than "D" are based on incorrect assumptions and/or interpretations of the law.

#35 (answer "D")

Upon entry of the court's final decree, Strong will be discharged from all of its debts and liabilities that arose before the confirmation of the plan, except as otherwise provided in the plan, the order of confirmation, or the Bankruptcy Code.

Answer choice "A" is incorrect because Strong will not necessarily be discharged from "all" its debts and liabilities. Some debts and/or liabilities may be expressly excepted in the plan, the order of confirmation, and/or the Bankruptcy Code.

Answer choice "B" is incorrect because Strong's discharge will not be limited to those debts owed to creditors who agreed to the plan. The discharge applies to all debts and liabilities that arose before confirmation of the plan and that are not exempted in the plan, the order of confirmation, and/or the Bankruptcy Code. Thus, debts owed to creditors who did not agree to the plan may be discharged by the court's final decree.

Answer choice "C" is incorrect because Strong will not be discharged from all its debts and liabilities that arose before the date of confirmation of the plan. Certain debts and/or liabilities that arose before confirmation of the plan may be exempted from discharge by the plan, the order of confirmation, and/or the Bankruptcy Code.

#36 (answer "D")

The Federal Unemployment Tax Act (FUTA) is a joint federal-state insurance program created to provide partial income replacement for a limited time to persons who lose their jobs through no fault of their own. Workers' compensation is a state insurance program to provide medical treatment, income maintenance, and death/disability benefits to employees for job-related injuries or illnesses. Both insurance programs are funded by employers. Thus, neither unemployment compensation insurance nor workers' compensation insurance is funded by employee salary deductions.

Answer choices other than "D" are based on incorrect assumptions and/or interpretations of the law.

#37 (answer "C")

The Federal Occupational and Safety Health Act (OSHA) imposes a general duty on private employers to provide a workplace "free from recognized hazards that are causing or are likely to cause death or serious physical harm" to employees. However, liability exists only where the employer actually knew or should have known of the danger. Employers must also comply with OSHA standards directed at specific industries.

OSHA's standards may be enforced by workplace inspections but such inspections are subject to constitutional safeguards, such as the Fourth Amendment's prohibition on unreasonable searches and seizures. Employers may, but are not required to, consent to an OSHA compliance officer's request for permission to conduct an inspection. If the employer does not consent, then the compliance officer must obtain a search warrant. To obtain the warrant, the compliance officer must show reasonable cause for selecting the particular workplace for an inspection. Thus, an on-site inspection of a workplace by an OSHA investigator would be permissible <u>at</u> <u>the</u> <u>request</u> <u>of</u> <u>employees</u> since such a request could show reasonable cause for conducting the inspection.

Answer choice "A" is incorrect because an OSHA investigator may conduct an on-site inspection of a workplace either with a warrant or with the permission of the employer.

Answer choice "B" is incorrect because an OSHA investigator is not limited to conducting inspections after working hours. Inspections may be legally conducted during working hours.

Answer choice "D" is incorrect because normally OSHA is prohibited from giving an employer advance notice of an inspection.

#38 (answer "A")

The provisions of the federal Americans With Disabilities Act (ADA) protect a disabled person from discrimination in employment, <u>public</u> <u>transportation</u>, telecommunications, <u>and</u> in <u>privately</u> <u>operated</u> <u>public</u> <u>accommodations</u>.

Answer choices other than "A" are based on incorrect assumptions and/or interpretations of the law.

#39 (answer "B")

The federal <u>Fair</u> <u>Labor</u> <u>Standards</u> <u>Act</u> (FLSA) mandates a minimum hourly wage as well as the payment of an overtime premium of time-and-a-half for work in excess of forty hours per week.

Answer choice "A" is incorrect because the National Labor Relations Act does not govern employees' wages and hours. The National Labor Relations Act governs collective bargaining and unionization in the private sector.

Answer choice "C" is incorrect because the Taft-Hartley Act does not govern employees' wages and hours. The Taft-Hartley Act governs unfair labor practices, both for management and for private sector unions.

Answer choice "D" is incorrect because the Americans With Disabilities Act does not govern employees' wages and hours. The Americans With Disabilities Act governs discrimination against the disabled by employers and providers of public transportation, telecommunications, and public accommodations.

#40 (answer "B")

The federal Employee Retirement Income Security Act of 1974 (ERISA) mandates recordkeeping, disclosure, and minimum vesting requirements for private sector pension plans. As a result of the minimum vesting requirements, <u>employers</u> <u>are</u> <u>prevented</u> <u>from</u> <u>unduly</u> <u>delaying</u> <u>an</u> <u>employee's</u> <u>participation</u> <u>in</u> <u>a</u> <u>pension</u> <u>plan</u>.

Answer choice "A" is incorrect because ERISA does not entitle employees to have an employer established pension plan. Instead, ERISA regulates those private pension plans that employers choose to offer to their employees.

Answer choice "C" is incorrect because ERISA does not prevent employers from managing retirement plans. Instead it permits an employer to act as the pension fund manager. ERISA does require pension plans to be written, and to name a pension fund manager. In addition, ERISA states that the pension fund manager is a fiduciary.

Answer choice "D" is incorrect because ERISA does not entitle employees to make investment decisions. Instead, ERISA permits a pension plan to grant employees the option to make investment decisions for their pension.

#41 (answer "A")

The basic types of commercial paper are (1) promissory notes and certificates of deposit that contain a promise by the maker to the payee, and (2) drafts and checks that contain an order by a drawer to the drawee.

Thus, under the Commercial Paper Article of the UCC, a <u>draft</u> <u>would</u> <u>be</u> <u>considered</u> <u>an</u> <u>order</u> <u>to</u> <u>pay</u>, while a certificate of deposit would be considered a promise to pay.

Answer choices other than "A" are based on incorrect assumptions and/or interpretations of the law.

#42 (answer "A")

A draft is an unconditional order in writing addressed by one person to another, signed by the person giving it, ordering the person to whom it is addressed to pay on demand or at a fixed or determinable future time, a sum certain in money to bearer or to order. A time draft is a draft that is payable at a specified future date. Thus, this instrument is a time draft.

Answer choice "B" is incorrect because a postdated check is created when a drawer writes a check and dates it with a future date. Dexter, the drawer, dated the draft as of the date of issuance but also ordered that the drawee not pay Robert Silver, the drawee, until several weeks after the draft was issued. Thus, this instrument is a time draft rather than a postdated check.

Answer choice "C" is incorrect because a trade acceptance is a credit device between merchants that is payable upon presentation by a seller of goods to the buyer of goods. This instrument was payable at a specified future date rather than upon presentation.

Answer choice "D" is incorrect because a promissory note contains a promise to pay, and this instrument contained an order to pay. Thus, this instrument is a draft rather than a note.

#43 (answer "A")

Under the Commercial Paper Article of the UCC, for an instrument to be negotiable it must:

1. Be in writing.
2. Be signed by the maker or drawer.
3. Be payable to order or to bearer.
4. Be payable at a fixed or determinable future time, or on demand.
5. Contain an unconditional promise or order.
6. Be payable in money only.
7. Be for a sum certain.

Answer choice "B" is incorrect because an instrument may be negotiable under the Commercial Paper Article of the UCC without being signed by the payee. To be negotiable, the instrument need only be signed by the maker or drawer of the instrument.

Answer choice "C" is incorrect because an instrument need not contain references to all agreements between the parties in order to be negotiable under the Commercial Paper Article of the

UCC. An instrument may be negotiable where it merely refers to the existence of an agreement(s) between the parties, but will not be negotiable if the obligation to pay is subject to, or conditioned upon, another agreement between the parties.

Answer choice "D" is incorrect because an instrument that places conditions on the maker's or drawer's obligation to honor the instrument is not negotiable. In order to be negotiable under the Commercial Paper Article of the UCC, the instrument must contain an unconditional promise or order to pay.

#44 (answer "D")

Under the Commercial Paper Article of the UCC, for an instrument to be negotiable it must:

1. Be in writing.
2. Be signed by the maker or drawer.
3. Be payable to order or to bearer.
4. Be payable at a fixed or determinable future time, or on demand.
5. Contain an unconditional promise or order.
6. Be payable in money only.
7. Be for a sum certain.

Thus, a clause that allows the maker to satisfy the note by the performance of services or the payment of money would prevent the note from being negotiable since the instrument would then not be payable in money only.

Answer choice "A" is incorrect because an instrument may be negotiable as long as it is payable at a determinable future time (e.g., where the instrument is payable at a definite time subject to extension by the obligor to a further definite time).

Answer choice "B" is incorrect because an instrument may be negotiable as long as it is payable at a determinable future time (e.g., where the instrument contains an acceleration clause that allows the holder to move up the maturity date of the note in the event of default).

Answer choice "C" is incorrect because, while negotiability requires that the instrument be signed by the maker or drawer of the instrument, the maker's signature may be made by a person having a power of attorney for the maker.

#45 (answer "C")

A holder of commercial paper is a party with both:

1. Possession of the instrument, and
2. All necessary endorsements.

Thus, under the Commercial Paper Article of the UCC, in order for a transferee of order paper to become a holder, the transferee must have possession of the instrument and the endorsement of the transferor.

Answer choices other than "C" are based on incorrect assumptions and/or interpretations of the law.

#46 (answer "B")

An "ordinary" holder of negotiable commercial paper takes it subject to all claims and/or defenses to the instrument. However, in a nonconsumer transaction, a holder in due course (HDC) takes negotiable commercial paper free of most claims and defenses to the instrument. In order to be a holder in due course, a transferee of an instrument must:

1. Be a holder of a negotiable instrument.
2. Take the instrument for value.
3. Take the instrument in good faith.
4. Take the instrument without notice that it is overdue, has been dishonored, or of any claims to or defenses against it.

Thus, under the Commercial Paper Article of the UCC, in order to be a holder in due course of a promissory note the note must be negotiable.

Answer choice "A" is incorrect because one can become a holder in due course of a note payable to a specific payee, rather than to bearer, as long as the note is negotiable.

Answer choice "C" is incorrect because a person can become a holder in due course where one or more prior holders were not holders in due course of the instrument.

Answer choice "D" is incorrect because a person can become a holder in due course without the holder also being the payee of the note.

#47 (answer "A")

In order to be a holder in due course, a transferee of an instrument must:

1. Be a holder of a negotiable instrument.
2. Take the instrument for value.
3. Take the instrument in good faith.
4. Take the instrument without notice that it is overdue, had been dishonored, or of any claims to or defenses against it.

Thus, under the Commercial Paper Article of the UCC, a person would be prevented from becoming a holder in due course of an instrument where the person was notified that payment was refused, since such information would provide notice that the instrument has been dishonored.

Answer choice "B" is incorrect because a person can become a holder in due course despite having notice that a prior endorser of the instrument was discharged from the instrument. Such information does not constitute notice of a defense against the instrument.

Answer choice "C" is incorrect because a person could become a holder in due course of a note that was collateral for a loan.

Answer choice "D" is incorrect because a person could become a holder in due course of a note that was purchased at a discount.

#48 (answer "B")

An endorsement that includes the wording "without recourse" is a qualified endorsement. A qualified endorsement disclaims the endorser's contract liability on the instrument but not the endorser's warranty liability. Thus, under the Commercial Paper Article of the UCC, the statement that best describes the effect of a person endorsing a check "without recourse" is that the person makes no promise or guarantee of payment on dishonor of the instrument.

Answer choice "A" is incorrect because endorsing a check "without recourse" does not affect the endorser's liability to prior endorsers. Check endorsers incur no liability to prior endorsers of that check. Instead (under his or her warranty liability), one who endorses a check "without recourse" agrees to pay the holder of the check, or a subsequent endorser who pays the check.

Answer choice "C" is incorrect because a person who endorses a check "without recourse" may still be providing warranty protection to later transferees, because such wording does not disclaim the warranty liability of the endorser.

Answer choice "D" is incorrect because a person who endorses a check "without recourse" does not automatically convert the check into order paper. In fact, bearer paper endorsed in blank and "without recourse" remains as bearer paper.

#49 (answer "B")

In a nonconsumer transaction, a party with the rights of a holder in due course takes negotiable commercial paper free of most claims to, and defenses against, the instrument. However, even a party with the rights of a holder in due course is subject to real defenses. The <u>real</u> <u>defenses</u> that are <u>available</u> against a holder in due course include:

1. Forgery.
2. <u>Material</u> <u>alteration</u>.
3. Minority, to the extent it is a defense to a simple contract.
4. Any other incapacity, duress, or illegality that renders the obligation void.
5. Fraud in the execution.
6. <u>Discharge</u> <u>in</u> <u>bankruptcy</u> or other insolvency proceedings.

All other defenses, such as <u>breach</u> <u>of</u> <u>contract</u>, are personal defenses that are <u>not</u> <u>available</u> against a holder in due course.

Answer choices other than "B" are based on incorrect assumptions and/or interpretations of the law.

#50 (answer "C")

A holder of an instrument may discharge the liability of any party to an instrument by destroying the instrument or by striking the signature of the party or parties to be discharged. Such discharge is effective without consideration. However, striking the signature of a prior endorser results in the discharge of subsequent endorsers who had a right of recourse against the discharged endorser. Thus, <u>Betty</u> <u>Ash</u> is the only endorser who will be completely discharged from secondary liability to later endorsers of the instrument.

Answer choice "A" is incorrect because striking the signature of an endorser of an instrument only discharges subsequent endorsers of that instrument who had a right of recourse against the discharged endorser. Ann Tyler endorsed the instrument prior to Betty Ash, rather than subsequent to her. Thus, when Susan Town struck Betty Ash's endorsement, Ann Tyler's secondary liability was not discharged.

Answer choice "B" is incorrect because striking the signature of an endorser of an instrument only discharges subsequent endorsers of that instrument who had a right of recourse against the

discharged endorser. Mary Thomas endorsed the instrument prior to Betty Ash, rather than subsequent to her. Thus, when Susan Town struck Betty Ash's endorsement, Mary Thomas' secondary liability was not discharged.

Answer choice "D" is incorrect because striking the signature of an endorser of an instrument only discharges subsequent endorsers of that instrument who had a right of recourse against the discharged endorser. Despite the fact that Susan Town is a subsequent endorser of the instrument, her secondary liability on the instrument is not discharged because by striking Betty Ash's endorsement, Susan Town waived the discharge.

#51 (answer "A")

A tenancy in common is a type of multiple ownership in which a co-tenant's interest is inheritable and in which the co-tenants need not have equal fractional interests. Thus, if Oak dies, the property will be owned ½ by <u>Tower</u>, ¼ by <u>Nolan</u>, <u>and</u> ¼ <u>by</u> Oak's <u>heirs</u>.

Answer choices other than "A" are based on incorrect assumptions and/or interpretations of the law.

#52 (answer "A")

A lease is a contract wherein the landlord makes an enforceable promise to give possession and control of real property to a tenant, usually for a specified period of time. In general, a lease for a term of more than one year must satisfy the writing requirement of the statute of frauds. A written lease such as a residential lease agreement must:

1. Identify the parties (i.e., landlord and tenant).
2. <u>Contain</u> <u>a</u> <u>description</u> <u>of</u> <u>the</u> <u>leased</u> <u>premises</u>.
3. Specify the term of the lease.
4. Specify the amount of rent.
5. Be signed by the parties.

Answer choice "B" is incorrect because a residential lease agreement is not required to specify the due date for the payment of rent by the tenant to the landlord. Where a lease fails to specify when rent must be paid, the rent is payable at the end of the lease term.

Answer choice "C" is incorrect because a residential lease agreement need not require that a tenant have public liability insurance. The duty to carry public liability insurance may be negotiated by the parties.

Answer choice "D" is incorrect because a residential lease agreement need not require that the landlord perform all structural repairs to the property. The duty to make repairs is normally negotiated by the parties.

#53 (answer "B")

A deed is a written document by which a grantor transfers an interest in land to a grantee. A valid deed does not require consideration but must:

1. Be signed by the grantor.
2. Be witnessed.
3. Include a description of the property.
4. Be delivered by the grantor to the grantee with an intent to transfer an interest in real property.

Thus, for a deed to be effective between a purchaser and seller of real estate, the deed must be delivered by the seller with an intent to transfer title.

Answer choice "A" is incorrect because a deed need not be recorded. A unrecorded deed is valid between the grantor and grantee.

Answer choice "C" is incorrect because a valid deed need not specify the actual sales price to be paid by the purchaser to the seller.

Answer choice "D" is incorrect because a valid deed need not be signed by both the seller and purchaser. A valid deed needs only to be signed by the seller.

#54 (answer "B")

The federal Real Estate Settlement Procedures Act (RESPA) applies to "federally related mortgages" and requires mortgage lenders to:

1. Provide prospective borrowers with good faith estimates of settlement costs.
2. Eliminate kickbacks and referral fees.
3. Reduce the amounts that purchasers of residential property pay into escrow accounts for taxes and insurance.

The Federal Trade Commission Act regulates "unfair methods of competition," which is an antitrust function, as well as "unfair and deceptive" trade practices, which is a consumer protection function. The main thrust of the Act's consumer protection provisions is to prevent fraudulent sales techniques.

Thus, generally, the federal Real Estate Settlement Procedures Act (RESPA) regulates mortgage lenders, while the Federal Trade Commission Act regulates sellers of real estate, goods, and services.

Answer choices other than "B" are based on incorrect assumptions and/or interpretations of the law.

#55 (answer "C")

Two factors are considered by the courts in determining whether an item of personal property has become a fixture:

1. The manner of affixation.
2. The intent of the annexor regarding the permanence of the attachment.

The value of the item is not considered in determining whether an item of personal property has become a fixture.

Answer choices other than "C" are based on incorrect assumptions and/or interpretations of the law.

#56 (answer "D")

Under the Comprehensive Environmental Response, Compensation, and Liability Act (CERCLA), commonly known as the Superfund law, the EPA is authorized to clean up a hazardous waste disposal site and then recover the cleanup cost from:

1. The party who deposited the hazardous waste.
2. The current owner or operator of the site.
3. The person who transported the wastes to the site.
4. The person who owned or operated the site at the time of the disposal.

Answer choices other than "D" are based on incorrect assumptions and/or interpretations of the law.

#57 (answer "D")

Property in the legal sense is the "bundle of rights" that entitles one to exclusively possess, use, and transfer a thing. Property may be real (e.g., land and all things permanently attached thereto) or personal (e.g., most things other than land). Personal property may be tangible because it exists in a physical form, or intangible because it does not exist in a physical form but merely represents one or more valuable legal rights. An oil painting is an item of tangible personal property.

Answer choices "A," "B," and "C" are incorrect because a share of stock, a trademark, and a promissory note are examples of intangible personal property; each represents valuable legal rights that do not have separate tangible physical existence.

#58 (answer "D")

Common carriers transport goods for a fee for all members of the public. A common carrier has strict liability for damages to the goods it transports, except where the damage is caused by:

1. An act of God.
2. The inherent or defective nature of the goods.
3. An act of a public authority (i.e., a government authority).
4. The consignor's (shipper's) negligence.
5. An act of a public enemy (i.e., terrorist group, but not a common criminal).

Answer choice "A" is incorrect because the standard of liability of a common carrier in a bailment relationship is imposed upon the common carrier without regard to fault on the carrier's part. A common carrier is strictly liable for damages to the goods it transports. Thus, reasonable care by the carrier does not characterize the carrier's obligation in a bailment relationship.

Answer choice "B" is incorrect because the standard of liability of a common carrier in a bailment relationship is imposed upon the common carrier without regard to fault on the carrier's part. A common carrier is strictly liable for damages to the goods it transports. Thus, the gross negligence of the carrier does not characterize the carrier's obligation in a bailment relationship.

Answer choice "C" is incorrect because the standard of liability of a common carrier in a bailment relationship is imposed upon the common carrier without regard to fault on the carrier's part. A common carrier is strictly liable for damages to the goods it transports and does not share that liability with others. Thus, shared liability does not characterize the carrier's obligation in a bailment relationship.

#59 (answer "B")

Under a coinsurance clause, the insured is required to maintain insurance on the insured's property up to a certain amount or a certain percentage of the value of the insured property. If the policyholder insures the policyholder's property for less than the required amount, the insurer is liable only for its appropriate share of the amount of insurance required to be carried. However, a coinsurance clause does not apply to a total loss. Thus, if a fire totally destroyed the warehouse, the total dollar amount that Clark would receive from Fair and Zone is $200,000, the current market value of the warehouse.

Answer choices other than "B" are based on incorrect assumptions and/or interpretations of the law.

#60 (answer "C")

An insurable interest must exist for the insured in order for a valid insurance contract to exist between the insurer and the insured. An insurable interest exists when the insured would suffer a pecuniary loss upon the happening of a specified peril. With property insurance, the insurable interest must exist at the time of the loss. With life insurance, the insurable interest need only exist when the policy is taken out by the insured.

An insurable interest exists for both a corporate retailer in its inventory and for a partner in the partnership property.

Answer choices other than "C" are based on incorrect assumptions and/or interpretations of the law.

OTHER OBJECTIVE FORMATS/ESSAY QUESTIONS

Answer 2

Part 2(a)

#61 (answer "A")

A partnership agreement need not be in writing unless the agreement cannot possibly be fully performed in one year or less. Anchor, Chain, and Hook agreed to work full time for the partnership and to distribute profits based on their capital contributions. This agreement could be fully performed in one year or less. The ACH Associates oral partnership agreement was valid.

#62 (answer "A")

A partnership results from an agreement, express or implied, between competent parties to combine talent, money, effort, and so on, to carry on as co-owners a business for profit. Anchor, Chain, and Hook jointly owning and conducting a business for profit establishes a partnership relationship.

#63 (answer "B")

In the absence of a contrary agreement, partners share profits equally. However, Anchor, Chain, and Hook agreed to distribute profits based on their capital contributions. Hook contributed $15,000 of the $30,000 of ACH Associates' capital contributions. In 1993, ACH Associates had profits of $60,000. Hook's share of ACH Associates' 1993 profits was one-half, or $30,000.

#64 (answer "B")

Unless the partnership agreement provides otherwise, partners share losses in the same proportion as they share profits. Anchor, Chain, and Hook agreed to share profits in proportion to their capital contributions and would therefore share losses in the same proportion. Hook contributed one-half of ACH Associates' total capital contributions. Therefore, Hook's capital account would be reduced by one-half of any 1994 losses.

#65 (answer "B")

Dissolution is that point in time when the partners agree to cease continuation of the partnership. Dissolution terminates each partner's actual, but not apparent, authority to create new obligations for the partnership. In September 1994, ACH dissolved. In October 1994, Hook contracted with Ace Automobile Co. to purchase a car for the partnership. Ace would win a suit brought against ACH Associates because Hook's apparent authority continues during dissolution.

#66 (answer "B")

ACH Associates was a general partnership. General partners have joint liability for partnership debts. Anchor Chain and Hook would be jointly liable to pay any judgment recovered by Ace Automobile Co. against the partnership.

Part 2(b)

#67 (answer "A")

In most states, a closely held corporation is formed under the general incorporation statutes governing all corporations. Amber Corp. was a closely held corporation when it was formed. Amber Corp. must be formed under a state's general corporation statute.

#68 (answer "C")

A corporation's bylaws are the rules and regulations that govern the management of its internal affairs. Once a corporation is formed, the adoption of bylaws by either the incorporators or the board of directors is one of the first items of business at the initial organizational meeting of the corporation. Amber Corp.'s initial bylaws ordinarily would be adopted by its directors.

#69 (answer "C")

An initial board of directors is usually named in the articles of incorporation and serves until the first meeting of the shareholders. At the first meeting of the shareholders, a new board of directors is elected. Amber Corp.'s directors are elected by its stockholders.

#70 (answer "B")

In most states, the board of directors either elects or appoints the corporate officers. Amber Corp.'s officers ordinarily would be elected by its directors.

#71 (answer "C")

Corporate officers manage the daily operations of the corporation while executing the policies of the board of directors. Amber Corp.'s day-to-day business ordinarily would be operated by its officers.

#72 (answer "C")

In most states, shareholders may agree in writing to vote in a specified manner on any issue, subject to shareholder approval. These agreements are enforceable and often utilized in closely held corporations. In addition, the agreements may be for an unlimited duration. Adams, Frank, and Berg executed a written voting agreement in which it was provided that they would vote for each other as directors and officers. Adams Frank and Berg must always vote for each other as directors because they have a voting agreement.

Answer 3

Part 3(a)

#73 (answer "A")

A shipment contract requires the seller to send the goods to the buyer without requiring that the goods be delivered to a specific destination. The contract between Grand Corp. and Axle Co. provided that Grand was to ship the custom-designed cabinets F.O.B. sellers loading dock. The contract between Grand and Axle was a shipment contract.

#74 (answer "C")

The Sales Article of the Uniform Commercial Code imposes upon the seller of goods the obligation to tender goods to the buyer that comply precisely with the terms of the contract, or to be in breach of contract. This is known as the "perfect tender" rule. When one party to a contract for the sale of goods breaches the contract, the risk of loss for those goods is placed upon the breaching party. Grand breached its contract with Axle by shipping 15 standard cabinets, when the contract called for all the cabinets to be custom-designed. The risk of loss for the 100 cabinets remained with Grand.

#75 (answer "B")

The Sales Article of the Uniform Commercial Code imposes a duty of "perfect tender" upon the seller (i.e., to tender to the buyer goods that comply precisely with the terms of the contract with the buyer). A buyer has the right to reject a non-conforming (i.e., less than perfect) tender of delivery, or to accept it in whole or in part. The contract between Grand and Axle was voidable because Grand shipped only 85 custom cabinets, which Axle had the right to accept or reject.

#76 (answer "A")

The Sales Article of the Uniform Commercial Code imposes a duty of "perfect tender" upon the seller (i.e., to tender to the buyer goods that comply precisely with the terms of the contract with the buyer). A seller who fails to make a "perfect tender" of goods is in breach of contract with the buyer. Grand's shipment of the standard cabinets was a breach of the contract with Axle.

#77 (answer "C")

Generally, title to goods passes from the seller to the buyer when the seller completes his/her obligation to deliver the goods. The substantial performance doctrine does not apply to contracts for the sale of goods. Therefore, the seller of goods must make a "perfect tender" (i.e., deliver the exact goods called for in the contract with the buyer) in order to satisfy the delivery obligation and transfer title of the goods to the buyer. Thus, had the cabinets been delivered title would not have transferred because the cabinets were nonconforming goods.

#78 (answer "A")

If the goods contracted for are unique and the buyer cannot cover, then the Sales Article of the Uniform Commercial Code grants the buyer of goods the remedy of specific performance. Axle is entitled to specific performance from Grand because of the unique nature of the goods.

Part 3(b)

#79 (answer "B")

Attachment provides the secured party with a legally enforceable security interest in one or more items of the debtor's property. Attachment occurs when: (1) the secured party has possession of collateral pursuant to an agreement with the debtor, or the debtor has signed a security agreement describing the collateral, (2) the creditor gives value, and (3) the debtor has rights in the collateral.

On January 2, 1994, the debtor (Gray Interiors Corp.) obtained rights in the collateral (i.e., sofas) by making a $50,000 cash downpayment. That same day, the debtor gave a security agreement covering the sofas to Shore, the secured party. However, the creditor (Shore Furniture Co.) did not give value to the debtor until the sofas were delivered to the debtor on March 1, 1994. Thus, Shore's security interest in the sofas attached on March 1 1994.

#80 (answer "C")

Under the Secured Transactions Article of the Uniform Commercial Code, filing a financial statement is the most common method of perfecting a security interest. Shore filed a financing statement on March 10, 1994; therefore, <u>Shore's</u> <u>security</u> <u>interest</u> <u>in the sofas</u> <u>was</u> <u>perfected</u> <u>on</u> <u>March 10 1994</u>.

#81 (answer "A")

Attachment provides the secured party with a legally enforceable security interest in one or more items of the debtor's property. Attachment occurs when: (1) the secured party has possession of collateral pursuant to an agreement with the debtor, or the debtor has signed a security agreement describing the collateral; (2) the creditor gives value; and (3) the debtor has rights in the collateral. Thus, <u>Float's</u> <u>security</u> <u>interest</u> <u>in Gray's</u> <u>inventory</u> <u>attached</u> <u>on</u> <u>February 1 1994</u>.

#82 (answer "C")

Under the Secured Transactions Article of the Uniform Commercial Code, filing a financial statement is the most common method of perfecting a security interest. Float filed a financing statement on March 5, 1994; therefore, <u>Float's</u> <u>se-</u><u>curity</u> <u>interest</u> <u>in</u> <u>Gray's</u> <u>inventory</u> <u>was</u> <u>perfected</u> <u>on March 5 1994</u>.

#83 (answer "B")

The priorities among conflicting security interests in the same collateral are normally determined by the chronological order of perfection. When two conflicting security interests are both perfected by filing a financing statement, the order of filing determines priority. Thus, <u>Float's</u> <u>security</u> <u>interest</u> <u>has</u> <u>priority</u> <u>because</u> <u>Float's</u> <u>fi-</u><u>nancing</u> <u>statement</u> <u>was</u> <u>filed</u> <u>before</u> <u>Shore's</u>.

#84 (answer "C")

A buyer in the ordinary course of business is not subject to a security interest created by the seller of those goods, despite the fact that the security interest was perfected and the buyer was aware of the seller's security interest. This is a common occurrence where inventory has been pledged as collateral for a loan. Dove was a consumer purchaser in the ordinary course of business. Thus, <u>Dove</u> <u>purchased</u> <u>the</u> <u>sofa</u> <u>free</u> <u>of</u> <u>either</u> <u>the</u> <u>Shore</u> <u>or Float</u> <u>security</u> <u>interests</u>.

Answer 4

Part 4 (a)

Stone will be successful in its negligence suit against Verge. Stone should argue the following elements of negligence shown in the fact situation:

1. <u>Duty</u> <u>of</u> <u>care</u>—As a result of the contract between Stone and Verge, Verge owed Stone a duty to provide consulting services for Stone with the level of care and competence of a professional computer consultant.
2. <u>Breach</u> <u>of</u> <u>the</u> <u>duty</u> <u>of</u> <u>care</u>—Since Verge prepared the software programs in a manner that allowed some of Stone's accounts receivables to be erroneously deleted from Stone's records, Verge failed to provide the consulting services with the requisite degree of care.
3. <u>Proximate</u> <u>cause</u>—Verge's lack of due care was the proximate cause of the erroneously deleted accounts.
4. <u>Damages</u>—Verge's lack of due care resulted in injury to Stone because Stone's collection costs for these accounts was greatly increased.

Part 4 (b)

Stone will be successful in its fraud suit against Verge. Stone should argue the following elements of fraud shown in the fact situation:

1. <u>A</u> <u>false</u> <u>representation</u> <u>of</u> <u>a</u> <u>material</u> <u>fact</u>—Verge made a material, false statement of fact to Stone when Verge recommended that Stone purchase computers that would be more expensive, knowing they would be obsolete within a year.
2. <u>Scienter</u>—Verge made the recommendation with the knowledge that the computers would be obsolete within a year and that a less expensive, more efficient computer was available. Thus, Verge made the recommendation with scienter.
3. <u>Intention</u> <u>to</u> <u>induce</u> <u>reliance</u>—Verge expected that Stone would rely on his recommendation and purchase the more expensive model. Verge's receipt of a commission from the computer company for inducing Stone to purchase the more expensive computer adds weight to the claim.

4. <u>Justifiable</u> <u>reliance</u>—Stone was justified in relying on Verge's recommendations, since Verge was contracted to advise Stone on the proper computers to purchase.
5. <u>Damages</u>—Stone was injured by its reliance on Verge's recommendation when it purchased a more expensive, less efficient computer that would be obsolete within a year.

Answer 5

Part 5 (a)

1. World Corp. is not correct in its contention that its stock offering is exempt from registration under Regulation D, Rule 505, of the Securities Act of 1933. Rule 505 permits securities offerings of up to $5 million within a 12-month period. Thus, World's offering was within the permissible dollar limitation and the permissible time limits of Rule 505. However, World's offering was made to 50 nonaccredited investors, while Rule 505 permits offerings to a maximum of 35 nonaccredited investors. Also, World's offering involved a general advertising while Rule 505 offerings must be made in a nonpublic manner. Lastly, World notified the SEC 30 days after the first sale of the offering, while Rule 505 mandates that notification to the SEC occur within 15 days after the first sale of unregistered securities.
2. World is not correct in its contention that on subsequent resale the securities are completely exempt from registration. The Securities Act of 1933 exempts resales by most individuals, except underwriters or issuers, sold over the counter or on an exchange. Securities, however, sold under a Regulation D, Rule 505, exemption are restricted, and resales generally require registration.

Thus, resales of securities initially sold under Regulation D, Rule 505, must be registered or must qualify for an exemption.

Part 5 (b)

1. Unity Corp. is not correct in its contention that it is not a covered corporation and is not required to comply with the reporting requirements of the Securities Exchange Act of 1934. Issuers with assets of at least $10 million and at least 500 shareholders, or whose shares are traded on a national exchange, are considered "reporting companies" that must register with and file periodic reports with the SEC. Unity's assets and number of shareholders both exceed the minimum thresholds for a "reporting company." In addition, Unity's stock is traded on a national exchange. Thus, Unity is a "reporting company" and must register with and comply with the reporting provisions of the Securities Exchange Act of 1934.
2. Corporations that qualify as "reporting companies" must register with the SEC and must file an annual report (Form 10-K) that contains certified financial statements and detailed financial information about the company. In addition, "reporting companies" must file quarterly reports (Form 10-Q) with the SEC. These quarterly reports contain unaudited financial statements and abbreviated financial reports. SEC Regulation S-X specifies the format for the financial statements, while Regulation S-K specifies the format and content for nonfinancial disclosures.

Auditing (AUDIT)

FOUR-OPTION MULTIPLE-CHOICE QUESTIONS

Answer 1

#1 (answer "D")

Procedures that an auditor may consider in planning the audit before implementation of the audit strategy usually involve a review of records relating to the entity and discussions with other firm and client personnel. Examples include the following:

1. Review correspondence file, prior year's working papers, permanent files, financial statements, and the auditor's report.
2. Discuss matters that may affect the audit with firm personnel responsible for nonaudit services.
3. Inquire about current business developments.
4. Read current year's interim financial statements.
5. Discuss the type, scope, and timing of the audit with the audit committee or its equivalent; e.g., the timing of inventory observation procedures to be performed.
6. Consider the effects of applicable accounting and auditing pronouncements, particularly new ones.
7. Coordinate the assistance of entity personnel, in data preparation.
8. Consider involvement of consultants, specialists, and internal auditors.
9. Establish the timing and staffing of the audit.

Answer choices other than "D" are incorrect because they represent elements of the audit planning process that the auditor most likely would implement based on auditor's judgment, rather than an agreement with the client.

#2 (answer "D")

Before accepting an engagement with a client that has been previously audited, the successor auditor should take the initiative to communicate with the predecessor auditor. Permission must be obtained from the client before communication can be made, because of the confidentiality requirement of the AICPA Code of Conduct.

If a client will not permit such communication, the successor should carefully consider the desirability of accepting the engagement.

The successor's inquiries should focus on the predecessor's understanding of the reasons for the change in auditors, and should include specific questions concerning facts that might bear on the integrity of management and disagreements the predecessor had with management as to auditing procedures, accounting principles, or other similarly significant matters.

Answer choices other than "D" are incorrect because they represent matters about which the successor auditor would not make specific inquiries of the predecessor auditor.

#3 (answer "D")

It is good professional practice to confirm the terms (i.e., contractual obligations) of each engagement in a written engagement letter. Of significant importance in an engagement letter is a clear statement of the nature of the audit and the responsibilities assumed by the auditor. Although its use is highly recommended, an engagement letter is not required under GAAS.

The engagement letter should specify whether, based upon observations made during the audit, the auditor will prepare a letter recommending improvements; this is known as a management letter.

The engagement letter should also state any restrictions that will be imposed on the auditor's work, deadlines for completing the audit, and any assistance to be provided by client personnel. References to preparation of the client's tax returns and audit fees should also be included in the engagement letter.

The engagement letter is also a means of informing the client that the auditor is not primarily responsible for the discovery of fraud (i.e., illegal acts).

Accordingly, the auditor would not ordinarily include a statement in an engagement letter that "after performing our preliminary analytical procedures we will discuss with you the other procedures we consider necessary to complete the engagement."

Answer choices other than "D" are incorrect because they represent statements that would ordinarily appear in an engagement letter.

#4 (answer "B")

The first standard of fieldwork indicates that the audit is to be adequately planned and assistants, if any, are to be properly supervised.

Planning the audit involves developing an overall strategy for the expected conduct and scope of the audit.

Adequate planning includes the auditor's acquiring an understanding of the client's business, its organization, the location of its facilities, the products sold or services rendered, and its financial structure. To acquire the requisite level of knowledge, the auditor makes use of any prior experience with the client or the industry, including the review of prior years' audit work papers, financial statements, and auditor's reports.

Discussions on matters that potentially could influence the audit should be held with audit and nonaudit personnel. Discussions with management personnel will prove to be an important source of information, as will a review of interim financial statements.

The auditor should coordinate the assistance of client personnel, including the internal auditor and any anticipated use of consultants. All planning should be well documented and should include an audit program.

The procedures that an auditor may consider in planning the audit include:

1. Review correspondence files, prior-year working papers, permanent files, financial statements, and auditor's reports.
2. Discuss matters that may affect the audit with firm personnel responsible for nonaudit services.
3. Inquire about current business developments.
4. Read current year's interim financial statements.
5. Discuss the type, scope, and timing of the audit with the audit committee or its equivalent.
6. Consider the effects of applicable accounting and auditing pronouncements, particularly new ones.
7. Coordinate the assistance of entity personnel, in data preparation.
8. Consider involvement of consultants, specialists, and internal auditors.
9. Establish the timing and staffing of the audit.

In light of the above, the auditor most likely would <u>compare the financial statements to anticipated results</u> when planning a financial statement audit.

Answer choices "A" and "D" are incorrect because they represent procedures to obtain audit evidence, and accordingly do not relate to audit planning.

Answer choice "C" is incorrect because it represents a procedure to obtain evidence regarding the effectiveness of internal control, and is therefore not part of the audit planning process.

#5 (answer "A")

Quality control standards apply to all auditing, attestation, accounting, review, and other services for which professional standards have been established.

The purpose of quality control is to provide reasonable assurance that a firm's personnel comply with professional standards and the firm's standards of quality.

<u>The nature and extent of a CPA firm's quality controls depend on</u> a number of factors, such as <u>its size</u>, the degree of operating autonomy allowed its personnel and its offices, <u>the nature of its practice</u>, its organization, <u>and</u> appropriate <u>cost-benefit considerations</u>.

Answer choices other than "A" represent incorrect assumptions and/or illogical combinations.

#6 (answer "A")

Quality control standards apply to all auditing, attestation, accounting, review, and other services for which professional standards have been established.

The purpose of quality control is to provide reasonable assurance that a firm's personnel comply with professional standards and the firm's standards of quality.

The interrelated elements of quality control include:

1. <u>Personnel management</u>
   a. <u>Hiring</u>—personnel possess the appropriate characteristics to perform competently.

b. Assigning personnel to engagements—work will be performed by persons having the degree of technical training and proficiency required by the circumstances.

c. Professional development—personnel will have the knowledge required to fulfill assigned responsibilities; includes continuing professional education.

d. Advancement—personnel selected will have qualifications necessary for fulfillment of the responsibility they will be called upon to assume.

2. Independence, integrity, and objectivity—Personnel maintain independence in fact and in appearance, perform with integrity, and maintain objectivity.

3. Client and engagement acceptance and continuance—Used for deciding whether to accept or continue a client relationship and whether to perform a specific engagement; minimizes the likelihood of association with a client whose management lacks integrity.

4. Monitoring—Involves an ongoing consideration and evaluation to provide reasonable assurance that the firm's system of quality control is suitably designed and is effective.

5. Engagement performance—Includes policies and procedures to ensure that professional standards, regulatory requirements, and the firm's standards of quality are satisfied.

The firm's approach to assigning personnel (human resources) (item "1.b." above) to audit engagements would ordinarily consider the following factors in achieving a balance of staffing requirements, personnel skills, individual development, and utilization:

1. Engagement size and complexity.
2. Personnel availability.
3. Special expertise required.
4. Timing of the work to be performed.
5. Continuity and periodic rotation of human resources.
6. Opportunities for on-the-job training.

Answer choices other than "A" represent incorrect assumptions and/or illogical combinations.

#7 (answer "B")

The first standard of fieldwork requires that the work is to be adequately planned and assistants, if any, are to be properly supervised. Supervision involves directing the efforts of assistants who are involved in accomplishing the objectives of the audit, and determining whether those objectives were accomplished. Elements of supervision include instructing assistants, keeping informed of significant problems encountered, reviewing the work performed, and dealing with differences of opinion among firm personnel.

Assistants should be informed of their responsibilities and the objectives of the procedures they are to perform. They should also be informed of matters that may affect the nature, extent, and timing of these procedures.

Accordingly, the in-charge auditor has a supervisory responsibility to explain to staff assistants the objectives of the procedures that they are to perform; i.e., how the results of various auditing procedures performed by the assistants should be evaluated.

Answer choice "A" is incorrect because immaterial fraud may be reported to the audit committee; therefore, the supervisor should be informed if immaterial fraud is discovered.

Answer choices "C" and "D" are incorrect because they do not represent specific supervisory responsibilities of the in-charge auditor.

#8 (answer "C")

Analytical procedures consist of evaluations of financial information made by a study of plausible relationships among both financial and nonfinancial data. A basic premise underlying the application of analytical procedures is that plausible relationships among data may reasonably be expected to exist and continue in the absence of known conditions to the contrary.

The purpose of applying analytical procedures in planning the audit is to assist in planning the nature, timing, and extent of auditing procedures that will be used to obtain evidential matter for specific account balances or classes of transactions.

Analytical procedures used in planning the audit should focus on (1) enhancing the auditor's understanding of the client's business and the transactions and events that have occurred since the last audit date, and (2) identifying areas that may represent specific risks relevant to the audit.

Answer choice "A" is incorrect because, although analytical procedures may be used in substantive testing, tests of controls and substantive testing are not the focus of analytical procedures used in planning the audit.

Answer choice "B" is incorrect because analytical procedures used in planning the audit will not necessarily provide assurance that potential material misstatements will be identified.

Answer choice "D" is incorrect because assessing the adequacy of the available evidential matter is part of the focus of analytical procedures used in the final review stage of the audit.

#9 (answer "A")

Illegal acts refer to violations of laws or governmental regulations by the audited entity or its management or by employees acting on behalf of the entity.

In applying audit procedures, the auditor may encounter specific information that may raise a question concerning possible illegal acts. When the auditor becomes aware of information concerning a possible illegal act, the auditor should inquire of management at a level at least one level above those involved.

If the auditor concludes that an illegal act has or is likely to have occurred, the auditor should consider the effect on the financial statements. In evaluating the materiality of an illegal act that comes to the auditor's attention, the auditor should consider both the quantitative and qualitative materiality of the act. For example, an illegal payment of an otherwise immaterial amount could be material if there is a reasonable possibility that it could lead to a material contingent liability or a material loss of revenue.

Accordingly, a relatively small misstatement that most likely could have a material effect on an entity's financial statements would be an illegal payment to a foreign official that was not recorded.

Answer choices other than "A" are incorrect because they represent relatively small misstatements that could not ordinarily have a material effect on an entity's financial statements.

#10 (answer "C")

The various types of risks in an audit include:

1. Audit risk—The risk that the auditor may unknowingly fail to appropriately modify his or her opinion on financial statements that are materially misstated. Audit risk consists of inherent risk, control risk, and detection risk.
2. Inherent risk—The susceptibility of an assertion to a material misstatement, assuming there are no related controls.
3. Control risk—The risk that a material misstatement that could occur in an assertion will not be prevented or detected on a timely basis by an entity's internal controls.
4. Detection risk—The risk that the auditor will not detect a material misstatement that exists in an assertion.

Detection risk should bear an inverse relationship to inherent and control risks. That is, the lesser the inherent and control risk the auditor believes exists, the greater the detection risk he or she can accept, and vice versa.

Control risk detection risk and inherent risk may be assessed in nonquantitative terms that range, for example, from a minimum to a maximum, or in quantitative terms, such as percentages.

Answer choices other than "C" are based on incorrect assumptions and/or illogical combinations.

#11 (answer "B")

The auditor's consideration of materiality is a matter of professional judgment and is influenced by the auditor's perception of the needs of a reasonable person who will rely on the financial statements. The auditor plans the audit to obtain reasonable assurance of detecting misstatements that the auditor believes could be large enough, individually or in the aggregate, to be quantitatively material to the financial statements.

The concept of materiality recognizes that some matters, either individually or in the aggregate, are important for fair presentation of financial statements in conformity with generally accepted accounting principles, while other matters are not important. The phrase "present fairly, in all material respects, in conformity with generally accepted accounting principles," indicates the auditor's belief that the financial statements taken as a whole are not materially misstated.

In planning the audit, the auditor should use his or her preliminary judgment about materiality levels in a manner that can be expected to provide the auditor, given the inherent limitations of the auditing process, with sufficient evidential matter to obtain reasonable assurance about whether the financial statements are free of material misstatements. That judgment may or may not be quantified.

The auditor's preliminary judgment about materiality might be based on the entity's annualized interim financial statements or the financial statements of one or more prior annual periods, as long as he or she gives recognition to the effects of major changes in the entity's circumstances (e.g., a significant merger) and relevant changes in the economy as a whole or the industry in which the entity operates.

Answer choice "A" is incorrect because materiality is a factor in determining sample size for substantive tests; the higher the materiality level (i.e., tolerable misstatement) for an assertion, the smaller the sample size required.

Answer choice "C" is incorrect because the determination of the preliminary judgment about materiality would precede the use of the internal control questionnaire.

Answer choice "D" is incorrect because the management representation letter is provided at the completion (rather than at the beginning) of the audit, and therefore would not affect the auditor's preliminary judgment about materiality, which is considered in planning the audit.

#12 (answer "B")

Detection risk is the risk that the auditor will not detect a material misstatement that exists in an assertion.

As the acceptable level of detection risk decreases, the assurance required from substantive tests increases. Accordingly, as the acceptable level of detection risk decreases, the auditor may change:

1. The nature of substantive tests from a less effective to a more effective procedure (e.g., obtaining evidence from independent sources outside the entity rather than from sources inside the entity).

2. The extent of substantive tests (e.g., using a larger sample size).
3. The timing of substantive tests (e.g., an auditor may postpone the planned timing of substantive tests from interim dates to the year-end).

Answer choice "A" is incorrect because as the acceptable level of detection risk decreases, an auditor would ordinarily increase substantive testing.

Answer choice "C" is incorrect because detection risk relates directly to substantive testing and not to the assessment of inherent risk, which precedes substantive testing.

Answer choice "D" is incorrect because the assessment of control risk precedes and, in part, determines the acceptable level of detection risk.

#13 (answer "B")

Illegal acts refer to violations of laws or governmental regulations by the audited entity, its management, or employees acting on behalf of the entity.

When the auditor becomes aware of information concerning a possible illegal act, the auditor should inquire of management at least one level above those involved.

If the auditor concludes that an illegal act has or is likely to have occurred, the auditor should:

1. Consider the effects on the financial statements.
2. Consider the implications for other aspects of the audit, particularly the reliability of management representations.
3. Inform the audit committee, or others with equivalent authority, about all but clearly inconsequential illegal acts. Oral communication is permissible but should be documented in the work papers.

The auditor should:

1. Express either a qualified or an adverse opinion if an illegal act has a material effect on the financial statements and has not been properly accounted for or disclosed.
2. Disclaim an opinion if the auditor is precluded by the client from obtaining sufficient competent evidential matter needed

to evaluate whether an illegal act that could be material has, or is likely to have, occurred.

3. Withdraw from the engagement if the client:
   a. Refuses to accept the auditor's report.
   b. Does not take the remedial action the auditor considers necessary in the circumstances, even when the illegal act is not material to the financial statements.

Answer choice "A" is incorrect because a disclaimer of opinion is only appropriate when a scope limitation exists, which is clearly not the case in this question.

Answer choice "C" is incorrect because a disclaimer of opinion is only appropriate when a scope limitation exists, which is clearly not the case in this question. Further, an unqualified opinion should generally not be expressed when a material item has not been properly accounted for or disclosed.

Answer choice "D" is incorrect because an unqualified opinion should generally not be expressed when a material item has not been properly accounted for or disclosed.

#14 (answer "C")

The auditor should assess the risk of material misstatements of the financial statements due to errors and fraud; such assessment should be considered in the design of audit procedures to be performed.

Factors to be considered in assessing the risk of material misstatement arising from fraudulent financial reporting include:

1. Management characteristics and influence over the control environment
   a. Management motivation—significant portion of management's compensation represented by bonuses (or other incentives) based on unduly aggressive financial targets, excessive management interest in maintaining or increasing stock price or earnings trend, management interest in seeking inappropriate means of minimizing taxable income.
   b. Management failure to display and communicate an appropriate attitude toward regarding internal control and the finan-
cial reporting process—ineffective communication of the entity's values or ethics, single-person dominance, inadequate monitoring of controls (including failure to correct reportable conditions), setting unduly aggressive financial targets and expectations of employees, disregard for regulatory authorities, and continued employment of ineffective accounting, information technology, or internal auditing staff.
   c. High management turnover
   d. Strained relationship between management and the current or predecessor auditor—frequent disputes on accounting, auditing, or reporting issues, unreasonable demands on the auditor (e.g., time constraints), formal and informal scope restrictions limiting auditor access to people or information, domineering management behavior.
   e. Known history of violations (or claims of alleged violations) of law
2. Industry conditions—new accounting, statutory, or regulatory requirements that could impair financial stability or profitability, increased competition or market saturation accompanied by declining margins, declining industry with increasing business failures, and rapid changes in the industry.
3. Operating characteristics and financial stability—significant and unusual related-party transactions, significant, unusual, or highly complex transactions especially close to year end, unusually rapid growth or profitability, especially high vulnerability to changes in interest rates, unrealistically aggressive sales or profitability incentive programs, threat of imminent bankruptcy or foreclosure, or hostile takeover.

Answer choice "A" is incorrect because low turnover of senior accounting personnel would likely lessen the auditor's concern about the risk of intentional manipulation of financial statements.

Answer choice "B" is incorrect because, by itself, insider purchases of stock would not heighten an auditor's concern about the risk of intentional manipulation of financial statements.

Answer choice "D" is incorrect because a slow rate of change in the entity's industry would likely lessen the auditor's concern about the risk of intentional manipulation of financial statements.

#15 (answer "D")

Errors refer to unintentional misstatements, or omissions of amounts or disclosures in financial statements, including mistakes, incorrect accounting estimates, and misinterpretations.

Fraud refers to intentional misstatements, or omissions of amounts or disclosures in financial statements (i.e., fraudulent financial reporting), and misappropriation of assets (i.e., defalcations). Fraud may involve acts such as manipulation, falsification, or alteration of accounting records (i.e., intentional misapplication of GAAP).

Therefore, the auditor should assess the risk that errors and fraud may cause the financial statements to contain material misstatements and, based on that assessment, design the audit to provide reasonable assurance of detecting errors and fraud that have a material effect on the financial statements.

Answer choice "A" is incorrect because an auditor's responsibility is broad; an auditor's responsibility is not limited to detecting employee errors and simple fraud.

Answer choice "B" is incorrect because departures from GAAP are a potential result of, rather than the cause of, errors and fraud.

Answer choice "C" is incorrect because the application of GAAS will not necessarily result in the detection of errors and fraud; the audit should be designed to provide reasonable assurance of detection based on the audit procedures considered necessary.

#16 (answer "C")

The first standard of fieldwork under GAAS indicates that the audit is to be adequately planned and assistants, if any, are to be properly supervised.

Planning the audit involves developing an overall strategy for the expected conduct and scope of the audit. Adequate planning includes the auditor's acquiring an understanding of the client's business, its organization, the location of its facilities, the products sold or services rendered, and its financial structure.

In planning the audit, the auditor should consider the nature, extent, and timing of work to be done, and should prepare a written audit program describing the necessary procedures to be performed. An audit program aids in instructing assistants in the work to be done. It should set forth in reasonable detail the audit procedures that the auditor believes are necessary to achieve the specific objectives of the audit.

Answer choice "A" is incorrect because the audit is not normally designed to test all material transactions. An audit includes examining, on a test basis, evidence supporting the amounts and disclosures in the financial statements.

Answer choice "B" is incorrect because the timing and extent of substantive tests prior to the balance sheet date depend on the auditor's judgment concerning audit risk.

Answer choice "D" is incorrect because an audit program will not necessarily be designed to provide that each account balance is subjected to substantive tests. Further, if an auditor initially assesses control risk at the maximum level, tests of controls may be eliminated, and would therefore not be included in the written audit program.

#17 (answer "A")

In planning the audit, the auditor should consider the nature, extent, and timing of work to be done, and should prepare a written audit program describing the necessary procedures to be performed. An audit program aids in instructing assistants in the work to be done.

It should set forth in reasonable detail the audit procedures that the auditor believes are necessary to accomplish the specific objectives of the audit.

The form of the audit program and the extent of its detail will vary. In developing the audit program, the auditor should be guided by the results of the auditor's planning considerations and procedures. As the audit progresses, changed conditions may make it necessary to modify planned audit procedures.

In planning the audit, an auditor should obtain a sufficient understanding of the entity's internal control. The understanding should include knowledge about the design of relevant controls and whether they have been placed in operation by the entity. In planning the audit, such knowledge should be used to:

1. Identify types of potential misstatements.
2. Consider factors that affect the risk of material misstatements.
3. Design substantive tests.

Accordingly, the audit program usually cannot be finalized until the <u>consideration</u> <u>of</u> <u>the</u> <u>entity's</u> <u>internal</u> <u>control</u> <u>has</u> <u>been</u> <u>completed</u>.

Answer choice "B" is incorrect because an engagement letter setting forth the conditions of the audit would be signed prior to the development of the audit program. Furthermore, although good practice, an engagement letter is not required documentation for an audit.

Answer choice "C" is incorrect because the audit program can be finalized before reportable conditions are actually communicated to the audit committee, as long as the requirement to communicate is noted in the audit program.

Answer choice "D" is incorrect because the audit program can be finalized before the search for unrecorded liabilities has been performed and documented; the audit program usually cannot, however, be finalized if it does not include such scheduled procedures.

#18 (answer "D")

Before accepting an engagement with a client that has been previously audited, the successor auditor should take the initiative to communicate with the predecessor auditor. Permission must be obtained from the client before communication can be made because of the confidentiality requirements of the Code of Conduct. If a client will not permit such communication, the successor should carefully consider the desirability of accepting the engagement.

In the communication, the successor auditor should make specific and reasonable inquiries of the predecessor about matters relevant to the audit, such as:

1. Facts that might bear on the integrity of management.
2. Disagreements with management on accounting principles and auditing procedures.
3. The predecessor's understanding for the change in auditors.

The predecessor auditor is expected to respond promptly and fully.

Information obtained may also be helpful in planning the initial audit. Specific inquiries of the former auditor might relate to:

1. Areas requiring a large amount of audit time.
2. Problems arising out of the condition of the information system.
3. A review of the predecessor's working papers.

If, during the audit, the successor auditor becomes aware of information that leads him to believe that financial statements reported on by the predecessor auditor may require revision, he should <u>request</u> <u>the</u> <u>client</u> <u>to</u> <u>arrange</u> <u>a</u> <u>meeting</u> <u>among</u> <u>the</u> <u>three</u> <u>parties</u> to discuss this information and attempt <u>to</u> <u>resolve</u> <u>the</u> <u>matter</u>. If the client refuses, or if the successor is not satisfied with the result, the successor auditor may be well advised to consult with legal counsel in determining an appropriate course of further action.

Answer choice "A" is incorrect because the prior year's financial statements are the responsibility of management and the opinion is that of the predecessor auditor.

Answer choice "B" is incorrect because the predecessor auditor is the appropriate party to make a request that the prior year's financial statements be revised and reissued.

Answer choice "C" is incorrect because the successor auditor must obtain permission from the client before notifying the predecessor auditor of the information. Further, inquiries about the integrity of management would be made in the initial communication with the predecessor auditor.

#19 (answer "B")

SAS #61, "Communication with Audit Committees," establishes a requirement for the auditor to determine that certain matters related to the conduct of the audit be communicated (orally or in writing) to the audit committee (or, in the absence of an audit committee, to other financial oversight groups, such as finance or budget committees). Such communication need not be made before the issuance of the auditor's report.

Matters to be communicated are as follows:

1. The level of responsibility an auditor assumes for internal control and the financial statements under GAAS.
2. The initial selection of and changes in significant policies, methods used to account for significant unusual transactions, and the effect of continuing accounting policies in controversial areas.
3. The processes used by management in formulating accounting estimates and the basis for the auditor's conclusions about the reasonableness of those estimates.
4. Any adjustments arising from the audit that could have a significant effect on the entity's reporting process.
5. The auditor's responsibility for information, other than the audited financial statements, in documents such as corporate annual reports.
6. Any disagreements between the auditor and management, whether or not satisfactorily resolved.
7. Significant matters that were the subject of consultations with other accountants.
8. Any major issues discussed by management and the auditor before the auditor was hired.
9. Any serious difficulties the auditor encountered that were detrimental to the effective completion of the audit.

It should be noted that an auditor would not likely initiate a discussion with a client's audit committee concerning the maximum dollar amount of misstatements that could exist without causing the financial statements to be materially misstated; this is generally a matter of the auditor's professional judgment.

Answer choices other than "B" are incorrect because they represent matters required to be communicated to the audit committee.

#20 (answer "B")

An accountant is precluded from issuing a review report on the financial statements of an entity with respect to which she is not independent. However, if the accountant is not independent, a compilation report may be issued, provided compilation standards are adhered to and the accountant discloses the lack of independence in her report.

In judging whether independence exists, the accountant should be guided by the AICPA Code of Professional Conduct. Rule 101 of the Code specifically indicates that independence will be considered to be impaired if the accountant has any direct or material indirect financial interest in the client during the period of the engagement or at the time the report is issued.

In the question situation, in view of the fact that the accountant has a direct financial interest in the client, even though it is immaterial, the accountant is not independent and therefore may not issue a review report.

Answer choice "A" is incorrect because even though the accountant is not independent, association with the financial statements through a compilation engagement is still permitted.

Answer choice "C" is incorrect because lack of independence precludes the issuance of a review report.

Answer choice "D" is incorrect because an immaterial direct financial interest results in a lack of independence.

#21 (answer "D")

An accountant may submit a written personal financial plan containing unaudited personal financial statements to a client without complying with SSARS #1, provided that the financial statements are

1. Used solely to assist the client and the client's advisors in developing the client's personal financial goals and objectives.
2. Not to be used to obtain credit, or for any purposes other than developing these goals and objectives.

When the accountant chooses not to comply with the requirements of SSARS #1, the accountant's report should state that the unaudited financial statements (1) are designed solely to help develop the financial plan; (2) may be incomplete, contain departures from GAAP, and are not to be used to obtain credit; and (3) have not been audited, reviewed, or compiled.

Answer choice "A" is incorrect because comparative financial statements are not precluded by the exemption from SSARS #1 for unaudited personal financial statements.

Answer choice "B" is incorrect because departures from GAAP, including the omission of material disclosures, do not preclude the exemption from SSARS #1 for unaudited personal financial statements.

Answer choice "C" is incorrect because the exemption from SSARS #1 for unaudited personal financial statements is applicable whether or not the financial planner who will be using the financial statements is a CPA.

#22 (answer "D")

Whenever an accountant submits, to a client or others, prospective financial statements (i.e., financial forecasts and financial projections) that he has assembled, or assisted in assembling, the accountant should perform an engagement to either examine, compile, or apply agreed-upon procedures to the prospective financial statements.

A financial forecast presents, to the best of the responsible party's (usually management's) knowledge and belief, an entity's expected financial position, results of operations, and cash flows. A financial forecast is based on assumptions reflecting conditions expected to exist and the course of action expected to be taken.

A financial projection presents to the best of the responsible party's knowledge and belief, given one or more hypothetical assumptions (i.e., assumptions used to present a condition or course of action that is not necessarily expected to occur), an entity's expected financial position, results of operations, and cash flows. A financial projection is therefore based on "what if" assumptions.

An examination of a financial forecast involves evaluating (1) the preparation of the financial forecast; (2) the support underlying management's assumptions; and (3) the presentation of the prospective financial statements for conformity with AICPA guidelines, and results in the issuance of an examination report.

Answer choice "A" is incorrect because a compilation represents a different type of engagement relating to prospective financial statements.

Answer choice "B" is incorrect because distribution of a forecast is not limited.

Answer choice "C" is incorrect because the auditor assumes no responsibility to update management on events subsequent to the report date.

#23 (answer "D")

The third general standard states that "due professional care is to be exercised in the planning and performance of the audit and the preparation of the report."

Due care imposes a responsibility upon the auditor and each professional within an independent auditor's organization to observe the standards of fieldwork and reporting. A CPA who undertakes an engagement assumes a duty to perform as a professional possessing the degree of skill commonly possessed by others in the field. Exercise of due care requires the exercise of professional skepticism. Professional skepticism is an attitude that involves a questioning mind and a critical assessment of audit evidence.

Answer choice "A" is incorrect because it relates to the second standard of field work, which pertains to the auditor's consideration of the client's internal control. Further, it is not an appropriate interpretation of that standard.

Answer choice "B" is incorrect because it relates to the third standard of fieldwork, which pertains to evidential matter, and is not an appropriate interpretation of that standard.

Answer choice "C" is incorrect because it relates to the first general standard of fieldwork, which pertains to the technical training and proficiency of the auditor.

#24 (answer "A")

The second standard of fieldwork states:

> A sufficient understanding of internal control is to be obtained to plan the audit and to determine the nature, timing, and extent of tests to be performed.

The understanding should include knowledge about the design of relevant controls and whether they have been placed in operation by the client.

Thus, the primary objective of procedures performed to obtain an understanding of internal control is to provide the auditor with the knowledge necessary for audit planning.

Answer choice "B" is incorrect because inherent risk is the susceptibility of an assertion to a material misstatement, assuming there are no related internal controls. As such, inherent risk is independent of internal control.

Answer choice "C" is incorrect because the auditor needs to obtain an understanding of internal control in order to determine if tests of controls are even necessary. Based on the understanding obtained, the auditor may assess control risk at the maximum level and entirely omit tests of controls.

Answer choice "D" is incorrect because it concerns the operating effectiveness of internal control, rather than obtaining an understanding of internal control.

#25 (this question is obsolete)

#26 (answer "D")

When considering internal control, an auditor should be aware of the following:

1. Management has the basic responsibility for the establishment and maintenance of internal control.
2. The concept of reasonable assurance recognizes that an entity's internal control will accomplish its objectives within the framework of a reasonable cost/benefit equation.
3. Limitations are inherent in internal control. Errors may be caused by misunderstandings, mistakes in judgment, individual carelessness, fatigue, and so on. Internal control may also be ineffective because of collusion among personnel, both within and outside the entity, and by management's override of certain policies and procedures.

In light of point "2" above, the concept of reasonable assurance recognizes that the cost of an entity's internal control should not exceed the benefits expected to be derived.

Answer choice "A" is incorrect because it represents the "inherent limitation" consideration (i.e., the potential effectiveness of an entity's internal control is subject to inherent limitations).

Answer choice "B" is incorrect because adequate safeguards over access to assets and records do not relate to the concept of reasonable assurance.

Answer choice "C" is incorrect because it represents the consideration of internal control concerning management's responsibility.

#27 (answer "C")

Assessing control risk is the process of evaluating the effectiveness of an entity's internal controls in preventing or detecting material misstatements in the financial statements.

Control risk is the risk that a material misstatement that could occur in an assertion will not be prevented or detected on a timely basis by an entity's internal controls.

Accordingly, control risk should be assessed in terms of financial statement assertions.

Answer choice "A" is incorrect because specific control activities are part of internal control for which control risk is assessed.

Answer choice "B" is incorrect because potential fraud relates to potential material misstatements in assertions for which control risk is assessed.

Answer choice "D" is incorrect because control environment factors are part of internal control related to specific assertions for which control risk is assessed.

#28 (answer "D")

When performing tests of controls, the auditor is concerned with two aspects of sampling risk. These are the risk of assessing control risk too low and the risk of assessing control risk too high.

The risk of assessing control risk too low is the risk that the sample supports the auditor's conclusions about the control, when the true deviation rate of the population does not justify this conclusion.

The risk of assessing control risk too high is the risk that the sample does not support the auditor's conclusions about the control, when the true deviation rate of the population supports such a conclusion.

When the deviation rate in the auditor's sample plus the allowance for sampling risk is less than the tolerable rate, the auditor would conclude that the sample could be relied upon. However, if the true deviation rate in the population was more than the deviation rate in the auditor's sample, the auditor would assess control risk too low.

Answer choices "A" and "C" are incorrect because when testing controls, an auditor does not compare the true deviation rate in the population with the risk of assessing control risk too low, based on the auditor's sample.

Answer choice "B" is incorrect because when the true deviation rate in the population is less than the deviation rate in the auditor's sample, the auditor would most likely assess control risk too high.

#29 (answer "C")

The auditor should document the auditor's understanding of the entity's internal control components which include:

1. Control environment.
2. Risk assessment.
3. Control activities.
4. Information and communication (inclusive of the entity's accounting system).
5. Monitoring.

Such documentation may include flowcharts, questionnaires, narrative memoranda, and/or decision tables.

In addition, for those financial statement assertions where control risk is assessed at the maximum level, documentation may be limited to this assessment. The auditor need not document the basis for concluding that control risk is at the maximum level.

Answer choices other than "C" are based on incorrect assumptions and/or illogical combinations.

#30 (answer "C")

A major concern in executing cash receipts transactions is the possible diversion of cash before there is any documentation of its receipt. Hence, internal controls should provide reasonable assurance that documentation is produced at the moment cash is received.

For mail receipts, documentation consists of remittance advices, checks, and prelistings of mail receipts. Upon receipt in the mailroom, all checks should be restrictively endorsed "for deposit only." Further, a responsible employee should prepare a list of all remittances.

For over-the-counter receipts, documentation consists of cash register tapes, checks, and remittance advices.

As noted above, immediately upon receipt of checks by mail a responsible employee should prepare a remittance listing (i.e., a duplicate listing of checks received). A copy of this listing should be sent to the accounts receivable bookkeeper for posting of remittances in order to update the accounts receivable records.

Answer choice "A" is incorrect because adding the checks to the daily cash summary is not a sound internal control for cash receipts.

Answer choice "B" is incorrect because the check should be supported by a remittance advice, rather than a prenumbered sales invoice.

Answer choice "D" is incorrect because sound internal controls would dictate that checks be recorded in the cash receipts journal by an individual in the accounting department, and not by an individual in the mail room. Persons who have access to the actual receipts (i.e., the checks) should not have access to the books and records pertaining to the receipts.

#31 (answer "A")

If an auditor wishes to assess control risk at below the maximum level, the auditor must perform tests of controls. Four types of procedures used in tests of controls are

1. Inquiries of appropriate entity personnel—Although an inquiry is not generally a strong source of evidence about the effective operation of controls, it is an appropriate source of evidence.
2. Inspection of documents, records, and reports—For example, the auditor examines a customer order and the related approved sales order to ensure that they are complete and properly matched, and that the required signatures or initials are present.
3. Observation—Segregation of duties relies on specific persons performing specific tasks. As such, the auditor generally observes them being applied.
4. Reperformance—Control-related activities for which there are related documents and records, but which contain insufficient data for the auditor's purpose of assessing whether the controls are operating effectively (i.e., client personnel fail to indicate if they have compared prices on a sales invoice to a standard price list). As such, the

auditor would reperform the control activity to ascertain that proper results were obtained.

Accordingly, an auditor tests the segregation of duties related to inventory by <u>personal</u> <u>inquiry</u> <u>and</u> <u>observation</u>.

Answer choices "B" and "C" are incorrect because they represent substantive tests, rather than tests of controls.

Answer choice "D" is incorrect because while inspection of documents is a test of controls for proper authorization, reconciliation is a substantive test rather than a test of controls.

#32 (answer "B")

The failure of a company to process and properly record all sales transactions may seriously affect not only its profitability, but also its customer relations, operating efficiency, and the accuracy of its financial statements. Most companies recognize sales when goods are shipped. A shipping document is prepared at the time of shipment. This document, which is frequently a multicopy bill of lading, is essential to the proper billing of shipments to customers.

In order to prevent the unintentional omission of transactions from the records, and to ensure that sales are recorded in the proper period, it is important that sales be billed and recorded as soon as possible after shipment takes place. Obviously, an effective procedure to verify that <u>shipments</u> <u>to</u> <u>customers</u> <u>were</u> <u>properly</u> <u>invoiced</u> is to trace transactions from selected shipping documents to prenumbered sales invoices. It is also common to compare the dates on selected shipping documents to the dates on related duplicate sales invoices, sales journal entries, and subsidiary ledger entries. Significant differences indicate a potential cutoff problem.

It should be understood that tracing from source documents to the journals represents a test for omitted transactions, whereas tracing from the journals back to supporting documents represents a test for invalid transactions.

Answer choices other than "B" are incorrect because tracing shipping documents to prenumbered sales invoices would not provide the evidence indicated.

#33 (answer "A")

Assessing control risk is the process of evaluating the effectiveness of an entity's internal controls in preventing or detecting material misstatements in the financial statements.

Control risk is the risk that a material misstatement that could occur in an assertion will not be prevented or detected on a timely basis by an entity's internal control.

After obtaining an understanding of internal control and assessing control risk of an entity, an auditor may decide to perform tests of controls. The auditor most likely decided that <u>it</u> <u>would</u> <u>be</u> <u>efficient</u> <u>to</u> <u>perform</u> <u>tests</u> <u>of</u> <u>controls</u> <u>that</u> <u>would</u> <u>result</u> <u>in</u> <u>a</u> <u>reduction</u> <u>in</u> <u>planned</u> <u>substantive</u> <u>tests</u> (i.e., it was cost-beneficial to obtain additional evidence to support a further reduction in control risk).

Answer choice "B" is incorrect because if an auditor decides to perform tests of control, she likely believes that additional evidence to support a further reduction in control risk is available.

Answer choice "C" is incorrect because an auditor generally performs tests of controls when she desires to decrease (and not increase) the assessed level of control risk for certain financial statement assertions.

Answer choice "D" is incorrect because it represents a situation in which the auditor would most likely assess control risk at the maximum level and therefore decide not to perform tests of controls.

#34 (answer "B")

A voucher system is often used to handle cash disbursements. A voucher system helps gain control over cash disbursements by providing a routine that: (1) permits only designated departments and individuals to incur obligations that will result in cash disbursements; (2) establishes procedures for incurring such obligations, and for their verification, approval, and recording; and (3) permits checks to be issued only in payment of properly verified, approved, and recorded obligations.

Typically, upon receipt of a vendor's invoice (which often includes an attached remittance advice), the invoice is checked for mathematical accuracy by the vouchers (accounts) payable department, and then matched against copies of the receiving report, inspection report, purchase order, and purchase requisition. This procedure provides the most effective assurance that recorded purchases are free of material misstatements.

The accounting department is then in a position to approve the invoice, and a voucher (i.e., a request for payment) is prepared. The entire voucher package is then checked and approved by a responsible individual in the vouchers (accounts) payable department, and the amount is posted to the ledger.

After being approved for payment and recorded, a voucher is filed until its due date, at which time it is sent to the company's cashier (i.e., treasurer's department) for payment. A check is then prepared and signed by the treasurer's department. In turn, the check signer should control the mailing of the check and the related remittance advice. The voucher package is then canceled (i.e., stamped "paid," by the treasurer's department) and sent back to the vouchers (accounts) payable department for filing.

Accordingly, to provide assurance that each voucher is submitted and paid only once, an auditor most likely would examine a sample of paid vouchers and determine whether each voucher is stamped "paid" by the check signer.

Answer choice "A" is incorrect because the voucher documentation is assembled prior to payment, and this alone would not preclude duplicate payment.

Answer choice "C" is incorrect because prenumbered and accounted-for vouchers would not prevent duplicate payment.

Answer choice "D" is incorrect because approval for authorized purchases relates to the documentation assembled prior to payment, and would not preclude duplicate payment.

#35 (answer "A")

The objective in determining the sample size for a test of controls is to obtain a sample that will meet desired statistical objectives for each control being tested. The factors that affect the determination of sample size are (1) tolerable deviation rate, (2) risk of assessing control risk too low (i.e.,

sampling risk), and (3) the expected population deviation rate.

The expected population deviation rate has a significant and direct effect on sample size. As the expected population deviation rate increases, more exact information is required and a larger sample size results. Conversely, a smaller sample size would result as the expected population deviation rate decreases.

On the other hand, the tolerable rate and the risk of assessing control risk too low are inversely related to sample size. Accordingly, as these two parameters increase, a decrease in sample size will result.

Answer choices "B" and "D" are incorrect because they are factors that affect the sample size for substantive tests.

Answer choice "C" is incorrect because the auditor would consider the nature and cause of deviations when evaluating the sample results.

#36 (answer "D")

In performing audit tests in accordance with GAAS, the auditor may use either nonstatistical (i.e., judgmental) or statistical sampling, or both. Both types of sampling require the exercise of judgment in planning and executing the sampling plan and evaluating the results. Additionally, both types can provide sufficient evidential matter as required by the third standard of fieldwork, and both are subject to risk.

In nonstatistical sampling, the auditor determines sample size and evaluates sample results entirely on the basis of subjective criteria growing out of his experience. Thus, the auditor may unknowingly use too large a sample in one area and too small a sample in another.

However, statistical sampling should benefit the auditor in designing an efficient sample and measuring the sufficiency of the evidence obtained. That is, statistical methods provide an objective basis for quantitatively evaluating sample risk.

Answer choice "A" is incorrect because use of the sample as a dual-purpose test (i.e., both as a test of controls and as a substantive test) can be done with either statistical or nonstatistical methods.

Answer choice "B" is incorrect because both statistical and nonstatistical methods require use of auditor judgment.

Answer choice "C" is incorrect because both statistical and nonstatistical methods involve risk.

#37 (answer "B")

Substantive tests are comprised of tests of transactions, tests of account balances, and analytical procedures.

Tests of transactions and balances are procedures designed to enable the auditor to obtain evidence as to the validity and propriety of their accounting treatment. Their purpose is to detect the existence of any monetary misstatements.

The tests of transactions of concern to the auditor are:

1. Tests for omitted transactions—Tracing from the source documents to the journals.
2. Tests for invalid transactions—Vouching from the journals back to the supporting source documents.

In the case of payroll, transactions for a pay period start with employees performing their assigned tasks and recording hours worked. The number of hours worked is then converted into gross payroll dollars and recorded along with the related deductions in the payroll journal (i.e., the book of original entry).

When tests of payroll transactions are made, the auditor might vouch the number of hours worked as shown in the payroll register to approved clock card data. This would provide assurance that employees did indeed work the number of hours for which they are paid.

Answer choices other than "B" are incorrect because they refer to assurances that cannot be provided by the procedure described.

#38 (answer "C")

Reportable conditions are those matters coming to the auditor's attention that, in the auditor's judgment, should be communicated to the audit committee (or its equivalent) because they represent significant deficiencies in the design or operation of internal control, which could adversely affect the organization's ability to record, process, summarize, and report financial data consistent with the assertions of management in the financial statements.

A material weakness is a reportable condition in which the design or operation of internal control does not reduce to a relatively low level the risk that material errors or fraud may occur and not be detected timely by employees while performing their assigned functions.

While the communication of reportable conditions is usually made after the audit is concluded, interim communication may be warranted and is acceptable. Accordingly, an auditor may communicate reportable conditions during an audit or after the audit's completion.

The auditor should not issue a report indicating that no reportable conditions were noted during the audit.

The communication may be oral or written. If the auditor chooses to communicate orally, the auditor should document the communication in the working papers.

A written report issued on reportable conditions should:

1. Indicate that the purpose of the audit was to report on the financial statements, and not to provide assurance on internal control.
2. Include the definition of reportable conditions.
3. Include a restriction on the distribution (i.e., the distribution is intended for the audit committee, management, others within the organization, or, under certain circumstances, specific regulatory agencies).
4. Describe the reportable conditions noted.

Answer choice "A" is incorrect because during an audit, an auditor is not required to search for reportable conditions.

Answer choice "B" is incorrect because not all reportable conditions are considered to be material weaknesses; a material weakness is a special type of reportable condition.

Answer choice "D" is incorrect because if no reportable conditions are noted during an audit, no communication concerning reportable conditions should take place.

#39 (answer "C")

The third standard of fieldwork states that sufficient competent evidential matter is to be obtained through inspection, observation, inquiries, and confirmations to afford a reasonable basis for an opinion regarding the financial statements under audit.

Accordingly, evidence must be (1) competent (i.e., it must be both valid (true) and relevant (pertaining to the matter under review)), and (2) sufficient enough to form a conclusion.

The following presumptions about the validity of evidential matter should be considered:

1. Evidential matter obtained from independent sources outside an entity provides greater assurance of reliability than evidence obtained solely from within the organization.
2. The more effective the internal control, the more assurance it provides about the reliability of the accounting data and financial statements.
3. The auditor's direct personal knowledge, obtained through physical examination, observation, computation, and inspection, is more persuasive than information obtained indirectly from independent outside sources.

Bank statements obtained from the client would be the most persuasive type of evidence because they represent evidential matter that was generated outside the entity.

Answer choices other than "C" are incorrect because they represent evidential matter that was generated from within the client organization.

#40 (answer "A")

Management assertions about presentation and disclosure address whether particular components of the financial statements are properly classified, described, and disclosed.

For inventory, management asserts that disclosures, such as flow assumptions used and pledges of inventories resulting from loan agreements, have been properly made in the basic financial statements, and/or the related notes to the financial statements.

For loan agreements, management asserts that restrictions resulting from such agreements have been properly disclosed. The auditor inspects loan agreements to ascertain the existence and

terms of pledges and other restrictions. Therefore, evidence is provided for management's assertion concerning proper presentation and disclosure.

Answer choice "B" is incorrect because management's assertion about valuation or allocation addresses whether the dollar amount of inventory was properly stated.

Answer choice "C" is incorrect because management's assertion about existence or occurrence addresses the validity of recorded inventory or loan balances, or whether transactions have actually occurred.

Answer choice "D" is incorrect because management's assertion about completeness addresses whether all transactions and accounts dealing with inventory or loans that should be reflected in the financial statements are properly included.

#41 (answer "A")

Assertions are representations by management that are embodied in financial statement components. They can be classified as to:

1. Existence or occurrence—addresses whether assets or liabilities of the entity exist at a given date, or whether recorded transactions have occurred during a given period.
2. Completeness—addresses whether all transactions and accounts that should be presented in the financial statements are so included.
3. Rights and obligations—addresses whether assets are the rights of the entity (i.e., owned) at a given time.
4. Valuation or allocation—addresses whether asset, liability, equity, revenue, or expense components have been included in the financial statements at the appropriate amounts.
5. Presentation and disclosure—addresses whether particular components of the financial statements are properly classified, described, and disclosed.

In light of point #4, an auditor most likely would review or recompute amortization and determine whether the amortization period is reasonable in support of management's financial statement assertion of valuation or allocation.

Answer choices other than "A" are incorrect because they represent assertions that are not supported by the auditor's review or recomputation of amortization and determination of the reasonableness of the amortization period.

#42 (answer "C")

Assertions are representations by management that are embodied in financial statement components. They can be classified as to:

1. Existence or occurrence—addresses whether assets or liabilities of the entity exist at a given date and whether recorded transactions have occurred during a given period.
2. Completeness—addresses whether all transactions and accounts that should be presented in the financial statements are so included.
3. Rights and obligations—addresses whether assets are the rights of the entity (i.e., owned) at a given time.
4. Valuation or allocation—addresses whether asset, liability, equity, revenue, or expense components have been included in the financial statements at the appropriate amounts.
5. Presentation and disclosure—addresses whether particular components of the financial statements are properly classified, described, and disclosed.

Purchase cutoff tests are designed to provide reasonable assurance that purchases and accounts payable are recorded in the accounting period in which title to the goods passes to the buyer.

A purchase cutoff test is usually made as of the balance sheet date and involves:

1. Examining receiving documents for several days before and after the cutoff date, as well as determining the date and terms of receipt.
2. Tracing receiving documents to purchases and inventory records to ascertain that entries were made in the correct accounting period.
3. Inspecting vendor invoices to ascertain the validity and propriety of receipts.

Therefore, cutoff tests designed to detect purchases made before the end of the year that have been recorded in the subsequent year most likely would provide assurance about management's assertion of completeness.

Answer choices other than "C" are incorrect because they represent assertions that would not be supported by performing cutoff tests.

#43 (answer "A")

Assertions are representations by management that are embodied in financial statement components. They can be classified as to:

1. Existence or occurrence—addresses whether assets or liabilities of the entity exist at a given date and whether recorded transactions have occurred during a given period.
2. Completeness—addresses whether all transactions and accounts that should be presented in the financial statements are so included.
3. Rights and obligations—addresses whether assets are the rights of the entity (i.e., owned) at a given time.
4. Valuation or allocation—addresses whether asset, liability, equity, revenue, or expense components have been included in the financial statements at the appropriate amounts.
5. Presentation and disclosure—addresses whether particular components of the financial statements are properly classified, described and disclosed.

An auditor's inquiries of production and sales personnel concerning possible obsolete or slow-moving inventory items provide assurance about management's financial statement assertion of valuation or allocation. Based on the responses received, an auditor would then review the write-off and/or write-down of inventory items, in order to gain satisfaction as to the carrying amount of inventory on the balance sheet.

Answer choices other than "A" are incorrect because they represent assertions that would not be supported by inquiries of personnel concerning possible obsolete or slow-moving inventory items.

#44 (answer "B")

Assertions are representations by management that are embodied in financial statement components. They can be classified as to:

1. Existence or occurrence—addresses whether assets or liabilities of the entity exist at a

given date and whether recorded transactions have occurred during a given period.

2. <u>Completeness</u>—addresses whether all transactions and accounts that should be presented in the financial statements are so included.
3. <u>Rights</u> <u>and</u> <u>obligations</u>—addresses whether assets are the rights of the entity (i.e., owned) at a given time.
4. <u>Valuation</u> <u>or</u> <u>allocation</u>—addresses whether asset, liability, equity, revenue, or expense components have been included in the financial statements at the appropriate amounts.
5. <u>Presentation</u> <u>and</u> <u>disclosure</u>—addresses whether particular components of the financial statements are properly classified, described, and disclosed.

Confirmations represent written evidence received directly by the auditor from an independent third party verifying the accuracy of requested information.

Since confirmations come from sources independent of the client, they are the most highly regarded type of evidential matter.

Confirmations provide primary evidence as to the assertions of existence or occurrence and <u>rights</u> <u>and</u> <u>obligations</u>.

Answer choices other than "B" are incorrect because they represent assertions that would not be supported by confirmations of investment securities held by an outside agent.

#45 (answer "A")

Confirmations represent written evidence received directly by the auditor from an independent third party verifying the accuracy of requested information. Since confirmations come from sources independent of the client, they are the most highly regarded type of evidential matter.

Accounts may be confirmed by using the positive form, the negative form, or a combination of both. With the positive form, the respondent is asked to reply directly to the auditor, stating whether the balance as indicated on the request is correct or, if it is incorrect, to indicate the correct balance and any possible explanation for the difference.

The positive form is usually used (1) for individual account balances that are material in amount; (2) when the internal control relating to the assertion is weak; (3) when there is reason to believe that the possibility of disputes or fraud in the accounts is greater than usual; and (4) when there is reason to believe that a negative form will not receive adequate consideration.

With the negative form, the respondent is asked to reply only if the balance, as stated on the request, is not in agreement with its records. This type of request is useful when (1) the assessed level of control risk relating to the assertion is low; (2) a small number of accounts may be in dispute; (3) there are many accounts with small balances; and (4) there are indications that the requests will receive proper consideration.

Although returned negative confirmations may provide evidence about the financial statement assertions, <u>unreturned</u> <u>negative</u> <u>confirmation</u> <u>requests</u> <u>rarely</u> <u>provide</u> <u>significant</u> <u>explicit</u> <u>evidence</u> concerning financial statement assertions, other than certain aspects of the existence assertion. For example, negative confirmations may provide some evidence of the existence of third parties if they are not returned with an indication that the addressees are unknown. However, unreturned negative confirmations do not provide explicit evidence that the intended third parties received the confirmation requests and verified that the information contained on them is correct.

Answer choice "B" is incorrect because the effectiveness of negative confirmation requests is unrelated to the level of detection risk. In any event, when detection risk is low, the auditor wants more audit satisfaction and most likely will want to use positive confirmation requests.

Answer choice "C" is incorrect because no alternative procedures are required when negative confirmation requests are unreturned.

Answer choice "D" is incorrect because positive confirmation requests are more effective than negative confirmation requests when understatements of account balances are suspected.

#46 (answer "C")

Confirmations represent written evidence received directly by the auditor from an independent third party verifying the accuracy of information. Confirmation of accounts receivable balances provides primary evidence as to the rights and obligations, and existence assertions.

Since confirmations come from sources independent of the client, they are the most highly regarded type of evidential matter.

Accounts receivable may be confirmed by using the positive form, the negative form, or a combination of both. With the positive form, the respondent is asked to reply directly to the auditor, stating whether the balance as indicated on the request is correct or, if it is incorrect, to indicate the correct balance and any possible explanation for the difference.

The positive form is usually used (1) for individual account balances that are material in amount; (2) when the internal control relating to the receivables is weak; (3) when there is reason to believe that the possibility of disputes or fraud in the accounts is greater than usual; and (4) when there is reason to believe that a negative form will not receive adequate consideration.

When the auditor has not received replies to positive confirmation requests, she should apply alternative procedures to the nonresponses to obtain evidence necessary to reduce audit risk to an acceptably low level. Accordingly, the auditor most likely would <u>ask the client to contact the customers to request that the confirmations be returned</u>.

Answer choices other than "C" are incorrect because they do not represent procedures that an auditor would perform when she does not receive replies to positive requests for year-end accounts receivable confirmations.

#47 (answer "C")

Analytical procedures consist of evaluations of financial information made by a study of plausible relationships among both financial and nonfinancial data. A basic premise underlying the application of analytical procedures is that plausible relationships among data may reasonably be expected to exist and continue in the absence of known conditions to the contrary.

Analytical procedures:

1. Should be used to assist the auditor in planning the nature, timing, and extent of other auditing procedures.
2. May be used as a substantive test to obtain evidential matter about particular asser-

tions related to account balances or classes of transactions.
3. Should be used to perform an overall review of the financial information in the final review stage of the audit.

The objective of using analytical procedures in the overall review stage of an audit is to assist the auditor in assessing the validity of the conclusions reached. The overall review would generally include reading the financial statements and notes and <u>considering</u> (1) the adequacy of evidence gathered in response to unusual or unexpected balances identified in the planning stage of the audit, and (2) <u>unusual</u> <u>or</u> <u>unexpected account balances</u> or relationships <u>that were not previously identified</u>. Results of an overall review may indicate that additional evidence may be needed.

Answer choices other than "C" are based on incorrect assumptions.

#48 (answer "B")

Analytical procedures involve comparisons of recorded amounts, or ratios developed from recorded amounts, to expectations developed by the auditor. The auditor develops such expectations by identifying and using plausible relationships that are reasonably expected to exist based on the auditor's understanding of the client and the industry in which the client operates.

Following are examples of sources of information for developing expectations:

1. Financial information for comparable prior period(s) giving consideration to known changes.
2. Anticipated results (e.g., budgets, forecasts including extrapolations from interim or annual data, or expected current-year sales).
3. Relationships among elements of financial information within the period (e.g., computing accounts receivable turnover or estimating payroll expense).
4. Information regarding the industry in which the client operates (e.g., gross margin information).
5. Relationships of financial information with relevant nonfinancial information.

Accordingly, <u>projecting an error rate by comparing the results of a statistical sample with the actual</u>

population characteristics is not considered an analytical procedure. Rather, it is a procedure used in statistical sampling to evaluate sample results.

Answer choices other than "B" are incorrect because they represent examples of analytical procedures.

#49 (answer "B")

When planning a particular sample, the auditor should consider the specific audit objective to be achieved and determine that the audit procedure, or combination of procedures, to be applied will achieve that objective. The auditor should determine that the population from which he draws the sample is appropriate for the specific audit objective.

The primary audit objectives met by confirmation of accounts receivable balances concern the existence, and rights and obligations assertions.

Accordingly, the sampling unit for confirmation of accounts receivable, based on the information provided, would be individual invoices.

In the prior year's audit, it appears that the invoices represented valid amounts, although recording errors in posting these invoices evidently occurred. Differences between the valid amounts and the recorded amounts apparently resulted. In the current year's audit, if the auditor chooses individual invoices as the sampling unit, the auditor should be able to identify the differences suspected. If the auditor chooses account balances as the sampling unit, he would not be able to identify the specific differences that relate to individual invoices.

Answer choices other than "B" are incorrect because account balances are chosen as the sampling unit, which is not appropriate in the question situation.

#50 (answer "B")

When using statistical sampling, the auditor should develop an efficient sampling plan. A sampling plan is more efficient if its objectives can be achieved with a smaller sample size. In general, the greater the variability in a population, the greater the sample size required to achieve the objectives of the sampling plan.

For tests of controls, the greater the expected population deviation rate, the larger the sample size required to meet the sampling objectives. For substantive testing, the greater the standard deviation rate, the greater the sample size required to meet the sampling objectives.

The purpose of stratified sampling is to reduce the variability within the population to be estimated. This is done by dividing the population, often by relative dollar amounts, into several groups (i.e., subpopulations or strata), and then sampling from each group, using techniques such as unrestricted random sampling within the strata.

Stratified sampling is particularly appropriate when the population characteristic is widely scattered, skewed in one direction, or clustered around a few points, such as large dollar amounts. In a given population, unusually large dollar-value items may be segregated and then a high percentage of items in this group tested. The purpose of this stratification is to achieve the smallest possible standard deviation in dollars.

Thus, the auditor would most likely stratify a population into meaningful groups (i.e., subpopulations) if the population has highly variable recorded amounts.

Answer choice "A" is incorrect because stratification of the population is built into PPS sampling; therefore, an auditor will not need to stratify the population into meaningful groups.

Answer choice "C" is incorrect because tolerable misstatement is used to determine the sample size once the (sub)population to be sampled is identified.

Answer choice "D" is incorrect because stratification is not necessary if the standard deviation (i.e., the variability) of recorded amounts is relatively small.

#51 (answer "A")

Ratio estimation is a variable sampling technique based on random item selection. Variable sampling is used in substantive testing when there are numerous errors, and will yield an answer in dollar amounts. In ratio estimation sampling, the auditor determines an audit value for each item in the sample. A ratio is then calculated by dividing the sum of the audit values by the sum of the book values to arrive at an estimate of the total population value.

Ratio estimation sampling is most effective when the calculated audit amounts (and the resultant dollar amount of errors) are approximately (i.e., expected to be) proportional to the client's book amounts (i.e., values).

Answer choices other than "A" are based on incorrect assumptions regarding the use of the ratio estimation sampling technique.

#52 (answer "D")

Observing a client's annual physical inventory is useful in determining whether recorded inventory actually exists at the balance sheet date and is properly counted by the client. Regardless of the client's inventory record-keeping method, there must be a periodic physical count of the inventory items on hand.

If the auditor recorded test counts for several items and noted that such counts were higher than the recorded quantities in the client's perpetual records, then goods are being added to inventory without being recorded. This situation could be the result of the client's acceptance of goods returned by customers along with a failure to record sales returns.

Answer choice "A" is incorrect because failure to record purchase discounts would not affect the physical balance of goods on hand.

Answer choices "B" and "C" are incorrect because failure to record either purchase returns or sales would result in test counts that are lower than the recorded amounts.

#53 (answer "C")

Assertions are representations by management that are embodied in financial statement components. They can be classified as to:

1. Existence or occurrence—addresses whether assets or liabilities of the entity exist at a given date, or whether recorded transactions have occurred during a given period.
2. Completeness—addresses whether all transactions and accounts that should be presented in the financial statements are so included.
3. Rights and obligations—addresses whether assets are the rights of the entity (i.e., owned) at a given time.

4. Valuation or allocation—addresses whether asset, liability, equity, revenue, or expense components have been included in the financial statements at the appropriate amounts.
5. Presentation and disclosure—addresses whether particular components of the financial statements are properly classified, described, and disclosed.

To gain assurance that all inventory items in a client's inventory listing schedule are valid (i.e., actually exist), an auditor most likely would trace items listed in the inventory listing schedule to inventory tags and the auditor's recorded count sheets.

Answer choices other than "C" are incorrect because they represent procedures that would not provide assurance regarding the validity (i.e., the existence) of inventory.

#54 (answer "D")

In auditing payroll, there is generally a minimal risk of material misstatement, even though payroll is frequently a significant expense.

The risk is generally low because employees will notify someone if they are underpaid, and payroll transactions are typically uniform.

In the audit, tests of transactions are often used to verify account balances for payroll. Tests of transactions are performed due to the lack of independent third-party evidence (such as confirmation) for verifying accrued wages, withheld income taxes, accrued payroll taxes, and other balance sheet accounts. In addition, amounts in the balance sheet accounts may be comparatively small and can be readily verified if the auditor assesses control risk at a low level for assertions related to payroll.

Accordingly, when control risk is assessed as low for assertions related to payroll, substantive tests of payroll balances most likely would be limited to applying analytical procedures and recalculating payroll accruals.

Answer choice "A" is incorrect because it represents a test of controls, rather than a substantive test of payroll balances.

Answer choice "B" is incorrect because footing and crossfooting the payroll register only provides evidence as to the mathematical validity of totals in the register and would not provide assurance about payroll balances.

Answer choice "C" is incorrect because the auditor's procedures would most likely include inspection of payroll tax returns when control risk is assessed as high for payroll assertions.

#55 (answer "A")

Audit procedures to search for unrecorded retirements of fixed assets would relate to management's assertion of existence (i.e., whether fixed assets of the entity exist). An auditor would most likely inspect the property ledger and the insurance and tax records and then tour the client's facilities to obtain evidence about assets that had been retired but that had not been removed from the accounting records.

Answer choice "B" is incorrect because a tour of the client's facilities, and then inspection of the property ledger and the insurance and tax records, is useful in searching for unrecorded additions of fixed assets (i.e., the completeness assertion).

Answer choice "C" is incorrect because analysis of the repair and maintenance account would not provide evidence pertaining to unrecorded retirements of fixed assets.

Answer choice "D" is incorrect because a tour of the client's facilities, and then analysis of the repair and maintenance account, only provides evidence concerning the reasonableness of the repair and maintenance expense.

#56 (answer "D")

The statement of cash flows should report:

1. Net cash provided or used by operating, investing, and financing activities and the net effect of those flows on cash and cash equivalents during the period. The total amount of cash and cash equivalents shown in the statement of cash flows should agree with the corresponding amount shown in the balance sheet.
2. A reconciliation of net income to net cash flows from operating activities, regardless of whether the direct or indirect method is used.

Accordingly, in auditing the statement of cash flows, an auditor would most likely reconcile the amounts included in the statement of cash flows to the other financial statements' (i.e., the balance sheet and income statement) balances and amounts.

Answer choices other than "D" are based on incorrect assumptions.

#57 (answer "C")

Substantive tests are comprised of tests of transactions, tests of account balances, and analytical procedures.

Tests of transactions and balances are procedures designed to enable the auditor to obtain evidence as to the validity and propriety of their accounting treatment. Their purpose is to detect the existence of any monetary misstatements.

The tests of transactions of concern to the auditor are:

1. Tests for omitted transactions—Tracing from the source documents to the journals.
2. Tests for invalid transactions—Vouching from the journals back to the supporting source documents.

Accordingly, in determining whether transactions have been recorded (i.e., in testing the completeness assertion), the direction of the audit testing should be from the original source documents.

Answer choices other than "C" are incorrect because they represent sources of audit testing for the existence or validity of transactions (i.e., existence or occurrence assertion).

#58 (answer "C")

A review engagement is not an audit. A review does not provide a basis for expressing an opinion on the fairness of financial statements since it is not conducted under GAAS. The purpose of a review is to provide the accountant with a basis for expressing limited assurance that the financial statements conform to GAAP (or another comprehensive basis of accounting).

During a review engagement, through inquiries and analytical procedures, the accountant should obtain an understanding of the entity's business that will provide her with a reasonable basis for expressing limited assurance that no material modifications should be made to the financial statements in order for the financial statements to be in conformity with GAAP. Such inquiries and analytical procedures involve the following areas:

1. Entity accounting principles and practices.
2. Financial recording and financial statement preparation practices.
3. Procedures designed to identify items that appear to be unusual (e.g., comparisons with prior statements, budgets, predictable patterns).
4. Stockholders' and directors' meetings.
5. Conformity to GAAP.
6. Reports from other accountants, when applicable.
7. Persons having responsibility for financial matters, including subsequent-event knowledge.
8. A representation letter must be obtained from the chief executive and financial officers.

In accordance with point #1 above, during a review of a nonpublic entity's financial statements, the accountant should obtain a sufficient level of knowledge and understand the accounting principles and practices of the industry in which the entity operates.

Answer choices other than "C" are incorrect because they represent procedures applicable to an audit engagement.

#59 (answer "C")

The independent auditor may consider using the work of internal auditors and using internal auditors to provide direct assistance to the auditor in an audit performed in accordance with GAAS.

The auditor should consider such factors as whether the internal auditors':

1. Scope of work is appropriate to meet the objectives.
2. Audit programs are adequate.
3. Working papers adequately document work performed, including evidence of supervision and review.
4. Conclusions are appropriate in the circumstances.
5. Reports are consistent with the results of the work performed.

Because the independent auditor has the ultimate responsibility to express an opinion on the finan-

cial statements, the independent auditor is responsible for judgments about assessments of inherent and control risks, the materiality of misstatements, the sufficiency of tests performed, the evaluation of significant accounting estimates, and other matters affecting the auditor's report.

For assertions related to material financial statement amounts, where the risk of material misstatement, or the degree of subjectivity involved in the evaluation of the audit evidence, is high, the consideration of the internal auditors' work cannot alone reduce the audit risk to a level that will eliminate the necessity to perform tests of those assertions directly by the independent auditor.

Assertions that might have a high risk of material misstatement or involve a high degree of subjectivity in the evaluation of audit evidence include the valuation of assets and liabilities involving significant accounting estimates, and the existence and disclosure of related-party transactions, contingencies, uncertainties, and subsequent events.

Accordingly, the internal auditors' work would most likely relate to assertions where the risk of material misstatement is not high or the degree of subjectivity in the evaluation of audit evidence is low (e.g., the existence of fixed asset additions).

Answer choices other than "C" are incorrect because they represent situations where the risk of material misstatement is high or situations that involve a high degree of subjectivity in the evaluation of audit evidence.

#60 (answer "D")

The independent auditor may consider using the work of internal auditors and using internal auditors to provide direct assistance to the auditor in an audit performed in accordance with GAAS.

The internal auditors' work may affect the nature, timing, and extent of the audit, including:

1. Obtaining an understanding of internal control.
2. Performing tests of controls when assessing risk.
3. Performing substantive tests.

Answer choices other than "D" are based on incorrect assumptions and/or illogical combinations.

#61 (answer "A")

The auditor may decide to use the work of a specialist when, in his judgment, complex or subjective matters that are material to the financial statements require special skill or knowledge to obtain competent evidential matter.

Areas that may require using the work of a specialist include:

1. Valuation (e.g., special-purpose inventories).
2. Determination of physical characteristics (e.g., mineral reserves).
3. Derivation of amounts by using specialized techniques (e.g., actuarial determinations).
4. Interpretation of technical requirements, regulations, or agreements (e.g., potential significance of contracts).

To determine the specialist's professional qualifications, the auditor should consider:

1. Professional certification.
2. Reputation and standing.
3. Experience in the type of work.

The auditor should obtain an understanding of the specialist's work. This understanding should cover:

1. Objective and scope.
2. Methods or assumptions used and a comparison with those used in the preceding period.
3. Appropriateness for the intended audit purpose.
4. Form and content of the specialist's findings for use in the audit.

When considering the use of a particular specialist, the auditor should evaluate the relationship, if any, of the specialist to the client, including circumstances that might impair the specialist's objectivity.

If the specialist has a relationship with the client, the auditor should assess the risk that the specialist's objectivity might be impaired. If objectivity might be impaired, the auditor should either perform additional procedures to determine the reasonableness of findings or engage another specialist.

Accordingly, the work of a specialist who is related to the client may be acceptable under certain circumstances.

The auditor will ordinarily use the work of a specialist unless the auditor's procedures lead to the belief that the specialist's findings are unreasonable, in which case the auditor should apply additional procedures that may include obtaining the opinion of another specialist.

If there is a material difference between the specialist's findings and the financial statement assertions, the auditor should:

1. Apply additional procedures.
2. Obtain the opinion of another specialist, if still not satisfied.

If the matter is still unresolved, the auditor should qualify or disclaim an opinion because of the inability to obtain sufficient competent evidential matter as to an assertion of material significance.

If the auditor concludes that the assertions in the financial statements are not in conformity with generally accepted accounting principles, a qualified or adverse opinion should be expressed.

Answer choice "B" is incorrect because if an auditor believes that the determinations made by a specialist are unreasonable, she should apply additional procedures, which may include obtaining the opinion of another specialist.

Answer choice "C" is incorrect because if there is a material difference between a specialist's findings and the assertions in the financial statements, the auditor may (1) apply additional procedures, (2) obtain the opinion of another specialist, or (3) issue a qualified or adverse opinion.

Answer choice "D" is incorrect because the determination of physical characteristics relating to inventories is an appropriate use of a specialist.

#62 (answer "A")

A specialist possesses special skill or knowledge in a field other than accounting or auditing (e.g., an actuary, appraiser, engineer, or attorney).

When expressing an unqualified opinion, the auditor should generally not refer to the work or findings of a specialist. Such reference might be construed as a qualification of the auditor's opinion or a division of responsibility, neither of which is intended.

If an auditor, as a result of the report or findings of the specialist, decides to (1) add an explanatory paragraph describing an uncertainty, (2) add an explanatory paragraph describing the auditor's substantial doubt about the entity's ability to continue as a going concern, (3) add an explanatory paragraph to emphasize a matter regarding the financial statements, or (4) depart from an unqualified opinion, reference to and identification of the specialist may be made in the auditor's report if the auditor believes such reference will facilitate an understanding of the reason for the explanatory paragraph or the departure from the unqualified opinion.

Answer choices other than "A" are incorrect because none of the circumstances support making a reference to the specialist in the auditor's report.

#63 (answer "B")

Since the events or conditions that should be considered in the financial accounting for and reporting of litigation, claims, and assessments are matters within the direct knowledge and, often, control of management of an entity, management is the primary source of information about litigation, claims, and assessments.

A letter of audit inquiry sent to the client's lawyer is the auditor's primary means of obtaining corroboration of the information furnished by management concerning litigation, claims, and assessments. Evidential matter obtained from the client's legal department may provide the auditor with some corroboration, but it is not a substitute for information that should be obtained from the outside counsel, which represents an independent source.

A lawyer may appropriately limit her response to matters to which the lawyer has given substantive attention.

A lawyer may also limit her response to matters considered individually or collectively material to financial statements.

A lawyer's refusal to furnish requested information would be a limitation on the scope of the audit, sufficient to preclude an unqualified opinion.

The lawyer may be unable to respond because of inherent uncertainties. The auditor, in turn, will conclude that the outcome of a future event is thus not susceptible to reasonable estimation. If substantial doubt remains, the audit report should include an explanatory paragraph, following the unqualified opinion paragraph, to reflect that conclusion. The report, although modified, is still unqualified.

Answer choice "A" is incorrect because the refusal of a client's attorney to provide information requested in an inquiry letter represents a scope limitation that will generally result in the expression of either a qualified opinion or a disclaimer of opinion.

Answer choice "C" is incorrect because the situation described is not a reason to withdraw from the engagement. Rather, it is appropriate to express either a qualified opinion or a disclaimer of opinion.

Answer choice "D" is incorrect because the refusal of a client's attorney to respond to an inquiry letter is unrelated to the client's internal control, and accordingly, would not be equivalent to a reportable condition.

#64 (this question is obsolete)

#65 (answer "D")

The auditor should perform auditing procedures with respect to the period after the balance sheet date for the purpose of ascertaining the occurrence of subsequent events that may require either adjustments to or disclosures in the financial statements in order for them to be in conformity with GAAP.

The procedures generally performed by the auditor to ascertain the existence of subsequent events occur at or near the completion of fieldwork, and include:

1. Reading the latest available interim statements.
2. Inquiring and discussing with officers and other executives having responsibility for financial and accounting matters, such as:
   a. Substantial contingent liabilities.
   b. Significant changes in capital stock, long-term debt, or working capital.
   c. Unusual adjustments.
3. Reading the available minutes of meetings of stockholders and the board of directors.
4. Inquiring of client's attorneys concerning any pending litigation, unasserted claims, or assessments.
5. Obtaining a letter of representation.
6. Any other additional inquiries or procedures considered necessary.

In light of point # 2.b. above, the auditor would most likely <u>investigate</u> <u>changes</u> <u>in</u> <u>long-term</u> <u>debt</u> <u>occurring</u> <u>after</u> <u>year-end</u>.

Answer choices other than "D" are incorrect because they refer to procedures that do not provide evidence about subsequent events.

<u>#66 (answer "A")</u>

As part of an audit performed under GAAS, the independent auditor is required to obtain certain written representations from management. Such representations are part of the evidential matter the independent auditor obtains, but they are not a substitute for the application of other auditing procedures necessary to afford a reasonable basis for an opinion on the financial statements. Representations cover such matters as:

1. Acknowledgment of management's responsibility for the financial statements.
2. Completeness and availability of the accounting records and minutes of meetings of stockholders, directors, and audit committees.
3. The absence of unrecorded transactions, and errors and fraud in the financial statements.
4. Noncompliance with aspects of contractual agreements or regulatory reporting practices that may affect the financial statements.
5. Information concerning related party transactions and related amounts receivable or payable.
6. Information concerning subsequent events.
7. Management's plans or intentions that may affect the carrying value or classification of assets or liabilities.
8. Disclosure of compensating balances or other arrangements involving restrictions on cash balances.
9. Fraud involving management or employees.
10. Satisfactory title to assets, liens on assets, and assets pledged as collateral.
11. Losses from purchase commitments for inventory quantities in excess of normal requirements or at prices in excess of market.
12. Losses from sales commitments.
13. Unasserted claims or assessments.

Management's representations may be limited to matters that are considered, either individually or collectively, material to the financial statements, provided management and the auditor have reached an understanding on the limits of materiality for this purpose.

Materiality limits would not apply to the representations in points #1 and #2 above (i.e., acknowledgment of management's responsibility for the financial statements, and completeness and <u>availability</u> <u>of</u> the accounting records and <u>minutes</u> <u>of</u> <u>meetings</u> <u>of</u> <u>stockholders</u> <u>directors</u>, and audit committees) because those representations are not directly related to amounts included in the financial statements.

In addition, because of the possible effects of fraud on other aspects of the audit, a materiality limit would not apply to fraud involving management or employees (i.e., point #9 above).

Answer choices other than "A" are incorrect because they refer to representations that would be subject to materiality limits.

<u>#67 (answer "C")</u>

As part of an audit performed under GAAS, the independent auditor is required to obtain certain written representations from management. Such representations are part of the evidential matter the independent auditor obtains, but they are not a substitute for the application of other auditing procedures necessary to afford a reasonable basis for an opinion on the financial statements.

The auditor may rely on the representation letter's truthfulness, unless evidential matter to the contrary is revealed.

The management representation letter is addressed to the auditor, with <u>dating</u> <u>to</u> <u>coincide</u> <u>with</u> <u>the</u> <u>date</u> <u>of</u> <u>the</u> <u>auditor's</u> <u>report</u>, and signed by responsible management, usually the chief executive and financial officers.

Answer choices other than "C" are incorrect because they refer to dates that are inappropriate for the management representation letter.

<u>#68 (answer "D")</u>

A related party relationship exists when one party, directly or indirectly, has the ability to influence the management or operating policies of another party so significantly that one of the parties might be prevented from fully pursuing its own separate interests.

Established accounting principles ordinarily do not require transactions with related parties to be accounted for on a basis different from that which would be appropriate if the parties were not related. The auditor should view related party transactions within the framework of existing pronouncements, placing primary emphasis on evaluating the adequacy of disclosure of the related party transactions. In addition, the auditor should be aware that the substance of a particular transaction could be significantly different from its form, and that the financial statements should recognize the substance of a particular transaction, rather than merely its legal form.

Answer choices other than "D" are incorrect because, although they represent valid procedures applicable to related party transactions, they are secondary in nature.

#69 (answer "D")

The auditor is responsible for evaluating the reasonableness of accounting estimates made by management (e.g., allowance for doubtful accounts, warranty expenses, and so on). When planning and performing procedures to evaluate accounting estimates, the auditor should consider, with an attitude of professional skepticism, both subjective and objective factors.

When evaluating accounting estimates, the auditor's objective is to obtain sufficient competent evidential matter to provide reasonable assurance that:

1. All accounting estimates that could be material to the financial statements have been developed.
2. The accounting estimates are reasonable in the circumstances.
3. The accounting estimates are presented in conformity with GAAP and are properly disclosed.

In evaluating management's accounting estimates for reasonableness, the auditor should obtain an understanding of how management developed its estimates. Based on that understanding, the auditor should consider:

1. Reviewing and testing the process used by management to develop the estimate.
2. Developing an independent expectation of the estimate to corroborate the reasonableness of management's estimate.

3. Reviewing subsequent events or transactions.

Answer choices other than "D" are incorrect because they represent procedures that the auditor would ordinarily perform after obtaining an understanding of how management developed its estimates.

#70 (answer "A")

The quantity, type, and content of working papers varies with the circumstances of the particular engagement.

The content of an individual working paper or group of related papers should include identification of (1) the source of the information presented (e.g., fixed assets ledger, cash disbursements journal), (2) the nature and extent of the work done and conclusions reached (by symbols and legend narrative, or a combination of both), and (3) appropriate cross-references to other working papers.

To save time and avoid unnecessary detail in working paper preparation, asset (or liability) accounts and their related expense or income accounts are often analyzed on the same working paper. Examples include property, plant, and equipment, accumulated depreciation and related depreciation expense; notes receivable, accrued interest receivable, and interest income; notes payable, accrued or prepaid interest, and interest expense; and accrued taxes and related provisions for tax expense.

Answer choices other than "A" are incorrect because they do not represent pairs of accounts that an auditor would likely analyze on the same working paper.

#71 (answer "A")

Working papers constitute the main record of the work performed and the conclusions reached by the auditor. As such they:

1. Provide the principal support for the auditor's report.
2. Document observance of fieldwork standards.
3. Aid in the conduct and supervision of the audit.

The working papers should be sufficient to show that the accounting records agree or reconcile with the financial statements, or other information reported on, and that the standards of fieldwork have been observed. The quantity, type, and content of working papers varies with the circumstances of the particular engagement.

Answer choice "B" is incorrect because the working papers document observance of fieldwork standards, rather than adherence to the Code of Professional Conduct.

Answer choice "C" is incorrect because the firm's quality control procedures include review of the audit working papers.

Answer choice "D" is incorrect because the auditor's level of independence is not documented in the working papers since the auditor must be independent in order to undertake the audit engagement.

#72 (answer "B")

The objective of using the test data approach is to determine whether the client's computer programs can correctly handle valid and invalid transactions as they arise. To fulfill this objective, the auditor-developed <u>test data</u> (i.e., input for different types of transactions) <u>are processed by the client's computer programs under the auditor's control</u>.

Answer choice "A" is incorrect because only one transaction of each type need be tested to ascertain that the program can identify the invalid transactions.

Answer choice "C" is incorrect because preparing test data consisting of all possible valid and invalid conditions would not be warranted, and probably would be impossible to do from a cost/benefit point of view.

Answer choice "D" is incorrect because the program tested must be the same as the program used throughout the year by the client.

#73 (answer "A")

Interim testing (i.e., testing before the balance sheet date) increases the risk that misstatements may exist at year-end and not be detected. The greater the time remaining to year-end, the greater the risk.

Difficulty in controlling incremental audit risk should be judged by:

1. The existence of rapidly changing business circumstances that might cause management-misstatement in the remaining period.
2. Whether account balances are reasonably predictable as to amount, composition, and relative significance.
3. Whether the accounting system will permit investigation of unusual transactions, fluctuations, or changes in composition.
4. Whether the entity's procedures for analyzing and adjusting accounts at interim dates and establishing proper cutoffs are appropriate.

Accounts payable are not reasonably predictable as to amount, composition, and relative significance.

Accordingly, <u>confirmation of accounts payable would least likely be performed before the balance sheet date</u>.

Answer choices other than "A" are incorrect because they represent procedures that could be performed before the balance sheet date.

#74 (answer "C")

Analytical procedures consist of evaluation of financial information made by a study of plausible relationships among both financial and nonfinancial data. A basic premise underlying the application of analytical procedures is that plausible relationships among data may reasonably be expected to exist and continue in the absence of known conditions to the contrary.

Analytical procedures involve comparisons of recorded amounts, or ratios developed from recorded amounts, to expectations developed by the auditor, including the following:

1. Comparison of financial information with information for comparable prior period(s).
2. Comparison of financial information with anticipated results (e.g., budgets and forecasts).
3. Study of the relationships among elements of financial information that would be expected to conform to a predictable pattern based on the entity's experience.
4. Comparison of financial information with similar information regarding the industry in which the entity operates.

5. Study of the relationships of the financial information with relevant nonfinancial information.

In view of point #3 above, <u>ratio analysis</u> would most likely be used by an auditor in developing relationships among balance sheet accounts (i.e., elements of financial information).

Answer choices other than "C" are incorrect because they do not represent analytical procedures the auditor is likely to apply to balance sheet accounts in reviewing financial statements.

#75 (answer "A")

During a compilation, the accountant is not required to make inquiries or perform other procedures (including analytical procedures), or to verify, corroborate, or review information supplied by the entity. Before issuing his report on compiled financial statements, the accountant should <u>read the financial statements to consider whether they are free of obvious</u> material <u>mistakes in the application of accounting principles</u>.

Answer choices other than "A" are incorrect because they represent procedures that the accountant is not required to perform in a compilation engagement of a nonpublic entity.

#76 (answer "B")

The additional reporting standards under "Government Auditing Standards" require the auditor to either (1) describe the scope of the auditor's testing of internal controls and present the results of those tests, or (2) refer to separate reports containing that information.

Accordingly, an auditor most likely would be responsible for communicating significant deficiencies in the design of internal control <u>to specific legislative and regulatory bodies when reporting under "Government Auditing Standards</u>."

Answer choices other than "B" are incorrect because they represent parties to which an auditor would not likely communicate significant deficiencies in the design of internal control.

#77 (answer "D")

When part of the audit is performed by another auditor, the principal auditor must be able to gain satisfaction as to the independence and professional reputation of the other CPA, as well as to the quality of the audit. Having done so, the principal auditor must then decide whether she is willing to express an opinion on the financial statements taken as a whole without referring to the audit of the other auditor. A standard audit report is issued when the principal auditor decides not to make reference to the other auditor.

Generally, no reference to the other auditor is necessary when:

1. The other auditor is associated with the principal auditor.
2. The principal auditor retained, supervised, or guided and controlled the other auditor.
3. The principal auditor is satisfied as to the work of the other auditor.
4. The work of the other auditor is not material in relation to the financial statements.

Based on the above, the principal auditor would be justified in her decision not to make reference to another CPA if the principal auditor is also satisfied as to the independence and professional reputation of the other CPA. The principal auditor would then consider whether to perform one or more of the following procedures:

1. <u>Contact the other auditor</u> and discuss the audit procedures followed and results thereof.
2. <u>Review the audit programs</u> of the other auditor. In some cases, it may be appropriate to issue instructions to the other auditor as to the scope of her audit work.
3. <u>Review the working papers</u> of the other auditor, including the understanding of internal control and the assessment of control risk.

Answer choice "A" is incorrect because the principal auditor would not add an explanatory paragraph for immaterial items, or otherwise modify the standard report, if the principal auditor decides not to refer to the audit of another CPA.

Answer choice "B" is incorrect because the principal auditor assumes responsibility for the other CPA's work when the principal auditor decides not to refer to the audit of another CPA.

Answer choice "C" is incorrect because the principal auditor decides whether or not to make reference to the work of another auditor; permission is needed only if the principal auditor wishes to name the other auditor in the principal auditor's report.

#78 (answer "B")

A compilation of financial statements is an accounting service, provided to a nonpublic entity, in which an accountant prepares or assists in preparing financial statements without expressing any assurance that the statements are accurate, complete, or in conformity with GAAP.

The accountant's compilation report, which should accompany the financial statements, should state that:

1. A compilation was performed by the accountant in accordance with Statements on Standards for Accounting and Review Services issued by the AICPA.
2. A compilation is limited to presenting, in the form of financial statements, information that is the representation of management.
3. No audit or review has taken place, and the accountant does not express an opinion or any other form of assurance on the statements.
4. The report date is the date on which the compilation was completed.

Furthermore, each page of the financial statements should be marked, "See Accountant's Compilation Report."

Answer choice "A" is incorrect because an audit, and not a compilation, includes assessing the accounting principles used and significant management estimates, as well as evaluating the overall financial statement presentation.

Answer choice "C" is incorrect because it represents a statement that is not appropriate for inclusion in a compilation report.

Answer choice "D" is incorrect because it refers to limited assurance, which is expressed in a review report. An accountant does not express limited assurance or any other form of assurance in a compilation report.

#79 (answer "B")

The accountant is required to issue a report whenever he completes a review of financial statements of a nonpublic entity. An accountant may issue a review report on one financial statement (such as a balance sheet) and not on other related financial statements (such as the statements of income, retained earnings, and cash flows), provided the scope of the inquiry and analytical procedures has not been restricted.

Answer choice "A" is incorrect because the balance sheet does not have to be presented in a prescribed form of an industry trade association in order for Moore to issue a review report on the balance sheet only.

Answer choice "C" is incorrect because the balance sheet may be used to obtain credit or distributed to creditors as long as it is accompanied by the appropriate review report.

Answer choice "D" is incorrect because Moore may issue the review report even if the specialized accounting principles and practices of Dover's industry are not disclosed, provided the review report is modified to indicate the lack of disclosure.

#80 (answer "C")

A review engagement is substantially less in scope than an audit conducted in conformity with GAAS, and does not provide a basis for expressing an opinion on the fairness of the financial statements.

The purpose of a review is to provide the accountant with a basis for expressing limited assurance that the financial statements conform to GAAP (or to a comprehensive basis of accounting other than GAAP).

A review report should state that:

1. A review was performed in accordance with Statements on Standards for Accounting and Review Services issued by the AICPA.
2. All information included in the financial statements is the representation of the management (owners) of the entity.
3. A review consists principally of inquiries of company personnel and analytical procedures applied to financial data.
4. A review is substantially less in scope than an audit, the objective of which is the expression of an opinion regarding the financial statements taken as a whole and, accordingly, no such opinion is expressed.
5. The accountant is not aware of any material modifications that should be made to the financial statements in order for them to be in conformity with GAAP.

In addition, each page of the financial statements should be marked "See Accountant's Review Report."

If the accountant believes that modification of the standard review report is not adequate to indicate the deficiencies in the financial statements taken as a whole, the accountant should <u>withdraw from the engagement</u> and provide no further services with respect to those financial statements. The accountant may wish to consult with legal counsel in those circumstances.

Answer choices other than "C" are incorrect because an accountant may not express any type of opinion, nor may she disclaim an opinion, when engaged to perform a review of financial statements.

#81 (answer "C")

A review engagement is substantially less in scope than an audit conducted in conformity with GAAS, and does not provide a basis for expressing an opinion on the fairness of the financial statements.

The purpose of a review is to provide the accountant with a basis for expressing limited assurance that the financial statements conform to GAAP (or to a comprehensive basis of accounting other than GAAP).

A review report should state that:

1. A review was performed in accordance with Statements on Standards for Accounting and Review Services issued by the AICPA.
2. All information included in the financial statements is the representation of the management (owners) of the entity.
3. A review consists principally of inquiries of company personnel and analytical procedures applied to financial data.
4. A review is substantially less in scope than an audit, the objective of which is the expression of an opinion regarding the financial statements taken as a whole and, accordingly, no such opinion is expressed.
5. The accountant is not aware of any material modifications that should be made to the financial statements in order for them to be in conformity with GAAP.

In addition, each page of the financial statements should be marked "See Accountant's Review Report."

Answer choices other than "C" are incorrect because they represent references that are not appropriate for reviewed financial statements.

#82 (answer "B")

When reporting on financial statements prepared in conformity with a comprehensive basis of accounting other than GAAP, such as the cash basis of accounting, an independent auditor should include the following paragraphs in a special report:

1. Paragraph stating that the financial statements:
   a. Identified in the report were audited.
   b. Are the responsibility of management; auditor is responsible for expressing an opinion.
2. Paragraph stating that the:
   a. Audit was conducted in accordance with GAAS.
   b. Auditor is required to plan and perform the audit to obtain reasonable assurance that financial statements are free of material misstatement.
   c. Audit includes examining, on a test basis, evidence supporting the amounts and disclosures in the financial statements, assessing accounting principles used, and significant estimates made by management, and evaluating overall presentation.
3. Paragraph stating the basis of presentation:
   a. Including a reference to the note to the financial statements describing the basis.
   b. Is a comprehensive basis of accounting other than GAAP.
4. Paragraph expressing the auditor's opinion (or disclaiming an opinion) on whether the financial statements are presented fairly, in all material respects, in conformity with the basis of accounting described in the relevant note to the financial statements.

Based on the above, the auditor's report on financial statements prepared on the cash receipts and disbursements basis of accounting <u>should not include a statement that the cash receipts and disbursements basis of accounting is not a comprehensive basis of accounting</u>.

Answer choices other than "B" are incorrect because they represent statements that should be included in an auditor's report on financial statements prepared on the cash receipts and disbursements basis of accounting.

#83 (answer "A")

A review of interim financial information of a public entity is substantially less in scope than an audit. It does not provide the basis for expressing an opinion, since it omits many standard audit procedures. Its objective is to provide an accountant with a basis for reporting to the board of directors or stockholders whether material modifications should be made for such information to conform with generally accepted accounting principles.

Answer choice "B" is incorrect because a review does not provide a reasonable basis for the expression of an updated opinion on financial statements that were previously audited.

Answer choice "C" is incorrect because a review does not provide a basis for determining what should be included in a registration statement.

Answer choice "D" is incorrect because only an audit would provide a basis for reporting whether the financial statements are presented fairly in accordance with generally accepted accounting principles.

#84 (answer "D")

In reporting on an entity's internal control over financial reporting, a practitioner should use the following report format:

1. A title that includes the word independent.
2. An identification of management's assertion concerning the entity's internal control effectiveness and the date to which the opinion relates.
3. A description of the scope of the engagement.
4. A statement that the practitioner believes the examination provides a reasonable basis for her opinion.
5. An explanation of the objectives and inherent limitations of internal control.
6. An opinion as to management's assertion about the entity's internal control effectiveness.

Answer choices other than "D" are incorrect because they represent paragraphs that should not be included in a report on an entity's internal control over financial reporting.

#85 (answer "C")

If, after issuing his report, the independent auditor concludes that an auditing procedure considered necessary at the time of the audit was omitted from such audit, the auditor should first assess the importance of the omitted procedure to his present ability to support the opinion expressed on the financial statements taken as a whole.

To accomplish this, the auditor should review the working papers, make necessary inquiries, and reevaluate the overall scope of the audit. The auditor need not apply the omitted procedure if the results of other procedures that were applied tend to compensate for the procedure omitted, or make its omission less important. Also, subsequent audits may provide audit evidence in support of the previously expressed opinion.

If the auditor concludes that his present ability to support the previously expressed opinion is impaired, the auditor should promptly undertake to apply the omitted procedure, or apply an alternative procedure that would provide a satisfactory basis for the opinion.

Answer choice "A" is incorrect because the distribution of the audit report does not determine whether an omitted audit procedure need be applied.

Answer choice "B" is incorrect because the type of opinion expressed does not determine whether an omitted audit procedure need be applied.

Answer choice "D" is incorrect because the auditor still needs to apply the omitted procedure if his ability to support the previously expressed opinion is impaired, even though the omission is due to unreasonable delays by client personnel in providing data on a timely basis.

#86 (answer "B")

A "comfort letter" is a letter written by the accountant and sent to an underwriter of securities during client registration procedures with the SEC. The letter is so named because it is designed to give comfort (i.e., assurance) to underwriters that the financial and accounting data not covered by the auditor's opinion on the financial statements, but included in the prospectus, are (1) in compliance with the Securities Act of 1933, and (2) in conformity with GAAP. Comfort letters are not required and are not provided to the SEC.

The <u>contents</u> <u>of</u> <u>a</u> typical <u>comfort</u> <u>letter</u> <u>include</u>:

1. A statement regarding the independence of the accountants.
2. An opinion as to whether the audited financial statements and financial schedules included in the registration statement comply, as to form, in all material respects with the applicable accounting requirements and related published rules and regulations of the SEC.
3. <u>Negative</u> <u>assurance</u> <u>on</u> whether:
   a. The <u>unaudited</u> condensed <u>interim</u> <u>financial</u> <u>information</u> included in the registration statement complies, as to form, in all material respects with the applicable accounting requirements of the Act and related published rules and regulations.
   b. Any material modifications should be made to the unaudited condensed financial statements included in the registration statement in order for them to be in conformity with generally accepted accounting principles.
   c. There has been any change in capital stock, increase in long-term debt, or decrease in other specified financial statement items during a specified period following the date of the latest financial statements included in the registration statement and prospectus.

The comfort letter should conclude with a statement indicating that the letter is solely for the use of the underwriter in connection with the specific security issue.

Furthermore, the letter should be dated at the time, or shortly before, the securities are delivered to the underwriter in exchange for the proceeds of the offering.

Answer choices other than "B" are based on incorrect assumptions regarding comfort letters.

#87 (answer "C")

When an auditor submits, to a client or others, a document containing the basic financial state-

ments and other accompanying information, she must report on all of the client representations in the document.

Examples of such representations are (1) additional details or explanations of items related to the financial statements, (2) consolidating information, (3) historical summaries, and (4) statistical data.

When such additional information is submitted, the auditor is required by the fourth standard of reporting to indicate the degree of responsibility she is taking. The auditor should either express an opinion as to the fairness of the additional information in relation to the financial statements taken as a whole, or disclaim an opinion, depending on whether the information has been subjected to the auditing procedures applied in the audit of the basic financial statements.

In the question situation, the auditor-submitted document has been subjected to audit procedures, and accordingly, the auditor may include in the auditor's report on the financial statements an opinion that the accompanying information is fairly stated in <u>all</u> <u>material</u> <u>respects</u> <u>in</u> <u>relation</u> <u>to</u> <u>the</u> <u>basic</u> <u>financial</u> <u>statements</u> <u>taken</u> <u>as</u> <u>a</u> <u>whole</u>.

Answer choices other than "C" are incorrect because they represent improper forms of reporting.

#88 (answer "B")

Certain matters related to the conduct of the audit must be communicated (orally or in writing) to the audit committee (or, in the absence of an audit committee, to other financial oversight groups, such as finance or budget committees). Such communication need not be made before the issuance of the auditor's report.

Matters to be communicated are as follows:

1. The level of responsibility an auditor assumes for internal control and the financial statements under GAAS.
2. The initial selection of, and changes in, significant accounting policies, methods used to account for significant unusual transactions, and the effect of continuing accounting policies in controversial areas.
3. The processes used by management in formulating accounting estimates, and the basis for the auditor's conclusions about the reasonableness of those estimates.

4. Any adjustments arising from the audit that could have a significant effect on the entity's reporting process.
5. The auditor's responsibility for information, other than the audited financial statements, in documents such as corporate annual reports.
6. Any disagreements between the auditor and management, whether or not satisfactorily resolved.
7. Significant matters that were the subject of consultations with other accountants.
8. Any major issues discussed by management and the auditor before the auditor was hired.
9. Any serious difficulties the auditor encountered that were detrimental to the effective completion of the audit.

As noted in point #2 above, the communication should include management changes in the application of significant accounting policies.

Answer choices other than "B" are incorrect because they represent incorrect assumptions regarding an auditor's required communication with an entity's audit committee.

#89 (answer "B")

Under "Government Auditing Standards," an auditor is required to report on compliance with applicable laws and regulations. An auditor may either (1) describe the scope of the auditor's testing of compliance with laws and regulations and present the results of those tests, or (2) refer to separate reports containing that information.

When an auditor concludes, based on evidence obtained, that an irregularity or illegal act either has occurred or is likely to have occurred, he should report relevant information. An auditor need not report information about an irregularity or illegal act that is clearly inconsequential.

Accordingly, an auditor should include in the auditor's report material instances of fraud and illegal acts that were discovered.

Answer choice "A" is incorrect because the scope of the auditor's tests should be sufficient to support an opinion; accordingly, the auditor would not test all controls over fraud and illegal acts.

Answer choice "C" is incorrect because there is no requirement to include the materiality criteria used.

Answer choice "D" is incorrect because there is no requirement to report whether compliance with laws and regulations affected the entity's goals and objectives.

#90 (answer "B")

Generally Accepted Government Auditing Standards (GAGAS) incorporate the Generally Accepted Auditing Standards (GAAS) of reporting for financial audits, and the following additional standards of reporting needed to satisfy the unique needs of government financial audits.

1. Communicating with audit committees or other responsible individuals—Communicate the following information to the audit committee or to the individuals with whom they contracted for the audit:
   a. The auditor's responsibilities in a financial statement audit, including responsibilities for testing and reporting on internal controls and compliance with laws and regulations.
   b. The nature of any additional testing of internal controls, and compliance required by laws and regulations.
2. Reporting on compliance with generally accepted government auditing standards—State that the audit was made in accordance with generally accepted government auditing standards.
3. Reporting on compliance with laws and regulations and on internal controls—Either (a) describe the scope of the auditor's testing of compliance with laws and regulations and internal controls and present the results of those tests, or (b) refer to separate reports containing that information.
4. Privileged and confidential information—If certain information is prohibited from general disclosure, the audit report should state the nature of the information omitted and the requirement that makes the omission necessary.
5. Report distribution—Submit written audit reports to the appropriate officials both inside and outside the audited organization. Unless restricted by law or regulation, copies should be made available for public inspection.

Answer choice "A" is incorrect because the assessment of valid and reliable measures of economy and efficiency relate to performance audits rather than to audits of financial statements.

Answer choice "C" is incorrect because specific audit procedures should not be described in the audit report.

Answer choice "D" is incorrect because the assessment of program results relates to performance audits rather than to financial statement audits.

OTHER OBJECTIVE FORMATS/ESSAY QUESTIONS

Answer 2

#91 (answer "C")

The report must contain a title that includes the word independent (e.g., "Independent Auditor's Report").

#92 (answer "I")

All the basic financial statements (i.e., the consolidated balance sheets, and related statements of income, retained earnings, and cash flows) are properly identified in the introductory paragraph.

#93 (answer "I")

A reference to the American Institute of Certified Public Accountants is not appropriate in any paragraph in the audit report.

#94 (answer "I")

When the principal auditor decides to assume responsibility for the work of another auditor as it relates to the expression of an opinion on the consolidated financial statements taken as a whole, there should be no reference to the other auditor.

#95 (answer "I")

Since Perry & Price decided to assume responsibility for the work of Larkin & Lake insofar as it relates to the expression of an opinion on the consolidated financial statements taken as a whole, no division of responsibility should be indicated in the report. Accordingly, the subsidiary BX Inc., and the magnitude of the portion of the financial statements audited by Larkin & Lake should not be disclosed in the introductory paragraph.

#96 (answer "I")

The scope paragraph of the auditor's report should not include a reference to any specific audit procedures (e.g., analytical procedures) performed in conducting the audit.

#97 (answer "I")

The scope paragraph of the auditor's report should not state that an audit includes assessing internal control.

#98 (answer "C")

The scope paragraph of the auditor's report should include the statement, "An audit also includes assessing the accounting principles used and significant estimates made by management, as well as evaluating the overall financial statement presentation."

#99 (answer "C")

If, in an updated report, the opinion is different from the opinion previously expressed on the financial statements of a prior period, the auditor should disclose all the substantive reasons for the different opinion in a separate explanatory paragraph(s) preceding the opinion paragraph of the auditor's report. The explanatory paragraph(s) should disclose (1) the date of the auditor's previous report, (2) the type of opinion previously expressed, (3) the circumstances or events that caused the auditor to express a different opinion, and (4) that the auditor's updated opinion on the financial statements of the prior period is different from the auditor's previous opinion on those statements.

#100 (answer "I")

If, in an updated report, the opinion is different from the opinion previously expressed on the financial statements of a prior period, the auditor should disclose all the substantive reasons for the different opinion in a separate explanatory paragraph(s) preceding the opinion paragraph of the auditor's report. The explanatory paragraph(s) should disclose (1) the date of the auditor's previous report, (2) the type of opinion previously expressed, (3) the circumstances or events that caused the auditor to express a different opinion, and (4) that the auditor's updated opinion on the financial statements of the prior period is different from the auditor's previous opinion on those statements.

#101 (answer "C")

The auditor's standard report implies that the auditor is satisfied that there have been no material changes affecting comparability; explicit concurrence with an accounting change is inappropriate.

#102 (answer "C")

When the financial statements are affected by uncertainties (e.g., litigation) concerning future events, the outcome of which is not susceptible of reasonable estimation at the date of the auditor's report, the auditor must decide whether to add an explanatory paragraph containing a reference to the (litigation) uncertainty. However, unless the uncertainty leads to a disclaimer of opinion, it is appropriate to issue an unqualified opinion in which the opinion paragraph is unaffected.

#103 (answer "C")

When, as a result of an uncertainty pertaining to litigation, an auditor decides to add an explanatory paragraph to the report, it should be presented following the opinion paragraph and should refer to the financial statement disclosure (i.e., note).

#104 (answer "I")

The auditor's report should not refer to the letter of inquiry to Bond's lawyer concerning litigation, claims, and assessments.

#105 (answer "I")

The auditor's report should not be "dual dated" because of the change in opinion. Rather, the date of the prior year's report should be indicated in the first explanatory paragraph (refer to the answer to #99).

Answer 3

#106 (answer "C")

Mailing monthly statements to all customers with outstanding balances could prevent invoices for goods sold from being posted to incorrect customer accounts.

#107 (answer "G")

Comparison of shipping documents with sales invoices when goods are shipped provides a control to ensure that shipments have been billed to customers. Any shipping document not supported by an invoice should be investigated.

#108 (answer "F")

Comparison of daily sales summaries with control totals of invoices provides an independent check that invoices for shipped goods are also recorded in the sales journal.

#109 (answer "K")

Comparison of control amounts posted to the accounts receivable ledger with control totals of invoices provides an independent check that the amounts recorded in the sales journal are also posted to a customer account in the accounts receivable ledger.

#110 (answer "I")

Comparison of customer orders with an approved customer list would reveal whether the customer has a satisfactory credit rating. Orders should be suspended for any customer not on the approved customer list.

#111 (answer "B")

To prevent goods from being removed from inventory for unauthorized orders, approved sales orders should be required for goods to be released from the warehouse.

#112 (answer "D")

Comparison by the shipping clerks of the goods received from the warehouse with approved sales orders provides an independent check that the items ordered by customers agrees with the goods shipped to customers. Any differences between the description of the goods to be shipped and the approved sales order should be investigated.

#113 (answer "L")

Comparison of sales invoices with shipping documents and approved customer orders before invoices are mailed provides a control to prevent the recording of fictitious transactions.

#114 (answer "P")

Comparison of total amounts posted to the accounts receivable ledger from remittance advices with the validated bank deposit slip provides an independent check on the recording process. Amounts posted to the customers' accounts in the accounts receivable ledger should be supported by the remittance advices in order to prevent the posting of amounts in excess of the actual amounts received.

#115 (answer "C")

Mailing monthly statements to all customers with outstanding balances could prevent customers' checks from being misappropriated before being forwarded to the cashier for deposit because customers could indicate that their accounts had not been properly credited for the checks remitted.

#116 (answer "C")

Mailing monthly statements to all customers with outstanding balances could prevent customers' checks from being credited to incorrect customer accounts. Customers could indicate that their accounts had not been properly credited for the checks remitted.

#117 (answer "P")

Comparison of the total amounts posted to the accounts receivable ledger from remittance advices with the validated bank deposit slip provides an independent check on the recording process. The total amounts posted to the accounts receivable ledger should be supported by the remittance advices. If different customer accounts are each credited for the same cash receipt, the total amount posted to the accounts receivable ledger would be different from the total amount on the validated bank deposit slip.

#118 (answer "S")

Periodic preparation of a bank reconciliation by an employee other than the bookkeeper should reveal errors in recording receipts in the cash receipts journal; differences between the amount deposited (i.e., per bank) and the cash recorded (i.e., per books) could easily be identified.

#119 (answer "P")

Comparison of total amounts posted to the accounts receivable ledger from remittance advices with the validated bank deposit slip provides an independent check on performance. The amounts posted to the accounts receivable ledger should be supported by remittance advices. If checks are misappropriated after being forwarded to the cashier for deposit, the total amount posted in the accounts receivable ledger would be higher than the amount of the deposit validated by the bank.

#120 (answer "N")

Proper approval by the supervisor of the sales department of goods returned for credit should preclude invalid transactions granting credit for sales returns from being recorded.

Answer 4

Part 4 (a)

Hart may accept an attest engagement to examine and report on management's assertion about the effectiveness of Unidyne's internal control if the following conditions are met:

1. Management accepts responsibility for the effectiveness of Unidyne's internal control.
2. Management evaluates the effectiveness of Unidyne's internal control using reasonable criteria (i.e., "control criteria") established by a recognized body, such as the AICPA or a regulatory agency.
3. Sufficient evidential matter exists, or could be developed, to support management's evaluation.
4. Management presents its written assertion about the effectiveness of Unidyne's internal control based upon the control criteria referred to in its report.

Part 4 (b)

The broad engagement activities that would be involved in Hart's performing an examination of management's assertion about the effectiveness of Unidyne's internal control include:

1. Planning the scope of the engagement.
2. Obtaining an understanding of internal control through inquiry, observation, and inspection.
3. Evaluating and testing the design and operating effectiveness of internal controls. Tests of relevant controls should concentrate on how policies and procedures are

applied, the consistency with which they are applied, and by whom they are applied.

4. Expressing an opinion about whether management's assertion regarding the effectiveness of the entity's internal control is fairly stated, in all material respects, based on the control criteria.

Part 4 (c)

Hart may also be engaged to perform agreed-upon procedures relating to management's assertion about the effectiveness of the entity's internal control. Hart should not provide negative assurance about whether management's assertion is fairly stated; rather, Hart's report should be in the form of procedures and findings.

Hart should not accept an engagement to review and report on management's assertion about the effectiveness of the entity's internal control.

Answer 5

Part 5 (a)

Wall has a responsibility to evaluate whether there is substantial doubt concerning Trendy's ability to continue as a going concern for a reasonable time period, not to exceed one year beyond the date of the audited financial statements.

Part 5 (b)

The audit procedures that Wall most likely would perform to identify conditions and events that may indicate that Trendy has a going concern problem are those procedures designed and performed to achieve other audit objectives, and include:

1. Analytical procedures.
2. Review of subsequent events.
3. Review of compliance with the terms of debt and loan agreements.
4. Reading of minutes of meetings of stockholders and board of directors.
5. Inquiry of an entity's legal counsel about litigation, claims, and assessments.
6. Confirmation with related and third parties of the details of arrangements to provide or maintain financial support.

Part 5 (c)

If Wall identified conditions and events that indicated a potential going concern problem, Wall should consider management's plans to mitigate the adverse effects of Trendy's financial difficulties. Wall should therefore consider Trendy's plans and ability to:

1. Dispose of assets.
2. Borrow money and/or restructure debt.
3. Reduce or delay expenditures.
4. Obtain new equity capital and reduce dividend payments.

Accounting & Reporting—Taxation, Managerial, and Governmental and Not-for-Profit Organizations (ARE)

FOUR-OPTION MULTIPLE-CHOICE QUESTIONS

Answer 1

#1 (answer "C")

Matriculated students (i.e., degree candidates) may exclude from gross income amounts received from qualified educational institutions, but only to the extent the amounts received are for tuition, course-related fees, books, and supplies. Nondegree candidates may not avail themselves of this exclusion.

Amounts received for teaching, research, or other services may not be excluded from gross income.

Answer choices other than "C" are based on incorrect assumptions and/or combinations.

#2 (answer "C")

All taxpayers except trusts, estates, and certain noncorporate lessors may elect to deduct certain assets (called Section 179 property) as an expense rather than capitalizing the asset and depreciating it under MACRS.

1. Annual dollar limitation—Section 179 property is personal property qualifying under MACRS and is acquired for trade or business use.
   The maximum amount that may be expensed is $18,000 per year. The amount that may be expensed is reduced by the amount by which the cost of Section 179 property placed into service during the taxable year exceeds $200,000.
   The amount that may be expensed is further limited to the taxable income (computed without regard to the Section 179 deduction) of the trade or business.
2. Dollar limitation in case of partnerships and S corporations—Both the partnership and each partner are subject to the annual dollar limitation. (The deduction passes through to the partners.) A similar rule shall apply in the case of an S corporation and its shareholders.

3. Recapture—There is recapture of expensed amounts as ordinary income if a disposition of the property results in a gain.

Since the cost of Browne's office machinery was clearly less than $200,000, Browne may elect to treat the maximum amount as an expense, rather than a capital expenditure. Browne's deduction under the Section 179 election is therefore $18,000.

Answer choice "A" is incorrect because it assumes that the Section 179 deduction is equal to 20 percent of the cost of the qualifying property.

Answer choice "B" is incorrect because it reflects the maximum Section 179 deduction that was allowed in tax years prior to 1993.

Answer choice "D" is incorrect because it presumes that the full cost of Browne's office machinery may be expensed, and therefore fails to consider the statutory limit of $18,000.

#3 (answer "A")

Questions #3 and #4 relate to losses between related parties.

A loss on a sale or exchange of property between members of the same family is governed by the rules applicable to related parties. Such a loss is, therefore, not deductible. If, however, the property is subsequently sold by the original transferee at a gain, such gain will be recognized only to the extent that it exceeds the loss previously disallowed the transferor. The loss previously disallowed the transferor may not be used to create or increase a loss incurred by the original transferee. This relief provision applies only to gains. A loss upon disposition by the original transferee is measured by the difference between the sales price and the adjusted basis of the property (unaffected by the previously disallowed loss).

Additionally, there is no effect on the holding period by virtue of the related-party rules. The rules applicable to ordinary purchases and sales of property determine the holding period.

In view of the above, while Conner realizes a loss from the sale of Zinco stock in 1994 in the amount of $10,000 (i.e., $30,000 − $20,000), the amount of the loss from the sale of Zinco stock that Conner can deduct in 1994 is $0, since the sale was to a related party.

Answer choice "B" is incorrect because it presumes that Conner's related-party loss may be recognized to the extent of the $3,000 limitation applicable to capital losses of an individual.

Answer choice "C" is clearly incorrect because it assumes that one-half of Conner's related-party loss is deductible.

Answer choice "D" is incorrect because it treats Conner's realized loss as fully deductible; it fails to consider that (1) related-party losses are not deductible and (2) a sale of stock between unrelated parties at a loss generally creates a capital loss, which is subject to a deduction limitation of $3,000.

#4 (answer "A")

See question #3 preceding for background relating to losses between related parties.

Alice's recognized gain on her sale is $0 because her $5,000 (i.e., $25,000 − $20,000) realized gain may be offset by $5,000 of Conner's previously disallowed related-party loss (i.e., $10,000).

Answer choice "B" is incorrect because it fails to take into account the fact that Alice may use Conner's previously disallowed related-party loss to eliminate her realized gain. Further, Alice's holding period is short-term, and not long-term, because she did not hold the stock for more than 12 months. There is no effect on the holding period by virtue of the related-party rules.

Answer choice "C" is incorrect because the loss previously disallowed Conner (i.e., the transferor) may not be used to create or increase a loss incurred by Alice (i.e., the original transferee).

Answer choice "D" is incorrect because the loss previously disallowed Conner (i.e., the transferor) may not be used to create or increase a loss incurred by Alice (i.e., the original transferee). In addition, Alice's holding period is short-term, and not long-term, because she did not hold the stock for more than 12 months. There is no effect on the holding period by virtue of the related-party rules.

SOURCE: LPR, MAY 1995, #4

#4 (answer "D")

When preparing a tax return, a CPA may, in good faith, rely on information furnished by the client or third parties. However, the CPA should make inquiries if the furnished information appears to be incorrect, incomplete, or inconsistent, either on its face or with other facts known to the CPA.

Kopel had no reason to believe that the information provided by Raff was incorrect. Thus, Kopel is not subject to the preparer penalty for willful understatement of tax liability because Kopel was justified in relying on Raff's representation.

Answer choice "A" is incorrect because Kopel was entitled to rely on the information provided by Raff and therefore was not obligated to examine the underlying documentation for Raff's deduction.

Answer choice "B" is incorrect because Kopel was entitled to rely on the information provided by Raff and was not required to obtain Raff's representation in writing.

Answer choice "C" is incorrect because Kopel was entitled to rely on the information provided by Raff; the relative size of the claimed deduction to the amount that should have been deducted has no significance.

#5 (answer "D")

Under the Modified Accelerated Cost Recovery System (MACRS) of depreciation, which is mandated for all assets placed into service after December 31, 1986, for regular tax purposes, the depreciation deduction for real property is generally based on the straight-line method over the following recovery periods:

Recovery Period	Type of Eligible Assets
27.5 years	Residential real property
31.5 years	Nonresidential real property placed into service before May 13, 1993
39.0 years	Nonresidential real property placed into service on or after May 13, 1993

The depreciation deduction is prorated by the number of months the property is placed into service. A mid-month convention is utilized so that property is treated as being placed into service in the middle of the month.

It should be obvious that land, although considered to be real property, is not depreciable.

In view of the above, Graham could only claim depreciation on the cost of the office building (i.e., $264,000 − $30,000, or $234,000) for 4½ months; Graham's MACRS deduction for the office building in 1994 was therefore $2,250 (i.e., ($234,000/39) × 4.5/12).

Answer choice "A" is incorrect because it (1) fails to prorate the deduction based on the number of months the building is placed into service, (2) fails to consider the mid-month convention, (3) includes the cost of the land in the depreciable base, and (4) reflects depreciation utilizing a 27.5-year recovery period, which is applicable to residential real property; depreciation is incorrectly determined to be $9,600 (i.e., $264,000/27.5).

Answer choice "B" is incorrect because it fails to (1) prorate the deduction based on the number of months the building is placed into service and (2) consider the mid-month convention; depreciation is incorrectly determined to be $6,000 (i.e., $234,000/39).

Answer choice "C" is incorrect because it reflects depreciation using a 32.5-year recovery period (which does not exist in the statute) and the half-year convention applicable to personal property; depreciation is incorrectly determined to be $3,600 (i.e., [$234,000/32.5] × ½).

#6 (answer "B")

In arriving at adjusted gross income, a deduction is allowed for certain expenses incurred in moving to a new residence, because of a new employer or place of work, if certain distance and time requirements are satisfied.

1. Distance requirement
   To deduct the cost of moving to a new residence, the distance between the new place of work and the former home must be at least 50 miles farther than the former home was from the former place of work.
2. Time requirement
   In order to qualify for a moving expense deduction:
   a. Employees are required to work full time for at least 39 weeks during the 12-month period immediately after their arrival in the general location of their new place of work.
   b. Self-employed individuals are required to perform services on a full-time basis

for at least 78 weeks during the 24-month period immediately after their arrival, of which 39 weeks must be within the first 12 months after arrival at the new place of work.

3. Deductible moving expenses only include unreimbursed costs of:
   a. Moving household goods and personal effects.
   b. Travel (including lodging but not meals) for all family members.

Accordingly, the amount deductible as moving expense on Grey's 1994 tax return is $2,800, which consists of the lodging and travel expense while moving (i.e., $1,000) and the costs of moving household furnishings and personal effects (i.e., $1,800).

Answer choice "A" is incorrect because it includes the $1,200 pre-move househunting costs, which are not deductible.

Answer choice "C" is incorrect because it fails to include the lodging and travel expenses (i.e., $1,000) while moving.

Answer choice "D" is incorrect because it fails to include the costs of moving household furnishings and personal effects (i.e., $1,800).

#7 (answer "C")

To be deductible, charitable contributions must be paid in cash or other property before the close of the tax year. Contributions charged to a bank credit card may be deducted in the year of the charge.

A donation of property other than cash is deductible to the extent of its fair market value at the time of the contribution, unless the donated property is appreciated property. A donation of appreciated long-term capital gain property is generally deductible at its fair market value. The deduction is limited to basis with respect to contributions of ordinary income property and short-term capital gain property.

Out-of-pocket expenses that are paid for rendering services without compensation to a charitable organization are deductible. Included are:

1. Transportation costs, including a personal automobile; optional use of a twelve-cents-per-mile rate is permissible.
2. Travel expenses, including necessary meals and lodging, provided there is no signifi-

cant element of personal pleasure, recreation, or vacation.
3. The cost and upkeep of required uniforms that have no general utility.

The deduction for contributions is generally subject to an overall limitation equal to 50 percent of adjusted gross income. However, donations of long-term capital gain property are generally limited to 30 percent of adjusted gross income.

Any charitable contributions made during the year in excess of the limitations above may be carried over 5 succeeding years. However, contributions actually made during the later years plus the carryover must fall within the annual limitations above. Any excess not used up within the 5-year period is lost forever.

It should be noted that if a taxpayer pays more than fair market value to a qualified charitable organization for merchandise, goods, or services, the amount in excess of fair market value is a deductible charitable contribution.

No deduction will be allowed for separate charitable contributions of $250 or more (whether in cash or in property) unless written substantiation is obtained from the charitable organization.

The maximum amount of properly substantiated charitable contributions that Moore could claim as an itemized deduction for 1994 was limited to 50% of her $50,000 adjusted gross income, or $25,000; this consisted of the $18,000 contributed to her church in 1994, plus $7,000 (out of the $18,000) carried over from 1993.

Answer choice "A" is incorrect because it only represents the charitable contribution carryover from 1993; it fails to consider the $18,000 Moore contributed to her church in 1994, which must be deducted before claiming any portion of the carryover from 1993.

Answer choice "B" is incorrect because it fails to include the $7,000 portion of the charitable contribution carryover available from 1993.

Answer choice "D" is incorrect because it reflects an amount in excess of 50% of adjusted gross income (i.e., $50,000 × 50%, or $25,000).

#8 (answer "C")

If a taxpayer itemizes her deductions, the following taxes paid during the year may be deducted.

1. State and local income taxes paid (including estimated tax payments) or withheld.
2. Real estate taxes on property owned by the taxpayer and used for personal or investment purposes.
3. Personal property taxes (state and local).

Nondeductible taxes include all federal taxes such as excise (including customs duties), income, social security, self-employment, gift taxes, as well as state and local sales taxes. Certain state and local taxes similarly are not deductible. Included in this category are dog license fees, fees for hunting licenses, driver's license fees, motor vehicle registration fees (unless based upon the value of the vehicle), as well as state and local gasoline taxes.

The total amount that Matthews was entitled to claim for taxes on her 1994 Schedule A of Form 1040 is $1,900, consisting of the 1994 state and local income taxes withheld (i.e., $1,500) and the 1994 state estimated income taxes paid December 30, 1994 (i.e., $400).

Answer choice "A" is incorrect because it includes the 1994 federal income taxes withheld (i.e., $2,500) and the 1994 state and local income taxes paid April 17, 1995 (i.e., $300); the former is never deductible while the latter is deductible in 1995.

Answer choice "B" is incorrect because it includes the 1994 state and local income taxes paid April 17, 1995 (i.e., $300); this amount is deductible in 1995 and not in 1994.

Answer choice "D" is incorrect because it fails to include the 1994 state estimated income taxes paid December 30, 1994 (i.e., $400).

#9 (answer "A")

In general, miscellaneous expenses are deductible as itemized deductions only if the aggregate amount of such expenses exceeds 2% of AGI. Included in this category of expenses are employee's unreimbursed business car (and other travel) expenses, tax return preparation fees, investment counsel fees, special apparel, and certain job search expenses.

If an employee is reimbursed by his employer for miscellaneous expenses, he (1) must only include in income the excess reimbursement or (2) may only deduct the excess of expenses over reimbursements.

Answer choices other than "A" are incorrect because they represent adjustments to gross income and therefore may not be claimed as itemized deductions.

#10 (answer "A")

A casualty is the damage, destruction, or loss of property resulting from an event that is sudden, unexpected, or unusual.

With respect to personal casualty losses, the loss is the lesser of the decrease in the fair market value of the property as a result of the casualty, or the adjusted basis of the property, reduced by any insurance recovery.

Personal casualty losses are deductible only to the extent that they exceed 10% of adjusted gross income after deducting a $100 floor amount for each loss.

The amount of the fire loss that Frazer was entitled to claim as an itemized deduction on her 1994 tax return is $2,900, computed as follows:

Loss	$130,000
Less: Insurance recovery	(120,000)
Deductible	(100)
Total casualty loss	9,900
Less: 10% of AGI (10% of $70,000)	(7,000)
Allowable deduction, 1994	$ 2,900

Answer choice "B" is incorrect because the total casualty loss (i.e., $9,900) is reduced by 2% of adjusted gross income (i.e., 2% × $70,000, or $1,400); the casualty loss deduction is therefore erroneously determined to be $9,900 − 1,400, or $8,500.

Answer choice "C" is incorrect because (1) the total casualty loss fails to reflect the $100 statutory floor amount and (2) the deductible amount reflects a reduction for 2% (instead of 10%) of AGI; the casualty loss deduction is therefore inaccurately determined to be $8,600 (i.e., [$130,000 − $120,000, or $10,000] − [2% × $70,000, or $1,400]).

Answer choice "D" is incorrect because it fails to reflect the $100 statutory floor amount and the reduction for 10% of AGI (i.e., $7,000).

#11 (answer "A")

Itemized deductions (other than medical expenses, investment interest, and casualty and theft losses) must be reduced by 3% of adjusted gross income (AGI) in excess of an "applicable amount." The "applicable amount" is based on the taxpayer's filing status and is adjusted annually for inflation. It should be noted that in no event may the reduction exceed 80%.

It should therefore be readily apparent that charitable contributions are subject to the phase out of itemized deductions that may be claimed by high-income individuals.

Answer choices other than "A" are based on assumptions not valid under current tax law.

#12 (answer "A")

Qualifying medical expenses are subject to a 7.5% of AGI floor.

Qualifying medical expenses include:

1. Medical insurance premiums.
2. Prescription drugs and insulin.
3. Fees paid to doctors, dentists, hospitals, and laboratories.
4. Transportation expenses. (In lieu of actual automobile expenses, a taxpayer may deduct nine cents per mile plus parking and tolls.)
5. Expenses for lodging while away from home primarily for and essential to medical care provided by a physician in a licensed hospital or its equivalent. A maximum of $50 per day, per individual (including a person accompanying the patient), is allowed and cannot include the cost of meals or any pleasure element.
6. Tuition for schooling at a special school for the physically or mentally handicapped. If an individual is in the educational facility primarily for the availability of medical care, the cost of meals and lodging, incident to that care, is also deductible.
7. The costs to purchase, repair, and maintain special equipment (e.g., wheelchairs and hearing aids) used to alleviate the effects of a medical condition.

A deduction for medical expenses of a child paid for by a legally divorced or separated parent is available even though the dependency exemption cannot be claimed by the payor. Thus, each parent can include in her medical expense deduction those payments attributable to her child.

The deduction for medical expenses includes expenses paid by the taxpayer for the benefit of dependents. Furthermore, the deduction includes those expenses paid for a person who would have qualified as a dependent except for the fact that they (1) had gross income from sources not exempt from tax equal to or greater than the exemption amount or (2) filed a joint return.

Logically, without regard to the 7.5% adjusted gross income threshold, the Whites may claim $8,600 as qualifying medical expenses (i.e., the $600 paid for repair and maintenance of the wheelchair and the $8,000 expense for special schooling for their physically handicapped dependent child).

Answer choices "B" and "C" are incorrect because either the $600 item or the $8,000 item is not included, and both should be.

Answer choice "D" is incorrect because neither the $600 item nor the $8,000 item is included, and both should be.

#13 (answer "D")

A taxpayer may be classified as a "qualifying widow(er)" (also known as a "surviving spouse") if (1) his spouse died within two tax years preceding the year for which the return is being filed, (2) he was entitled to file a joint return for the year in which his spouse died, (3) he did not remarry during the tax year, (4) he has a dependent child, and (5) he paid more than one-half the cost of keeping up a home that is the principal residence for him and the dependent child for the entire year, except for temporary absences. (A qualifying widow[er] is subject to the same tax rates as on a joint return.)

Therefore, based on the preceding information, neither I nor II is among the requirements to enable a taxpayer to be classified as a "qualifying widow(er)."

Answer choices other than "D" are based on incorrect assumptions and/or combinations.

#14 (answer "C")

There are five tests that must be met to permit a deduction for dependency exemptions. These are the tests for (1) support, (2) gross income, (3) relationship, (4) citizenship, and (5) whether or not dependent and spouse filed a joint return, as explained below.

1. The support test generally means that more than one-half of the dependent's total support must be provided by the taxpayer. (Social security payments, like other nontaxable income used for support, are considered as having been contributed by the recipient for her support.)
2. The gross income test generally means that the dependent's gross income from sources not exempt from tax is less than the appropriate exemption amount, except for a child under 19, or a child under the age of 24 who is a full-time student for five months of the calendar year.
3. The relationship test generally provides that a person who is a relative in any of the following ways does not have to live with the taxpayer in order for the exemption to be claimed: a child, grandchild, great-grandchild, stepchild, brother, sister, half brother, half sister, stepbrother, stepsister, parent, grandparent or other direct ancestor, stepfather or stepmother, aunt or uncle, niece or nephew, father-in-law, mother-in-law, son-in-law, daughter-in-law, brother-in-law, or sister-in-law. Any other person would have to live with the taxpayer to qualify as a dependent.

   A custodial parent (i.e., one who has custody of a child or stepchild, pursuant to a decree of divorce or agreement of separate maintenance) is entitled to the exemption for her child unless she elects not to claim it.
4. The citizenship test requires that the dependent be a U.S. citizen, resident or national, or a resident of Canada or Mexico for some part of the tax year.
5. The joint return test precludes dependency status for a person who files a joint return. However, if the sole purpose of filing a joint return is to obtain a refund, even though no return is required to be filed, the joint return test is considered satisfied.

No exemption is allowed to a taxpayer who is claimed as a dependent on another taxpayer's return.

In light of the preceding discussion, it should be evident that only Ruth may be claimed as a dependent. Clay may not be claimed as a dependent by Smith because the joint return test is not satisfied since the joint return filed by Clay was required because an additional $500 in taxes was due on his wife's income. In any event, the question fails to indicate (1) Clay's age, and (2) for how many months Clay is a full-time student.

Accordingly, the number of exemptions that Smith was entitled to claim on his 1994 tax return is two (i.e., one each for himself and his widowed mother, Ruth).

Answer choice "A" is incorrect because it includes exemptions for Clay and his wife, neither of whom qualifies as a dependent.

Answer choice "B" is incorrect because it includes an exemption for Clay, who, as previously indicated, does not qualify as a dependent.

Answer choice "D" is incorrect because it fails to include an exemption for Smith's widowed mother, Ruth, who clearly qualifies as Smith's dependent.

#15 (answer "D")

A cash basis taxpayer should report gross income for the year in which income is either actually or constructively received, whether in cash or in property. (The fair market value of the property governs the amount includible in income.)

An individual has constructively received income when it is credited without restriction and made available to him. For example, interest credited to a taxpayer's savings account is deemed to be constructively received. Accordingly, income need not be in the taxpayer's possession for it to be considered received.

Answer choices "A" and "C" are incorrect because income need not be received in cash only.

Answer choice "B" is incorrect in light of the doctrine of constructive receipt.

#16 (answer "C")

In general, an accuracy-related penalty will be assessed in the amount of 20% of an underpayment attributable to any of the following actions:

1. Negligent or intentional (but not fraudulent) disregard of tax rules or regulations

(e.g., failure to keep adequate books and records).
2. Substantial understatement of income tax; i.e., the greater of 10% of the tax required to be shown or $5,000 ($10,000 for most corporations).
3. Substantial income tax valuation misstatement (i.e., 200% or more of the proper value).
4. Substantial pension liability overstatement (i.e., 200% or more of the proper amount, and the resulting tax underpayment is at least $1,000).

It should be noted that the accuracy-related penalty will be doubled to 40% if there is a gross income tax valuation misstatement (i.e., 400% or more of the proper value) or a gross pension liability misstatement (i.e., 400% or more of the proper amount).

Answer choices other than "C" are based on incorrect assumptions and/or combinations.

#17 (answer "C")

The imposition of the alternative minimum tax (AMT) is intended to prevent a taxpayer with significant income from avoiding significant tax liability through the use of tax preference items.

The AMT, computed on Form 6251, is payable to the extent that it exceeds the taxpayer's regular income tax before tax credits.

The AMT is calculated as follows:

Taxable income before exemptions (computed using regular income tax rules)
Add or subtract adjustments to taxable income
Add tax preferences
Equals alternative minimum taxable income
Subtract exemption amount
Multiply by AMT rate
Subtract AMT foreign tax credit
Equals tentative minimum tax
Subtract regular income tax
Equals AMT

Some of the more common adjustments to taxable income are

1. The standard deduction.
2. Certain itemized deductions, which include:
   a. State and local income taxes (refunds should be subtracted).

b. Most miscellaneous deductions.
c. Medical expenses—the smaller of 2.5% of AGI or the amount claimed as an itemized deduction for regular income tax purposes.
3. Excess depreciation on personal property placed into service after 1986.
4. Passive activity losses; passive activity gains must be recalculated taking into account all AMT rules.

Some of the more common tax preference items are:

1. Tax-exempt interest on private activity bonds issued after August 7, 1986, reduced by any deductions (e.g., interest expense) that would have been allowable if the interest were includible in income for regular tax purposes.
2. Excess percentage depletion for coal and iron ore.
3. Excess accelerated depreciation on certain real property.

For 1996, the AMT exemption amount is generally:

1. $45,000 for married filing jointly or qualifying widow(er).
2. $33,750 for single or head of household.
3. $22,500 for married filing separately.

The AMT exemption amounts start to phase out at the rate of 25% when AMTI exceeds:

1. $150,000 for married filing jointly or qualifying widow(er).
2. $112,500 for single or head of household.
3. $75,000 for married filing separately.

For 1996, the amount that Mills reported as alternative minimum taxable income before the AMT exemption was $77,000, computed as follows:

Taxable income before personal exemptions		$70,000
Add adjustments for state and local income taxes	$5,000	
Miscellaneous deductions that exceed 2% of adjusted gross income	2,000	7,000
Alternative minimum taxable income before the AMT exemption, 1996		$77,000

Answer choice "A" is incorrect because it fails to include the state and local income taxes ($5,000)

as an adjustment in arriving at alternative minimum taxable income before the exemption amount.

Answer choice "B" is incorrect because it fails to include the miscellaneous deductions that exceed 2% of adjusted gross income (i.e., $2,000) as an adjustment in arriving at alternative minimum taxable income before the exemption amount.

Answer choice "D" is incorrect because it treats the home mortgage interest on loan to acquire residence (i.e., $6,000) as an adjustment (or tax preference item) in arriving at alternative minimum taxable income before the exemption amount when, in fact, it has no effect at all.

#18 (answer B")

Refer to question #17 for background material pertaining to the alternative minimum tax applicable to individuals.

As indicated in the answer, tax-exempt interest from private activity bonds issued after August 7, 1986, is considered an alternative minimum tax preference.

It should be noted that, in general, charitable contributions have no effect on the calculation of alternative minimum taxable income; no adjustment or tax preference is created.

Answer choices other than "B" are based on incorrect assumptions and/or combinations.

#19 (answer "A")

In general, an individual is required to make quarterly estimated tax payments if she expects her estimated income tax (including the alternative minimum tax) after credits to be $500 or more. The first three estimated tax payments are due by the 15th day of the 4th, 6th, and 9th months of the tax year. The last estimated tax payment is due on the 15th day of the first month of the following year.

If an individual does not pay estimated tax when due, an underpayment penalty may be charged for the period of underpayment, at a rate that is periodically determined by the Internal Revenue Service.

The underpayment penalty, like all other penalties imposed by taxing authorities, is not deductible.

However, an individual generally will not be liable for the penalty if her actual tax liability is $500 or more and she timely paid 90% of the tax liability for the year through withholding or estimated tax payments.

Alternatively, an individual with AGI in excess of $150,000 may avoid the underpayment penalty by paying 110% of the actual tax liability of the preceding year. If an individual's AGI does not exceed $150,000, the applicable percentage, to avoid the penalty, is 100%.

An individual may be able to reduce or eliminate the underestimated tax penalty by using the annualized income method. This method, under which the required installment for one or more periods may be less than one-fourth of the required annual payment, generally may be used if the individual's income varies during the year.

Further, no penalty will be imposed on an individual for underpayment of estimated tax for a particular year if the tax for that year is less than $500, since the required estimated tax payment threshold has not been reached.

Answer choices other than "A" are clearly based on incorrect assumptions and/or combinations.

#20 (answer "C")

Under the general rule, a claim for refund of erroneously paid taxes must be filed within three years from the date the return was filed or within two years from the date the tax was paid, whichever is later. Returns filed before the due date are considered to have been filed on the due date. If a return was not filed, a claim for refund must be filed within two years from the date the tax was paid.

An exception to the general rule exists for claims relating to deductions of bad debts and worthless securities. In these cases, the three-year limitation is extended to seven years.

The claim for refund by an individual is submitted on Form 1040X.

Answer choice "A" is incorrect because Form 1139, "Corporation Application for Tentative Refund," is generally used to apply for a quick refund of corporate income taxes from the carryback of a net operating loss or an unused general business credit.

Answer choice "B" is incorrect because Form 1045, "Application for Tentative Refund," is generally used to apply for a quick refund of individual income taxes from the carryback of a net operating loss or an unused general business credit.

Answer choice "D" is incorrect because Form 843, "Claim for Refund and Request for Abatement," may not be used to claim a refund of income taxes. Form 843 may be used to claim refunds of employment, estate, gift, and excise taxes.

#21 (answer "B")

To be eligible for the Subchapter S election, a corporation must:

1. Be a domestic corporation.
2. Not be an active member of an affiliated group.
3. Have one class of stock. (Differences in the voting power attached to shares of stock will not be deemed to create more than one class of stock.)
4. Have no more than 35 (75, beginning in 1997) shareholders who are individuals or estates (or trusts under certain circumstances). (All stockholdings, whether jointly or individually held, of a husband, wife, or their estates, are counted as one shareholder.)

Given proper election, there will be no federal tax except for the tax on "built-in" gains (which is beyond the scope of the CPA examination) and the tax on excessive passive investment income.

The election may be made at any time during the previous taxable year or at any time on or before the 15th day of the third month of the current taxable year. An invalid or a late-filed election may be treated as a timely-filed valid election if the Internal Revenue Service determines that there is reasonable cause. This is clearly not the case in the question situation.

Since Village's S Corporation election was made on December 5, 1993, which is after the 15th day of the third month of the 1993 taxable year (i.e., March 15, 1993), Village's election is effective on January 1, 1994, which is the first day of the next taxable year.

Answer choice "A" is incorrect because it represents the date on which Village's S status would have been effective had Village made a valid S Corporation election on or before March 15, 1993.

Answer choices "C" and "D" are based on assumptions that are not valid under current tax law.

#22 (answer "D")

The basis of a shareholder's stock in an S corporation is increased by his ratable share of all items of corporate income that are passed through to him, whether or not separately stated.

His basis will be reduced by (1) all items of corporate loss and deduction, whether or not separately stated, (2) all nontaxable distributions that represent return of capital, and (3) all expenses not deducted in computing taxable income and not properly chargeable to the capital account.

Property distributions reduce the basis of the shareholder's stock by the fair market value of the property.

The reduction in basis is first applied against stock, and then against any indebtedness owed to the shareholder by the corporation.

Accordingly, a shareholder's basis in the stock of an S corporation is increased by the shareholder's pro rata share of income from both tax-exempt interest and taxable interest.

Answer choices other than "D" are based on incorrect assumptions and/or combinations.

#23 (answer "B")

Determination of whether a corporation is to be treated as a personal holding company, and therefore subject to a 39.6% tax on undistributed income in addition to other corporate taxes, is based on two tests: income and stock ownership.

The income test provides that a corporation is a personal holding company when 60% of adjusted gross income consists of dividends (including those received from an unrelated domestic corporation), taxable interest, certain royalties, annuities, certain rents, personal service contract income, and certain income from estates and trusts. Interest earned on tax-exempt obligations is not considered when determining if the income requirements for a personal holding company have been satisfied.

As to stock ownership, if during the period of the last half of the taxable year more than 50% of the value of the outstanding stock is owned by or for not more than five individuals, the corporation is deemed to be a personal holding company. For purposes of determining the five individuals, the rules of constructive stock ownership apply.

Under the constructive stock ownership rules:

1. Stock owned, directly or indirectly, by or for a corporation, partnership, estate, or trust shall be considered as being owned proportionately by its shareholders, partners, or beneficiaries.
2. An individual shall be considered as owning the stock owned, directly or indirectly, by or for her family or by or for her partner. Family includes only brothers, sisters, spouse, ancestors, and lineal descendants.

It should be noted that if a corporation is liable for the tax on undistributed income, it should be self-assessed by filing a separate schedule (Form 1120-PH) along with the regular tax return.

Since the tax is imposed on undistributed personal holding company income, sufficient distribution of dividends can mitigate the tax.

Based on the above, in determining if the income requirements for a personal holding company have been met, Edge should consider the dividends received from an unrelated domestic corporation, but should not consider the interest earned on tax-exempt obligations.

Answer choices other than "B" are based on incorrect assumptions and/or combinations.

#24 (answer "C")

Generally, any distribution made by a corporation to its shareholders is considered a dividend to the extent of earnings and profits, both accumulated and for the current year. In determining the source of a distribution, current-year earnings and profits are considered before accumulated earnings and profits. In the event that a corporation has current-year earnings and profits but has a deficit in accumulated earnings and profits at the beginning of the year, the distribution will be considered a dividend, but only to the extent of the current-year earnings and profits.

Any distribution that is not taxed as a dividend will first reduce the shareholder's basis in the stock, and then result in a capital gain.

It should be noted that, in general, the amount of dividend income resulting from a property distribution received by a shareholder is the fair market value of the property received.

Accordingly, the amount of the nonliquidating distribution made by Kent was $200,000 (i.e., the fair market value of the property distributed); the amount of the distribution that was taxable as dividend income to Reed is limited to $185,000, which is the sum of the current earnings and profits (i.e., $60,000) and the accumulated earnings and profits at January 1, 1994 (i.e., $125,000).

Answer choice "A" is incorrect because it fails to consider any portion of the accumulated earnings and profits at January 1, 1994, in determining the amount of the distribution taxable as dividend income to Reed.

Answer choice "B" is incorrect because it reflects the $150,000 adjusted basis of the distributed property. Rather, the amount of the distribution must take into account the $200,000 fair market value of the distributed property. Further, the effect of earnings and profits on the taxability of the distribution is not considered.

Answer choice "D" is incorrect because it treats the entire amount of the distribution (i.e., $200,000) as a taxable dividend. As such, it ignores the effect of earnings and profits on the taxability of the distribution.

#25 (answer "B")

The Internal Revenue Code specifically defines seven types of corporate reorganizations:

1. A statutory merger or consolidation (type "A" reorganization).
2. The acquisition by one corporation, in exchange solely for all or a part of its (or its parent's) voting stock, of stock of another corporation (i.e., target), if, immediately after the acquisition, the acquiring corporation has control of such other corporation (type "B" reorganization).
3. The acquisition by one corporation, in exchange solely for all or a part of its voting stock, of substantially all of the properties of another corporation (type "C" reorganization).
4. A transfer by a corporation of all or a part of its assets to another corporation if, immediately after the transfer, the transferor, or one or more of its shareholders, or any combination thereof, is in control of the corporation to which the assets are transferred (type "D" reorganization).
5. A recapitalization (type "E" reorganization).
6. A mere change in identity, form, or place of organization (type "F" reorganization).
7. A reorganization pursuant to Title 11 of the Bankruptcy Code (type "G" reorganization).

For purposes of corporate reorganizations, control generally means ownership of at least 80% of the total combined voting power of all voting stock and at least 80 percent of all nonvoting stock.

It should be noted that a stock redemption (which occurs when a corporation cancels or redeems its own stock) is not a corporate reorganization.

The requirements for each type of reorganization are generally beyond the scope of the CPA examination.

An examination question that contains the phrase "pursuant to a corporate reorganization" should be answered utilizing the following general rules:

1. No gain will be recognized by the shareholders unless "boot" is received in addition to the receipt of stock. In addition, no gain will be recognized by the corporation(s) involved.
2. Three types of "boot" may trigger recognition of gain:
   a. Cash.
   b. Bonds—gain will be recognized if the principal amount of the bonds received exceeds the principal amount of the bonds surrendered, or if bonds are received and none are surrendered.
      The fair market value of the bonds will be utilized in measuring the gain.
   c. Payments equivalent to a dividend when one of the parties to the reorganization has accumulated earnings and profits.

In the question situation, the transaction involves the acquisition by King, in exchange solely for

50% of its voting stock, of 90% of Jaxson stock. It should be evident that immediately after the acquisition, King has control of Jaxson; the transaction will qualify as a tax-free reorganization (i.e., type "B").

Answer choice "A" is incorrect because King need not acquire 100 percent of Jaxson for the transaction to be a tax-free reorganization; rather, King must only acquire at least 80 percent control of Jaxson, which in fact it did.

Answer choice "C" is incorrect because King need not issue at least 60 percent of its voting common stock for the transaction to qualify as a tax-free reorganization (i.e., type "B").

Answer choice "D" is incorrect because Jaxson need not surrender assets for the transaction to qualify as a tax-free reorganization. A type "B" reorganization, as is described in the question situation, only involves the exchange of stock.

#26 (answer "C")

The basis of a partner's interest in a partnership is the original basis and subsequent adjustments thereto.

When one receives a partnership interest in exchange for services, the value of the interest is ordinary income and the basis is its fair market value.

The original basis equals the amount of money paid plus the adjusted basis of any contributed property, reduced by the portion of indebtedness on such property, if any, assumed by the other partners. (In general, no gain or loss is recognized either to the partnership or any partner upon a contribution of property in exchange for a partnership interest.)

Subsequent increases to a partner's basis in a partnership result from further contributions, the sum of the partner's distributive shares of partnership income (whether or not taxable), and increases in partnership liabilities that increase each partner's share of the liabilities.

Subsequent decreases in basis result from the amount of money and the adjusted basis of property distributed, the sum of distributive shares of partnership losses, and nondeductible, noncapital expenditures. The adjusted basis for an interest in a partnership can never be less than zero.

Accordingly, Dean's tax basis in Target on December 31, 1994, must reflect Dean's distributive share of all partnership items of income for 1994; Dean's tax basis in Target on December 31, 1994, is therefore equal to $20,000 plus $13,000 (i.e., 25% × [$12,000 + $40,000]) minus $8,000, or $25,000.

Answer choice "A" is incorrect because it fails to include Dean's 25% share of Target's ordinary income (i.e., 25% × $40,000, or $10,000).

Answer choice "B" is incorrect because it fails to (1) include Dean's share of Target's ordinary income (i.e., 25% × $40,000, or $10,000) and (2) deduct the $8,000 nonliquidating cash distribution from Target.

Answer choice "D" is incorrect because it fails to (1) include Dean's share of Target's municipal bond interest income (i.e., 25% × $12,000, or $3,000) and (2) deduct the $8,000 nonliquidating cash distribution from Target.

#27 (answer "A")

The original basis of a partner's interest includes the amount of money paid, plus the adjusted basis of any contributed property, reduced by the portion of any indebtedness on such property assumed by the other partners.

(In general, no gain or loss is recognized either by the partnership or any partner upon a contribution of property in exchange for a partnership interest. Gain, however, will be recognized by a partner to the extent that any indebtedness on contributed property assumed by the other partners exceeds the contributing partner's adjusted basis in such property.)

The adjusted basis for an interest in a partnership, however, can never be less than zero.

Strom's basis in Ace is $0:

Adjusted basis of property contributed	$16,000
Less: Portion of mortgage assumed by other partners; 75% × $24,000	18,000
Strom's basis in Ace	$ 0

Answer choice "B" is incorrect because it assumes that Strom's basis in Ace is equal to the adjusted basis of the property contributed (i.e., $16,000); therefore, it fails to consider the effect of the mortgage assumed by the partnership.

Answer choice "C" is incorrect because it assumes that Strom's basis in Ace is equal to the fair market value of the land contributed by Strom (i.e., $50,000) reduced by the full amount of the $24,000 mortgage assumed by the partnership.

Answer choice "D" is incorrect because it reduces the fair market value of the contributed property (i.e., $50,000), rather than reducing Strom's adjusted basis of the contributed property (i.e., $16,000) by the portion of the mortgage assumed by the other partners (i.e., 75% × $24,000, or $18,000). This results in the incorrect answer choice of $32,000.

#28 (answer "B")

A partnership's organization costs may be amortized over a period of not less than 60 months (the "minimum period") by a newly created partnership that elects to do so. Failing the election, the amount is deductible only upon liquidation.

Organization costs do not include expenses to sell or the promotion to sell a partnership interest.

Alt's only amortizable organization costs are the $12,000 of legal fees to prepare the partnership agreement.

Since Alt began business on October 1, 1994, it is entitled to deduct amortization for three months. Accordingly, the maximum amount that Alt could deduct on the 1994 partnership return is $600 (i.e., 3/60 × $12,000) for the amortization of organizational costs on the 1994 partnership return.

Answer choice "A" is incorrect because it fails to recognize that the legal fees to prepare the partnership agreement are considered amortizable organization costs.

Answer choice "C" is incorrect because it (1) reflects amortization for a full year of the accounting fees to prepare the representations in offering materials, when in fact, such expenses may not be amortized, and (2) fails to recognize that the legal fees to prepare the partnership agreement are considered amortizable organization costs.

Answer choice "D" is incorrect because it reflects amortization over a four-year period of both the legal fees to prepare the partnership agreement (which are properly amortizable over a 60-month

period) and the accounting fees to prepare the representations in offering materials (which are not amortizable).

#29 (answer "A")

Certain partnership items, which are not deductible by a partnership, retain their identities and flow through to the returns of the individual partners. The distributive items to be considered separately by each partner are those that are subject to special handling or limitation on the individual returns of the partner, and include contributions to recognized charities and capital gains and losses.

In computing the ordinary income of a partnership, a deduction is allowed for fixed salaries, determined without regard to the income of the partnership, paid to partners for services. Similarly, a partnership may deduct fixed payments, determined without regard to the income of the partnership, paid to partners for the use of their capital. Such payments, frequently called "guaranteed payments," merely alter the manner in which respective partners share profits.

Thus, guaranteed payments are deductible expenses on Form 1065, "U.S. Partnership Return of Income," in order to arrive at partnership income (loss), and are included on schedule K-1 to be taxed as ordinary income to the partners.

In view of the above, a guaranteed payment by a partnership to a partner for services rendered may include an agreement to pay a salary of $5,000 monthly without regard to partnership income, but may not include an agreement to pay a 25% interest in partnership profits.

Answer choices other than "A" are based on incorrect assumptions and/or combinations.

#30 (answer "C")

The basis of property distributed as a current nonliquidating distribution is equal to the lower of (1) the adjusted basis of the property in the hands of the partnership immediately prior to the distribution, or (2) the adjusted basis of the partner's partnership interest immediately prior to the distribution, reduced by any money distributed simultaneously.

Curry's basis in the land distributed by Vantage is $5,000, which is the lower of (1) $6,000, the adjusted basis of the property to the partnership, or (2) $5,000, the adjusted basis of Curry's partnership interest.

Answer choice "A" is incorrect because it represents the fair market value of the property distributed, which is never considered in determining a partner's basis in property distributed by a partnership.

Answer choice "B" is incorrect because it reflects the adjusted basis of the property distributed (i.e., $6,000), when in fact it should reflect Curry's adjusted basis of his partnership interest (i.e., $5,000), which is the lesser amount.

Answer choice "D" is incorrect because it merely represents the difference between the adjusted basis of the land (i.e., $6,000) and Curry's adjusted basis in Vantage (i.e., $5,000).

#31 (answer "A")

The distribution deduction that may be claimed on an estate's fiduciary income tax return is equal to the amount of income required to be distributed currently plus any amount of income or principal actually paid, credited, or otherwise required to be distributed for that year. Generally, in no event may the distribution deduction be greater than distributable net income (DNI). In essence, DNI (1) fixes the limit on the amount of the deduction for an estate's distributions to its beneficiaries and (2) establishes the amounts and character of the income items reportable by the beneficiaries.

In general, DNI is equal to the taxable income of the estate with certain modifications. Some of the more common modifications are as follows:

1. No distribution deduction is permitted.
2. Tax-exempt interest is included, net of any related expenses.
3. Capital gains allocable to corpus (i.e., principal) are not included; similarly excluded are capital gains that are not paid, credited, or required to be currently distributed to any beneficiary or charity.
4. Capital losses are not included except to the extent of capital gains that are paid, credited, or required to be distributed.

In the question situation, for the calendar year 1994, the estate's distributable net income (DNI) was $15,000 (i.e., the taxable interest $20,000

less the administrative expenses attributable to taxable income $5,000). (The estate's distribution deduction, however, is limited to the required periodic distribution [i.e., $9,000] made by the estate in 1994.)

Answer choice "B" is incorrect because it fails to reflect the allowable $5,000 deduction for administrative expenses attributable to taxable income.

Answer choice "C" is incorrect because it includes the $10,000 net long-term capital gains allocable to corpus.

Answer choice "D" is incorrect because it (1) includes the $10,000 net long-term capital gains allocable to corpus, and (2) fails to reflect the allowable $5,000 deduction for administrative expenses attributable to taxable income.

#32 (answer "B")

An executor of a decedent's estate that has only U.S. citizens as beneficiaries is required to file a fiduciary income tax return if the estate's gross income for the year is at least $600.

If a decedent's estate has one or more beneficiaries who are nonresident aliens, then a fiduciary income tax return must be filed, regardless of the estate's gross income.

Estates must generally file Form 1041, "U.S. Fiduciary Income Tax Return," by the 15th day of the fourth month following the close of the tax year. If the due date falls on a Saturday, Sunday, or legal holiday, the return is due on the next business day.

A request by an estate for an extension of time to file generally extends the due date 60 days, unless the IRS is satisfied that sufficient need is demonstrated.

In view of the above, since Lyon's executor does not intend to file an extension request for the estate fiduciary income tax return, the executor must file the Form 1041, for the estate's 1994 calendar year, by Monday, April 17, 1995.

Answer choice "A" is incorrect because it represents the unextended due date for a corporation's 1994 calendar-year income tax return.

Answer choice "C" is incorrect because it represents the normal extended due date for an estate's 1994 calendar-year fiduciary income tax return.

Answer choice "D" is incorrect because it represents the extended due date for a corporation's 1994 calendar-year income tax return.

#33 (answer "C")

The distribution deduction that may be claimed on an estate's fiduciary income tax return is equal to the amount of income required to be distributed currently plus any amount of income or principal actually paid, credited, or otherwise required to be distributed for that year. Generally, in no event may the distribution deduction be greater than distributable net income (DNI). In essence, DNI (1) fixes the limit on the amount of the deduction for an estate's distributions to its beneficiaries and (2) establishes the amounts and character of the income items reportable by the beneficiaries.

In general, DNI is equal to the taxable income of the estate with certain modifications. Some of the more common modifications are as follows:

1. No distribution deduction is permitted.
2. Tax-exempt interest is included, net of any related expenses.
3. Capital gains allocable to corpus (i.e., principal) are not included; similarly excluded are capital gains that are not paid, credited, or required to be currently distributed to any beneficiary or charity.
4. Capital losses are not included except to the extent of capital gains that are paid, credited, or required to be distributed.

In view of the above, the maximum amount of the distribution to be included in the beneficiary's gross income is limited to the estate's distributable net income.

Answer choices other than "C" are incorrect because the maximum amount of an estate's distribution to be included in the beneficiary's gross income is not limited to the amounts referred to in these answer choices.

#34 (answer "A")

A private foundation is an exempt organization other than (1) an individual bound by the 50% of adjusted gross income limitation applicable to deductions for charitable contributions, (2) an organization that normally receives more than one-third of its support from its members or the public and not more than one-third of its support

from gross investment income and the excess of unrelated business taxable income over the tax on unrelated business taxable income, (3) an organization that actively functions in a supporting relationship, and (4) an organization formed for the purpose of testing public safety.

Accordingly, the private foundation status of an exempt organization will automatically terminate if it becomes a public charity.

Answer choice "B" is incorrect since an organization formed under foreign law may qualify as an exempt organization if it meets the exemption tests specified in the Internal Revenue Code.

Answer choice "C" is incorrect because a private foundation is not required to distribute its net assets.

Answer choice "D" is incorrect because the charter may limit its exempt purposes to specific areas.

#35 (answer "C")

In general, an annual information return must be filed by all exempt organizations. Two of the more common exceptions to the general rule are (1) churches and their integrated auxiliaries, and (2) an entity, other than a private foundation, whose annual gross receipts do not exceed $25,000. Thus, private foundations must file annual information returns.

Answer choices other than "C" are based on assumptions that are invalid under current tax law.

#36 (answer "A")

Generally, total cost contains both fixed and variable elements. Given total costs and a measure of activity (such as orders), it is possible to separate the fixed and variable elements of total cost. A simple technique to accomplish this is known as the "high-low point" method.

1. The first step is to determine the variable cost per unit of activity.

	ORDERS	COST
High (March)	1,800	$4,320
Low (January)	1,200	3,120
Difference	600	$1,200

Therefore, the estimated variable rate is $1,200/600, or $2.00 per order.

2. The second step is to determine the total fixed costs.

Total cost	$4,320
Variable cost; 1,800 orders × $2.00 per order	3,600
Fixed cost for orders	$ 720

Answer choice "B" is incorrect because it uses the total rates of all four months (i.e., $14,520/6,000 equals $2.42); it erroneously treats all costs as variable costs.

Answer choice "C" is incorrect because it treats the total costs of January and March as variable (i.e., [$3,120 + $4,320]/[1,200 + 1,800] equals $2.48); not all of the costs are variable.

Answer choice "D" is not logical based on the facts presented.

#37 (answer "C")

The following should be noted.

1. Estimated cash disbursements for inventories would include amounts needed for projected sales, and an increase in inventory, if any.
2. A decrease in inventories would reduce disbursements necessary for projected sales.
3. A decrease in accounts payable represents payments for prior purchases; as such, cash disbursements would increase.
4. Since purchases will be made in 12 equal monthly amounts, and paid for in the following month, cash will be required for 11/12.

The estimated cash disbursements are $306,000:

Required for projected sales;	
$300,000 × 11/12	$275,000
Increase in inventory;	
$12,000 × 11/12	11,000
Decrease in accounts payable for inventories	20,000
Budgeted cash payment for purchases	$306,000

Answer choice "A" is incorrect because the $11,000 increase in inventory is not included, and should be (i.e., [$300,000 × 11/12] + $20,000 equals $295,000).

Answer choice "B," which represents the total cost of goods sold, is incorrect for several reasons.

First, only 11/12 of the $300,000, or $275,000, should be included. In addition, the $11,000 inventory increase and the $20,000 decrease in accounts payable are not included; both should be.

Answer choice "D" is incorrect for several reasons. First, it considers the total cost of goods sold of $300,000, rather than $275,000 (i.e., $300,000 × 11/12), and the $12,000 total increase in inventory, rather than 11/12, or $11,000. In addition, the $20,000 decrease in accounts payable is not included, and should be.

#38 (answer "C")

The net present value method of capital budgeting holds that at a desired rate of return, the discounted cash flow (i.e., present value) generated is equal to the original investment. Discounted cash flows are generated by annual savings (i.e., additional revenue and/or decreased costs) plus the anticipated residual value of the investment, if any.

Any excess of the discounted cash flow (i.e., present value) over the original investment is positive net present value, which indicates a rate of return higher than the desired rate; any excess of the original investment over the discounted cash flow indicates negative net present value and a lesser return. (The desired rate of return is built into the tables that are used.)

Discounted cash flow (i.e., present value) is determined by applying the desired rate of return to cash inflows for each period. When the inflows are uniform for each period, an annuity table is used. When the inflows are not uniform, they must be discounted separately by using the present value of $1.

As such, the present value of these future savings is $62,900.

Years 1 and 2; $30,000 × 1.65	$49,500
Year 3; $20,000 × .67 (i.e., 2.32 less 1.65)	13,400
Present value of future savings	$62,900

It should be noted that if the rate for three periods is 2.32, and the rate for two periods is 1.65, the rate for the third period standing alone is 2.32 − 1.65, or .67, as noted above.

Answer choices "A" and "B" are not logical in view of the facts presented.

Answer choice "D" is incorrect because, while the present value of the first two years is handled appropriately (i.e., $30,000 × 1.65 equals $49,500), the total cash savings of $20,000 is included for year three (i.e., $49,500 + $20,000 equals $69,500); the $13,400 present value of the $20,000 should be included.

#39 (answer "A")

Breakeven sales in dollars is equal to fixed costs and expenses divided by the contribution margin percentage (i.e., contribution margin divided by sales).

The $100,000 fixed costs divided by breakeven sales of $800,000 yields a contribution margin of 12.5%. Hence, 12.5 percent of $400,000 (i.e., $1,200,000 budgeted less $800,000 breakeven sales) yields a projected profit of $50,000.

Answer choices "B" and "C" are not logical in view of the explanation provided.

Answer choice "D" is incorrect because $400,000 is the "margin of safety," which is the excess of budgeted sales of $1,200,000 less breakeven sales of $800,000.

#40 (answer "D")

The main distinction between direct (variable) costing and conventional (absorption) costing lies in the fact that direct costing inventory consists of variable costs only (i.e., direct materials, direct labor, and variable overhead); conventional costing consists of direct materials, direct labor, and both fixed and variable overhead costs.

Hence, using the variable costing method, variable factory overhead costs would be assigned to inventory, while variable selling and administrative costs would be treated as a period cost and not as a product cost.

Answer choices other than "D" are based on incorrect assumptions and/or combinations.

#41 (answer "D")

The treatment of spoilage in a cost accounting system other than standard costing may be summarized as follows:

1. Normal spoilage—Normal spoilage arises under efficient operating conditions; it is an unavoidable result of the manufacturing process. Costs of normal spoilage are treated as factory overhead and a provision is made for such costs in the predetermined factory overhead rate. In this manner, the costs are prorated over all production of a period.
2. Abnormal spoilage—Generally, abnormal spoilage is spoilage that is not expected to arise under efficient operating conditions. Losses from abnormal spoilage should not be included in production costs (inventoriable cost). Rather, they are removed from production costs and accounted for as a "loss from abnormal spoilage," which is appropriately treated as a period cost.

   It should also be noted that if abnormal spoilage is caused by a particular job's exacting specifications or other unusual factors, such spoilage would be charged to that job.

In this situation, there is no indication that the abnormal cost is associated with a particular job. Accordingly, the $60,000 of normal spoilage is inventoriable (i.e., charged to production), and the $30,000 of abnormal spoilage is a period cost.

(Parenthetically, it should be noted that in a standard cost system, spoilage losses would be accounted for as a function of variance analysis.)

Answer choice "A" is incorrect because the $60,000 of normal spoilage should be accounted for as an inventoriable cost, not a period cost.

Answer choice "B" is incorrect because the $30,000 of abnormal spoilage should be accounted for as a period cost, and not as inventoriable cost.

Answer choice "C" is incorrect because the costs are reversed (i.e., $60,000 should be inventoriable, and $30,000 should be a period cost).

#42 (answer "A")

Standard costs are scientifically predetermined costs that serve as a target for performance. In addition, they can help put together product costs and operating budgets. Their presence allows for the exercise of management by exception and the control of costs.

A standard cost system may be used in conjunction with either a mass production industry or a service industry.

Answer choices other than "A" are based on incorrect assumptions and/or combinations.

#43 (answer "B")

A by-product is the secondary result of manufacturing operations.

When inventory of a by-product is recorded at net realizable value (i.e., sales price less the costs of completion and disposal) when produced, it implies that the cost of the major product has been reduced by that amount, or $3 per unit (i.e., selling price of $4 per unit less the additional selling cost of $1 per unit).

However, if Kode were to change its method of accounting for May from a by-product to a joint product, the selling cost of $1 per unit would become a period, rather than a product, cost. Hence Kode's overall gross margin (i.e., sales less cost of goods sold) would increase by $1 for each unit of May sold.

Answer choices other than "B" are not logical based on the facts presented.

#44 (answer "B")

The following relevant background should be understood:

1. Costs are assigned on the basis of activities performed to produce, distribute, or support products (i.e., purchasing, administrative, and engineering functions). In this sense, costs are not accumulated by department or function, as they are in traditional systems such as job order costing or process costing, etc. In a traditional cost system, the basis for cost allocation is usually direct labor hours, direct labor costs, or machine hours, and so on.
2. Cost drivers are actions or conditions that directly influence and create costs; they are used as a basis for cost allocation. (For example, cost drivers for the purchasing activity would include the number of purchase orders, the number of supplier contracts, and the number of shipments received.)
3. Activity-based costing allows management to identify value-adding and nonvalue-adding activities. Clearly, a value-adding activity increases the worth (i.e., "value") of a product, while a nonvalue-adding ac-

tivity increases the time spent on a product or service, but does not increase its worth. The objective therefore is to ensure that activities that do not add value to the product are identified and reduced to the extent possible.

As such, activity-based costing is a process that uses multiple cost drivers to predict and allocate costs to products and services. Hence, a department's manufacturing overhead costs are assigned to products based on multiple cause and effect relationships.

Answer choice "A" is incorrect because costs are assigned on a multiple, and not a single, cause and effect relationship.

Answer choices "C" and "D" are not logical based on the facts provided.

#45 (answer "D")

The following relationships should be understood in order to arrive at an answer to this question.

1. Classically, percentage return on assets is equal to net income divided by average total assets (i.e., "average invested capital").
2. Asset turnover (i.e., "capital turnover rate") is equal to net sales divided by average total assets.
3. Profit margin on sales (i.e., "net income on net sales," or "return on sales") is equal to net income divided by net sales.

Based on interpolation of the facts provided, the rate of percentage return on assets can be arrived at by multiplying asset turnover by the profit margin on sales; the answer is therefore 5 × 2%, or 10.0%.

It should be noted that the answer has effectively been arrived at by the elimination of the remaining answer choices on the basis of logical examination of the facts.

Answer choices other than "D" are not logical based on the facts provided.

#46 (answer "D")

Responsibility accounting relates income, costs, and expenses to positions and people in the organizational structure who control and are directly responsible for creating them; it fixes responsibility for performance.

Measures of performance can be either financial or nonfinancial in nature.

Financial measures of performance include division profits, achievement of budget objectives, individual and total variances from budget or standard, and cash flows.

Nonfinancial measures of performance may be used to evaluate either the effectiveness (i.e., product quality inclusive of rework units) or efficiency (i.e., time) of managers' performance. They rely on data outside of a conventional cost system, such as production cycle time (i.e., inclusive of set-up time and unscheduled down time), throughput time, delivery time, warranty expenses, total number of units completed, service calls, returns and allowances, and customer complaints.

Thus, all the measures indicated should be considered in evaluating the performance of a manufacturing system.

Answer choices other than "D" are based on incorrect assumptions and/or combinations.

#47 (answer "B")

The basic principle of a "just-in-time" production system is to receive raw materials as needed, rather than building up inventories. Fewer goods on hand requires less warehouse space and storage equipment, resulting in cost savings.

Since inventory levels would be greatly reduced, or eliminated entirely, a change from a traditional manufacturing philosophy to a "just-in-time" philosophy, would be most conducive when cost per purchase order decreases and inventory unit carrying costs increase.

Answer choices other than "B" are based on incorrect assumptions and/or combinations.

#48 (answer "C")

The term "expected value of Dough's decision, etc.," relates to "probability." In probability theory, for a range of variables and occurrences, the "estimated probabilities" yield the "expected values" as weighted averages.

The following definitions are relevant.

1. Estimated probabilities—An estimated probability is the chance of an event happening. Further, the probability of an event is defined as the number of trials. Therefore, one must accept that the sum of several probabilities must equal one, or 100%.
2. Random variables—Those amounts of cost revenue, etc., in the estimated range that are multiplied by the estimated probability to arrive at an expected value (weighted amount).
3. Expected value—The random variable is multiplied by its probability of occurrence to become an "expected value," which in essence is a weighted average as to what may be expected from future events.

In this question, there are two events or random variables. These are (1) selling 60 additional boxes, which has a 60% chance of happening, and (2) selling an additional 100 boxes, which has a 40% chance of happening.

The random variables are a profit of $20 if 60 boxes are sold (i.e., [60 × $3] + [40 × $1] − [100 × $2] equals $20), and a profit of $100 if all the boxes are sold (i.e., 100 × [$3 − $2]).

The expected value of the decision to buy 100 additional boxes is $52.

EVENT (RANDOM VARIABLE)	PROBABILITY	VALUE OF RANDOM VARIABLE (CONDITIONAL VALUE)	EXPECTED VALUE)
60 additional boxes	.6	$ 20	$12
100 additional boxes	.4	$100	40
Expected value of the decision			$52

Answer choice "A" is incorrect because it is the result of subtracting the $12 expected value from the $40 expected value, rather than adding them together.

Answer choice "B" is incorrect because it represents the expected value of selling the additional 100 boxes, and excludes the expected value of selling the additional 60 boxes.

Answer choice "D" is not logical in view of the explanation provided for "C."

#49 (answer "D")

Contribution margin is the difference between total revenues and total variable costs (both manufacturing and nonmanufacturing) for all units sold. Total contribution margin identifies the amount available to "contribute" to the coverage of all fixed expenses, both manufacturing and nonmanufacturing. After fixed expenses are covered, any remaining contribution provides profit to the company.

Thus, for short-run profit maximization, Jago should manufacture the product with the greater contribution margin per hour of manufacturing capacity.

Answer choice "A" is incorrect because it does not consider the nonmanufacturing variable costs, and it should; these are a factor in contribution margin. In addition, variable, not total manufacturing, costs are a factor in contribution margin.

Answer choice "B" is incorrect because it does not consider the nonmanufacturing variable costs, and should.

Answer choice "C" is incorrect because gross profit is the difference between revenues and the total cost of goods sold. It does not consider the nonmanufacturing variable costs (i.e., period costs), and it should. In addition, fixed manufacturing costs are included in determination of gross profit; these are not a factor in contribution margin.

#50 (answer "C")

This question can be solved either by expressing the information in algebraic terms, or by the use of trial and error.

It must be considered that the price of food is equal to the quoted $60 per person less the 15% service charge on the food, and less the 6% sales tax on the food plus the service charge.

The following answer is expressed in an equation.

Let "X" equal the price of food.

$$
\begin{aligned}
\text{Then, } X &= \$60 - (.15X + .06\,[X + .15X]) \\
X &= \$60 - (.15X + .06X + .009X) \\
X &= \$60 - .219X \\
1.219X &= \$60 \\
X &= \underline{\$49.22} \text{ (rounded)}
\end{aligned}
$$

The answer may also be arrived at by trial and error.

Answer "A": $56.40 + (15% × $56.40) + 6% ($56.40 + [15% × $56.40]) = $56.40 + $8.46 + $3.89 = $68.75 $68.75 is not $60.00.

Answer "B": $51.00 + (15% × $51.00) + 6% ($51.00 + [15% × $51.00]) = $51.00 + $7.65 + $3.52 = $62.17 $62.17 is not $60.00.

Answer "C": $49.22 + (15% × $49.22) + 6% ($49.22 + [15% × $49.22]) = $49.22 + $7.38 + $3.40 = $60.00.

As can be seen, the answer would have been arrived at on the third trial.

(Where necessary, numbers have been rounded to two decimal places, which would be appropriate in the circumstances.)

Answer choices other than "C" are based on incorrect assumptions.

#51 (answer "B")

The nature of fund accounting lies in its non-profit orientation. There is no profit motive and what is measured is accountability, rather than profitability. The main objective is stewardship of financial resources received and expended in compliance with legal requirements (i.e., flows of financial resources), and on determination of financial position (i.e., balances of financial resources).

Fund accounting concepts are a feature of accounting for governmental units (as well as other not-for-profit institutions, such as hospitals, universities, and voluntary health and welfare organizations). These concepts adhere to generally accepted accounting principles as applicable to not-for-profit institutions. Legal/contractual compliances, if at odds with GAAP, would be reported in supplementary information.

Answer choice "A" is incorrect because fund accounting measures accountability rather than profitability (i.e., income determination).

Answer choice "C" is incorrect because the focus is on financial resources rather than economic resources (i.e., capital maintenance is not a primary concern of fund accounting and reporting).

Answer choice "D" is incorrect because cash flows and balances are not the measurement focus of fund accounting.

#52 (answer "C")

A summary of financial reporting objectives for government entities is as follows:

1. Accountability
   a. Should provide information to <u>determine whether current-year revenues were sufficient to pay for current-year services</u>.
   b. Should demonstrate whether resources were obtained and used in accordance with the entity's legally adopted budget. Should also demonstrate compliance with other finance-related legal or contractual requirements.
   c. Should provide information to assist in assessing the service efforts, costs, and accomplishments of the governmental entity; i.e., to help assess the economy, efficiency, and effectiveness of government and to help form a basis for voting or funding decisions (i.e., <u>making social and political decisions</u>).
2. <u>Evaluating</u> the <u>operating</u> results
   a. Should provide information about sources and uses of financial resources.
   b. Should provide information about how the governmental entity financed its activities and met its cash requirements.
   c. Should provide information necessary to determine whether the entity's financial position improved or deteriorated as a result of the year's operations.
3. <u>Assessing the level of governmental services and the entity's ability to meet its obligations as they become due</u>
   a. Should provide information about the financial position and condition of a governmental entity.
   b. Should provide information about a governmental entity's physical and other nonfinancial resources having useful lives that extend beyond the current year.
   c. Should disclose legal or contractual restriction on resources and risks of potential loss of resources.

Additionally, it should be noted that "interperiod equity" is a concept that implies that a government should operate within its budget, and not shift the burden of paying for current-year services to future taxpayers.

Answer choices other than "C" are based on incorrect assumptions and/or combinations.

#53 (answer "C")

In general, combined financial statements for a governmental entity constitute the basic financial statements necessary for fair presentation in accordance with GAAP.

Total columns are optional (as memorandum notations only), but commonly shown, for combined financial statements showing the various fund types. As such, the various funds types are combined (i.e., added together) rather than consolidated.

Accordingly, because each fund is a fiscal and accounting entity, the amount due to one fund from other funds, as well as the amounts owed to other funds (i.e., <u>interfund receivables and payables</u>), <u>should be reported as amounts due to and due from other funds</u>.

Answer choice "A" is incorrect because the reservations of fund balance do not involve interfund receivables and payables.

Answer choice "B" is incorrect because receivables and payables are not shown as adjustments to the unrestricted fund balance.

Answer choice "D" is incorrect because governmental fund types are combined rather than eliminated.

#54 (answer "A")

The major accounting classifications of expenditures are:

1. <u>Function or program</u>—information on the overall purposes of expenditures.
2. <u>Organization</u>—information on the organization unit making the expenditures.
3. <u>Activity</u>—information to aid evaluation of economy and efficiency of operations.
4. <u>Character</u>—information on the basis of the fiscal period presumed to benefit from the expenditures (e.g., "current" or "capital outlay").
5. <u>Object</u>—information on the types of items purchased, or services obtained (e.g., "<u>salaries and wages</u>").

Answer choices other than "A" do not represent the appropriate expenditure classification categories for "salaries and wages."

#55 (answer "C")

GASB Statement #18 establishes standards of accounting and financial reporting for Municipal Solid Waste Landfill (MSWLF) closure and postclosure care costs. MSWLF owners and operators are required to incur a variety of costs to provide for protection of the environment during the postclosure period. The numerous cost components of the closure care costs include the cost of infrastructure, the cost of capping the landfill, and the cost of monitoring and maintaining the expected usable MSWLF area during the postclosure period. Current cost is the amount that would be paid if all equipment, facilities, and services included in the estimate were acquired during the current period.

Accordingly, current expenses would include:

1. Cost of a final cover to be applied to the landfill.
2. Cost of equipment to be installed to monitor the landfill (i.e., the methane gas build-up).

Answer choices other than "C" are based on incorrect assumptions and/or illogical combinations.

#56 (answer "D")

In governmental accounting, there are three broad types of funds and two "account groups." The three broad types are governmental funds, proprietary funds, and fiduciary funds. The two account groups are the general fixed assets account group and the general long-term debt account group.

Governmental-type funds include general funds, special revenue funds, capital projects funds, and debt service funds.

Proprietary funds are enterprise funds and internal service funds.

Fiduciary funds include trust and agency funds.

The two account groups are self-balancing sets of accounts and not "funds" in the strict sense.

The question refers to "nonexpendable trust funds" and "expendable trust funds" as two of the answer choices.

In an expendable trust fund, both principal and earnings may be expended; in a nonexpendable trust fund, only earnings may be expended.

Nonexpendable trust funds use the same accounting basis (i.e., accrual) as a proprietary fund.

Expendable trust funds use the same accounting basis (i.e., modified accrual) as a governmental-type fund.

Answer choice "A" is incorrect because an enterprise fund is a proprietary fund.

Answer choice "B" is incorrect because an internal service fund is a proprietary fund.

Answer choice "C" is incorrect because a nonexpendable trust fund is accounted for in the same manner as a proprietary fund.

#57 (answer "C")

In accordance with FASB Statement #117, the term used for equity is net assets, which represents the excess of assets over liabilities.

The financial statements focus on the entity taken as a whole rather than on individual funds.

Net assets (i.e., resources) are classified in groups within three categories: permanently restricted, temporarily restricted, or unrestricted.

1. Permanently restricted—These are resources with a donor-imposed restriction that stipulates that resources be maintained permanently, but permits the organization to use up, or expend, all or part of the income generated from the donated assets.
2. Temporarily restricted—These are resources with a donor-imposed restriction that permits the organization to use up, or expend, the donated assets as specified, and is satisfied either by the passage of time or by actions of the organization.
3. Unrestricted—These are resources that have no external restrictions as to use or purpose. They can be used for any purpose designated by the governing board as distinguished from funds restricted externally (i.e., by donors, for specific purposes or time periods).

Reclassification to or from net asset categories may occur.

Revenues, including contributions, are recognized as increases in unrestricted net assets, unless the use of such assets is limited by donor-imposed restrictions, in which event there would be an increase in either temporarily restricted net assets, or permanently restricted net assets.

As a rule, revenue associated with restricted gifts is classified as unrestricted if the restrictions are met in the same period in which the resources are received.

Accordingly, the receipt of the $7,000,000 contribution should be reported as follows: $5,000,000 as temporarily restricted net assets; $2,000,000 as permanently restricted net assets.

Answer choice "A" is incorrect because $5,000,000 is temporarily restricted.

Answer choice "B" is incorrect because $2,000,000 is permanently restricted.

Answer choice "D" is incorrect because it includes the permanently restricted amount with the temporarily restricted amount (i.e., $5,000,000 + $2,000,000 equals $7,000,000).

#58 (answer "B")

Net assets (i.e., resources) are classified in groups within three categories: permanently restricted, temporarily restricted, or unrestricted.

1. Permanently restricted—These are resources with a donor-imposed restriction that stipulates that resources be maintained permanently, but permits the organization to use up, or expend, all or part of the income generated from the donated assets.
2. Temporarily restricted—These are resources with a donor-imposed restriction that permits the organization to use up, or expend, the donated assets as specified, and is satisfied either by the passage of time or by actions of the organization.
3. Unrestricted—These are resources that have no external restrictions as to use or purpose. They can be used for any purpose designated by the governing board, as distinguished from funds restricted externally (i.e., by donors for specific purposes or time periods).

Reclassification to or from net asset categories may occur.

Revenues, including contributions, are recognized as increases in unrestricted net assets, un-

less the use of such assets is limited by donor-imposed restrictions, in which event there would be an increase in either temporarily restricted net assets, or permanently restricted net assets.

As a rule, revenue associated with restricted gifts is classified as unrestricted, if the restrictions are met in the same period in which the resources are received.

Accordingly, the receipt of the money should be reported as a temporarily restricted contribution.

Answer choice "A" is incorrect because the donor stipulated a purpose restriction for the contribution.

Answer choice "C" is incorrect because the organization can release the restriction by meeting the stipulation made by the donor.

Answer choice "D" is incorrect because the receipt of the money should be reported as a contribution (i.e., support received), not as a liability.

#59 (answer "B")

"Collections" are "works of art, historical treasures, etc., that are held for public exhibition, education, or research in furtherance of public service rather than financial gain." If such assets are cared for and preserved, and subject to an organizational policy that requires the proceeds from the sale of such items to be used to acquire other items, the capitalization of collections is optional for not-for-profit organizations.

Answer choices other than "B" represent situations where contributions of items would be recognized as revenue (i.e., support).

#60 (answer "D")

When a not-for-profit organization receives a donation of materials and/or supplies, the donation should be recorded at its fair value if there is a clearly objective and measurable basis for determining such value.

It should be noted that while revenue results from such a donation, it is recorded with an offset to expense. Thus, while the transaction nets out, both elements are recorded for reporting purposes.

There are two revenue captions of a not-for-profit hospital: patient service revenues and other operating revenues.

Patient service revenues are those directly related to patient care. They are presented net, with optional disclosure of related allowances. Bad debts are reported as an operating expense.

Other operating revenues include sources indirectly related to providing patient services (e.g., tuition from educational programs, cafeteria revenues, parking fees and gift shop revenues). Also included are transfers from specific purpose funds, and donated materials and supplies.

Nonoperating gains include revenue sources that are neither patient service revenues nor other operating revenues. Included are general contributions, unrestricted income from endowment funds, income from investments, unrestricted income earmarked for specific purposes, and so on. Also included is the value of donated services.

Clearly, then, the donation should be valued at $5,000. Based on the background provided above, the donation is recorded as other operating revenue of $5,000.

Answer choice "A" is incorrect because the transaction is not recorded as a memorandum entry only.

Answer choices "B" and "C" are incorrect because they result in a netting of the transaction; both revenue and expense should be reported.

OTHER OBJECTIVE FORMATS QUESTIONS

Answer 2

#61 (answer "N")

In this situation, the journal entry to record the adoption of the budget is as follows:

Dr. Estimated
    revenues—control   6,000,000
    Cr. Appropriations—
      control   5,600,000
    Cr. Budgetary fund
      balance   400,000

Accordingly, the budgetary fund balance increased by $400,000, not by $50,000.

#62 (answer "Y")

The general fund budgetary entry to record appropriations should include an operating transfer out for the amount expected to be transferred to the capital projects fund.

#63 (answer "N")

Transfers of resources to establish funds (e.g., the general fund contribution to help establish the water utility fund—a proprietary fund) should be reported as residual equity transfers, rather than operating transfers.

#64 (answer "N")

When bonds are issued for the construction of a capital project, the proceeds are recorded in the capital projects fund in a nominal account termed "bond issue proceeds," which is reported as an element of "other financing sources." Any bond premium received is transferred to the debt service fund, and not to the general fund.

#65 (answer "N")

The payment from the general fund for water received should be treated as an expenditure. It is a quasi-external transaction and should be recorded in the general fund in the same way that it would be if an organization external to the governmental unit were involved.

It is not an operating transfer out in the general fund.

#66 (answer "N")

For governmental funds, revenue is recognized on the modified accrual basis (i.e., when it becomes available and measurable). For property tax revenues, "available" means then due, or past due and receivable within the current period, and collected within the current period or expected to be collected soon enough thereafter to be used to pay liabilities of the current period. Such time thereafter shall not exceed 60 days.

Since, by definition, property taxes receivable would include amounts in revenue, such amounts would not include those expected to be collected after 60 days; March 15, 1995, is more than 60 days after December 31, 1994.

#67 (answer "N")

In this situation, closing the budgetary accounts involves a reversal of the entry to record the budget at the beginning of the year (see answer to #61 above) as follows:

Dr. Appropriations—control 5,600,000
Dr. Budgetary fund balance   400,000

Cr. Estimated revenues—
control   6,000,000

Accordingly, the fund balance would <u>decrease</u>, <u>not increase</u>, by $400,000.

#68 (answer "Y")

In this situation, closing the actual accounts increases the fund balance $50,000 as follows:

Dr. Revenues—control 5,750,000
 Cr. Expenditures—control   5,700,000
 Cr. Fund balance   50,000

As shown above, the closing entry in answer #67 reduces the fund balance by $400,000. Accordingly, the interaction between budgetary and actual amounts causes the fund balance to <u>decrease by $350,000</u> (credit of $50,000 less debit of $400,000).

#69 (answer "Y")

The general fixed assets account group is used to account for all fixed assets other than those specifically associated with and carried in a proprietary fund or a trust fund. In this situation, the capital projects fund recorded $1,080,000 in expenditures for construction of the civic center. Accordingly, the entry in the general fixed assets account group is:

Dr. Construction in progress 1,080,000
 Cr. <u>Investment in general</u>
   <u>fixed assets</u>—
    <u>capital project fund</u>   1,080,000

#70 (answer "Y")

While there is no requirement that depreciation be recorded in general fixed assets, <u>it may be recorded as an optional procedure</u>.

(Where this option is exercised, depreciation is recorded as a debit to the "investment in fixed assets" account and not as an expenditure.)

#71 (answer "N")

The general fixed assets account group is used to account for all fixed assets other than those specifically associated with and carried in a proprietary fund (i.e., the water utility fund) or trust fund. Depreciation is recognized in the proprietary and/or nonexpendable trust funds that have depreciable fixed assets.

Depreciation on proprietary fund fixed assets <u>could not be recorded by the general fund (in the general fixed assets account group</u>) in any manner.

#72 (answer "Y")

In general, combined financial statements for each fund type constitute the basic financial statements necessary for fair presentation in accordance with GAAP. Included is a "combined statement of revenues, expenditures, and changes in fund balances—all governmental fund types and discretely presented component units." Accordingly, <u>the capital project fund should be included</u> as a governmental fund.

#73 (answer "Y")

In general, combined financial statements for each fund type constitute the basic financial statements necessary for fair presentation in accordance with GAAP. Included is a "combined balance sheet—all fund types, account groups and discretely presented component units." Accordingly, <u>the water utility enterprise fund should be included</u>.

#74 (answer "N")

A combined statement of cash flows is reported for proprietary fund types (and nonexpendable trust funds) and discretely presented component units. The presentation of cash flows requires that cash receipts and payments be classified in four categories:

 a. <u>Operating activities</u>—generally include the cash effects of transactions that enter into the determination of operating income.
 b. <u>Noncapital financing activities</u>—generally include grants, subsidies, and interfund transactions.
 c. <u>Capital and related financing activities</u>—generally include the acquisition, construction, and improvements of capital assets, as well as the related financing transactions, inclusive of debt service (both principal and interest).
 d. <u>Investing activities</u>—generally include the purchases and sales of investments, and cash flows resulting from investment income.

As the debt service fund is not a proprietary fund or a nonexpendable trust fund, <u>no statement of cash flows is prepared for the fund</u>.

#75 (answer "N")

See the explanation for #74 above. As the capital project fund is not a proprietary fund or a nonexpendable trust fund, no statement of cash flows is prepared for this fund.

#76 (answer "Y")

See the explanation for #74 above. As the water utility enterprise fund is a proprietary fund, the statement of cash flows with the category "capital and related financing activities" for the proceeds of the revenue bond issue should be reported.

#77 (answer "5,600,000")

In this situation, the journal entry to record the adoption of the budget is as follows:

Dr. Estimated revenues—
control   6,000,000
    Cr. Appropriations—
    control   5,600,000
    Cr. Budgetary fund balance   400,000

Accordingly, $5,600,000 was recorded for appropriations (i.e., the budgeted expenditures).

#78 (answer "4,750,000")

In this situation, based on the information provided, the entry to record the property tax levy would be as follows:

Dr. Property taxes receivable   4,750,000
    Cr. Allowance for estimated
     uncollectible taxes—current   50,000
    Cr. Property tax revenue   4,700,000

(It should be noted that the revenue is recorded net of the allowance for uncollectibles.)

#79 (answer "1,200,000")

The general long-term debt account group is used to account for the principal on all unmatured long-term debt (inclusive of lease-purchase agreements, etc.), except debt payable from a proprietary fund or a trust fund. In this situation, the principal amount to be included is the $1,200,000 par value of bonds issued for the civic center. The $4,000,000 in revenue bonds should be reported in the water utility enterprise fund (i.e., a proprietary fund).

#80 (answer "1,080,000")

As noted in the explanation to #69 above, the credit to "investment in general fixed assets—capital project fund" should be recorded as $1,080,000.

#81 (answer "2,473,000")

The completed cost of the civic center is derived as follows:

Total resources available 1994–1995:		
Revenues		$ 800,000
Bond proceeds	$1,230,000	
Less: Bond premium (operating transfer out)	(30,000)	1,200,000
Operating transfer in		500,000
Total available		2,500,000
Residual equity transfer out		(27,000)
Total expenditures		$2,473,000

(It should be noted that the residual equity transfer out was made when the project was closed, which is appropriate.)

#82 (answer "800,000")

Based on the information provided, the capital project fund received financing from a combination of general fund transfers, a state grant, and an issue of general obligation bonds. The only revenue item not otherwise accounted for, and thus assumed to be from the state capital grant, was $800,000.

#83 (answer "2,422,000")

Based on the information provided, the total encumbrances recorded during 1994 consist of the following:

Expenditures previously encumbered during 1994	$1,080,000
Purchase orders and commitments outstanding at December 31, 1994	1,300,000
Excess of total encumbrances over corresponding expenditures in 1994	42,000
Total encumbrances recorded during 1994	$2,422,000

#84 (answer "120,000")

The unreserved fund balance reported in the capital project fund at December 31, 1994, is determined as follows:

Unreserved fund balance from closing	$1,420,000
Less: Encumbrances outstanding closed out and establishment of a reserve for encumbrances	1,300,000
Unreserved fund balance at December 31, 1994	$ 120,000

Answer 3

#85 (answer "15,000, I")

Only 50% of meals and entertainment is deductible in arriving at a corporation's taxable income. Accordingly, Reliant's Schedule M-1 adjustment for the nondeductible portion of the business meals (i.e., 50% × $30,000, or $15,000) increases its 1994 taxable income. It should be noted that travel expenses are fully deductible.

#86 (answer "7,000, I")

Premiums for keyman life insurance policies are not deductible if the corporation is the beneficiary. As a result, Reliant's $7,000 expense for the term life insurance premiums on the corporate officers is nondeductible and increases its 1994 taxable income on Schedule M-1.

#87 (answer "0, N")

State franchise tax is deductible by a corporation in arriving at federal taxable income. Accordingly, Reliant's state franchise tax expense for 1994 has no effect on its 1994 taxable income on Schedule M-1.

#88 (answer "6,000, D")

Under the Modified Accelerated Cost Recovery System (MACRS), computers represent five-year recovery property; depreciation is calculated using the 200% declining-balance method, with a switch to the straight-line method at the point when deductions will be maximized (i.e., generally at the midpoint of the recovery period). A half-year convention is used for (1) the first year an asset is placed service, and (2) the year of disposition of an asset before the end of the recovery period.

Reliant's 1993 tax depreciation is $10,000 (i.e., $50,000 × ⅕ × 200% × ½); the tax depreciation for 1994 is $16,000 (i.e., ($50,000 − $10,000) × ⅕

× 200%). Since Reliant's book depreciation on computers for 1994 was $10,000, Reliant must make a Schedule M-1 adjustment to decrease its taxable income by $6,000 (i.e., $16,000 − $10,000).

#89 (answer "1,000, I")

Corporations may deduct capital losses only to the extent of capital gains. Capital losses may never offset ordinary income.

The $4,000 short-term capital gain distribution from a mutual fund corporation received by Reliant in 1994, when netted with the $5,000 loss on the sale of Retro stock, results in a $1,000 net loss. As a result, Reliant must make a $1,000 Schedule M-1 adjustment, which increases its taxable income.

#90 (answer "0, N")

A corporation may claim a deduction for charitable contributions made in cash or property. The deduction is limited to 10% of taxable income without taking into account (1) the deduction for contributions, (2) the dividends-received deduction, (3) any net operating loss carryback to the tax year, and (4) any capital loss carryback to the tax year.

Reliant's $15,000 expense for charitable contributions is fully deductible because it is less than Reliant's $50,000 limit (i.e., 10% × $500,000) for deducting charitable contributions.

Accordingly, in preparing its schedule M-1, Reliant's charitable contributions will have no effect on taxable income.

#91 (answer "P")

Reliant's purchase of theater tickets for its out-of-town clients is partially deductible, because only 50% of meals and entertainment is deductible in arriving at a corporation's taxable income.

#92 (answer "F")

In general, advertising expenses, like other selling expenses, represent ordinary and necessary business expenses; advertising expenses should generally not be capitalized as part of inventory.

Accordingly, <u>advertising expenses to promote a new product line are fully deductible</u>, even if part of the new product line remains in ending inventory.

#93 (answer "N")

Interest on indebtedness to purchase municipal bonds is not deductible because the interest income derived from these bonds is not taxable.

#94 (answer "N")

In general, a C corporation is required to make estimated tax payments when its expected tax liability (after tax credits) for the year is at least $500. The required estimated tax payments are due on the 15th day of the 4th, 6th, 9th, and 12th months of the tax year.

Failure to pay sufficient estimated tax may result in an underpayment penalty for the period of underpayment, at a rate that is periodically determined by the Internal Revenue Service.

<u>The penalty for the underpayment of estimated taxes is nondeductible.</u>

#95 (answer "F")

<u>The bonuses declared by Reliant's board of directors on December 9, 1994, and that were paid on February 3, 1995, are fully deductible.</u>

An accrual-basis corporation may accrue and deduct salaries (including bonuses and vacation pay) for non-stockholder employees if paid on or before the due date of the corporation's tax return (which is generally the 15th day of the third month following the close of the taxable year).

#96 (answer "N")

<u>The portion of Reliant's refund that represented the overpayment of the 1992 federal taxes is nontaxable</u>, because federal taxes are nondeductible.

It should be noted that refunds of state franchise tax are includible in income, based on the tax-benefit rule. Under the tax-benefit rule, a refund of state franchise tax is taxable to the extent that (1) the state franchise tax had been previously deducted for tax purposes, and (2) the income tax liability had been reduced in a previous year.

#97 (answer "F")

<u>The portion of Reliant's refund that is attributable to the interest on the overpayment of federal taxes is fully taxable.</u>

In general, only interest income on municipal bonds is nontaxable.

#98 (answer "N")

<u>The dividend income received by Reliant from a mutual fund that invests solely in municipal bonds is nontaxable.</u>

It should be noted that the dividends-received deduction generally available to a C corporation is not applicable to dividend income received from a mutual fund that invests solely in interest-paying securities.

#99 (answer "F")

<u>The value of the capital improvements made by the lessee of Reliant's property is fully taxable to Reliant in 1994.</u>

Amounts received as rent must be included in gross income. Capital improvements made in lieu of rent are includible in gross income to the extent of their fair market value in the year in which the improvements are made.

Advance rental receipts must also be included in gross income regardless of the period covered or the method of accounting used (i.e., cash basis or accrual basis).

#100 (answer "P")

<u>The proceeds collected by Reliant on the term life insurance policy on the life of a debtor who was not a shareholder are partially taxable.</u>

Proceeds collected on a life insurance policy, which is pledged or assigned to an insured's creditor as collateral for debt, are taxable to the extent that the proceeds are in excess of the debt.

#101 (answer "N")

The 70% dividends-received deduction used by Reliant for regular tax purposes has no effect on Reliant's 1994 alternative taxable income (AMTI) prior to the adjusted current earnings (ACE) adjustment.

It should be noted that the 70% dividends-received deduction is not allowed in the determination of ACE; the 80% dividends-received deduction (applicable to 20%-or-more-owned corporations), however, is allowable in determining ACE.

#102 (answer "N")

The interest received by Reliant from a state's general obligation bonds has no effect on AMTI prior to the ACE adjustment because municipal bond interest, other than from private activity bonds, is not includible income to arrive at AMTI prior to the ACE adjustment.

#103 (answer "I")

Depreciation on personal property to arrive at AMTI prior to the ACE adjustment is computed under the Alternative Depreciation System, except that personal property is depreciated using the 150% declining-balance method. Further, under the Alternative Depreciation System, recovery periods are longer than those utilized for deductions under MACRS.

(For regular tax purposes, seven-year personal property is generally depreciated using the 200% declining-balance method.)

In view of the above, Reliant will be required to make an adjustment for depreciation on the seven-year personal property; this will effectively increase its AMTI prior to the ACE adjustment.

#104 (answer "I")

In determining AMTI prior to the ACE adjustment, a depreciation adjustment may be necessary because the Alternative Depreciation System must be utilized. Commercial real property, as well as residential rental property, must be depreciated using the straight-line method over a recovery period of 40 years. For regular tax purposes, the recovery period for real property placed into service on or after May 13, 1993, is 39 years. The applicable depreciation adjustment generally increases AMTI prior to the ACE adjustment.

#105 (answer "N")

Reliant's cash charitable contributions for 1994 have no effect on AMTI prior to the ACE adjustment.

In calculating AMTI prior to the ACE adjustment, there is no tax preference or adjustment for charitable contributions of cash or appreciated tangible personal property.

(It should be noted that ACE is also unaffected by charitable contributions.)

#106 (answer "F")

A corporation's alternative minimum tax is equal to 20% of AMTI (in excess of the exemption amount) reduced by the corporation's regular tax liability. The corporate exemption amount, which therefore reduces AMTI, is equal to $40,000, but must be reduced by 25% of the excess of AMTI over $150,000.

#107 (answer "F")

An assessment may be made at any time for filing a false or fraudulent return or for failing to file a tax return.

Accordingly, the statute of limitations on Reliant's fraudulent 1990 federal income tax return never expires.

#108 (answer "F")

The general rule is that the statute of limitations will expire three years after the later of either the due date of the return or the date the return was filed.

A major exception to the general rule relates to the "substantial omission of items" from the return. Simply stated, the three-year period will be extended to six years if the taxpayer omits from gross income an amount in excess of 25% of the amount of gross income as reported on the return (prior to the deduction for cost of goods sold).

Additionally, an assessment may be made at any time for filing a false or fraudulent return or for failing to file a tax return.

In view of the above, the statute of limitations on Reliant's 1991 federal income tax return, which omitted in excess of 25% of gross receipts, expires six years after the later of either the due date of the return or the date the return was filed.

#109 (answer "T")

The general business credit, which may be claimed on Form 3800—General Business Credit, is a combination of several tax credits to provide uniform rules for the current and carryback-carryover years. The general business credit consists of the following components: the investment tax credit, the target jobs credit (and its replacement, the work opportunity credit), the alcohol fuel credit, the incremental research credit, the low-income housing credit, the enhanced oil recovery credit, and the disabled access credit.

#110 (answer "T")

As a small business, Reliant qualifies for the disabled access credit because it incurred qualifying expenditures to remove existing barriers (to disabled individuals) at the place of employment in 1994.

A business qualifies as a small business if, during the preceding tax year, it either had (1) gross receipts that were not in excess of $1,000,000 or (2) no more than 30 full-time employees.

The disabled access credit, which is a component of the general business credit, is generally equal to 50% of the eligible access expenditures in excess of $250 (but not in excess of $10,250).

#111 (answer "T")

A tax return preparer may be liable for a $250 civil penalty for improper disclosure or use of tax return information.

In general, in order to avoid the imposition of the penalty, a tax return preparer must obtain the consent of the taxpayer to disclose or use tax return information. No consent, however, is necessary if the disclosure or use of the tax return information is in connection with the quality or peer review of the tax return preparer. Consent is also not required if a tax return preparer uses information from one taxpayer in preparing the tax return of another taxpayer, but only if (1) the taxpayers are related (e.g., a corporation and its shareholders), (2) the taxpayers do not have any adverse interest, and (3) disclosure is not expressly prohibited by the first taxpayer.

Accordingly, Reliant's tax preparer may use the 1994 corporate tax return information to prepare corporate officers' tax returns without the consent of the corporation.

#112 (answer "F")

An amended tax return is a tax return that (1) is filed after the due date of the original tax return, and (2) either increases or decreases a tax liability.

An amended tax return that decreases a tax liability is considered to be a claim for a refund. Under the general rule, a claim for refund must be filed within three years from the date the return was filed or within two years from the date the tax was paid, whichever is later. Returns filed before the due date are considered to have been filed on the due date. An exception to the general rule exists for claims relating to deductions of bad debts and worthless securities. In these cases, the three-year limitation is extended to seven years.

In general, there is no limitation of time to file an amended tax return that increases a tax liability.

In view of the rules above, it should be apparent that Reliant need not file an amended return for 1994 within one year of the filing date.

Financial Accounting & Reporting—Business Enterprises (FARE)

FOUR-OPTION MULTIPLE-CHOICE QUESTIONS

Answer 1

#1 (answer "D")

Statement of Financial Accounting Concepts #2, "Qualitative Characteristics of Accounting Information," identifies qualitative characteristics that make accounting information useful.

The primary qualities of information presented are relevance and reliability, which are described as follows:

1. Relevance—Capable of making a difference in the user's decision-making.
   a. Timeliness—availability of information before it loses its decision making value.
   b. Predictive value—helping users form predictions about outcomes past, present, and future.
   c. Feedback value—providing information on earlier expectations.
2. Reliability—Assures that information is reasonably free from error and bias and thus faithfully portrays what it purports to represent.
   a. Verifiability—the ability, through consensus among measurers, to ensure that information portrays what it purports to represent, or that the chosen method of measurement has been used without error or bias.
   b. Representational faithfulness—agreement between a portrayal (i.e., description) and the item it is supposed to represent (also called validity).
   c. Neutrality—absence of bias intended to attain a predetermined result.

As such, a situation in which financial statements include property with a carrying amount increased to management's estimate of market value violates the concept of reliability (i.e., the information is biased).

Answer choice "A" is incorrect because it is related to relevance (i.e., predictive value), not reliability; further, it does not indicate a violation in any event.

Answer choice "B" is incorrect because late issuance of financial statements would violate relevance (i.e., timeliness), but not reliability.

Answer choice "C" is incorrect because it is related to relevance (i.e., feedback value), and not reliability.

#2 (answer "C")

According to Statement of Financial Accounting Concepts #6, "Elements of Financial Statements," comprehensive income includes all changes in equity during the period from transactions, events, and circumstances, other than investments, by owners and distributions to owners (i.e., dividends paid to stockholders).

Comprehensive income consists of the basic components of earnings (i.e., revenues, expenses, gains, and losses); further, it includes other things not included in earnings, such as corrections of prior period errors and unrealized gains and losses on investments in available-for-sale marketable securities.

Answer choice "A" is incorrect because losses from discontinued operations is an element of comprehensive income and earnings.

Answer choice "B" is incorrect because a prior period error correction is an element of comprehensive income, even though it is not an element of earnings.

Answer choice "D" is incorrect because an unrealized loss on investments in noncurrent marketable (i.e., available-for-sale) equity securities is an element of comprehensive income, even though it is not an element of earnings. This unrealized loss is reported as a separate component of stockholders' equity.

#3 (this question is obsolete)

#4 (answer "A")

FASB Statement #105, "Disclosure of Information About Financial Instruments with Off-Balance Sheet Risk and Financial Instruments with Concentrations of Credit Risk," requires the disclosure of:

1. The extent, nature, and terms of financial instruments with off-balance sheet risk.

2. The credit risk of financial instruments with off-balance sheet risk.
3. The concentrations of credit risk in financial instruments with or without off-balance sheet risk of accounting loss (i.e., all financial instruments).

Answer choice "B" is incorrect because disclosure is required for financial instruments, with or without off-balance sheet credit risk.

Answer choice "C" is incorrect because disclosure is required of those financial instruments with credit risk, not those with market risk only.

Answer choice "D" is incorrect because disclosure is required of all financial instruments, not only those with risk of accounting loss.

#5 (answer "C")

FASB Statement #6, "Classification of Short-Term Obligations Expected to be Refinanced," provides background relative to this question. In accordance with that Statement:

1. Short-term obligations arising from transactions in the normal course of business and due in customary terms shall be classified as current liabilities.
2. Short-term obligations other than those covered by "1" above shall be excluded from current liabilities only if:
   a. The enterprise intends to refinance them on a long-term basis.
   b. The intent to refinance is supported by an ability to do so as demonstrated by either:
      (1) Post-balance sheet issuance of long-term debt or equity securities.
      (2) Before the balance sheet is issued, the entry into a financing agreement that clearly permits the refinancing of the short-term obligation on a long-term basis on terms that are readily determinable, and all of the following conditions are met.
         (a) Agreement does not expire within one year.
         (b) No violation of any provision in the financing agreement exists.
         (c) The lender, or investors, is expected to be financially capable of honoring the agreement.

Since the $4,000,000 note payable was refinanced prior to the issuance of its 1994 financial statements, it should be classified as a noncurrent liability, with separate disclosure of the note refinancing.

Answer choice "A" is incorrect because the note should be classified as a noncurrent liability.

Answer choice "B" is incorrect because the note should be classified as a noncurrent liability, and because separate disclosure of all significant post-balance sheet investing and financing events is required.

Answer choice "D" is incorrect because separate disclosure is required of all significant post-balance sheet investing and financing events.

#6 (answer "D")

This question is based on FASB Statement #115, "Accounting for Certain Investments in Debt and Equity Securities." Under the Statement, investments in both trading debt and equity securities, and available-for-sale debt and equity securities, are reported on the balance sheet at market value at the date of the financial statements. The only difference between the two categories of securities is the placement of holding gains and losses in the financial statements. For trading securities, such gains and losses are recognized in earnings; for available-for-sale securities, such gains and losses are included as a separate component of shareholders' equity. Held-to-maturity debt securities are generally carried at amortized cost.

Trading securities are those that are bought and held principally for the purposes of selling them in the near future. Held-to-maturity debt securities are those that the entity has the positive intent and ability to hold to maturity. Available-for-sale securities are those that are not classified as either trading or held-to-maturity securities.

Accordingly, securities classified as trading should be reported at fair value, with holding gains and losses included in earnings.

Answer choice "A" is incorrect because lower of cost or market is not an appropriate basis for valuing marketable securities.

Answer choice "B" is incorrect because lower of cost or market is not an appropriate basis for valuing marketable securities, and because all holding gains and losses from trading securities are included in earnings.

Answer choice "C" is incorrect because all holding gains and losses from trading securities are included in earnings.

#7 (answer "D")

When a receivable is factored (i.e., sold) without recourse, the seller is relieved of any contingent liability with respect to the receivable; if the receivable becomes uncollectible, the buyer must recognize the loss.

Accordingly, the situation described in the question is a sale of Gar's accounts receivable to Ross, with the risk of uncollectible accounts transferred to Ross.

Answer choice "A" is incorrect because it describes a loan where the accounts receivable were pledged (not factored).

Answer choice "B" is incorrect because it describes a loan where the accounts receivable were assigned (not factored).

Answer choice "C" is incorrect because it describes a factoring transaction on a with-recourse basis, since the risk of uncollectible accounts was retained by Gar, the seller of the accounts.

#8 (answer "C")

Under APB Opinion #21, "Interest on Receivables and Payables," interest must be imputed on transactions of a term of one year or more where no interest rate is specified in the contract, or where the specified interest rate is not realistic.

Here, no interest rate is specified; therefore interest at the market rate of 8% must be imputed. The contract called for ten payments of $10,000 each, with the first payment made on December 30, 1994; thus, only nine ordinary annuity payments will be received, with the next scheduled for December 30, 1995.

In its December 31, 1994, balance sheet, Chang should report the note receivable at $62,500, which results from application of the annuity factor for nine periods (i.e., $10,000 × 6.25 equals $62,500).

Answer choice "A" is incorrect because it results from application of the present value of $1 factor to the total of the nine payments (i.e., [$10,000 ×

9] × .50 equals $45,000); the annuity factor applied to the constant payment should be used.

Answer choice "B" is incorrect because it results from application of the present value of $1 factor to the total of the ten payments (i.e., [$10,000 × 10] × .46 equals $46,000). Not only should the annuity factor applied to the constant payment be used, but the number of future payments is nine, not ten.

Answer choice "D" is incorrect because it includes all ten payments in the receivable; one payment was received on December 30, 1994 (i.e., $10,000 × 6.71 equals $67,100).

#9 (answer "A")

The amount of the allowance for doubtful accounts is subtracted from gross accounts receivable in order to present them at their net realizable value. The balance in the allowance for uncollectible accounts at December 31, 1994, is $115,000:

Balance, December 31, 1993	$260,000
Uncollectible account expense;	
$9,000,000 × 2%	180,000
Accounts written off in 1994	(325,000)
Allowance for uncollectible accounts, December 31, 1994	$115,000

Answer choice "B" is incorrect because it is the amount of uncollectible accounts expense for 1994 (i.e., $9,000,000 × 2% equals $180,000), not the balance in the allowance for uncollectible accounts at December 31, 1994.

Answer choice "C" is not a feasible combination of the amounts presented.

Answer choice "D" is incorrect because it is the sum of the balance in the allowance for uncollectible accounts at December 31, 1993, and the uncollectible accounts expense for 1994 (i.e., $260,000 + [2% × $9,000,000] equals $440,000); it excludes the accounts written off in 1994.

#10 (answer "C")

Under the relative sales value method, costs are allocated based on the sales value of any one item in proportion to the total sales value.

The total costs are $1,200,000 plus $300,000, or $1,500,000, of which $600,000 should be allocated to the Class A lots:

LOT CLASS	NUMBER OF LOTS	SALES PRICE PER LOT	TOTAL SALES VALUE OF LOTS
A	100	$24,000	$2,400,000
B	100	16,000	1,600,000
C	200	10,000	2,000,000
Total sales value			$6,000,000

Allocated to class A lots;
$2,400,000/$6,000,000
× $1,500,000 $600,000

Answer choice "A" is incorrect because it allocates an equal amount of cost to each lot without regard to the sales value of the lot; also, it does not consider the additional costs incurred in preparing the land for sale, which are part of the cost of the land (i.e., [$1,200,000/400] × 100 equals $300,000).

Answer choice "B" is incorrect because it allocates an equal amount of cost to each lot without regard to its sales value (i.e., [$1,500,000/400] × 100 equals $375,000).

Answer choice "D" is incorrect because it allocates the costs to the lots based upon the sum of the sales value of one lot from each class, rather than the total sales value of all the lots (i.e., $1,500,000 × [$24,000/$50,000] equals $720,000).

#11 (answer "B")

Generally, for background, the procedures to be utilized in connection with the dollar-value LIFO inventory method are:

1. Deflate ending inventory to base-period prices by using an appropriate external or internal index number that measures the specific price changes for inventory from the base period.
2. Subtract the beginning inventory at base-period prices from the ending inventory at base-period prices. The difference is the new layer at base-period prices.
3. Reinflate the new layer by multiplying it by the current-period index. This establishes the new layer at the current-period prices.
4. Add the new layer to the dollar-value LIFO cost of the beginning inventory to arrive at the dollar-value LIFO cost of the ending inventory.

This question is easy to deal with since the ending inventory at base year cost is given. One merely has to multiply the current year's layer by the index to reinflate the layer to current prices. Thus, the dollar-value LIFO inventory at December 31, 1994, is $527,500:

Inventory, January 1, 1994,
  at dollar-value LIFO cost $500,000
1994 layer; ($525,000 − $500,000)
  × 1.10   27,500
Dollar-value LIFO inventory,
  December 31, 1994 $527,500

Answer choice "A" is incorrect because it is the ending inventory at base year cost, not dollar-value LIFO cost.

Answer choice "C" is incorrect because it takes as the 1994 layer the excess of the ending inventory at current year cost (i.e., $577,500) over the ending inventory at base year cost (i.e., $525,000), and ignores the relevant price index (i.e., [$577,500 − $525,000] + $500,000 equals $552,500).

Answer choice "D" is incorrect because it is merely the ending inventory at current year cost, not dollar-value LIFO cost.

#12 (answer "A")

Theoretically, all costs necessary to be incurred in order to get an asset ready for its intended end use should be capitalized as part of the cost of the asset. Included in these costs are insurance on a machine while in transit, and testing and preparation of the machine for use.

Additional costs that could be capitalized include the freight costs to transport the asset to the place of end use, the costs of installing the asset, and the labor and material costs incurred in the testing process. Excluded are those costs that could have been avoided, such as damage during the installation process, and prompt payment discounts not taken.

Answer choices other than "A" are based on incorrect assumptions and/or combinations.

#13 (answer "A")

The cost of a patent purchased from outsiders, along with legal costs incurred in connection with the successful defense of the patent, and the legal fees and other costs incurred in connection with securing or registering an internally developed patent, should be capitalized.

Such costs are amortized over the 17-year legal life of a patent, or its economic life, if less. When the economic life changes, the remaining un-amortized cost is amortized over the remaining life.

Further, in accordance with FASB Statement #2, "Accounting for Research and Development Costs," all research and development costs must be expensed as incurred, unless such costs are contractually reimbursable; this includes both internal and external research and development costs.

Accordingly, Jase should expense the research and development costs associated with the patent, and capitalize the $34,000 cost of registering the patent. The $34,000 cost should be amortized over its 10-year economic life. Jase should report the patent in its December 31, 1994, balance sheet at $32,300:

Cost of patent	$34,000
Less: Amortization for 1994;	
$34,000 × 10% × ½ year	(1,700)
Patent, net of accumulated amortization	$32,300

Answer choices other than "A" are not logical in view of the explanation provided.

#14 (answer "B")

The following considerations are relevant in arriving at an answer to this question.

1. Since the facts are based on an "unadjusted trial balance," and no other information was provided with respect to any other insurance policies, it may be assumed that the only prepaid insurance was the amount associated with the payment made on March 1, 1995.
2. Since insurance expense had a $7,200 balance before adjustment, it is likewise safe to assume that the March 1, 1995, payment was charged to that account.

Accordingly, the amount to be reported for prepaid insurance at March 31, 1995, is $7,200 × 35/36, or $7,000.

By the same token, insurance expense should include the $300 balance of prepaid insurance in the unadjusted trial balance since it was clearly expired, and 1/36 of the $7,200 paid on March 31 (i.e., $200), for a total of $500.

Answer choices other than "B" are based on incorrect assumptions and/or combinations.

#15 (answer "B")

Sales taxes collected by a retail store do not represent revenue to the seller; rather, the seller is acting in an agency capacity to collect the taxes. Accordingly, sales taxes should not be included in sales revenue. Here, Ivy did include the 6% state sales taxes in revenue, and accounted for the payment of the sales taxes as a reduction of revenue.

Since the total credits to sales included sales taxes, sales before sales taxes amounted to $25,000 (i.e., $26,500/1.06). As such, the sales tax collected was $25,000 × 6%, or $1,500. Therefore, if the total sales tax collected was $1,500, and $600 was paid in February, the sales taxes payable at March 31, 1995, should be reported as $900.

Answer choice "A" is incorrect because $600 is the amount of sales taxes remitted to the state, not the sales tax liability at March 31, 1995.

Answer choice "C" is incorrect because $1,500 is the total amount of sales taxes collected in the first quarter of 1995, not the sales tax liability at March 31, 1995.

Answer choice "D" is incorrect because it is 6% of the total credit to sales revenue (i.e., 6% × $26,500 equals $1,590), which is inclusive of the sales tax collected on $25,000 of sales.

#16 (answer "D")

This question is based upon FASB Statement #109, "Accounting for Income Taxes." The following items should be noted.

1. The net current and the net noncurrent deferred tax assets and liabilities are separately disclosed. Such assets and liabilities are classified as current or noncurrent, based upon the classification of the related asset or liability for financial reporting. That is, a liability resulting from using accelerated depreciation for tax purposes will result in a noncurrent deferred tax liability, since the depreciable asset is a noncurrent asset. An asset resulting from accruing a warranty liability for book purposes will result in a current deferred tax asset, since the warranty liability is a current liability.

It should be noted that while a current deferred tax asset can be offset by a current deferred tax liability, a current deferred tax asset cannot be offset by a noncurrent deferred tax liability, and so on.

2. Deferred tax assets or liabilities that are not related to an asset or liability for financial purposes, such as a deferred tax asset related to a loss carryforward, are classified according to their expected reversal dates (i.e., those expected to reverse within one year are current).

3. The total provision for income taxes is the sum of the amount of tax currently payable (i.e., current tax expense) and the net change in the deferred tax assets and deferred tax liabilities (i.e., deferred tax expense or benefit).

   a. The amount of tax currently payable is the current year's taxable income multiplied by the current year's tax rate.

   b. The net change in the deferred tax assets and liabilities is generally the result of changes in the amount of temporary differences.

Obviously, if the financial reporting basis exceeded the tax basis, depreciation for tax purposes would have been higher, giving rise to a deferred tax liability, since future taxable income will be higher. Thus, the temporary difference related to depreciable assets would be classified as a liability of $100,000, the excess of the financial reporting basis of the asset over its tax basis multiplied by the tax rate scheduled to be in effect when the temporary difference is scheduled to reverse (i.e., $250,000 × 40%).

Answer choice "A" is incorrect because the temporary difference is a taxable difference that will result in additional taxes being paid in the future; thus, it results in a liability, not an asset. Further, the deferred taxes should be measured at the 40% tax rate scheduled to be in effect when the difference reverses, and not the current rate of 30% (i.e., $250,000 × 30% equals $75,000).

Answer choice "B" is incorrect because the temporary difference will result in a liability, not an asset.

Answer choice "C" is incorrect because the deferred tax liability should be measured at the 40% tax rate scheduled to be in effect when the difference is scheduled to reverse, not the current

tax rate of 30 percent (i.e., $250,000 × 30% equals $75,000).

#17 (answer "B")

Under FASB Statement #109, "Accounting for Income Taxes," the net current and the net noncurrent deferred tax assets and liabilities are separately disclosed. Such assets and liabilities are classified as current or noncurrent, based upon the classification of the related asset or liability for financial reporting purposes. That is, a deferred tax liability resulting from using accelerated depreciation for tax purposes will result in a noncurrent deferred tax liability, because the depreciable asset is a noncurrent asset. An asset resulting from accruing a warranty liability for book purposes will result in a current deferred tax asset, since the warranty liability is a current liability.

Also, a current deferred tax asset can be offset by a current deferred tax liability, but a current deferred tax asset cannot be offset by a noncurrent deferred tax liability, etc.

Deferred tax assets or liabilities that are not related to an asset or liability for financial purposes, such as a deferred tax asset related to a loss carryforward, are classified according to their expected reversal dates (i.e., those expected to reverse within one year are current, etc.).

Based on the preceding discussion, Bren should offset the $3,000 deferred income tax asset against the $15,000 deferred income tax liability, and report a net noncurrent liability of $12,000, since the items were both noncurrent.

Answer choices other than "B" are inconsistent with the explanation provided.

#18 (answer "A")

An accrued or prepaid pension cost results from differences between the amount of pension expense recognized and the amount of contributions to the pension fund. Under FASB Statement #87, "Employers' Accounting for Pensions," net periodic pension cost (expense) is typically composed of the following five items:

1. Service cost.
2. Interest cost.
3. Return on plan assets (reduces pension expense).

4. Amortization of unrecognized prior service costs.
5. Amortization of unrecognized net gain or loss (if any).

The unfunded accrued pension cost at December 31, 1994, is $45,000:

Pension expense for 1994:

Service cost	$19,000
Interest cost	38,000
Actual return on plan assets	(22,000)
Amortization of unrecognized prior service cost	52,000
	87,000

Less: Prepaid pension cost, January 1, 1994	$ 2,000	
Employer contributions, 1994	40,000	(42,000)
Unfunded accrued pension cost, December 31, 1994		$45,000

Answer choice "B" is incorrect because it treats the prepaid pension cost at January 1, 1994, as a credit, not a debit.

Answer choice "C" is incorrect because it ignores the actual return on plan assets in determining the net periodic pension cost.

Answer choice "D" is incorrect because it is the amount of net periodic pension expense for 1994, not the unfunded accrued pension cost at December 31, 1994 (i.e., $19,000 + $38,000 + $52,000 − $22,000 equals $87,000).

#19 (answer "D")

When bonds are issued between interest dates, the purchaser of the bonds must pay the accrued interest from the last interest date to the date of the trade.

Since the last semiannual interest date was April 1, 1994, the buyer of the bonds on July 1, 1994, must pay interest for the three months (i.e., April 1, 1994, through June 30, 1994) that the bonds were not held by the buyer.

Eagle received $609,000:

Bond proceeds; $600,000 × 99%	$594,000
Accrued interest; $600,000 × 10% × 3/12	15,000
Cash received	$609,000

Answer choice "A" is incorrect because the accrued interest is deducted from the bond pro-

ceeds, and it should be added (i.e., $594,000 less $15,000 equals $579,000).

Answer choice "B" is incorrect because the accrued interest is not included, and it should be.

Answer choice "C" is incorrect because it represents the maturity value of the bonds; the bond premium and accrued interest are ignored, and should not be.

#20 (answer "B")

According to APB Opinion #21, "Interest on Receivables and Payables," the interest method of bond premium or discount amortization is to be used any time the difference between that method and the straight-line method is material.

Under the effective interest method, bond premium or discount amortization is such that a constant yield rate is maintained. As a result, amortization of the premium or discount begins at a low amount and increases as the maturity date approaches. At the maturity date, the premium or discount is fully amortized under either the interest method or straight-line amortization method.

It should also be noted that amortization of premium decreases the carrying amount of bonds, and amortization of discount increases the carrying amount.

Nast issued the bonds at a discount, and the discount was incorrectly amortized using the straight-line method. At December 31, 1994, the carrying amount of the bonds is overstated, because the amortization by the straight-line method was more than it would have been under the interest method; thus, the carrying value under the straight-line method was higher.

At January 2, 2000, the discount would be fully amortized under either the interest or straight-line method; therefore, on that date there would be no effect on the carrying amount of the bonds; it would equal the maturity value of the bonds.

Answer choices other than "B" are based on incorrect assumptions and/or combinations.

#21 (answer "A")

The estimated liability for coupons at December 31, 1994, is $3,960:

Total coupons issued	110,000
Proportion expected to be redeemed	60%
To be redeemed	66,000

Number of toys to be distributed;
66,000/5 coupons   13,200

Liability for coupons,
December 31, 1994; 13,200 × $.30 $3,960

The liability is 80 cents each less the 50 cents to be received, or 30 cents per toy.

Answer choice "B" is incorrect because it does not consider the amount received ($.50) when the coupons are redeemed (i.e., 13,200 × $.80 equals $10,560).

Answer choice "C" is incorrect because it does not consider that five coupons must be exchanged in order to receive the toy (i.e., 66,000 × $.30 equals $19,800).

Answer choice "D" is incorrect for two reasons. First, it does not consider that five coupons must be exchanged to receive one toy. In addition, it is based on the cost of the toy ($.80), rather than the $.30 net cost of redemption (i.e., 66,000 × $.80 equals $52,800).

#22 (answer "A")

This question relates to FASB Statement #5, "Accounting for Contingencies," which provides the following.

1. In order for an estimated loss to be accrued as a charge against income, the loss must be both probable at the date of the financial statements, and the amount of the loss must be reasonably estimated.
2. Where a range of estimates is involved, the best estimate within the range should be used. When no amount within the range is a better estimate than any other amount, the minimum amount should be accrued.
3. When a loss contingency is reasonably possible, but not probable, footnote disclosure is required. The disclosure shall indicate the nature of the contingency and give an estimate of the possible loss, or range of loss, or state that an estimate cannot be made.

The question indicates that an unfavorable outcome is probable and, clearly, it can be reasonably estimated in the range of $200,000 to $300,000.

Since a range of loss is involved, the appropriate amount for Haft to report as accrued liability at December 31, 1994, is the minimum amount, or $200,000.

Answer choice "B" is incorrect because $250,000 represents the midpoint of the range; the minimum amount should be accrued unless another amount within the range is a better estimate.

Answer choice "C" is incorrect because $275,000 is the amount of the eventual settlement; this amount was unknown at the date the financial statements were issued.

Answer choice "D" is incorrect because $300,000 is the maximum amount within the range; the minimum amount should be accrued unless another amount within the range is a better estimate.

#23 (answer "D")

An incoming partner may be admitted by contributing assets to the partnership, or by purchasing the interest of one of the existing partners. When assets are contributed, both the total assets and total capital of the partnership are increased by the fair value of the assets contributed.

To effect recording of the new partner's interest, either the "bonus" or "goodwill" method may be used if the amount to be credited to the new partner's capital account is not equal to the fair value of the assets contributed. The following should be noted.

1. Bonus—A "bonus" is created when the increase in partnership capital is equal to the assets contributed, and the new partner's capital is credited with an amount different than his investment.
2. Goodwill—Goodwill is created when the total partnership capital, after admission, exceeds the old capital plus the net assets contributed by the new partner.
3. Investment with "bonus" or goodwill to the old partners—If there is a "bonus" and goodwill is not recorded, any excess of the new partner's asset contribution over the capital account credit he is to receive is credited to the old partners, based on their respective profit and loss ratios prior to admission of the new partner.
   If goodwill is to be recorded, the asset increase results in an increase in the capital balances of the old partners.
4. Investment with "bonus" or goodwill to the new partner—If there is a "bonus" and

goodwill is not recorded, any excess of the capital account credit the new partner is to receive over his net asset contribution is charged to the old partners, based on their respective profit and loss ratios prior to admission of the new partner.

If goodwill is to be recorded, the asset increase results in an increase in the capital balance of the new partner.

Here, no goodwill or bonus is to be recorded; therefore, the assets contributed by Capp should equal Capp's 20% share of the net assets of the new partnership. The amount to be contributed by Capp is <u>$145,000</u>:

Total existing capital; $348,000 plus $232,000	$580,000
Proportion of equity allocated to Alfa and Beda	÷ 80%
Total capital of new partnership	725,000
Capp's interest	× 20%
<u>Capp's contribution</u>	<u>$145,000</u>

Answer choice "A" is incorrect for two reasons. First, it nets the Beda loan with the partners' capital; the loan should not be considered a reduction of capital for purposes of admitting a new partner. Second, it is simply 20% of the old partnership's existing net capital (i.e., [$348,000 + $232,000 − $30,000] × 20% equals $110,000).

Answer choice "B" is incorrect because it is 20% of the old partnership's capital, not 20% of the new partnership's capital (i.e., [$348,000 + $232,000] × 20% equals $116,000).

Answer choice "C" is incorrect because it is simply 20% of total liabilities and equity of the existing partnership, not 20% of the equity of the new partnership (i.e., $700,000 × 20% equals $140,000).

#24 (answer "B")

Upon the liquidation of a partnership, assets are sold and any gains or losses are divided among the partners according to their profit-sharing ratios.

Any available cash is first used to pay off liabilities. Before cash may be distributed to any partner, her capital account (net of loans, if any) must first have been reduced by losses realized upon liquidation.

If, in the process of assigning liquidation losses, a debit balance exists in any partner's account, that deficiency must be eliminated by a charge to the remaining partner(s) in their respective profit and loss ratios.

With the foregoing as background, available cash in the amount of $273,000 should be distributed to Alfa:

	ALFA	BEDA	TOTAL
Capital balance before liquidation	$348,000	$232,000	$580,000
Reclassification of Beda loan	—	(30,000)	(30,000)
Allocation of loss on assets sold (60/40); $625,000 − $500,000 = $125,000	(75,000)	(50,000)	(125,000)
<u>Available cash to be distributed to Alfa</u>	<u>$273,000</u>	<u>$152,000</u>	<u>$425,000</u>

Answer choice "A is incorrect because it assumes that 60% of the loan to Beda should be written off against Alfa's capital account (i.e., $273,000 − [$30,000 × 60%] equals $255,000).

Answer choice "C" is incorrect because it is 60% of the available cash after sale of the assets (i.e., [$45,000 + $500,000] × 60% equals $327,000). The amount distributed to the partners should be based upon the balances in their respective capital accounts.

Answer choice "D" is incorrect because it is simply the balance in Alfa's capital account before the liquidation of the other assets; the gain or loss on other assets must be distributed among the partners before the amount to be distributed to each partner can be determined.

#25 (answer "C")

Since fees were recorded on the cash basis, and financial statement fees should be converted to the accrual basis, the beginning point is the cash basis amount given, which would be modified as follows:

1. The beginning balance on accounts receivable should be subtracted from cash collections; it represents cash collections that do not represent accrual basis revenue for the current period.

2. The ending balance of accounts receivable should be added to cash collections; it represents an increase in revenue for which no cash was received.
3. Clearly, unearned fees should not be included in accrual basis revenue.

Accrual basis service revenue is $215,000:

Cash basis fees, 1994 (net of $5,000 unearned fees)	$195,000
Add: Accounts receivable, December 31, 1994	60,000
Less: Accounts receivable, December 31, 1993	(40,000)
Service revenue for the year ended December 31, 1994	$215,000

Answer choice "A" is incorrect because the $60,000 of accounts receivable at December 31, 1994, were subtracted and should have been added, and because the $40,000 of accounts receivable at December 31, 1993, were not subtracted, and should have been (i.e., [$195,000 − $60,000] + $40,000 equals $175,000).

Answer choice "B" is incorrect because the $60,000 of accounts receivable at December 31, 1994, were subtracted and should have been added, and because the $40,000 of accounts receivable at December 31, 1993, were added, and should have been subtracted. Also, the unearned fees were inappropriately included in service revenue (i.e., [$200,000 − $60,000] + $40,000 equals $180,000).

Answer choice "D" is incorrect because the $5,000 of unearned fees were added to cash received from clients and should have been subtracted to determine the service fees earned.

#26 (answer "A")

Under the percentage-of-completion method of accounting for long-term contracts, revenue is determined by the following formula:

$$\frac{\text{Costs incurred to date}}{\text{Total estimated costs}} \times \text{Contract price} = \text{Cumulative Revenue}$$

Any revenue that had been recognized in a prior period is subtracted from the cumulative revenue total to arrive at the current period's revenue. Income for the period is simply revenue recognized less costs for the period; therefore, income is obviously a cumulative consideration.

In the final year of a contract, the actual total costs would be known and would be used in the determination of income.

Accordingly, actual total costs and income previously recognized would be used to calculate the income recognized in the fourth and final year of a contract accounted for by the percentage-of-completion method.

Answer choices other than "A" are based on incorrect assumptions and/or combinations.

#27 (answer "C")

The installment sales method, as well as the cost recovery method, is appropriate in financial accounting only when there is reason to doubt collection of the full sales price.

Generally, under the installment method of accounting, gross profit is recognized in income in proportion to the cash collection.

Answer choice "A" is incorrect because under the installment method, revenue is not recognized at the point of sale. Under accrual accounting, income is recognized at the point of sale.

Answer choice "B" is incorrect because under the installment method, it is not necessary to defer the recognition of income until the final cash is received.

Answer choice "D" is incorrect because it is under the cost recovery method, not the installment method, that income is not recognized until after cash collections equal to the cost of sales have been received.

#28 (answer "C")

This question relates to sales-type leases. In essence, a lease that is a capital lease to the lessee is either a direct financing or sales-type lease to the lessor.

The difference between a direct financing and a sales-type lease is that under a sales-type lease, the lessor, who is a dealer or a manufacturer of the product, recognizes a profit or a loss on the sale of the leased asset as well as interest income over the term of the lease. In a direct financing lease, only interest income is recognized over the term of the lease.

The sales price in a sales-type lease is an amount equal to the present value of the minimum lease payments discounted at the implicit rate of interest to be earned by the lessor. The cost of the asset leased is charged against income in the period of sale. The gross profit recognized at the inception of the lease is the difference between the sales price and the cost of the asset sold.

Farm should report interest revenue from the lease in the amount of $5,750:

Present value of minimum lease payments	$135,000
Less: Payment received July 3, 1994	(20,000)
Net investment in lease, 7/3/94 to 12/31/94	$115,000
Interest revenue, 1994; $115,000 × 10% × ½	$5,750

Answer choice "A" is incorrect because interest revenue should be recognized for both a direct financing and sales-type lease; only under an operating lease is interest revenue not recognized.

Answer choice "B" is incorrect because it bases interest on the cost of the equipment, not the present value of the lease payments (i.e., $110,000 × 10% × ½ equals $5,500).

Answer choice "D" is incorrect because it bases interest revenue on the original present value of the lease payments (i.e., $135,000 × 10% × ½ equals $6,750). Since a $20,000 payment was received on July 3, 1994, this amount must be subtracted from the original present value of the minimum lease payments to determine the correct amount of interest for the period 7/1/94 to 12/31/94.

#29 (answer "C")

Generally, when an investment in a corporation's stock does not involve either a controlling interest or the ability to exercise significant influence (i.e., the equity method as per APB Opinion #18), cash dividends received represent revenue. Stock dividends, however, do not represent revenue because they do not represent a distribution of assets.

Since Wood owns 10% of Arlo's preferred stock, it will receive 10% of any preferred dividends declared. While the total annual dividend on the preferred would be only $120,000 (i.e., $100 × 6% × 20,000 shares), the fact that total preferred dividends of $240,000 were declared suggests that dividends in arrears on the cumulative preferred stock must also have been declared. Since no cash dividend was declared on the common stock, no revenue would be recognized; stock dividends do not result in the recognition of dividend revenue.

As such, the dividend income in Wood's 1994 income statement would be $24,000 (i.e., $240,000 × 10%).

Answer choice "A" is incorrect because it ignores the dividends in arrears on cumulative preferred stock.

Answer choice "B" is incorrect for two reasons. First, it ignores dividends in arrears on the cumulative preferred stock. Second, it includes the fair value of the stock dividends received as income; stock dividends do not result in income.

Answer choice "D" is incorrect because it includes the fair value of the stock dividends received as income (i.e., $24,000 + [1,000 × 5% × $10] equals $24,500); stock dividends do not result in income.

#30 (answer "B")

The treatment of exchanges involving nonmonetary assets is set forth in APB Opinion #29, "Accounting for Nonmonetary Transactions."

An exchange is a reciprocal transfer between an enterprise and another entity that results in the enterprise's acquiring assets or services, or satisfying liabilities by surrendering other assets or services, or incurring other obligations.

The specific treatment of an exchange differs as between an exchange of dissimilar assets (i.e., nonreciprocal transfers), and an exchange of similar assets (that are not considered to result in the culmination of an earnings process). The following should be noted.

1. For dissimilar assets, the accounting should be based on the fair values of the assets involved, recognizing any gain or loss on the exchange.
2. For similar assets, exchanges of inventory items or assets employed in production should be based on the recorded amounts of the nonmonetary items given up, without recognition of gain. However, losses should be recognized. (Similar productive assets are those that are of the same general type, that perform the same function, or

that are employed in the same line of business.)

3. Further, when monetary consideration is involved in an exchange of similar assets, the recipient has realized gain on the exchange to the extent that the cash received exceeds a proportionate share of the recorded amount of the asset surrendered. The portion of the cost (i.e., recorded amount) applicable to the realized amount should be based on the ratio of monetary consideration to the total consideration received, with the nonmonetary item at fair value. If a loss is thus indicated, that should be recognized.

The monetary asset received, less any realized gain, reduces the carrying (i.e, recorded) amount of the nonmonetary asset exchanged.

4. The entity paying monetary consideration (i.e., cash) should not recognize any gain; however, losses should be recognized.

The transaction in this question is an exchange of similar assets. Since the recipient (Slate) has received monetary consideration, plus land with fair values in excess of carrying amounts of the assets surrendered, <u>a gain in an amount determined by the ratio of cash received to total consideration</u> should be recognized.

Answer choice "A" is incorrect because it is the appropriate accounting treatment for exchanges of dissimilar assets, not similar assets.

Answer choice "C" is incorrect because a gain, and not a loss, is recognized (i.e., Slate has received total consideration in excess of the carrying amounts of the assets surrendered).

Answer choice "D" is incorrect because a gain may be recognized when similar assets are exchanged and monetary consideration is received.

<u>#31 (answer "B")</u>

In general, the method used to translate foreign currency items depends on the determination of the functional currency.

The following background should be considered.

1. If the entity maintains its accounting records in a currency (i.e., German marks) other than the functional currency (i.e., Swiss francs), remeasurement (i.e., "restatement") of a subsidiary's foreign financial statements is required before translation can be accomplished. When such is the case, a gain or loss is recognized in the income statement.

2. When the foreign currency is the functional currency, the translation process does not result in a gain or loss being recognized on the income statement. Rather, a cumulative translation adjustment is recognized as a separate component of stockholders' equity.

3. Translation process if the foreign currency is the functional currency:
   a. Assets and liabilities are translated using the current exchange rate at the balance sheet date.
   b. Income statement items are translated using a weighted-average exchange rate for the period.

4. Remeasurement process if the accounting records are maintained in a currency other than the functional currency:
   a. Cash, receivables, and payables are converted at the foreign exchange rate in effect at the balance sheet date. Other assets and liabilities are converted at the foreign exchange rate in effect at the time of the transaction (i.e., historical rate), except that the exchange rate in effect at the balance sheet date is used to translate assets and liabilities that are accounted for on the basis of current prices (i.e., estimated warranty obligations, etc.)
   b. Income statement items are translated using a weighted-average exchange rate for the period, except that items that relate to assets and liabilities translated at historical rates should be translated at such rates (i.e., depreciation).

The question states that remeasurement resulted in a $7,600 gain, and translation resulted in an $8,100 gain. While the remeasurement gain should be included in income, the $8,100 translation gain should be included in the cumulative translation adjustment, which is a separate component of stockholders' equity.

Answer choice "A" is incorrect because there is a foreign exchange gain.

Answer choice "C" is incorrect because $8,100 represents the translation gain, which is reported as a separate component of stockholders' equity, and not on the income statement.

Answer choice "D" is incorrect because the $8,100 translation gain is included, and should not be (i.e., $7,600 plus $8,100 equals $15,700). The translation gain is reported as a separate component of stockholders' equity, and not on the income statement.

#32 (answer "D")

This question is based on FASB Statement #52, "Foreign Currency Translation."

Gains and losses on transactions denominated in a currency other than the functional currency are generally included in determining net income for the period in which the exchange rates change. Likewise, a transaction gain or loss realized upon settlement of a foreign currency transaction generally should be included in determining net income for the period in which the transaction is settled.

When the balance sheet falls between the date of the transaction and the date of settlement, any receivable or payable must be adjusted to its dollar equivalent as of the balance sheet date. The difference between the current balance and the new balance is an exchange rate gain or loss. Obviously, upon settlement of the transaction, the gain or loss will be finalized.

This question deals with a transaction recognized on September 22, 1994, and settled on March 20, 1995. At December 31, 1994, the account payable must be adjusted for changes in exchange rates.

Liability at 12/31/94; 10,000 at $.70	$7,000
Liability at 9/22/94; 10,000 at $.55	5,500
Foreign currency transaction loss at 12/31/94; 10,000 at $.15	$1,500

Answer choice "A" is incorrect because when exchange rates change, a gain or loss must be recognized on transactions denominated in a currency other than the functional currency.

Answer choice "B" is incorrect because it represents the amount of gain that will be recognized in 1995 when the transaction is settled (i.e., [$.70 − $.65] × 10,000 equals $500).

Answer choice "C" is incorrect because $1,000 is the total amount of loss that will be recognized on this transaction (i.e., [$.65 − $.55] × 10,000

equals $1,000); however, that amount will be partly recognized in 1994 and the remainder in 1995.

#33 (answer "B")

This question simply requires a computation of cost of goods sold for 1994; all information necessary to make the computation is provided in a straightforward manner. The only complication relates to the goods out on consignment.

Title to consigned goods remains with the consignor and is included in inventory. Inventory costs for the consigned goods include all normal costs related to purchase or production, inclusive of freight out associated with shipment to the consignee.

Accordingly, Kam should include the cost of the consigned goods, and the transportation to consignees in its determination of 1994 cost of goods sold. Freight out is a selling expense and should be excluded from the computation of cost of goods sold.

In its 1994 income statement, Kam should report cost of goods sold as $512,000:

Beginning inventory		$122,000
Purchases		540,000
Freight in		10,000
Transportation to consignees		5,000
Cost of goods available for sale		677,000
Less: Ending inventory		
− held by Kam	$145,000	
− held by consignees	20,000	(165,000)
Cost of goods sold, 1994		$512,000

Answer choice "A" is incorrect because it excludes the $5,000 cost of transportation to consignees.

Answer choice "C" is incorrect because the $5,000 cost of transportation to consignees is not included, and should be, and because the $20,000 of inventory held by consignees is not deducted, and should be (i.e., $122,000 + $540,000 + $10,000 − $145,000 equals $527,000).

Answer choice "D" is incorrect because it includes the $35,000 cost of freight out in the computation of cost of goods sold; freight out is a selling expense, and should not be included.

#34 (answer "D")

General and administrative expenses include all items connected with the administrative functions of the organization and/or such items that are not included in the cost of goods sold, selling expenses, or other revenues and expenses.

Inclusions in the cost of goods sold are obvious; these are costs directly associated with the product. Selling expenses include items connected with the sales function. Other revenues and expenses typically include interest revenue, interest expense, and gains and losses on the disposal of assets.

Accordingly, interest expense is not included in general and administrative expenses; it is included in other expenses. Likewise, advertising expense is not included in general and administrative expenses; it is a selling expense.

Answer choices other than "D" are based on incorrect assumptions and/or combinations.

#35 (answer "B")

Under accrual accounting, revenue is recognized when it is earned and measurable, and expenses are recognized when they are incurred and measurable; this is consistent with the matching concept.

When goods are sold on credit, one of the costs that should be matched with revenue is the estimated uncollectible accounts expense. Using the allowance method, uncollectible accounts expense is recorded in the period in which the related revenue is recognized. Under the direct write-off method, uncollectible accounts expense is recognized when the receivable is determine to be uncollectible, not in the period of sale.

Therefore, the allowance method is consistent with accrual accounting, and the direct write-off method is not consistent with accrual accounting.

Answer choices other than "B" are the result of inappropriate assumptions and/or combinations.

#36 (answer "B")

Depletion is similar to depreciation, except that it relates to a natural resource rather than a fixed asset. The amount of depletion is determined by dividing all costs associated with a property by the estimated recoverable reserves contained in the property. The depletable costs of the property include those incurred in preparing the property for production, and any expected reclamation costs, and are reduced by any residual value.

It should be observed that the basis for depletion at the end of any period is the remaining depletable cost (i.e., unrecovered carrying value) allocated over the most updated estimates of recoverable reserves. In effect, therefore, any resulting change is a change in estimate that is accounted for prospectively only (i.e., in the year of change, and any future years that may be affected).

Depletion for 1994 is $144,000:

Acquisition cost	$2,640,000
Restoration (reclamation) cost	180,000
Development costs	360,000
Estimated salvage value	(300,000)
Total depletable cost	$2,880,000
1994 production	60,000 tons
Depletion rate; $2,880,000/ 1,200,000 tons	$2.40/ton
Depletion, 1994	$144,000

Answer choice "A" is incorrect because it excludes the reclamation cost from the total depletable cost (i.e., [$2,640,000 + $360,000 − $300,000]/1,200,000 × 60,000 equals $135,000).

Answer choice "C" is incorrect because it excludes both the reclamation cost and the estimated salvage value from the determination of the total depletable cost (i.e., [$2,640,000 + $360,000]/1,200,000 × 60,000 equals $150,000).

Answer choice "D" is incorrect because it excludes the estimated salvage value from the determination of the total depletable cost (i.e., [$2,640,000 + $180,000 + $360,000]/1,200,000 × 60,000 equals $159,000).

#37 (answer "B")

Under the declining-balance method of depreciation, salvage value is ignored and depreciation is based on the declining book value of the asset. (When the method is double-declining-balance, depreciation is at twice the straight-line rate.)

Since 1994 is the third year of the asset's use, depreciation expense must consider the effect of depreciation in the first two years.

Rye would report $10,000 as the depreciation expense for 1994 using the double-declining-balance method:

Cost of machine	$80,000
Depreciation, 1992; $80,000 × 50%	(40,000)
Book value, December 31, 1992	40,000
Depreciation, 1993; $40,000 × 50%	(20,000)
Book value, December 31, 1993	$20,000
Depreciation expense, 1994;	
$20,000 × 50%	$10,000

It should be noted that the machine may not be depreciated below its expected salvage value (i.e., $8,000); the carrying value of the machine at December 31, 1994, was $10,000. Therefore, depreciation for 1995 may not exceed $2,000 (i.e., $10,000 less $8,000).

Answer choice "A" is incorrect because it represents depreciation expense for six months of 1994 under the straight-line method (i.e., [$80,000 − $8,000]/4 × 6/12 equals $9,000).

Answer choice "C" is incorrect because it represents depreciation expense for 1994 under the straight-line method (i.e., [$80,000 − $8,000]/4 equals $18,000).

Answer choice "D" is incorrect because it is the double-declining-balance depreciation for 1993, the second year the assets were held (i.e., $80,000 − [$80,000 × 50%] × 50% equals $20,000).

#38 (answer "B")

When two parties enter into a royalty agreement, the assignor permits the assignee to use the patented item for a period of time in exchange for a periodic royalty; the royalty may be fixed or variable depending upon the pattern of use of the patented item. Regardless, accrual accounting applies; the assignor will recognize royalty revenue when it has been earned and measurable, and the assignee (Wand) will recognize royalty expense in the period incurred.

Answer choice "A" is incorrect because it is based upon cash-basis accounting, rather than accrual-basis accounting.

Answer choice "C" is incorrect because the expense has not been incurred at the date the royalty agreement began but, rather, will accrue as the object of the agreement is used.

Answer choice "D" is incorrect because the expense should be recognized as it is incurred, in order to match the cost of using the patent with the benefit derived from it.

#39 (answer "B")

According to FASB Statement #87, "Employers' Accounting for Pensions," the difference between the amount of pension cost recognized, and the amount funded with the pension trustee represents an adjustment to the accrued, or prepaid, pension cost.

An expense in excess of funding results in an accrued pension cost (i.e., a liability), while funding in excess of pension expense results in a prepaid pension cost (i.e., an asset).

Under Statement #87, net periodic pension cost is the sum of the following components.

1. Service cost—The increase in the projected benefit obligation resulting from services rendered by employees in the current period. (Will increase the periodic cost.)
2. Interest cost—The increase in the projected benefit obligation due to the passage of time. It is measured by applying the discount rate to the projected benefit obligation as of the beginning of the year. (Will increase the periodic cost.)
3. Amortization of prior service cost—The amount allocated to the current period resulting from retroactive amendments to the pension plan. (Will generally increase the periodic cost.)
   Prior service costs are generally the result of a plan adoption or amendment; while they relate to the past, they are allocated to future earnings. Further, these costs are recognized only as they are amortized; they are not booked as liabilities.
4. Return on plan assets—Generally a decrease in the net periodic pension cost based on either expected or actual return.
   a. Expected return—The fair value of the plan assets as of the beginning of the year, multiplied by the expected rate of return.
   b. Actual return—The change in the fair value of the plan assets during the year, adjusted for employer contributions and benefits paid to retired employees.
5. Amortization of unrecognized gains and losses—The amount added to, or subtracted

from, the net periodic pension cost when the actual return on plan assets is materially different than the expected return. The difference between actual and expected return is deferred and amortized when the cumulative unrecognized gains or losses exceed 10% of the greater of the beginning of year balances of either the fair value of plan assets or projected benefit obligation; this excess is referred to as the "corridor" amount.

The amount of amortization is the excess of the unrecognized gain or loss over the corridor amount divided by the average remaining service period of active employees.

The amount that Gali should use as actual return on plan assets is $150,000:

Fair value of plan assets, end of year		$525,000
Fair value of plan assets, beginning of year		350,000
Change in plan assets		175,000
Adjusted for:		
Employer contributions	$110,000	
Benefits paid	85,000	25,000
Actual return on plan assets, 1994		$150,000

It should be noted that employer contributions (which increased assets) are deducted from the change, and benefits paid (which decreased assets) are added back.

Answer choice "A" is incorrect because it excludes the impact of benefits paid to retirees, which should be added back.

Answer choice "C" is incorrect because it is simply the change in the fair value of the plan assets during the year (i.e., $525,000 − $350,000 equals $175,000). The impact of both the employer contributions and the benefits paid to retirees is ignored.

Answer choice "D" is incorrect because $260,000 is the sum of the change in the fair value of the plan assets and the benefits paid. Employer contributions should be subtracted from the change in the fair value of the assets.

#40 (answer "D")

In accordance with APB Opinion #30, "Reporting the Results of Operations," an item that is

both unusual in nature and infrequent in occurrence should be classified as an extraordinary item and reported as a separate component of income after income from continuing operations. Specifically, an extraordinary gain or loss is reported, net of tax effect, after discontinued operations (net of tax), and before any cumulative effects of changes in accounting principle (net of tax).

A material loss should be presented separately as a component of income from continuing operations (on a before-tax basis) when it is either unusual or infrequent, but not both (i.e., when it is not unusual in nature but infrequent in occurrence).

Answer choice "A" is incorrect because an extraordinary item should be shown as a separate component of income (net of taxes), after income from continuing operations.

Answer choice "B" is incorrect because a cumulative effect type change in accounting principle is shown as a separate component of income (net of taxes).

Answer choice "C" is incorrect because it describes an extraordinary item, which is shown as a separate component of income (net of taxes).

#41 (answer "C")

The total provision for income taxes is the sum of the amount of tax currently payable (i.e., current tax expense) and the net change in the deferred tax assets and deferred liabilities (i.e., deferred tax expense or benefit).

1. The amount of tax currently payable is the current year's taxable income multiplied by the current year's tax rate.
2. The net change in the deferred tax assets and liabilities is the result of changes in the amount of temporary differences.

Based on the preceding, the current income tax expense is the taxable income for 1994 multiplied by the 1994 effective income tax rate, or $195,000 (i.e., $650,000 × 30%).

Answer choice "A" is incorrect because it is the current income tax liability at December 31, 1994 (i.e., [$650,000 × 30%] − $90,000 equals $105,000), which results from reducing the expense by the estimated payments. As such, it is not the expense.

Answer choice "B" is incorrect because it is based on pretax financial statement income rather than taxable income (i.e., $750,000 × 30% equals $225,000), and because the expense is reduced by the amount of prepayments (i.e., $225,000 − $90,000 equals $135,000).

Answer choice "D" is incorrect because it is based on pretax financial statement income (i.e., $750,000 × 30% equals $225,000); current income tax expense should be based on taxable income.

#42 (answer "C")

The deferred income tax expense or benefit is the net change in the deferred tax assets and/or deferred tax liabilities for the year. Deferred tax assets and deferred tax liabilities are generally the result of temporary differences.

At December 31, 1993, Quinn reported a net deferred tax asset of $9,000. At December 31, 1994, Quinn should report a deferred tax liability of $21,000 (i.e., $70,000 × 30%). It should be noted that a taxable temporary difference will give rise to additional taxes in the future; hence, it gives rise to a liability.

Quinn should report deferred income tax expense in its December 31, 1994, income statement as $30,000 (i.e., $9,000 plus $21,000).

Answer choice "A" is incorrect because it is the difference between the deferred tax asset at the beginning of the year and the deferred tax liability at the end of the year (i.e., $21,000 less $9,000 equals $12,000); obviously, the amounts should be added.

Answer choice "B" is incorrect because $21,000 is the amount of the deferred tax liability at December 31, 1994, not the deferred tax expense for 1994.

Answer choice "D" is incorrect because it is the current income tax expense for 1994 (i.e., $200,000 × 30% equals $60,000), and not the deferred income tax expense.

#43 (answer "C")

Under present law, net operating losses are carried back three (3) years and forward fifteen (15) years. (A corporation may elect to forgo the carryback.)

In accordance with FASB Statement #109, "Accounting for Income Taxes," the tax benefit of a net operating loss is generally recognized in the year in which the loss is incurred. The following should be noted.

1. Carrybacks—The tax benefit of a loss carryback is recognized as a receivable (i.e., refundable income taxes) if the loss is carried back to a profitable year. The tax benefit (i.e., expense reduction) is measured at the tax rate(s) in effect in the carryback period.
2. Carryforwards—The tax benefit of a loss carryforward is recognized as a deferred tax asset if the loss is to be carried forward to offset future amounts of taxable income. The tax benefit is measured at the tax rate(s) scheduled to be in effect for the carryforward period. However, the amount of the deferred tax asset is reduced by a valuation allowance if it is more likely than not that some or all of the benefit of the loss carryforward will not be realized (that is, sufficient taxable income will not be earned in the carryforward period).

In the year in which the net operating loss is incurred, the recognition of the deferred tax asset reduces the income tax expense. In subsequent years, as income is realized, the deferred tax asset is reduced.

Simply put, $300,000 of the 1993 loss would logically have been carried back to 1992 to generate a refund. Consequently, $400,000 (i.e., $700,000 less $300,000) would have been available to carry forward to 1994. Therefore, the 1994 income subject to tax would have been $800,000 (i.e., $1,200,000 less $400,000). As such, given no deferred income taxes, Mobe should report 30% × $800,000, or $240,000, as total income tax expense in 1994.

Answer choice "A" is incorrect because it is the amount of the loss carryforward realized in 1994 (i.e., $400,000 × 30% equals $120,000), not total income tax expense.

Answer choice "B" is incorrect because it is the amount of income tax expense that would have been recognized for 1994 had the entire 1993 net operating loss been carried forward, rather than carried back to the maximum extent possible (i.e., [($1,200,000 less $700,000] × 30% equals $150,000).

Answer choice "D" is incorrect because it is the amount of income tax expense that would have been recognized for 1994 without regard to the carryforward (i.e., $1,200,000 × 30% equals $360,000).

#44 (answer "B")

APB Opinion #30, "Reporting the Results of Operations," provides guidelines for the treatment of gains and losses that arise on the disposal of a segment of a business.

There are two elements of gain and loss with respect to a disposed segment, each of which is presented separately, net of tax.

1. <u>Income or loss from operations</u>—In the year that includes the measurement date (i.e., management's commitment to a formal plan of action), the results of discontinued operations are those from the beginning of the year up to and including the date prior to the measurement date. The results will include appropriate estimates.
   (When comparative statements are presented, which include periods prior to the measurement date, all information is separate from the results of continuing operations.)

2. <u>Gain or loss on disposal</u>—Presented in the year of disposal, except that if losses are anticipated, these must be provided for in the year that includes the measurement date, even if the disposal is not completed. Also includes (a) costs directly associated with the decision to dispose of a segment, and (b) actual and/or expected net losses from operations between the measurement date and disposal date.

The following should be noted.

1. As indicated above, the results of operations are presented separately, net of tax; however, the question required an answer before tax effect.

2. In accordance with Opinion #30, it is appropriate to include actual and/or estimated operating losses from operations subsequent to the measurement date (i.e., October 1, 1994) in the disposal loss; this is the case in the information provided.

In 1994, the loss on disposal of the segment would be $250,000:

Operating losses during phase-out period:

10/1/94–12/31/94	($200,000)	
1/1/95–3/31/95	(400,000)	($600,000)
Estimated gain on disposal of segment		350,000
Loss recognized in 1994 (before income taxes)		($250,000)

Answer choice "A" is incorrect because $200,000 is the amount of operating loss from the measurement date to the end of 1994; the loss on disposal should include the entire operating loss for the phase-out period (i.e., the losses after the measurement date of October 1, 1994), in addition to the gain or loss on disposal.

Answer choice "C" is incorrect because it is the total operating loss for 1994 (i.e., $300,000 plus $200,000 equals $500,000). The operating loss up to the measurement date is not part of the loss on disposal of the segment. Also, the expected gain on disposal of assets, as well as the expected operating losses for the period 1/1/95 to 3/31/95, should be recognized in 1994.

Answer choice "D" is incorrect because $600,000 excludes the gain on disposal of the segment's assets. Since the net effect of the disposal is a loss, the $350,000 estimated gain on disposal of assets should be recognized in 1994.

#45 (answer "C")

The "cumulative effect of an accounting change" is a separate income statement item provided for in APB Opinion #20, "Accounting Changes." "Cumulative effect" type items appear on the income statement (net of tax effect) after extraordinary items.

In accordance with Opinion #20, "cumulative effect" items arise from changes in accounting principle (including changes in accounting methods). Not only is the new principle to be used in current and future periods, there is additional disclosure of the "cumulative effect," the measure of which is the difference between beginning retained earnings and the retained earnings balance had the method been retroactively applied.

Changes in accounting estimate, as opposed to changes in principle, require presentation only in current and future years, if the change affects both. There is no "cumulative effect" involved.

The cumulative effect of the change from the FIFO method of inventory valuation to the weighted-average method is the after-tax difference in the opening balance of retained earnings that would have existed if the weighted-average method had been used since inception.

The cumulative effect should be $4,200:

Inventory valuation, 1/1/94:	
Weighted-average method	$77,000
FIFO method	71,000
Cumulative effect before taxes	$ 6,000
Cumulative effect, net of taxes;	
$6,000 × 70%	$4,200

Answer choice "A" is incorrect because it is the amount of the cumulative effect that would have been recognized had the change been effective December 31, 1994, rather than January 1, 1994 (i.e., [$83,000 − $79,000] × 70% equals $2,800).

Answer choice "B" is incorrect for two reasons. First, it is the difference between the valuation of the inventory under FIFO and weighted-average at December 31, 1994 (i.e., $83,000 less $79,000 equals $4,000), rather than the January 1, 1994, balances. In addition, it is presented before tax and should be net of tax effect.

Answer choice "D" is incorrect because it excludes the tax effect of the change in accounting principle (i.e., $77,000 less $71,000 equals $6,000).

#46 (answer "D")

See question #45 for background on cumulative effect type changes.

As noted in the explanation to question #45, the change involved is a change in accounting principle, which is a cumulative effect type change.

The "cumulative effect of an accounting change" is a separate income statement item provided for in APB Opinion #20, "Accounting Changes." "Cumulative effect" type changes appear on the income statement as a component of income after extraordinary items.

Answer choice "A" is incorrect because the change involved is not a prior period adjustment, which is usually the result of the correction of a theoretical or mechanical error in the preparation of a prior year's financial statements; it is presented as an adjustment of the opening balance of retained earnings.

Answer choice "B" is incorrect because the effect of a change in accounting principle should be reported after income from continuing operations (net of income tax), not as a component of income from continuing operations.

Answer choice "C" is incorrect because a cumulative effect type accounting change is not an extraordinary item; rather, it is reported after extraordinary items (if any). An extraordinary item is an event that occurs infrequently, and is unusual in nature.

#47 (answer "A")

This question is based on the provisions of FASB Statement #95, "Statement of Cash Flows."

The Statement classifies cash receipts and cash payments as cash inflows and cash outflows from investing activities, financing activities, and operating activities.

The following should be noted for background.

1. Cash flows from investing activities
   a. Making and collecting loans (but not related interest).
   b. Acquiring and disposing of debt or equity instruments of other entities, except for investments in "trading securities," as per FASB Statement #115, which are treated as operating cash flows (but not related interest or dividends).
   c. Acquiring and disposing of property, plant, and equipment and other productive assets.
2. Cash flows from financing activities
   a. Obtaining resources from owners and providing them with a return on, and a return of, their investment (but not related interest).
   b. Borrowing money and repaying amounts involved, or otherwise settling the obligation (but not related interest).
   c. Obtaining and paying for other resources obtained from creditors on long-term credit (but not related interest).
3. Cash flows from operating activities—Operating activities include the cash effects of all transactions and other events that are neither investing activities nor financing activities; essentially, operating activities relate to income statement items. They generally involve producing and delivering goods and providing services.

It should be noted that receipts of interest and dividends from all sources, and interest paid to creditors, represent operating activities.

4. Noncash activities—Information about investing and financing activities not resulting in cash receipts or cash payments, such as issuing a mortgage note in exchange for a building, converting debt to equity, or exchanging common stock for plant and equipment, should be reported separately (as supplementary information) and not be included in the body of the statement.

5. Direct and indirect methods—Statement #95 encourages use of the direct method of presenting cash flow information, but also permits use of the indirect method.

Under the direct method, individual income statement items are presented as gross cash receipts and gross cash payments. In addition, a reconciliation of net income and net cash flows from operating activities is presented as a separate schedule; this schedule has the same net result as gross cash receipts and cash payments from operating activities.

Under the indirect method, the reconciliation of net income and net cash flows from operating activities is the key element in the statement. It is presented either in the body of the statement, or in a separate schedule. If presented in a separate schedule, the net cash flow from operating activities is presented as a single line item. There is no presentation of gross cash receipts and gross cash payments from operating activities.

The net cash used in investing activities was $170,000:

Purchase of A.S., Inc. bonds (i.e., cash outflow)	$180,000
Proceeds from sale of equipment (i.e., cash inflow)	(10,000)
Net cash used (i.e., net cash outflow) in investing activities	$170,000

The following should be noted.

1. Cash inflows and outflows, and not carrying amounts, are reported in the statement of cash flows. Thus, the sale of equipment would have resulted in a cash inflow equal to the proceeds from the sale; the $5,000

gain should be added back to income to arrive at cash flows from operations.

2. Proceeds from the sale of treasury stock is a financing transaction, not an investing transaction.

3. The amortization of the bond discount (related to the bond investment) should be subtracted from income to arrive at cash flows from operations.

Answer choices other than "A" are not logical in view of the explanation provided.

#48 (answer "D")

In accordance with FASB Statement #95, cash flows from financing activities include:

1. Obtaining resources from owners and providing them with a return on, and a return of, their investment (but not related interest).

2. Borrowing money and repaying amounts involved, or otherwise settling the obligation (but not related interest).

3. Obtaining and paying for other resources obtained from creditors on long-term credit (but not related interest).

Based on the preceding, the net cash provided by financing activities should be $37,000:

Proceeds from sale of treasury stock (i.e., cash inflow)	$75,000
Cash dividends paid in 1994 (i.e., cash outflow)	(38,000)
Net cash provided (i.e., net cash inflow) by financing activities, 1994	$37,000

Additionally, the following should be observed.

1. Dividends paid, not dividends declared, result in an outflow of cash.

2. The carrying amount of the treasury stock is not relevant; the proceeds from the sale result in a cash inflow.

Answer choices other than "D" are inconsistent with the information provided.

#49 (answer "C")

FASB Statement #95, "Statement of Cash Flows," provides that information on cash flow per share should not be reported in either the body of the statement of cash flows or as supplemental information. However, information about investing and financing activities not resulting in cash receipts or cash payments, such as <u>conversion of debt to equity</u>, or exchanging common stock for plant and equipment, <u>should be reported as supplemental information</u> and not in the body of the statement.

Answer choices other than "C" are the result of incorrect assumptions and/or combinations.

#50 (answer "D")

When preparing consolidated financial statements, all intercompany transactions must be eliminated so that only those transactions with parties outside of the consolidated entity are included in the financial statements.

The amount of intercompany revenues must be determined based upon information about Pare's revenues, Shel's revenues, and consolidated revenues. It should be noted that Pare's revenues (i.e., $400,000) include intercompany sales to Shel. Intercompany sales from Pare to Shel, which would have been eliminated in consolidation, were <u>$64,000</u>:

Total combined revenues;	
$400,000 + $280,000	$680,000
Consolidated revenues	(616,000)
<u>Intercompany sales during 1994</u>	<u>$ 64,000</u>

Answer choice "A" is incorrect because it is the amount of unrealized gross profit in the ending inventory, which would have been eliminated in consolidation (i.e., the $110,000 combined inventory of Pare and Shel less $104,000 of consolidated inventory equals $6,000).

Answer choice "B" is incorrect because it is the amount of intercompany accounts receivable at December 31, 1994, which would have been eliminated in consolidation (i.e., the $90,000 combined accounts receivable of Pare and Shel less $78,000 of consolidated accounts receivable equals $12,000).

Answer choice "C" is incorrect because it represents the adjustment needed to arrive at consolidated cost of sales (i.e., the $520,000 combined cost of sales of Pare and Shel less $462,000 of consolidated cost of sales equals $58,000).

#51 (answer "B")

The basic premise underlying this question is that in preparing consolidated financial statements, all intercompany transactions are eliminated; the balance sheet should include only amounts due to or from those outside of the consolidated entity.

As such, since the combined accounts receivable of Pare and Shel are $90,000 (i.e., $52,000 plus $38,000), and consolidated accounts receivable are $78,000, it must logically follow that <u>$12,000</u> <u>represents the amount of Shel's payable to Pare for intercompany sales</u>.

Answer choice "A" is incorrect because it is the amount of unrealized gross profit in the ending inventory, which would have been eliminated in consolidation (i.e., the $110,000 combined inventory of Pare and Shel less $104,000 of consolidated inventory equals $6,000).

Answer choice "C" is incorrect because it represents the adjustment to arrive at consolidated cost of goods sold (i.e., the $520,000 combined cost of sales of Pare and Shel less $462,000 of consolidated cost of sales equals $58,000).

Answer choice "D" is incorrect because it represents intercompany sales (i.e., the $680,000 combined revenues of Pare and Shel less $616,000 of consolidated revenues equals $64,000).

#52 (answer "A")

On a consolidated balance sheet, the inventory purchased by one constituent part of the consolidated entity from another must be stated at historical cost to the consolidated entity, which is the acquisition cost to the selling party.

The difference between the selling price and the historical cost of inventory at the date of the consolidated financial statements is unrealized intercompany profit, which must be eliminated in consolidation.

Thus, it is easy to determine <u>the unrealized intercompany</u> (gross) <u>profit</u> in ending inventory that <u>was eliminated</u>. It is merely the difference between the $110,000 combined inventory (i.e., $60,000 plus $50,000), and the $104,000 consolidated inventory, or <u>$6,000</u>.

Answer choice "B" is incorrect because it represents the combined accounts receivable/payable less the consolidated accounts receivable/payable (i.e., $90,000 less $78,000 equals $12,000).

Answer choice "C" is incorrect because it represents the adjustment to arrive at consolidated cost of goods sold (i.e., the $520,000 combined cost of sales of Pare and Shel less $462,000 of consolidated cost of sales equals $58,000).

Answer choice "D" is incorrect because it is the amount of intercompany sales eliminated in the consolidation process (i.e., [$400,000 + $280,000] − $616,000 equals $64,000).

#53 (answer "D")

The purchase and pooling of interests methods are both acceptable methods of accounting for business combinations; however, they are not alternatives for the same transaction.

Generally, a pooling of interests is accomplished by an exchange of voting common stock for at least 90% of the voting common stock of another company. Since it is deemed to be a combination of shareholders' equity, the assets and liabilities of the acquired company do not change, and goodwill is not recognized. All costs incurred with the business combination are charged against income as they are incurred.

A purchase is generally deemed to be an acquisition of assets; thus, a new basis of accountability is established. Assets and liabilities acquired are recognized at their respective fair values, with goodwill recognized at an amount equal to the difference between the cost of the investment and the fair value of the net identifiable assets acquired. The direct cost of the combination, other than registration and issuance costs of equity securities, should be <u>included in the acquisition cost to be allocated to identifiable assets according to their fair values</u>.

Answer choice "A" is incorrect because the direct costs of a purchase are not deferred and amortized, but are considered part of the cost of the net assets acquired.

Answer choice "B" is incorrect because the direct costs of a purchase are not deducted directly from retained earnings. It should be noted that the costs associated with registering and issuing equity securities issued to effect the purchase are deducted from additional paid-in capital.

Answer choice "C" is incorrect because the direct costs of a pooling of interests, not a purchase, are deducted in determining the net income of the combined corporation for the period in which the costs were incurred.

#54 (answer "A")

The purchase and pooling of interests methods are both acceptable methods of accounting for business combinations; however, they are not alternatives for the same transaction.

Generally, a pooling of interests is accomplished by an exchange of voting common stock for at least 90% of the voting common stock of another company. Since it is deemed to be a combination of shareholders' equity, the assets and liabilities of the acquired company do not change, and goodwill is not recognized. Regardless of when the pooling actually occurred, it is assumed that the two companies had always been combined. Accordingly, dividends paid by the acquired company (Shaw) prior to the combination would be deemed paid to the shareholders of the combined entity under a pooling.

A purchase is an acquisition of assets; thus, a new basis of accountability is established. Assets and liabilities acquired are recognized at their respective fair values, with goodwill recognized at an amount equal to the difference between the cost of the investment and the fair value of the net identifiable assets acquired. Since the assets of the acquired company are recognized at fair value at the date of the combination, dividends paid to the shareholders of the acquired company are not recognized in the consolidated financial statements.

In the December 31, 1994, consolidated statement of retained earnings, dividends declared <u>under the purchase method</u> would be <u>$100,000</u> (those paid by Poe, only). <u>Under the pooling of interests method</u>, dividends declared would be <u>$130,000</u> (those paid by Poe; i.e., $100,000, plus those paid by Shaw prior to the business combination; i.e., $10,000 × 3, or $30,000).

Answer choices other than "A" are based upon incorrect assumptions and/or combinations.

#55 (answer "C")

Personal financial statements may be prepared for an individual, a husband, a wife, or a family. Generally, accrual accounting is used, assets are measured at estimated current values, and liabilities are measured at the estimated current amounts. A set of personal financial statements usually consists of <u>a statement of financial condition and a statement of changes in net worth</u> (optional).

Answer choice "A" is incorrect because a statement of net worth is not presented in personal financial statements.

Answer choice "B" is incorrect because neither an income statement nor a statement of net worth is presented in personal financial statements.

Answer choice "D" is incorrect because a statement of cash flows is not required in a set of personal financial statements.

#56 (answer "A")

FASB Statement #14, "Financial Reporting for Segments of a Business Enterprise," requires that publicly owned entities provide segment information as to different industries, foreign operations, export sales, and/or major customers.

An industry segment is reportable if its sales, operating profit, or identifiable assets are 10% or more of all combined amounts. Foreign operations must be disclosed if their revenues from unaffiliated customers, or their total assets, are 10% or more of the respective consolidated amounts. Further, separate disclosure is required if sales to a single customer or export sales are 10% or more of total revenue.

Answer choices other than "A" are based upon incorrect assumptions and/or combinations.

#57 (answer "D")

Under FASB Statement #87, "Employers' Accounting for Pensions," the minimum disclosure requirements include:

1. A description of the plan, including type of benefit formula and funding policy.
2. The components of net periodic pension cost for the period.
3. Assumptions including the discount rate and the return rate on plan assets.
4. A reconciliation of the funded status of the pension plan with the accrued or prepaid pension cost reported in the balance sheet, showing separately:
   a. The fair value of plan assets.
   b. The projected benefit obligation, separately identifying the accumulated benefit obligation and vested benefit obligation.
   c. The amount of unrecognized prior service cost.

d. The amount of unrecognized gain or loss.
e. The amount of any remaining unrecognized net obligation.
f. The amount of unconditional liability equal to (1) the unfunded accumulated benefit obligation plus any prepaid pension cost, (2) the unfunded accumulated benefit obligation reduced by any unfunded accrued pension cost, or (3) the amount of the unfunded accumulated benefit obligation.
g. The amount of the net pension asset or liability that has been recognized in the employer's balance sheet.

Answer choices other than "D" are inconsistent with the explanation provided.

#58 (this question is obsolete)

#59 (this question is obsolete)

#60 (this question is obsolete)

OTHER OBJECTIVE FORMATS/ESSAY QUESTIONS

Answer 2

#61 (answer "14,000")

Generally, a prior period adjustment is the result of the correction of a theoretical or mechanical error in the preparation of the financial statement of a prior year. The failure to amortize the patent that was purchased on July 1, 1993, is an accounting error that requires treatment as a prior period adjustment, which is reported net of applicable income taxes.

The amount of the prior period adjustment is determined as follows:

Cost of patent	$320,000
Useful life	8 years
Annual amortization	40,000
Portion of year not amortized	50%
Gross error	20,000
Less: Income tax (30%)	(6,000)
Prior period adjustment	$ 14,000

#62 (answer "12,000")

Dividends on cumulative preferred stock become liabilities only when they are declared by the board of directors. Since there is no information about dividends in arrears, only the current year's dividends were declared on the preferred shares. The amount of the preferred dividends was $12,000; the $6 dividend rate per share (i.e., $100 par value @ 6%) multiplied by the 2,000 shares of preferred stock outstanding on the declaration date (i.e., December 20, 1994).

#63 (answer "165,000")

The cash dividend on common stock is based upon the number of shares outstanding on the record date (i.e., November 15, 1994). On the record date, the number of shares outstanding was as follows:

Outstanding at December 31, 1993	100,000
Issued on February 1, 1994	13,000
Less: Treasury shares on record date; 5,000 − 2,000	(3,000)
Shares outstanding on November 15, 1994	110,000
Dividend rate	$1.50
Common dividends—cash	$165,000

#64 (answer "720,000")

According to APB Opinion #29, "Nonmonetary Transactions," a property dividend is a nonreciprocal transfer of assets that should be measured at the fair market value of the asset to be distributed as measured on the date of declaration. Therefore, the amount of the common dividends—property was $720,000, the fair value of the marketable securities that were distributed on the date of declaration (i.e., May 10, 1994).

#65 (answer "113,000")

The number of shares issued are those shares that have been sold and not subsequently retired. Accordingly, shares that are held as treasury shares are considered issued but not outstanding. The number of common shares issued at December 31, 1994, was 113,000; i.e., those outstanding at the end of the prior year (i.e., 100,000) plus the shares issued on February 1, 1994 (i.e., 13,000).

#66 (answer "113,000")

The amount of the common stock issued is simply the par (or stated) value of the shares issued. As indicated in the answer to item #65, there were 113,000 issued at December 31, 1994, and

the par value of the common shares was $1; thus, the amount of the common stock issued is $113,000.

#67 (answer "934,000")

In general, additional paid-in capital is the excess of the issue price of stock over the par value of the stock issued, plus or minus any differences between the reissue price and cost of treasury shares sold. Additional paid-in capital at December 31, 1994, is determined as follows:

Balance at December 31, 1993		$800,000
Fair value of shares issued 2/1/94; 13,000 @ $11	$143,000	
Less: Par value of shares issued	(13,000)	130,000
Treasury stock transactions:		
Proceeds of shares sold on 10/1/94; 2,000 @ $16	$32,000	
Less cost of shares sold; 2,000 @ $14	(28,000)	4,000
Additional paid-in capital, including treasury stock transactions		$934,000

#68 (answer "42,000")

Treasury stock are those issued shares that have been reacquired by the corporation but not formally retired. Under the cost method, the cost of the treasury shares is reported as a contra-equity item.

The cost of the treasury shares at December 31, 1994, was $42,000 (3,000 shares @ $14).

#69 (answer "24.86")

The book value of common stock is equal to total common stockholders' equity (total equity less preferred equity at par or liquidation value) divided by the number of shares outstanding on the balance sheet date. Book value per share at December 31, 1993, is determined as follows, considering that 100,000 shares were outstanding:

Total stockholders' equity at December 31, 1993	$2,686,000
Less: Preferred equity; 2,000 shares @ $100	(200,000)
Common equity at December 31, 1993	$2,486,000

Book value per share at
December 31, 1993;
$2,486,000/100,000   **$24.86**

#70 (answer "826,000")

The numerator used in calculating earnings per share is the amount of net income that is applicable to common stock (net income less preferred stock dividends). Accordingly, at December 31, 1994, the numerator is determined as follows:

Net income, 1994	$838,000
Less: Preferred dividends declared;	
2,000 shares @ $6 per share	(12,000)
Earnings applicable to common stock	$826,000

Answer 3

#71 (answer "B, 73,000")

A material gain or loss from the extinguishment of debt is classified as an extraordinary item without regard to frequency of occurrence or usual nature. The amount of the gain or loss is the difference between the carrying value of the debt and the amount paid to retire it, excluding accrued interest. Accordingly, the amount of the loss from the extinguishment of the 8% bonds is determined as follows:

Redemption price;			
$1,000,000 × 1.02			$1,020,000
Less carrying amount,			
June 30, 1994:			
Carrying amount at			
January 1, 1994		$940,000	
Add discount			
amortization,			
1/1/94—6/30/94:			
Interest at effective			
rate; $940,000 ×			
10% × 6/12	$47,000		
Interest at stated			
rate; $1,000,000 ×			
8% × 6/12	(40,000)	7,000	947,000
Loss on extinguishment			
(before taxes)			$ 73,000

#72 (answer "C, 100,000")

A change from one generally accepted accounting principle to another is a change in accounting principle that is reported using the cumulative effect method. The cumulative effect of this change is the difference between accumulated depreciation at January 1, 1994, under the old method (sum-of-the-years'-digits) and the new method (straight-line). The amount of the change is determined as follows:

Accumulated depreciation,	
1/1/94, under sum-of-the-	
years'-digits method;	
([$520,000—20,000] × 12/15)	$400,000
Accumulated depreciation,	
1/1/94 under straight-line	
method; ([520,000—20,000] × 3/5)	(300,000)
Cumulative effect (before taxes)	$100,000

#73 (answer "A, 125,000")

The result of the settlement of a lawsuit should be reported as an element of income from continuing operations, since it is a change in the estimated liability recognized in the prior year's financial statements. It is not a correction of an error; therefore, it is not a prior-period adjustment. It is probably not infrequent in occurrence nor unusual in nature; therefore, it is not an extraordinary item.

Under FASB Statement #5, "Accounting for Contingencies," a liability should be accrued when it is probable that an asset has been impaired as of the date of the financial statements, and the amount can be reasonably estimated. When the estimate is a range, the most likely amount within that range should be accrued; when no amount within the range is more likely than another, the minimum amount within the range should be accrued.

Accordingly, Hake accrued a liability of $250,000 at December 31, 1993. When the lawsuit was settled in 1994 for $375,000, Hake would need to record an additional loss of $125,000.

#74 (answer "A, 10,000")

Under FASB Statement #115, "Accounting for Certain Investments in Debt and Equity Securities," investments that are held principally to sell in the near term are classified as trading securities. Trading securities are valued at their market value at the date of the balance sheet, with any unrealized gains and losses recognized as a component of income from continuing operations. Thus, the difference between the total cost of both investments (i.e., $360,000) and their fair values at 12/31/94 (i.e., $350,000), or $10,000, will be recognized as a holding loss in the 1994 income statement.

#75 (answer "B, 255,000")

The loss from the hurricane should be classified as an <u>extraordinary item</u> in Hake's 1994 income statement. An extraordinary item is one that is both infrequent in occurrence and unusual in nature. The event is infrequent because this was the first hurricane ever to strike the area. Most acts of God, such as hurricanes, are unusual in nature.

<u>The loss is</u> equal to the difference between the proceeds received from the insurance company and the carrying amount of the assets lost, determined as follows:

Warehouse	$ 470,000
Equipment	250,000
Inventory	535,000
Total	1,255,000
Less: Proceeds received from insurance company	(1,000,000)
<u>Extraordinary</u> <u>loss</u> (<u>before</u> <u>taxes</u>)	$ 255,000

#76 (answer "E, 41,000")

Under FASB Statement #52 "Foreign Currency Translation," the cumulative translation adjustment arising from translating a foreign subsidiary's financial statements from the functional currency to the reporting currency (dollars) is recognized as a <u>separate component of stockholders' equity.</u>

Where the functional currency is the foreign currency, all assets and liabilities are translated at the exchange rate in effect on the balance sheet date, and all income statement elements are translated at the weighted-average exchange rate for the year.

Thus, the cumulative foreign currency translation adjustment must consider the beginning of year balance of net assets (in this case, the date of acquisition), the end of year balance, and the translated net income. As such, <u>the adjustment is</u> $429,000 less $388,000, or <u>$41,000</u>.

(It should be noted that the $429,000 figure is the sum of the beginning balance and translated net income, which represents an appropriate "cumulative" consideration.)

Answer 4

Part 4 (a)

Bing should account for its investment in Latt by the equity method if it can exercise significant influence over the operating, investing, and financing policies of Latt. There is a presumption of the ability to exercise significant influence if 20% or more of the outstanding voting common stock is owned by the investor. However, the equity method may be appropriate at levels of ownership of less than 20% if the ability to exercise influence can be demonstrated. Examples of ways to demonstrate the ability to exercise influence include membership on the board of directors, participation in the investee's policy making process, material intercompany transactions, interchange of managerial personnel, technological dependency, or widely dispersed ownership of the remaining outstanding shares.

The equity method is consistent with accrual accounting because the investor recognizes income when it is earned by the investee, rather than when it is realized through the receipt of dividends. Therefore, the equity method better matches revenue and expenses in the period of benefit.

Part 4 (b)

Bing <u>Co.</u>
<u>Schedule of Investment Income from Latt</u>
<u>on Income Statement</u>
<u>For the year ended December 31, 1994</u>

Equity in reported earnings of Latt;		
$400,000 × (39,000/200,000)		$78,000
Less amortization of goodwill:		
Cost of investment	$585,000	
Carrying amount of shares acquired	405,000	
Goodwill	$180,000	
Amortization, 1994;		
$180,000/10		18,000
Equity in earnings of Latt, 1994		$60,000

Bing <u>Co.</u>
<u>Schedule of Investment in Latt</u>
<u>on Balance Sheet</u>
<u>As at December 31, 1995</u>

Cost of investment	$585,000
Equity in earnings of Latt for 1994 (from above)	60,000
Less: Dividends received;	
$100,000 × (39,000/200,000)	(19,500)
Balance, December 31, 1994	$625,500

Answer 5

Part 5 (a)

Certain long-term leases are required to be capitalized because in economic substance, if not in legal form, they represent the acquisition of assets and the incurrence of liabilities.

The lease represents an asset because it is a probable future economic benefit that is controlled by the lessee as the result of a past transaction.

The lease is a liability because it is a probable future sacrifice of an economic benefit by the lessee as the result of a past transaction.

It may also be viewed that capitalization is consistent with the transfer of substantial ownership benefits to the lessee, along with the related uncertainties and risks.

Part 5 (b)

Dr. Cash	864,000	
Cr. Equipment		540,000
Cr. Deferred gross profit		
on sale-leaseback		324,000

To record capital lease at present value of minimum lease payments; $150,000 (net of executory costs) $\times$ 5.76, or $864,000. Deferred gross profit equals $864,000 − $540,000 of cost, or $324,000.

Dr. Leased equipment		
under capital lease	864,000	
Cr. Liability under		
capital lease		864,000

To record leaseback at present value of minimum lease payments.

Part 5 (c)

Dr. Liability under capital lease	63,600	
Dr. Interest expense	86,400	
Dr. Executory cost expense	3,000	
Cr. Cash		153,000

To record lease payment at December 31, 1994:

Total payment, net of executory costs	$150,000
Applicable to interest expense;	
$864,000 $\times$ 10%	86,400
Reduction of liability	$ 63,600

Dr. Depreciation expense	96,000	
Cr. Accumulated depreciation		96,000

To record depreciation of leased asset; $864,000/9

Dr. Deferred gross profit on		
sale-leaseback	36,000	
Cr. Depreciation expense		36,000

To record amortization of deferred gross profit; $324,000/9

Answer Sheet

November 1995 CPA Examination

LPR

AUDIT

LPR

1. Ⓐ Ⓑ Ⓒ Ⓓ	31. Ⓐ Ⓑ Ⓒ Ⓓ
2. Ⓐ Ⓑ Ⓒ Ⓓ	32. Ⓐ Ⓑ Ⓒ Ⓓ
3. Ⓐ Ⓑ Ⓒ Ⓓ	33. Ⓐ Ⓑ Ⓒ Ⓓ
4. Ⓐ Ⓑ Ⓒ Ⓓ	34. Ⓐ Ⓑ Ⓒ Ⓓ
5. Ⓐ Ⓑ Ⓒ Ⓓ	35. Ⓐ Ⓑ Ⓒ Ⓓ
6. obsolete	36. Ⓐ Ⓑ Ⓒ Ⓓ
7. obsolete	37. Ⓐ Ⓑ Ⓒ Ⓓ
8. Ⓐ Ⓑ Ⓒ Ⓓ	38. Ⓐ Ⓑ Ⓒ Ⓓ
9. Ⓐ Ⓑ Ⓒ Ⓓ	39. Ⓐ Ⓑ Ⓒ Ⓓ
10. Ⓐ Ⓑ Ⓒ Ⓓ	40. Ⓐ Ⓑ Ⓒ Ⓓ
11. Ⓐ Ⓑ Ⓒ Ⓓ	41. Ⓐ Ⓑ Ⓒ Ⓓ
12. Ⓐ Ⓑ Ⓒ Ⓓ	42. Ⓐ Ⓑ Ⓒ Ⓓ
13. Ⓐ Ⓑ Ⓒ Ⓓ	43. Ⓐ Ⓑ Ⓒ Ⓓ
14. Ⓐ Ⓑ Ⓒ Ⓓ	44. Ⓐ Ⓑ Ⓒ Ⓓ
15. Ⓐ Ⓑ Ⓒ Ⓓ	45. Ⓐ Ⓑ Ⓒ Ⓓ
16. Ⓐ Ⓑ Ⓒ Ⓓ	46. Ⓐ Ⓑ Ⓒ Ⓓ
17. Ⓐ Ⓑ Ⓒ Ⓓ	47. Ⓐ Ⓑ Ⓒ Ⓓ
18. Ⓐ Ⓑ Ⓒ Ⓓ	48. Ⓐ Ⓑ Ⓒ Ⓓ
19. Ⓐ Ⓑ Ⓒ Ⓓ	49. Ⓐ Ⓑ Ⓒ Ⓓ
20. Ⓐ Ⓑ Ⓒ Ⓓ	50. Ⓐ Ⓑ Ⓒ Ⓓ
21. Ⓐ Ⓑ Ⓒ Ⓓ	51. Ⓐ Ⓑ Ⓒ Ⓓ
22. Ⓐ Ⓑ Ⓒ Ⓓ	52. Ⓐ Ⓑ Ⓒ Ⓓ
23. Ⓐ Ⓑ Ⓒ Ⓓ	53. Ⓐ Ⓑ Ⓒ Ⓓ
24. Ⓐ Ⓑ Ⓒ Ⓓ	54. Ⓐ Ⓑ Ⓒ Ⓓ
25. Ⓐ Ⓑ Ⓒ Ⓓ	55. Ⓐ Ⓑ Ⓒ Ⓓ
26. Ⓐ Ⓑ Ⓒ Ⓓ	56. Ⓐ Ⓑ Ⓒ Ⓓ
27. Ⓐ Ⓑ Ⓒ Ⓓ	57. Ⓐ Ⓑ Ⓒ Ⓓ
28. Ⓐ Ⓑ Ⓒ Ⓓ	58. Ⓐ Ⓑ Ⓒ Ⓓ
29. Ⓐ Ⓑ Ⓒ Ⓓ	59. Ⓐ Ⓑ Ⓒ Ⓓ
30. Ⓐ Ⓑ Ⓒ Ⓓ	60. Ⓐ Ⓑ Ⓒ Ⓓ

AUDIT

1. Ⓐ Ⓑ Ⓒ Ⓓ	31. Ⓐ Ⓑ Ⓒ Ⓓ	61. Ⓐ Ⓑ Ⓒ Ⓓ
2. Ⓐ Ⓑ Ⓒ Ⓓ	32. Ⓐ Ⓑ Ⓒ Ⓓ	62. Ⓐ Ⓑ Ⓒ Ⓓ
3. Ⓐ Ⓑ Ⓒ Ⓓ	33. Ⓐ Ⓑ Ⓒ Ⓓ	63. Ⓐ Ⓑ Ⓒ Ⓓ
4. Ⓐ Ⓑ Ⓒ Ⓓ	34. Ⓐ Ⓑ Ⓒ Ⓓ	64. obsolete
5. Ⓐ Ⓑ Ⓒ Ⓓ	35. Ⓐ Ⓑ Ⓒ Ⓓ	65. Ⓐ Ⓑ Ⓒ Ⓓ
6. Ⓐ Ⓑ Ⓒ Ⓓ	36. Ⓐ Ⓑ Ⓒ Ⓓ	66. Ⓐ Ⓑ Ⓒ Ⓓ
7. Ⓐ Ⓑ Ⓒ Ⓓ	37. Ⓐ Ⓑ Ⓒ Ⓓ	67. Ⓐ Ⓑ Ⓒ Ⓓ
8. Ⓐ Ⓑ Ⓒ Ⓓ	38. Ⓐ Ⓑ Ⓒ Ⓓ	68. Ⓐ Ⓑ Ⓒ Ⓓ
9. Ⓐ Ⓑ Ⓒ Ⓓ	39. Ⓐ Ⓑ Ⓒ Ⓓ	69. Ⓐ Ⓑ Ⓒ Ⓓ
10. Ⓐ Ⓑ Ⓒ Ⓓ	40. Ⓐ Ⓑ Ⓒ Ⓓ	70. obsolete
11. Ⓐ Ⓑ Ⓒ Ⓓ	41. Ⓐ Ⓑ Ⓒ Ⓓ	71. Ⓐ Ⓑ Ⓒ Ⓓ
12. Ⓐ Ⓑ Ⓒ Ⓓ	42. obsolete	72. Ⓐ Ⓑ Ⓒ Ⓓ
13. Ⓐ Ⓑ Ⓒ Ⓓ	43. Ⓐ Ⓑ Ⓒ Ⓓ	73. Ⓐ Ⓑ Ⓒ Ⓓ
14. Ⓐ Ⓑ Ⓒ Ⓓ	44. Ⓐ Ⓑ Ⓒ Ⓓ	74. Ⓐ Ⓑ Ⓒ Ⓓ
15. Ⓐ Ⓑ Ⓒ Ⓓ	45. Ⓐ Ⓑ Ⓒ Ⓓ	75. Ⓐ Ⓑ Ⓒ Ⓓ
16. Ⓐ Ⓑ Ⓒ Ⓓ	46. Ⓐ Ⓑ Ⓒ Ⓓ	76. Ⓐ Ⓑ Ⓒ Ⓓ
17. Ⓐ Ⓑ Ⓒ Ⓓ	47. Ⓐ Ⓑ Ⓒ Ⓓ	77. Ⓐ Ⓑ Ⓒ Ⓓ
18. Ⓐ Ⓑ Ⓒ Ⓓ	48. Ⓐ Ⓑ Ⓒ Ⓓ	78. Ⓐ Ⓑ Ⓒ Ⓓ
19. Ⓐ Ⓑ Ⓒ Ⓓ	49. Ⓐ Ⓑ Ⓒ Ⓓ	79. Ⓐ Ⓑ Ⓒ Ⓓ
20. Ⓐ Ⓑ Ⓒ Ⓓ	50. Ⓐ Ⓑ Ⓒ Ⓓ	80. Ⓐ Ⓑ Ⓒ Ⓓ
21. Ⓐ Ⓑ Ⓒ Ⓓ	51. Ⓐ Ⓑ Ⓒ Ⓓ	81. Ⓐ Ⓑ Ⓒ Ⓓ
22. Ⓐ Ⓑ Ⓒ Ⓓ	52. Ⓐ Ⓑ Ⓒ Ⓓ	82. Ⓐ Ⓑ Ⓒ Ⓓ
23. Ⓐ Ⓑ Ⓒ Ⓓ	53. Ⓐ Ⓑ Ⓒ Ⓓ	83. Ⓐ Ⓑ Ⓒ Ⓓ
24. Ⓐ Ⓑ Ⓒ Ⓓ	54. Ⓐ Ⓑ Ⓒ Ⓓ	84. Ⓐ Ⓑ Ⓒ Ⓓ
25. Ⓐ Ⓑ Ⓒ Ⓓ	55. Ⓐ Ⓑ Ⓒ Ⓓ	85. Ⓐ Ⓑ Ⓒ Ⓓ
26. Ⓐ Ⓑ Ⓒ Ⓓ	56. Ⓐ Ⓑ Ⓒ Ⓓ	86. Ⓐ Ⓑ Ⓒ Ⓓ
27. Ⓐ Ⓑ Ⓒ Ⓓ	57. Ⓐ Ⓑ Ⓒ Ⓓ	87. Ⓐ Ⓑ Ⓒ Ⓓ
28. Ⓐ Ⓑ Ⓒ Ⓓ	58. Ⓐ Ⓑ Ⓒ Ⓓ	88. Ⓐ Ⓑ Ⓒ Ⓓ
29. Ⓐ Ⓑ Ⓒ Ⓓ	59. Ⓐ Ⓑ Ⓒ Ⓓ	89. Ⓐ Ⓑ Ⓒ Ⓓ
30. Ⓐ Ⓑ Ⓒ Ⓓ	60. Ⓐ Ⓑ Ⓒ Ⓓ	90. Ⓐ Ⓑ Ⓒ Ⓓ

Answer Sheet

ARE

1. Ⓐ Ⓑ Ⓒ Ⓓ   31. Ⓐ Ⓑ Ⓒ Ⓓ
2. Ⓐ Ⓑ Ⓒ Ⓓ   32. Ⓐ Ⓑ Ⓒ Ⓓ
3. Ⓐ Ⓑ Ⓒ Ⓓ   33. Ⓐ Ⓑ Ⓒ Ⓓ
4. Ⓐ Ⓑ Ⓒ Ⓓ   34. Ⓐ Ⓑ Ⓒ Ⓓ
5. Ⓐ Ⓑ Ⓒ Ⓓ   35. Ⓐ Ⓑ Ⓒ Ⓓ
6. Ⓐ Ⓑ Ⓒ Ⓓ   36. Ⓐ Ⓑ Ⓒ Ⓓ
7. Ⓐ Ⓑ Ⓒ Ⓓ   37. Ⓐ Ⓑ Ⓒ Ⓓ
8. Ⓐ Ⓑ Ⓒ Ⓓ   38. Ⓐ Ⓑ Ⓒ Ⓓ
9. Ⓐ Ⓑ Ⓒ Ⓓ   39. Ⓐ Ⓑ Ⓒ Ⓓ
10. Ⓐ Ⓑ Ⓒ Ⓓ   40. Ⓐ Ⓑ Ⓒ Ⓓ
11. Ⓐ Ⓑ Ⓒ Ⓓ   41. Ⓐ Ⓑ Ⓒ Ⓓ
12. Ⓐ Ⓑ Ⓒ Ⓓ   42. Ⓐ Ⓑ Ⓒ Ⓓ
13. Ⓐ Ⓑ Ⓒ Ⓓ   43. Ⓐ Ⓑ Ⓒ Ⓓ
14. Ⓐ Ⓑ Ⓒ Ⓓ   44. Ⓐ Ⓑ Ⓒ Ⓓ
15. Ⓐ Ⓑ Ⓒ Ⓓ   45. Ⓐ Ⓑ Ⓒ Ⓓ
16. Ⓐ Ⓑ Ⓒ Ⓓ   46. Ⓐ Ⓑ Ⓒ Ⓓ
17. Ⓐ Ⓑ Ⓒ Ⓓ   47. Ⓐ Ⓑ Ⓒ Ⓓ
18. Ⓐ Ⓑ Ⓒ Ⓓ   48. Ⓐ Ⓑ Ⓒ Ⓓ
19. Ⓐ Ⓑ Ⓒ Ⓓ   49. Ⓐ Ⓑ Ⓒ Ⓓ
20. Ⓐ Ⓑ Ⓒ Ⓓ   50. Ⓐ Ⓑ Ⓒ Ⓓ
21. Ⓐ Ⓑ Ⓒ Ⓓ   51. Ⓐ Ⓑ Ⓒ Ⓓ
22. Ⓐ Ⓑ Ⓒ Ⓓ   52. Ⓐ Ⓑ Ⓒ Ⓓ
23. Ⓐ Ⓑ Ⓒ Ⓓ   53. Ⓐ Ⓑ Ⓒ Ⓓ
24. Ⓐ Ⓑ Ⓒ Ⓓ   54. Ⓐ Ⓑ Ⓒ Ⓓ
25. Ⓐ Ⓑ Ⓒ Ⓓ   55. Ⓐ Ⓑ Ⓒ Ⓓ
26. Ⓐ Ⓑ Ⓒ Ⓓ   56. Ⓐ Ⓑ Ⓒ Ⓓ
27. Ⓐ Ⓑ Ⓒ Ⓓ   57. Ⓐ Ⓑ Ⓒ Ⓓ
28. Ⓐ Ⓑ Ⓒ Ⓓ   58. Ⓐ Ⓑ Ⓒ Ⓓ
29. Ⓐ Ⓑ Ⓒ Ⓓ   59. Ⓐ Ⓑ Ⓒ Ⓓ
30. Ⓐ Ⓑ Ⓒ Ⓓ   60. Ⓐ Ⓑ Ⓒ Ⓓ

FARE

1. Ⓐ Ⓑ Ⓒ Ⓓ   31. Ⓐ Ⓑ Ⓒ Ⓓ
2. Ⓐ Ⓑ Ⓒ Ⓓ   32. Ⓐ Ⓑ Ⓒ Ⓓ
3. Ⓐ Ⓑ Ⓒ Ⓓ   33. Ⓐ Ⓑ Ⓒ Ⓓ
4. Ⓐ Ⓑ Ⓒ Ⓓ   34. Ⓐ Ⓑ Ⓒ Ⓓ
5. Ⓐ Ⓑ Ⓒ Ⓓ   35. Ⓐ Ⓑ Ⓒ Ⓓ
6. Ⓐ Ⓑ Ⓒ Ⓓ   36. Ⓐ Ⓑ Ⓒ Ⓓ
7. Ⓐ Ⓑ Ⓒ Ⓓ   37. Ⓐ Ⓑ Ⓒ Ⓓ
8. Ⓐ Ⓑ Ⓒ Ⓓ   38. Ⓐ Ⓑ Ⓒ Ⓓ
9. Ⓐ Ⓑ Ⓒ Ⓓ   39. Ⓐ Ⓑ Ⓒ Ⓓ
10. Ⓐ Ⓑ Ⓒ Ⓓ   40. Ⓐ Ⓑ Ⓒ Ⓓ
11. Ⓐ Ⓑ Ⓒ Ⓓ   41. Ⓐ Ⓑ Ⓒ Ⓓ
12. Ⓐ Ⓑ Ⓒ Ⓓ   42. Ⓐ Ⓑ Ⓒ Ⓓ
13. Ⓐ Ⓑ Ⓒ Ⓓ   43. Ⓐ Ⓑ Ⓒ Ⓓ
14. Ⓐ Ⓑ Ⓒ Ⓓ   44. Ⓐ Ⓑ Ⓒ Ⓓ
15. Ⓐ Ⓑ Ⓒ Ⓓ   45. Ⓐ Ⓑ Ⓒ Ⓓ
16. Ⓐ Ⓑ Ⓒ Ⓓ   46. Ⓐ Ⓑ Ⓒ Ⓓ
17. Ⓐ Ⓑ Ⓒ Ⓓ   47. Ⓐ Ⓑ Ⓒ Ⓓ
18. Ⓐ Ⓑ Ⓒ Ⓓ   48. Ⓐ Ⓑ Ⓒ Ⓓ
19. Ⓐ Ⓑ Ⓒ Ⓓ   49. Ⓐ Ⓑ Ⓒ Ⓓ
20. Ⓐ Ⓑ Ⓒ Ⓓ   50. Ⓐ Ⓑ Ⓒ Ⓓ
21. Ⓐ Ⓑ Ⓒ Ⓓ   51. Ⓐ Ⓑ Ⓒ Ⓓ
22. Ⓐ Ⓑ Ⓒ Ⓓ   52. Ⓐ Ⓑ Ⓒ Ⓓ
23. Ⓐ Ⓑ Ⓒ Ⓓ   53. Ⓐ Ⓑ Ⓒ Ⓓ
24. Ⓐ Ⓑ Ⓒ Ⓓ   54. Ⓐ Ⓑ Ⓒ Ⓓ
25. Ⓐ Ⓑ Ⓒ Ⓓ   55. Ⓐ Ⓑ Ⓒ Ⓓ
26. Ⓐ Ⓑ Ⓒ Ⓓ   56. Ⓐ Ⓑ Ⓒ Ⓓ
27. Ⓐ Ⓑ Ⓒ Ⓓ   57. Ⓐ Ⓑ Ⓒ Ⓓ
28. Ⓐ Ⓑ Ⓒ Ⓓ   58. Ⓐ Ⓑ Ⓒ Ⓓ
29. Ⓐ Ⓑ Ⓒ Ⓓ   59. Ⓐ Ⓑ Ⓒ Ⓓ
30. Ⓐ Ⓑ Ⓒ Ⓓ   60. Ⓐ Ⓑ Ⓒ Ⓓ

9. November 1995 CPA Examination

This chapter includes the second of two practice examinations that you were to take. This examination is the actual AICPA examination given in November 1995.*

By this time, you should have taken the Preliminary Readiness Tests in Chapter 7 and the May 1995 CPA Examination in Chapter 8, and you should have seen steady improvement. If not, you should spend more time reviewing those topical areas in which you have performed poorly. In order to do this, analyze your weak areas in Chapter 6—Chart Your Progress and Plan Your Course of Action. Then review using one of the recommended methods described in Chapter 3.

Be sure to take each of the four sections of this examination just as you would the actual test. *Allow no more time than each examination section indicates. Take each section in one sitting, and do no more than two sections in a day.* You will then become accustomed to concentrating for the duration of a test period and to working efficiently during this time.

Before beginning this practice examination, be sure to review the test tactics outlined in Chapter 5—How to Approach CPA Examination Questions. After completing this examination, turn to Chapter 6—Chart Your Progress and Plan Your Course of Action for guidance in analyzing your score and in planning your review program.

Remember: Read directions carefully!

---

*Note: All answer explanations are the author's.

UNIFORM CERTIFIED PUBLIC ACCOUNTANT EXAMINATION
Business Law & Professional Responsibilities

The point values for each question, and estimated time allotments based primarily on point value, are as follows:

	Point Value	Estimated Minutes Minimum	Estimated Minutes Maximum
No. 1	60	90	100
No. 2	10	10	15
No. 3	10	10	15
No. 4	10	15	25
No. 5	10	15	25
Totals	100	140	180

CANDIDATE NUMBER

Record your 7-digit candidate number in the boxes.

Print your **STATE** name here.

LPR

November 1, 1995; 9:00 A.M. to 12:00 NOON

INSTRUCTIONS TO CANDIDATES *Failure to follow these instructions may have an adverse effect on your Examination grade.*

1. Do not break the seal around *Examination Questions* (pages 3 through 18) until you are told to do so.

2. Question Numbers 1, 2, and 3 should be answered on the *Objective Answer Sheet*, which is pages 27 and 28. You should attempt to answer all objective items. There is no penalty for incorrect responses. Since the objective items are computer-graded, your comments and calculations associated with them are not considered. Be certain that you have entered your answers on the *Objective Answer Sheet* before the examination time is up. The objective portion of your examination will not be graded if you fail to record your answers on the *Objective Answer Sheet*. You will not be given additional time to record your answers.

3. Question Numbers 4 and 5 should be answered beginning on page 19. If you have not completed answering a question on a page, fill in the appropriate spaces in the wording on the bottom of the page "**QUESTION NUMBER ____ CONTINUES ON PAGE ____.**" If you have completed answering a question, fill in the appropriate space in the wording on the bottom of the page "**QUESTION NUMBER ____ ENDS ON THIS PAGE.**" Always begin the start of an answer to a question on the top of a new page (which may be the reverse side of a sheet of paper).

4. Although the primary purpose of the examination is to test your knowledge and application of the subject matter, selected essay responses will be graded for writing skills.

5. You are required to turn in by the end of each session:

   a. Attendance Record Form, page 1;
   b. *Examination Questions*, pages 3 through 18;
   c. *Essay Ruled Paper*, pages 19 through 26;
   d. *Objective Answer Sheet*, pages 27 and 28; and
   e. All unused examination materials.

   Your examination will not be graded unless the above listed items are handed in before leaving the examination room.

6. Unless otherwise instructed, if you want your *Examination Questions* mailed to you, write your name and address in both places indicated on page 18 and place 55 cents postage in the space provided. *Examination Questions* will be distributed no sooner than the day following the administration of this examination.

Examination Questions Booklet No.

303

Test Cover 2

2 72272 Q

BUSINESS LAW & PROFESSIONAL RESPONSIBILITIES (LPR)

Number 1

Instructions

Select the **best** answer for each of the following items. Use a No. 2 pencil to blacken the appropriate ovals on the Objective Answer Sheet to indicate your answers. **Mark only one answer for each item. Answer all items.** Your grade will be based on the total number of correct answers.

1. According to the ethical standards of the profession, which of the following acts is generally prohibited?
   A. Purchasing a product from a third party and reselling it to a client.
   B. Writing a financial management newsletter promoted and sold by a publishing company.
   C. Accepting a commission for recommending a product to an audit client.
   D. Accepting engagements obtained through the efforts of third parties.

2. According to the ethical standards of the profession, which of the following acts is generally prohibited?
   A. Issuing a modified report explaining a failure to follow a governmental regulatory agency's standards when conducting an attest service for a client.
   B. Revealing confidential client information during a quality review of a professional practice by a team from the state CPA society.
   C. Accepting a contingent fee for representing a client in an examination of the client's federal tax return by an IRS agent.
   D. Retaining client records after an engagement is terminated prior to completion and the client has demanded their return.

3. According to the standards of the profession, which of the following activities may be required in exercising due professional care?

	Consulting with experts	Obtaining specialty accreditation
A.	Yes	Yes
B.	Yes	No
C.	No	Yes
D.	No	No

4. According to the standards of the profession, which of the following activities would most likely **not** impair a CPA's independence?
   A. Providing extensive advisory services for a client.
   B. Contracting with a client to supervise the client's office personnel.
   C. Signing a client's checks in emergency situations.
   D. Accepting a luxurious gift from a client.

5. Under the Statements on Standards for Consulting Services, which of the following statements best reflects a CPA's responsibility when undertaking a consulting services engagement? The CPA must
   A. Not seek to modify any agreement made with the client.
   B. Not perform any attest services for the client.
   C. Inform the client of significant reservations concerning the benefits of the engagement.
   D. Obtain a written understanding with the client concerning the time for completion of the engagement.

6. This question is obsolete.

7. This question is obsolete.

8. Under the "Ultramares" rule, to which of the following parties will an accountant be liable for negligence?

	Parties in privity	Foreseen parties
A.	Yes	Yes
B.	Yes	No
C.	No	Yes
D.	No	No

9. When performing an audit, a CPA will most likely be considered negligent when the CPA fails to
   A. Detect all of a client's fraudulent activities.
   B. Include a negligence disclaimer in the client engagement letter.
   C. Warn a client of known internal control weaknesses.
   D. Warn a client's customers of embezzlement by the client's employees.

10. Which of the following is the best defense a CPA firm can assert in a suit for common law fraud based on its unqualified opinion on materially false financial statements?
  A. Contributory negligence on the part of the client.
  B. A disclaimer contained in the engagement letter.
  C. Lack of privity.
  D. Lack of scienter.

11. Under the anti-fraud provisions of Section 10(b) of the Securities Exchange Act of 1934, a CPA may be liable if the CPA acted
  A. Negligently.
  B. With independence.
  C. Without due diligence.
  D. Without good faith.

12. Under Section 11 of the Securities Act of 1933, which of the following standards may a CPA use as a defense?

	Generally accepted accounting principles	Generally accepted fraud detection standards
A.	Yes	Yes
B.	Yes	No
C.	No	Yes
D.	No	No

13. Ocean and Associates, CPAs, audited the financial statements of Drain Corporation. As a result of Ocean's negligence in conducting the audit, the financial statements included material misstatements. Ocean was unaware of this fact. The financial statements and Ocean's unqualified opinion were included in a registration statement and prospectus for an original public offering of stock by Drain. Sharp purchased shares in the offering. Sharp received a copy of the prospectus prior to the purchase but did not read it. The shares declined in value as a result of the misstatements in Drain's financial statements becoming known. Under which of the following Acts is Sharp most likely to prevail in a lawsuit against Ocean?

	Securities Exchange Act of 1934, Section 10(b), Rule 10b-5	Securities Act of 1933, Section 11
A.	Yes	Yes
B.	Yes	No
C.	No	Yes
D.	No	No

14. Which of the following statements is correct regarding a CPA's working papers? The working papers must be
  A. Transferred to another accountant purchasing the CPA's practice even if the client hasn't given permission.
  B. Transferred permanently to the client if demanded.
  C. Turned over to any government agency that requests them.
  D. Turned over pursuant to a valid federal court subpoena.

15. Thorp, CPA, was engaged to audit Ivor Co.'s financial statements. During the audit, Thorp discovered that Ivor's inventory contained stolen goods. Ivor was indicted and Thorp was subpoenaed to testify at the criminal trial. Ivor claimed accountant-client privilege to prevent Thorp from testifying. Which of the following statements is correct regarding Ivor's claim?
  A. Ivor can claim an accountant-client privilege only in states that have enacted a statute creating such a privilege.
  B. Ivor can claim an accountant-client privilege only in federal courts.
  C. The accountant-client privilege can be claimed only in civil suits.
  D. The accountant-client privilege can be claimed only to limit testimony to audit subject matter.

16. Generally, under the Uniform Partnership Act, a partnership has which of the following characteristics?

	Unlimited duration	Obligation for payment of federal income tax
A.	Yes	Yes
B.	Yes	No
C.	No	Yes
D.	No	No

17. Which of the following statements is(are) usually correct regarding general partners' liability?
  I. All general partners are jointly and severally liable for partnership torts.
  II. All general partners are liable only for those partnership obligations they actually authorized.

  A. I only.
  B. II only.
  C. Both I and II.
  D. Neither I nor II.

18. Which of the following statements is correct regarding the division of profits in a general partnership when the written partnership agreement only provides that losses be divided equally among the partners? Profits are to be divided

A. Based on the partners' ratio of contribution to the partnership.
B. Based on the partners' participation in day to day management.
C. Equally among the partners.
D. Proportionately among the partners.

19. Which of the following statements best describes the effect of the assignment of an interest in a general partnership?

A. The assignee becomes a partner.
B. The assignee is responsible for a proportionate share of past and future partnership debts.
C. The assignment automatically dissolves the partnership.
D. The assignment transfers the assignor's interest in partnership profits and surplus.

20. Park and Graham entered into a written partnership agreement to operate a retail store. Their agreement was silent as to the duration of the partnership. Park wishes to dissolve the partnership. Which of the following statements is correct?

A. Park may dissolve the partnership at any time.
B. Unless Graham consents to a dissolution, Park must apply to a court and obtain a decree ordering the dissolution.
C. Park may **not** dissolve the partnership unless Graham consents.
D. Park may dissolve the partnership only after notice of the proposed dissolution is given to all partnership creditors.

21. Which of the following facts is(are) generally included in a corporation's articles of incorporation?

	Name of registered agent	Number of authorized shares
A.	Yes	Yes
B.	Yes	No
C.	No	Yes
D.	No	No

22. Which of the following statements best describes an advantage of the corporate form of doing business?

A. Day to day management is strictly the responsibility of the directors.
B. Ownership is contractually restricted and is **not** transferable.
C. The operation of the business may continue indefinitely.
D. The business is free from state regulation.

23. To which of the following rights is a stockholder of a public corporation entitled?

A. The right to have annual dividends declared and paid.
B. The right to vote for the election of officers.
C. The right to a reasonable inspection of corporate records.
D. The right to have the corporation issue a new class of stock.

24. Carr Corp. declared a 7% stock dividend on its common stock. The dividend

A. Must be registered with the SEC pursuant to the Securities Act of 1933.
B. Is includable in the gross income of the recipient taxpayers in the year of receipt.
C. Has **no** effect on Carr's earnings and profits for federal income tax purposes.
D. Requires a vote of Carr's stockholders.

25. Which of the following statements is a general requirement for the merger of two corporations?

A. The merger plan must be approved unanimously by the stockholders of both corporations.
B. The merger plan must be approved unanimously by the boards of both corporations.
C. The absorbed corporation must amend its articles of incorporation.
D. The stockholders of both corporations must be given due notice of a special meeting, including a copy or summary of the merger plan.

26. Which of the following statements is(are) correct regarding debtors' rights?

 I. State exemption statutes prevent all of a debtor's personal property from being sold to pay a federal tax lien.
 II. Federal social security benefits received by a debtor are exempt from garnishment by creditors.

 A. I only.
 B. II only.
 C. Both I and II.
 D. Neither I nor II.

27. Which of the following liens generally require(s) the lienholder to give notice of legal action before selling the debtor's property to satisfy the debt?

	Mechanic's lien	Artisan's lien
A.	Yes	Yes
B.	Yes	No
C.	No	Yes
D.	No	No

28. Which of the following rights does one co-surety generally have against another co-surety?
 A. Exoneration.
 B. Subrogation.
 C. Reimbursement.
 D. Contribution.

29. Which of the following acts always will result in the total release of a compensated surety?
 A. The creditor changes the manner of the principal debtor's payment.
 B. The creditor extends the principal debtor's time to pay.
 C. The principal debtor's obligation is partially released.
 D. The principal debtor's performance is tendered.

30. When a principal debtor defaults and a surety pays the creditor the entire obligation, which of the following remedies gives the surety the best method of collecting from the debtor?
 A. Exoneration.
 B. Contribution.
 C. Subrogation.
 D. Attachment.

31. Under the Federal Insurance Contributions Act (FICA), which of the following acts will cause an employer to be liable for penalties?

	Failure to supply taxpayer identification numbers	Failure to make timely FICA deposits
A.	Yes	Yes
B.	Yes	No
C.	No	Yes
D.	No	No

32. Taxes payable under the Federal Unemployment Tax Act (FUTA) are
 A. Calculated as a fixed percentage of all compensation paid to an employee.
 B. Deductible by the employer as a business expense for federal income tax purposes.
 C. Payable by employers for all employees.
 D. Withheld from the wages of all covered employees.

33. Which of the following claims is(are) generally covered under workers' compensation statutes?

	Occupational disease	Employment aggravated preexisting disease
A.	Yes	Yes
B.	Yes	No
C.	No	Yes
D.	No	No

34. Generally, which of the following statements concerning workers' compensation laws is correct?
 A. The amount of damages recoverable is based on comparative negligence.
 B. Employers are strictly liable without regard to whether or **not** they are at fault.
 C. Workers' compensation benefits are **not** available if the employee is negligent.
 D. Workers' compensation awards are payable for life.

35. Under the Age Discrimination in Employment Act, which of the following remedies is(are) available to a covered employee?

	Early retirement	Back pay
A.	Yes	Yes
B.	Yes	No
C.	No	Yes
D.	No	No

36. Which of the following Acts prohibit(s) an employer from discriminating among employees based on sex?

	Equal Pay Act	Title VII of the Civil Rights Act
A.	Yes	Yes
B.	Yes	No
C.	No	Yes
D.	No	No

37. Under the Fair Labor Standards Act, which of the following pay bases may be used to pay covered, nonexempt employees who earn, on average, the minimum hourly wage?

	Hourly	Weekly	Monthly
A.	Yes	Yes	Yes
B.	Yes	Yes	No
C.	Yes	No	Yes
D.	No	Yes	Yes

38. Under the Fair Labor Standards Act, if a covered, nonexempt employee works consecutive weeks of 45, 42, 38, and 33 hours, how many hours of overtime must be paid to the employee?
    A. 0
    B. 7
    C. 18
    D. 20

39. Under the Employee Retirement Income Security Act of 1974 (ERISA), which of the following areas of private employer pension plans is(are) regulated?

	Employee vesting	Plan funding
A.	Yes	Yes
B.	Yes	No
C.	No	Yes
D.	No	No

40. Which of the following employee benefits is(are) exempt from the provisions of the National Labor Relations Act?

	Sick pay	Vacation pay
A.	Yes	Yes
B.	Yes	No
C.	No	Yes
D.	No	No

41. Under the Sales Article of the UCC, a firm offer will be created only if the
    A. Offer states the time period during which it will remain open.
    B. Offer is made by a merchant in a signed writing.
    C. Offeree gives some form of consideration.
    D. Offeree is a merchant.

42. Under the Sales Article of the UCC, when a written offer has been made without specifying a means of acceptance but providing that the offer will only remain open for ten days, which of the following statements represent(s) a valid acceptance of the offer?

    I. An acceptance sent by regular mail the day before the ten-day period expires that reaches the offeror on the eleventh day.
    II. An acceptance faxed the day before the ten-day period expires that reaches the offeror on the eleventh day, due to a malfunction of the offeror's printer.

    A. I only.
    B. II only.
    C. Both I and II.
    D. Neither I nor II.

43. Under the Sales Article of the UCC, the warranty of title
    A. Provides that the seller cannot disclaim the warranty if the sale is made to a bona fide purchaser for value.
    B. Provides that the seller deliver the goods free from any lien of which the buyer lacked knowledge when the contract was made.
    C. Applies only if it is in writing and signed by the seller.
    D. Applies only if the seller is a merchant.

44. To establish a cause of action based on strict liability in tort for personal injuries that result from the use of a defective product, one of the elements the injured party must prove is that the seller
    A. Was aware of the defect in the product.
    B. Sold the product to the injured party.
    C. Failed to exercise due care.
    D. Sold the product in a defective condition.

45. Under the Sales Article of the UCC, which of the following factors is most important in determining who bears the risk of loss in a sale of goods contract?
    A. The method of shipping the goods.
    B. The contract's shipping terms.
    C. Title to the goods.
    D. How the goods were lost.

46. Under the Sales Article of the UCC, in an F.O.B. place of shipment contract, the risk of loss passes to the buyer when the goods
    A. Are identified to the contract.
    B. Are placed on the seller's loading dock.
    C. Are delivered to the carrier.
    D. Reach the buyer's loading dock.

47. Under the Sales Article of the UCC, which of the following rights is(are) available to the buyer when a seller commits an anticipatory breach of contract?

	Demand assurance of performance	Cancel the contract	Collect punitive damages
A.	Yes	Yes	Yes
B.	Yes	Yes	No
C.	Yes	No	Yes
D.	No	Yes	Yes

48. Under the Sales Article of the UCC, and unless otherwise agreed to, the seller's obligation to the buyer is to
    A. Deliver the goods to the buyer's place of business.
    B. Hold conforming goods and give the buyer whatever notification is reasonably necessary to enable the buyer to take delivery.
    C. Deliver all goods called for in the contract to a common carrier.
    D. Set aside conforming goods for inspection by the buyer before delivery.

49. Under the Sales Article of the UCC, which of the following statements regarding liquidated damages is(are) correct?
    I. The injured party may collect any amount of liquidated damages provided for in the contract.
    II. The seller may retain a deposit of up to $500 when a buyer defaults even if there is no liquidated damages provision in the contract.

    A. I only.
    B. II only.
    C. Both I and II.
    D. Neither I nor II.

50. Under the Sales Article of the UCC, which of the following rights is available to a seller when a buyer materially breaches a sales contract?

	Right to cancel the contract	Right to recover damages
A.	Yes	Yes
B.	Yes	No
C.	No	Yes
D.	No	No

51. Long, Fall, and Pear own a building as joint tenants with the right of survivorship. Long gave Long's interest in the building to Green by executing and delivering a deed to Green. Neither Fall nor Pear consented to this transfer. Fall and Pear subsequently died. After their deaths, Green's interest in the building would consist of
    A. A ⅓ interest as a joint tenant.
    B. A ⅓ interest as a tenant in common.
    C. No interest because Fall and Pear did **not** consent to the transfer.
    D. Total ownership due to the deaths of Fall and Pear.

52. A method of transferring ownership of real property that most likely would be considered an arm's-length transaction is transfer by
    A. Inheritance.
    B. Eminent domain.
    C. Adverse possession.
    D. Sale.

53. Which of the following provisions must be included to have an enforceable written residential lease?

	A description of the leased premises	A due date for the payment of rent
A.	Yes	Yes
B.	Yes	No
C.	No	Yes
D.	No	No

54. Which of the following elements must be contained in a valid deed?

	Purchase price	Description of the land
A.	Yes	Yes
B.	Yes	No
C.	No	Yes
D.	No	No

55. Rich purchased property from Sklar for $200,000. Rich obtained a $150,000 loan from Marsh Bank to finance the purchase, executing a promissory note and a mortgage. By recording the mortgage, Marsh protects its

   A. Rights against Rich under the promissory note.
   B. Rights against the claims of subsequent bona fide purchasers for value.
   C. Priority against a previously filed real estate tax lien on the property.
   D. Priority against all parties having earlier claims to the property.

56. Which of the following facts help determine whether an item of personal property is a fixture?

   I. Degree of the item's attachment to the property.
   II. Intent of the person who had the item installed.

   A. I only.
   B. II only.
   C. Both I and II.
   D. Neither I nor II.

57. Which of the following activities is(are) regulated under the Federal Water Pollution Control Act (Clean Water Act)?

	Discharge of heated water by nuclear power plants	Dredging of wetlands
A.	Yes	Yes
B.	Yes	No
C.	No	Yes
D.	No	No

58. Which of the following methods of obtaining personal property will give the recipient ownership of the property?

	Lease	Finding abandoned property
A.	Yes	Yes
B.	Yes	No
C.	No	Yes
D.	No	No

59. A common carrier bailee generally would avoid liability for loss of goods entrusted to its care if the goods are

   A. Stolen by an unknown person.
   B. Negligently destroyed by an employee.
   C. Destroyed by the derailment of the train carrying them due to railroad employee negligence.
   D. Improperly packed by the party shipping them.

60. Which of the following statements correctly describes the requirements of insurable interest relating to property insurance? An insurable interest

   A. Must exist when any loss occurs.
   B. Must exist when the policy is issued and when any loss occurs.
   C. Is created only when the property is owned in fee simple.
   D. Is created only when the property is owned by an individual.

Number 2

Number 2 consists of two unrelated parts.

Instructions—Number 2a

Question Number 2a consists of five items. Select the **best** answer for each item. Use a No. 2 pencil to blacken the appropriate ovals on the Objective Answer Sheet to indicate your answers. **Answer all items.** Your grade will be based on the total number of correct answers.

a. Items 61 through 65 are based on the following:

Lace Computer Sales Corp. orally contracted with Banks, an independent consultant, for Banks to work part-time as Lace's agent to perform Lace's customers' service calls. Banks, a computer programmer and software designer, was authorized to customize Lace's software to the customers' needs, on a commission basis, but was specifically told not to sell Lace's computers.

On September 15, Banks made a service call on Clear Co. to repair Clear's computer. Banks had previously called on Clear, customized Lace's software for Clear, and collected cash payments for the work performed. During the call, Banks convinced Clear to buy an upgraded Lace computer for a price much lower than Lace would normally charge. Clear had previously purchased computers from other Lace agents and had made substantial cash down payments to the agents. Clear had no knowledge that the price was lower than normal. Banks received a $1,000 cash down payment and promised to deliver the computer the next week. Banks never turned in the down payment and left town. When Clear called the following week to have the computer delivered, Lace refused to honor Clear's order.

Required:

Items 61 through 65 relate to the relationships between the parties. For each item, select from List I whether only statement I is correct, whether only statement II is correct, or whether both statements I and II are correct, or whether neither statement I nor II is correct. Blacken the corresponding oval on the Objective Answer Sheet.

List I
(A) I only.
(B) II only.
(C) Both I and II.
(D) Neither I nor II.

61. I. Lace's agreement with Banks had to be in writing for it to be a valid agency agreement.
II. Lace's agreement with Banks empowered Banks to act as Lace's agent.

62. I. Clear was entitled to rely on Banks' implied authority to customize Lace's software.
II. Clear was entitled to rely on Banks' express authority when buying the computer.

63. I. Lace's agreement with Banks was automatically terminated by Banks' sale of the computer.
II. Lace must notify Clear before Banks' apparent authority to bind Lace will cease.

64. I. Lace is **not** bound by the agreement made by Banks with Clear.
II. Lace may unilaterally amend the agreement made by Banks to prevent a loss on the sale of the computer to Clear.

65. I. Lace, as a disclosed principal, is solely contractually liable to Clear.
II. Both Lace and Banks are contractually liable to Clear.

Instructions—Number 2b

Question Number 2b consists of five items. Select the **best** answer for each item. Use a No. 2 pencil to blacken the appropriate ovals on the Objective Answer Sheet to indicate your answers. **Answer all items.** Your grade will be based on the total number of correct answers.

b. Items 66 through 70 are based on the following:

Under the provisions of Glenn's testamentary trust, after payment of all administrative expenses and taxes, the entire residuary estate was to be paid to Strong and Lake as trustees. The trustees were authorized to invest the trust assets, and directed to distribute income annually to Glenn's children for their lives, then distribute the principal to Glenn's grandchildren, per capita. The trustees were also authorized to make such principal payments to the income beneficiaries that the trustees determined to be reasonable for the beneficiaries' welfare. Glenn died in 1992. On Glenn's death there were two surviving children, aged 21 and 30, and one two-year-old grandchild.

On June 15, 1995, the trustees made the following distributions from the trust:

- Paid the 1992, 1993, and 1994 trust income to Glenn's children. This amount included the proceeds from the sale of stock received by the trust as a stock dividend.
- Made a $10,000 principal payment for medical school tuition to one of Glenn's children.
- Made a $5,000 principal payment to Glenn's grandchild.

Required:

Items 66 through 70 relate to the above fact pattern. For each item, select from List II whether only statement I is correct, whether only statement II is correct, whether both statements I and II are correct, or whether neither statement I nor II is correct. Blacken the corresponding oval on the Objective Answer Sheet.

List II
(A) I only.
(B) II only.
(C) Both I and II.
(D) Neither I nor II.

66.   I. Glenn's trust was valid because it did **not** violate the rule against perpetuities.
      II. Glenn's trust was valid even through it permitted the trustees to make principal payments to income beneficiaries.

67.   I. Glenn's trust would be terminated if both of Glenn's children were to die.
      II. Glenn's trust would be terminated because of the acts of the trustees.

68.   I. Strong and Lake violated their fiduciary duties by making any distributions of principal.
      II. Strong and Lake violated their fiduciary duties by failing to distribute the trust income annually.

69.   I. Generally, stock dividends are considered income and should be distributed.
      II. Generally, stock dividends should be allocated to principal and remain as part of the trust.

70.   I. The $10,000 principal payment was an abuse of the trustees' authority.
      II. The $5,000 principal payment was valid because of its payment to a non-income beneficiary.

Number 3

Number 3 consists of two unrelated parts.

Instructions—Number 3a

Question Number 3a consists of five items. Select the **best** answer for each item. Use a No. 2 pencil to blacken the appropriate ovals on the Objective Answer Sheet to indicate your answers. **Answer all items.** Your grade will be based on the total number of correct answers.

a. Items 71 through 75 are based on the following:

On June 1, 1995, Rusk Corp. was petitioned involuntarily into bankruptcy. At the time of the filing, Rusk had the following creditors:

- Safe Bank, for the balance due on the secured note and mortgage on Rusk's warehouse.
- Employee salary claims.
- 1994 federal income taxes due.
- Accountant's fees outstanding.
- Utility bills outstanding.

Prior to the bankruptcy filing, but while insolvent, Rusk engaged in the following transactions:

- On February 1, 1995, Rusk repaid all corporate directors' loans made to the corporation.
- On May 1, 1995, Rusk purchased raw materials for use in its manufacturing business and paid cash to the supplier.

Required:

Items 71 through 75 relate to Rusk's creditors and the February 1 and May 1 transactions. For each item, select from List I whether only statement I is correct, whether only statement II is correct, whether both statements I and II are correct, or whether neither statement I nor II is correct. Blacken the corresponding oval on the Objective Answer Sheet.

List I
(A) I only.
(B) II only.
(C) Both I and II.
(D) Neither I nor II.

71.   I. Safe Bank's claim will be the first paid of the listed claims because Safe is a secured creditor.
    II. Safe Bank will receive the entire amount of the balance of the mortgage due as a secured creditor regardless of the amount received from the sale of the warehouse.

72.   I. The employee salary claims will be paid in full after the payment of any secured party.
    II. The employee salary claims up to $4,000 per claimant will be paid before payment of any general creditors' claims.

73.   I. The claim for 1994 federal income taxes due will be paid as a secured creditor claim.
    II. The claim for 1994 federal income taxes due will be paid prior to the general creditor claims.

74.   I. The February 1 repayments of the directors' loans were preferential transfers even through the payments were made more than 90 days before the filing of the petition.
    II. The February 1 repayments of the directors' loans were preferential transfers because the payments were made to insiders.

75.   I. The May 1 purchase and payment was **not** a preferential transfer because it was a transaction in the ordinary course of business.
    II. The May 1 purchase and payment was a preferential transfer because it occurred within 90 days of the filing of the petition.

Instructions—Number 3b

Question Number 3b consists of five items. Select the **best** answer for each item. Use a No. 2 pencil to blacken the appropriate ovals on the Objective Answer Sheet to indicate your answers. **Answer all items.** Your grade will be based on the total number of correct answers.

b. Items 76 through 80 are based on the following:

Coffee Corp., a publicly held corporation, wants to make an $8,000,000 exempt offering of its shares as a private placement offering under Regulation D, Rule 506, of the Securities Act of 1933. Coffee has more than 500 shareholders and assets in excess of $1 billion, and has its shares listed on a national securities exchange.

Required:

Items 76 through 80 relate to the application of the provisions of the Securities Act of 1933 and the Securities Exchange Act of 1934 to Coffee Corp. and the offering. For each item, select from List II whether only statement I is correct, whether only statement II is correct, whether both statements I and II are correct, or whether neither statement I nor II is correct. Blacken the corresponding oval on the Objective Answer Sheet.

List II
(A) I only.
(B) II only.
(C) Both I and II.
(D) Neither I nor II.

76.   I. Coffee Corp. may make the Regulation D, Rule 506, exempt offering.
    II. Coffee Corp., because it is required to report under the Securities Exchange Act of 1934, may **not** make an exempt offering.

77.   I. Shares sold under a Regulation D, Rule 506, exempt offering may only be purchased by accredited investors.
    II. Shares sold under a Regulation D, Rule 506, exempt offering may be purchased by any number of investors provided there are **no** more than 35 non-accredited investors.

78. I. An exempt offering under Regulation D, Rule 506, must **not** be for more than $10,000,000.
II. An exempt offering under Regulation D, Rule 506, has **no** dollar limit.

79. I. Regulation D, Rule 506, requires that all investors in the exempt offering be notified that for nine months after the last sale **no** resale may be made to a nonresident.
II. Regulation D, Rule 506, requires that the issuer exercise reasonable care to assure that purchasers of the exempt offering are buying for investment and are **not** underwriters.

80. I. The SEC must be notified by Coffee Corp. within five days of the first sale of the exempt offering securities.
II. Coffee Corp. must include an SEC notification of the first sale of the exempt offering securities in Coffee's next filed Quarterly Report (Form 10-Q).

Number 4

On July 5, 1995, Korn sent Wilson a written offer to clear Wilson's parking lot whenever it snowed through December 31, 1995. Korn's offer stated that Wilson had until October 1 to accept.

On September 28, 1995, Wilson mailed Korn an acceptance with a request that the agreement continue through March 1996. Wilson's acceptance was delayed and didn't reach Korn until October 3.

On September 29, 1995, Korn saw weather reports indicating the snowfall for the season would be much heavier than normal. This would substantially increase Korn's costs to perform under the offer.

On September 30, 1995, Korn phoned Wilson to insist that the terms of the agreement be changed. When Wilson refused, Korn orally withdrew the offer and stated that Korn would not perform.

Required:

a. State and explain the points of law that Korn would argue to show that there was **no** valid contract.
b. State and explain the points of law that Wilson would argue to show that there was a valid contract.
c. Assuming that a valid contract existed:

1. Determine whether Korn breached the contract and the nature of the breach, and

2. State the common law remedies available to Wilson.

Number 5

On October 30, 1995, Dover, CPA, was engaged to audit the financial records of Crane Corp., a tractor manufacturer. During the review of notes receivable, Dover reviewed a promissory note given to Crane by Jones Corp., one of its customers, in payment for a tractor. The note appears below.

(Face)

July 18, 1995

Sixty (60) days from date, the undersigned promises to

Pay to the order of _____Jones Corp._____
Twenty Thousand and 00/100 ($20,000) dollars
at West Bank

OVAL CORP.
___G. J. Small___
By: G. J. Small, Pres.

(Back)

Jones Corp.
Without Recourse
___R. Mall___
By: R. Mall, Pres.

Crane Corp.
For Collection

Payment Refused

On the note's due date, Crane deposited the note for collection and was advised by the bank that Oval had refused payment. After payment was refused, Crane contacted Oval. Oval told Crane that Jones fraudulently induced Oval into executing the note and that Jones knew about Oval's claim before Jones endorsed the note to Crane.

Dover also reviewed a security agreement signed by Harper, a customer, given to Crane to finance Harper's purchase of a tractor for use in Harper's farming business. On October 1, 1995, Harper made a down payment and gave Crane a purchase money security interest for the balance of the price of the tractor. Harper executed a financing statement that was filed on October 10, 1995. The tractor had been delivered to Harper on October 5, 1995. On October 8, 1995, Harper gave Acorn Trust a security agreement covering all of Harper's business equipment, including the tractor. Harper executed a financing statement that Acorn filed on October 9, 1995.

Required:

As the auditor on this engagement, write a memo to the partner-in-charge identifying, explaining, and stating your conclusions about the legal issues pertaining to the note and the security interest.

The memo should address the following:

- Whether Crane is a holder in due course
- Whether Oval will be required to pay the note
- Whether Jones is liable to pay the note
- When Crane's security interest was perfected and whether it had priority over Acorn's security interest.

UNIFORM CERTIFIED PUBLIC ACCOUNTANT EXAMINATION
Auditing

The point values for each question, and estimated time allotments based primarily on point value, are as follows:

	Point Value	Estimated Minutes Minimum	Estimated Minutes Maximum
No. 1	60	140	150
No. 2	10	15	25
No. 3	10	15	25
No. 4	10	25	35
No. 5	10	25	35
Totals	100	220	270

CANDIDATE NUMBER

Record your 7-digit candidate number in the boxes.

Print your **STATE** name here.

AUDIT

November 1, 1995; 1:30 P.M. to 6:00 P.M.

INSTRUCTIONS TO CANDIDATES *Failure to follow these instructions may have an adverse effect on your Examination grade.*

1. Do not break the seal around *Examination Questions* (pages 3 through 22) until you are told to do so.

2. Question Numbers 1, 2, and 3 should be answered on the *Objective Answer Sheet*, which is pages 31 and 32. You should attempt to answer all objective items. There is no penalty for incorrect responses. Since the objective items are computer-graded, your comments and calculations associated with them are not considered. Be certain that you have entered your answers on the *Objective Answer Sheet* before the examination time is up. The objective portion of your examination will not be graded if you fail to record your answers on the *Objective Answer Sheet*. You will not be given additional time to record your answers.

3. Question Numbers 4 and 5 should be answered beginning on page 23. If you have not completed answering a question on a page, fill in the appropriate spaces in the wording on the bottom of the page "**QUESTION NUMBER ___ CONTINUES ON PAGE ___.**" If you have completed answering a question, fill in the appropriate space in the wording on the bottom of the page "**QUESTION NUMBER ___ ENDS ON THIS PAGE.**" Always begin the start of an answer to a question on the top of a new page (which may be the reverse side of a sheet of paper).

4. Although the primary purpose of the examination is to test your knowledge and application of the subject matter, selected essay responses will be graded for writing skills.

5. You are required to turn in by the end of each session:

    a. Attendance Record Form, page 1;
    b. *Examination Questions*, pages 3 through 22;
    c. *Essay Ruled Paper*, pages 23 through 30;
    d. *Objective Answer Sheet*, pages 31 and 32; and
    e. All unused examination materials.

    Your examination will not be graded unless the above listed items are handed in before leaving the examination room.

6. Unless otherwise instructed, if you want your *Examination Questions* mailed to you, write your name and address in both places indicated on page 22 and place 55 cents postage in the space provided. *Examination Questions* will be distributed no sooner than the day following the administration of this examination.

Prepared by the Board of Examiners of the American Institute of Certified Public Accountants and adopted by the examining boards of all states, the District of Columbia, Guam, Puerto Rico, and the Virgin Islands of the United States.

Copyright © 1995 by the American Institute of Certified Public Accountants, Inc.

Examination Questions Booklet No.

1 70982 Q

Audit (AUDIT)

Number 1

Instructions

Select the **best** answer for each of the following items. Use a No. 2 pencil to blacken the appropriate ovals on the Objective Answer Sheet to indicate your answers. **Mark only one answer for each item. Answer all items.** Your grade will be based on the total number of correct answers.

1. In assessing the objectivity of internal auditors, an independent auditor should
   A. Evaluate the quality control program in effect for the internal auditors.
   B. Examine documentary evidence of the work performed by the internal auditors.
   C. Test a sample of the transactions and balances that the internal auditors examined.
   D. Determine the organizational level to which the internal auditors report.

2. In planning an audit, the auditor's knowledge about the design of relevant internal controls should be used to
   A. Identify the types of potential misstatements that could occur.
   B. Assess the operational efficiency of internal control.
   C. Determine whether controls have been circumvented by collusion.
   D. Document the assessed level of control risk.

3. Able Co. uses an online sales order processing system to process its sales transactions. Able's sales data are electronically sorted and subjected to edit checks. A direct output of the edit checks most likely would be a
   A. Report of all missing sales invoices.
   B. File of all rejected sales transactions.
   C. Printout of all user code numbers and passwords.
   D. List of all voided shipping documents.

4. Which of the following auditor concerns most likely could be so serious that the auditor concludes that a financial statement audit **cannot** be conducted?
   A. The entity has **no** formal written code of conduct.
   B. The integrity of the entity's management is suspect.
   C. Controls requiring segregation of duties are subject to management override.
   D. Management fails to modify prescribed controls for changes in conditions.

5. Management philosophy and operating style most likely would have a significant influence on an entity's control environment when
   A. The internal auditor reports directly to management.
   B. Management is dominated by one individual.
   C. Accurate management job descriptions delineate specific duties.
   D. The audit committee actively oversees the financial reporting process.

6. Which of the following is a management control method that most likely could improve management's ability to supervise company activities effectively?
   A. Monitoring compliance with internal control requirements imposed by regulatory bodies.
   B. Limiting direct access to assets by physical segregation and protective devices.
   C. Establishing budgets and forecasts to identify variances from expectations.
   D. Supporting employees with the resources necessary to discharge their responsibilities.

Items 7 and 8 are based on the following flowchart of a client's revenue cycle:

7. Symbol A most likely represents
   A. Remittance advice file.
   B. Receiving report file.
   C. Accounts receivable master file.
   D. Cash disbursements transaction file.

8. Symbol B most likely represents
   A. Customer orders.
   B. Receiving reports.
   C. Customer checks.
   D. Sales invoices.

9. In an audit of financial statements in accordance with generally accepted auditing standards, an auditor is required to
   A. Document the auditor's understanding of the entity's internal control.
   B. Search for significant deficiencies in the operation of internal control.
   C. Perform tests of controls to evaluate the effectiveness of the entity's accounting system.
   D. Determine whether controls are suitably designed to prevent or detect material misstatements.

10. Which of the following is an example of a validity check?

    A. The computer ensures that a numerical amount in a record does **not** exceed some predetermined amount.

    B. As the computer corrects errors and data are successfully resubmitted to the system, the causes of the errors are printed out.

    C. The computer flags any transmission for which the control field value did **not** match that of an existing file record.

    D. After data for a transaction are entered, the computer sends certain data back to the terminal for comparison with data originally sent.

11. Which of the following types of evidence would an auditor most likely examine to determine whether internal controls are operating as designed?

    A. Gross margin information regarding the client's industry.

    B. Confirmations of receivables verifying account balances.

    C. Client records documenting the use of EDP programs.

    D. Anticipated results documented in budgets or forecasts.

12. Which of the following internal controls most likely would reduce the risk of diversion of customer receipts by an entity's employees?

    A. A bank lockbox system.

    B. Prenumbered remittance advices.

    C. Monthly bank reconciliations.

    D. Daily deposit of cash receipts.

13. In obtaining an understanding of an entity's internal controls that are relevant to audit planning, an auditor is required to obtain knowledge about the

    A. Design of the controls for each component of internal control.

    B. Effectiveness of the controls that have been placed in operation.

    C. Consistency with which the controls are currently being applied.

    D. Controls related to each principal transaction class and account balance.

14. Which of the following controls most likely could prevent EDP personnel from modifying programs to bypass programmed controls?

    A. Periodic management review of computer utilization reports and systems documentation.

    B. Segregation of duties within EDP for computer programming and computer operations.

    C. Participation of user department personnel in designing and approving new systems.

    D. Physical security of EDP facilities in limiting access to EDP equipment.

15. Which of the following is a control that most likely could help prevent employee payroll fraud?

    A. The personnel department promptly sends employee termination notices to the payroll supervisor.

    B. Employees who distribute payroll checks forward unclaimed payroll checks to the absent employees' supervisors.

    C. Salary rates resulting from new hires are approved by the payroll supervisor.

    D. Total hours used for determination of gross pay are calculated by the payroll supervisor.

16. Which of the following controls would a company most likely use to safeguard marketable securities when an independent trust agent is **not** employed?

    A. The investment committee of the board of directors periodically reviews the investment decisions delegated to the treasurer.

    B. Two company officials have joint control of marketable securities, which are kept in a bank safe-deposit box.

    C. The internal auditor and the controller independently trace all purchases and sales of marketable securities from the subsidiary ledgers to the general ledger.

    D. The chairman of the board verifies the marketable securities, which are kept in a bank safe-deposit box, each year on the balance sheet date.

17. The diagram below depicts an auditor's estimated maximum deviation rate compared with the tolerable rate, and also depicts the true population deviation rate compared with the tolerable rate.

Auditor's estimate based on sample results	True state of population	
	Deviation rate is less than tolerable rate	Deviation rate exceeds tolerable rate
Maximum deviation rate is less than tolerable rate	I.	III.
Maximum deviation rate exceeds tolerable rate	II.	IV.

As a result of tests of controls, the auditor assesses control risk too low and thereby decreases substantive testing. This is illustrated by situation
- A. I.
- B. II.
- C. III.
- D. IV.

18. In assessing control risk, an auditor ordinarily selects from a variety of techniques, including
- A. Inquiry and analytical procedures.
- B. Reperformance and observation.
- C. Comparison and confirmation.
- D. Inspection and verification.

19. The risk of incorrect acceptance and the likelihood of assessing control risk too low relate to the
- A. Allowable risk of tolerable misstatement.
- B. Preliminary estimates of materiality levels.
- C. Efficiency of the audit.
- D. Effectiveness of the audit.

20. Which of the following statements is correct concerning an auditor's assessment of control risk?
- A. Assessing control risk may be performed concurrently during an audit with obtaining an understanding of the entity's internal control.
- B. Evidence about the operation of controls in prior audits may **not** be considered during the current year's assessment of control risk.
- C. The basis for an auditor's conclusions about the assessed level of control risk need **not** be documented unless control risk is assessed at the maximum level.
- D. The lower the assessed level of control risk, the less assurance the evidence must provide that the controls are operating effectively.

21. An auditor assesses control risk because it
- A. Is relevant to the auditor's understanding of control environment.
- B. Provides assurance that the auditor's materiality levels are appropriate.
- C. Indicates to the auditor where inherent risk may be the greatest.
- D. Affects the level of detection risk that the auditor may accept.

22. Assessing control risk at below the maximum level most likely would involve
- A. Performing more extensive substantive tests with larger sample sizes than originally planned.
- B. Reducing inherent risk for most of the assertions relevant to significant account balances.
- C. Changing the timing of substantive tests by omitting interim-date testing and performing the tests at year end.
- D. Identifying specific internal controls relevant to specific assertions.

23. After assessing control risk at below the maximum level, an auditor desires to seek a further reduction in the assessed level of control risk. At this time, the auditor would consider whether
    A. It would be efficient to obtain an understanding of the entity's control activities.
    B. The entity's internal controls have been placed in operation.
    C. The entity's internal controls pertain to any financial statement assertions.
    D. Additional evidential matter sufficient to support a further reduction is likely to be available.

24. When assessing control risk below the maximum level, an auditor is required to document the auditor's

	Understanding of the entity's control environment	Basis of concluding that control risk is below the maximum level
A.	Yes	No
B.	No	Yes
C.	Yes	Yes
D.	No	No

25. An auditor who uses statistical sampling for attributes in testing internal controls should reduce the planned reliance on a prescribed control when the
    A. Sample rate of deviation plus the allowance for sampling risk equals the tolerable rate.
    B. Sample rate of deviation is less than the expected rate of deviation used in planning the sample.
    C. Tolerable rate less the allowance for sampling risk exceeds the sample rate of deviation.
    D. Sample rate of deviation plus the allowance for sampling risk exceeds the tolerable rate.

26. In addition to evaluating the frequency of deviations in tests of controls, an auditor should also consider certain qualitative aspects of the deviations. The auditor most likely would give broader consideration to the implications of a deviation if it was
    A. The only deviation discovered in the sample.
    B. Identical to a deviation discovered during the prior year's audit.
    C. Caused by an employee's misunderstanding of instructions.
    D. Initially concealed by a forged document.

27. When there are numerous property and equipment transactions during the year, an auditor who plans to assess control risk at a low level usually performs
    A. Tests of controls and extensive tests of property and equipment balances at the end of the year.
    B. Analytical procedures for current year property and equipment transactions.
    C. Tests of controls and limited tests of current year property and equipment transactions.
    D. Analytical procedures for property and equipment balances at the end of the year.

28. An auditor suspects that a client's cashier is misappropriating cash receipts for personal use by lapping customer checks received in the mail. In attempting to uncover this embezzlement scheme, the auditor most likely would compare the
    A. Dates checks are deposited per bank statements with the dates remittance credits are recorded.
    B. Daily cash summaries with the sums of the cash receipts journal entries.
    C. Individual bank deposit slips with the details of the monthly bank statements.
    D. Dates uncollectible accounts are authorized to be written off with the dates the write-offs are actually recorded.

29. In testing controls over cash disbursements, an auditor most likely would determine that the person who signs checks also
   A. Reviews the monthly bank reconciliation.
   B. Returns the checks to accounts payable.
   C. Is denied access to the supporting documents.
   D. Is responsible for mailing the checks.

30. For effective internal control, the accounts payable department generally should
   A. Stamp, perforate, or otherwise cancel supporting documentation after payment is mailed.
   B. Ascertain that each requisition is approved as to price, quantity, and quality by an authorized employee.
   C. Obliterate the quantity ordered on the receiving department copy of the purchase order.
   D. Establish the agreement of the vendor's invoice with the receiving report and purchase order.

31. In determining the effectiveness of an entity's controls relating to the existence or occurrence assertion for payroll transactions, an auditor most likely would inquire about and
   A. Observe the segregation of duties concerning personnel responsibilities and payroll disbursements.
   B. Inspect evidence of accounting for prenumbered payroll checks.
   C. Recompute the payroll deductions for employee fringe benefits.
   D. Verify the preparation of the monthly payroll account bank reconciliation.

32. In obtaining an understanding of a manufacturing entity's internal control concerning inventory balances, an auditor most likely would
   A. Analyze the liquidity and turnover ratios of the inventory.
   B. Perform analytical procedures designed to identify cost variances.
   C. Review the entity's descriptions of inventory controls.
   D. Perform test counts of inventory during the entity's physical count.

33. Which of the following factors is(are) considered in determining the sample size for a test of controls?

	Expected deviation rate	Tolerable deviation rate
A.	Yes	Yes
B.	No	No
C.	No	Yes
D.	Yes	No

34. A weakness in internal control over recording retirements of equipment may cause an auditor to
   A. Inspect certain items of equipment in the plant and trace those items to the accounting records.
   B. Review the subsidiary ledger to ascertain whether depreciation was taken on each item of equipment during the year.
   C. Trace additions to the "other assets" account to search for equipment that is still on hand but **no** longer being used.
   D. Select certain items of equipment from the accounting records and locate them in the plant.

35. An auditor's letter issued on reportable conditions relating to an entity's internal control observed during a financial statement audit should
   A. Include a brief description of the tests of controls performed in searching for reportable conditions and material weaknesses.
   B. Indicate that the reportable conditions should be disclosed in the annual report to the entity's shareholders.
   C. Include a paragraph describing management's assertion concerning the effectiveness of the internal control.
   D. Indicate that the audit's purpose was to report on the financial statements and **not** to provide assurance on internal control.

36. Brown, CPA, has accepted an engagement to examine and report on Crow Company's written assertion about the effectiveness of Crow's internal control. In what form may Crow present its written assertions?

   I. In a separate report that will accompany Brown's report.
  II. In a representation letter to Brown.

    A. I only.
    B. II only.
    C. Either I or II.
    D. Neither I nor II.

37. Computer Services Company (CSC) processes payroll transactions for schools. Drake, CPA, is engaged to report on CSC's controls placed in operation as of a specific date. These controls are relevant to the schools' internal control, so Drake's report will be useful in providing the schools' independent auditors with information necessary to plan their audits. Drake's report expressing an opinion on CSC's controls placed in operation as of a specific date should contain a(an)
    A. Description of the scope and nature of Drake's procedures.
    B. Statement that CSC's management has disclosed to Drake all design deficiencies of which it is aware.
    C. Opinion on the operating effectiveness of CSC's controls.
    D. Paragraph indicating the basis for Drake's assessment of control risk.

38. An auditor may achieve audit objectives related to particular assertions by
    A. Performing analytical procedures.
    B. Adhering to a system of quality control.
    C. Preparing auditor working papers.
    D. Increasing the level of detection risk.

39. The confirmation of customers' accounts receivable rarely provides reliable evidence about the completeness assertion because
    A. Many customers merely sign and return the confirmation without verifying its details.
    B. Recipients usually respond only if they disagree with the information on the request.
    C. Customers may **not** be inclined to report understatement errors in their accounts.
    D. Auditors typically select many accounts with low recorded balances to be confirmed.

40. Which of the following sets of information does an auditor usually confirm on one form?
    A. Accounts payable and purchase commitments.
    B. Cash in bank and collateral for loans.
    C. Inventory on consignment and contingent liabilities.
    D. Accounts receivable and accrued interest receivable.

41. An auditor's analytical procedures most likely would be facilitated if the entity
    A. Segregates obsolete inventory before the physical inventory count.
    B. Uses a standard cost system that produces variance reports.
    C. Corrects material weaknesses in internal control before the beginning of the audit.
    D. Develops its data from sources solely within the entity.

42. This question is obsolete.

43. How would increases in tolerable misstatement and assessed level of control risk affect the sample size in a substantive test of details?

	Increase in tolerable misstatement	Increase in assessed level of control risk
A.	Increase sample size	Increase sample size
B.	Increase sample size	Decrease sample size
C.	Decrease sample size	Increase sample size
D.	Decrease sample size	Decrease sample size

44. An advantage of statistical sampling over nonstatistical sampling is that statistical sampling helps an auditor to
    A. Eliminate the risk of nonsampling errors.
    B. Reduce the level of audit risk and materiality to a relatively low amount.
    C. Measure the sufficiency of the evidential matter obtained.
    D. Minimize the failure to detect errors and fraud.

45. The usefulness of the standard bank confirmation request may be limited because the bank employee who completes the form may
    A. Not believe that the bank is obligated to verify confidential information to a third party.
    B. Sign and return the form without inspecting the accuracy of the client's bank reconciliation.
    C. Not have access to the client's cutoff bank statement.
    D. Be unaware of all the financial relationships that the bank has with the client.

46. An auditor most likely would limit substantive audit tests of sales transactions when control risk is assessed as low for the existence or occurrence assertion concerning sales transactions and the auditor has already gathered evidence supporting
    A. Opening and closing inventory balances.
    B. Cash receipts and accounts receivable.
    C. Shipping and receiving activities.
    D. Cutoffs of sales and purchases.

47. Which of the following procedures would an auditor most likely perform in searching for unrecorded liabilities?
    A. Trace a sample of accounts payable entries recorded just before year end to the unmatched receiving report file.
    B. Compare a sample of purchase orders issued just after year end with the year-end accounts payable trial balance.
    C. Vouch a sample of cash disbursements recorded just after year end to receiving reports and vendor invoices.
    D. Scan the cash disbursements entries recorded just before year end for indications of unusual transactions.

48. An auditor traced a sample of purchase orders and the related receiving reports to the purchases journal and the cash disbursements journal. The purpose of this substantive audit procedure most likely was to
    A. Identify unusually large purchases that should be investigated further.
    B. Verify that cash disbursements were for goods actually received.
    C. Determine that purchases were properly recorded.
    D. Test whether payments were for goods actually ordered.

49. Which of the following explanations most likely would satisfy an auditor who questions management about significant debits to the accumulated depreciation accounts?
    A. The estimated remaining useful lives of plant assets were revised upward.
    B. Plant assets were retired during the year.
    C. The prior year's depreciation expense was erroneously understated.
    D. Overhead allocations were revised at year end.

50. Which of the following circumstances most likely would cause an auditor to suspect an employee payroll fraud scheme?
    A. There are significant unexplained variances between standard and actual labor cost.
    B. Payroll checks are disbursed by the same employee each payday.
    C. Employee time cards are approved by individual departmental supervisors.
    D. A separate payroll bank account is maintained on an imprest basis.

51. The objective of tests of details of transactions performed as substantive tests is to
    A. Comply with generally accepted auditing standards.
    B. Attain assurance about the reliability of the accounting system.
    C. Detect material misstatements in the financial statements.
    D. Evaluate whether management's policies and procedures operated effectively.

52. A primary advantage of using generalized audit software packages to audit the financial statements of a client that uses an EDP system is that the auditor may
    A. Access information stored on computer files while having a limited understanding of the client's hardware and software features.
    B. Consider increasing the use of substantive tests of transactions in place of analytical procedures.
    C. Substantiate the accuracy of data through self-checking digits and hash totals.
    D. Reduce the level of required tests of controls to a relatively small amount.

53. The work of internal auditors may affect the independent auditor's

   I. Procedures performed in obtaining an understanding of internal control.
  II. Procedures performed in assessing the risk of material misstatement.
 III. Substantive procedures performed in gathering direct evidence.

    A. I and II only.
    B. I and III only.
    C. II and III only.
    D. I, II, and III.

54. Which of the following statements is correct concerning an auditor's use of the work of a specialist?

    A. The auditor need **not** obtain an understanding of the methods and assumptions used by the specialist.
    B. The auditor may **not** use the work of a specialist in matters material to the fair presentation of the financial statements.
    C. The reasonableness of the specialist's assumptions and their applications are strictly the auditor's responsibility.
    D. The work of a specialist who has a contractual relationship with the client may be acceptable under certain circumstances.

55. Which of the following is an audit procedure that an auditor most likely would perform concerning litigation, claims, and assessments?

    A. Request the client's lawyer to evaluate whether the client's pending litigation, claims, and assessments indicate a going concern problem.
    B. Examine the legal documents in the client's lawyer's possession concerning litigation, claims, and assessments to which the lawyer has devoted substantive attention.
    C. Discuss with management its policies and procedures adopted for evaluating and accounting for litigation, claims, and assessments.
    D. Confirm directly with the client's lawyer that all litigation, claims, and assessments have been recorded or disclosed in the financial statements.

56. Which of the following procedures would an auditor most likely perform to obtain evidence about the occurrence of subsequent events?

    A. Confirming a sample of material accounts receivable established after year end.
    B. Comparing the financial statements being reported on with those of the prior period.
    C. Investigating personnel changes in the accounting department occurring after year end.
    D. Inquiring as to whether any unusual adjustments were made after year end.

57. Which of the following matters would an auditor most likely include in a management representation letter?

    A. Communications with the audit committee concerning weaknesses in internal control.
    B. The completeness and availability of minutes of stockholders' and directors' meetings.
    C. Plans to acquire or merge with other entities in the subsequent year.
    D. Management's acknowledgment of its responsibility for the detection of employee fraud.

58. Which of the following auditing procedures most likely would assist an auditor in identifying related party transactions?

    A. Inspecting correspondence with lawyers for evidence of unreported contingent liabilities.
    B. Vouching accounting records for recurring transactions recorded just after the balance sheet date.
    C. Reviewing confirmations of loans receivable and payable for indications of guarantees.
    D. Performing analytical procedures for indications of possible financial difficulties.

59. Cooper, CPA, believes there is substantial doubt about the ability of Zero Corp. to continue as a going concern for a reasonable period of time. In evaluating Zero's plans for dealing with the adverse effects of future conditions and events, Cooper most likely would consider, as a mitigating factor, Zero's plans to
   A. Discuss with lenders the terms of all debt and loan agreements.
   B. Strengthen internal controls over cash disbursements.
   C. Purchase production facilities currently being leased from a related party.
   D. Postpone expenditures for research and development projects.

60. The permanent (continuing) file of an auditor's working papers most likely would include copies of the
   A. Lead schedules.
   B. Attorney's letters.
   C. Bank statements.
   D. Debt agreements.

61. Harris, CPA, has been asked to audit and report on the balance sheet of Fox Co. but not on the statements of income, retained earnings, or cash flows. Harris will have access to all information underlying the basic financial statements. Under these circumstances, Harris may
   A. Not accept the engagement because it would constitute a violation of the profession's ethical standards.
   B. Not accept the engagement because it would be tantamount to rendering a piecemeal opinion.
   C. Accept the engagement because such engagements merely involve limited reporting objectives.
   D. Accept the engagement but should disclaim an opinion because of an inability to apply the procedures considered necessary.

62. Which of the following statements is a basic element of the auditor's standard report?
   A. The disclosures provide reasonable assurance that the financial statements are free of material misstatement.
   B. The auditor evaluated the overall internal control.
   C. An audit includes assessing significant estimates made by management.
   D. The financial statements are consistent with those of the prior period.

63. An auditor may **not** issue a qualified opinion when
   A. An accounting principle at variance with GAAP is used.
   B. The auditor lacks independence with respect to the audited entity.
   C. A scope limitation prevents the auditor from completing an important audit procedure.
   D. The auditor's report refers to the work of a specialist.

64. This question is obsolete.

65. An auditor would express an unqualified opinion with an explanatory paragraph added to the auditor's report for

	An unjustified accounting change	A material weakness in internal control
A.	Yes	Yes
B.	Yes	No
C.	No	Yes
D.	No	No

66. Under which of the following circumstances would a disclaimer of opinion **not** be appropriate?
   A. The auditor is unable to determine the amounts associated with an employee fraud scheme.
   B. Management does **not** provide reasonable justification for a change in accounting principles.
   C. The client refuses to permit the auditor to confirm certain accounts receivable or apply alternative procedures to verify their balances.
   D. The chief executive officer is unwilling to sign the management representation letter.

67. Digit Co. uses the FIFO method of costing for its international subsidiary's inventory and LIFO for its domestic inventory. Under these circumstances, the auditor's report on Digit's financial statements should express an
   A. Unqualified opinion
   B. Opinion qualified because of a lack of consistency.
   C. Opinion qualified because of a departure from GAAP.
   D. Adverse opinion.

68. The fourth standard of reporting requires the auditor's report to contain either an expression of opinion regarding the financial statements taken as a whole or an assertion to the effect that an opinion cannot be expressed. The objective of the fourth standard is to prevent
   A. An auditor from expressing different opinions on each of the basic financial statements.
   B. Restrictions on the scope of the audit, whether imposed by the client or by the inability to obtain evidence.
   C. Misinterpretations regarding the degree of responsibility the auditor is assuming.
   D. An auditor from reporting on one basic financial statement and **not** the others.

69. In which of the following circumstances would an auditor **not** express an unqualified opinion?
   A. There has been a material change between periods in accounting principles?
   B. Quarterly financial data required by the SEC has been omitted.
   C. The auditor wishes to emphasize an unusually important subsequent event.
   D. The auditor is unable to obtain audited financial statements of a consolidated investee.

70. This question is obsolete.

71. Which of the following phrases would an auditor most likely include in the auditor's report when expressing a qualified opinion because of inadequate disclosure?
   A. Subject to the departure from generally accepted accounting principles, as described above.
   B. With the foregoing explanation of these omitted disclosures.
   C. Except for the omission of the information discussed in the preceding paragraph.
   D. Does **not** present fairly in all material respects.

72. Kane, CPA, concludes that there is substantial doubt about Lima Co.'s ability to continue as a going concern for a reasonable period of time. If Lima's financial statements adequately disclose its financial difficulties, Kane's auditor's report is required to include an explanatory paragraph that specifically uses the phrase(s)

	"Possible discontinuance of operations"	"Reasonable period of time, **not** to exceed one year"
A.	Yes	Yes
B.	Yes	No
C.	No	Yes
D.	No	No

73. Mead, CPA, had substantial doubt about Tech Co.'s ability to continue as a going concern when reporting on Tech's audited financial statements for the year ended June 30, 1994. That doubt has been removed in 1995. What is Mead's reporting responsibility if Tech is presenting its financial statements for the year ended June 30, 1995, on a comparative basis with those of 1994?
   A. The explanatory paragraph included in the 1994 auditor's report should **not** be repeated.
   B. The explanatory paragraph in the 1994 auditor's report should be repeated in its entirety.
   C. A different explanatory paragraph describing Mead's reasons for the removal of doubt should be included.
   D. A different explanatory paragraph describing Tech's plan for financial recovery should be included.

74. In the first audit of a new client, an auditor was able to extend auditing procedures to gather sufficient evidence about consistency. Under these circumstances, the auditor should
   A. Not report on the client's income statement.
   B. Not refer to consistency in the auditor's report.
   C. State that the consistency standard does **not** apply.
   D. State that the accounting principles have been applied consistently.

75. When reporting on comparative financial statements, an auditor ordinarily should change the previously issued opinion on the prior-year's financial statements if the
    A. Prior year's financial statements are restated to conform with generally accepted accounting principles.
    B. Auditor is a predecessor auditor who has been requested by a former client to reissue the previously issued report.
    C. Prior year's opinion was unqualified and the opinion on the current year's financial statements is modified due to a lack of consistency.
    D. Prior year's financial statements are restated following a pooling of interests in the current year.

76. Jewel, CPA, audited Infinite Co.'s prior-year financial statements. These statements are presented with those of the current year for comparative purposes without Jewel's auditor's report, which expressed a qualified opinion. In drafting the current year's auditor's report, Crain, CPA, the successor auditor, should

    I. Not name Jewel as the predecessor auditor.
    II. Indicate the type of report issued by Jewel.
    III. Indicate the substantive reasons for Jewel's qualification.

    A. I only.
    B. I and II only.
    C. II and III only.
    D. I, II, and III.

77. The introductory paragraph of an auditor's report contains the following sentences:

We did not audit the financial statements of EZ Inc., a wholly owned subsidiary, which statements reflect total assets and revenues constituting 27 and 29%, respectively, of the related consolidated totals. Those statements were audited by other auditors whose report has been furnished to us, and our opinion, insofar as it relates to the amounts included for EZ Inc., is based solely on the report of the other auditors.

These sentences
    A. Indicate a division of responsibility.
    B. Assume responsibility for the other auditor.
    C. Require a departure from an unqualified opinion.
    D. Are an improper form of reporting.

78. March, CPA, is engaged by Monday Corp., a client, to audit the financial statements of Wall Corp., a company that is not March's client. Monday expects to present Wall's audited financial statements with March's auditor's report to First Federal Bank to obtain financing in Monday's attempt to purchase Wall. In these circumstances, March's auditor's report would usually be addressed to
    A. Monday Corp., the client that engaged March.
    B. Wall Corp., the entity audited by March.
    C. First Federal Bank.
    D. Both Monday Corp. and First Federal Bank.

79. Financial statements of a nonpublic entity that have been reviewed by an accountant should be accompanied by a report stating that a review
    A. Provides only limited assurance that the financial statements are fairly presented.
    B. Includes examining, on a test basis, information that is the representation of management.
    C. Consists principally of inquiries of company personnel and analytical procedures applied to financial data.
    D. Does **not** contemplate obtaining corroborating evidential matter or applying certain other procedures ordinarily performed during an audit.

80. Financial statements of a nonpublic entity compiled without audit or review by an accountant should be accompanied by a report stating that
    A. The scope of the accountant's procedures has **not** been restricted in testing the financial information that is the representation of management.
    B. The accountant assessed the accounting principles used and significant estimates made by management.
    C. The accountant does **not** express an opinion or any other form of assurance on the financial statements.
    D. A compilation consists principally of inquiries of entity personnel and analytical procedures applied to financial data.

81. A CPA's report on agreed-upon procedures related to management's assertion about an entity's compliance with specified requirements should contain
   A. A statement of limitations on the use of the report.
   B. An opinion about whether management's assertion is fairly stated.
   C. Negative assurance that control risk has **not** been assessed.
   D. An acknowledgment of responsibility for the sufficiency of the procedures.

82. When an accountant examines projected financial statements, the accountant's report should include a separate paragraph that
   A. Describes the limitations on the usefulness of the presentation.
   B. Provides an explanation of the differences between an examination and an audit.
   C. States that the accountant is responsible for events and circumstances up to one year after the report's date.
   D. Disclaims an opinion on whether the assumptions provide a reasonable basis for the projection.

83. Field is an employee of Gold Enterprises. Hardy, CPA, is asked to express an opinion on Field's profit participation in Gold's net income. Hardy may accept this engagement only if
   A. Hardy also audits Gold's complete financial statements.
   B. Gold's financial statements are prepared in conformity with GAAP.
   C. Hardy's report is available for distribution to Gold's other employees.
   D. Field owns controlling interest in Gold.

84. Which of the following statements is correct about an auditor's required communication with an entity's audit committee?
   A. Any matters communicated to the entity's audit committee also are required to be communicated to the entity's management.
   B. The auditor is required to inform the entity's audit committee about significant errors discovered by the auditor and subsequently corrected by management.
   C. Disagreements with management about the application of accounting principles are required to be communicated in writing to the entity's audit committee.
   D. Weaknesses in internal control previously reported to the entity's audit committee are required to be communicated to the audit committee after each subsequent audit until the weaknesses are corrected.

85. Which of the following events occurring after the issuance of an auditor's report most likely would cause the auditor to make further inquiries about the previously issued financial statements?
   A. An uninsured natural disaster occurs that may affect the entity's ability to continue as a going concern.
   B. A contingency is resolved that had been disclosed in the audited financial statements.
   C. New information is discovered concerning undisclosed lease transactions of the audited period.
   D. A subsidiary is sold that accounts for 25% of the entity's consolidated net income.

86. A registration statement filed with the SEC contains the reports of two independent auditors on their audits of financial statements for different periods. The predecessor auditor who audited the prior-period financial statements generally should obtain a letter of representation from the
   A. Successor independent auditor.
   B. Client's audit committee.
   C. Principal underwriter.
   D. Securities and Exchange Commission.

87. An auditor is engaged to report on selected financial data that are included in a client-prepared document containing audited financial statements. Under these circumstances, the report on the selected data should

    A. Be limited to data derived from the audited financial statements.

    B. Be distributed only to senior management and the board of directors.

    C. State that the presentation is a comprehensive basis of accounting other than GAAP.

    D. Indicate that the data are **not** fairly stated in all material respects.

88. In auditing a not-for-profit entity that receives governmental financial assistance, the auditor has a responsibility to

    A. Issue a separate report that describes the expected benefits and related costs of the auditor's suggested changes to the entity's internal control.

    B. Assess whether management has identified laws and regulations that have a direct and material effect on the entity's financial statements.

    C. Notify the governmental agency providing the financial assistance that the audit is **not** designed to provide any assurance of detecting errors and fraud.

    D. Render an opinion concerning the entity's continued eligibility for the governmental financial assistance.

89. In auditing compliance with requirements governing major federal financial assistance programs under the Single Audit Act, the auditor's consideration of materiality differs from materiality under generally accepted auditing standards. Under the Single Audit Act, materiality is

    A. Calculated in relation to the financial statements taken as a whole.

    B. Determined separately for each major federal financial assistance program.

    C. Decided in conjunction with the auditor's risk assessment.

    D. Ignored, because all account balances, regardless of size, are fully tested.

90. Which of the following statements represents a quality control requirement under government auditing standards?

    A. A CPA who conducts government audits is required to undergo an annual external quality control review when an appropriate internal quality control system is **not** in place.

    B. A CPA seeking to enter into a contract to perform an audit should provide the CPA's most recent external quality control review report to the party contracting for the audit.

    C. An external quality control review of a CPA's practice should include a review of the working papers of each government audit performed since the prior external quality control review.

    D. A CPA who conducts government audits may **not** make the CPA's external quality control review report available to the public.

Number 2

Question Number 2 consists of 15 items. Select the **best** answer for each item. Use a No. 2 pencil to blacken the appropriate ovals on the Objective Answer Sheet to indicate your answers. **Answer all items.** Your grade will be based on the total number of correct answers.

Required:

Items 91 through 105 represent a series of unrelated statements, questions, excerpts, and comments taken from various parts of an auditor's working paper file. Below the items is a list of the likely sources of the statements, questions, excerpts, and comments. Select, as the best answer for each item, the most likely source. Select only one source for each item. A source may be selected once, more than once, or not at all.

Statements, Questions, Excerpts, and Comments

91. There are no material transactions that have not been properly recorded in the accounting records underlying the financial statements.
92. In connection with an audit of our financial statements, management has prepared, and furnished to our auditors, a description and evaluation of certain contingencies.
93. Provision has been made for any material loss to be sustained in the fulfillment of, or from the inability to fulfill, any sales commitments.
94. Fees for our services are based on our regular per diem rates, plus travel and other out-of-pocket expenses.
95. The objective of our audit is to express an unqualified opinion on the financial statements, although it is possible that facts or circumstances encountered may preclude us from expressing an unqualified opinion.
96. There has been no fraud involving employees that could have a material effect on the financial statements.
97. Are you aware of any facts or circumstances that may indicate a lack of integrity by any member of senior management?
98. If a difference of opinion on a practice problem existed between engagement personnel and a specialist or other consultant, was the difference resolved in accordance with firm policy and appropriately documented?
99. Although we have not conducted a comprehensive, detailed search of our records, no other deposit or loan accounts have come to our attention except as noted below.

100. At the conclusion of our audit, we will request certain written representations from you about the financial statements and related matters.
101. We have no plans or intentions that may materially affect the carrying value or classification of assets and liabilities.
102. As discussed in Note 14 to the financial statements, the Company has had numerous dealings with businesses controlled by, and people who are related to, the officers of the Company.
103. There were unreasonable delays by management in permitting the commencement of the audit and in providing needed information.
104. If this statement is not correct, please write promptly, using the enclosed envelope, and give details of any differences directly to our auditors.
105. The Company has suffered recurring losses from operations and has a net capital deficiency that raises substantial doubt about its ability to continue as a going concern.

List of Sources

(A) Partner's engagement review program.
(B) Communication with predecessor auditor.
(C) Auditor's engagement letter.
(D) Management representation letter.
(E) Standard financial institution confirmation request.
(F) Auditor's communication with the audit committee.
(G) Auditor's report.
(H) Letter for underwriters.
(I) Audit inquiry letter to legal counsel.
(J) Accounts receivable confirmation.

Number 3

Question Number 3 consists of 15 items. Select the **best** answer for each item. Use a No. 2 pencil to blacken the appropriate ovals on the Objective Answer Sheet to indicate your answers. **Answer all items.** Your grade will be based on the total number of correct answers.

Required:

Items **106 through 120** represent a series of unrelated procedures that an accountant may consider performing in separate engagements to review the financial statements of a nonpublic entity (a review) and to compile the financial statements of a nonpublic entity (a compilation). Select, as the best answer for each item, whether the procedure is required (R) or not required (N) for both review and compilation engagements. Make two selections for each item.

Procedures

106. The accountant should establish an understanding with the entity regarding the nature and limitations of the services to be performed.
107. The accountant should make inquiries concerning actions taken at the board of directors' meetings.
108. The accountant, as the entity's successor accountant, should communicate with the predecessor accountant to obtain access to the predecessor's working papers.
109. The accountant should obtain a level of knowledge of the accounting principles and practices of the entity's industry.
110. The accountant should obtain an understanding of the entity's internal control.
111. The accountant should perform analytical procedures designed to identify relationships that appear to be unusual.
112. The accountant should make an assessment of control risk.
113. The accountant should send a letter of inquiry to the entity's attorney to corroborate the information furnished by management concerning litigation.
114. The accountant should obtain a management representation letter from the entity.
115. The accountant should study the relationships of the financial statement elements that would be expected to conform to a predictable pattern.
116. The accountant should communicate to the entity's senior management illegal employee acts discovered by the accountant that are clearly inconsequential.
117. The accountant should make inquiries about events subsequent to the date of the financial statements that would have a material effect on the financial statements.
118. The accountant should modify the accountant's report if there is a change in accounting principles that is adequately disclosed.
119. The accountant should submit a hard copy of the financial statements and accountant's report when the financial statements and accountant's report are submitted on a computer disk.
120. The accountant should perform specific procedures to evaluate whether there is substantial doubt about the entity's ability to continue as a going concern.

Number 4

Recently there has been a significant number of highly publicized cases of alleged or actual management fraud involving the misstatement of financial statements. Although most client managements possess unquestioned integrity, a very small number, given sufficient incentive and opportunity, may be predisposed to fraudulently misstate reported financial condition and operating results.

Required:

a. What distinguishes management fraud from a defalcation?

b. What are an auditor's responsibilities under generally accepted auditing standards to detect management fraud?

c. What are the characteristics of management fraud that an auditor should consider to fulfill the auditor's responsibilities under generally accepted auditing standards related to detecting management fraud?

d. Three factors that heighten an auditor's concern about the existence of management fraud include (1) an intended public placement of securities in the near future, (2) management remuneration dependent on operating results, and (3) a weak internal control environment evidenced by lack of concern for basic controls and disregard of the auditor's recommendations.

What other factors should heighten an auditor's concern about the existence of management fraud?

Number 5

Most of an auditor's work in forming an opinion on financial statements consists of obtaining and evaluating evidential matter concerning the financial statement assertions.

Required:

a. What is the definition of "financial statement assertions?"

Do not list the assertions.

b. What is the relationship between audit objectives and financial statement assertions?

c. What should an auditor consider in developing the audit objectives of a particular engagement?

d. What is the relationship between audit objectives and audit procedures?

e. What are an auditor's primary considerations when selecting particular substantive tests to achieve audit objectives?

E X A M I N A T I O N   Q U E S T I O N S

UNIFORM CERTIFIED PUBLIC ACCOUNTANT EXAMINATION
Accounting & Reporting—Taxation, Managerial, and
Governmental and Not-for-Profit Organizations

The point values for each question, and estimated time allotments based primarily on point value, are as follows:

	Point Value	Estimated Minutes Minimum	Estimated Minutes Maximum
No. 1	60	120	130
No. 2	5	5	10
No. 3	20	25	40
No. 4	5	5	10
No. 5	10	15	20
Totals	100	170	210

ARE

November 2, 1995; 8:30 A.M. to 12:00 NOON

INSTRUCTIONS TO CANDIDATES *Failure to follow these instructions may have an adverse effect on your Examination grade.*

1. Do not break the seal around the *Examination Questions* (pages 3 through 26) until you are told to do so.

2. All questions should be answered on the *Objective Answer Sheet*, which is pages 27 and 28. You should attempt to answer all objective items. There is no penalty for incorrect responses. Work space to solve the objective questions is provided in the *Examination Questions* on pages 5 through 19. Since the objective items are computer-graded, your comments and calculations associated with them are not considered. Be certain that you have entered your answers on the *Objective Answer Sheet* before the examination time is up. Your examination will not be graded if you fail to record your answers on the *Objective Answer Sheet*. You will not be given additional time to record your answers.

3. You are required to turn in by the end of each session:
   a. Attendance Record and Calculator Sign-off Record Form, page 1;
   b. *Examination Questions*, pages 3 through 26;
   c. *Objective Answer Sheet*, pages 27 and 28;
   d. Calculator; and
   e. All unused examination materials.

   Your examination will not be graded unless the above listed items are handed in before leaving the examination room.

4. Unless otherwise instructed, if you want your *Examination Questions* mailed to you, write your name and address in both places indicated on page 26 and place 55 cents postage in the space provided. *Examination Questions* will be distributed no sooner than the day following the administration of this examination.

Prepared by the Board of Examiners of the American Institute of Certified Public Accountants and adopted by the examining boards of all states, the District of Columbia, Guam, Puerto Rico, and the Virgin Islands of the United States.

Copyright © 1995 by the American Institute of Certified Public Accountants, Inc.

Examination Questions Booklet No.

4 74372 Q

Accounting & Reporting— Taxation, Managerial, and Governmental and Not-for-Profit Organizations (ARE)

Number 1

Instructions

Select the **best** answer for each of the following items. Use a No. 2 pencil to blacken the appropriate ovals on the Objective Answer Sheet to indicate your answers. **Mark only one answer for each item. Answer all items.** Your grade will be based on the total number of correct answers.

1. In 1994, Starke Corp., an accrual-basis calendar year corporation, reported book income of $380,000. Included in that amount was $50,000 municipal bond interest income, $170,000 for federal income tax expense, and $2,000 interest expense on the debt incurred to carry the municipal bonds. What amount should Starke's taxable income be as reconciled on Starke's Schedule M-1 of Form 1120, U.S. Corporation Income Tax Return?
   - A. $330,000
   - B. $500,000
   - C. $502,000
   - D. $550,000

2. Lake Corp., an accrual-basis calendar year corporation, had the following 1994 receipts:

1995 advanced rental payments where the lease ends in 1996	$125,000
Lease cancellation payment from a five-year lease tenant	50,000

Lake had no restrictions on the use of the advanced rental payments and renders no services. What amount of income should Lake report on its 1994 tax return?
   - A. $0
   - B. $ 50,000
   - C. $125,000
   - D. $175,000

3. A C corporation's net capital losses are
   - A. Carried forward indefinitely until fully utilized.
   - B. Carried back three years and forward five years.
   - C. Deductible in full from the corporations's ordinary income.
   - D. Deductible from the corporation's ordinary income only to the extent of $3,000.

4. In 1994, Best Corp., an accrual-basis calendar year C corporation, received $100,000 in dividend income from the common stock that it held in an unrelated domestic corporation. The stock was not debt-financed, and was held for over a year. Best recorded the following information for 1994:

Loss from Best's operations	($ 10,000)
Dividends received	100,000
Taxable income (before dividends-received deduction)	$ 90,000

Best's dividends-received deduction on its 1994 tax return was
   - A. $100,000
   - B. $ 80,000
   - C. $ 70,000
   - D. $ 63,000

5. Data Corp., a calendar year corporation, purchased and placed into service office equipment during November 1994. No other equipment was placed into service during 1994. Under the general MACRS depreciation system, what convention must Data use?
   - A. Full-year.
   - B. Half-year.
   - C. Mid-quarter.
   - D. Mid-month.

6. Capital assets include
   - A. A corporation's accounts receivable from the sale of its inventory.
   - B. Seven-year MACRS property used in a corporation's trade or business.
   - C. A manufacturing company's investment in U.S. Treasury bonds.
   - D. A corporate real estate developer's unimproved land that is to be subdivided to build homes, which will be sold to customers.

SOURCE: LPR, NOVEMBER 1995, #6

6. According to the standards of the profession, which of the following sources of information should a CPA consider before signing a client's tax return?

I. Information actually known to the CPA from the tax return of another client.
II. Information provided by the client that appears to be correct based on the client's returns from prior years.

    A. I only.
    B. II only.
    C. Both I and II.
    D. Neither I nor II.

7. Baker Corp., a calendar year C corporation, realized taxable income of $36,000 from its regular business operations for calendar year 1994. In addition, Baker had the following capital gains and losses during 1994:

Short-term capital gain	$8,500
Short-term capital loss	(4,000)
Long-term capital gain	1,500
Long-term capital loss	(3,500)

Baker did not realize any other capital gains or losses since it began operations. What is Baker's total taxable income for 1994?

    A. $46,000
    B. $42,000
    C. $40,500
    D. $38,500

SOURCE: LPR, NOVEMBER 1995, #7

7. According to the standards of the profession, which of the following statements is(are) correct regarding the action to be taken by a CPA who discovers an error in a client's previously filed tax return?

I. Advise the client of the error and recommend the measures to be taken.
II. Withdraw from the professional relationship regardless of whether or not the client corrects the error.

    A. I only.
    B. II only.
    C. Both I and II.
    D. Neither I nor II.

8. In 1994, Cable Corp., a calendar year C corporation, contributed $80,000 to a qualified charitable organization. Cable's 1994 taxable income before the deduction for charitable contributions was $820,000 after a $40,000 dividends-received deduction. Cable also had carryover contributions of $10,000 from the prior year. In 1994, what amount can Cable deduct as charitable contributions?

    A. $90,000
    B. $86,000
    C. $82,000
    D. $80,000

9. If a corporation's charitable contributions exceed the limitation for deductibility in a particular year, the excess

    A. Is **not** deductible in any future or prior year.
    B. May be carried back or forward for one year at the corporation's election.
    C. May be carried forward to a maximum of five succeeding years.
    D. May be carried back to the third preceding year.

10. In 1994, Stewart Corp. properly accrued $5,000 for an income item on the basis of a reasonable estimate. In 1995, after filing its 1994 federal income tax return, Stewart determined that the exact amount was $6,000. Which of the following statements is correct?

    A. No further inclusion of income is required as the difference is less than 25% of the original amount reported and the estimate had been made in good faith.
    B. The $1,000 difference is includible in Stewart's 1995 income tax return.
    C. Stewart is required to notify the IRS within 30 days of the determination of the exact amount of the item.
    D. Stewart is required to file an amended return to report the additional $1,000 of income.

11. The uniform capitalization method must be used by

   I. Manufacturers of tangible personal property.
  II. Retailers of personal property with $2 million dollars in average annual gross receipts for the 3 preceding years.

    A. I only.
    B. II only.
    C. Both I and II.
    D. Neither I nor II.

12. Kane Corp. is a calendar year domestic personal holding company. Which deduction(s) must Kane make from 1994 taxable income to determine undistributed personal holding company income prior to the dividend-paid deduction?

	Federal income taxes	Net long-term capital gain less related federal income taxes
A.	Yes	Yes
B.	Yes	No
C.	No	Yes
D.	No	No

13. Bank Corp. owns 80% of Shore Corp.'s outstanding capital stock. Shore's capital stock consists of 50,000 shares of common stock issued and outstanding. Shore's 1994 net income was $140,000. During 1994, Shore declared and paid dividends of $60,000. In conformity with generally accepted accounting principles, Bank recorded the following entries in 1994:

	Debit	Credit
Investment in Shore Corp.		
common stock	$112,000	
Equity in earnings of		
subsidiary		$112,000
Cash	48,000	
Investment in Shore Corp.		
common stock		48,000

In its 1994 consolidated tax return, Bank should report dividend revenue of

    A. $48,000
    B. $14,400
    C. $ 9,600
    D. $0

14. Dart Corp., a calendar year domestic C corporation, is not a personal holding company. For purposes of the accumulated earnings tax, Dart has accumulated taxable income for 1994. Which step(s) can Dart take to eliminate or reduce any 1994 accumulated earnings tax?

   I. Demonstrate that the "reasonable needs" of its business require the retention of all or part of the 1994 accumulated taxable income.
  II. Pay dividends by March 15, 1995.

    A. I only.
    B. II only.
    C. Both I and II.
    D. Neither I nor II.

15. Eastern Corp., a calendar year corporation, was formed January 3, 1994, and on that date placed five-year property in service. The property was depreciated under the general MACRS system. Eastern did not elect to use the straight-line method. The following information pertains to Eastern:

Eastern's 1994 taxable income	$300,000
Adjustment for the accelerated depreciation taken on 1994 five-year property	1,000
1994 tax-exempt interest from specified private activity bonds issued after August 7, 1986	5,000

What was Eastern's 1994 alternative minimum taxable income before the adjusted current earnings (ACE) adjustment?

    A. $306,000
    B. $305,000
    C. $304,000
    D. $301,000

16. A civil fraud penalty can be imposed on a corporation that underpays tax by

    A. Omitting income as a result of inadequate recordkeeping.
    B. Failing to report income it erroneously considered **not** to be part of corporate profits.
    C. Filing an incomplete return with an appended statement, making clear that the return is incomplete.
    D. Maintaining false records and reporting fictitious transactions to minimize corporate tax liability.

17. A corporation may reduce its regular income tax by taking a tax credit for
   A. Dividends-received exclusion.
   B. Foreign income taxes.
   C. State income taxes.
   D. Accelerated depreciation.

18. The accumulated earnings tax can be imposed
   A. On both partnerships and corporations.
   B. On companies that make distributions in excess of accumulated earnings.
   C. On personal holding companies.
   D. Regardless of the number of stockholders in a corporation.

19. The following information pertains to Dahl Corp.:

Accumulated earnings and profits at January 1, 1994	$120,000
Earnings and profits for the year ended December 31, 1994	160,000
Cash distributions to individual stockholders during 1994	360,000

What is the total amount of distributions taxable as dividend income to Dahl's stockholders in 1994?
   A. $0
   B. $160,000
   C. $280,000
   D. $360,000

20. Ridge Corp., a calendar year C corporation, made a nonliquidating cash distribution to its shareholders of $1,000,000 with respect to its stock. At that time, Ridge's current and accumulated earnings and profits totaled $750,000 and its total paid-in capital for tax purposes was $10,000,000. Ridge had no corporate shareholders. Ridge's cash distribution

   I. Was taxable as $750,000 in ordinary income to its shareholders.
   II. Reduced its shareholders' adjusted bases in Ridge stock by $250,000.

   A. I only.
   B. II only.
   C. Both I and II.
   D. Neither I nor II.

21. Clark and Hunt organized Jet Corp. with authorized voting common stock of $400,000. Clark contributed $60,000 cash. Both Clark and Hunt transferred other property in exchange for Jet stock as follows:

	Other property		
	Adjusted basis	Fair market value	Percentage of Jet stock acquired
Clark	$ 50,000	$100,000	40%
Hunt	120,000	240,000	60%

What was Clark's basis in Jet stock?
   A. $0
   B. $100,000
   C. $110,000
   D. $160,000

22. Ace Corp. and Bate Corp. combine in a qualifying reorganization and form Carr Corp., the only surviving corporation. This reorganization is tax-free to the

	Shareholders	Corporation
A.	Yes	Yes
B.	Yes	No
C.	No	Yes
D.	No	No

23. Bass Corp., a calendar year C corporation, made qualifying 1994 estimated tax deposits based on its actual 1993 tax liability. On March 15, 1995, Bass filed a timely automatic extension request for its 1994 corporate income tax return. Estimated tax deposits and the extension payment totalled $7,600. This amount was 95% of the total tax shown on Bass' final 1994 corporate income tax return. Bass paid $400 additional tax on the final 1994 corporate income tax return filed before the extended due date. For the 1994 calendar year, Bass was subject to pay

   I. Interest on the $400 tax payment made in 1995.
   II. A tax delinquency penalty.

   A. I only.
   B. II only.
   C. Both I and II.
   D. Neither I nor II.

24. Edge Corp., a calendar year C corporation, had a net operating loss and zero tax liability for its 1994 tax year. To avoid the penalty for underpayment of estimated taxes, Edge could compute its first quarter 1995 estimated income tax payment using the

	Annualized income method	Preceding year method
A.	Yes	Yes
B.	Yes	No
C.	No	Yes
D.	No	No

25. A corporation's tax year can be reopened after all statutes of limitations have expired if

  I. The tax return has a 50% nonfraudulent omission from gross income.
 II. The corporation prevails in a determination allowing a deduction in an open tax year that was taken erroneously in a closed tax year.

    A. I only.
    B. II only.
    C. Both I and II.
    D. Neither I nor II.

26. A penalty for understated corporate tax liability can be imposed on a tax preparer who fails to

    A. Audit the corporate records.
    B. Examine business operations.
    C. Copy all underlying documents.
    D. Make reasonable inquiries when taxpayer information appears incorrect.

27. Barker acquired a 50% interest in Kode Partnership by contributing $20,000 cash and a building with an adjusted basis of $26,000 and a fair market value of $42,000. The building was subject to a $10,000 mortgage that was assumed by Kode. The other partners contributed cash only. The basis of Barker's interest in Kode is

    A. $36,000
    B. $41,000
    C. $52,000
    D. $62,000

28. At partnership inception, Black acquires a 50% interest in Decorators Partnership by contributing property with an adjusted basis of $250,000. Black recognizes a gain if

  I. The fair market value of the contributed property exceeds its adjusted basis.
 II. The property is encumbered by a mortgage with a balance of $100,000.

    A. I only.
    B. II only.
    C. Both I and II.
    D. Neither I nor II.

29. Evan, a 25% partner in Vista Partnership, received a $20,000 guaranteed payment in 1994 for deductible services rendered to the partnership. Guaranteed payments were not made to any other partner. Vista's 1994 partnership income consisted of:

Net business income before guaranteed payments	$80,000
Net long-term capital gains	10,000

What amount of income should Evan report from Vista Partnership on her 1994 tax return?

    A. $37,500
    B. $27,500
    C. $22,500
    D. $20,000

30. On January 4, 1994, Smith and White contributed $4,000 and $6,000 in cash, respectively, and formed the Macro General Partnership. The partnership agreement allocated profits and losses 40% to Smith and 60% to White. In 1994, Macro purchased property from an unrelated seller for $10,000 cash and a $40,000 mortgage note that was the general liability of the partnership. Macro's liability

    A. Increases Smith's partnership basis by $16,000.
    B. Increases Smith's partnership basis by $20,000.
    C. Increases Smith's partnership basis by $24,000.
    D. Has **no** effect on Smith's partnership basis.

31. Hart's adjusted basis in Best Partnership was $9,000 at the time he received the following nonliquidating distributions of partnership property:

Cash	$ 5,000
Land	
Adjusted basis	7,000
Fair market value	10,000

What was the amount of Hart's basis in the land?
A. $0
B. $ 4,000
C. $ 7,000
D. $10,000

32. Stone's basis in Ace Partnership was $70,000 at the time he received a nonliquidating distribution of partnership capital assets. These capital assets had an adjusted basis of $65,000 to Ace, and a fair market value of $83,000. Ace had no unrealized receivables, appreciated inventory, or properties that had been contributed by its partners. What was Stone's recognized gain or loss on the distribution?
A. $18,000 ordinary income.
B. $13,000 capital gain.
C. $ 5,000 capital loss.
D. $0.

33. On January 3, 1994, the partners' interests in the capital, profits, and losses of Able Partnership were:

	% of capital, profits and losses
Dean	25
Poe	30
Ritt	45

On February 4, 1994, Poe sold her entire interest to an unrelated party. Dean sold his 25 percent interest in Able to another unrelated party on December 20, 1994. No other transactions took place in 1994. For tax purposes, which of the following statements is correct with respect to Able?
A. Able terminated as of February 4, 1994.
B. Able terminated as of December 20, 1994.
C. Able terminated as of December 31, 1994.
D. Able did **not** terminate.

34. Curry's sale of her partnership interest causes a partnership termination. The partnership's business and financial operations are continued by the other members. What is(are) the effect(s) of the termination?
I. There is a deemed distribution of assets to the remaining partners and the purchaser.
II. There is a hypothetical recontribution of assets to a new partnership.

A. I only.
B. II only.
C. Both I and II.
D. Neither I nor II.

35. A distribution to an estate's sole beneficiary for the 1994 calendar year equalled $15,000, the amount currently required to be distributed by the will. The estate's 1994 records were as follows:

Estate income	
$40,000	Taxable interest

Estate disbursements	
$34,000	Expenses attributable to taxable interest

What amount of the distribution was taxable to the beneficiary?
A. $40,000
B. $15,000
C. $ 6,000
D. $0

36. Steve and Kay Briar, U.S. citizens, were married for the entire 1994 calendar year. In 1994, Steve gave a $30,000 cash gift to his sister. The Briars made no other gifts in 1994. They each signed a timely election to treat the $30,000 gift as made one-half by each spouse. Disregarding the unified credit and estate tax consequences, what amount of the 1994 gift is taxable to the Briars?
A. $30,000
B. $20,000
C. $10,000
D. $0

37. The organizational test to qualify a public service charitable entity as tax exempt requires the articles of organization to

I. Limit the purpose of the entity to the charitable purpose.
II. State that an information return should be filed annually with the Internal Revenue Service.

    A. I only.
    B. II only.
    C. Both I and II.
    D. Neither I nor II.

38. Which of the following activities regularly conducted by a tax exempt organization will result in unrelated business income?

I. Selling articles made by handicapped persons as part of their rehabilitation, when the organization is involved exclusively in their rehabilitation.
II. Operating a grocery store almost fully staffed by emotionally handicapped persons as part of a therapeutic program.

    A. I only.
    B. II only.
    C. Both I and II.
    D. Neither I nor II.

39. Sender, Inc. estimates parcel mailing costs using data shown on the chart below.

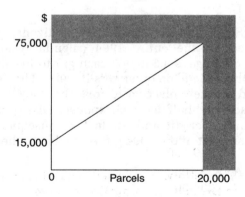

What is Sender's estimated cost for mailing 12,000 parcels?
    A. $36,000
    B. $45,000
    C. $51,000
    D. $60,000

40. Mien Co. is budgeting sales of 53,000 units of product Nous for October 1995. The manufacture of one unit of Nous requires 4 kilos of chemical Loire. During October 1995, Mien plans to reduce the inventory of Loire by 50,000 kilos and increase the finished goods inventory of Nous by 6,000 units. There is no Nous work-in-process inventory. How many kilos of Loire is Mien budgeting to purchase in October 1995?
    A. 138,000
    B. 162,000
    C. 186,000
    D. 238,000

41. The basic difference between a master budget and a flexible budget is that a master budget is
    A. Only used before and during the budget period and a flexible budget is only used after the budget period.
    B. For an entire production facility and a flexible budget is applicable to single departments only.
    C. Based on one specific level of production and a flexible budget can be prepared for any production level within a relevant range.
    D. Based on a fixed standard and a flexible budget allows management latitude in meeting goals.

42. For the next two years, a lease is estimated to have an operating net cash inflow of $7,500 per annum, before adjusting for $5,000 per annum tax basis lease amortization, and a 40% tax rate. The present value of an ordinary annuity of $1 per year at 10% for 2 years is $1.74. What is the lease's after-tax present value using a 10% discount factor?
    A. $ 2,610
    B. $ 4,350
    C. $ 9,570
    D. $11,310

43. Product Cott has sales of $200,000, a contribution margin of 20%, and a margin of safety of $80,000. What is Cott's fixed cost?
    A. $16,000
    B. $24,000
    C. $80,000
    D. $96,000

44. Break-even analysis assumes that over the relevant range
   A. Unit revenues are nonlinear.
   B. Unit variable costs are unchanged.
   C. Total costs are unchanged.
   D. Total fixed costs are nonlinear.

45. Gram Co. develops computer programs to meet customers' special requirements. How should Gram categorize payments to employees who develop these programs?

	Direct costs	Value-adding costs
A.	Yes	Yes
B.	Yes	No
C.	No	No
D.	No	Yes

46. The Forming Department is the first of a two-stage production process. Spoilage is identified when the units have completed the Forming process. Costs of spoiled units are assigned to units completed and transferred to the second department in the period spoilage is identified. The following information concerns Forming's conversion costs in May 1995:

Conversion

	Units	Costs
Beginning work-in-process (50% complete)	2,000	$10,000
Units started during May	8,000	75,500
Spoilage—normal	500	
Units completed & transferred	7,000	
Ending work-in-process (80% complete)	2,500	

Using the weighted average method, what was Forming's conversion cost transferred to the second production department?
   A. $59,850
   B. $64,125
   C. $67,500
   D. $71,250

47. The standard direct material cost to produce a unit of Lem is 4 meters of material at $2.50 per meter. During May 1995, 4,200 meters of material costing $10,080 were purchased and used to produce 1,000 units of Lem. What was the material price variance for May 1995?
   A. $400 favorable.
   B. $420 favorable.
   C. $ 80 unfavorable.
   D. $480 unfavorable.

48. For purposes of allocating joint costs to joint products, the sales price at point of sale, reduced by cost to complete after split-off, is assumed to be equal to the
   A. Joint costs.
   B. Total costs.
   C. Net sales value at split-off.
   D. Sales price less a normal profit margin at point of sale.

49. Parat College allocates support department costs to its individual schools using the step method. Information for May 1995 is as follows:

	Support departments	
	Maintenance	Power
Costs incurred	$99,000	54,000
Service percentages provided to:		
Maintenance	—	10%
Power	20%	—
School of Education	30%	20%
School of Technology	50%	70%
	100%	100%

What is the amount of May 1995 support department costs allocated to the School of Education?
   A. $40,500
   B. $42,120
   C. $46,100
   D. $49,125

50. The following selected data pertain to the Darwin Division of Beagle Co. for 1994:

Sales	$400,000
Operating income	40,000
Capital turnover	4
Imputed interest rate	10%

What was Darwin's 1994 residual income?
   A. $0
   B. $ 4,000
   C. $10,000
   D. $30,000

51. Key Co. changed from a traditional manufacturing operation with a job order costing system to a just-in-time operation with a back-flush costing system. What is(are) the expected effect(s) of these changes on Key's inspection costs and recording detail of costs tracked to jobs in process?

	Inspection costs	Detail of costs tracked to jobs
A.	Decrease	Decrease
B.	Decrease	Increase
C.	Increase	Decrease
D.	Increase	Increase

52. The economic order quantity formula assumes that
A. Periodic demand for the good is known.
B. Carrying costs per unit vary with quantity ordered.
C. Costs of placing an order vary with quantity ordered.
D. Purchase costs per unit differ due to quantity discounts.

53. Under frost-free conditions, Cal Cultivators expects its strawberry crop to have a $60,000 market value. An unprotected crop subject to frost has an expected market value of $40,000. If Cal protects the strawberries against frost, then the market value of the crop is still expected to be $60,000 under frost-free conditions and $90,000 if there is a frost. What must be the probability of a frost for Cal to be indifferent to spending $10,000 for frost protection?
A. .167
B. .200
C. .250
D. .333

54. During 1994, Deet Corp. experienced the following power outages:

Number of outages per month	Number of months
0	3
1	2
2	4
3	3
	12

Each power outage results in out-of-pocket costs of $400. For $500 per month, Deet can lease an auxiliary generator to provide power during outages. If Deet leases an auxiliary generator in 1995, the estimated savings (or additional expenditures) for 1995 would be
A. ($3,600)
B. ($1,200)
C. $1,600
D. $1,900

55. Based on potential sales of 500 units per year, a new product has estimated traceable costs of $990,000. What is the target price to obtain a 15 percent profit margin on sales?
A. $2,329
B. $2,277
C. $1,980
D. $1,935

56. Lynn Manufacturing Co. prepares income statements using both standard absorption and standard variable costing methods. For 1994, unit standard costs were unchanged from 1993. In 1994, the only beginning and ending inventories were finished goods of 5,000 units. How would Lynn's ratios using absorption costing compare with those using variable costing?

	Current ratio	Return on stockholders' equity
A.	Same	Same
B.	Same	Smaller
C.	Greater	Same
D.	Greater	Smaller

57. Which of the following fund types of a governmental unit has(have) income determination as a measurement focus?

	General funds	Expendable trust funds
A.	Yes	Yes
B.	Yes	No
C.	No	No
D.	No	Yes

58. Fixed assets donated to a governmental unit should be recorded
A. At the donor's carrying amount.
B. At estimated fair value when received.
C. At the lower of the donor's carrying amount or estimated fair value when received.
D. As a memorandum entry only.

59. Which event(s) is(are) supportive of inter-period equity as a financial reporting objective of a governmental unit?

  I. A balanced budget is adopted.
  II. Residual equity transfers out equals residual equity transfers in.

   A. I only.
   B. II only.
   C. Both I and II.
   D. Neither I nor II.

60. Fund accounting is used by governmental units with resources that must be
   A. Composed of cash or cash equivalents.
   B. Incorporated into combined or combining financial statements.
   C. Segregated for the purpose of carrying on specific activities or attaining certain objectives.
   D. Segregated physically according to various objectives.

61. Vale City legally adopts a cash-basis budget. What basis should be used in Vale's combined statement of revenues, expenditures, and changes in fund balances—budget and actual?
   A. Cash.
   B. Modified accrual.
   C. Accrual.
   D. Modified cash.

62. What is the basic criterion used to determine the reporting entity for a governmental unit?
   A. Special financing arrangement.
   B. Geographic boundaries.
   C. Scope of public services.
   D. Financial accountability.

63. Which event(s) should be included in a statement of cash flows for a governmental entity?

  I. Cash inflow from issuing bonds to finance city hall construction.
  II. Cash outflow from a city utility representing payments in lieu of property taxes.

   A. I only.
   B. II only.
   C. Both I and II.
   D. Neither I nor II.

64. Fish Road property owners in Sea County are responsible for special assessment debt that arose from a storm sewer project. If the property owners default, Sea has no obligation regarding debt service, although it does bill property owners for assessments and uses the monies it collects to pay debt holders. What fund type should Sea use to account for these collection and servicing activities?
   A. Agency.
   B. Debt service.
   C. Expendable trust funds.
   D. Capital projects.

65. The revenues control account of a governmental unit is increased when
   A. The encumbrance account is decreased.
   B. Appropriations are recorded.
   C. Property taxes are recorded.
   D. The budget is recorded.

66. Tuston Township issued the following bonds during the year ended June 30, 1995:

Bonds issued for the garbage collection enterprise fund that will service the debt	$700,000
Revenue bonds to be repaid from admission fees collected by the Township zoo enterprise fund	500,000

What amount of these bonds should be accounted for in Tuston's general long-term debt account group?
   A. $1,200,000
   B. $ 700,000
   C. $ 500,000
   D. $0

67. Frome City signed a 20-year office property lease for its general staff. Frome could terminate the lease at any time after giving one year's notice, but termination is considered a remote possibility. The lease meets the criteria for a capital lease. What is the effect of the lease on the asset amount in Frome's general fixed assets account group and the liability amount in Frome's general long-term debt account group?

	Asset amount	Liability amount
A.	Increase	Increase
B.	Increase	No effect
C.	No effect	Increase
D.	No effect	No effect

68. Polk County's solid waste landfill operation is accounted for in a governmental fund. Polk used available cash to purchase equipment that is included in the estimated current cost of closure and post-closure care of this operation. How would this purchase affect the asset amount in Polk's general fixed assets account group and the liability amount in Polk's general long-term debt account group?

	Asset amount	Liability amount
A.	Increase	Decrease
B.	Increase	No effect
C.	No effect	Decrease
D.	No effect	No effect

69. Financial statements for which fund type generally report retained earnings?
   A. Capital projects.
   B. Enterprise.
   C. Special revenue.
   D. Expendable pension trust.

70. Lys City reports a compensated absences liability in its combined balance sheet. The salary rate used to calculate the liability should normally be the rate in effect
   A. When the unpaid compensated absences were earned.
   B. When the compensated absences are to be paid.
   C. At the balance sheet date.
   D. When the compensated absences were earned or are to be paid, or at the balance sheet date, whichever results in the lowest amount.

71. Which account should Spring Township credit when it issues a purchase order for supplies?
   A. Appropriations control.
   B. Vouchers payable.
   C. Encumbrance control.
   D. Reserve for encumbrances.

72. The estimated revenues control account of a governmental unit is debited when
   A. Actual revenues are recorded.
   B. Actual revenues are collected.
   C. The budget is recorded.
   D. The budget is closed at the end of the year.

73. The billings for transportation services provided to other governmental units are recorded by the internal service fund as
   A. Transportation appropriations.
   B. Operating revenues.
   C. Interfund exchanges.
   D. Intergovernmental transfers.

74. A large not-for-profit organization's statement of activities should report the net change for net assets that are

	Unrestricted	Permanently restricted
A.	Yes	Yes
B.	Yes	No
C.	No	No
D.	No	Yes

75. Which of the following should normally be considered ongoing or central transactions for a not-for-profit hospital?

   I. Room and board fees from patients.
   II. Recovery room fees.

   A. Neither I nor II.
   B. Both I and II.
   C. II only.
   D. I only.

Number 2

Question Number 2 consists of six items. Select the **best** answer for each item. Use a No. 2 pencil to blacken the appropriate ovals on the Objective Answer Sheet to indicate your answers. **Answer all items.** Your grade will be based on the total number of correct answers.

Lan Corp., an accrual-basis calendar year repair-service corporation, began business on Monday, January 3, 1994. Lan's valid S corporation election took effect retroactively on January 3, 1994.

Required:

a. For **Items 76 through 79,** determine the amount, if any, using the fact pattern for each item. To record your answer, blacken the ovals on the Objective Answer Sheet. If zeros precede your numerical answer, blacken the zeros in the ovals preceding your answer. **You cannot receive credit for your answers if you fail to blacken an oval in each column.** You may write the numbers in the boxes provided to facilitate blackening the ovals; however, the numbers written in the boxes will **not** be graded.

76. Assume the following facts:

Lan's 1994 books recorded the following items:

Gross receipts	$7,260
Interest income on investments	50
Charitable contributions	1,000
Supplies	1,120

What amount of net business income should Lan report on its 1994 Form 1120S, U.S. Income Tax Return for an S corporation, Schedule K?

77. Assume the following facts:

As of January 3, 1994, Taylor and Barr each owned 100 shares of the 200 issued shares of Lan stock. On January 31, 1994, Taylor and Barr each sold 20 shares to Pike. No election was made to terminate the tax year. Lan had net business income of $14,520 for the year ended December 31, 1994, and made no distributions to its shareholders. Lan's 1994 calendar year had 363 days.

What amount of net business income should have been reported on Pike's 1994 Schedule K-1 from Lan? (1994 is a 363-day tax year.) Round the answer to the nearest hundred.

78. Assume the following facts:

Pike purchased 40 Lan shares on January 31, 1994, for $4,000. Lan made no distributions to shareholders, and Pike's 1994 Schedule K-1 from Lan reported:

Ordinary business loss	($1,000)
Municipal bond interest income	150

What was Pike's basis in his Lan stock at December 31, 1994?

79. Assume the following facts:

On January 3, 1994, Taylor and Barr each owned 100 shares of the 200 issued shares of Lan stock. Taylor's basis in Lan shares on that date was $10,000. Taylor sold all of his Lan shares to Pike on January 31, 1994, and Lan made a valid election to terminate its tax year. Taylor's share of ordinary income from Lan prior to the sale was $2,000. Lan made a cash distribution of $3,000 to Taylor on January 30, 1994.

What was Taylor's basis in Lan shares for determining gain or loss from the sale to Pike?

Required:

b. For **Items 80 and 81,** indicate if the statement is true (T) or false (F) regarding Lan's S corporation status. Blacken the corresponding oval on the Objective Answer Sheet.

80. Lan issues shares of both preferred and common stock to shareholders at inception on January 3, 1994. This will **not** affect Lan's S corporation eligibility.

81. Lan, an S corporation since inception, has passive investment income for three consecutive years following the year a valid S corporation election takes effect. Lan's S corporation election is terminated as of the first day of the fourth year.

Number 3

Question Number 3 consists of 29 items. Select the **best** answer for each item. Use a No. 2 pencil to blacken the appropriate ovals on the Objective Answer Sheet to indicate your answers. **Answer all items.** Your grade will be based on the total number of correct answers.

Tom and Joan Moore, both CPAs, filed a joint 1994 federal income tax return showing $70,000 in taxable income. During 1994, Tom's daughter Laura, age 16, resided with Tom's former spouse. Laura had no income of her own and was not Tom's dependent.

Required:

a. For **Items 82 through 91,** determine the amount of income or loss, if any, that should be included on page one of the Moores' 1994 Form 1040. To record your answer, blacken the ovals on the Objective Answer Sheet. If zeros precede your numerical answer, blacken the zeros in the ovals preceding your answer. **You cannot receive credit for your answers if you fail to blacken an oval in each column.** You may write the numbers in the boxes provided to facilitate blackening the ovals; however, the numbers written in the boxes will **not** be graded.

82. The Moores had no capital loss carryovers from prior years. During 1994 the Moores had the following stock transactions which resulted in a net capital loss:

	Date acquired	Date sold	Sales price	Cost
Revco	2-1-93	3-17-94	$15,000	$25,000
Abbco	2-18-94	4-1-94	8,000	4,000

83. In 1992, Joan received an acre of land as an inter-vivos gift from her grandfather. At the time of the gift, the land had a fair market value of $50,000. The grandfather's adjusted basis was $60,000. Joan sold the land in 1994 to an unrelated third party for $56,000.

84. The Moores received a $500 security deposit on their rental property in 1994. They are required to return the amount to the tenant.

85. Tom's 1994 wages were $53,000. In addition, Tom's employer provided group-term life insurance on Tom's life in excess of $50,000. The value of such excess coverage was $2,000.

86. During 1994, the Moores received a $2,500 federal tax refund and a $1,250 state tax refund for 1993 overpayments. In 1993, the Moores were not subject to the alternative minimum tax and were not entitled to any credit against income tax. The Moores' 1993 adjusted gross income was $80,000 and itemized deductions were $1,450 in excess of the standard deduction. The state tax deduction for 1993 was $2,000.

87. In 1994, Joan received $1,300 in unemployment compensation benefits. Her employer made a $100 contribution to the unemployment insurance fund on her behalf.

88. The Moores received $8,400 in gross receipts from their rental property during 1994. The expenses for the residential rental property were:

Bank mortgage interest	$1,200
Real estate taxes	700
Insurance	500
MACRS depreciation	3,500

89. The Moores received a stock dividend in 1994 from Ace Corp. They had the option to receive either cash or Ace stock with a fair market value of $900 as of the date of distribution. The par value of the stock was $500.

90. In 1994, Joan received $3,500 as beneficiary of the death benefit that was provided by her brother's employer. Joan's brother did not have a nonforfeitable right to receive the money while living.

91. Tom received $10,000, consisting of $5,000 each of principal and interest, when he redeemed a Series EE savings bond in 1994. The bond was issued in his name in 1987 and the proceeds were used to pay for Laura's college tuition. Tom had not elected to report the yearly increases in the value of the bond.

Required:

b. For **Item 92,** determine the amount of the adjustment, if any, to arrive at adjusted gross income. To record your answer, blacken the ovals on the Objective Answer Sheet. If zeros precede your numerical answer, blacken the zeros in the ovals preceding your answer. **Your cannot receive credit for your answers if you fail to blacken an oval in each column.** You may write the numbers in the boxes provided to facilitate blackening the ovals; however, the numbers written in the boxes will **not** be graded.

92. As required by a 1990 divorce agreement, Tom paid an annual amount of $8,000 in alimony and $10,000 in child support during 1994.

Required:

c. During 1994, the following events took place. For **Items 93 to 104,** select the appropriate tax treatment and blacken the corresponding oval on the Objective Answer Sheet. A tax treatment may be selected once, more than once, or not at all.

Required:

d. For **Items 105 to 110,** indicate if the statement is true (T) or false (F) regarding the Moores' 1994 tax return. Blacken the corresponding oval on the Objective Answer Sheet.

Event

93. On March 23, 1994, Tom sold 50 shares of Zip stock at a $1,200 loss. He repurchased 50 shares of Zip on April 15, 1994.
94. Payment of a personal property tax based on the value of the Moores' car.
95. Used clothes were donated to church organizations.
96. Premiums were paid covering insurance against Tom's loss of earnings.
97. Tom paid for subscriptions to accounting journals.
98. Interest was paid on a $10,000 home-equity line of credit secured by the Moores' residence. The fair market value of the home exceeded the mortgage by $50,000. Tom used the proceeds to purchase a sailboat.
99. Amounts were paid in excess of insurance reimbursement for prescription drugs.
100. Funeral expenses were paid by the Moores for Joan's brother.
101. Theft loss was incurred on Joan's jewelry in excess of insurance reimbursement. There were no 1994 personal casualty gains.
102. Loss on the sale of the family's sailboat.
103. Interest was paid on the $300,000 acquisition mortgage on the Moores' home. The mortgage is secured by their home.
104. Joan performed free accounting services for the Red Cross. The estimated value of the services was $500.

Tax Treatment

(A) Not deductible on Form 1040.
(B) Deductible in full in Schedule A-Itemized Deductions.
(C) Deductible in Schedule A-Itemized Deductions, subject to a threshold of 7.5% of adjusted gross income.
(D) Deductible in Schedule A-Itemized Deductions, subject to a limitation of 50% of adjusted gross income.
(E) Deductible in Schedule A-Itemized Deductions, subject to a $100 floor and a threshold of 10% of adjusted gross income.
(F) Deductible in Schedule A-Itemized Deductions, subject to a threshold of 2% of adjusted gross income.

105. For 1994, the Moores were subject to the phaseout of half their personal exemptions for regular tax because their adjusted gross income was $75,000.

106. The Moores' unreimbursed medical expenses for AMT had to exceed 10% of adjusted gross income.

107. The Moores' personal exemption amount for regular tax was not permitted for determining 1994 AMT.

108. The Moores paid $1,200 in additional 1994 taxes when they filed their return on Friday, April 14, 1995. Their 1994 federal tax withholdings equaled 100% of 1993 tax liability. Therefore, they were not subject to the underpayment of tax penalty.

109. The Moores, both being under age 50, were subject to an early withdrawal penalty on their IRA withdrawals used for medical expenses.

110. The Moores were allowed an earned income credit against their 1994 tax liability equal to a percentage of their wages.

Number 4

Question Number 4 consists of six items. Select the **best** answer for each item. Use a No. 2 pencil to blacken the appropriate ovals on the Objective Answer Sheet to indicate your answers. **Answer all items.** Your grade will be based on the total number of correct answers.

Alpha Hospital, a large not-for-profit organization, has adopted an accounting policy that does not imply a time restriction on gifts of long-lived assets.

Required:

For **Items 111 through 116,** indicate, by blackening the corresponding oval on the Objective Answer Sheet, the manner in which the transaction affects Alpha's financial statements.

(A) Increase in unrestricted revenues, gains, and other support.
(B) Decrease in an expense.
(C) Increase in temporarily restricted net assets.
(D) Increase in permanently restricted net assets.
(E) No required reportable event.

111. Alpha's board designates $1,000,000 to purchase investments whose income will be used for capital improvements.

112. Income from investments in item 111 above, which was not previously accrued, is received.

113. A benefactor provided funds for building expansion.

114. The funds in item 113 above are used to purchase a building in the fiscal period following the period the funds were received.

115. An accounting firm prepared Alpha's annual financial statements without charge to Alpha.

116. Alpha received investments subject to the donor's requirement that investment income be used to pay for outpatient services.

Number 5

Question Number 5 consists of 10 items. Select the **best** answer for each item. Use a No. 2 pencil to blacken the appropriate ovals on the Objective Answer Sheet to indicate your answers. **Answer all items.** Your grade will be based on the total number of correct answers.

The following information relates to Dane City during its fiscal year ended December 31, 1994:

* On October 31, 1994, to finance the construction of a city hall annex, Dane issued 8% 10-year general obligation bonds at their face value of $600,000. Construction expenditures during the period equaled $364,000.
* Dane reported $109,000 from hotel room taxes, restricted for tourist promotion, in a special revenue fund. The fund paid $81,000 for general promotions and $22,000 for a motor vehicle.
* 1994 general fund revenues of $104,500 were transferred to a debt service fund and used to repay $100,000 of 9% 15-year term bonds, and to pay $4,500 of interest. The bonds were used to acquire a citizens' center.
* At December 31, 1994, as a consequence of past services, city firefighters had accumulated entitlements to compensated absences valued at $86,000. General fund resources available at December 31, 1994, are expected to be used to settle $17,000 of this amount, and $69,000 is expected to be paid out of future general fund resources.

- At December 31, 1994, Dane was responsible for $83,000 of outstanding general fund encumbrances, including the $8,000 for supplies indicated below.
- Dane uses the purchases method to account for supplies. The following information relates to supplies:

Inventory—	1/1/94	$ 39,000
	12/31/94	42,000
Encumbrances outstanding—		
1/1/94		6,000
12/31/94		8,000
Purchase orders during 1994		190,000
Amounts credited to vouchers payable during 1994		181,000

Required:

For **Items 117 through 126,** determine the amounts based solely on the preceeding information. To record your answer, blacken the ovals on the Objective Answer Sheet. If zeros precede your numerical answer, blacken the zeros in the ovals preceding your answer. **You cannot receive credit for your answers if you fail to blacken an oval in each column.** You may write the numbers in the boxes provided to facilitate blackening the ovals; however, the numbers written in the boxes will **not** be graded.

117. What is the amount of 1994 general fund operating transfers out?

118. How much should be reported as 1994 general fund liabilities from entitlements for compensated absences?

119. What is the 1994 reserved amount of the general fund balance?

120. What is the 1994 capital projects fund balance?

121. What is the 1994 fund balance on the special revenue fund for tourist promotion?

122. What is the amount of 1994 debt service fund expenditures?

123. What amount should be included in the general fixed assets account group for the cost of assets acquired in 1994?

124. What amount stemming from 1994 transactions and events decreased the liabilities reported in the general long-term debt account group?

125. Using the purchases method, what is the amount of 1994 supplies expenditures?

126. What was the total amount of 1994 supplies encumbrances?

UNIFORM CERTIFIED PUBLIC ACCOUNTANT EXAMINATION
Financial Accounting & Reporting—Business Enterprises

The point values for each question, and estimated time allotments based primarily on point value, are as follows:

	Point Value	Estimated Minutes Minimum	Estimated Minutes Maximum
No. 1	60	130	140
No. 2	10	15	25
No. 3	10	15	25
No. 4	10	30	40
No. 5	10	30	40
Totals	100	220	270

FARE

November 2, 1995; 1:30 P.M. to 6:00 P.M.

INSTRUCTIONS TO CANDIDATES *Failure to follow these instructions may have an adverse effect on your Examination grade.*

1. Do not break the seal around the *Examination Questions* (pages 3 through 26) until you are told to do so.

2. Question Numbers 1, 2, and 3 should be answered on the *Objective Answer Sheet*, which is pages 35 and 36. You should attempt to answer all objective items. There is no penalty for incorrect responses. Work space to solve the objective questions is provided in the *Examination Questions* on pages 5 through 21. Since the objective items are computer-graded, your comments and calculations associated with them are not considered. Be certain that you have entered your answers on the *Objective Answer Sheet* before the examination time is up. The objective portion of your examination will not be graded if you fail to record your answers on the *Objective Answer Sheet*. You will not be given additional time to record your answers.

3. Question Numbers 4 and 5 should be answered beginning on page 27. Support **all** answers with properly labeled and legible calculations that can be identified as sources of amounts used to derive your final answer. If you have not completed answering a question on a page, fill in the appropriate spaces in the wording on the bottom of the page **"QUESTION NUMBER ___ CONTINUES ON PAGE ___ ."** If you have completed answering a question, fill in the appropriate space in the wording on the bottom of the page **"QUESTION NUMBER ___ ENDS ON THIS PAGE."** Always begin the start of an answer to a question on the top of a new page (which may be the reverse side of a sheet of paper). Use the entire width of the page to answer requirements of a noncomputational nature. To answer requirements of a computational nature, you may wish to use the three vertical columns provided on the right side of each page.

4. Although the primary purpose of the examination is to test your knowledge and application of the subject matter, selected essay responses will be graded for writing skills.

5. You are required to turn in by the end of each session:

   a. Attendance Record and Calculator Sign-off Record Form, page 1;
   b. *Examination Questions*, pages 3 through 26;
   c. *Essay Ruled Paper*, pages 27 through 34;
   d. *Objective Answer Sheet*, pages 35 and 36;
   e. Calculator; and
   f. All unused examination materials.

Your examination will not be graded unless the above listed items are handed in before leaving the examination room.

Examination Questions Booklet No.

3 73922 Q

Financial Accounting & Reporting (FARE)

Number 1

Instructions

Select the **best** answer for each of the following items. Use a No. 2 pencil to blacken the appropriate ovals on the Objective Answer Sheet to indicate your answers. **Mark only one answer for each item. Answer all items.** Your grade will be based on the total number of correct answers.

1. According to the FASB conceptual framework, the objectives of financial reporting for business enterprises are based on
   A. Generally accepted accounting principles.
   B. Reporting on management's stewardship.
   C. The need for conservatism.
   D. The needs of the users of the information.

2. According to the FASB conceptual framework, the usefulness of providing information in financial statements is subject to the constraint of
   A. Consistency.
   B. Cost-benefit.
   C. Reliability.
   D. Representational faithfulness.

3. What is the underlying concept governing the generally accepted accounting principles pertaining to recording gain contingencies?
   A. Conservatism.
   B. Relevance.
   C. Consistency.
   D. Reliability.

4. A development state enterprise should use the same generally accepted accounting principles that apply to established operating enterprises for

	Revenue recognition	Deferral of expenses
A.	Yes	Yes
B.	Yes	No
C.	No	No
D.	No	Yes

5. According to the FASB conceptual framework, which of the following attributes would **not** be used to measure inventory?
   A. Historical cost.
   B. Replacement cost.
   C. Net realizable value.
   D. Present value of future cash flows.

6. Conceptually, interim financial statements can be described as emphasizing
   A. Timeliness over reliability.
   B. Reliability over relevance.
   C. Relevance over comparability.
   D. Comparability over neutrality.

7. For which type of material related-party transactions does Statement of Financial Accounting Standard No. 57, "Related Party Disclosures," require disclosure?
   A. Only those not reported in the body of the financial statements.
   B. Only those that receive accounting recognition.
   C. Those that contain possible illegal acts.
   D. All those other than compensation arrangements, expense allowances, and other similar items in the ordinary course of business.

8. Terra Co.'s total revenue from its three business segments were as follows:

Segment	Sales to unaffiliated customers	Inter-segment sales	Total revenues
Lion	$ 70,000	$30,000	$100,000
Monk	22,000	4,000	26,000
Nevi	8,000	16,000	24,000
Combined	$100,000	$50,000	$150,000
Elimination	—	(50,000)	(50,000)
Consolidation	$100,000	$ —	$100,000

Which business segment(s) is(are) deemed to be reportable segments?
   A. None.
   B. Lion only.
   C. Lion and Monk only.
   D. Lion, Monk, and Nevi.

9. A company decided to change its inventory valuation method from FIFO to LIFO in a period of rising prices. What was the result of the change on ending inventory and net income in the year of the change?

	Ending Inventory	*Net income*
A.	Increase	Increase
B.	Increase	Decrease
C.	Decrease	Decrease
D.	Decrease	Increase

10. Lang Co. uses the installment method of revenue recognition. The following data pertain to Lang's installment sales for the years ended December 31, 1993 and 1994:

	1993	1994
Installment receivables at year-end on 1993 sales	$60,000	$30,000
Installment receivables at year-end on 1994 sales	—	69,000
Installment sales	80,000	90,000
Cost of sales	40,000	60,000

What amount should Lang report as deferred gross profit in its December 31, 1994, balance sheet?

A. $23,000
B. $33,000
C. $38,000
D. $43,000

11. In a sale-leaseback transaction, a gain resulting from the sale should be deferred at the time of the sale-leaseback and subsequently amortized when

I. The seller-lessee has transferred substantially all the risks of ownership.
II. The seller-lessee retains the right to substantially all of the remaining use of the property.

A. I only.
B. II only.
C. Both I and II.
D. Neither I nor II.

12. A six-year capital lease entered into on December 31, 1994, specified equal minimum annual lease payments due on December 31 of each year. The first minimum annual lease payment, paid on December 31, 1994, consists of which of the following?

	Interest expense	*Lease liability*
A.	Yes	Yes
B.	Yes	No
C.	No	Yes
D.	No	No

13. Lime Co.'s payroll for the month ended January 31, 1995, is summarized as follows:

Total wages	$10,000
Federal income tax withheld	1,200

All wages paid were subject to FICA. FICA tax rates were 7% each for employee and employer. Lime remits payroll taxes on the 15th of the following month. In its financial statements for the month ended January 31, 1995, what amount should Lime report as total payroll tax liability and as payroll tax expense?

	Liability	*Expense*
A.	$1,200	$1,400
B.	$1,900	$1,400
C.	$1,900	$ 700
D.	$2,600	$ 700

Items 14 and 15 are based on the following:

The following information pertains to Hall Co.'s defined-benefit pension plan at December 31, 1994:

Unfunded accumulated benefit obligation	$25,000
Unrecognized prior service cost	12,000
Net periodic pension cost	8,000

Hall made no contributions to the pension plan during 1994.

14. At December 31, 1994, what amount should Hall record as additional pension liability?

A. $ 5,000
B. $13,000
C. $17,000
D. $25,000

15. In its December 31, 1994, statement of stockholders' equity, what amount should Hall report as excess of additional pension liability over unrecognized prior service cost?

A. $ 5,000
B. $13,000
C. $17,000
D. $25,000

16. On March 1, 1993, Fine Co. borrowed $10,000 and signed a two-year note bearing interest at 12% per annum compounded annually. Interest is payable in full at maturity on February 28, 1995. What amount should Fine report as a liability for accrued interest at December 31, 1994?

A. $0
B. $1,000
C. $1,200
D. $2,320

17. Eagle Co. has cosigned the mortgage note on the home of its president, guaranteeing the indebtedness in the event that the president should default. Eagle considers the likelihood of default to be remote. How should the guarantee be treated in Eagle's financial statements?

A. Disclosed only.
B. Accrued only.
C. Accrued and disclosed.
D. Neither accrued nor disclosed.

18. Nest Co. issued 100,000 shares of common stock. Of these, 5,000 were held as treasury stock at December 31, 1993. During 1994, transactions involving Nest's common stock were as follows:

May 3	—1,000 shares of treasury stock were sold.
August 6	—10,000 shares of previously unissued stock were sold.
November 18	—A 2-for-1 stock split took effect.

Laws in Nest's state of incorporation protect treasury stock from dilution. At December 31, 1994, how many shares of Nest's common stock were issued and outstanding?

	Shares	
	Issued	Outstanding
A.	220,000	212,000
B.	220,000	216,000
C.	222,000	214,000
D.	222,000	218,000

19. Cyan Corp. issued 20,000 shares of $5 par common stock at $10 per share. On December 31, 1993, Cyan's retained earnings were $300,000. In March 1994, Cyan reacquired 5,000 shares of its common stock at $20 per share. In June 1994, Cyan sold 1,000 of these shares to its corporate officers for $25 per share. Cyan uses the cost method to record treasury stock. Net income for the year ended December 31, 1994, was $60,000. At December 31, 1994, what amount should Cyan report as retained earnings?

A. $360,000
B. $365,000
C. $375,000
D. $380,000

20. Asp Co. was organized on January 2, 1994, with 30,000 authorized shares of $10 par common stock. During 1994 the corporation had the following capital transactions:

January 5	—issued 20,000 shares at $15 per share.
July 14	—purchased 5,000 shares at $17 per share.
December 27	—reissued the 5,000 shares held in treasury at $20 per share.

Asp used the par value method to record the purchase and reissuance of the treasury shares. In its December 31, 1994, balance sheet, what amount should Asp report as additional paid-in-capital in excess of par?

A. $100,000
B. $125,000
C. $140,000
D. $150,000

21. A company issued rights to its existing shareholders without consideration. The rights allowed the recipients to purchase unissued common stock for an amount in excess of par value. When the rights are issued, which of the following accounts will be increased?

	Common stock	Additional paid-in capital
A.	Yes	Yes
B.	Yes	No
C.	No	No
D.	No	Yes

22. In September 1989, West Corp. made a dividend distribution of one right for each of its 120,000 shares of outstanding common stock. Each right was exercisable for the purchase of 1/100 of a share of West's $50 variable rate preferred stock at an exercise price of $80 per share. On March 20, 1993, none of the rights had been exercised, and West redeemed them by paying each stockholder $0.10 per right. As a result of this redemption, West's stockholders' equity was reduced by
A. $ 120
B. $ 2,400
C. $12,000
D. $36,000

23. During 1994, Young and Zinc maintained average capital balances in their partnership of $160,000 and $100,000, respectively. The partners received 10% interest on average capital balances, and residual profit or loss is divided equally. Partnership profit before interest was $4,000. By what amount should Zinc's capital account change for the year?
A. $ 1,000 decrease.
B. $ 2,000 increase.
C. $11,000 decrease.
D. $12,000 increase.

24. On February 1, 1995, Tory began a service proprietorship with an initial cash investment of $2,000. The proprietorship provided $5,000 of services in February and received full payment in March. The proprietorship incurred expenses of $3,000 in February, which were paid in April. During March, Tory drew $1,000 against the capital account. In the proprietorship's financial statements for the two months ended March 31, 1995, prepared under the cash basis method of accounting, what amount should be reported as capital?
A. $1,000
B. $3,000
C. $6,000
D. $7,000

25. The stockholders' equity section of Brown Co.'s December 31, 1994, balance sheet consisted of the following:

Common stock, $30 par, 10,000 shares authorized and outstanding	$ 300,000
Additional paid-in capital	150,000
Retained earnings (deficit)	(210,000)

On January 2, 1995, Brown put into effect a stockholder-approved quasi-reorganization by reducing the par value of the stock to $5 and eliminating the deficit against additional paid-in capital. Immediately after the quasi-reorganization, what amount should Brown report as additional paid-in capital?
A. $ (60,000)
B. $150,000
C. $190,000
D. $400,000

Items 26 through 28 are based on the following:

Grant, Inc. acquired 30% of South Co.'s voting stock for $200,000 on January 2, 1993. Grant's 30% interest in South gave Grant the ability to exercise significant influence over South's operating and financial policies. During 1993, South earned $80,000 and paid dividends of $50,000. South reported earnings of $100,000 for the six months ended June 30, 1994, and $200,000 for the year ended December 31, 1994. On July 1, 1994, Grant sold half of its stock in South for $150,000 cash. South paid dividends of $60,000 on October 1, 1994.

26. Before income taxes, what amount should Grant include in its 1993 income statement as a result of the investment?
A. $15,000
B. $24,000
C. $50,000
D. $80,000

27. In Grant's December 31, 1993, balance sheet, what should be the carrying amount of this investment?
A. $200,000
B. $209,000
C. $224,000
D. $230,000

28. In its 1994 income statement, what amount should Grant report as gain from the sale of half of its investment?
- A. $24,500
- B. $30,500
- C. $35,000
- D. $45,500

29. Glade Co. leases computer equipment to customers under direct-financing leases. The equipment has no residual value at the end of the lease and the leases do not contain bargain purchase options. Glade wishes to earn 8% interest on a five-year lease of equipment with a fair value of $323,400. The present value of an annuity due of $1 at 8% for five years is 4.312. What is the total amount of interest revenue that Glade will earn over the life of the lease?
- A. $ 51,600
- B. $ 75,000
- C. $129,360
- D. $139,450

30. Rill Co. owns a 20% royalty interest in an oil well. Rill receives royalty payments on January 31 for the oil sold between the previous June 1 and November 30, and on July 31 for oil sold between the previous December 1 and May 31. Production reports show the following oil sales:

June 1, 1993—November 30, 1993	$300,000
December 1, 1993—December 31, 1993	50,000
December 1, 1993—May 31, 1994	400,000
June 1, 1994—November 30, 1994	325,000
December 1, 1994—December 31, 1994	70,000

What amount should Rill report as royalty revenue for 1994?
- A. $140,000
- B. $144,000
- C. $149,000
- D. $159,000

31. It is proper to recognize revenue prior to the sale of merchandise when

I. The revenue will be reported as an installment sale.
II. The revenue will be reported under the cost recovery method.

- A. I only.
- B. II only.
- C. Both I and II.
- D. Neither I nor II.

32. Fogg Co., a U.S. company, contracted to purchase foreign goods. Payment in foreign currency was due one month after the goods were received at Fogg's warehouse. Between the receipt of goods and the time of payment, the exchange rates changed in Fogg's favor. The resulting gain should be included in Fogg's financial statements as a(an)
- A. Component of income from continuing operations.
- B. Extraordinary item.
- C. Deferred credit.
- D. Separate component of stockholders' equity.

33. Gray Co. was granted a patent on January 2, 1991, and appropriately capitalized $45,000 of related costs. Gray was amortizing the patent over its estimated useful life of 15 years. During 1994, Gray paid $15,000 in legal costs in successfully defending an attempted infringement of the patent. After the legal action was completed, Gray sold the patent to the plaintiff for $75,000. Gray's policy is to take no amortization in the year of disposal. In its 1994 income statement, what amount should Gray report as gain from sale of patent?
- A. $15,000
- B. $24,000
- C. $27,000
- D. $39,000

34. When should a lessor recognize in income a nonrefundable lease bonus paid by a lessee on signing an operating lease?
- A. When received.
- B. At the inception of the lease.
- C. At the expiration of the lease.
- D. Over the life of the lease.

35. Upon the death of an officer, Jung Co. received the proceeds of a life insurance policy held by Jung on the officer. The proceeds were not taxable. The policy's cash surrender value had been recorded on Jung's books at the time of payment. What amount of revenue should Jung report in its statements?
- A. Proceeds received.
- B. Proceeds received less cash surrender value.
- C. Proceeds received plus cash surrender value.
- D. None.

36. On its December 31, 1994, balance sheet, Shin Co. had income taxes payable of $13,000 and a current deferred tax asset of $20,000 before determining the need for a valuation account. Shin had reported a current deferred tax asset of $15,000 at December 31, 1993. No estimated tax payments were made during 1994. At December 31, 1994, Shin determined that it was more likely than not that 10% of the deferred tax asset would not be realized. In its 1994 income statement, what amount should Shin report as total income tax expense?

 A. $ 8,000
 B. $ 8,500
 C. $10,000
 D. $13,000

Items 37 and 38 are based on the following:

Zeff Co. prepared the following reconciliation of its pretax financial statement income to taxable income for the year ended December 31, 1994, its first year of operations:

Pretax financial income	$160,000
Nontaxable interest received on municipal securities	(5,000)
Long-term loss accrual in excess of deductible amount	10,000
Depreciation in excess of financial statement amount	(25,000)
Taxable income	$140,000

Zeff's tax rate for 1994 is 40 percent.

37. In its 1994 income statement, what amount should Zeff report as income tax expense—current portion?

 A. $52,000
 B. $56,000
 C. $62,000
 D. $64,000

38. In its December 31, 1994, balance sheet, what should Zeff report as deferred income tax liability?

 A. $2,000
 B. $4,000
 C. $6,000
 D. $8,000

39. During January 1993, Doe Corp. agreed to sell the assets and product line of its Hart division. The sale was completed on January 15, 1994, and resulted in a gain on disposal of $900,000. Hart's operating losses were $600,000 for 1993 and $50,000 for the period January 1 through January 15, 1994. Disregarding income taxes, what amount of net gain (loss) should be reported in Doe's comparative 1994 and 1993 income statements?

	1994	1993
A.	$0	$ 250,000
B.	$250,000	$ 0
C.	$850,000	$(600,000)
D.	$900,000	$(650,000)

40. On April 30, 1994, Deer Corp. approved a plan to dispose of a segment of its business. For the period January 1 through April 30, 1994, the segment had revenues of $500,000 and expenses of $800,000. The assets of the segment were sold on October 15, 1994, at a loss for which no tax benefit is available. In its income statement for the year ended December 31, 1994, how should Deer report the segment's operations from January 1 to April 30, 1994?

 A. $500,000 and $800,000 should be included with revenues and expenses, respectively, as part of continuing operations.
 B. $300,000 should be reported as part of the loss on disposal of a segment.
 C. $300,000 should be reported as an extraordinary loss.
 D. $300,000 should be reported as a loss from operations of a discontinued segment.

41. In open market transactions, Gold Corp. simultaneously sold its long-term investment in Iron Corp. bonds and purchased its own outstanding bonds. The broker remitted the net cash from the two transactions. Gold's gain on the purchase of its own bonds exceeded its loss on the sale of the Iron bonds. Gold should report the
  A. Net effect of the two transactions as an extraordinary gain.
  B. Net effect of the two transactions in income before extraordinary items.
  C. Effect of its own bond transaction gain in income before extraordinary items, and report the Iron bond transaction as an extraordinary loss.
  D. Effect of its own bond transaction as an extraordinary gain, and report the Iron bond transaction loss in income before extraordinary items.

42. During 1994 both Raim Co. and Cane Co. suffered losses due to the flooding of the Mississippi River. Raim is located two miles from the river and sustains flood losses every two to three years. Cane, which has been located fifty miles from the river for the past twenty years, has never before had flood losses. How should the flood losses be reported in each company's 1994 income statement?

	Raim	Cane
A.	As a component of income from continuing operations	As an extraordinary item
B.	As a component of income from continuing operations	As a component of income from continuing operations
C.	As an extraordinary item	As a component of income from continuing operations
D.	As an extraordinary item	As an extraordinary item

43. Lore Co. changed from the cash basis of accounting to the accrual basis of accounting during 1994. The cumulative effect of this change should be reported in Lore's 1994 financial statements as a
  A. Prior period adjustment resulting from the correction of an error.
  B. Prior period adjustment resulting from the change in accounting principle.
  C. Component of income before extraordinary item.
  D. Component of income after extraordinary item.

44. Oak Co. offers a three-year warranty on its products. Oak previously estimated warranty costs to be 2% of sales. Due to a technological advance in production at the beginning of 1994, Oak now believes 1% of sales to be a better estimate of warranty costs. Warranty costs of $80,000 and $96,000 were reported in 1992 and 1993, respectively. Sales for 1994 were $5,000,000. What amount should be disclosed in Oak's 1994 financial statements as warranty expense?
  A. $ 50,000
  B. $ 88,000
  C. $100,000
  D. $138,000

45. Ute Co. had the following capital structure during 1993 and 1994:

Preferred stock, $10 par, 4% cumulative, 25,000 shares issued and outstanding	$250,000
Common stock, $5 par, 200,000 shares issued and outstanding	1,000,000

Preferred stock is not convertible into common stock. Ute reported net income of $500,000 for the year ended December 31, 1994. Ute paid no preferred dividends during 1993 and paid $16,000 in preferred dividends during 1994. Assume Ute adopted FASB Statement #128, "Earnings Per Share." In its December 31, 1994, income statement, what amount should Ute report as basic earnings per share?
  A. $2.42
  B. $2.45
  C. $2.48
  D. $2.50

46. West Co. had basic earnings per share of $15.00 for 1994 before considering the effects of any convertible securities. No conversion or exercise of convertible securities occurred during 1994. However, possible conversion of convertible bonds would have reduced earnings per share by $0.75. The effect of possible exercise of common stock options would have increased earnings per share by $0.10. According to FASB Statement #128, "Earnings Per Share," what amount should West report as diluted earnings per share for 1994?

    A. $14.25
    B. $14.35
    C. $15.00
    D. $15.10

47. Mend Co. purchased a three-month U.S. Treasury bill. Mend's policy is to treat as cash equivalents all highly liquid investments with an original maturity of three months or less when purchased. How should this purchase be reported in Mend's statement of cash flows?

    A. As an outflow from operating activities.
    B. As an outflow from investing activities.
    C. As an outflow from financing activities.
    D. Not reported.

48. Which of the following is **not** disclosed on the statement of cash flows when prepared under the direct method, either on the face of the statement or in a separate schedule?

    A. The major classes of gross cash receipts and gross cash payments.
    B. The amount of income taxes paid.
    C. A reconciliation of net income to net cash flow from operations.
    D. A reconciliation of ending retained earnings to net cash flow from operations.

Items 49 through 51 are based on the following:

On January 2, 1994, Pare Co. purchased 75% of Kidd Co.'s outstanding common stock. Selected balance sheet data at December 31, 1994, is as follows:

	Pare	Kidd
Total assets	$420,000	$180,000
Liabilities	$120,000	$ 60,000
Common stock	100,000	50,000
Retained earnings	200,000	70,000
	$420,000	$180,000

During 1994, Pare and Kidd paid cash dividends of $25,000 and $5,000, respectively, to their shareholders. There were no other intercompany transactions.

49. In its December 31, 1994, consolidated statement of retained earnings, what amount should Pare report as dividends paid?

    A. $ 5,000
    B. $25,000
    C. $26,250
    D. $30,000

50. In Pare's December 31, 1994, consolidated balance sheet, what amount should be reported as minority interest in net assets?

    A. $0
    B. $ 30,000
    C. $ 45,000
    D. $105,000

51. In its December 31, 1994, consolidated balance sheet, what amount should Pare report as common stock?

    A. $ 50,000
    B. $100,000
    C. $137,500
    D. $150,000

52. In a business combination, how should long-term debt of the acquired company generally be reported under each of the following methods?

	Pooling of interest	Purchase
A.	Fair value	Carrying amount
B.	Fair value	Fair value
C.	Carrying amount	Fair value
D.	Carrying amount	Carrying amount

53. In a business combination accounted for as a purchase, the appraised values of the identifiable assets acquired exceeded the acquisition price. How should the excess appraised value be reported?

    A. As negative goodwill.
    B. As additional paid-in capital.
    C. As a reduction of the values assigned to noncurrent assets and a deferred credit for any unallocated portion.
    D. As positive goodwill.

54. A business interest that constitutes a large part of an individual's total assets should be presented in a personal statement of financial condition as

- A. A separate listing of the individual assets and liabilities at cost.
- B. Separate line items of both total assets and total liabilities at cost.
- C. A single amount equal to the proprietorship equity.
- D. A single amount equal to the estimated current value of the business interest.

55. Quinn is preparing a personal statement of financial condition as of April. 30, 1995. Included in Quinn's assets are the following:

- 50% of the voting stock of Ink Corp. A stockholders' agreement restricts the sale of the stock and, under certain circumstances, requires Ink to repurchase the stock. Quinn's tax basis for the stock is $430,000, and at April 30, 1995, the buyout value is $675,000.
- Jewelry with a fair value aggregating $70,000 based on an independent appraisal on April 30, 1995, for insurance purposes. This jewelry was acquired by purchase and gift over a 10-year period and has a total tax basis of $40,000.

What is the total amount at which the Ink stock and jewelry should be reported in Quinn's April 30, 1995, personal statement of financial condition?

- A. $470,000
- B. $500,000
- C. $715,000
- D. $745,000

56. In financial statements prepared on the income-tax basis, how should the nondeductible portion of expenses such as meals and entertainment be reported?

- A. Included in the expense category in the determination of income.
- B. Included in a separate category in the determination of income.
- C. Excluded from the determination of income but included in the determination of retained earnings.
- D. Excluded from the financial statements.

57. Financial statements prepared under which of the following methods include adjustments for both specific price changes and general price-level changes?

- A. Historical cost/nominal dollar.
- B. Current cost/nominal dollar.
- C. Current cost/constant dollar.
- D. Historical cost/constant dollar.

58. What effect would the sale of a company's trading securities at their carrying amounts for cash have on each of the following ratios?

	Current ratio	Quick ratio
A.	No effect	No effect
B.	Increase	Increase
C.	No effect	Increase
D.	Increase	No effect

59. Barr Co. has total debt of $420,000 and stockholders' equity of $700,000. Barr is seeking capital to fund an expansion. Barr is planning to issue an additional $300,000 in common stock, and is negotiating with a bank to borrow additional funds. The bank is requiring a debt-to-equity ratio of .75. What is the maximum additional amount Barr will be able to borrow?

- A. $225,000
- B. $330,000
- C. $525,000
- D. $750,000

60. The following data pertain to Cowl, Inc., for the year ended December 31, 1994:

Net sales	$ 600,000
Net income	150,000
Total assets, January 1, 1994	2,000,000
Total assets, December 31, 1994	3,000,000

What was Cowl's rate of return on assets for 1994?

- A. 5%
- B. 6%
- C. 20%
- D. 24%

Number 2

Question Number 2 consists of 10 items. Select the **best** answer for each item. Use a No. 2 pencil to blacken the appropriate ovals on the Objective Answer Sheet to indicate your answers. **Answer all items.** Your grade will be based on the total number of correct answers.

Items 61 through 64 are based on the following:

Camp Co. purchased various securities during 1994 to be classified as held-to-maturity securities, trading securities, or available-for-sale securities.

Required:

Items 61 through 64 describe various securities purchased by Camp. For each item, select from the following list the appropriate category for each security and blacken the corresponding oval on the Objective Answer Sheet. A category may be used once, more than once, or not at all.

Categories	
(H)	Held-to-maturity
(T)	Trading
(A)	Available-for-sale

61. Debt securities bought and held for the purpose of selling in the near term.

62. U.S. Treasury bonds that Camp has both the positive intent and the ability to hold to maturity.

63. $3 million debt security bought and held for the purpose of selling in three years to finance payment of Camp's $2 million long-term note payable when it matures.

64. Convertible preferred stock that Camp does not intend to sell in the near term.

The following information pertains to Dayle, Inc.'s portfolio of marketable investments for the year ended December 31, 1994:

	COST	FAIR VALUE, 12/31/93	1994 ACTIVITY PURCHASES	1994 ACTIVITY SALES	FAIR VALUE 12/31/94
Held-to-maturity securities					
Security ABC			$100,000		$ 95,000
Trading securities					
Security DEF	$150,000	$160,000			155,000
Available-for-sale securities					
Security GHI	190,000	165,000		$175,000	
Security JKL	170,000	175,000			160,000

Security ABC was purchased at par. All declines in fair value are considered to be temporary.

Items 65 through 70 are based on the above table.

Required:

Items 65 through 70 describe amounts to be reported in Dayle's 1994 financial statements. For each item, select from the following list the correct numerical response and blacken the corresponding oval on the Objective Answer Sheet. An amount may be selected once, more than once, or not at all. Ignore income tax considerations.

65. Carrying amount of security ABC at December 31, 1994.

66. Carrying amount of security DEF at December 31, 1994.

67. Carrying amount of security JKL at December 31 1994.

Items 68 through 70 require a second response. For each item, indicate whether a gain (G) or a loss (L) is to be reported and blacken the corresponding oval on the Objective Answer Sheet.

68. Recognized gain or loss on sale of security GHI.

69. Unrealized gain or loss to be reported in 1994 income statement.

70. Unrealized gain or loss to be reported at December 31, 1994, as a separate component of stockholders' equity.

Answer List	
(A)	$0
(B)	$ 5,000
(C)	$ 10,000
(D)	$ 15,000
(E)	$ 25,000
(F)	$ 95,000
(G)	$100,000
(H)	$150,000
(I)	$155,000
(J)	$160,000
(K)	$170,000

Number 3

Question Number 3 consists of 13 items. Select the **best** answer for each item. Use a No. 2 pencil to blacken the appropriate ovals on the Objective Answer Sheet to indicate your answers. **Answer all items.** Your grade will be based on the total number of correct answers.

Items 71 through 77 are based on the following:

On January 2, 1994, North Co. issued bonds payable with a face value of $480,000 at a discount. The bonds are due in 10 years and interest is payable semiannually every June 30 and December 31. On June 30, 1994, and on December 31, 1994, North made the semiannual interest payments due, and recorded interest expense and amortization of bond discount.

Required:

Items 71 through 77, contained in the partially completed amortization table that follows, represent information needed to complete the table. For each item, select from the following boxed lists (A–X) the correct numerical response and blacken the corresponding oval on the Objective Answer Sheet. A response may be selected once, more than once, or not at all.

Rates	
(A)	3.0%
(B)	4.5%
(C)	5.0%
(D)	6.0%
(E)	9.0%
(F)	10.0%

Amounts			
(G)	$ 3,420	(P)	$ 21,600
(H)	$ 3,600	(Q)	$116,400
(I)	$ 3,780	(R)	$120,000
(J)	$ 3,960	(S)	$123,600
(K)	$14,400	(T)	$360,000
(L)	$17,820	(U)	$363,600
(M)	$18,000	(V)	$367,200
(N)	$18,180	(W)	$467,400
(O)	$18,360	(X)	$480,000

	CASH	INTEREST EXPENSE	AMORTIZATION	DISCOUNT	CARRYING AMOUNT
1/2/94					**(73)**
6/30/94	**(72)**	18,000	3,600	**(71)**	363,600
12/31/94	$14,400	**(76)**	**(77)**		
Annual Interest Rates: Stated		**(74)**			
Effective		**(75)**			

Items 78 through 83 are based on the following:

Town, Inc. is preparing its financial statements for the year ended December 31, 1994.

Required:

Items 78 through 83 represent various commitments and contingencies of Town at December 31, 1994, and events subsequent to December 31, 1994, but prior to the issuance of the 1994 financial statements. For each item, select from the following list the reporting requirement and blacken the corresponding oval on the Objective Answer Sheet. A reporting requirement may be selected once, more than once, or not at all.

Reporting Requirement	
(D)	Disclosure only.
(A)	Accrual only.
(B)	Both accrual and disclosure.
(N)	Neither accrual nor disclosure.

78. On December 1, 1994, Town was awarded damages of $75,000 in a patent infringement suit it brought against a competitor. The defendant did not appeal the verdict, and payment was received in January 1995.

79. A former employee of Town has brought a wrongful-dismissal suit against Town. Town's lawyers believe the suit to be without merit.

80. At December 31, 1994, Town had outstanding purchase orders in the ordinary course of business for purchase of a raw material to be used in its manufacturing process. The market price is currently higher than the purchase price and is not anticipated to change within the next year.

81. A government contract completed during 1994 is subject to renegotiation. Although Town estimates that it is reasonably possible that a refund of approximately $200,000—$300,000 may be required by the government, it does not wish to publicize this possibility.

82. Town has been notified by a governmental agency that it will be held responsible for the cleanup of toxic materials at a site where Town formerly conducted operations. Town estimates that it is probable that its share of remedial action will be approximately $500,000.

83. On January 5, 1995, Town redeemed its outstanding bonds and issued new bonds with a lower rate of interest. The reacquisition price was in excess of the carrying amount of the bonds.

Number 4

The following information pertains to Village Flowers, a calendar-year sole proprietorship, which maintained its books on the cash basis during the year.

Village Flowers
TRIAL BALANCE
December 31, 1994

	DR.	CR.
Cash	$ 25,600	
Accounts receivable, 12/31/93	16,200	
Inventory, 12/31/93	62,000	
Furniture & fixtures	118,200	
Land improvements	45,000	
Accumulated depreciation, 12/31/93		$ 32,400
Accounts payable, 12/31/93		17,000
Village, Drawings		
Village, Capital, 12/31/93		124,600
Sales		653,000
Purchases	305,100	
Salaries	174,000	
Payroll taxes	12,400	
Insurance	8,700	
Rent	34,200	
Utilities	12,600	
Living expenses	13,000	
	$827,000	$827,000

Village has developed plans to expand into the wholesale flower market and is in the process of negotiating a bank loan to finance the expansion. The bank is requesting 1994 financial statements prepared on the accrual basis of accounting from Village. During the course of a review engagement, Carson, Village's accountant, obtained the following additional information.

1. Amounts due from customers totaled $32,000 at December 31, 1994.

2. An analysis of the above receivables revealed that an allowance for uncollectible accounts of $3,800 should be provided.

3. Unpaid invoices for flower purchases totaled $30,500 and $17,000, at December 31, 1994, and December 31, 1993, respectively.

4. The inventory totaled $72,800 based on a physical count of the goods at December 31, 1994. The inventory was priced at cost, which approximates market value.

5. On May 1, 1994, Village paid $8,700 to renew its comprehensive insurance coverage for one year. The premium on the previous policy, which expired on April 30, 1994, was $7,800.

6. On January 2, 1994, Village entered into a 25-year operating lease for the vacant lot adjacent to its retail store for use as a parking lot. As agreed in the lease, Village paved and fenced in the lot at a cost of $45,000. The improvements were completed on April 1, 1994, and have an estimated useful life of 15 years. No provision for depreciation or amortization has been recorded. Depreciation on furniture and fixtures was $12,000 for 1994.

7. Accrued expenses at December 31, 1993 and 1994, were as follows:

	1993	1994
Utilities	$ 900	$1,500
Payroll taxes	1,100	1,600
	$2,000	$3,100

8. Village is being sued for $400,000. The coverage under the comprehensive insurance policy is limited to $250,000. Village's attorney believes that an unfavorable outcome is probable and that a reasonable estimate of the settlement is $300,000.

9. The salaries account includes $4,000 per month paid to the proprietor. The proprietor also receives $250 per week for living expenses.

Required:

a. Using the worksheet below, prepare the adjustments necessary to convert the trial balance of Village Flowers to the accrual basis of accounting for the year ended December 31, 1994. Formal journal entries are not required to support your adjustments. However, use the numbers given with the additional information to cross-reference the postings in the adjustment columns on the worksheet.

b. Write a brief memo to Village's proprietor explaining why the bank would require financial statements prepared on the accrual basis instead of the cash basis.

Village Flowers
WORKSHEET TO CONVERT TRIAL BALANCE TO ACCRUAL BASIS
December 31, 1994

ACCOUNT TITLE	CASH BASIS DR.	CASH BASIS CR.	ADJUSTMENTS DR.	ADJUSTMENTS CR.	ACCRUAL BASIS* DR.*	ACCRUAL BASIS* CR.*
Cash	25,600					
Accounts receivable	16,200					
Inventory	62,000					
Furniture & fixtures	118,200					
Land improvements	45,000					
Accumulated depreciation & amortization		32,400				
Accounts payable		17,000				
Village, Drawings						
Village, Capital		124,600				
Sales		653,000				
Purchases	305,100					
Salaries	174,000					
Payroll taxes	12,400					
Insurance	8,700					
Rent	34,200					
Utilities	12,600					
Living expenses	13,000					
	827,000	827,000				

*Completion of these columns is not required.

Number 5

During 1994, Broca Co. had the following transactions:

- On January 2, Broca purchased the net assets of Amp Co. for $360,000. The fair value of Amp's identifiable net assets was $172,000. Broca believes that, due to the popularity of Amp's consumer products, the life of the resulting goodwill is unlimited.
- On February 1, Broca purchased a franchise to operate a ferry service from the state government for $60,000 and an annual fee of 1% of ferry revenues. The franchise expires after five years. Ferry revenues were $20,000 during 1994. Broca projects future revenues of $40,000 in 1995, and $60,000 per annum for the three years thereafter.
- On April 5, Broca was granted a patent that had been applied for by Amp. During 1994, Broca incurred legal costs of $51,000 to register the patent and an additional $85,000 to successfully prosecute a patent infringement suit against a competitor. Broca estimates the patent's economic life to be ten years.

Broca's accounting policy is to amortize all intangibles on the straight-line basis over the maximum period permitted by generally accepted accounting principles, taking a full year's amortization in the year of acquisition.

Required:

a. 1. Describe the characteristics of intangible assets. Discuss the accounting for the purchases or internal development of intangible assets with an indeterminable life, such as goodwill.

2. Over what period should intangible assets be amortized? How should this period be determined? Discuss the justification for amortization of intangible assets with indeterminable lives.

3. Describe the financial statement disclosure requirements relating to Broca's intangible assets and expenses. Do not write the related footnotes.

b. Prepare a schedule showing the intangibles section of Broca's balance sheet at December 31, 1994, and a schedule showing the related expenses that would appear on Broca's 1994 income statement. Show supporting computations.

ANSWER KEY—FOUR-OPTION MULTIPLE-CHOICE QUESTIONS

Be sure to read Chapter 6—Chart Your Progress and Plan Your Course of Action. It will help you analyze your test and plan your study program.

Business Law & Professional Responsibilities (LPR)

QUESTION #	ANSWER	TOPICAL AREA
1	C	Professional Responsibilities
2	D	Professional Responsibilities
3	B	Professional Responsibilities
4	A	Professional Responsibilities
5	C	Professional Responsibilities
6	—	This question is obsolete
7	—	This question is obsolete
8	B	Accountants' Legal Responsibility
9	C	Accountants' Legal Responsibility
10	D	Accountants' Legal Responsibility
11	D	Accountants' Legal Responsibility
12	B	Accountants' Legal Responsibility
13	C	Accountants' Legal Responsibility
14	D	Accountants' Legal Responsibility
15	A	Accountants' Legal Responsibility
16	D	Partnerships
17	A	Partnerships
18	C	Partnerships
19	D	Partnerships
20	A	Partnerships
21	A	Corporations
22	C	Corporations
23	C	Corporations
24	C	Corporations
25	D	Corporations
26	B	Suretyship and Creditor's Rights
27	A	Suretyship and Creditor's Rights

QUESTION #	ANSWER	TOPICAL AREA
28	D	Suretyship and Creditor's Rights
29	D	Suretyship and Creditor's Rights
30	C	Suretyship and Creditor's Rights
31	A	Employment Regulations
32	B	Employment Regulations
33	A	Employment Regulations
34	B	Employment Regulations
35	C	Employment Regulations
36	A	Employment Regulations
37	A	Employment Regulations
38	B	Employment Regulations
39	A	Employment Regulations
40	D	Employment Regulations
41	B	Sales
42	C	Sales
43	B	Sales
44	D	Sales
45	B	Sales
46	C	Sales
47	B	Sales
48	B	Sales
49	B	Sales
50	A	Sales
51	B	Property
52	D	Property
53	B	Property
54	C	Property
55	B	Property
56	C	Property
57	A	Property
58	C	Property
59	D	Property
60	A	Insurance

Auditing (AUDIT)

QUESTION #	ANSWER	TOPICAL AREA
1	D	Audit Planning
2	A	Audit Planning
3	B	Electronic Data Processing (EDP)
4	B	Audit Planning
5	B	Internal Control
6	C	Internal Control

QUESTION #	ANSWER	TOPICAL AREA	QUESTION #	ANSWER	TOPICAL AREA
7	C	Internal Control	55	C	Audit Evidence
8	D	Internal Control	56	D	Audit Reporting Standards
9	A	Internal Control	57	B	Audit Evidence
10	C	Electronic Data Processing (EDP)	58	C	Audit Evidence
			59	D	Audit Evidence
11	C	Internal Control	60	D	Audit Planning
12	A	Internal Control	61	C	Audit Reporting Standards
13	A	Internal Control	62	C	Audit Reporting Standards
14	B	Electronic Data Processing (EDP)	63	B	Audit Reporting Standards
			64	—	This question is obsolete
15	A	Internal Control	65	D	Audit Reporting Standards
16	B	Internal Control	66	B	Audit Reporting Standards
17	C	Statistical Sampling	67	A	Audit Reporting Standards
18	B	Internal Control	68	C	Auditing Concepts and Standards
19	D	Statistical Sampling			
20	A	Internal Control	69	D	Audit Reporting Standards
21	D	Internal Control	70	—	This question is obsolete
22	D	Internal Control	71	C	Audit Reporting Standards
23	D	Internal Control	72	D	Audit Evidence
24	C	Internal Control	73	A	Audit Reporting Standards
25	D	Statistical Sampling	74	B	Audit Reporting Standards
26	D	Internal Control	75	A	Audit Reporting Standards
27	C	Internal Control	76	D	Audit Reporting Standards
28	A	Audit Evidence	77	A	Audit Reporting Standards
29	D	Internal Control	78	A	Audit Reporting Standards
30	D	Internal Control	79	C	Other Reporting Areas
31	A	Internal Control	80	C	Other Reporting Areas
32	C	Internal Control	81	A	Other Reporting Areas
33	A	Statistical Sampling	82	A	Other Reporting Areas
34	D	Internal Control	83	A	Other Reporting Areas
35	D	Internal Control	84	B	Internal Control
36	C	Internal Control	85	C	Audit Reporting Standards
37	A	Internal Control	86	A	Other Reporting Areas
38	A	Audit Evidence	87	A	Audit Reporting Standards
39	C	Audit Evidence	88	B	Other Reporting Areas
40	B	Audit Evidence	89	B	Other Reporting Areas
41	B	Audit Planning	90	B	Other Reporting Areas
42	—	This question is obsolete			
43	C	Statistical Sampling			
44	C	Statistical Sampling			
45	D	Audit Evidence			
46	B	Audit Evidence			
47	C	Audit Evidence			
48	C	Audit Evidence			
49	B	Audit Evidence			
50	A	Audit Evidence			
51	C	Audit Evidence			
52	A	Electronic Data Processing (EDP)			
53	D	Audit Planning			
54	D	Audit Planning			

Accounting & Reporting— Taxation, Managerial, and Governmental and Not-for-Profit Organizations (ARE)

QUESTION #	ANSWER	TOPICAL AREA
1	C	Federal Income Taxes— Corporations
2	D	Federal Income Taxes— Tax Accounting Methods

QUESTION #	ANSWER	TOPICAL AREA	QUESTION #	ANSWER	TOPICAL AREA
3	B	Federal Income Taxes—Corporations	24	B	Federal Income Taxes—Tax Procedures & Administration
4	D	Federal Income Taxes—Corporations	25	B	Federal Income Taxes—Tax Procedures & Administration
5	C	Federal Income Taxes—Depreciation & Depreciation Recapture	26	D	Federal Income Taxes—Tax Preparers' Responsibilities
6	C	Federal Income Taxes—Capital Gains & Losses	27	B	Federal Income Taxes—Partnerships
LPR #6	C	Federal Income Taxes—Tax Preparers' Responsibilities	28	D	Federal Income Taxes—Partnerships
7	D	Federal Income Taxes—Corporations	29	A	Federal Income Taxes—Partnerships
LPR #7	A	Federal Income Taxes—Tax Preparers' Responsibilities	30	A	Federal Income Taxes—Partnerships
8	B	Federal Income Taxes—Corporations	31	B	Federal Income Taxes—Partnerships
9	C	Federal Income Taxes—Corporations	32	D	Federal Income Taxes—Partnerships
10	B	Federal Income Taxes—Tax Procedures & Administration	33	B	Federal Income Taxes—Partnerships
11	A	Federal Income Taxes—Tax Accounting Methods	34	C	Federal Income Taxes—Partnerships
12	A	Federal Income Taxes—Corporations	35	C	Federal Income Taxes—Estates & Trusts
13	D	Federal Income Taxes—Corporations	36	C	Federal Income Taxes—Estates & Trusts
14	C	Federal Income Taxes—Corporations	37	A	Federal Income Taxes—Exempt Organizations
15	A	Federal Income Taxes—Corporations	38	D	Federal Income Taxes—Exempt Organizations
16	D	Federal Income Taxes—Tax Procedures & Administration	39	C	Managerial Accounting and Quantitative Methods
17	B	Federal Income Taxes—Corporations	40	C	Cost Accounting
18	D	Federal Income Taxes—Corporations	41	C	Managerial Accounting and Quantitative Methods
19	C	Federal Income Taxes—Corporations	42	D	Managerial Accounting and Quantitative Methods
20	C	Federal Income Taxes—Corporations	43	B	Managerial Accounting and Quantitative Methods
21	C	Federal Income Taxes—Corporations	44	B	Managerial Accounting and Quantitative Methods
22	A	Federal Income Taxes—Corporations	45	A	Managerial Accounting and Quantitative Methods
23	A	Federal Income Taxes—Tax Procedures & Administration	46	C	Cost Accounting
			47	B	Cost Accounting
			48	C	Cost Accounting
			49	C	Cost Accounting
			50	D	Managerial Accounting and Quantitative Methods

QUESTION #	ANSWER	TOPICAL AREA
51	A	Managerial Accounting and Quantitative Methods
52	A	Managerial Accounting and Quantitative Methods
53	B	Managerial Accounting and Quantitative Methods
54	C	Managerial Accounting and Quantitative Methods
55	A	Managerial Accounting and Quantitative Methods
56	D	Cost Accounting
57	C	Not-for-Profit Accounting—Governmental Units
58	B	Not-for-Profit Accounting—Governmental Units
59	A	Not-for-Profit Accounting—Governmental Units
60	C	Not-for-Profit Accounting—Governmental Units
61	A	Not-for-Profit Accounting—Governmental Units
62	D	Not-for-Profit Accounting—Governmental Units
63	B	Not-for-Profit Accounting—Governmental Units
64	A	Not-for-Profit Accounting—Governmental Units
65	C	Not-for-Profit Accounting—Governmental Units
66	D	Not-for-Profit Accounting—Governmental Units
67	A	Not-for-Profit Accounting—Governmental Units
68	C	Not-for-Profit Accounting—Governmental Units
69	B	Not-for-Profit Accounting—Governmental Units
70	C	Not-for-Profit Accounting—Governmental Units
71	D	Not-for-Profit Accounting—Governmental Units
72	C	Not-for-Profit Accounting—Governmental Units
73	B	Not-for-Profit Accounting—Governmental Units
74	A	Not-for-Profit Accounting—Other Than Governmental Units
75	B	Not-for-Profit Accounting—Other Than Governmental Units

Financial Accounting & Reporting—Business Enterprises (FARE)

QUESTION #	ANSWER	TOPICAL AREA
1	D	Accounting Concepts
2	B	Accounting Concepts
3	A	Accounting Concepts
4	A	Financial Statements
5	D	Accounting Concepts
6	A	Accounting Concepts
7	D	Financial Statements
8	D	Financial Statements
9	C	Inventories
10	C	Installment Sales
11	B	Leases
12	C	Leases
13	D	Liabilities
14	C	Pension Costs
15	A	Pension Costs
16	D	Liabilities
17	A	Liabilities
18	A	Stockholders' Equity
19	A	Stockholders' Equity
20	B	Stockholders' Equity
21	C	Stockholders' Equity
22	C	Stockholders' Equity
23	A	Partnerships
24	C	Accounting Fundamentals
25	C	Stockholders' Equity
26	B	Investments
27	B	Investments
28	B	Investments
29	A	Leases
30	C	Accounting Fundamentals
31	D	Installment Sales
32	A	Foreign Currency Translation
33	B	Intangibles
34	D	Leases
35	D	Investments
36	C	Income Taxes, Accounting for
37	B	Income Taxes, Accounting for
38	C	Income Taxes, Accounting for
39	B	Financial Statements
40	D	Financial Statements
41	D	Financial Statements

QUESTION #	ANSWER	TOPICAL AREA	QUESTION #	ANSWER	TOPICAL AREA
42	A	Financial Statements	52	C	Consolidation and Business Combination
43	A	Financial Statements	53	C	Consolidation and Business Combination
44	A	Financial Statements	54	D	Financial Statements
45	B	Stockholders' Equity	55	D	Financial Statements
46	C	Stockholders' Equity	56	A	Financial Statements
47	D	Cash Flows	57	C	Inflation Accounting
48	D	Cash Flows	58	A	Financial Statement Analysis
49	B	Consolidation and Business Combination			
50	B	Consolidation and Business Combination	59	B	Liabilities
51	B	Consolidation and Business Combination	60	B	Financial Statement Analysis

SOLUTIONS AND EXPLAINED ANSWERS

Business Law & Professional Responsibilities (LPR)

FOUR-OPTION MULTIPLE-CHOICE QUESTIONS

Answer 1

#1 (answer "C")

According to Rule 503 of the AICPA Code of Professional Conduct, a CPA may accept a commission for recommending or referring to a client a product or service if the CPA does not also perform (1) an audit or review of historical financial statements, (2) an examination of prospective financial information, or (3) a compilation of a financial statement when the CPA expects that a third party will or might use the financial statement, and the compilation report fails to indicate the lack of independence.

Additionally, the acceptance of a commission must be disclosed to the party to which the CPA recommends or refers a product or service.

Thus, <u>accepting a commission for recommending a product to an audit client</u> is generally prohibited by the ethical standards of the profession.

Answer choice "A" is incorrect because the ethical standards of the profession permit a CPA to purchase a product from a third party and resell it to the client. This transaction creates no conflict of interest for the CPA.

Answer choice "B" is incorrect because the ethical standards of the profession permit a CPA to write a financial management newsletter promoted and sold by a publishing company.

Answer choice "D" is incorrect because the ethical standards of the profession permit a CPA to accept engagements obtained through the efforts of third parties.

#2 (answer "D")

Rule 501 of the AICPA Code of Professional Conduct provides that a CPA should not commit an act in the CPA's personal or professional life that discredits the profession. Interpretations of Rule 501 require a CPA to return client books and records upon the request of the client even where the client has not yet paid the CPA's fee. Thus, the ethical standards of the profession generally prohibit a CPA from <u>retaining client records after an engagement is terminated prior to completion and the client has demanded their return</u>.

Answer choice "A" is incorrect because the ethical standards of the profession permit a CPA to issue a modified report explaining a failure to follow a governmental regulatory agency's standards when conducting an attest service for a client. In fact, such an explanation is expected.

Answer choice "B" is incorrect because the ethical standards of the profession permit a CPA to reveal confidential client information during a quality review of a professional practice by a team from the state CPA society. Disclosure of confidential client information is considered unethical unless the disclosure is at the client's request, pursuant to a validly issued subpoena, or in accordance with AICPA or state CPA society requirements, such as a state CPA-society-sponsored quality review of a CPA's practice.

Answer choice "C" is incorrect because the ethical standards of the profession permit a CPA to accept a contingent fee for representing a client in an examination of the client's federal tax return by an IRS agent. While generally a CPA's professional services should not be rendered under a contingent fee arrangement, certain tax-related matters constitute exceptions to the general rule.

#3 (answer "B")

Article Five of the Principles of the Code of Professional Conduct requires a CPA to observe the profession's technical and ethical standards, continually strive to improve personal competence and the quality of services, and discharge professional responsibility to the best of the CPA's ability. Competence requires a CPA to understand the CPA's limitations and to seek consultation when a professional engagement exceeds the CPA's personal competence. Thus, the standards of the profession <u>may require consulting with experts</u> in exercising due professional care but <u>not obtaining specialty accreditation</u>.

Answer choices other than "B" are based on incorrect assumptions and/or interpretations of the law.

#4 (answer "A")

Article Four of the Principles of the Code of Professional Conduct requires a CPA to maintain objectivity and independence in discharging the CPA's professional responsibilities, especially when providing attestation services. Further, Rule 101 provides that a CPA shall be independent in the rendering of professional services. However, a CPA is not required to maintain independence in the provision of consulting services, but only to maintain objectivity and integrity. Thus, providing extensive advisory services for a client would most likely not impair a CPA's independence.

Answer choice "B" is incorrect because contracting with a client to supervise the client's office personnel is equivalent to being an employee or member of the management group of a client. Such a relationship could at minimum create the appearance of a conflict of interest for the CPA.

Answer choice "C" is incorrect because signing a client's checks, even in emergency situations, could create the appearance of a conflict of interest for the CPA.

Answer choice "D" is incorrect because a CPA may only accept a gift from a client if the gift is a mere token. A luxurious gift is more than a token.

#5 (answer "C")

Consulting services provided by a CPA typically include activities relating to the determination of client objectives, fact-finding, the definition of problems or opportunities, evaluation of alternatives, formulation of proposed actions, communication of results, and follow-up. The following compliance standards address the distinctive nature of consulting services. The CPA shall:

1. Serve the client's interests, to meet stated objectives, while maintaining integrity and objectivity.
2. Obtain a written or oral understanding with the client concerning the responsibilities of the parties and the nature, scope, and limitations of services to be performed.
3. Inform client of conflicts of interests, significant reservations of the engagement, and/or significant findings or events.

Thus, a CPA undertaking a consulting services engagement must inform the client of significant reservations concerning the benefits of the engagement.

Answer choice "A" is incorrect because a CPA undertaking a consulting services engagement is free to seek to modify any agreement made with the client.

Answer choice "B" is incorrect because a CPA undertaking a consulting services engagement may also perform attest services for the client, but must maintain independence as well as objectivity and integrity and must comply with all other AICPA rules.

Answer choice "D" is incorrect because a CPA undertaking a consulting services engagement must obtain an understanding with the client concerning the responsibilities of the parties and the nature, scope, and limitations of services to be performed. However, the understanding need not be in writing.

#6 (this answer is obsolete)

#7 (this answer is obsolete)

#8 (answer "B")

The "Ultramares" rule exempts accountants from liability for ordinary negligence to nonclients who were not known to the accountant. Thus, under the "Ultramares" rule, an accountant will be liable for negligence to parties in privity with the accountant but not to foreseen parties.

Answer choices other than "B" are based on incorrect assumptions and/or interpretations of the law.

#9 (answer "C")

A CPA is negligent if the CPA fails to exercise the degree of care a reasonably competent accountant would exercise under similar circumstances. Thus, a CPA performing an audit will most likely be considered negligent when the CPA fails to warn a client of known internal control weaknesses.

Answer choice "A" is incorrect because a CPA does not guarantee to detect all of a client's fraudulent activities but only those fraudulent activities that should be detected by diligently performing the audit.

Answer choice "B" is incorrect because a CPA should not include a negligence disclaimer in the client's engagement letter. Such disclaimers are unenforceable as a matter of public policy.

Answer choice "D" is incorrect because a CPA may not disclose confidential client information without the consent of the client.

#10 (answer "D")

Actions for fraud require proof of the following:

1. A material, false statement or omission.
2. Scienter—knowledge of the falsity or omission.
3. Intention that plaintiff rely.
4. Justifiable reliance by plaintiff.
5. Damages caused by plaintiff's reliance.

Thus, the best defense a CPA firm can assert in a suit for common law fraud based on its unqualified opinion on materially false financial statements is lack of scienter.

Answer choice "A" is incorrect because a client's contributory negligence is not a valid defense to a suit for common law fraud.

Answer choice "B" is incorrect because a disclaimer of liability for damages resulting from a CPA's fraud is unenforceable because it violates public policy.

Answer choice "C" is incorrect because privity is not required for a plaintiff to succeed in a suit for common law fraud. A CPA who commits common law fraud is liable to clients, known third parties, and reasonably foreseeable third parties.

#11 (answer "D")

SEC Rule 2(e) authorizes the SEC to sanction an accountant for acting in bad faith. The sanctions may be imposed where the accountant:

1. Lacks the qualifications necessary to represent others.
2. Lacks character or integrity.
3. Engaged in unethical or improper professional conduct.
4. Willfully violated or aided and abetted in the violation of federal securities laws.

Private litigants often bring civil actions for damages against an accountant who is sanctioned by the SEC under Rule 2(e). Thus, under the antifraud provisions of Section 10(b) of the Securities Exchange Act of 1934, a CPA may be liable if the CPA acted without good faith.

Answer choice "A" is incorrect because a CPA may not be liable for acting negligently under the antifraud provisions of Section 10(b) of the Securities Exchange Act of 1934. A successful plaintiff must prove fraud under the 1934 Act, but may recover for negligence under the 1933 Securities Act.

Answer choice "B" is incorrect because a CPA may not be held liable under the antifraud provisions of Section 10(b) of the Securities Exchange Act of 1934 for acting with independence. A successful plaintiff must prove fraud under the 1934 Act.

Answer choice "C" is incorrect because a CPA may not be liable under the antifraud provisions of Section 10(b) of the Securities Exchange Act of 1934 for acting without due diligence. A successful plaintiff must prove fraud under the 1934 Act. Due diligence is a defense for a CPA sued under the provisions of the 1933 Securities Act.

#12 (answer "B")

Under Section 11 of the Securities Act of 1933, a CPA may be civilly liable for damages for negligence in the conduct of an audit or in the preparation of financial statements used in a registration statement. Thus, under Section 11 of the Securities Act of 1933, a CPA may use the CPA's compliance with generally accepted accounting principles as a defense. However, the use of generally accepted fraud detection standards is not a viable defense for a CPA under Section 11 of the Securities Act of 1933. For a CPA, the appropriate standards are generally accepted auditing standards.

Answer choices other than "B" are based on incorrect assumptions and/or interpretations of the law.

#13 (answer "C")

Under the Securities Act of 1933, a CPA may be held liable for negligence in the preparation of a registration statement, while under the Securities Exchange Act of 1934 a CPA is liable only for fraud. Since Ocean was negligent in conducting its audit of Drain's financial statements, but was unaware that the financial statements included material misstatements, Sharp is most likely to prevail in a lawsuit against Ocean under Section 11 of the Securities Act of 1933. Accountants are <u>not</u> <u>liable</u> for mere negligence <u>under</u> <u>Section</u> <u>10(b),</u> <u>Rule</u> <u>10b-5,</u> <u>of</u> <u>the</u> <u>Securities</u> <u>Ex-</u> <u>change</u> <u>Act</u> <u>of</u> <u>1934</u>.

Answer choices other than "C" are based on incorrect assumptions and/or interpretations of the law.

#14 (answer "D")

A CPA's working papers are the property of the CPA and need not be given to the client. In addition, a CPA may not disclose the contents of working papers unless the client consents or a court so orders. Thus, working papers must be <u>turned</u> <u>over</u> <u>pursuant</u> <u>to</u> <u>a</u> <u>valid</u> <u>federal</u> <u>court</u> <u>subpoena</u>.

Answer choice "A" is incorrect because the contents of working papers are confidential. Thus, working papers may not be transferred to another accountant purchasing the CPA's practice unless the client has given permission for the transfer.

Answer choice "B" is incorrect because a CPA's working papers belong to the CPA and need not be surrendered to the CPA's client.

Answer choice "C" is incorrect because the contents of a CPA's working papers are confidential. Therefore, they may not be turned over to any government agency that requests them, but only pursuant to a court order mandating that the working papers be turned over to a specific agency.

#15 (answer "A")

Generally, communications between a CPA and a client are not privileged. The common law does not recognize the privilege nor does federal law. However, some states have adopted statutes creating an accountant-client privilege for the client. Thus, <u>Ivor</u> <u>can</u> <u>claim</u> <u>an</u> <u>accountant-client</u> <u>privi-</u> <u>lege</u> <u>only</u> <u>in</u> <u>states</u> <u>that</u> <u>have</u> <u>enacted</u> <u>a</u> <u>statute</u> <u>cre-</u> <u>ating</u> <u>such</u> <u>a</u> <u>privilege</u>.

Answer choice "B" is incorrect because the federal courts do not recognize the accountant-client privilege.

Answer choice "C" is incorrect because the accountant-client privilege may be claimed in both civil and criminal suits in those states that have enacted a statute creating such a privilege.

Answer choice "D" is incorrect because in those states that have enacted a statute creating such a

privilege, the accountant-client privilege can be claimed to limit testimony on all types of communications between the accountant and the client, rather than only testimony on the subject matter of an audit.

#16 (answer "D")

A partnership results from an agreement between competent parties to combine talent, money, effort, and so on, to carry on as co-owners a business for profit. A partnership dissolves whenever the partners cease to carry on the business together. In addition, a partnership is not a legal entity for purposes of federal taxation. Thus, <u>a</u> <u>partnership</u> <u>does</u> <u>not</u> <u>have</u> <u>the</u> <u>characteristics</u> <u>of</u> <u>unlimited</u> <u>duration</u> <u>or</u> <u>an</u> <u>obligation</u> <u>to</u> <u>pay</u> <u>federal</u> <u>income</u> <u>taxes</u>.

Answer choices other than "D" are based on incorrect assumptions and/or interpretations of the law.

#17 (answer "A")

In a general partnership, each partner has unlimited, personal liability for partnership debts and for the business-related acts of all partners. Each partner's tort liability is joint and several, which means that all the partners may be sued together in one suit, or they may be sued separately in separate suits leading to several individual judgments.

In a general partnership, each partner is an agent for the firm and for the other partners for carrying on partnership business in the normal manner. The firm and the partners are jointly liable for the contracts of a partner made within the partner's actual and apparent authority. Thus, in general, <u>all</u> <u>general</u> <u>partners</u> <u>are</u> <u>jointly</u> <u>and</u> <u>severally</u> <u>liable</u> <u>for</u> <u>partnership</u> <u>torts</u>. Furthermore, general partners are liable for partnership obligations they actually authorized, as well as those obligations they apparently authorized.

Answer choices other than "A" are based on incorrect assumptions and/or interpretations of the law.

#18 (answer "C")

In the absence of a contrary agreement, the Uniform Partnership Act provides that profits are shared equally among the partners. Thus, when the written partnership agreement provides only for losses to be divided equally among the partners, profits are also to be divided <u>equally</u> <u>among</u> <u>the</u> <u>partners</u>.

Answer choice "A" is incorrect because, in the absence of a contrary agreement, the profits of a general partnership are divided equally, rather than in proportion to the partners' ratio of contributions to the partnership.

Answer choice "B" is incorrect because, in the absence of a contrary agreement, the profits of a general partnership are divided equally, rather than in proportion to the partners' participation in day to day management.

Answer choice "D" is incorrect because, in the absence of a contrary agreement, the profits of a general partnership are divided equally, rather than proportionately among the partners.

#19 (answer "D")

A partner may assign his interest in the partnership but the assignee does not automatically become a partner with the right to participate in the management of the firm. The assignee obtains the right to receive the assignor's share of the partnership's profits and, upon liquidation, the assignor's share of any surplus. Thus, when a partner assigns an interest in a general partnership, <u>the</u> <u>assignment</u> <u>transfers</u> <u>the</u> <u>assignor's</u> <u>interest</u> <u>in</u> <u>partnership</u> <u>profits</u> <u>and</u> <u>surplus</u>.

Answer choice "A" is incorrect because the assignee of an interest in a general partnership does not become a partner. Instead, the assignee is entitled to the assignor's share of profits and a share of any surplus remaining after liquidation of the firm.

Answer choice "B" is incorrect because the assignee of an interest in a general partnership is not responsible for a proportionate share of past and future partnership debts. Instead, the assignee is entitled to the assignor's share of profits and a share of any surplus remaining after liquidation of the firm. The assignee has no liability for partnership debts unless the assignee consciously assumes such liability.

Answer choice "C" is incorrect because an assignment does not automatically dissolve the partnership. The assigning partner continues as a partner with the same rights and duties. Thus, the composition of the firm is unchanged by an assignment of a partner's interest.

#20 (answer "A")

A dissolution occurs at that point in time when the partners cease to carry on the business together. A dissolution can occur by an act of the partners, by operation of law, or by order of a court.

Each partner always has the power to dissolve a partnership by the partner's acts, but the partnership agreement determines whether or not the partner has the legal right to dissolve it. If a partner withdraws from the partnership in violation of the partnership agreement, the partner is liable to the other partners for damages for wrongful dissolution.

The partnership agreement between Park and Graham was silent as to the partnership's duration. Thus, <u>Park</u> <u>may</u> <u>dissolve</u> <u>the</u> <u>partnership</u> <u>at</u> <u>any</u> <u>time</u> and will not incur liability for wrongful dissolution.

Answer choice "B" is incorrect because Park always has the power to withdraw from the partnership and thereby to dissolve it, without either Graham's consent or a court order.

Answer choice "C" is incorrect because Park always has the power to withdraw from the partnership and thus to dissolve it without Graham's consent.

Answer choice "D" is incorrect because Park always has the power to withdraw from the partnership and may do so without first notifying all partnership creditors of the proposed dissolution. Dissolution does not terminate the rights of the partnership's creditors.

#21 (answer "A")

A corporation's articles of incorporation normally include:

1. Corporate name (required).
2. Corporate purpose.
3. Duration (may be perpetual).
4. <u>Number</u> <u>of</u> <u>authorized</u> <u>shares</u> (required).
5. Number and names of initial directors.
6. Names and addresses of each incorporator (required).
7. Corporate powers.
8. Street address for the initial registered office and the <u>name</u> <u>of</u> <u>the</u> initial <u>registered</u> <u>agent</u> at that office (required).

Answer choices other than "A" are based on incorrect assumptions and/or interpretations of the law.

#22 (answer "C")

A corporation has the following powers:

1. To buy and sell property.
2. To make contracts.
3. To have exclusive use of its corporate name.
4. To sue and be sued in its corporate name.
5. To have perpetual existence.
6. To borrow or lend money.

Thus, an advantage of the corporate form of doing business is that the operation of the business may continue indefinitely.

Answer choice "A" is incorrect because the day to day management of the corporation is the responsibility of the corporate officers, rather than the board of directors.

Answer choice "B" is incorrect because ownership of a corporation is transferable. Normally, the shares in a corporation can be freely transferred.

Answer choice "D" is incorrect because corporations are created through compliance with a state incorporation statute. Incorporation is a privilege granted by the states and, in return, the states may regulate corporations as deemed necessary to promote the health, safety, and welfare of its citizens.

#23 (answer "C")

Corporate shareholders have the following rights:

1. To vote.
2. To share in profits.
3. To participate in distribution of capital upon dissolution.
4. Preemptive right with respect to additional issues.
5. To make a reasonable inspection of corporate records.
6. To bring a shareholder's derivative suit when necessary.

Thus, a stockholder of a public corporation is entitled to the right to a reasonable inspection of corporate records.

Answer choice "A" is incorrect because a stockholder in a public corporation has no right to have annual dividends declared and paid. The stockholders may compel the declaration and payment of dividends only when the board of directors has abused its discretion concerning the declaration of dividends.

Answer choice "B" is incorrect because a stockholder in a public corporation has no right to vote for the election of corporate officers. Instead, they have the right to vote for the election of the corporation's board of directors, and the board of directors appoints the corporate officers.

Answer choice "D" is incorrect because a stockholder in a public corporation has no right to have the corporation issue a new class of stock. The board of directors is the group that determines if and when a new class of stock should and will be issued. The decision to issue a new class of stock requires an amendment to the corporation's articles of incorporation and therefore the approval of the stockholders.

#24 (answer "C")

A stock dividend is a distribution of stock to shareholders, with each shareholder receiving a ratable share according to the shareholder's holdings. The declaration of a stock dividend has no effect on Carr's earnings and profits for federal income tax purposes.

Answer choice "A" is incorrect because a stock dividend does not constitute a sale of securities and thus is not required to be registered with the SEC pursuant to the Securities Act of 1933.

Answer choice "B" is incorrect because, while cash or property dividends are includible in the gross income of the recipient taxpayers in the year of receipt, a stock dividend is not includible in the gross income of the recipient taxpayers.

Answer choice "D" is incorrect because the declaration of a dividend is a matter within the discretion of the board of directors and therefore does not require a vote of Carr's stockholders.

#25 (answer "D")

A merger is an extraordinary action, which requires approval from a majority of each corporation's voting shares. Under the Revised Model Business Corporation Act, the stockholders of both corporations must be given due notice of a special meeting, including a copy or summary of the merger plan. The sole agenda for the special meeting is the proposed merger.

Answer choice "A" is incorrect because a merger plan need only be approved by a majority of the stockholders of both corporations. Stockholder unanimity is not required.

Answer choice "B" is incorrect because a merger plan need only be approved by a majority of the directors of both corporations. Unanimous approval is not required.

Answer choice "C" is incorrect because the merger of two corporations does not require that the absorbed corporation amend its articles of incorporation. Instead, the absorbed corporation is dissolved and its articles of incorporation rescinded.

#26 (answer "B")

Title III of the Federal Consumer Credit Protection Act protects debtors from abusive and excessive garnishment. The Act permits debtors subjected to garnishment to retain the larger of 75% of their weekly disposable earnings, or an amount equal to 30 hours of work payable at the federal minimum wage rate. States may impose more stringent limits on garnishments.

Federal statutes exempt certain property from the reach of creditors. In general these statutes exempt social benefits such as social security or veterans' benefits. Thus, federal social security benefits received by a debtor are exempt from garnishment by creditors. State exemption statutes prevent the sale of some but not all of a debtor's personal property.

Answer choices other than "B" are based on incorrect assumptions and/or interpretations of the law.

#27 (answer "A")

The common law gives certain service providers a possessory lien on personal property belonging to the debtor in order to secure payment for services rendered with the debtor's consent. In order to foreclose and sell property subject to the lien, lienholders must normally notify the debtor of a proposed foreclosure and advertise a proposed foreclosure sale. Thus, both a mechanic's lien and an artisan's lien require the lienholder to give notice of legal action before selling the debtor's property to satisfy the debt.

Answer choices other than "A" are based on incorrect assumptions and/or interpretations of the law.

#28 (answer "D")

Co-suretyship exists when two or more sureties are liable for the same debt of the same debtor. co-sureties need not be liable for the same amount; they need not know of each other's existence; and they need not assume their obligations at the same time. co-sureties are jointly and severally liable to the lender if the debtor defaults. When a co-surety has paid more than her proportionate share of the debtor's obligation, then that co-surety may require her co-sureties to contribute their proportionate shares of the debtor's obligation. Thus, one co-surety has the right of contribution against another co-surety.

Answer choice "A" is incorrect because a co-surety seeks exoneration against the debtor. Exoneration is the co-surety's right to seek an equitable decree ordering the debtor to pay his debt to the lender/creditor.

Answer choice "B" is incorrect because a co-surety seeks subrogation against the debtor. Once the co-surety pays the lender/creditor, then the co-surety becomes entitled to the lender's rights against the debtor and in essence "steps into the lender's shoes."

Answer choice "C" is incorrect because a co-surety seeks reimbursement against the debtor. After the co-surety pays the creditor, the co-surety may seek reimbursement from the debtor.

#29 (answer "D")

A compensated surety is a party who is paid for serving as a surety. A compensated surety is usually a professional, such as a bonding company. The courts are somewhat less protective of compensated sureties than noncompensated sureties, but generally their liability is the same.

A surety is discharged from liability if:

1. The creditor fails to inform the surety of matters material to the risk, when the creditor has reason to believe that the surety does not possess such information.
2. A material modification of the original contract is made, to which the surety does not consent.

3. Release of the debtor by the creditor occurs without the consent of the surety.
4. The creditor releases or impairs the value of the security; the surety then is discharged up to the value of the released or impaired security.
5. The debtor tenders performance to the creditor.

Thus, a compensated surety will always be totally released from his obligation to the creditor when the principal debtor's performance is tendered.

Answer choices "A" and "B" are incorrect because a compensated surety is not released by a modification of the principal debtor's contract unless the modification is material, and it materially increases the risk to the compensated surety.

Answer choice "C" is incorrect because the creditor's partial release of the principal debtor's obligation will not release a surety (compensated or not) if the creditor reserves his rights against the surety. In such a situation, the surety retains reimbursement rights against the debtor, which may be enforced if the surety is forced to pay the debtor's obligation to the creditor.

#30 (answer "C")

The right of subrogation permits the surety to pay the creditor the entire obligation of the debtor and then "step into the shoes of" the creditor. As a result, the surety is entitled to all the rights the creditor had against the debtor. Thus, when a principal debtor defaults and a surety pays the creditor the entire obligation, subrogation gives the surety the best method of collecting from the debtor.

Answer choice "A" is incorrect because exoneration gives the surety a prejudgment method of forcing the debtor to honor her obligation to the creditor. However, it does not provide the surety with a method of collecting from the debtor after the debtor has already defaulted.

Answer choice "B" is incorrect because contribution provides the surety with a method of collecting a pro-rata share from co-sureties after the debtor has defaulted and the surety has paid the entire debt. Contribution does not provide the surety with a method of collecting from the debtor.

Answer choice "D" is incorrect because attachment is a prejudgment remedy ordering a sheriff to seize nonexempt property of the debtor, which can be sold, if necessary, to satisfy a judgment against the debtor. Attachment is not favored by the courts and is granted sparingly. Thus, it is not the surety's best method of collecting from the debtor.

#31 (answer "A")

The Federal Insurance Contributions Act (FICA) is jointly funded by employee and matching employer contributions. The employer is responsible for withholding the employee's contribution and forwarding it to the IRS. Under FICA, an employer will be liable for penalties for failure to supply taxpayer identification numbers and failure to make timely FICA deposits.

Answer choices other than "A" are based on incorrect assumptions and/or interpretations of the law.

#32 (answer "B")

The Federal Unemployment Tax Act (FUTA) provides partial income replacement for a limited time for workers who lose their jobs through no fault of their own. FUTA is funded solely by employer contributions. Thus, the taxes payable under FUTA are deductible by the employer as a business expense for federal income tax purposes.

Answer choice "A" is incorrect because FUTA is calculated as a fixed percentage of an employee's salary up to a stated maximum salary. The FUTA tax is not calculated against all compensation paid to an employee.

Answer choice "C" is incorrect because FUTA taxes are payable by employers only for nonexempt employees. Certain types of employees such as federal, state, and local government employees are exempted from FUTA coverage.

Answer choice "D" is incorrect because FUTA taxes are paid exclusively by employers and thus are not withheld from employees' wages.

#33 (answer "A")

All states have adopted workers' compensation schemes to provide medical treatment, income maintenance, and death and disability benefits to employees for job-related injuries and/or illnesses. Generally, workers' compensation statutes will cover a claim for an <u>occupational</u> <u>disease</u> <u>and</u> an <u>employment</u> <u>aggravated</u> <u>preexisting</u> <u>disease</u>.

Answer choices other than "A" are based on incorrect assumptions and/or interpretations of the law.

#34 (answer "B")

Workers' compensation laws are based upon a strict liability theory so that the employee is not required to prove wrongful conduct by the employer. Thus, <u>employers</u> <u>are</u> <u>strictly</u> <u>liable</u> <u>without</u> <u>regard</u> <u>to</u> <u>whether</u> <u>or</u> <u>not</u> <u>they</u> <u>are</u> <u>at</u> <u>fault</u>.

Answer choice "A" is incorrect because workers' compensation is a no-fault liability system. Damage awards are based on strict liability, rather than comparative negligence.

Answer choice "C" is incorrect because workers' compensation benefits are available without regard to fault. Thus contributory negligence by an otherwise eligible employee does not preclude that employee from receiving workers' compensation benefits.

Answer choice "D" is incorrect because generally workers' compensation awards are one-time payments, rather than payable for life. Compensation for permanent disability is the only lifetime award.

#35 (answer "C")

The Age Discrimination in Employment Act (ADEA) prohibits employment discrimination based solely on an employee's age. A covered employee's <u>remedies</u> <u>include</u> <u>back</u> <u>pay</u>, injunctive relief, and affirmative action. <u>Early</u> <u>retirement</u> <u>is</u> <u>not</u> <u>a</u> <u>remedy</u>.

Answer choices other than "C" are based on incorrect assumptions and/or interpretations of the law.

#36 (answer "A")

The <u>Equal</u> <u>Pay</u> <u>Act</u> prohibits employers from discriminating based on sex by paying differential wages for substantially equal work. Similarly, <u>Title</u> <u>VII</u> <u>of</u> <u>the</u> <u>Civil</u> <u>Rights</u> <u>Act</u> of 1964 prohibits employment discrimination based upon race, color, religion, sex, or national origin.

Answer choices other than "A" are based on incorrect assumptions and/or interpretations of the law.

#37 (answer "A")

The Fair Labor Standards Act (FLSA) mandates a minimum hourly wage for covered employees, as well as the payment of a premium of time-and-a-half for work in excess of forty hours per week. Professionals, managers, and outside salespersons are exempted from the provisions of the Act. Under FLSA, <u>hourly</u>, <u>weekly</u>, or <u>monthly</u> pay bases may be used to pay covered, nonexempt employees who earn, on average, the minimum hourly wage.

Answer choices other than "A" are based on incorrect assumptions and/or interpretations of the law.

#38 (answer "B")

The Fair Labor Standards Act (FLSA) mandates a minimum hourly wage for covered employees, as well as the payment of a premium of time-and-a-half for work in excess of forty hours per week. Overtime is payable for each and every week in which a covered employee exceeds forty hours, without regard to the employee's average weekly hours. Thus, if a covered nonexempt employee works consecutive weeks of 45, 42, 38, and 33 hours, <u>7</u> <u>hours</u> <u>of</u> <u>overtime</u> must be paid to the employee.

Answer choices other than "B" are based on incorrect assumptions and/or interpretations of the law.

#39 (answer "A")

The Employee Retirement Income Security Act of 1974 (ERISA) establishes recordkeeping and disclosure requirements for private pension plans. ERISA also regulates <u>plan</u> <u>funding</u>, participation, <u>and</u> <u>employee</u> <u>vesting</u> requirements for private employer pension plans but does not require employers to offer pensions.

Answer choices other than "A" are based on incorrect assumptions and/or interpretations of the law.

#40 (answer "D")

The National Labor Relations Act (NLRA) provides covered employees with the right to unionize and bargain collectively with their employers. Section 8(d) requires bargaining on "wages, hours, and other terms and conditions of work." The Act does not define the phrase "other terms and conditions of work," but the courts have interpreted it to include sick pay and vacation pay. Thus, <u>neither</u> <u>sick</u> <u>pay</u> <u>nor</u> <u>vacation</u> <u>pay</u> <u>is</u> <u>exempt</u> from the provisions of the NLRA.

Answer choices other than "D" are based on incorrect assumptions and/or interpretations of the law.

#41 (answer "B")

In general, an offeror has the right to withdraw his offer any time prior to acceptance. Under the Sales Article of the UCC, an exception exists for a merchant's firm offer, which is irrevocable for the period stated by the offeror (not to exceed three months) or, if no time is stated, for a reasonable time not to exceed three months. A firm offer is

1. An offer to buy or sell goods.
2. Made by a merchant.
3. In a signed writing.
4. One that gives assurance it will be held open.

Thus, under the Sales Article of the UCC, a firm offer will be created only if the <u>offer</u> <u>is</u> <u>made</u> <u>by a</u> <u>merchant</u> <u>in</u> <u>a</u> <u>signed</u> <u>writing</u>.

Answer choice "A" is incorrect because a firm offer may exist without stating the precise time period during which it will remain open. The offer need only give assurance that it will be held open. If no precise period of time is specified, the offer will remain open for a reasonable period of time not to exceed three months.

Answer choice "C" is incorrect because the creation of a firm offer does not require that the offeree give the offeror some form of consideration. A firm offer is irrevocable without consideration from the offeree.

Answer choice "D" is incorrect because the creation of a firm offer does not require that the offeree be a merchant. Instead, the offeror must be a merchant in order for a firm offer to be created.

#42 (answer "C")

The Sales Article of the UCC provides that an offer to create a contract invites acceptance in any manner and by any reasonable medium, unless the language of the offer or the circumstances surrounding the offer clearly indicate otherwise. Also, an acceptance is effective when dispatched.

When a written offer has been made without specifying a means of acceptance but providing that the offer will only remain open for ten days, <u>an acceptance</u> <u>sent</u> <u>by</u> <u>regular</u> <u>mail</u> <u>the</u> <u>day</u> <u>before</u> <u>the</u> <u>ten-day</u> <u>period</u> <u>expires</u> <u>that</u> <u>reaches</u> <u>the</u> <u>offeror</u> <u>on</u> <u>the</u> <u>eleventh</u> <u>day</u> is valid because it is effective when sent. <u>Also</u> valid is <u>an</u> <u>acceptance</u> <u>faxed</u> <u>the</u> <u>day</u> <u>before</u> <u>the</u> <u>ten-day</u> <u>period</u> <u>expires</u> <u>that</u> <u>reaches</u> <u>the</u> <u>offeror</u> <u>on</u> <u>the</u> <u>eleventh</u> <u>day,</u> <u>due</u> <u>to</u> <u>a</u> <u>malfunction</u> <u>of</u> <u>the</u> <u>offeror's</u> <u>printer</u>. This acceptance is also effective when sent, rather than when received.

Answer choices other than "C" are based on incorrect assumptions and/or interpretations of the law.

#43 (answer "B")

Under the Sales Article of the UCC, implied warranties from a seller of goods to the buyer of those goods exist by operation of law. The implied warranty of title is normally merged with the implied warranty against encumbrances to <u>provide</u> <u>that</u> <u>the</u> <u>seller</u> <u>deliver</u> <u>the</u> <u>goods</u> <u>free</u> <u>from</u> <u>any</u> <u>lien</u> <u>of</u> <u>which</u> <u>the</u> <u>buyer</u> <u>lacked</u> <u>knowledge</u> <u>when</u> <u>the</u> <u>contract</u> <u>was</u> <u>made</u> and that the title conveyed is good and its transfer rightful.

Answer choice "A" is incorrect because the warranty of title does not preclude the seller from disclaiming it to a bona fide purchaser for value. However, the implied warranty of title may only be excluded by specific language or circumstances that give the buyer reason to know that the seller does not claim title to the goods or is only purporting to sell whatever rights or title the seller has.

Answer choice "C" is incorrect because the warranty of title is implied and therefore exists in a contract for the sale of goods automatically by operation of law. Thus, a writing signed by the seller is not required to create the warranty of title.

Answer choice "D" is incorrect because it occurs automatically by operation of law regardless of whether the seller is a merchant or a nonmerchant.

#44 (answer "D")

Strict liability is no-fault liability imposed upon a retailer, wholesaler, or manufacturer (i.e., a merchant seller) for personal injuries or property damage suffered by the product user or purchaser. To establish a cause of action for strict liability for personal injuries that resulted from the use of a defective product, the injured party must prove that:

1. The seller was engaged in the business of selling the defective product.
2. The seller sold the product in a defective condition.
3. The product was unreasonably dangerous because of its defective condition.
4. The use of the defective product caused the plaintiff's injury.
5. The product was expected to and did reach customers without substantial changes in the condition in which it was sold.

Answer choice "A" is incorrect because the injured party suing on the theory of strict liability does not need to prove that the seller was aware of the defect in the product that caused the plaintiff's injuries. Such awareness is not an element of strict liability.

Answer choice "B" is incorrect because the injured party suing on the theory of strict liability is not required to prove that the seller sold the product to the injured party. Strict liability may be imposed upon a retailer, wholesaler, or manufacturer regardless of who sold the product to the injured party. Privity is not an element of strict liability.

Answer choice "C" is incorrect because negligence is not an element of strict liability. Strict liability does not require the injured party to establish fault.

#45 (answer "B")

The common law places the risk of loss upon the party who had title at the time of the loss. The Sales Article of the UCC allocates risk of loss independently from title and provides a detailed set of rules for determining the risk of loss during a sale of goods. One such rule governs risk of loss where the parties have agreed that a common carrier will transport the goods for the parties. In such situations, the contract's shipping terms determine who bears the risk of loss.

Answer choice "A" is incorrect because the contract's shipping terms, rather than the method of shipping the goods, determine who bears the risk of loss in a contract for the sale of goods.

Answer choice "C" is incorrect because the contract's shipping terms, rather than title to the goods, determine who bears the risk of loss in a contract for the sale of goods. Under the Sales Article of the UCC, title and risk of loss are independent.

Answer choice "D" is incorrect because the contract's shipping terms, rather than how the goods were lost, determine who bears the risk of loss in a contract for the sale of goods.

#46 (answer "C")

Where a sales contract calls for the shipment of goods via common carrier (F.O.B. shipping point), the risk of loss passes to the buyer when the goods are delivered to the carrier.

Answer choice "A" is incorrect because the process of identification of goods to a contract for the sale of goods is a necessary prerequisite for title to pass from a seller of goods to a buyer, but is not determinative of when risk of loss passes in an F.O.B. place of shipment contract.

Answer choice "B" is incorrect because in an F.O.B. place of shipment contract, the risk of loss passes to the buyer when the goods are delivered to the carrier, rather than when the goods are placed on the seller's loading dock.

Answer choice "D" is incorrect because in an F.O.B. place of shipment contract, the risk of loss passes to the buyer when the goods are delivered to the carrier, rather than when the goods reach the buyer's loading dock.

#47 (answer "B")

An anticipatory repudiation is a repudiation made before the repudiating party's performance was due under that contract. When either party repudiates a contract for the sale of goods before performance was due, and the repudiation substantially impairs the value of the contract to the other party, the nonbreaching party may wait a commercially reasonable period of time for the other party to perform or immediately seek a remedy for breach of contract. Thus, when a seller commits an anticipatory breach of contract, the buyer <u>may</u> <u>cancel</u> <u>the</u> <u>contract</u> and recover or seek damages. However, public policy precludes collecting punitive damages in breach of contract cases.

When either party has reasonable grounds to question whether the other party will perform his contractual obligations, the questioning party <u>may</u> in writing <u>demand</u> <u>assurance</u> <u>of</u> <u>performance</u> and suspend his performance until such assurance is forthcoming. An anticipatory repudiation by a seller provides the buyer with reasonable grounds to question the seller's intent to perform and thus seek this remedy.

Answer choices other than "B" are based on incorrect assumptions and/or interpretations of the law.

#48 (answer "B")

Under the Sales Article of the UCC, the rights and obligations of the parties are determined by the terms of their contract. If the contract does not address a particular issue, then the UCC, common law, custom, and/or usage of trade will supplement the contract of the parties.

Thus, unless otherwise agreed to, the seller's obligation to the buyer is to <u>hold</u> <u>conforming</u> <u>goods</u> <u>and</u> <u>give</u> <u>the</u> <u>buyer</u> <u>whatever</u> <u>notification</u> <u>is</u> <u>reasonably</u> <u>necessary</u> <u>to</u> <u>enable</u> <u>the</u> <u>buyer</u> <u>to</u> <u>take</u> <u>delivery</u>. Once a tender of conforming goods occurs, then the seller is entitled to acceptance of the goods by the buyer and to payment of the contract price.

Answer choice "A" is incorrect because unless otherwise agreed, the seller is not obligated to deliver the goods to the buyer's place of business. Instead, the seller need only hold conforming goods and notify the buyer to come to the seller's place of business to pick up the goods.

Answer choice "C" is incorrect because, unless otherwise agreed, the seller is not obligated to deliver all the goods called for in the contract to a common carrier for transport to the buyer. Instead the buyer must go to the seller's place of business to pick up of the goods.

Answer choice "D" is incorrect because, unless otherwise agreed, the seller is not obligated to set aside conforming goods for inspection by the buyer prior to delivery. While the buyer has the right to inspect the goods before accepting them,

the seller has no obligation to deliver the goods to the buyer. The seller need only hold conforming goods and notify the buyer to come to the seller's place of business to pick up the goods.

#49 (answer "B")

The Sales Article of the UCC permits the parties to a contract for the sale of goods to specify in advance (i.e., to liquidate) the damages payable if a breach occurs. Liquidated damages clauses are valid as long as the amount specified bears a reasonable relationship to the damages that would actually occur in the event of a breach. A term fixing unreasonably large liquidated damages is void. Thus, an injured party may not collect any amount of liquidated damages provided for in a contract, but only an amount that bears a reasonable relationship to actual damages.

Where a seller justifiably withholds delivery of goods because of the buyer's breach, and no liquidated damages clause exists, the seller is entitled to keep the <u>smaller</u> of 20% of the purchase price or $500; the excess must be returned to the purchaser. Thus, <u>the</u> <u>seller</u> <u>may</u> <u>retain</u> <u>a</u> <u>deposit</u> <u>of</u> <u>up</u> <u>to</u> <u>$500</u> <u>when</u> <u>a</u> <u>buyer</u> <u>defaults</u> <u>even</u> <u>if</u> <u>there</u> <u>is</u> <u>no</u> <u>liquidated</u> <u>damages</u> <u>provision</u> <u>in</u> <u>the</u> <u>contract</u>.

Answer choices other than "B" are based on incorrect assumptions and/or interpretations of the law.

#50 (answer "A")

When a buyer materially breaches a sales contract, a seller has the following rights:

1. Withhold delivery to an insolvent buyer except for cash.
2. Stop delivery of goods in transit or in possession of a bailee.
3. Reclaim goods from the buyer if demand made within ten days of insolvent buyer's receipt (unless resold to an innocent purchaser).
4. Cure the defect(s) and proceed with the contract.
5. Complete manufacture of unfinished goods and identify them to the contract, or cease their manufacture and use remainder for scrap.
6. <u>Recover</u> <u>damages</u>.
7. <u>Cancel</u> <u>the</u> <u>contract</u>.
8. Recover contract price.

Answer choices other than "A" are based on incorrect assumptions and/or interpretations of the law.

#51 (answer "B")

In a joint tenancy, each joint tenant has the right of survivorship (i.e., automatically inherits the interest of a co-tenant who predeceases her). A joint tenant may convey her interest to a third party and thereby terminate the joint tenancy. The new owner becomes a tenant in common with the remaining joint tenants. Where Long conveyed Long's interest in the building by deed to Green, and Fall and Pear subsequently died, Green's interest in the building would consist of a ⅓ interest as a tenant in common.

Answer choices other than "B" are based on incorrect assumptions and/or interpretations of the law.

#52 (answer "D")

An arm's-length transaction is one in which the parties deal with each other on equal terms. Most everyday business transactions are arm's-length transactions. Thus, a transfer by sale is most likely to be considered an arm's-length transaction.

Answer choice "A" is incorrect because the parties to an inheritance do not deal with each other on equal terms. The testator has complete power to decide whether to grant an inheritance and, if so, to whom.

Answer choice "B" is incorrect because the doctrine of eminent domain allows the government to force an owner of private property to sell it to the government. Thus, no equality exists between the parties in a transfer of title by eminent domain.

Answer choice "C" is incorrect because title to property is transferred involuntarily via adverse possession. Thus, no equality exists between the parties in a transfer of title by adverse possession.

#53 (answer "B")

A lease is a contract between the owner of the land (i.e., the lessor) and another party (i.e., the tenant) whereby the lessor transfers to the lessee the right to use and control the property. Normally a lease for more than one year must satisfy the statute of frauds. An enforceable written residential lease must include:

1. The parties to the lease.
2. A description of the leased premises.
3. The term of the lease.
4. The amount of rent.
5. The signatures of the parties.

However, an enforceable written residential lease need not include a due date for the payment of rent.

Answer choices other than "B" are based on incorrect assumptions and/or interpretations of the law.

#54 (answer "C")

A deed is a written document by which a grantor transfers an interest in land to a grantee. Consideration is not required, and the purchase price need not be specified in the deed. However, a valid deed must:

1. Be signed by the grantor.
2. Be witnessed and delivered to the grantee with an intent to transfer an interest in real property.
3. Include a description of the land.

Answer choices other than "C" are based on incorrect assumptions and/or interpretations of the law.

#55 (answer "B")

Recording a mortgage protects a mortgagee's claim by giving public notice of the claim to third parties. While recordation is not necessary to protect the mortgagee's claim against the mortgagor, a subsequent good faith purchaser for value of land will take title to the land free of the mortgagee's claim if the mortgage is unrecorded. Thus, by recording the mortgage, Marsh protects its rights against the claims of subsequent bona fide purchasers for value.

Answer choice "A" is incorrect because Marsh's rights under the promissory note are not affected by Marsh's recordation of its mortgage. Marsh can enforce its rights under the promissory note against Rich without recording the mortgage.

Answer choice "C" is incorrect because Marsh's recordation of its mortgage gives it priority over subsequently filed claims against Rich's property.

However, Marsh's recordation does not give it priority over a previously filed real estate tax lien on the property.

Answer choice "D" is incorrect because Marsh's recordation of its mortgage gives it priority over subsequently filed claims against Rich's property but not priority against all parties having earlier claims to the property.

#56 (answer "C")

A fixture is a piece of personal property that has been attached to real property in a manner by which it becomes part of the real property. Two factors are considered by the courts to help determine whether an item of personal property has become a fixture:

1. The degree of the item's attachment to the property.
2. The intent of the person who had the item installed.

Answer choices other than "C" are based on incorrect assumptions and/or interpretations of the law.

#57 (answer "A")

The Federal Water Pollution Control Act (Clean Water Act) authorizes the Environmental Protection Agency to establish water quality criteria regulating concentrations of pollutants that are permissible in a body of water, and effluent limitations regulating the amount of pollutants that are discharged from a particular source. The Clean Water Act also regulates:

1. Point sources of water pollution (establishes standards for water pollution from sources such as utilities and manufacturing plants).
2. Thermal pollution (forbids the discharge of heated water by nuclear power plants).
3. Wetlands (forbids the filling or dredging of wetlands).
4. Hazardous substances (forbids the discharge of hazardous substances in harmful quantities).

Answer choices other than "A" are based on incorrect assumptions and/or interpretations of the law.

#58 (answer "C")

Property may be classified as either real property (land and all permanently attached personal property) or personal property (mobile things other than land and fixtures). While the process of transferring title (i.e., ownership) to real property is relatively formal, the transfer of title to personal property may be relatively informal. Ownership of personal property may be acquired in a variety of ways including:

1. By purchase.
2. By gift.
3. By taking possession (i.e., finding lost or abandoned property).
4. By production (i.e., producing a finished product from raw materials).

However, ownership is not acquired by leasing personal property, since a lease only transfers the right to use and possess property for the term of the lease.

Answer choices other than "C" are based on incorrect assumptions and/or interpretations of the law.

#59 (answer "D")

Common carriers transport goods for a fee for all members of the public. The consignor delivers goods to the carrier for shipment, while the consignee is the person designated by the consignor to receive the shipment. A common carrier is strictly liable for damages to the goods it transports, except where the damage is caused by:

1. An act of God.
2. The inherent or defective nature of the goods.
3. An act of a public authority (i.e., a government official).
4. Consignor's negligence.
5. An act of a public enemy (i.e., a terrorist group, but not an ordinary criminal).

Thus, a common carrier bailee generally would avoid liability for the loss of goods entrusted to its care if the goods are improperly packed by the party shipping them. Improper packaging of goods for shipment constitutes negligence by the consignor.

Answer choice "A" is incorrect because a common carrier is generally liable where goods entrusted to it are stolen by an unknown person (i.e., an ordinary criminal).

Answer choices "B" and "C" are incorrect because a common carrier is generally liable under the rules of agency (respondent superior) for damage to the goods entrusted to it resulting from the negligence of an employee of the carrier.

#60 (answer "A")

An insurable interest is an interest such that, upon the happening of peril against the insured, a pecuniary loss will be suffered by the insured. With property insurance, the insurable interest <u>must exist when any loss occurs</u>.

Answer choice "B" is incorrect because an insurable interest related to property insurance need only exist when a loss occurs. It is not required to also exist when the policy is issued.

Answer choice "C" is incorrect because an insurable interest related to property insurance may be created when property is owned for durations other than in fee simple (i.e., a life estate) and even where the insured does not own the insured property (i.e., the interest of a tenant and/or a mortgagee).

Answer choice "D" is incorrect because an insurable interest related to property insurance may exist where property is owned by multiple owners, such as by tenants in common.

OTHER OBJECTIVE FORMATS/ESSAY QUESTIONS

Answer 2

Part 2 (a)

#61 (answer "B")

Normally, no formality such as a written contract is required to create a valid agency relationship. Thus, <u>Lace's agreement with Banks was not required to be in writing to be valid</u>.

Further, <u>the oral agreement between Lace and Banks empowered Banks to act as Lace's agent</u>.

#62 (answer "A")

An agent's actual authority may be express or implied. Express authority derives from the principal's written or oral communications to the agent, directing the agent to accomplish a specific task. Implied authority is the authority the agent reasonably believes the agent has in light of the principal's conduct, as well as the surrounding circumstances, which are known or should be known by the agent. Banks' authority to cus-

tomize Lace's software was implied from Banks' express authority to perform customer service calls. Thus, <u>Clear was entitled to rely on Banks' implied authority to customize Lace's software</u>.

Banks was specifically told not to sell Lace's computers. Thus, <u>Clear was not entitled to rely on Banks' express authority when buying the computer</u>. Instead, Banks' authority to sell a Lace computer to Clear resulted from Banks' apparent authority; Clear was entitled to rely on Banks' apparent authority to sell computers since Clear had previously purchased computers from other Lace agents and was not aware that the price Banks offered was lower than normal.

#63 (answer "B")

An agent's authority is derived from the principal. An agency relationship may be terminated automatically by operation of law or by an act of one or both of the parties. However, an agency relationship is not automatically terminated where an agent breaches his duty of obedience to the principal by violating an instruction from the principal. Thus, <u>Lace's agreement with Banks was not automatically terminated by Banks' sale of the computer</u>.

Apparent authority is the authority that a third party reasonably assumes the agent has in light of the communications and conduct of a disclosed principal. The acts of an agent within the agent's apparent authority bind the principal to third parties who rely on such. In order to terminate an agent's apparent authority, actual notice must be given to all third parties with whom the agent had prior dealings and constructive notice must be given to all other third parties. Thus, <u>Lace must notify Clear before Banks' apparent authority to bind Lace will cease</u>.

#64 (answer "D")

A disclosed principal is bound by the agreements made by the principal's agent within the agent's actual and/or apparent authority. The agreement made by Banks with Clear was within Banks' apparent authority. Thus, <u>Lace is bound by the agreement made by Banks with Clear</u>.

The agreement made by Banks with Clear was a contract, which can only be amended with the mutual consent of the contracting parties. Thus, <u>Lace may not unilaterally amend the agreement</u>

made by Banks to prevent a loss on the sale of the computer to Clear.

#65 (answer "A")

An agent for a disclosed principal is not normally a party to the contracts the agent negotiates with third parties for the principal and is not personally liable on those contracts. Similarly, where an agent has apparent but not actual authority, the agent is not liable to the third party, but is liable to the principal for losses caused by exceeding the agent's actual authority. Thus, Lace, as a disclosed principal, is solely contractually liable to Clear. Banks, however, is not contractually liable to Clear.

Part 2(b)

#66 (answer "C")

The purpose of the rule against perpetuities is to limit the length of time a grantor may restrict the transfer and vesting of property interests through the use of contingent remainders. Generally, the rule provides that a grant of a contingent remainder in property is valid only if the contingent interest will vest within 21 years after the death of the person named in the grant. Glenn's testamentary trust did not include a contingent remainder. Thus, Glenn's trust was valid because it did not violate the rule against perpetuities.

A trust is a legal, taxable entity to hold property for the benefit of some named beneficiary. A trustee may be authorized to make distributions of the trust principal to the trust's income beneficiaries. Thus, Glenn's trust was valid even though it permitted the trustees to make principal payments to income beneficiaries.

#67 (answer "A")

The duration of a trust is specified by the creator of the trust and may be determined by the lifetime of one or more named persons. Glenn directed that the trustees distribute the income from the trust to Glenn's children for their lives and then distribute the trust principal to Glenn's grandchildren. Thus, Glenn's trust would be terminated if both of Glenn's children were to die.

Absent a contrary provision in the trust document, a trustee's actions will not terminate a trust. Thus, Glenn's trust would not be terminated because of the acts of the trustees.

#68 (answer "B")

A fiduciary duty arises out of a relationship involving trust and confidence, and a fiduciary duty is owed by a trustee to a beneficiary. A trustee's fiduciary duty imposes the obligation to act primarily for the benefit of the beneficiary. This includes the duty to obey the terms of the trust document. Glenn authorized Strong and Lake to make distributions of principal to the income beneficiaries as they determined were reasonable for the beneficiaries' welfare. Thus, Strong and Lake did not violate their fiduciary duties by making some distributions of principal.

Glenn directed Strong and Lake to make annual distributions of the trust income to Glenn's children during their lifetimes. Thus, Strong and Lake violated their fiduciary duties by failing to distribute the trust income annually.

#69 (answer "B")

Changes in the form of the trust property, such as insurance proceeds or stock dividends, are considered principal. Thus, generally, stock dividends are not considered income and should not be distributed.

Since they are considered changes in the form of the trust property, generally, stock dividends should be allocated to principal and remain as part of the trust.

#70 (answer "D")

Glenn, as creator of the trust, authorized Strong and Lake to make principal payments to the trust's income beneficiaries (i.e., Glenn's children) as the trustees determined to be reasonable for the beneficiaries' welfare Thus, the $10,000 principal payment was not an abuse of the trustees' authority.

Glenn did not authorize Strong and Lake to make principal payments to his grandchild. Thus, the $5,000 principal payment was not valid.

Answer 3

Part 3 (a)

#71 (answer "A")

A creditor with a secured claim against specific property of a debtor has the first priority of claim to the proceeds from the sale of that property. Thus, Safe Bank's claim will be the first paid of the listed claims because Safe is a secured creditor.

If the proceeds from the sale of the secured asset are insufficient to fully satisfy the secured party's claim, the secured party is treated as a general unsecured creditor for the deficiency. Thus, Safe Bank will not receive the entire amount of the balance of the mortgage due it as a secured creditor regardless of the amount received from the sale of the warehouse. If the sale of the warehouse does not produce an amount sufficient to pay the entire mortgage debt, then Safe Bank may not be able to recover the deficiency but may attempt to do so as a general unsecured creditor.

#72 (answer "B")

Once secured claims are satisfied, any remaining assets are applied to the claims of unsecured creditors. Some unsecured claims may have priority; if so, they are paid in full before a distribution can be made to satisfy claims with lesser priority. Unsecured claims for wages earned within 90 days before the filing of a bankruptcy petition have a priority over other unsecured claims, but the priority is limited to $4,000 for each employee. Thus, Rusk's employee salary claims may not be paid in full after the payment of any secured party; whether or not these claims are paid in full will depend on the level of the proceeds generated by the sale of the remaining assets.

However, the employee salary claims up to $4,000 per claimant will be paid before payment of any general creditors' claims.

#73 (answer "B")

Claims for unpaid taxes are unsecured claims, which are given a priority. Thus, the claim for 1994 federal income taxes due will not be paid as a secured creditor claim.

However, the claim for 1994 federal income taxes will be paid prior to the general creditor claims.

#74 (answer "C")

A bankruptcy trustee has the power to avoid a preferential transfer. A preferential transfer has the following elements:

1. Made to or for the benefit of a creditor.
2. Enables a creditor to obtain a preference over other creditors.

3. Made in connection with an antecedent debt.
4. Made within 90 days of petition filing (one year if transferee is an insider; i.e., one with whom the debtor has close ties).
5. Made while the debtor is insolvent (in the balance sheet sense). A debtor is presumed to have been insolvent during the 90 days immediately preceding the date the petition was filed.

A preferential transfer to an insider is one made within one year from the filing of a bankruptcy petition. Corporate directors are insiders. Thus, the February 1 repayments of the directors' loans were preferential transfers even though the payments were made more than 90 days before the filing of the petition for involuntary bankruptcy.

Also, the February 1 repayments of the directors' loans were preferential transfers because the payments were made to insiders; this fact extended the period within which a transfer is considered preferential from 90 days to one year.

#75 (answer "A")

Certain transfers made within 90 days of filing a bankruptcy petition are not deemed preferential, including:

1. Cash purchases and other substantially contemporaneous exchanges for new value.
2. Enabling loans where the creditor gives the debtor "new value" to acquire property; the debtor signs a security agreement giving the creditor a security interest in the property; the debtor uses the "new value" to actually acquire the property; and the creditor perfects her security interest within 20 days after the debtor receives possession of the property.
3. Transfers that are in payment of a debt incurred in the ordinary course of business of the debtor and transferee; made in the ordinary course of business of the debtor and transferee; and made according to ordinary business terms.
4. Any transfer of property valued at less than $600 where the debtor is an individual whose debts are primarily "consumer" debts.
5. A transfer that was for payment of child support or alimony.

Thus, the May 1 purchase and payment was not a preferential transfer because it was a transaction in the ordinary course of business.

As explained above, not all transfers made within 90 days of the filing of a bankruptcy petition are voidable preferences. Thus, the May 1 purchase and payment was not a preferential transfer even though it occurred within 90 days of the filing of the bankruptcy petition.

Part 3 (b)

#76 (answer "A")

Generally, Rule 505 and 506 of Regulation D of the 1933 Securities Act requires: (1) a private placement and (2) filing of a report with the SEC within 15 days of the sale of exempt securities. In addition, Rule 506 places no ceiling on the size of the offering and permits offerings to an unlimited number of accredited investors, but a maximum of 35 nonaccredited investors who are financially sophisticated. Thus, Coffee Corp. may make the Regulation D, Rule 506, exempt offering.

A "reporting company" under the Securities and Exchange Act of 1934 is one with more than $10 million in assets and a minimum of 500 shareholders or one whose securities are listed on a national exchange. Reporting companies are not precluded from taking advantage of the registration exemptions of the 1933 Securities Act. Thus, Coffee Corp. may make an exempt offering and is not disqualified by the fact that it is required to report to the SEC under the Securities Exchange Act of 1934.

#77 (answer "B")

Shares sold under a Regulation D, Rule 506, exempt offering may be purchased by any number of investors provided there are no more than 35 nonaccredited investors. Thus, shares sold under a Regulation D, Rule 506, exempt offering are not limited only to accredited investors but the offering may also include nonaccredited investors.

#78 (answer "B")

An exempt offering under Regulation D, Rule 506, has no dollar limit. Thus, an exempt offering may be for more than $10,000,000.

#79 (answer "B")

All purchases under Regulation D, Rule 506, result in ownership of "restricted securities," which must be held for two years or registered with the SEC before resale. An issuer who uses the Regulation D exemption must take reasonable care to assure against nonexempt, unregistered resales of these restricted securities. Reasonable care includes:

1. Making a reasonable inquiry to determine if the purchaser is acquiring the securities for himself or for other investors.
2. Providing written disclosure prior to the sale to each purchaser that the securities have not been registered and thus cannot be resold unless either registered with the SEC or an exemption is secured.
3. Placing a legend on the securities stating that they have not been registered and are restricted securities.

Thus, Regulation D, Rule 506, does not require notification to all investors in the exempt offering of a nine-month resale restriction applicable to nonresidents. However, Rule 506 does require that the issuer exercise reasonable care to assure that purchasers of the exempt offering are buying for investment and are not underwriters.

#80 (answer "D")

Regulation D, Rule 506, requires that the SEC be notified within 15 days of the sale of the first exempt securities. Thus, the SEC need not be notified by Coffee Corp. within 5 days of the first sale of the exempt offering securities.

When a Regulation D, Rule 506, exemption is used, the issuer notifies the SEC by filing a Form D within 15 days of the first sale of exempt securities. Thus, Coffee Corp. is not required to include an SEC notification of the first sale of the exempt offering securities in its next filed Quarterly Report (Form 10-Q).

Answer 4

Part 4 (a)

Korn would argue the following points of law to show that there was no valid contract:

1. Revocation—Korn would argue that Korn revoked Korn's offer to Wilson during their

phone conversation on September 30, 1995. An offeror may withdraw the offer any time prior to its acceptance, even where the offeror promised to hold the offer open for a specified period.

2. Counteroffer—Korn would argue that Wilson's letter of September 28 requesting to extend the agreement through March 1996, was a counteroffer. A counteroffer rejects the offeror's offer and communicates a willingness to contract but on different terms from those contained in the other party's offer.

Part 4 (b)

Wilson would argue the following points of law to show that there was a valid contract:

1. Acceptance effective upon dispatch—Wilson mailed Korn an acceptance on September 28, 1995. Normally an acceptance is effective upon dispatch. Thus, Wilson will argue that a contract was formed with Korn when Wilson mailed Wilson's letter of acceptance on September 28, which was several days before the offer was withdrawn.

2. Acceptance—A valid acceptance assents to the terms of the offer. Wilson will argue that Wilson accepted Korn's offer on September 28, 1995, and that Wilson's request to extend the terms of the contract through March 1996 did not constitute a counteroffer because it was immaterial and merely an inquiry to determine Korn's willingness to reopen the contract and modify its duration.

Part 4 (c)

1. Korn did breach the contract by orally repudiating it during the phone call to Wilson on September 30, 1995. A repudiation before the performance date specified in the contract is an anticipatory repudiation, which permits the nonbreaching party to either sue immediately or wait until the performance due date to sue.

2. The common law remedy available to Wilson is cancellation and/or the recovery of money damages. Money damages will place Wilson economically in the same position Wilson would have occupied if no breach had occurred, and will permit Wilson to

contract with another comparably priced snow removal contractor.

Answer 5

TO: Bill Smith, Partner-in-Charge

FROM: William Dover, Staff Auditor

SUBJECT: Audit of Crane Corp.

During the course of my audit of the financial records of Crane Corp., I became aware of several legal issues that I feel compelled to bring to your attention as partner-in-charge. Each issue is separately identified and explained below. In addition, I have provided for your consideration my conclusions on each issue.

Issue #1:   Is Crane a holder in due course?

Conclusion: Yes

Explanation: In order to be a holder in due course, a party must:

1. Be a holder of a negotiable instrument.
2. Take the instrument for value.
3. Take the instrument in good faith and before maturity.
4. Take the instrument without notice of any claims or defenses.

Thus, Crane is a holder in due course of the promissory note because Crane satisfied the requirements for such. The subsequent disclosure that Oval has a personal defense of fraud in the inducement against Jones does not affect Crane's status as a holder in due course.

Issue #2:   Can Crane compel Oval to honor the note?

Conclusion: Yes

Explanation: A holder in due course is not subject to personal defenses, such as fraud in the inducement. Oval Corp.'s defense to Crane's request for payment of the note is that Jones fraudulently induced Oval to execute the promissory note. Thus, Crane can compel Oval to honor the note.

Issue #3:   Is Jones Corp. liable on the note?

Conclusion: Yes

Explanation: All parties who transfer commercial paper in return for value, including those who endorse "without recourse," make certain implied transfer warranties on the instrument. A party who transfers commercial paper by endorsing it "without recourse" implicitly warrants that he has no knowledge of a defense of any party that is good against him.

Jones transferred the note to Crane Corp. for value (i.e., in exchange for a tractor). Oval contends that when Jones Corp. endorsed the note to Crane "without recourse," Jones knew about Oval's defense of fraud in the inducement. If Oval's claim is correct, then Jones is liable to pay the note to Crane because of Jones' breach of its implied transfer warranty.

Issue #4:   When was Crane's security interest perfected?

Conclusion: October 5, 1995

Explanation: Attachment of a security interest occurs when all of the following events happen:

1. The secured party has possession of the collateral pursuant to an agreement with the debtor, or the debtor has signed a security agreement describing the collateral.
2. The creditor has given value.
3. The debtor has property rights in the collateral.

Perfection occurs after attachment and when all the applicable steps required for perfection have been taken. Perfection may be accomplished in several ways, including filing a financial statement with the appropriate public official.

Crane's security interest in the tractor it sold to Harper attached on October 5, 1995, since Harper, the debtor, signed a security agreement on October 1, 1995, for the tractor; Crane gave value to Harper by delivering the tractor to Harper on October 5, 1995, and Harper already had rights in the tractor since Harper had made a down payment on the tractor on October 1, 1995.

Crane filed a financing statement covering the tractor on October 10, 1995, thereby perfecting its security interest in the tractor. The perfection relates back to the date that Harper took possession of the tractor (i.e., the collateral), which was on October 5, 1995. Thus, Crane's security interest in the tractor was perfected on October 5, 1995.

Issue #5:   Does Crane's security interest have priority over Acorn's security interest?

Conclusion: Yes

Explanation: Normally the chronological order of perfection determines priority among competing security interests. However, a purchase money security interest in collateral other than inventory has priority over a conflicting security interest in the same collateral if the purchase money security interest is perfected at the time the debtor receives possession of the collateral or within ten days thereafter.

On October 1, 1995, Crane provided partial financing to Harper to facilitate Harper's purchase of the tractor for use in Harper's farming business (i.e., as equipment). As a result, Crane had a purchase money security interest in the tractor. Harper, the debtor, took possession of the tractor on October 5, 1995. Crane filed its financing statement for the tractor on October 10, 1995, which was within ten days of the date that Harper, the debtor, took possession of the tractor. Thus, Crane's security interest has priority over Acorn's security interest because Crane's security interest is treated as perfected as of October 5, 1995 (i.e., the perfection relates back to the date the debtor took possession of the collateral), while Acorn's was not perfected until it filed a financing statement covering the tractor on October 9, 1995.

Auditing (AUDIT)

FOUR-OPTION MULTIPLE-CHOICE QUESTIONS

Answer 1

#1 (answer "D")

The objectivity of internal auditors may be judged in part by <u>determining the organizational level to which the internal auditors report</u> the results of their work. This indicates the degree to which the internal auditors can act independently of the people responsible for the functions being audited.

When the internal audit staff is independent of both the operating and the accounting departments and reports directly to top management, the internal control is enhanced. Reliance on the work of internal auditors depends on their competence, integrity, and independence from accounting and operating departments.

Answer choices other than "D" are incorrect because they represent procedures utilized to evaluate the competence of the internal auditor.

#2 (answer "A")

The auditor should obtain a sufficient understanding of the entity's internal control to properly plan the audit of the entity's financial statements. The understanding should include knowledge about the design of relevant controls, and records and whether they have been placed in operation by the entity. In planning the audit, such knowledge should be used to:

1. <u>Identify types of potential misstatements that could occur</u>.
2. Consider factors that affect the risk of material misstatements.
3. Design substantive tests.

Answer choice "B" is incorrect because the auditor has no responsibility to assess the operational efficiency of internal control.

Answer choice "C" is incorrect because collusion represents an inherent limitation of internal control. The auditor has no responsibility to determine whether controls have been circumvented by collusion since it may be impossible to detect.

Answer choice "D" is incorrect because the auditor must evaluate the effectiveness of the relevant internal controls before the auditor can document the assessed level of control risk.

#3 (answer "B")

Online processing is an EDP technique whereby processing procedures provide for concurrent input and recording of data. During processing, the data are subjected to record input controls to ensure that transaction data are authorized, accurate, and complete. The record input controls include an edit control or check, which detects whether input data are incomplete, invalid, or in error.

Therefore, a direct output of the edit checks most likely would be a <u>file of all rejected sales transactions</u>.

Answer choice "A" is incorrect because an online sales order processing system would generate a report of all missing sales invoices, but not as a direct output of the edit checks.

Answer choice "C" is incorrect because a printout of all user code numbers and passwords would not be a direct output of the edit checks.

Answer choice "D" is incorrect because a list of all voided shipping documents would not be generated by the edit checks of sales orders.

#4 (answer "B")

An auditor has a responsibility to comply with GAAS in conducting an audit. The auditor's understanding of internal control may sometimes <u>raise doubts about</u> the auditability of an entity's financial statements. Further, concerns about <u>the integrity of the entity's management</u> may be so serious as to cause the auditor to conclude that the risk of management misrepresentations in the financial statements is such that an audit cannot be conducted.

Answer choice "A" is incorrect because the lack of a formal written code of conduct would not preclude an audit from being conducted.

Answer choice "C" is incorrect because management override is an inherent limitation of any internal control.

Answer choice "D" is incorrect because management's failure to modify prescribed controls for changes in conditions may be due to cost-benefit considerations and would not ordinarily prevent an audit from being conducted.

#5 (answer "B")

For purposes of an audit of financial statements, an entity's internal control consists of (1) control environment, (2) risk assessment, (3) control activities, (4) information and communication, and (5) monitoring.

"Control environment" sets the tone of an organization, influencing the control consciousness of its people. It is the function for all other components of internal control, providing discipline and structure.

Specific control environment factors include:

1. Commitment to competence.
2. Participation of the board of directors or audit committee.
3. Assignment of authority and responsibility.
4. Human resource policies and practices.
5. Organizational structure.
6. Management's philosophy and operating style.
7. Ethical values and integrity.

Management's philosophy and operating style encompass a broad range of characteristics. Such characteristics may include management's approach to taking and monitoring business risks, management's attitudes and actions toward financial reporting, and management's emphasis on meeting budget, profit, and other financial and operating goals. These characteristics have significant influence on the control environment, particularly when management is dominated by one or a few individuals, regardless of the consideration given to the other control environment factors.

Answer choices other than "B" are incorrect because they reflect favorable control environment factors.

#6 (answer "C")

Management control methods include:

1. Establishing planning and reporting systems that set forth management's plan and the results of actual performance. Such systems may include business planning, budgeting, forecasting, profit planning, and responsibility accounting.

2. Establishing methods that identify the status of actual performance and exceptions from planned performance, as well as communicating them to the appropriate levels of management.
3. Using such methods at appropriate management levels to investigate variances from expectations and to take appropriate and timely corrective action.

In view of the above, establishing budgets and forecasts to identify variances from expectations is a management control method that most likely could improve management's ability to supervise company activities effectively.

Answer choices other than "C" are based on incorrect assumptions.

#7 (answer "C")

A flowchart is a schematic representation of the flow of data through a sequence of operations.

In the question situation, the flowchart is for a revenue cycle. The flowchart indicates that order and shipping data, remittances from customers, and sales return and write-off authorizations are entered into application programs.

The application programs process the data using several data files. These data files consist of the sales transaction file, the cash receipts transaction file, the general ledger transaction file, the general ledger master file, and the accounts receivable master file (i.e., symbol "A").

Answer choice "A" is incorrect because remittance advice information is contained in the cash receipts transaction file.

Answer choices "B" and "D" are incorrect because they represent files applicable to a client's expenditure cycle.

#8 (answer "D")

A flowchart is a schematic representation of the flow of data through a sequence of operations.

In the question situation, the flowchart is for a revenue cycle. The flowchart indicates that order and shipping data, remittances from customers, and sales return and write-off authorizations are entered into application programs.

The application programs process the data using several data files. These data files consist of the sales transaction file, the cash receipts transaction file, the general ledger transaction file, the general ledger master file, and the accounts receivable master file.

In the revenue cycle, output includes updated files and records, and documents such as credit memos and sales invoices.

Answer choice "A" is incorrect because customer orders represent input data rather than output data.

Answer choice "B" is incorrect because receiving reports are not an output of revenue cycle processing.

Answer choice "C" is incorrect because customer checks are part of the remittance data input.

#9 (answer "A")

As part of an audit, an auditor is required to document the auditor's understanding of the entity's internal control. Such documentation may include flowcharts, questionnaires, narrative memoranda, and/or decision tables. In addition, for those financial statement assertions where control risk is assessed at the maximum level (i.e., 100%, which is the greatest probability that a material misstatement in a financial statement assertion will not be prevented or detected by an entity's internal control), the auditor should document the auditor's conclusion that control risk is at the maximum level, but need not document the basis for that conclusion.

Answer choice "B" is incorrect because an auditor is not required to search for significant deficiencies in the operation of internal control.

Answer choices "C" and "D" are incorrect because they represent controls that would not be required when the auditor assesses control risk at the maximum level.

#10 (answer "C")

Controls in an electronic data processing (EDP) system can be classified as general controls and application controls. General controls relate to all parts of the EDP system and must, therefore, be evaluated early in the audit. Application controls, however, apply to specific use of the system and should be evaluated specifically for every audit area in which the client uses the computer.

General controls include the plan of organization and operation of the EDP activity, the procedures for documenting, reviewing, testing, and approving systems and programs and changes therein, as well as controls built into the equipment by the manufacturer (i.e., hardware controls) that will detect and sometimes correct machine-based errors.

Application controls include input, processing, and output controls.

Input controls should be designed to provide reasonable assurance that information accepted from other parts of the accounting system is authorized, accurate, and complete.

Processing controls should be designed to provide reasonable assurance that accounting information generated by the application is accurate. Two of the more common processing controls are a limit test and a validity check test. The former is designed to ascertain that information fits within prescribed limits and control totals. The latter involves the CPU checking whether data are classified appropriately as allowed by the system.

Output controls should be designed to ensure the accuracy of the processing result, and to ensure that only authorized personnel receive the output.

In view of the above, an example of a validity check is a computer flag of any transmission for which the control field value did not match that of an existing file record.

Answer choice "A" is incorrect because it is representative of a limit test.

Answer choice "B" is incorrect because it is representative of a report.

Answer choice "D" is incorrect because it is representative of a machine-based check.

#11 (answer "C")

In obtaining an understanding of internal controls that are relevant to audit planning, the auditor should perform procedures to provide sufficient knowledge of the design of the relevant controls pertaining to each of the five internal control components and whether they have been placed in operation.

Inquiries of appropriate entity personnel and inspection of documents and records, such as source documents, journals, and ledgers, may provide an understanding of the accounting records designed to process those transactions and whether they have been placed in operation. Similarly, in obtaining an understanding of the design of computer-programmed control procedures and whether they have been placed in operation, the auditor may make inquiries of appropriate entity personnel and examine client records documenting the use of EDP programs.

Answer choices "A" and "D" are incorrect because they represent evidence derived from analytical procedures. Analytical procedures are not relevant to an auditor's consideration of internal control.

Answer choice "B" is incorrect because it represents evidence from a substantive test.

#12 (answer "A")

Most entities request customers to pay by check in order to minimize the likelihood of diversion of mail receipts. Entities with a large volume of mail receipts should use a bank lockbox system. A lockbox is a post office box that is controlled by the company's bank. The bank picks up the mail daily, credits the entity for cash, and sends remittance advices to the entity's accounts receivable clerk. This system expedites the depositing of checks and permits the company to receive credit sooner.

Accordingly, a bank lockbox system reduces the risk of employee misappropriation (i.e., diversion) of cash receipts.

Answer choices other than "A" are incorrect because they would not be as effective as a bank lockbox system in reducing the risk of diversion of customer receipts by an entity's employees.

#13 (answer "A")

In obtaining an understanding of internal controls that are relevant to audit planning, the auditor should perform procedures to provide sufficient knowledge of the design of the relevant controls for each component of internal control and whether they have been placed in operation.

Answer choices other than "A" are incorrect because they represent knowledge obtained in assessing control risk rather than in obtaining an understanding of internal control.

#14 (answer "B")

Control procedures are those controls, in addition to the control environment and information system, that management has established to provide reasonable assurance that an entity's established objectives will be achieved.

Control procedures include segregation of functions designed to avoid a position that can both perpetrate and conceal an error and/or fraud.

In an EDP environment, duties should be assigned as follows:

1. Systems analyst—Evaluates existing systems, designs new systems, and provides specifications for programmers.
2. Programmer—Flow charts programs, develops, debugs, and documents programs.
3. Computer operator—Operates the computer (console) following program operating instructions.
4. Data entry operator—Translates data into machine-readable media.

In light of the above, segregation of duties within EDP for computer programming and computer operations could most likely prevent EDP personnel from modifying programs to bypass programmed controls.

Answer choices other than "B" are incorrect because they represent control procedures that could not prevent EDP personnel from modifying programs to bypass programmed controls.

#15 (answer "A")

Control activities are the policies and procedures that help ensure that management directives are carried out. They help ensure that necessary actions are taken to address risks to achievement of the entity's objectives.

Control activities relevant to an audit include policies and procedures that pertain to:

1. Performance reviews—include comparisons of actual performance to budgets and forecasts.
2. Information processing—controls should be performed to check accuracy, completeness, and authorization of transactions:
   a. General controls—include controls over data center operations, access security, and system development.

b. <u>Application</u> <u>controls</u>—apply to the processing of individual applications and help ensure that transactions are valid, properly authorized, and completely and accurately processed.
3. <u>Physical</u> <u>controls</u>—include adequate safeguards over access to assets and records, and periodic counting and comparison with amounts shown on control records.
4. <u>Segregation</u> <u>of</u> <u>duties</u>—involves assigning different people the responsibilities of authorizing transactions, recording transactions, and maintaining custody of assets in order to reduce the opportunity to allow any person to both perpetrate and conceal errors or fraud in the normal course of his duties.

In view of the above, a control whereby <u>the personnel</u> <u>department</u> <u>promptly</u> <u>sends</u> <u>employee</u> <u>termination</u> <u>notices</u> <u>to</u> <u>the</u> <u>payroll</u> <u>supervisor</u> most likely could help prevent employee payroll fraud.

Answer choices other than "A" are incorrect because they represent poor controls that could enhance the opportunity for employee payroll fraud, rather than prevent it.

#16 (answer "B")

Proper safeguarding of securities held as investments requires segregation of:

1. The custody of, or access to, securities from the accounting or record keeping responsibility for the securities.
2. The proper authorization of transactions from the custody of, or access to, the securities.
3. Operational responsibility from record keeping responsibility.

In addition, requiring the signatures and presence of two designated officials is a dual-access procedure that would require collusion to remove the assets. Dual access is generally used to provide assurance that marketable securities held as investments are safeguarded.

Accordingly, a control whereby <u>two</u> <u>company</u> <u>officials</u> <u>have</u> <u>joint</u> <u>control</u> <u>of</u> <u>marketable</u> <u>securities,</u> <u>which</u> <u>are</u> <u>kept</u> <u>in</u> <u>a</u> <u>bank</u> <u>safe-deposit</u> <u>box,</u> employs the dual-access procedure to safeguard marketable securities.

Answer choices other than "B" are incorrect because they refer to procedures that would not provide assurance that marketable securities are safeguarded.

#17 (answer "C")

Sampling risk arises from the possibility that, when a test of controls or a substantive test is limited to a sample, the auditor's conclusions may be different from the conclusions that would have been drawn had the test been applied to all of the items in the population.

The auditor is concerned with two aspects of sampling risk in conducting tests of controls. They are

1. <u>The</u> <u>risk</u> <u>of</u> <u>assessing</u> <u>control</u> <u>risk</u> <u>too</u> <u>low</u>—In performing tests of controls, the risk that the assessed level of control risk based on the sample is less than the true operating effectiveness of the controls.
2. <u>The</u> <u>risk</u> <u>of</u> <u>assessing</u> <u>control</u> <u>risk</u> <u>too</u> <u>high</u>—In performing tests of controls, the risk that the assessed level of control risk based on the sample is greater than the true operating effectiveness of the controls.

The two aspects of sampling risk with which the auditor is concerned in conducting substantive tests of details are

1. <u>The</u> <u>risk</u> <u>of</u> <u>incorrect</u> <u>acceptance</u>—The sample supports the conclusion that the recorded account balances are not materially misstated when, in fact, they are.
2. <u>The</u> <u>risk</u> <u>of</u> <u>incorrect</u> <u>rejection</u>—The sample supports the conclusion that the recorded account balances are materially misstated when, in fact, they are not.

The risk of incorrect rejection and the risk of assessing control risk too high relate to the efficiency of the audit.

The risk of incorrect acceptance and the risk of assessing control risk too low relate to the effectiveness of the audit.

Accordingly, the risk of assessing control risk too low exists when the <u>auditor's</u> <u>estimate</u> <u>based</u> <u>on</u> <u>sample</u> <u>results</u> indicates that the <u>maximum</u> <u>deviation</u> <u>rate</u> <u>is</u> <u>less</u> <u>than</u> <u>the</u> <u>tolerable</u> <u>rate</u> when, in fact, the <u>true</u> <u>state</u> <u>of</u> <u>the</u> <u>population</u> <u>deviation</u> <u>rate</u> <u>exceeds</u> <u>the</u> <u>tolerable</u> <u>rate.</u>

Answer choices other than "C" are based on incorrect assumptions.

#18 (answer "B")

If an auditor wishes to assess control risk at below the maximum level, the auditor must perform tests of controls. The auditor selects such tests from a variety of techniques, such as inquiry, <u>observation</u>, inspection, <u>and</u> <u>reperformance</u> of a control that pertains to an assertion. No one specific test of controls is always necessary, applicable, or equally effective in every circumstance.

The following describes the appropriate circumstances in which each of these tests should be used.

1. Inquiries of appropriate entity personnel. Although an inquiry is generally not a strong source of evidence about the effective operation of controls, it is an appropriate form of evidence (e.g., inquiries of computer librarian).
2. Inspection of documents, records, and reports is appropriate when a clear trail of documentary evidence exists (e.g., the auditor examines a customer order and the related approved sales order to ensure that they are complete and properly matched, and that the required signatures or initials are present).
3. Observation is appropriate when there is no complete transaction trail (e.g., separation of duties relies on specific persons performing specific tasks, and there is typically no documentation of the separate performances). As such, for controls that leave no documentary evidence, the auditor generally observes them being applied.
4. Reperformance involves control-related activities for which there are related documents and records, but that contain insufficient data for the auditor's purpose of assessing whether the controls are operating effectively (e.g., client personnel fail to indicate if they have compared prices on a sales invoice to a standard price list). As such, the auditor would reperform the control activity to ascertain that proper results were obtained.

Answer choice "A" is incorrect because analytical procedures are not relevant to tests of controls that are performed in assessing control risk.

Answer choice "C" is incorrect because comparison and confirmation are relevant to substantive testing and not to tests of controls that are performed in assessing control risk.

Answer choice "D" is incorrect because verification is relevant to substantive testing and not to tests of controls that are performed in assessing control risk.

#19 (answer "D")

Sampling risk arises from the possibility that, when a test of controls or a substantive test is limited to a sample, the auditor's conclusions may be different from the conclusions that would have been drawn had the test been applied to all of the items in the population.

The auditor is concerned with two aspects of sampling risk in conducting tests of controls. They are

1. The <u>risk</u> <u>of</u> <u>assessing</u> <u>control</u> <u>risk</u> <u>too</u> <u>low</u>— In performing tests of controls, the risk that the assessed level of control risk based on the sample is less than the true operating effectiveness of the controls.
2. The <u>risk</u> <u>of</u> <u>assessing</u> <u>control</u> <u>risk</u> <u>too</u> <u>high</u>— In performing tests of controls, the risk that the assessed level of control risk based on the sample is greater than the true operating effectiveness of the controls.

The two aspects of sampling risk with which the auditor is concerned in conducting substantive tests of details are:

1. The <u>risk</u> <u>of</u> <u>incorrect</u> <u>acceptance</u>—The sample supports the conclusion that the recorded account balances are not materially misstated when, in fact, they are.
2. The <u>risk</u> <u>of</u> <u>incorrect</u> <u>rejection</u>—The sample supports the conclusion that the recorded account balances are materially misstated when, in fact, they are not.

The risk of incorrect rejection and the risk of assessing control risk too high relate to the efficiency of the audit. This is so because although the auditor will draw correct conclusions, the auditor performs more procedures than necessary.

The risk of incorrect acceptance and the likelihood of assessing control risk too low relate to the <u>effectiveness</u> <u>of</u> <u>the</u> <u>audit</u>. That is, based upon the finding of the sample, the auditor will draw incorrect conclusions regarding the population under audit.

Answer choices "A" and "B" are clearly based on incorrect assumptions.

Answer choice "C" is incorrect because the risk of incorrect rejection and the likelihood of assessing control risk too high relate to the efficiency of the audit.

#20 (answer "A")

Assessing control risk may be performed concurrently during an audit with obtaining an understanding of the entity's internal control. The objective of tests of controls is to provide the auditor with evidential matter to use in assessing control risk. The objective of procedures performed to obtain an understanding of internal control is to provide the auditor with knowledge necessary for audit planning. Procedures performed to achieve one objective may also pertain to the other objective.

Answer choice "B" is incorrect because evidence about the operation of controls in prior audits may be considered during the current year's assessment of control risk.

Answer choice "C" is incorrect because the basis for an auditor's conclusions about the assessed level of control risk need not be documented only if control risk is assessed at the maximum level.

Answer choice "D" is incorrect because the lower the assessed level of control risk, the greater assurance the evidence must provide that the control procedures are operating effectively.

#21 (answer "D")

Audit risk and materiality affect the application of GAAS, in particular the standards of fieldwork and reporting.

Audit risk—The risk that the auditor may unknowingly fail to modify the auditor's opinion on financial statements that are materially misstated. Inherent, control, and detection risks are the constituent parts of audit risk as follows:

1. Inherent risk—The susceptibility of an assertion to a material misstatement, assuming there are no related controls.
2. Control risk—Risk that a material misstatement that could occur in an assertion will not be prevented or detected on a timely basis by an entity's internal controls.

3. Detection risk—Risk that the auditor will not detect a material misstatement that exists in an assertion.

Inherent and control risks exist independently of the audit of financial statements. Detection risk relates to the auditor's procedures and can be altered at the auditor's discretion.

An auditor uses the knowledge provided by the understanding of internal control and the assessed level of control risk primarily to determine the nature, timing, and extent of substantive tests for financial statement assertions.

The substantive tests that the auditor performs reduce detection risk. Accordingly, an auditor assesses control risk (and uses the assessed level of control risk, together with the assessed level of inherent risk) because it affects the level of detection risk that the auditor may accept.

Answer choice "A" is incorrect because the auditor's understanding of control environment precedes the assessment of control risk.

Answer choice "B" is incorrect because materiality levels are established prior to the assessment of control risk. In subsequent stages of the audit, the auditor may lower materiality levels because of audit findings.

Answer choice "C" is incorrect because inherent risk is independent of the assessment of control risk.

#22 (answer "D")

Assessing control risk is the process of evaluating the effectiveness of an entity's internal controls in preventing or detecting material misstatements in the financial statements.

Control risk is the risk that a material misstatement that could occur in an assertion will not be prevented or detected on a timely basis by an entity's internal controls.

After obtaining an understanding of internal control, the auditor may assess control risk at the maximum level (i.e., 100%, which is the greatest probability that a material misstatement in a financial statement assertion will not be prevented or detected by an entity's internal control) for some or all assertions because the auditor believes that:

1. Controls are unlikely to pertain to an assertion.

2. Controls are unlikely to be effective.
3. Evaluating the effectiveness of the controls would be inefficient.

Assessing control risk at below the maximum level involves:

1. <u>Identifying</u> <u>specific</u> <u>internal</u> <u>controls</u> <u>relevant</u> <u>to</u> <u>specific</u> <u>assertions</u> that are likely to detect or prevent material misstatements in those assertions.
2. Performing tests of controls to evaluate the effectiveness of such controls.

Answer choices "A" and "C" are incorrect because they involve substantive testing, and would not be used in assessing control risk.

Answer choice "B" is incorrect because inherent risk is independent of the assessment of control risk.

#23 (answer "D")

Control risk is the risk that a material misstatement that could occur in an assertion will not be prevented or detected on a timely basis by an entity's internal controls.

After obtaining the understanding of internal control and assessing control risk at below the maximum level, the auditor may desire to seek a further reduction in the assessed level of control risk for certain assertions. In such cases, the auditor considers whether <u>additional</u> <u>evidential</u> <u>matter</u> <u>sufficient</u> <u>to</u> <u>support</u> <u>a</u> <u>further</u> <u>reduction</u> <u>is</u> <u>likely</u> <u>to</u> <u>be</u> <u>available</u>, and whether it would be efficient to perform tests of controls to obtain that evidential matter. The results of the procedures performed to obtain the understanding of internal control, as well as pertinent information from other sources, help the auditor to evaluate those two factors.

Answer choice "A" is incorrect because the auditor obtains an understanding of the entity's control activities prior to assessing control risk.

Answer choice "B" is incorrect because an auditor determines whether internal controls have been placed in operation as part of obtaining an understanding of internal control.

Answer choice "C" is incorrect because the auditor must consider whether the entity's internal controls pertain to any financial statement assertions prior to assessing control risk at below the maximum level.

#24 (answer "C")

Assessing control risk is the process of evaluating the effectiveness of an entity's internal controls in preventing or detecting material misstatements in the financial statements. This assessment is required after the auditor obtains and documents her understanding of an entity's internal control components.

Accordingly, the auditor should document the auditor's <u>understanding</u> <u>of</u> <u>the</u> <u>entity's</u> <u>control</u> <u>environment</u>. Generally, the more complex the internal control and the more extensive the procedures performed, the more extensive the auditor's documentation should be.

In addition, the auditor should document her conclusions about the assessed level of control risk.

For those financial statement assertions where control risk is assessed at the maximum level, the auditor should document her conclusion that control risk is at the maximum level, but need not document the basis for that conclusion. <u>For</u> <u>those</u> <u>assertions</u> <u>where</u> <u>the</u> <u>assessed</u> <u>level</u> <u>of</u> <u>control</u> <u>risk</u> <u>is</u> <u>below</u> <u>the</u> <u>maximum</u> <u>level</u>, the auditor is required to <u>document</u> the <u>basis</u> <u>for</u> the auditor's <u>conclusions</u> that the effectiveness of the design and operation of the internal controls support that assessed level.

Answer choices other than "C" are based on incorrect assumptions and/or illogical combinations.

#25 (answer "D")

Attribute sampling is a statistical method used to estimate the upper limit deviation rate (the upper precision limit) for an attribute (i.e., a specific type of deviation in the control being tested).

The required sample size is based on three factors:

1. Sampling risk.
2. Expected population deviation rate.
3. Tolerable deviation rate.

Once the sample size is determined, the sample is selected and audited.

The achieved upper limit deviation rate is based on the sum of two factors:

1. The sample deviation rate (i.e., the actual rate found in the sample).

402 November 1995 CPA Examination

2. The allowance for sampling risk.

If the achieved upper limit deviation rate does not exceed the tolerable deviation rate, then the sample results are normally satisfactory (that is, control risk may be assessed at less than the maximum level).

However, if the <u>sample rate of deviation plus the allowance for sampling risk exceeds the tolerable</u> deviation <u>rate</u>, then the sample results are not satisfactory and the auditor should normally reduce the planned reliance on a prescribed control.

Answer choices other than "D" are based on incorrect assumptions.

#26 (answer "D")

The deviation rate (i.e., the frequency of deviations in tests of controls) in the sample is the auditor's best estimate of the deviation rate in the population from which it was selected.

In addition to evaluating the frequency of deviations from pertinent procedures, consideration should be given to the qualitative aspects of the deviations. These include (1) the nature and cause of the deviations, such as whether they are errors or fraudulent acts or are due to the misunderstanding of instructions or to carelessness, and (2) the possible relationship of the deviations to other phases of the audit. The discovery of fraud ordinarily requires a broader consideration of possible implications than does the discovery of an error.

Accordingly, the auditor most likely would give broader consideration to the implications of a deviation if it was <u>initially concealed by a forged document</u>.

Answer choices other than "D" are based on incorrect conclusions.

#27 (answer "C")

In planning to assess control risk at a low level for specific assertions, an auditor will first obtain an understanding of internal control and then assess control risk. To seek a further reduction in the assessed level of control risk, the auditor will test the effectiveness of the internal controls through tests of controls.

When the results of tests of controls support the design of internal controls as expected, the audi-

tor will then use the assessed level of control risk as planned, resulting in decreased substantive testing during the audit.

Thus, when the auditor plans to assess control risk at a low level for property and equipment, the auditor should (1) obtain an understanding of internal control, (2) perform <u>tests of controls</u> and, if supportive of the internal controls as expected, (3) perform <u>limited</u> substantive <u>tests of current year property and equipment transactions</u>.

Answer choice "A" is incorrect because the assessment of control risk at a low level would result in limited, rather than extensive, tests of property and equipment balances.

Answer choices "B" and "D" are incorrect because analytical procedures are substantive tests and not tests of controls used to support the assessment of control risk at a low level.

#28 (answer "A")

For proper functioning of internal controls, there must be a segregation of:

1. The custody of, or access to, assets from the accounting or record keeping responsibility for the assets.
2. The proper authorization of transactions from the custody of, or access to, the related assets.
3. Duties within the accounting function.
4. Operational responsibility from record keeping responsibility.

Lapping involves the postponement of entries for the collection of receivables to conceal cash shortages. Cash receipts from one customer that are unrecorded are covered by the receipts from another customer; these receipts in turn are covered by other receipts. This type of fraud can be perpetrated by a person who records receipts of cash in both the cash receipts journal and the accounts receivable ledger. Therefore, comparison of the <u>dates checks are deposited per bank statements with the dates remittance credits are recorded</u> would most likely reveal the delay caused by lapping.

Answer choices "B" and "C" are incorrect because they do not consider the accounts receivable ledger.

Answer choice "D" is incorrect because comparison of dates for authorization of write-offs of uncollectible accounts with dates of recorded write-offs does not involve cash receipts.

#29 (answer "D")

A voucher system is often used to handle cash disbursements. A voucher system helps gain control over cash disbursements by providing a routine that: (1) permits only designated departments and individuals to incur obligations that will result in cash disbursements; (2) establishes procedures for incurring such obligations, and for their verification, approval, and recording; and (3) permits checks to be issued only in payment of properly verified, approved, and recorded obligations.

Typically, upon receipt of a vendor's invoice (which often includes an attached remittance advice), the invoice is checked for mathematical accuracy by the vouchers (accounts) payable department, and then matched against copies of the receiving report, inspection report, purchase order, and purchase requisition. This procedure provides the most effective assurance that recorded purchases are free of material misstatements.

The accounting department is then in a position to approve the invoice, and a voucher (i.e., a request for payment) is prepared. The entire voucher package is then checked and approved by a responsible individual in the vouchers (accounts) payable department, and the amount is posted to the ledger.

After being approved for payment and recorded, a voucher is filed until its due date, at which time it is sent to the company's cashier (i.e., treasurer's department) for payment. A check is then prepared and signed by the treasurer. In turn, the check signer should control the mailing of the check and the related remittance advice.

The voucher package is then canceled by the treasurer and sent back to the vouchers (accounts) payable department for filing.

Thus, the person who signs checks should also be responsible for mailing checks and remittance advices.

Answer choice "A" is incorrect because reviewing the monthly bank reconciliation is not a responsibility of the individual who signs checks.

Answer choice "B" is incorrect because signed checks are not returned to accounts payable.

Answer choice "C" is incorrect because the supporting documentation provides the basis for signing checks.

#30 (answer "D")

A voucher system is often used to handle cash disbursements. A voucher system helps gain control over cash disbursements by providing a routine that: (1) permits only designated departments and individuals to incur obligations that will result in cash disbursements; (2) establishes procedures for incurring such obligations, and for their verification, approval, and recording; and (3) permits checks to be issued only in payment of properly verified, approved, and recorded obligations.

Typically, upon receipt of a vendor's invoice (which often includes an attached remittance advice), the invoice is checked for mathematical accuracy by the vouchers (accounts) payable department, and then matched against copies of the receiving report, inspection report, purchase order, and purchase requisition. This procedure provides the most effective assurance that recorded purchases are free of material misstatements.

The accounting department is then in a position to approve the invoice, and a voucher (i.e., a request for payment) is prepared. The entire voucher package is then checked and approved by a responsible individual in the vouchers (accounts) payable department, and the amount is posted to the expense ledger.

After being approved for payment and recorded, a voucher is filed until its due date, at which time it is sent to the company's cashier (i.e., treasurer's department) for payment. A check is then prepared and signed by the treasurer. In turn, the check signer should control the mailing of the check and the related remittance advice. The voucher package is then canceled by the treasurer and sent back to the vouchers (accounts) payable department for filing.

For effective internal control, the vouchers (accounts) payable department generally should establish the agreement of the vendor's invoice with the receiving report, inspection report, purchase order, and purchase requisition.

Answer choice "A" is incorrect because the voucher package is canceled in the treasurer's department, not in the vouchers (accounts) payable department.

Answer choices "B" and "C" are incorrect because they represent functions of the purchasing department, not the vouchers (accounts) payable department.

#31 (answer "A")

To determine the effectiveness of an entity's controls relating to assertions, the auditor will perform tests of controls. The auditor selects such tests from a variety of techniques, such as inquiry, observation, inspection, and reperformance of a policy or procedure that pertains to an assertion. No one specific test of controls is always necessary, applicable, or equally effective in every circumstance.

The following describes the appropriate circumstances in which each of these tests may be used.

1. Inquiries of appropriate entity personnel. Although an inquiry is generally not a strong source of evidence about the effective operation of controls, it is an appropriate form of evidence (e.g., inquiries of computer librarian).
2. Inspection of documents, records, and reports is appropriate when there is a clear trail of documentary evidence (e.g., the auditor examines a customer order and the related approved sales order to ensure that they are complete and properly matched, and that the required signatures or initials are present).
3. Observation is appropriate when there may not be a clear or complete transaction trail (e.g., separation of duties relies on specific persons performing specific tasks and there is typically no documentation of the separate performances, such as computer processing of the transaction). For controls that leave no documentary evidence, or incomplete documentary evidence, the auditor generally observes them being applied.
4. Reperformance involves control-related activities for which there are related documents and records, but they contain insufficient data for the auditor's purpose of assessing whether the controls are operating effectively (e.g., client personnel fail to indicate if they have compared prices on a

sales invoice to a standard price list). As such, the auditor would reperform the control activity to ascertain that proper results were obtained.

In determining the effectiveness of an entity's controls relating to the existence or occurrence assertion for payroll transactions, an auditor most likely would inquire about and <u>observe</u> the <u>segregation</u> <u>of</u> <u>duties</u> <u>concerning</u> <u>personnel</u> <u>responsibilities</u> <u>and</u> <u>payroll</u> <u>disbursement</u>.

Answer choice "B" is incorrect because inspection is used when a clear trail of documentary evidence exists; the existence of such a trail cannot be determined from the facts presented.

Answer choices "C" and "D" are incorrect because they represent substantive tests.

#32 (answer "C")

The auditor should obtain a sufficient understanding of the entity's internal control to properly plan the audit of the entity's financial statements. The understanding should include knowledge about the design of relevant controls, and whether they have been placed in operation by the client. This knowledge is obtained through previous experience with the entity, inquiry, observation, client descriptions, and so on.

An auditor should obtain an understanding of an entity's internal control in planning an audit in order to:

1. Identify the types of potential misstatements that can occur.
2. Design substantive tests.
3. Consider factors that affect the risk of material misstatements.

The auditor need not obtain knowledge regarding operating effectiveness as part of the understanding of the internal control. The auditor's concern at this point is whether controls have been placed in service (i.e., utilized).

In obtaining an understanding of a manufacturing entity's internal control concerning inventory balances, an auditor most likely would <u>review</u> <u>the</u> <u>entity's</u> <u>descriptions</u> <u>of</u> <u>inventory</u> <u>controls</u>.

Answer choices other than "C" are incorrect because they represent substantive tests, and therefore are not useful in obtaining an understanding of an entity's internal control.

#33 (answer "A")

The objective of determining the sample size for a test of controls is to obtain a sample that will meet desired statistical objectives for each control being tested.

The factors that affect the determination of sample size are (1) <u>tolerable</u> <u>deviation</u> <u>rate</u>, (2) the <u>allowable</u> <u>risk</u> <u>of</u> <u>assessing</u> <u>control</u> <u>risk</u> <u>too</u> <u>low</u> (i.e., the sampling risk), <u>and</u> (3) the <u>expected</u> <u>deviation</u> <u>rate</u>.

The expected deviation rate has a significant and direct effect on sample size. This effect recognizes that as the expected deviation rate increases, more exact information is required and a larger sample size results. Conversely, a smaller sample size would result as the expected deviation rate decreases.

However, tolerable deviation rate and the allowable risk of assessing control risk too low are inversely related to sample size. Accordingly, as these two parameters increase, a decrease in sample size will result.

Answer choices other than "A" are based on incorrect assumptions and/or illogical combinations.

#34 (answer "D")

Audit procedures to search for unrecorded retirements of equipment would relate to management's assertion of existence (i.e., whether the equipment of the entity exists). A weakness in internal control over recording retirements of equipment may cause an auditor to <u>select</u> <u>certain</u> <u>items</u> <u>of</u> <u>equipment</u> <u>from</u> <u>the</u> <u>accounting</u> <u>records</u> <u>and</u> <u>locate</u> <u>them</u> <u>in</u> <u>the</u> <u>plant</u> to ascertain whether the equipment still exists or has been retired. This would provide evidence about assets that had been retired but that had not been removed from the accounting records.

Answer choice "A" is incorrect because inspecting certain items of equipment in the plant and tracing those items to the accounting records provides evidence of unrecorded additions of equipment (i.e., the completeness assertion).

Answer choices "B" and "C" are incorrect because they represent controls that would not provide evidence pertaining to unrecorded retirements of equipment.

#35 (answer "D")

Reportable conditions are those matters coming to the auditor's attention that, in the auditor's judgment, should be communicated to the audit committee (or its equivalent) because they represent significant deficiencies in the design or operation of internal control, which could adversely affect the organization's ability to record, process, summarize, and report financial data consistent with the assertions of management in the financial statements.

Such deficiencies may involve aspects of internal control procedures (e.g., the lack of segregation of duties, and the absence of approvals of transactions).

While the communication is usually made after the audit is concluded, interim communication may be warranted and is acceptable. The auditor should not issue a report indicating that no reportable conditions were noted during the audit.

The communication may be oral or written. If the auditor chooses to communicate orally, the auditor should document the communication in the working papers.

A written report issued on reportable conditions should:

1. <u>Indicate</u> <u>that</u> <u>the</u> <u>purpose</u> <u>of</u> <u>the</u> <u>audit</u> <u>was</u> <u>to</u> <u>report</u> <u>on</u> <u>the</u> <u>financial</u> <u>statements</u> <u>and</u> <u>not</u> <u>to</u> <u>provide</u> <u>assurance</u> <u>on</u> <u>internal</u> <u>control</u>.
2. Include the definition of reportable conditions.
3. Describe the reportable conditions noted.
4. Include a restriction on the distribution (i.e., the distribution is intended for the audit committee, management, others within the organization, or, under certain circumstances, specific regulatory agencies).

Answer choices other than "D" are incorrect because they represent items that are not includible in an auditor's letter on reportable conditions.

#36 (answer "C")

SSAE #2, "Reporting on an Entity's Internal Control over Financial Reporting," provides guidance for performing attestation engagements to examine and report on management's written assertion about the effectiveness of an entity's internal control as of a point in time or during a period of time.

The practitioner's objective in an attestation engagement to examine and report on management's assertions about the effectiveness of the entity's internal control is to express an opinion about whether management's assertion regarding the effectiveness of the entity's internal control is fairly stated, in all material respects, based upon the control criteria used.

Management may present its written assertion about the effectiveness of the entity's internal control in a separate report that will accompany the practitioner's report, or in a representation letter to the practitioner.

Answer choices other than "C" are based on incorrect assumptions and/or illogical combinations.

#37 (answer "A")

An entity may use the services of other organizations to process significant transactions or to handle significant assets or liabilities. The internal control of the service organization may be considered part of the user organization's internal control and thus be subject to audit planning and control risk assessment considerations by the user organization auditor. In planning the audit, the user auditor should consider available information about the service organization's internal control, including reports by service auditors.

A report on controls placed in operation may be useful to a user auditor in providing a sufficient understanding to plan the audit of the user organization. Such a report is not intended to provide any evidence of the operating effectiveness of the relevant controls that would allow the user auditor to reduce the assessed level of control risk below the maximum. Such evidence may be derived from a service auditor's report on controls placed in operation and tests of operating effectiveness.

A service auditor's report expressing an opinion on a description of controls placed in operation at a service organization and tests of operating effectiveness should contain, among other items:

1. A specific reference to the applications, services, products, or other aspects of the service organization covered.

2. A description of the scope and nature of the service auditor's procedures.

3. Identification of the party specifying the control objectives.

4. An indication that the purpose of the service auditor's engagement was to obtain reasonable assurance about whether (a) the service organization's description presents fairly, in all material respects, the aspects of the service organization's controls that may be relevant to a user organization's internal control, (b) the controls were suitably designed to achieve specified control objectives, and (c) such controls had been placed in operation as of a specific date.

5. The service auditor's opinion on whether the description presents fairly, in all material respects, the relevant aspects of the service organization's controls that had been placed in operation as of a specific date. The opinion should also state whether the controls were suitably designed to provide reasonable assurance that the specified control objectives would be achieved if those controls were complied with satisfactorily.

6. The service auditor's opinion on whether the controls that were tested were operating with sufficient effectiveness to provide reasonable, but not absolute, assurance that the related control objectives were achieved during the period specified.

7. A statement of inherent limitations of the potential effectiveness of controls at the service organization and of the risk of projecting to the future any evaluation of the description or any conclusions about the effectiveness of controls in achieving control objectives.

8. Identification of the parties for whom the report is intended.

Answer choices other than "A" are based on incorrect assumptions.

#38 (answer "A")

Analytical procedures are used for the following purposes:

1. To assist the auditor in planning the nature, timing, and extent of other auditing procedures.

2. As a substantive test to obtain evidential matter about particular assertions related

to account balances or classes of transactions.

3. As an overall review of the financial information in the final review stage of the audit.

An auditor may achieve audit objectives related to particular assertions by <u>performing analytical procedures</u>, tests of transactions, tests of details of account balances, or a combination thereof. The decision about which procedure or procedures to use to achieve a particular audit objective is based on the auditor's judgment about the expected effectiveness and efficiency of the available procedures.

Answer choices other than "A" are incorrect because they represent actions that do not assist an auditor to achieve audit objectives.

#39 (answer "C")

Assertions are representations by management that are embodied in financial statement components. They can be classified as to:

1. <u>Existence</u> or <u>occurrence</u>—addresses whether assets or liabilities of the entity exist at a given date, or whether recorded transactions have occurred during a given period.
2. <u>Completeness</u>—addresses whether all transactions and accounts that should be presented in the financial statements are so included.
3. <u>Rights</u> <u>and</u> <u>obligations</u>—addresses whether assets are the rights of the entity (i.e., owned) at a given time.
4. <u>Valuation</u> or <u>allocation</u>—addresses whether asset, liability, equity, revenue, or expense components have been included in the financial statements at the appropriate amounts.
5. <u>Presentation</u> <u>and</u> <u>disclosure</u>—addresses whether particular components of the financial statements are properly classified, described, and disclosed.

Accounts may be confirmed by using the positive form, the negative form, or a combination of both. With the positive form, the respondent is asked to reply directly to the auditor, stating whether the balance as indicated on the request is correct or, if it is incorrect, to indicate the correct balance and any possible explanation for the difference.

With the negative form, the respondent is asked to reply only if the balance, as stated on the request, is not in agreement with its records. This type of request is useful when (1) the assessed level of control risk relating to the assertion is low, (2) a small number of accounts may be in dispute, (3) there are many accounts with small balances, and (4) there are indications that the requests will receive proper consideration.

It should be noted that the confirmation of customers' accounts receivable rarely provides reliable evidence about the completeness assertion because <u>customers</u> <u>may</u> <u>not</u> <u>be</u> <u>inclined</u> to <u>report understatement errors in their accounts</u>.

Answer choices other than "C" are based on incorrect assumptions regarding the confirmation process as it relates to the completeness assertion.

#40 (answer "B")

A standard confirmation request should be sent to all banks in which the client has an account, including those accounts that may have a zero balance at the end of the year. Such communications may disclose the existence of a balance in the account. The standard confirmation request extends beyond the verification of the actual cash balances. The confirmation requests not only the cash balances on deposit as of the balance sheet date, and any applicable interest rate(s), but also information pertaining to direct indebtedness to the bank.

Accordingly, a standard confirmation request would be used to confirm <u>cash</u> <u>in</u> <u>bank</u> <u>and</u> information about <u>collateral</u> <u>for</u> <u>loans</u> from the bank.

Answer choices other than "B" are incorrect because they represent sets of information that would not be confirmed on one form.

#41 (answer "B")

Analytical procedures may be performed as substantive tests designed to evaluate the reasonableness of financial information. They are performed by studying and comparing relationships among data.

Analytical procedures include the following:

1. Comparison of the current-year financial information with the financial information of a comparable prior period or periods.

2. Comparison of financial information with anticipated results (e.g., budgets and forecasts, including the use of a standard cost system that produces variance reports).
3. Study of the relationships of elements of financial information that would be expected to conform to a predictable pattern based on the entity's experience.
4. Comparison of financial information with similar information regarding the industry in which the entity operates.
5. Study of relationships of financial information with relevant nonfinancial information.

In light of point "2" above, an auditor's analytical procedures most likely would be facilitated if the entity uses a standard cost system that produces variance reports.

Answer choices other than "B" are based on incorrect assumptions about analytical procedures.

#42 (this answer is obsolete)

#43 (answer "C")

Factors influencing sample size in a substantive test of details are as follows:

| | Sample Size | |
Factor	Increased by	Decreased by
1. Assessment of inherent risk	High assessed level	Low assessed level
2. Assessment of control risk	High assessed level	Low assessed level
3. Assessment of risk for other substantive tests related to the same assertion	High assessed risk	Low assessed risk
4. Expected amount and frequency of misstatements	Greater amount and frequency	Lower amount and frequency
5. Measure of tolerable misstatement	Decrease in	Increase in
6. Number of items in population	Increase in items	Decrease in items
7. Sampling risk	Decrease in risk	Increase in risk

Answer choices other than "C" are based on incorrect assumptions and/or combinations.

#44 (answer "C")

In performing audit tests in accordance with GAAS, the auditor may use nonstatistical (subjective) sampling, statistical sampling, or both. Sampling, in general, requires the exercise of judgment in planning and executing the sampling plan and evaluating the results. Additionally, sampling can provide sufficient evidential matter as required by the third standard of fieldwork, but is subject to risk. The critical difference is the use, in statistical sampling, of the laws of probability in measuring risk.

In nonstatistical sampling, the auditor determines sample size and evaluates sample results entirely on the basis of subjective criteria growing out of the auditor's own experience. Thus, the auditor may unknowingly use too large a sample in one area and too small a sample in another.

However, statistical sampling should benefit the auditor in designing an efficient sample, measuring the sufficiency of the evidential matter obtained, and evaluating sample results. Most importantly, statistical sampling enables the auditor to quantify and control sampling risk.

Answer choice "A" is incorrect because nonsampling errors result from human mistakes (e.g., failing to recognize errors included in documents that the auditor examined, applying auditing procedures inappropriate to the audit objectives, or misinterpreting the results of the sample). Statistical sampling will not help eliminate the risk of nonsampling errors.

Answer choice "B" is incorrect because the use of statistical sampling does not imply that the level of audit risk and materiality is reduced to a relatively low amount.

Answer choice "D" is incorrect because statistical sampling does not necessarily minimize the failure to detect errors and fraud.

#45 (answer "D")

A standard confirmation request should be sent to all banks in which the client has an account, including those accounts that may have a zero balance at the end of the year. Such communication may disclose the existence of a balance in the account. The standard confirmation request extends beyond the verification of the actual cash balances. The confirmation requests not only the cash balances on deposit as of the balance sheet date, and any applicable interest rate(s), but also information pertaining to direct indebtedness to the bank.

To confirm a client's oral and written guarantees with a financial institution, the auditor should direct the request to a financial institution official who is responsible for the financial institution's relationship with the client or is knowledgeable about the transactions or arrangements.

However, "Standard Form to Confirm Account Balance Information with Financial Institutions" is designed to substantiate information that is stated on the confirmation request; the form is not designed to provide assurance that information about accounts not listed on the form will be reported.

It should be apparent that the usefulness of the standard bank confirmation request may be limited because the bank employee who completes the form may be unaware of all the financial relationships that the bank has with the client.

Answer choices other than "D" are based on incorrect assumptions.

#46 (answer "B")

The auditor should design substantive tests by relating financial statement assertions to specific audit objectives.

Assertions are representations by management that are embodied in financial statement components. They can be classified as to:

1. Existence or occurrence—addresses whether assets or liabilities of the entity exist at a given date, or whether recorded transactions have occurred during a given period.
2. Completeness—addresses whether all transactions and accounts that should be presented in the financial statements are so included.
3. Rights and obligations—addresses whether assets are the rights of the entity (i.e., owned) at a given time.
4. Valuation or allocation—addresses whether asset, liability, equity, revenue, or expense

components have been included in the financial statements at the appropriate amounts.
5. Presentation and disclosure—addresses whether particular components of the financial statements are properly classified, described, and disclosed.

Generally, a single assertion will lead to more than one audit objective. After an audit objective is identified, audit procedures are selected to achieve the particular audit objective. Of course, an audit objective may require that more than one audit procedure be performed. Likewise, a single audit procedure may, in part, contribute evidence regarding other audit objectives.

Accordingly, an auditor most likely would limit substantive audit tests of sales transactions when control risk is assessed as low for the existence or occurrence assertion concerning sales transactions and the auditor has already gathered evidence supporting related cash receipts and accounts receivable.

Answer choices other than "B" are incorrect because they refer to evidence that does not support the existence or occurrence assertion for sales transactions.

#47 (answer "C")

The best audit procedure that could assist in determining the existence of unrecorded liabilities is to vouch a sample of cash disbursements recorded just after year end to receiving reports and vendor invoices, because the disbursements clearly indicate the liquidation of liabilities. The auditor needs to ascertain in which time period the liability arose (i.e., the period under audit or the period subsequent thereto).

Answer choice "A" is incorrect because it deals with investigation of payables recorded prior to year end and a determination of whether they are supported by receiving reports. This will not enable detection of unrecorded liabilities. Rather, it might reveal liabilities recorded in the period under audit that belong in the subsequent period.

Answer choice "B" is incorrect because it refers to a procedure that would not enable an auditor to determine unrecorded liabilities of the period under audit.

Answer choice "D" is incorrect because it relates to recorded cash payments and not to unrecorded liabilities.

#48 (answer "C")

Substantive tests are comprised of tests of transactions, tests of account balances, and analytical procedures.

Tests of transactions and account balances are procedures designed to enable the auditor to obtain evidence as to the validity and propriety of their accounting treatment. Their purpose is to detect the existence of any monetary misstatements.

The tests of transactions of concern to the auditor are:

1. Tests for omitted transactions—Tracing from the source documents to the journals.
2. Tests for invalid transactions—Vouching from the journals back to the supporting source documents.

Accordingly, the purpose of a substantive audit procedure involving the tracing of a sample of purchase orders and related receiving reports to the purchases journal and the cash disbursements journal was to test for omitted transactions (that is, to determine that purchases were properly recorded).

Answer choices other than "C" are incorrect because they do not satisfy the objective of a test for omitted transactions.

#49 (answer "B")

In performing auditing procedures and gathering evidential matter, the auditor continually maintains an attitude of professional skepticism. The performance of auditing procedures during the audit may result in the detection of conditions or circumstances that should cause the auditor to consider whether material misstatements exist.

Circumstances likely to cause an auditor to consider whether material misstatements exist include:

1. Analytical procedures that disclose unexpected differences.
2. Unreconciled differences that are not appropriately investigated and corrected on a timely basis.

3. Confirmation requests that disclose significant differences or yield fewer responses than expected.
4. Transactions selected for testing that are not supported by proper documentation or are not appropriately authorized.
5. Supporting records or files that are not readily available.
6. Audit tests that indicate errors that apparently were known to client personnel but were not voluntarily disclosed to the auditor.

An auditor who discovers significant debits to the accumulated depreciation accounts most likely would be satisfied by an explanation that plant assets were retired during the year and such retirements were supported by proper documentation.

Answer choice "A" is incorrect because upward revisions in remaining useful lives of plant assets would not result in significant debits to accumulated depreciation accounts.

Answer choice "C" is incorrect because correction of an understatement of the prior year's depreciation expense would result in credits, rather than debits, to accumulated depreciation accounts in the current period.

Answer choice "D" is incorrect because overhead allocation revisions would likely not affect the total amount of depreciation taken during the year; therefore, accumulated depreciation accounts would not likely be affected.

#50 (answer "A")

In performing auditing procedures and gathering evidential matter, the auditor continually maintains an attitude of professional skepticism. The performance of auditing procedures during the audit may result in the detection of conditions or circumstances that should cause the auditor to consider whether material misstatements exist.

Circumstances likely to cause an auditor to consider whether material misstatements exist include:

1. Analytical procedures that disclose unexpected differences.
2. Unreconciled differences that are not appropriately investigated and corrected on a timely basis.

3. Confirmation requests that disclose significant differences or yield fewer responses than expected.
4. Transactions selected for testing that are not supported by proper documentation or are not appropriately authorized.
5. Supporting records or files that are not readily available.
6. Audit tests that indicate errors that apparently were known to client personnel but were not voluntarily disclosed to the auditor.

Analytical procedures consist of evaluations of financial information made by a study of plausible relationships among both financial and nonfinancial data. A basic premise underlying the application of analytical procedures is that these plausible relationships among data may reasonably be expected to exist and continue in the absence of known conditions to the contrary.

In light of point "1" above, an auditor would most likely suspect an employee payroll fraud scheme when <u>there</u> <u>are</u> <u>significant</u> <u>unexplained</u> <u>variances</u> <u>between</u> <u>standard</u> <u>and</u> <u>actual</u> <u>labor</u> <u>cost</u>.

Answer choice "B" is incorrect because disbursement of payroll checks by the same employee each payday, in and of itself, would not cause suspicion of fraud; additional factors would have to be considered.

Answer choices "C" and "D" are incorrect because they represent aspects of sound internal control over payroll; accordingly, fraud would not be suspected.

#51 (answer "C")

Tests of details of transactions are substantive tests designed to provide evidence about the validity and propriety of the accounting treatment of transactions. The objective of tests of details of transactions is to <u>detect</u> <u>material</u> <u>misstatements</u> <u>in</u> <u>the</u> <u>financial</u> <u>statements</u>. For example, a substantive test of the details of a transaction occurs when the auditor traces a sales invoice to the accounting records to determine whether any monetary errors have occurred in journalizing and posting. These tests may be performed during the year under audit or at or near the balance sheet date.

Answer choice "A" is incorrect because generally accepted auditing standards (GAAS) do not re-

quire an auditor to perform tests of details of transactions. The substantive tests performed by an auditor are a matter of professional judgment.

Answer choices "B" and "D" are incorrect because they relate to an entity's internal control. Substantive tests, including tests of details of transactions, do not pertain to an entity's internal control.

#52 (answer "A")

Generalized audit software packages commonly consist of individual computer programs, or routines, designed to perform a variety of functions. Typically, the software can perform all of the normal data handling and processing functions provided by the client's own software. Information can be sorted, stratified, sampled, evaluated, included or excluded, and summarized as desired. The software also has the capability of processing transactions, updating master files for current transactions, generating printed reports, and performing data search and retrieval. In addition, data files may be reviewed for completeness, reasonableness, and mathematical accuracy.

A primary advantage of using generalized audit software packages is that the auditor may <u>access</u> <u>information</u> <u>stored</u> <u>on</u> <u>computer</u> <u>files</u> <u>while</u> <u>having</u> <u>a</u> <u>limited</u> <u>understanding</u> <u>of</u> <u>the</u> <u>client's</u> <u>hardware</u> <u>and</u> <u>software</u> <u>features</u>.

Answer choice "B" is incorrect because generalized audit software packages may assist in performing analytical procedures as a substantive test, as well as aiding substantive tests of transactions.

Answer choice "C" is incorrect because it is secondary and not primary in nature. Once computer files are accessed, all other functions, such as verifying data accuracy, can be performed.

Answer choice "D" is incorrect because the use of a generalized audit software program, in and of itself, would not necessarily reduce the level of required tests of controls to a relatively small amount.

#53 (answer "D")

The independent auditor may consider using the work of internal auditors and using internal auditors to provide direct assistance to the auditor in an audit performed in accordance with GAAS.

The internal auditors' work may affect the nature, timing, and extent of the audit, including:

1. <u>Obtaining an understanding of internal control</u>.
2. <u>Performing tests of controls when assessing risk</u>.
3. <u>Performing substantive tests</u>.

Answer choices other than "D" are based on incorrect assumptions and/or illogical combinations.

#54 (answer "D")

The auditor may decide to use the work of a specialist when, in the auditor's judgment, complex or subjective matters that are material to the financial statements require special skill or knowledge to obtain competent evidential matter.

Areas that may require using the work of a specialist include:

1. Valuation; e.g., special-purpose inventories.
2. Determination of physical characteristics; e.g., mineral reserves.
3. Derivation of amounts by using specialized techniques; e.g., actuarial determinations.
4. Interpretation of technical requirements, regulations, or agreements (e.g., potential significance of contracts).

To determine the specialist's professional qualifications, the auditor should consider:

1. Professional certification.
2. Reputation and standing.
3. Experience in the type of work.

The auditor should obtain an understanding of the specialist's work. This understanding should cover:

1. Objective and scope.
2. Methods or assumptions used and a comparison with those used in the preceding period.
3. Appropriateness for the intended audit purpose.
4. Form and content of the specialist's findings for use in the audit.

When considering the use of a particular specialist, the auditor should evaluate the relationship, if any, of the specialist to the client, including circumstances that might impair the specialist's objectivity.

If the specialist has a relationship with the client, the auditor should assess the risk that the specialist's objectivity might be impaired. If objectivity might be impaired, the auditor should either perform additional procedures to determine the reasonableness of findings or engage another specialist.

Accordingly, <u>the work of a specialist</u> who is related to the client or <u>who has a contractual relationship with the client may be acceptable under certain circumstances</u>.

Answer choice "A" is incorrect because when using the work of a specialist, the auditor should obtain an understanding of the methods and assumptions used by the specialist.

Answer choice "B" is incorrect because the auditor generally uses the work of a specialist only in matters material to the fair presentation of the financial statements.

Answer choice "C" is incorrect because the reasonableness of the specialist's assumptions and their applications are not the auditor's responsibility.

#55 (answer "C")

A concern to the auditor is the determination of whether litigation, claims, and assessments have been properly reflected in the financial statements.

Management is the primary source of information about the existence of such matters. The independent auditor's procedures with respect to litigation, claims, and assessments should include the following:

1. Inquire and <u>discuss with management its policies and procedures adopted for</u> identifying, <u>evaluating, and accounting for litigation, claims, and assessments</u>.
2. Obtain from management a description and evaluation of litigation, claims, and assessments existing at the balance sheet date.
3. Examine documents in the client's possession concerning litigation, claims, and assessments, including correspondence and invoices from lawyers.
4. Obtain assurance from management that it has disclosed all unasserted claims that the lawyer has advised are probable of assertion and must be disclosed.

Since the auditor ordinarily does not possess legal skills, the auditor cannot make legal judgments. As such, the auditor should request that management send a letter of inquiry to those lawyers with whom it consulted concerning litigation, claims, and assessments. A letter of audit inquiry sent to the client's lawyers is the auditor's primary means of obtaining corroboration of the information furnished by management concerning litigation, claims, and assessments. Evidential matter obtained from the client's legal department may provide the auditor with some corroboration, but it is not a substitute for information that should be obtained from the outside counsel, which represents an independent source.

The ability of the auditor to confirm directly with the client's lawyers does not provide assurance that all claims have been recorded in the financial statements. A review of the financial statements by the auditor would provide audit satisfaction as to this assertion.

Answer choice "A" is incorrect because the auditor, and not the client's lawyer, must evaluate whether there is substantial doubt concerning the entity's ability to continue as a going concern.

Answer choice "B" is incorrect because the auditor cannot make legal judgments.

Answer choice "D" is incorrect because the auditor, and not the client's lawyer, must determine that all material litigation, claims, and assessments have been recorded or disclosed in the financial statements.

#56 (answer "D")

The auditor should perform auditing procedures with respect to the period after the balance sheet date for the purpose of ascertaining the occurrence of subsequent events that may require either adjustments to or disclosures in the financial statements in order for them to be in conformity with GAAP.

The procedures generally performed by the auditor to ascertain the existence of subsequent events occur at or near the completion of fieldwork, and include:

1. Reading the latest available interim statements.

2. Inquiring and discussing with officers and other executives having responsibility for financial and accounting matters, such as:
   a. Substantial contingent liabilities.
   b. Significant changes in capital stock, long-term debt, or working capital.
   c. Unusual adjustments.
3. Reading the available minutes of meetings of stockholders and the board of directors.
4. Inquiring of client's attorneys concerning any pending litigation, unasserted claims, or assessments.
5. Obtaining a letter of representation.
6. Any other additional inquiries or procedures considered necessary.

In light of point #2c above, the auditor would most likely <u>inquire as to whether any unusual adjustments were made after year end</u>.

Answer choices other than "D" are incorrect because they refer to procedures that do not provide evidence about subsequent events.

#57 (answer "B")

As part of an audit performed under GAAS, the independent auditor is required to obtain certain written representations from management. Such representations are part of the evidential matter the independent auditor obtains, but they are not a substitute for the application of other auditing procedures necessary to afford a reasonable basis for an opinion on the financial statements.

Representations cover such matters as:

1. Acknowledgment of management's responsibility for the financial statements.
2. <u>Completeness and availability of</u> the accounting records and <u>minutes of stockholders', directors',</u> and audit committees' <u>meetings</u>.
3. The absence of unrecorded transactions, and errors and fraud in the financial statements.
4. Noncompliance with aspects of contractual agreements or regulatory reporting practices that may affect the financial statements.
5. Information concerning related party transactions and related amounts receivable or payable.
6. Information concerning subsequent events.

7. Management's plans or intentions that may affect the carrying value or classification of assets or liabilities.
8. Disclosure of compensating balances or other arrangements involving restrictions on cash balances.
9. Fraud involving management or employees.
10. Satisfactory title to assets, liens on assets, and assets pledged as collateral.
11. Losses from purchase commitments for inventory quantities in excess of normal requirements, or at prices in excess of market.
12. Violations or possible violations of laws or regulations whose effects should be considered for disclosure in the financial statements or as a basis for recording a loss contingency.

Answer choices other than "B" are incorrect because they do not represent matters ordinarily included in a management representation letter.

#58 (answer "C")

A related party relationship exists when one party, directly or indirectly, has the ability to influence the management or operating policies of another party so significantly that one of the parties might be prevented from fully pursuing its own separate interests.

Auditing procedures to identify related party transactions include:

1. Emphasizing the auditing of material transactions with known related parties.
2. Reviewing minutes, proxy material, and management conflict-of-interest statements.
3. Considering whether transactions are occurring and are not being given accounting recognition (e.g., services at no charge).
4. Examining unusual or large transactions.
5. Reviewing confirmations of compensating balance arrangements, and loans receivable and payable for indications of guarantees.

Answer choices "A" and "B" are incorrect because they represent procedures that would not likely assist an auditor in identifying related party transactions.

Answer choice "D" is incorrect because analytical procedures focus on plausible relationships, rather than on individual transactions (inclusive of related party transactions).

#59 (answer "D")

If the auditor believes there is substantial doubt about the ability of the entity to continue as a going concern for a reasonable period of time, the auditor should consider management's plans for dealing with the adverse effects of the conditions and events. The auditor should obtain information about the plans and consider whether it is likely that the adverse effects will be mitigated for a reasonable period of time and that such plans can be effectively implemented. The auditor's considerations may include management's plans to:

1. Dispose of assets.
2. Borrow money or restructure debt.
3. Reduce or delay expenditures (e.g., plans to reduce overhead or administrative expenditures, to postpone expenditures for research and development projects, or to lease rather than purchase assets).
4. Increase ownership equity.

Answer choice "A" is incorrect because discussing terms of all debt and loan agreements would not, in and of itself, represent a mitigating factor.

Answer choice "B" is incorrect because strengthening internal controls over cash disbursements would not necessarily reduce negative cash flow; accordingly, it does not necessarily represent a mitigating factor.

Answer choice "C" is incorrect because a purchase, rather than a lease, would likely have an adverse effect on the entity.

#60 (answer "D")

Working papers are generally filed under two categories: (1) current files and (2) permanent (continuing) files. The current files contain corroborating information pertaining only to the execution of the current year's audit. The permanent (continuing) files contain data that are expected to be useful to the auditor during the current and future engagements.

Items contained in the current files include:

1. Schedules and analyses of accounts (e.g., lead schedules and supporting schedules).
2. An audit program.
3. Correspondence with third parties confirming balances, transactions, and other data.

4. Schedule of time spent on the engagement by each individual auditor.
5. A copy of the current year's financial statements.
6. Review notes pertaining to questions and comments regarding the audit work performed.
7. Letters from attorneys.

Items contained in the permanent files include:

1. Copies of articles of incorporation and by-laws.
2. Organization charts.
3. Plant layouts and descriptions of manufacturing processes.
4. Details (analyses) of capital stock (and other owners' equity accounts) and bond issues.
5. Charts of accounts.
6. Narrative descriptions and flowcharts of the client's internal control.
7. Copies of pension plans, lease agreements, and bond and note indentures (e.g., debt agreements).
8. Summaries of accounting principles used by the client.

As noted above, the permanent file generally should include copies of the debt agreements.

Answer choices other than "D" are incorrect because they represent items that should be included in the current file, and not in the permanent file, of an auditor's working papers.

#61 (answer "C")

The auditor may be asked to report on one basic financial statement and not on the others. These engagements do not involve scope limitations if the auditor's access to information underlying the basic financial statements is not limited, and all procedures considered necessary in the circumstances are appropriately applied. As such, these types of engagements involve limited reporting objectives.

In a limited reporting engagement, the auditor must employ procedures to determine whether accounting principles have been applied consistently with those used in the previous year. If there has been a violation of the consistency standard, an explanatory paragraph should be added to the auditor's report (after the opinion paragraph). An unqualified opinion, however, is expressed on the financial statement(s).

In view of the above, Harris may accept the engagement (to audit and report on the balance sheet of Fox Co.) because such engagements merely involve limited reporting objectives.

Answer choice "A" is incorrect because accepting a limited reporting engagement to audit and report on one financial statement would not constitute a violation of the profession's ethical standards.

Answer choice "B" is incorrect because reporting on one financial statement would not be tantamount to rendering a piecemeal opinion (i.e., expressing an opinion as to certain identified items in financial statements); piecemeal opinions should not be rendered.

Answer choice "D" is incorrect because Harris would not have to disclaim an opinion on the balance sheet of Fox Co. as long as Harris was able to apply the procedures considered necessary for the limited reporting engagement.

#62 (answer "C")

When the auditor reports on single-year or comparative financial statements, the auditor's standard report implies that the auditor is satisfied that there have been no material changes in GAAP affecting comparability.

Furthermore, the auditor's standard report on single-year or comparative financial statements explicitly states in the scope paragraph that:

1. The audit was conducted in accordance with GAAS.
2. GAAS requires the auditor to plan and perform the audit to obtain reasonable assurance about whether the financial statements are free of material misstatements.
3. An audit includes:
   a. Examining, on a test basis, evidence supporting the amounts and disclosures in the financial statements.
   b. Assessing the accounting principles used and significant estimates made by management.
   c. Evaluating the overall financial statement presentation.
4. The auditor believes that the audit provides a reasonable basis for the auditor's opinion.

Answer choices other than "C" are incorrect because they do not represent basic elements of the auditor's standard report.

#63 (answer "B")

Generally accepted auditing standards (GAAS) require independence in fact and in appearance. It is essential that CPAs maintain an independent attitude in fulfilling their responsibilities. It is also important that the users of financial statements have confidence in the existence of that independence. These two objectives are identified, respectively, as independence in fact and independence in appearance.

Independence in fact exists when the auditor is able to maintain an unbiased attitude throughout the audit. Independence in appearance is dependent on how others perceive this independence. Independence in appearance enhances public confidence in the profession.

If the auditor lacks independence with respect to the audited entity, the auditor may not issue a qualified opinion, since only a disclaimer of opinion may be issued.

Answer choice "A" is incorrect because a qualified opinion may be issued when an accounting principle at variance with GAAP is used.

Answer choice "C" is incorrect because a scope limitation that prevents the auditor from completing an important audit procedure may result in a qualified opinion.

Answer choice "D" is incorrect because a matter that has not been resolved between the auditor and the specialist may lead to a qualified (adverse, or disclaimer of) opinion.

#64 (this question is obsolete)

#65 (answer "D")

The auditor adds an explanatory paragraph to the standard audit report, but still renders an unqualified opinion, in the following circumstances:

1. Departure from GAAP—When the financial statements contain a departure from GAAP, but the auditor can demonstrate that due to unusual circumstances, the financial statements would be misleading had the client followed GAAP.
2. Lack of consistency— When there is a change in accounting principle with which the auditor concurs, the auditor's report should include an explanatory paragraph following the opinion paragraph.

3. Emphasis of a matter—When the auditor wishes to emphasize a matter regarding the financial statements, an additional paragraph may be included.
4. Supplementary information—Supplementary information required by FASB or GASB need not be referred to in the audit report except if it is omitted. The auditor need not present the omitted supplementary information, but must identify it in a separate paragraph, the result of which is still an unqualified opinion.

Neither an unjustified accounting change nor a material weakness in internal control represents a circumstance in which the auditor would express an unqualified opinion with an explanatory paragraph added to the report. An unjustified accounting change would result in the expression of a qualified or adverse opinion. A material weakness in internal control generally has no effect on the type of opinion that the auditor may express.

Answer choices other than "D" are based on incorrect assumptions and/or illogical combinations.

#66 (answer "B")

A disclaimer of opinion states that the auditor is unable to express an opinion on the fairness of the financial statements taken as a whole. This type of report is appropriate when:

1. The auditor is unable to obtain sufficient evidence concerning the statements taken as a whole; this is referred to as a scope limitation.
2. There are significant uncertainties affecting the financial statements taken as a whole and, in the auditor's judgment, the expression of an unqualified opinion is not warranted.

If management does not provide reasonable justification for a change in accounting principles, the auditor should express either a qualified or adverse opinion; a disclaimer of opinion would not be appropriate.

Answer choices other than "B" are incorrect because they represent severe scope limitations; as such, in each case a disclaimer of opinion may be appropriate.

#67 (answer "A")

The auditor's opinion that financial statements "present fairly," in all material respects, an entity's financial position, results of operations, and cash flows should be based on professional judgment as to whether the accounting principles selected and applied are within the framework of GAAP.

Using one GAAP inventory-costing method for one portion of the inventory and a different GAAP method for the remainder is an acceptable procedure, provided there is a basis for doing so and such use is consistently applied.

Assuming the auditor is satisfied in all other respects, there is no basis for anything other than an <u>unqualified</u> <u>opinion</u>.

Answer choices other than "A" are based on incorrect reporting practices.

#68 (answer "C")

The fourth standard of reporting prevents <u>misinterpretations</u> <u>regarding</u> <u>the</u> <u>degree</u> <u>of</u> <u>responsibility</u> <u>the</u> <u>auditor</u> <u>is</u> <u>assuming</u> when her name is associated with the financial statements.

Answer choice "A" is incorrect because an auditor may express different opinions on each of the basic financial statements.

Answer choice "B" is incorrect because preventing restrictions on the scope of an audit is not an objective of the fourth standard of reporting.

Answer choice "D" is incorrect since reference in this standard to "financial statements taken as a whole" applies equally to a complete set of financial statements and to the individual statements that comprise a complete set.

#69 (answer "D")

Scope limitations occur when there is a lack of sufficient competent evidential matter. Scope limitations may lead to a qualified opinion or may warrant a disclaimer of an opinion.

If <u>the</u> <u>auditor</u> <u>is</u> <u>unable</u> <u>to</u> <u>obtain</u> <u>audited</u> <u>financial</u> <u>statements</u> <u>of</u> <u>a</u> <u>consolidated</u> <u>investee</u>, a scope limitation sufficient to preclude an unqualified opinion will usually result.

Answer choice "A" is incorrect because, although a material change between periods in accounting principles will result in an explanatory paragraph being added to the auditor's report, the opinion is still unqualified.

Answer choice "B" is incorrect because quarterly financial data required by the SEC are not part of the basic financial statements and their omission would not preclude an unqualified opinion.

Answer choice "C" is incorrect because, although the emphasis of a matter adds an explanatory paragraph to the auditor's report, the opinion is still unqualified.

#70 (this question is obsolete)

#71 (answer "C")

When the auditor expresses a qualified opinion, the auditor should disclose all of the substantive reasons in one or more explanatory paragraph(s) preceding the opinion paragraph of the auditor's report.

The auditor should also include, in the opinion paragraph, the appropriate qualifying language and a reference to the explanatory paragraph. A qualified opinion should include a phrase such as "except for" or "with the exception of."

Accordingly, the auditor would most likely include the phrase "<u>except</u> <u>for</u> <u>the</u> <u>omission</u> <u>of</u> <u>the</u> <u>information</u> <u>discussed</u> <u>in</u> <u>the</u> <u>preceding</u> <u>paragraph</u>" in the auditor's report when expressing a qualified opinion because of inadequate disclosure.

Answer choices "A" and "B" are incorrect because phrases such as "subject to" and "with the foregoing explanation" are not clear or forceful enough and should not be used.

Answer choice "D" is incorrect because it refers to language that is appropriate for an adverse opinion.

#72 (answer "D")

A special type of significant uncertainty concerns the ability of an entity to continue as a going concern. During the course of an audit, an auditor may become aware of events that seriously threaten the entity's continued existence. Questions of continued existence usually hinge upon a company's ability to meet its financial obligations, but may also involve such factors as loss of key employees or major customers. If, after considering identified conditions and events and management's plans, the auditor concludes that substantial doubt about the entity's ability to continue as a going concern for a reasonable period of time remains, the audit report should include an explanatory paragraph (following the opinion paragraph) to reflect that conclusion. The auditor's conclusion about the entity's ability to continue as a going concern should be expressed through the use of the phrase "substantial doubt about its ability to continue as a going concern."

In light of the above, neither the phrase "possible discontinuance of operations" nor "reasonable period of time, not to exceed one year" is required to be included in the explanatory paragraph.

Answer choices other than "D" are based on incorrect assumptions and/or illogical combinations.

#73 (answer "A")

During the course of an audit, an auditor may become aware of events that seriously threaten the entity's continued existence. Questions of continued existence usually hinge upon a company's ability to meet its financial obligations, but may also involve such factors as loss of key employees or major customers.

If, after considering identified conditions and events and management's plans, the auditor concludes that substantial doubt about the entity's ability to continue as a going concern for a reasonable period of time remains, the audit report should include an explanatory paragraph (following the opinion paragraph) to reflect that conclusion. The auditor's conclusion about the entity's ability to continue as a going concern should be expressed through the use of the phrase "substantial doubt about its ability to continue as a going concern."

If substantial doubt about the entity's ability to continue as a going concern for a reasonable period of time existed at the date of prior period financial statements that are presented on a comparative basis, and that doubt has been removed in the current period, the explanatory paragraph included in the auditor's report (following the opinion paragraph) on the financial statements of the prior period should not be repeated.

Answer choices other than "A" are based on incorrect reporting practices.

#74 (answer "B")

The auditor's standard report implies that the auditor is satisfied that there have been no material changes in GAAP affecting consistency. When lack of consistency exists (i.e., when there is a change in accounting principle), with which the auditor concurs, the auditor's report should include an explanatory paragraph following the opinion paragraph. The auditor's opinion is, however, still unqualified. If the auditor does not concur with the change, the auditor should render a qualified opinion. Otherwise, there is no reference to consistency in the auditor's report.

In the question situation, no circumstances regarding lack of consistency are presented and, accordingly, the auditor should not refer to consistency in the auditor's report.

Answer choice "A" is incorrect because under the circumstances described, the auditor may report on the client's financial statements (inclusive of the income statement).

Answer choice "C" is incorrect because the consistency standard is applicable even in the first audit of a new client.

Answer choice "D" is incorrect because the auditor should not state that the accounting principles have been applied consistently; the consistent application of accounting principles is implicit in the auditor's report.

#75 (answer "A")

If an auditor has previously issued a qualified or adverse opinion on the financial statements of a prior period because of a departure from GAAP, and the prior year's financial statements are restated in the current period to conform with GAAP, the auditor's updated report on the financial statements of the prior period should indicate that the statements have been restated, and should express an unqualified opinion with respect to the restated financial statements.

In the updated report, the auditor should indicate in a separate paragraph(s), preceding the opinion paragraph of the auditor's report:

1. The date of the auditor's previous report (note that the updated report is dated currently).
2. The type of opinion previously expressed.

3. The circumstances that caused the auditor to express a different opinion.
4. That the auditor's updated opinion on the financial statements of the prior period is different from the auditor's previous opinion on these statements.

Answer choices other than "A" are incorrect because they do not represent circumstances that would cause a change to the previously issued opinion.

#76 (answer "D")

When comparative financial statements are presented, and there has been a change in auditors between years, the predecessor's audit report may or may not be presented. When the predecessor's audit report is not presented, regardless of the type of opinion expressed, the successor auditor should specify in the introductory paragraph that the prior year's financial statements were audited by another auditor.

The introductory paragraph should also indicate the date of the predecessor's report, the type of report issued and, if other than an unqualified opinion was issued, the substantive reasons for such an opinion. However, the successor auditor should not name the predecessor auditor.

Answer choices other than "D" are based on incorrect assumptions and/or illogical combinations.

#77 (answer "A")

When part of the audit is performed by another auditor, the principal auditor must be able to gain satisfaction as to the independence and professional reputation of the other auditor, as well as to the quality of the audit. Having done so, the principal auditor must then decide whether he is willing to express an opinion on the financial statements taken as a whole without referring to the audit of the other auditor. If the principal auditor decides to do so, it should not be stated that part of the audit was performed by another auditor, because to do so may cause a reader to misinterpret the degree of responsibility being assumed. As such, a standard audit report is issued when the principal auditor decides not to make reference to the other auditor.

Generally, the principal auditor decides to refer to the other auditor because the other auditor's work was material in relation to the total, or because it was impractical to review that work.

When reference is made to the other auditor, the report should indicate clearly, in the introductory, the scope, and the opinion paragraphs, the division of responsibility. In addition, the introductory paragraph should indicate the magnitude of the portion of the financial statements audited by the other auditor.

Hence, the sentences presented in the question are part of the introductory paragraph included in the auditor's report; specifically, the sentences indicate a division of responsibility.

Answer choices other than "A" are based on incorrect assumptions.

#78 (answer "A")

The auditor's standard report includes the following elements and paragraphs:

1. Title—The report must contain a title that includes the word *independent.*
2. Addressee—The report should ordinarily be addressed to the company, its board of directors, or the stockholders.
3. Introductory paragraph—Includes statements that the financial statements:
   a. Were audited.
   b. Are the responsibility of management and that the auditor's responsibility is to express an opinion on the audited financial statements.
4. Scope paragraph—Includes statements that:
   a. The audit was conducted in accordance with GAAS.
   b. GAAS requires that the auditor plan and perform the audit to obtain reasonable assurance about whether the financial statements are free of material misstatements.
   c. An audit includes:
      (1) Examining, on a test basis, evidence supporting the amounts and disclosures in the financial statements.
      (2) Assessing the accounting principles used and significant estimates made by management.
      (3) Evaluating the overall financial statement presentation.
   d. The auditor believes that her audit provides a reasonable basis for an opinion.

5. Opinion paragraph—An opinion as to whether the financial statements are presented fairly, in all material respects, in conformity with GAAP.
6. Signature—Manual or printed signature of the auditor.
7. Date—Usually the completion of fieldwork.

Occasionally, an auditor is retained to audit the financial statements of a company that is not the auditor's client; in such cases, the report is customarily addressed to the client and not to the directors or stockholders of the company whose financial statements are being audited.

Answer choices other than "A" are based on incorrect reporting practices.

#79 (answer "C")

A review engagement is substantially less in scope than an audit conducted in conformity with GAAS and does not provide a basis for expressing an opinion on the fairness of the financial statements.

The purpose of a review is to provide the accountant with a basis for expressing limited assurance that the financial statements conform either to GAAP or to a comprehensive basis of accounting other than GAAP.

A standard review report should state that:

1. A review was performed in accordance with Statements on Standards for Accounting and Review Services issued by the American Institute of Certified Public Accountants.
2. All information included in the financial statements is the representation of the management (owners) of the entity.
3. A review consists principally of inquiries of company personnel and analytical procedures applied to financial data.
4. A review is substantially less in scope than an audit, the objective of which is the expression of an opinion regarding the financial statements taken as a whole and, accordingly, no such opinion is expressed.
5. The accountant is not aware of any material modifications that should be made to the financial statements in order for them to be in conformity with GAAP.

Furthermore, each page of the financial statements should be marked "See Accountant's Review Report."

Answer choices other than "C" are incorrect because they represent statements that are not appropriate for inclusion in a review report on financial statements.

#80 (answer "C")

A compilation of financial statements is a service, provided to a nonpublic entity, in which an accountant prepares or assists in preparing financial statements without expressing any assurance that the statements are in conformity with GAAP.

The accountant's compilation report, which should accompany the financial statements, states that:

1. The accountant has compiled the financial statements in accordance with Statements on Standards for Accounting and Review Services issued by the American Institute of Certified Public Accountants.
2. A compilation is limited to presenting, in the form of financial statements, information that is the representation of management.
3. No audit or review of the financial statements has taken place and the accountant does not express an opinion or any other form of assurance on the financial statements.
4. The report date is the date on which the compilation was completed.

Furthermore, each page of the financial statements should be marked "See Accountant's Compilation Report."

Answer choices other than "C" are incorrect because they represent statements that are not appropriate for inclusion in a compilation report on financial statements.

#81 (answer "A")

The objective in an agreed-upon-procedures engagement is to present specific findings about an entity's compliance with specified requirements or about the effectiveness of an entity's internal control over compliance based on procedures agreed upon by the users of the report.

The practitioner's report, which is usually addressed to the entity, should include the following elements:

1. A title that includes the word <u>independent</u>.
2. A statement that the procedures were performed to assist the users in evaluating management's assertion about compliance with specified requirements.
3. A reference to management's assertion about compliance with specified requirements, including the period or point in time addressed in management's assertion.
4. A statement that the sufficiency of the procedures is solely the responsibility of the parties specifying the procedures, and a disclaimer of responsibility for the sufficiency of those procedures.
5. A list of the procedures performed (or reference thereto) and related findings.
6. A statement that the work performed was less in scope than an examination of management's assertion about compliance with specified requirements, a disclaimer of opinion, and a statement that if additional procedures had been performed, other matters might have come to the practitioner's attention that would have been reported.
7. <u>A statement of limitations on the use of the report</u> because it is intended solely for the use of specified parties.
8. The report date, which should be the date of completion of the agreed-upon procedures.

The practitioner should not provide negative assurance about whether management's assertion is fairly stated.

Answer choices other than "A" are based on incorrect reporting practices.

#82 (answer "A")

Whenever an accountant submits, to a client or others, prospective financial statements (i.e., financial forecasts and financial projections) that the accountant has assembled, or assisted in assembling, the accountant should perform an engagement to examine, compile, or apply agreed-upon procedures to the prospective financial statements.

A financial forecast presents, to the best of the responsible party's (usually management's) knowl-edge and belief, an entity's expected financial position, results of operations, and cash flows. A financial forecast is based on assumptions reflecting conditions expected to exist and the course of action expected to be taken.

A financial projection presents to the best of the responsible party's knowledge and belief, given one or more hypothetical assumptions (i.e., assumptions used to present a condition or course of action that is not necessarily expected to occur), an entity's expected financial position, results of operations, and cash flows. A financial projection is therefore based on "what if" assumptions.

An examination of a financial projection provides the accountant with a basis for expressing an opinion that (1) the financial projection is presented in conformity with AICPA guidelines, and (2) the assumptions provide a reasonable basis for the projection given the hypothetical assumptions. Further, the accountant's report should include a separate paragraph that <u>describes the limitations on the usefulness of the presentation</u>.

Answer choice "B" is incorrect because no reference to an audit is made in the accountant's report on projected financial statements that were examined.

Answer choice "C" is incorrect because the auditor assumes no responsibility to update the report for events and circumstance subsequent to the report date.

Answer choice "D" is incorrect because when an accountant examines projected financial statements, the accountant provides an opinion on whether the assumptions provide a reasonable basis for the projection.

#83 (answer "A")

Auditor's reports issued in connection with the following criteria constitute special reports.

1. Financial statements prepared in accordance with a comprehensive basis of accounting other than GAAP. A comprehensive basis of accounting other than GAAP may be a basis prescribed by a regulatory body, a basis used for income-tax purposes, the cash or modified-cash basis, or a basis having substantial support, such as the constant-dollar or replacement-cost basis.

2. Specified elements, accounts, or items of a financial statement. Examples include rentals, royalties, accounts receivable, profit participation, or a provision for income taxes.
3. Compliance with contractual agreements or regulatory requirements related to audited financial statements.
4. Financial presentations to comply with contractual agreements or regulatory provisions that are incomplete or are not in conformity with GAAP or another comprehensive basis of accounting.
5. Financial information and/or auditor's report required in a prescribed form.

In connection with point #2 above, if a specified element, account, or item is based upon an entity's net income or stockholders' equity or the equivalent thereof, the auditor should have audited the complete financial statements to express an opinion on the specified element, account, or item.

Accordingly, Hardy may accept an engagement to express an opinion on Field's profit participation in Gold's net income only if <u>Hardy</u> <u>also</u> <u>audits</u> <u>Gold's</u> <u>complete</u> <u>financial</u> <u>statements</u>.

Answer choice "B" is incorrect because Hardy may accept the engagement to express an opinion on Field's profit participation in Gold's net income even if Gold's financial statements are prepared in conformity with a comprehensive basis of accounting other than GAAP.

Answer choice "C" is incorrect because Hardy's report on Field's profit participation in Gold's net income need not be available for distribution to Gold's other employees.

Answer choice "D" is incorrect because Field need not own a controlling interest in Gold in order for Hardy to accept an engagement to report on Field's profit participation in Gold's net income.

#84 (answer "B")

SAS #61, "Communication with Audit Committees," establishes a requirement for the auditor to determine that certain matters related to the conduct of the audit be communicated (orally or in writing) to the audit committee (or, in the absence of an audit committee, to other financial oversight groups, such as finance or budget com-

mittees). Such communication need not be made before the issuance of the auditor's report.

Matters to be communicated include:

1. The level of responsibility an auditor assumes for internal control and the financial statements under GAAS.
2. The initial selection of and changes in significant policies, methods used to account for significant unusual transactions, and the effect of continuing accounting policies in controversial areas.
3. The process used by management in formulating sensitive accounting estimates, and the basis for the auditor's conclusions about the reasonableness of those estimates.
4. Any adjustments arising from the audit that could have a significant effect on the entity's reporting process.
5. The auditor's responsibility for information, other than the audited financial statements, in documents such as corporate annual reports.
6. Any disagreements between the auditor and management, whether or not satisfactorily resolved.
7. Significant matters that were the subject of consultations with other accountants.
8. Any major issues discussed by management and the auditor before the auditor was hired.
9. Any serious difficulties the auditor encountered that were detrimental to the effective completion of the audit.

In light of point #4 above, <u>the auditor is required to inform the entity's audit committee about significant errors discovered by the auditor and subsequently corrected by management</u>.

Answer choices other than "B" are incorrect because they are based on incorrect assumptions about the auditor's required communication with the entity's audit committee.

#85 (answer "C")

After the financial statements and the auditor's report are released, the auditor continues to have a responsibility with respect to the subsequent discovery of facts (i.e., the discovery of material facts existing at the audit report date that were not known to the auditor when the report was issued).

Upon such discovery, the auditor should determine whether the information is reliable and whether the facts actually existed at the date of the auditor's report. If so, the auditor should discuss the matter with the client's management, including the board of directors.

When the subsequently discovered information is found to be both reliable and to have existed at the date of the auditor's report, the auditor should determine if:

1. The audit report would have been affected had the information been known to the auditor at the date of the report.
2. The auditor believes there are persons who currently rely, or are likely to rely, on the financial statements and who would attach importance to the information.

When the auditor has concluded that action should be taken, the auditor should advise the client to make appropriate disclosure of the newly discovered facts. In addition, the client should issue revised financial statements and the auditor should issue a revised report.

In view of the above, the auditor would need to make further inquiries about the previously issued financial statements if <u>new information concerning undisclosed lease transactions of the audited period</u> is discovered.

Answer choices other than "C" are incorrect because they involve subsequent events, rather than the subsequent discovery of facts. Accordingly, the auditor would not have to make further inquiries after the issuance of the financial statements and the auditor's report.

#86 (answer "A")

A registration statement filed with the Securities and Exchange Commission may contain the reports of two or more independent auditors on their audits of the financial statements for different periods. An auditor who has audited the financial statements for prior periods but has not audited the financial statements for the most recent audited period included in the registration statement has a responsibility relating to events subsequent to the date of the prior-period financial statements, and extending to the effective date, that bear materially on the prior-period financial statements on which the auditor reported. Generally, the auditor should:

1. Read pertinent portions of the prospectus and of the registration statement.
2. Obtain a letter of representation from the <u>successor</u> <u>independent</u> <u>auditor</u> regarding whether the audit revealed any matters that, in the auditor's opinion, might have a material effect on the financial statements reported on by the predecessor auditor or would require disclosure.

Answer choices other than "A" are incorrect because they represent inappropriate sources of a letter of representation.

#87 (answer "A")

An auditor may be engaged to report on selected financial data that are included in a client-prepared document containing audited financial statements. Selected financial data are not a required part of the basic financial statements, and the entity's management is responsible for determining the specific selected financial data to be presented.

If an auditor is engaged to report on selected financial data, the report should <u>be</u> <u>limited</u> <u>to</u> <u>data</u> <u>derived</u> <u>from</u> <u>the</u> <u>audited</u> <u>financial</u> <u>statements</u>. If selected financial data that management presents include both data derived from audited financial statements and other information, the auditor's report should specifically identify the data on which the auditor is reporting.

The auditor's report should indicate (1) that the auditor has audited and expressed an opinion on the complete financial statements, (2) the type of opinion expressed, and (3) whether, in the auditor's opinion, the information set forth in the selected financial data is fairly stated in all material respects in relation to the complete financial statements from which it has been derived.

If the selected financial data for any of the years presented are derived from financial statements that were audited by another independent auditor, the report on the selected financial data should state that fact, and the auditor should not express an opinion on that data.

Answer choices other than "A" are based on incorrect assumptions.

#88 (answer "B")

An auditor performing an audit in accordance with "Government Auditing Standards" is required to report on compliance with laws and regulations and on internal control, in addition to fulfilling the reporting responsibilities under GAAS.

Under GAAS, an auditor should design the audit to provide reasonable assurance of detecting (1) fraud that is material to the financial statements and (2) misstatements resulting from direct and material illegal acts.

An auditor is responsible for being aware of the characteristics and types of potential fraud that could be associated with the area being audited so that the auditor can plan the audit to provide the reasonable assurance of detecting material fraud.

In auditing a not-for-profit entity that receives governmental financial assistance, the auditor has a responsibility to assess whether management has identified laws and regulations that have a direct and material effect on the entity's financial statements.

Answer choices other than "B" are incorrect because they do not represent responsibilities of the auditor under either GAAS or "Government Auditing Standards."

#89 (answer "B")

The Single Audit Act of 1984 requires the auditor to report on compliance with:

1. Laws and regulations that may have a material effect on the financial statements.
2. General requirements that may have a material effect on major programs.
3. Specific requirements that may have a material effect on major programs.
4. Certain laws and regulations applicable to nonmajor federal financial assistance programs.

Accordingly, the auditor's consideration of materiality in auditing compliance with requirements governing major federal financial assistance programs differs from that in an audit of financial statements in accordance with generally accepted auditing standards. Under the Single Audit Act, materiality is determined separately for each major federal financial assistance program.

Answer choice "A" is incorrect because the Single Audit Act deals with material effects on major programs, rather than on the financial statements.

Answer choice "C" is incorrect because the Single Audit Act does not specify that materiality should be decided in conjunction with the auditor's risk assessment.

Answer choice "D" is incorrect because materiality is not ignored under the Single Audit Act.

#90 (answer "B")

The General Accounting Office prescribes generally accepted government auditing standards (GAGAS) for the audit of governmental organizations, programs, activities, and functions. These standards, commonly referred to as the "Yellow Book," cover governmental financial, compliance, and performance audits. These standards also apply to audits of government assistance received by contractors, nonprofit organizations, and other nongovernment organizations. They include general standards, fieldwork standards, and reporting standards.

General standards include:

1. Qualifications—Adequate professional proficiency for the tasks required.
2. Independence—Free from personal and external impairments to independence; organizationally independent; and maintains an independent attitude and appearance.
3. Due professional care—Should be exercised in conducting the audit and in preparing related reports.
4. Quality control—Have an internal quality control system and undergo an external quality control review.

Further, under the quality control general standards, a CPA seeking to enter into a contract to perform an audit in accordance with these standards should provide the CPA's most recent external quality control review report to the party contracting for the audit. Information in the external quality control review report often would be relevant to decisions on procuring audit services. CPAs also should make their external quality control review reports available to auditors using their work and to appropriate oversight bodies. It is recommended that the report be made available to the public.

Answer choices other than "B" are based on incorrect assumptions about the quality control requirements under government auditing standards.

OTHER OBJECTIVE FORMATS/ESSAY QUESTIONS

Answer 2

#91 (answer "D")

The source of this statement is a <u>management representation letter</u>.

SAS #19, "Client Representations," requires the independent auditor to obtain certain written representations from management as part of an audit made under GAAS. Refusal to furnish representations constitutes a scope limitation sufficient to preclude an unqualified opinion.

#92 (answer "I")

The source of this excerpt is the <u>audit inquiry letter to legal counsel</u>.

A letter of inquiry to legal counsel is the primary means of obtaining corroboration concerning litigation, claims, and assessments. Evidential matter obtained from the client's own legal department may be corroborating, but is not a substitute for information obtained from outside counsel.

#93 (answer "D")

The source of this statement is a <u>management representation letter</u>.

SAS #19, "Client Representations," requires the independent auditor to obtain certain written representations from management as part of an audit made under GAAS. Refusal to furnish representations constitutes a scope limitation sufficient to preclude an unqualified opinion.

#94 (answer "C")

The source of this statement is an <u>auditor's engagement letter</u>.

Although not required under GAAS, an engagement letter should be used to confirm the understanding reached with a client as to the scope and terms of an audit engagement.

#95 (answer "C")

The source of this statement is an <u>auditor's engagement letter</u>.

Although not required under GAAS, an engagement letter should be used to confirm the understanding reached with a client as to the scope and terms of an audit engagement.

#96 (answer "D")

The source of this statement is a <u>management representation letter</u>.

SAS #19, "Client Representations," requires the independent auditor to obtain certain written representations from management as part of an audit made under GAAS. Refusal to furnish representations constitutes a scope limitation sufficient to preclude an unqualified opinion.

#97 (answer "B")

The source of this question is a <u>communication with the predecessor auditor</u>.

Before accepting an engagement with a client that has been previously audited, the successor auditor should take the initiative to communicate with the predecessor auditor. Permission must be obtained from the client before communication can be made because of the confidentiality requirement of the Code of Conduct. If a client will not permit such communication, the successor should carefully consider the desirability of accepting the engagement.

In the communication, the successor auditor should make specific and reasonable inquiries of the predecessor about matters relevant to the audit, such as:

1. Facts that might bear on the integrity of management.
2. Disagreements with management on accounting principles and auditing procedures.
3. The predecessor's understanding regarding the change in auditors.

#98 (answer "A")

The source of this question is a <u>partner's engagement review program</u>.

SAS #73, "Using the Work of a Specialist," provides guidance when the work of a specialist, who is not a member of the auditor's staff, is used in performing an audit under GAAS. A specialist possesses special skill or knowledge in a particular field other than accounting or auditing. The auditor will ordinarily use the work of a specialist unless the auditor's procedures lead to the belief that the specialist's findings are unreasonable, in which case the auditor should apply additional procedures, which may include obtaining the opinion of another specialist.

#99 (answer "E")

The source of this comment is the <u>standard finan-cial institution confirmation request</u>.

In an audit, evidential matter for cash requires the auditor to obtain and review confirmations at year-end. The "Standard Form to Confirm Account Balance Information with Financial Institutions" includes:

1. The balances in all accounts.
2. The interest rate on interest-bearing accounts.
3. Information on direct indebtedness to the financial institution for notes, mortgages, or other debt, including the amount of the loan, the date of the loan, its due date, interest rate, and the existence of collateral.

#100 (answer "C")

The source of this excerpt is the <u>auditor's engagement letter</u>.

Although not required under GAAS, an engagement letter should be used. The purpose of this excerpt is to clarify that the financial statements are the client's and not the auditor's.

#101 (answer "D")

The source of this statement is a <u>management representation letter</u>.

SAS #19, "Client Representations," requires the independent auditor to obtain certain written representations from management as part of an audit made under GAAS. Refusal to furnish representations constitutes a scope limitation sufficient to preclude an unqualified opinion.

#102 (answer "G")

The source of this excerpt is the <u>auditor's report</u>.

The auditor adds an explanatory paragraph to the standard audit report, but still renders an unqualified opinion, when the auditor may wish to emphasize a matter regarding the financial statements. Emphasis that the entity being reported on had significant transactions with related parties is a situation that may be presented in an additional paragraph.

#103 (answer "F")

The source of this comment is the <u>auditor's communication with the audit committee</u>.

SAS #61, "Communication with Audit Committees," establishes a requirement for the auditor to determine that certain matters related to the conduct of the audit be communicated (orally or in writing) to the audit committee (or, in the absence of an audit committee, to other financial oversight groups, such as finance or budget committees). Such communication need not be made before the issuance of the auditor's report.

Matters to be communicated include any serious difficulties the auditor encountered that were detrimental to the effective completion of the audit. This may include unreasonable delays by management in permitting the commencement of the audit or in providing needed information, and whether the timetable set by management was unreasonable under the circumstances.

#104 (answer "J")

The source of this excerpt is an <u>accounts receivable confirmation</u>.

Confirmation is the process of obtaining and evaluating a direct communication from a third party in response to a request for information about an item affecting financial statement assertions.

Confirmation requests may use the positive form, which may be:

1. Filled-in forms, which request the recipient to indicate agreement with the stated information.
2. Blank forms, which request the recipient to fill in the balance and/or provide other information.

Confirmation requests may also use the negative form, which requests the recipient to respond only if there is a disagreement with information on the request.

#105 (answer "G")

The source of this excerpt is the <u>auditor's report</u>.

As part of an audit, an auditor must evaluate whether there is substantial doubt concerning an entity's ability to continue as a going concern for a reasonable time period, not to exceed one year beyond the date of the audited financial statements.

If substantial doubt remains, the audit report should include an explanatory paragraph (following the unqualified opinion paragraph) to reflect that conclusion.

Answer 3

#106 (answer "R,R")

The accountant is <u>required</u> to establish an understanding with the entity, regarding the nature and limitations of the services to be performed in <u>both</u> <u>review</u> <u>and</u> <u>compilation</u> engagements. The understanding, which should preferably be in writing, should also include a description of the report that the accountant expects to issue.

#107 (answer "R,N")

A review involves performing inquiry and analytical procedures intended to provide a reasonable basis for expressing limited assurance that financial statements conform to GAAP or another comprehensive basis of accounting.

Accordingly, as part of a <u>review</u> engagement, the accountant is <u>required</u> to make inquiries concerning actions taken at stockholders' and board of directors' meetings.

However, as part of a <u>compilation</u> engagement, the accountant is <u>not</u> <u>required</u> to make inquiries or perform procedures to verify information supplied by management.

#108 (answer "N,N")

For <u>both</u> <u>review</u> <u>and</u> <u>compilation</u> <u>engagements</u>, the successor accountant is <u>not</u> <u>required</u> to communicate with the predecessor accountant concerning acceptance of an engagement. However, the successor accountant may decide to do so because of such matters as frequent changes in accountants and limited information obtained from the prospective client.

#109 (answer "R,R")

In <u>both</u> <u>review</u> and <u>compilation</u> engagements, the accountant is <u>required</u> to obtain a level of knowledge of the accounting principles and practices of the industry in which the entity operates.

#110 (answer "N,N")

Obtaining an understanding of internal control is <u>not</u> <u>required</u> for <u>both</u> <u>review</u> and <u>compilation</u> engagements of a nonpublic entity.

(Obtaining an understanding of internal control is required as part of an audit. Further, the accountant must have sufficient knowledge of a client's internal control as part of a review of a public entity's interim financial information.)

#111 (answer "R,N")

As part of a <u>review</u>, the accountant is <u>required</u> to perform analytical procedures designed to identify relationships that appear to be unusual, e.g., comparisons with prior statements, budgets, or predictable patterns.

The accountant, however, is <u>not</u> <u>required</u> to perform analytical procedures as part of a <u>compilation</u> engagement.

#112 (answer "N,N")

An assessment of control risk is <u>not</u> <u>required</u> for <u>both</u> <u>review</u> and <u>compilation</u> engagements.

(An assessment of control risk is, however, required as part of an audit engagement.)

#113 (answer "N,N")

For <u>both</u> <u>review</u> <u>and</u> <u>compilation</u> engagements, the accountant is <u>not</u> <u>required</u> to send a letter of inquiry to the entity's attorney to corroborate the information furnished by management concerning litigation.

(It should be noted that the accountant is required to send a letter of inquiry to the entity's attorney as part of an audit.)

#114 (answer "R,N")

As part of a <u>review</u> engagement, the accountant is <u>required</u> to obtain a management representation letter from the entity. Normally, the chief executive officer and chief financial officer should sign the representation letter.

The accountant, however, is <u>not</u> <u>required</u>, as part of a <u>compilation</u> engagement, to obtain a management representation letter from the entity.

#115 (answer "R,N")

As part of a <u>review</u>, the accountant is <u>required</u> to perform analytical procedures designed to study the relationships of the financial statement elements that would be expected to conform to a predictable pattern; the study of these relationships, however, is not required for compilation engagements.

#116 (answer "N,N")

When performing a review or compilation engagement, the accountant should inform the appropriate level of management of any material errors, fraud, or illegal acts that come to his attention, unless they are clearly inconsequential. Accordingly, communication of clearly inconsequential matters is not required for both review and compilation engagements.

#117 (answer "R,N")

During a review, the accountant performs inquiry and analytical procedures intended to provide a reasonable basis for expressing limited assurance that financial statements conform to GAAP or another comprehensive basis of accounting. Accordingly, as part of a review engagement, the accountant is required to make inquiries about events subsequent to the date of the financial statements that would have a material effect on the financial statements; the accountant, however, is not required to make such inquiries as part of a compilation engagement.

#118 (answer "N,N")

As long as a change in accounting principles is adequately disclosed, the accountant, as part of a review or compilation engagement is not required to modify the accountant's report. Lack of adequate disclosure (like any other departure from generally accepted accounting principles), however, would necessitate modification of the accountant's report.

#119 (answer "N,N")

For both review and compilation engagements, the accountant should not submit unaudited financial statements of a nonpublic entity to her client, unless the accountant issues a report prepared in accordance with the standards applicable to the engagement.

Submission of unaudited financial statements includes presenting to a client, or others, financial statements that the accountant has generated, either manually or by computer software, or has modified by materially changing account classifi-

cations, amounts, or disclosures directly on client-prepared financial statements.

The accountant is not required as part of a review or compilation engagement to submit a hard (paper) copy of the financial statements and accountant's report if the financial statements and accountant's report are submitted on a computer disk; in this case, the standards have been adhered to.

#120 (answer "N,N")

The accountant is not required, as part of a review or compilation engagement, to perform specific procedures to evaluate whether there is substantive doubt about the entity's ability to continue as a going concern.

(Only as part of an audit must an accountant evaluate whether there is substantial doubt about the entity's ability to continue as a going concern. However, no specific procedures must be performed.)

Answer 4

Part 4 (a)

Irregularities may involve both management fraud and defalcations.

1. Management fraud involves intentional misstatements or omissions of amounts or disclosures from financial statements that render the financial statements misleading.

2. Defalcations involve misappropriation of assets through embezzlement, falsification of documents, or violation of policy.

Part 4 (b)

Under generally accepted audit standards, the auditor has a responsibility to assess the risk that management fraud (as well as other irregularities and errors) may cause the financial statements to contain a material misstatement. An assessment of the risk of material misstatement should be made while planning the audit. Based on that assessment, the auditor should design the audit to provide reasonable assurance of detecting management fraud (as well as other irregularities and errors) that is material to the financial statements.

Accordingly, the auditor should exercise due care and adopt an attitude of professional skepticism.

Part 4 (c)

The auditor's understanding of internal control should either increase or diminish the auditor's concern about the risk of material misstatements. Further, factors to be considered in assessing the risk of material misstatements caused by management fraud include the materiality of the effect on the financial statements, the level of management involved, the extent and skillfulness of any concealment, and the particular financial statements affected.

Part 4 (d)

Other factors that should heighten an auditor's concern about the existence of management fraud include:

1. The potential sale or exchange of the entity.
2. Indications that earnings and sales forecasts will not be met.
3. Negative industry considerations.
4. The existence of related party transactions.
5. A board of directors dominated by a single individual.
6. Indications of going concern problems.

Answer 5

Part 5 (a)

"Financial statement assertions" are management representations that are explicitly or implicitly embodied in the components of financial statements.

Part 5 (b)

In obtaining evidential matter in support of financial statement assertions, the auditor develops specific audit objectives in the light of those assertions.

Part 5 (c)

In developing the audit objectives of a particular engagement, the auditor should consider the specific circumstances of the entity, including the nature of its economic activity and the accounting practices unique to its industry.

Part 5 (d)

Audit procedures are actions or activities performed by the auditor to gather evidential matter to satisfy audit objectives. The procedures to be applied on a particular engagement are a matter of professional judgment based on the specific circumstances. However, the procedures adopted should be adequate to achieve the audit objectives developed by the auditor. In turn, the evidential matter obtained should be sufficient for the auditor to form conclusions about the validity of the individual assertions embodied in the components of financial statements.

There is not necessarily a one-to-one relationship between audit objectives and procedures. Some auditing procedures may relate to more than one objective. Further, a combination of auditing procedures may be necessary to achieve a particular audit objective.

Part 5 (e)

In selecting particular substantive tests to achieve the audit objectives developed, the auditor, in part, considers the risk of material misstatement of the financial statements. The auditor considers the assessed levels of control risk and the expected effectiveness and efficiency of substantive tests, which may include tests of transactions, tests of account balances, and analytical procedures.

The auditor also considers the nature and materiality of the items being tested, the kinds and competence of available evidential matter, and the nature of the audit objective to be achieved.

Accounting & Reporting—Taxation, Managerial, and Governmental and Not-for-Profit Organizations (ARE)

FOUR-OPTION MULTIPLE-CHOICE QUESTIONS

Answer 1

#1 (answer "C")

Schedule M-1 of the U.S. Corporation Income Tax Return (Form 1120) is used to show the reconciliation of income per books with income per the tax return.

In preparing Schedule M-1, the starting point is net income per books. Items to be added are (1) federal income tax, (2) the excess of capital losses over capital gains, (3) income subject to tax but not recorded on the books in the tax year, and (4) expenses recorded on the books but not deducted on the tax return in the tax year (e.g., interest expense to carry municipal bonds). Items to be subtracted are (1) income recorded on the books but not includible on the return in the tax year (e.g., municipal bond interest income), and (2) deductions on the return not charged against book income in the tax year.

In view of the above, the amount that Starke's taxable income should be as reconciled on Starke's Schedule M-1 of Form 1120, U.S. Corporation Income Tax Return, is $502,000:

Book income	$380,000
Add: Federal income tax expense	170,000
Interest expense to carry municipal bonds	2,000
Less: Municipal bond interest income	(50,000)
Taxable income, Schedule M-1	$502,000

Answer choice "A" is incorrect because it fails to include both the federal income tax expense and the interest expense on the debt incurred to carry municipal bonds.

Answer choice "B" is incorrect because it fails to include the interest expense to carry municipal bonds.

Answer choice "D" is incorrect because it fails to (1) include the interest expense on the debt to carry municipal bonds, and (2) reflect a reduction for the municipal bond interest income.

#2 (answer "D")

Amounts received as rent must be included in income. Advance rental receipts must also be included in income regardless of the period covered or the method of accounting used (i.e., cash basis or accrual basis).

Receipt of a security deposit is not included in income if the lessor plans to return it to the tenant at the end of the lease. If, during the course of the lease, the lessor keeps part or all of the security deposit because the tenant breaks a term of the lease, then the amount retained is treated as rental income.

Further, if an amount called a security deposit is to be used as a final payment of the rent, it is considered to be advance rent and therefore includible in income in the year received.

Finally, receipt of a lease cancellation payment is includible in income because it is received in lieu of rental income.

It should be clear, then, that the amount of income that Lake should report on its 1994 tax return is $125,000 + $50,000, or $175,000.

Answer choice "A" is incorrect because it treats both the advanced rental payments and the lease cancellation payment as nontaxable; in fact, both represent taxable income.

Answer choice "B" is incorrect because it fails to include the advanced rental payments, which represent taxable income.

Answer choice "C" is incorrect because it fails to include the lease cancellation payment, which represents taxable income.

#3 (answer "B")

Corporations may deduct capital losses only to the extent of capital gains. Capital losses may never offset ordinary income.

Any capital loss that exceeds capital gains is carried back to the three years preceding the year of the loss, and, if not completely absorbed, is then carried forward for up to five years succeeding the loss year (as a short-term loss).

Answer choice "A" is incorrect because it refers to the capital loss carry forward rule applicable to individuals.

Answer choice "C" is incorrect because it fails to consider the general rule that capital losses may never offset a corporation's ordinary income.

Answer choice "D" is incorrect because it refers to the $3,000 capital loss limitation applicable to individuals.

#4 (answer "D")

The dividends-received deduction is generally 70% (80% as to dividends received from a 20%-or-more-owned corporation) of dividends received from taxable domestic corporations limited to 70% (80% as noted) of the corporation's taxable income computed without regard to the dividends-received deduction and net operating loss deduction.

If a corporation sustains a net operating loss for the year, the limitation of 70% (80% as noted) of taxable income does not apply.

The 70% (80% as noted) of taxable income limitation will not apply if the full dividends-received deduction results in a net operating loss.

Dividends-received deductions for "affiliated corporations" are subject to different rules. Under certain circumstances, 100% of such dividends may be excluded.

It should be noted that the corporate dividends-received deduction is allowed only if the investor corporation owns the investee's stock for a specified minimum holding period, which in general is at least 46 days.

In view of the above, Best's dividends-received deduction on its 1994 tax return was limited to 70% of the $90,000 taxable income (before the dividends-received deduction), or $63,000, because (1) an 80% dividends-received deduction may not be claimed since there is no indication that the dividends were received from a 20%-or-more-owned corporation, (2) Best did not sustain a net operating loss for the year, and (3) the full dividends-received deduction will not result in a net operating loss.

Answer choice "A" is incorrect because it presumes that the dividends-received deduction is equal to 100% of the dividends received, with the result that the dividends will not be taxed. In general, only affiliated corporations that file a consolidated tax return will not be taxed on dividends paid from one includible corporation to another.

Answer choice "B" is incorrect because it (1) reflects an 80% dividends-received deduction and (2) fails to consider the taxable income limitation.

Answer choice "C" is incorrect because it fails to consider the taxable income limitation.

#5 (answer "C")

With regard to depreciation computations for personal property made under the general MACRS method, the half-year convention provides that one-half of the first year's depreciation is allowed in the year in which the property is placed into service, regardless of when the property is placed into service during the year, and a half-year's depreciation is allowed for the year in which the property is disposed of.

An exception to the general rule is the mid-quarter convention, which is applicable if more than 40% of the aggregate value of personal property is placed into service during the last three months of the year. Accordingly, assets acquired during the first quarter would generate 10.5 months of cost recovery; the second quarter, 7.5 months; the third quarter, 4.5 months; and the fourth quarter, 1.5 months.

In view of the above, Data must use the mid-quarter convention because it placed into service all the office equipment during the month of November (i.e., during the last three months of the year).

Answer choice "A" is incorrect because a full-year convention does not exist under current tax law.

Answer choice "B" is incorrect because it reflects the general rule, which is clearly not applicable in Data's case in view of the explanation to answer choice "C."

Answer choice "D" is incorrect because the mid-month convention is applicable to real property only.

#6 (answer "C")

A capital asset is any property owned and used for personal purposes, pleasure, or investment except:

1. Stock in trade or other property properly includible in inventory or held for sale to customers in the ordinary course of a trade or business.
2. Accounts or notes receivable acquired in the ordinary course of a trade or business for services rendered, or from the sale of any properties described in item #1 above, or for services rendered as an employee.
3. Real property, or depreciable personal property used in a trade or business.
4. A copyright, a literary, musical or artistic composition, or similar property:
   a. Created by one's own effort.
   b. In whose possession the basis of such property is the same as the basis of the creator of such property.

A Section 1231 asset is any property held for the long-term holding period that is:

1. Held for the production of rent or royalties.
2. Depreciable property used in a trade or business.
3. Real property used in a trade or business.
4. Any "involuntarily converted" capital asset held in connection with a trade or business, or a transaction entered into for profit.

In view of the above, capital assets include a manufacturing company's investment in U.S. Treasury bonds.

Answer choice "A" is incorrect because accounts receivable are specifically excluded from the definition of a capital asset.

Answer choice "B" is incorrect because it refers to depreciable property used in a trade or business, which is specifically excluded from the definition of a capital asset. This property, if held for the long-term holding period, would be classified as a Section 1231 asset.

Answer choice "D" is incorrect because a real estate developer's unimproved land that is to be subdivided to build homes for sale to customers represents inventory, which is specifically excluded from the definition of a capital asset.

SOURCE: LPR, NOVEMBER 1995, #6

#6 (answer "C")

When preparing a client's tax return, a CPA may rely on information provided by the client and should consider information from another client's return, as long as confidentiality is not breached and no law is violated. Thus, according to the standards of the profession, a CPA should consider information actually known to the CPA from the tax return of another client and information provided by the client that appears correct based on the client's returns from prior years.

Answer choices other than "C" are based on incorrect assumptions and/or interpretations of the law.

#7 (answer "D")

Corporations may deduct capital losses only to the extent of capital gains. Any capital loss that exceeds capital gains is carried back to the three years preceding the year of the loss and, if not completely absorbed, is then carried forward for up to five years succeeding the loss year (as a short-term loss).

By inspection of the figures presented, it is clear that the net long-term loss of $2,000 (i.e., $1,500 gain less $3,500 loss) would reduce the net short-term gain of $4,500 (i.e., $8,500 gain less $4,000 loss) to yield a taxable short-term gain of $2,500.

Baker's total taxable income for 1994 is $38,500:

Taxable income from regular business operations	$36,000
Add: Net short-term capital gain	2,500
Total taxable income, 1994	$38,500

Answer choice "A" is incorrect because while it includes the short- and long-term capital gains, it does not reflect the short- and long-term capital losses, which may be used to offset such gains.

Answer choice "B" is incorrect because it fails to reflect the long-term capital loss, which may be used to offset the net taxable capital gain.

Answer choice "C" is incorrect because it fails to consider both the long-term capital gain and the long-term capital loss.

SOURCE: LPR, NOVEMBER 1995, #7

#7 (answer "A")

A CPA who discovers an error in a client's previously filed tax return must advise the client of the error and recommend the measures to be taken.

However, the CPA need not withdraw from the relationship if the client corrects the error.

Answer choices other than "A" are based on incorrect assumptions and/or interpretations of the law.

#8 (answer "B")

A corporation may claim a deduction for charitable contributions made in cash or property. The deduction is limited to 10% of taxable income without taking into account:

1. The deduction for contributions.
2. The dividends-received deduction.
3. Any net operating loss carryback to the tax year.
4. Any capital loss carryback to the tax year.

Any charitable contributions made during the year in excess of the 10% limitation may be carried forward to a maximum of five succeeding years. However, contributions actually made during the later years plus the carryover must fall within the 10% limit. Any excess not used up within the five-year period is lost forever. Also, a contributions carryover is not allowed to the extent that it increases a net operating loss carryover.

An accrual basis taxpayer may elect to deduct contributions authorized by the Board of Directors but not paid during the tax year if payment is made within two and a half months after the close of the tax year.

The maximum allowable deduction that Cable may claim in 1994 for contributions is $86,000:

Taxable income before deduction for charitable contributions	$820,000
Add: Dividends-received deduction	40,000
Amount subject to 10% limitation	$860,000
Maximum allowable deduction;	
$860,000 × 10%	$86,000

In view of the above, Cable can deduct $86,000 as charitable contributions, which includes the $80,000 contributed in 1994 to a qualified charitable organization and $6,000 (of the $10,000) carryover contributions from the prior year.

Answer choice "A" is incorrect because it fails to consider the 10%-of-taxable-income limitation.

Answer choice "C" is incorrect because it fails to add back the dividends-received deduction in computing the base to which the 10% limitation should be applied.

Answer choice "D" is incorrect because it fails to include the allowable part of the carryover contributions from the prior year.

#9 (answer "C")

Refer to the answer to question #8 for background material pertaining to a corporation's deduction for charitable contributions.

As indicated in the answer to question #8, any charitable contributions made during the year in excess of the 10% limitation may be carried forward to a maximum of five succeeding years.

Answer choices other than "C" are based on incorrect assumptions.

#10 (answer "B")

Under the accrual method of accounting, income must be reported in the year in which all events have occurred that determine the taxpayer's right to receive it, and the amount is estimable with reasonable accuracy.

If a taxpayer, in good faith, accrues an estimated amount of income, and subsequently determines that the exact amount is different, the taxpayer should:

1. In the case of an underaccrual, include the difference in income for the year in which the exact amount is determined.
2. In the case of an overaccrual, reduce the income for the year in which the exact amount is determined, by the difference.

In view of the above, the $1,000 difference is includible in Stewart's 1995 income tax return.

Answer choices "A" and "C" are based on assumptions that are not valid under current tax law.

Answer choice "D" is incorrect because an amended return should only be filed by Stewart to correct an intentional omission of income, which is clearly not the case, since the estimated accrual was reasonable and was made in good faith (i.e., proper).

#11 (answer "A")

In general, under the uniform capitalization rules applicable to real and personal property acquired for resale, certain costs, referred to as allocable costs (or Sec. 263A costs), must be capitalized with respect to inventory.

It should be noted that the uniform capitalization rules are also applicable to self-constructed (manufactured) real and personal property. The uniform capitalization rules do not apply to retailers (and wholesalers) of personal property with no more than $10,000,000 average annual gross receipts for the three preceding years.

Allocable costs include both the direct costs of the property and the property's share of certain indirect costs. Accordingly, allocable indirect costs include certain depreciation and interest deductions, taxes, and on-site and off-site inventory storage costs.

Allocable costs do not include selling, marketing, advertising and distribution expenses, and deductible research and experiment expenditures.

Answer choices other than "A" are based on incorrect assumptions and/or combinations.

#12 (answer "A")

Determination of whether a corporation is to be treated as a personal holding company, and therefore subject to a 39.6% tax on undistributed income in addition to other corporate taxes, is based on two tests—as to income and stock ownership.

The income test provides that a corporation is a personal holding company when 60% of adjusted gross income consists of dividends, interest, certain royalties, annuities, certain rents, personal service contract income, and certain income from estates and trusts.

As to stock ownership, if during the period of the last half of the taxable year more than 50% of the value of the outstanding stock is owned by or for not more than five individuals, the corporation is deemed to be a personal holding company. (For purposes of determining the five individuals, the rules of constructive stock ownership apply.)

Should the corporation be liable for the tax on undistributed income, it should be self-assessed by filing a separate schedule (Form 1120-PH) along with the regular tax return.

The tax is imposed on "undistributed personal holding company income," which is taxable income with the following adjustments, minus the dividend-paid deduction:

1. Deduction is allowed for federal and foreign income and taxes on excess profits.
2. Deduction is allowed for excess charitable contributions; instead of the normal 10% limit, the deduction may be as high as 50% of taxable income.
3. Deduction is allowed for net long-term capital gain less related federal income taxes.
4. No deduction is allowed for dividends received.
5. Except for a special one-year net operating loss carryover deduction, no net operating loss deduction is allowed.

The deduction for dividends paid includes the following:

1. Dividends actually paid during the tax year.
2. Consent dividends, which represent amounts not actually paid out as dividends but that are includible in the shareholder's income because such an election was made by consenting shareholders on the last day of the corporation's tax year.
3. With certain limitations, "late-paid" dividends. "Late-paid" dividends are dividends paid after year-end, but no later than the 15th day of the third month of the following year. In order to claim the deduction for "late-paid" dividends, a proper election must be made.

In view of the above, to determine undistributed personal holding company income prior to the dividend-paid deduction, Kane must deduct from taxable income both federal income taxes and net long-term capital gain less related federal income taxes.

Answer choices other than "A" are based on incorrect assumptions and/or combinations.

#13 (answer "D")

A group of affiliated corporations may file consolidated tax returns for the period that they are affiliated, but only if all the corporations that were members of the affiliated group at any time during the tax year consent before the last day for filing the return.

An affiliated group may be defined as one or more chains of includible corporations connected through stock ownership with a common parent corporation that is an includible corporation, but only if (1) the common parent owns stock possessing at least 80% of the total voting power and at least 80% of the total value of the stock of at least one includible corporation, and (2) stock meeting the 80% requirement in each of the includible corporations (except the common parent) is owned directly by one or more of the other includible corporations.

An "includible corporation" means all corporations except: (1) exempt corporations, (2) life insurance or mutual insurance companies, (3) foreign corporations, (4) corporations with 80% income from U.S. possessions, (5) regulated investment companies, (6) real estate investment trusts, and (7) certain domestic international sales corporations (DISCs).

Logically, affiliated corporations that file a consolidated tax return will not be taxed on dividends paid from one includible corporation to another. (Practically, this is as a result of the intercompany eliminations necessary to prevent double taxation.)

(Affiliated corporations that do not file a consolidated tax return similarly are entitled to a 100%-dividends-received deduction for qualifying dividends received from members of the affiliated group.)

In view of the preceding, since Bank Corp. and Shore Corp. are members of an affiliated group that files a consolidated tax return, Bank should report $0 of dividend revenue received from Shore.

Answer choice "A" is incorrect because it fails to consider the elimination of dividends paid between members of an affiliated group.

Answer choices "B" and "C" are not logical in view of the background provided.

#14 (answer "C")

In addition to liability for regular income taxes, every corporation (other than a domestic or foreign personal holding company, a domestic international sales corporation, or an exempt organization) is liable for an extra tax (in the nature of a penalty) if it is formed or availed of for the purpose of preventing the imposition of income tax upon its shareholders, or the shareholders of any

other corporation, by permitting earnings and profits to accumulate instead of being divided or distributed.

The rate of tax is 39.6%.

The tax is imposed on "accumulated taxable income" of the taxable year, which is taxable income with the following adjustments, minus the sum of the dividends-paid deduction and the accumulated earnings credit.

1. Deduction is allowed for federal income taxes and income and profit taxes of foreign countries and U.S. possessions (but not including the accumulated earnings tax or personal holding company tax).
2. The deduction for charitable contributions is unlimited.
3. No deduction is allowed for dividends received.
4. The net operating loss deduction is not allowed.
5. Deduction is allowed for net capital losses.
6. Deduction is allowed for the net capital gain for the year, minus the taxes attributed thereto.
7. No capital loss carryback or carryover is allowed.

The accumulated earnings credit is measured by the reasonable retained earnings (undistributed earnings and profits) of the business. There is a minimum credit of $250,000, limited to $150,000 for personal service corporations. Accordingly, if a corporation can demonstrate that the "reasonable needs" of its business require the retention of all or part of its current-year accumulated taxable income, the corporation can eliminate or reduce its liability for the accumulated earnings tax.

The dividends-paid deduction includes (1) dividends paid during the taxable year, (2) dividends paid on or before the 15th day of the third month following the close of the taxable year, and (3) consent dividends.

The accumulated earnings tax can be imposed regardless of the number of stockholders of a corporation.

Answer choices other than "C" are based on incorrect assumptions and/or combinations.

#15 (answer "A")

The alternative minimum tax is equal to 20% of alternative minimum taxable income (in excess of the exemption amount) reduced by the corporation's regular tax liability. The exemption amount is $40,000, but must be reduced by 25% of the excess of AMTI over $150,000.

Alternative minimum taxable income is equal to taxable income, after certain adjustments, plus tax preference items. The adjustments to taxable income are complex and are generally beyond the scope of the CPA examination.

Tax preferences and adjustments may be "deferral adjustments and preferences." It should be understood that "deferral adjustments and preferences" represent items that are taxed for AMT purposes in one year and for regular tax purposes in a future year.

In order to prevent "deferral adjustments and preferences" from being taxed twice (i.e., first under the AMT system and then in a future year under the regular tax system), a minimum tax credit is available. The minimum tax credit, which reduces the regular tax (and not the alternative minimum tax) liability in a later year by the amount of AMT liability attributable to "deferral preferences and adjustments" in the earlier year, may be carried forward indefinitely.

In computing the alternative minimum tax, the following are some of the more general types of tax preference items and adjustments to be considered:

1. Excess accelerated depreciation on real property.
2. Excess percentage depletion for coal and iron ore.
3. Excess amortization of pollution control facilities.
4. With respect to personal property placed into service after 1986, the excess of accelerated depreciation over the amount calculated using the 150%-declining-balance method with a switch to straight-line.
5. The adjusted current earnings (ACE) adjustment. The ACE adjustment is generally equal to 75% of the amount by which adjusted current earnings exceed AMTI. However, if AMTI exceeds adjusted current earnings, a reduction in AMTI equal to 75% of the difference is allowed. Accord-

ingly, the ACE adjustment can be a positive or negative amount.

Adjusted current earnings is equal to AMTI (before the ACE adjustment and the AMTI net operating loss deduction) plus or minus certain adjustments. The calculation of adjusted current earnings is based on tax concepts similar to those used in determining earnings and profits (i.e., E & P) for regular tax purposes. Accordingly, adjustments may be necessary for (a) depreciation, (b) certain items excluded from gross income but that are properly includible in E & P, and (c) items of deduction that are allowed in arriving at regular taxable income, but are not allowed in arriving at E & P.

For example, in determining adjusted current earnings, (a) all municipal bond interest is includible income, (b) all costs to purchase and carry municipal bonds are deductible, and (c) the 70%-dividends-received deduction is not allowable, but the 80%-dividends-received deduction is allowable. Further, the method of depreciation for personal property placed in service after 1989 for determining ACE is governed by the Alternative Depreciation system. Accordingly, the straight-line method must be used.

6. Tax-exempt interest on private activity bonds issued after August 7, 1986.

In view of the preceding, Eastern's 1994 alternative minimum taxable income before the adjusted current earnings (ACE) adjustment is $306,000:

1994 taxable income	$300,000
Add: Adjustment for the accelerated depreciation taken on 1994 five-year property	1,000
1994 tax-exempt interest from specified private activity bonds issued after August 7, 1986	5,000
Alternative minimum taxable income, 1994	$306,000

Answer choice "B" is incorrect because it does not include the adjustment for the accelerated depreciation taken on 1994 five-year property.

Answer choice "C" is incorrect because it treats the accelerated depreciation taken on 1994 five-year property as a reduction of, rather than an addition to, taxable income in arriving at alternative minimum taxable income.

Answer choice "D" is incorrect because it does not include the 1994 tax-exempt interest from specified private activity bonds issued after August 7, 1986.

#16 (answer "D")

A civil fraud penalty will be imposed on a taxpayer if any part of an underpayment of tax that is required to be shown on a tax return is due to fraud. The penalty is equal to 75% of the tax underpayment attributable to civil tax fraud. Civil tax fraud generally involves (1) a knowing falsehood, (2) an underpayment of tax, and (3) an intent to evade tax.

In view of the above, a civil fraud penalty can be imposed on a corporation that underpays tax by maintaining false records and reporting fictitious transactions to minimize corporate tax liability.

Answer choice "A" is incorrect because the omission of income as a result of inadequate record keeping is due to carelessness rather than an intent to evade tax.

Answer choice "B" is incorrect because failing to report income erroneously considered not to be part of corporate profits is an honest mistake; accordingly, the civil fraud penalty may not be assessed.

Answer choice "C" is incorrect because filing an incomplete return with an appended statement, making clear that the return is incomplete, does not involve fraud. In this situation, it appears that the taxpayer acted in good faith and did not intend to evade tax; accordingly, the civil fraud penalty may not be assessed.

#17 (answer "B")

In general, foreign income taxes paid by a corporation may be claimed either as a deduction or as a credit, at the election of the corporation. If the foreign tax credit is elected, the credit may not reduce the U.S. tax liability on income from U.S. sources. The computation to determine the allowable credit is:

$$\frac{\text{Foreign source income}}{\text{Worldwide income}} \times$$

Tentative U.S. liability = Foreign Tax Credit

It should be understood that the election to claim the foreign tax credit is usually more advantageous, since a tax credit reduces a corporation's liability on a dollar-for-dollar basis. Note, however, that the credit is limited to the amount paid.

Answer choice "A" is incorrect because a dividends-received "exclusion" does not exist under current tax law. It should be noted, however, that under certain circumstances, a C corporation may claim a dividends-received "deduction," which may reduce its regular income tax.

Answer choices "C" and "D" are incorrect because they represent valid deductions, but not credits, which may be claimed by a corporation.

#18 (answer "D")

In addition to liability for regular income taxes, every corporation (other than a domestic or foreign personal holding company, a domestic international sales corporation, or an exempt organization) is liable for an extra tax (in the nature of a penalty) if it is formed or availed of for the purpose of preventing the imposition of income tax upon its shareholders, or the shareholders of any other corporation, by permitting earnings and profits to accumulate instead of being divided or distributed.

The rate of tax is 39.6%.

The tax is imposed on "accumulated taxable income" of the taxable year, which is taxable income with the following adjustments, minus the sum of the dividends-paid deduction and the accumulated earnings credit.

1. Deduction is allowed for federal income taxes and income and profit taxes of foreign countries and U.S. possessions (but not including the accumulated earnings tax or personal holding company tax).
2. The deduction for charitable contributions is unlimited.
3. No deduction is allowed for dividends received.
4. The net operating loss deduction is not allowed.
5. Deduction is allowed for net capital losses.
6. Deduction is allowed for the net capital gain for the year, minus the taxes attributed thereto.
7. No capital loss carryback or carryover is allowed.

The accumulated earnings credit is measured by the reasonable retained earnings (undistributed earnings and profits) of the business. There is a minimum credit of $250,000, limited to $150,000 for personal service corporations. For any taxable year, the accumulated earnings credit is the amount by which the minimum credit exceeds the accumulated earnings and profits at the close of the preceding taxable year.

The dividends-paid deduction includes dividends paid during the taxable year, plus those paid on or before the 15th day of the third month following the close of the taxable year, and consent dividends.

The accumulated earnings tax can be imposed regardless of the number of stockholders in a corporation.

Answer choice "A" is incorrect because partnerships are not subject to any tax on earnings.

Answer choice "B" is incorrect because distributions in excess of accumulated earnings cannot possibly result in a taxable base.

Answer choice "C" is incorrect because a personal holding company cannot be treated as a corporation subject to the accumulated earnings tax. Otherwise, two "penalty" taxes could be levied against the same corporation.

#19 (answer "C")

Generally, any distribution made by a corporation to its shareholders is considered a dividend to the extent of earnings and profits, both accumulated and for the current year. (However, a distribution is not a taxable dividend if it constitutes a return of capital to the stockholder.)

It should be noted that in general, the amount of dividend income resulting from a property distribution received by a shareholder is the fair market value of the property received.

Accordingly, the total amount of distributions taxable as dividend income to Dahl's stockholders is $280,000 (i.e., to the extent of accumulated earnings and profits ($120,000) and current earnings and profits ($160,000)).

The balance of the distribution (i.e., $80,000) will be treated as a return of capital to the stockholders.

Answer choices other than "C" are based on incorrect assumptions and/or combinations that are not valid under current tax law.

#20 (answer "C")

Generally, any distribution made by a corporation to its shareholders is considered a dividend to the extent of earnings and profits, both accumulated and for the current year. (However, a distribution is not a taxable dividend if it constitutes a return of capital to the stockholder.)

It should be noted that in general, the amount of dividend income resulting from a property distribution received by a shareholder is the fair market value of the property received.

Accordingly, Ridge's cash distribution was taxable as $750,000 in ordinary income to its shareholders (i.e., limited to its current and accumulated earnings and profits) and reduced its shareholders' adjusted bases in Ridge stock by $250,000.

Answer choices other than "C" are based on incorrect assumptions and/or combinations.

#21 (answer "C")

If property is transferred to a corporation by one or more persons (individuals, trusts, estates, partnerships, or corporations) solely in exchange for stock in that corporation, and immediately after the exchange such person or persons are in control of the corporation to which the property was transferred, ordinarily no gain or loss will be recognized.

To be in control of the corporation, the person or persons making the transfer must own, immediately after the exchange, at least 80% of the total combined voting power of all classes of stock entitled to vote, and at least 80% of the total number of shares in each class of nonvoting stock outstanding.

The term property does not include services rendered, or to be rendered, to the issuing corporation. Stock received for services is taxable income to the recipient to the extent of the stock's fair market value.

If, in addition to stock, the persons transferring property to the corporation receive other property or cash, gain is recognized, but only to the extent of the cash and fair market value of the other property received. No loss, however, will be recognized.

The assumption of liabilities by a corporation is not regarded as the receipt of cash or other property in determining the gain or loss recognized. However, when the liabilities exceed the adjusted basis of the property transferred, gain is recognized to the extent of this excess.

A corporation's basis in the property is generally the same as the shareholder's basis immediately before the transfer, increased by any gain recognized by the shareholder as a result of the transfer.

The shareholder's basis in the stock received is equal to the cash plus the adjusted basis of the property transferred to the corporation, increased by any gain recognized. The basis is decreased to the extent of the cash and the fair market value of the other property, if any, received by the shareholder.

Accordingly, Clark's basis in Jet stock was $110,000, consisting of the $60,000 cash contribution plus the $50,000 adjusted basis of the other property contributed.

Answer choice "A" is clearly incorrect because Clark must have a basis in the Jet stock by virtue of Clark's transfers to the corporation of property with an existing adjusted basis solely in exchange for Jet stock.

Answer choice "B" is incorrect because it (1) fails to include the $60,000 cash contribution and (2) reflects the fair market value (rather than the adjusted basis) of the other property contributed.

Answer choice "D" is incorrect because it includes the fair market value (rather than the adjusted basis) of the other property contributed.

#22 (answer "A")

The Internal Revenue Code specifically defines seven types of corporate reorganizations.

1. A statutory merger or consolidation. (A type "A" reorganization.)
2. The acquisition by one corporation, in exchange solely for all or a part of its voting stock, of stock of another corporation if immediately after the acquisition, the acquiring corporation has control of such other corporation. (A type "B" reorganization.)
3. The acquisition by one corporation, in exchange solely for all or a part of its voting stock, of substantially all of the properties of another corporation. (A type "C" reorganization.)

4. A transfer by a corporation of all or a part of its assets to another corporation if immediately after the transfer the transferor, or one or more of its shareholders, or any combination thereof, is in control of the corporation to which the assets are transferred. (A type "D" reorganization.)
5. A recapitalization. (A type "E" reorganization.)
6. A mere change in identity, form, or place of organization. (A type "F" reorganization.)
7. A reorganization pursuant to Title 11 of the Bankruptcy Code. (A type "G" reorganization.)

It should be noted that a stock redemption (which occurs when a corporation cancels or redeems its own stock) is not a corporate reorganization.

The requirements for each type of reorganization are beyond the scope of the CPA examination.

An examination question that contains the phrase "pursuant to a corporate reorganization" should be answered utilizing the following general rules.

1. No gain will be recognized by the shareholders unless "boot" is received in addition to the receipt of stock. In addition, no gain will be recognized by the corporation(s) involved.
2. Three types of "boot" may trigger recognition of gain.
   a. Cash.
   b. Bonds—gain will be recognized if the principal amount of the bonds received exceeds the principal amount of the bonds surrendered, or if bonds are received and none are surrendered.
      The fair market value of the bonds will be utilized in measuring the gain.
   c. Payments equivalent to a dividend when one of the parties to the reorganization has accumulated earnings and profits.

In the question situation, Ace Corp. and Bate Corp. combine and form Carr Corp., the only surviving corporation. It should be readily apparent that this is a consolidation, which is a type "A" reorganization. Accordingly, the reorganization is tax-free to the shareholders and the corporation.

Answer choices other than "A" are based on incorrect assumptions and/or combinations.

#23 (answer "A")

Interest is normally charged on underpayments or late payments of tax at the rate of three percentage points above the applicable federal short-term rate (which is determined quarterly). Interest begins accumulating from the due date of the tax, and is compounded daily.

A corporation that fails to pay tax timely may be subject to a tax delinquency penalty in the amount of 0.5% per month, or part thereof, but not to exceed 25%.

A corporation that files an automatic extension request must in good faith (1) make an estimate of its tax liability and (2) pay any balance of tax due with the automatic extension request. Failure to pay the entire tax due by the due date for filing the automatic extension request will result in the imposition of interest and may result in the imposition of a tax delinquency penalty.

It should be noted, however, that a tax delinquency penalty will not be imposed if the amount of tax paid on or before the regular due date of the return (i.e., the due date for the filing of the automatic extension request) is at least 90% of the amount of tax shown on the final corporate income tax return, and any balance due shown on the final corporate return is paid on or before the due date of the return, including any extensions of time for filing.

It should therefore be apparent that Bass was subject to pay interest on the $400 tax payment made after the original due date of the return in 1995. Bass will not be subject to a tax delinquency penalty because it paid (1) in excess of 90% of the amount of tax shown on the final corporate return by the original due date of the return and (2) the $400 balance due by the extended due date.

Answer choices other than "A" are based on incorrect assumptions and/or combinations.

#24 (answer "B")

In general, a C corporation is required to make quarterly estimated tax payments if it expects its estimated tax (i.e., income tax less credits) to be $500 or more. Required estimated tax payments are due by the 15th day of the 4th, 6th, 9th, and 12th months of the tax year.

A corporation that does not pay estimated tax when due may be charged an underpayment penalty, for the period of underpayment, at a rate that is periodically determined by the Internal Revenue Service.

The underpayment penalty, like all other penalties imposed by taxing authorities, is not deductible.

However, a corporation generally will not be liable for the penalty if its tax liability is $500 or more and it timely paid either 100% of its tax liability for the year or 100% of its actual tax liability for the preceding year (if the corporation filed a return that showed a liability for at least some amount of tax, and the return covered a full 12 months).

A corporation may also be able to reduce or eliminate the underestimated tax penalty by using the annualized income method. This method, under which the required installment for one or more periods may be less than one-fourth of the required annual payment, generally may be used if the corporation's income varies during the year.

Further, no penalty will be imposed on a corporation for underpayment of estimated tax for a particular year if the tax for that year is less than $500, since the required estimated tax payment threshold has not been reached.

It should be noted that the underpayment penalty rules apply to a corporation's total income tax, which includes the alternative minimum tax.

In this question, Edge filed a tax return that showed no tax liability for its 1994 tax year. Accordingly, Edge could not use the 100% of the preceding tax year method in 1995. However, to avoid the penalty for underpayment of estimated taxes, Edge could compute its first quarter 1995 estimated income tax payment using the annualized income method.

Answer choices other than "B" are based on incorrect assumptions and/or combinations.

#25 (answer "B")

In its broadest terms, a "deficiency" is the difference between the correct tax liability and the tax liability as reported on the tax return as filed.

Once the Internal Revenue Service determines that a deficiency exists, it mails a "notice of deficiency" or "90-day letter" to the taxpayer. The taxpayer then has 90 days to either pay the tax or petition the Tax Court.

The Service must mail the "notice of deficiency" prior to the expiration of the statute of limitations.

The general rule is that the statute of limitations will expire three years after the later of either the due date of the return or the date the return was filed. It should be noted that the statute of limitations normally begins on the day after the later of the due date of the return or the date the return was filed. A return filed before the due date is considered to have been filed on the due date.

A major exception to the general rule relates to the "substantial omission of items" from the return. Simply stated, the three-year period will be extended to six years if the taxpayer omits from gross income an amount in excess of 25% of the amount of gross income as reported on the return (prior to the deduction for costs of goods sold).

It should be noted that under certain circumstances, to prevent inequities, a corporation's tax year can be reopened after all statutes of limitations have expired. Accordingly, <u>if a corporation prevails in a determination allowing a deduction in an open tax year that was taken erroneously in a closed tax year, the corporation's tax year can be reopened</u>. This will prevent the corporation from claiming the same deduction twice.

Additionally, an assessment may be made at any time for filing a false or fraudulent return, or for failing to file a tax return.

Answer choices other than "B" are based on incorrect assumptions and/or combinations.

#26 (answer "D")

When preparing a tax return, an income tax return preparer has no obligation to audit the taxpayer's records. The tax return preparer must exercise professional judgment. Accordingly, the tax return preparer must (1) be advised that adequate documentation exists, and (2) make inquiries when the information appears to be inaccurate or incomplete. Further, a tax return preparer must advise a client regarding errors or omissions in previously filed returns.

In preparing tax returns, a tax practitioner must adhere to the Internal Revenue Code and the regulations thereunder. Failure to do so may result in the imposition of civil and/or criminal penalties.

Some of the more common civil penalties that may be imposed on an income tax return preparer are

1. $1,000 ($10,000 with respect to a corporate tax return) for knowingly aiding in the preparation of a tax return that results in an understatement of the taxpayer's liability.
2. $250 for claiming a position that (a) has no realistic possibility of being sustained, and (b) is not disclosed on the return, or is frivolous.
3. $1,000 for willful understatement of the taxpayer's liability on a return or claim for refund.
4. $500 for endorsing or negotiating a taxpayer's income tax refund check.
5. $250 for improper disclosure or use of tax return information.
6. $50 for failure to:
   a. Sign a return.
   b. Report the preparer's identification number on the return.
   c. Give a copy of the return to the taxpayer.
   d. Keep a copy (or a list) of the returns prepared.
   e. Keep a list of tax return preparers employed.

Federal statutes also provide that a criminal action can be brought against the tax return preparer in the following circumstances:

1. Willfully delivering documents that are known by the preparer to be fraudulent.
2. Fraudulently executing documents required by provisions of the Internal Revenue Code.
3. Removing or concealing goods with the intent to evade any tax imposed by the Internal Revenue Code.

It should therefore be obvious that a penalty for understated corporate tax liability can be imposed on a tax preparer who fails to <u>make reasonable inquiries when taxpayer information appears incorrect</u>.

Answer choices other than "D" are incorrect because they represent actions that are not required of a tax return preparer.

#27 (answer "B")

The original basis of a partner's interest includes the amount of money paid, plus the adjusted basis of any contributed property, reduced by the portion of any indebtedness on such property assumed by the other partners.

The adjusted basis of Barker's interest in Kode is $41,000:

Cash contributed	$20,000
Adjusted basis of property contributed	26,000
	46,000
Less: Portion of mortgage assumed by other partners; 50% × $10,000	5,000
Adjusted basis of Barker's 50% interest	$41,000

Answer choice "A" is incorrect because, while it properly includes the $20,000 cash contribution and the building's $26,000 adjusted basis, it reflects a reduction for the total mortgage assumed by the partnership (i.e., $10,000), rather than a reduction for the $5,000 portion of the mortgage assumed by the other partners; this results in the incorrect answer choice of $36,000.

Answer choice "C" is incorrect because, while it properly includes the $20,000 cash contribution, it includes the $42,000 fair market value of the building (rather than its adjusted basis), reduced by the $10,000 mortgage assumed by the partnership (rather than the portion of the mortgage assumed by the other partners); this results in the incorrect answer choice of $52,000.

Answer choice "D" is clearly incorrect because, while it properly includes the $20,000 cash contribution, (1) it includes the $42,000 fair market value of the property, which is irrelevant in determining the adjusted basis of Barker's partnership interest, and (2) no adjustment is made for the portion of the mortgage assumed by the other partners; this results in the incorrect answer choice of $62,000.

#28 (answer "D")

In general, no gain or loss is recognized by either the partnership or any partner upon the contribution of property in exchange for a partnership interest. Gain, however, will be recognized by a partner to the extent that any indebtedness on contributed property assumed by the other partners exceeds the contributing partner's adjusted basis in such property.

Answer choice "A" is incorrect because, by itself, the fact that the fair market value of the contributed property exceeds its adjusted basis does not result in the recognition of a gain by the contributing partner.

Answer choice "B" is incorrect because the indebtedness on the contributed property assumed by the other partners (i.e., 50% × $100,000, or $50,000) does not exceed the contributing partner's (i.e., Black's) adjusted basis in such property (i.e., $250,000).

Answer choice "C" is clearly based on incorrect assumptions and/or incorrect combinations.

#29 (answer "A")

Even though partnership profits are not taxable to the partnership, the partnership must file an information return on Form 1065 showing the results of the partnership's operations for its tax year and the items of income, gain, loss, deduction, or credit affecting its partners' individual income tax returns.

Each partner, in determining his income for the year, must take into account, separately, his distributive share (whether or not distributed) of various items, including, of course, ordinary income.

Income or loss, and so on., will be allocable to a partner only for the portion of the year he is a member of the partnership.

A partnership may deduct fixed salaries, determined without regard to the income of the partnership, paid to partners for services.

Similarly, a partnership may deduct fixed payments, determined without regard to the income of the partnership, paid to partners for the use of their capital. Such payments, frequently called "guaranteed payments," merely alter the manner in which respective partners share profits. Thus, guaranteed payments are deductible expenses on the U.S. Partnership Return of Income, Form 1065, in order to arrive at partnership income (loss), and are taxed as ordinary income to the recipient partners.

In view of the above, the amount of income that Evan should report from Vista Partnership is $37,500, consisting of (1) the guaranteed payment received by Evan (i.e., $20,000), (2) Evan's distributive share of the net long-term capital gains (i.e., 25% × $10,000, or $2,500), and (3) Evan's distributive share of the net business income after guaranteed payments (i.e., 25% × [$80,000 − $20,000], or $15,000).

Answer choice "B" is clearly based on incorrect assumptions; the incorrect answer of $27,500 is arrived at by taking 25% of the sum of the (1) $20,000 guaranteed payment to Evan, (2) $80,000 net business income before guaranteed payments, and (3) $10,000 net long-term capital gains.

Answer choice "C" is incorrect because, while it includes the guaranteed payment (i.e., $20,000) received by Evan and his distributive share of the net long-term capital gain (i.e., 25% × $10,000, or $2,500), it fails to include Evan's distributive share of net business income after guaranteed payments (i.e., 25% × [$80,000 − $20,000], or $15,000).

Answer choice "D" is incorrect because it only reflects the guaranteed payment received by Evan. As such, it fails to include Evan's distributive share of both the (1) net business income after guaranteed payments, and (2) net long-term capital gains.

#30 (answer "A")

The basis of a partner's interest in a partnership is the original basis and subsequent adjustments thereto.

When one receives a partnership interest in exchange for services, the value of the interest is ordinary income and the basis is its fair market value.

The original basis equals the amount of money paid plus the adjusted basis of any contributed property reduced by the portion of indebtedness on such property, if any, assumed by the other partners. (In general, no gain or loss is recognized either to the partnership or any partner upon a contribution of property in exchange for a partnership interest.)

Subsequent increases to a partner's basis in a partnership result from further contributions, the sum of the partner's distributive shares of partnership income, and increases in partnership liabilities that increase each partner's share of the liabilities.

Subsequent decreases in basis result from the amount of money and the adjusted basis of prop-

erty distributed, the sum of distributive shares of partnership losses, and nondeductible, noncapital expenditures. The adjusted basis for an interest in a partnership can never be less than zero.

In view of the above, Macro's liability increases Smith's partnership basis by $16,000 (i.e., 40% × $40,000).

Answer choice "B" is incorrect because it assumes that Smith's partnership basis is increased by 50% of the $40,000 mortgage, or $20,000; in fact, Smith's basis should only by increased by 40% of the $40,000 mortgage, or $16,000.

Answer choice "C" is incorrect because it assumes that Smith's partnership basis is increased by 60% of the $40,000 mortgage, or $24,000; this actually represents the increase in White's partnership basis.

Answer choice "D" is incorrect because the basis of a partner's interest is affected by partnership liabilities.

#31 (answer "B")

The basis of property distributed as a current nonliquidating distribution is equal to the lower of (1) the adjusted basis of the property in the hands of the partnership immediately prior to the distribution, or (2) the adjusted basis of the partner's partnership interest immediately prior to the distribution, reduced by any money distributed simultaneously.

Hart's basis in the distributed property is $4,000, which is the lower of (1) $7,000, the adjusted basis of the property to the partnership, or (2) $4,000, the adjusted basis of Hart's partnership interest (i.e, $9,000) reduced by the cash (i.e., $5,000) distributed in the same transaction.

Answer choices other than "B" are based on assumptions that are not valid under current tax law.

#32 (answer "D")

When property is distributed as a current nonliquidating distribution (as in the question situation), no gain is recognized by the partner until she sells or otherwise disposes of the property.

The receipt of unrealized receivables and inventory items will result in ordinary income when sold, except when inventory items representing a capital asset are held by the partner in excess of five years. In that instance, any gain or loss will be treated as a capital asset transaction.

Accordingly, Stone's recognized gain or loss on the distribution is $0.

Answer choices other than "D" are clearly based on incorrect assumptions.

#33 (answer "B")

For tax purposes, a partnership terminates (1) when no part of the business continues to be carried on by any of its partners in the form of a partnership, or (2) if within a period of 12 months there is a sale or exchange of 50% or more of the total interest in the partnership capital and profits.

In a two-person partnership, termination of the partnership occurs on the date that the final liquidating payment is made to the retiring partner or to the deceased partner's successor in interest.

It should be noted that the taxable year of the partnership will close if there has been a termination of the partnership.

In the circumstances presented, within a 12-month period, Poe sold her 30% interest in Able and Dean sold his 25% interest in Able; accordingly, there was a sale of 55% of the total interest in the partnership capital and profits. As a result, Able terminated as of December 20, 1994, the day on which Dean sold his interest.

Answer choice "A" is incorrect because only 30% of the total interest in the partnership capital and profits was sold on February 4, 1994; termination will not result until more than 50% of the partnership interest is sold.

Answer choices "C" and "D" are clearly based on assumptions that are not valid under current tax law.

#34 (answer "C")

For tax purposes, a partnership terminates (1) when no part of the business continues to be carried on by any of its partners in the form of a partnership, or (2) if within a period of 12 months there is a sale or exchange of 50% or more of the total interest in the partnership capital and profits.

If a sale of a partnership interest results in a partnership termination and the partnership's business and financial operations are continued by the other members, there is a deemed distribution of assets to the remaining partners and the purchaser, and a hypothetical recontribution of assets to a new partnership.

It should be noted that where there is a division of a partnership into multiple partnerships, the resulting partnerships are considered a continuation of the prior partnership if the members of any new partnership had more than a 50% interest in the capital and profits of the prior partnership.

Answer choices other than "C" are based on incorrect assumptions and/or combinations.

#35 (answer "C")

The distribution deduction that may be claimed on an estate's fiduciary income tax return is equal to the amount of income required to be distributed currently plus any amount of income or principal actually paid, credited, or otherwise required to be distributed for that year. Generally, in no event may the distribution deduction be greater than distributable net income (DNI). In essence, DNI (1) fixes the limit on the amount of the deduction for an estate's distributions to its beneficiaries, and (2) establishes the amounts and character of the income items reportable by the beneficiaries.

In general, DNI is equal to taxable income of the estate with certain modifications. Some of the more common modifications are as follows:

1. No distribution deduction is permitted.
2. Tax-exempt interest is included, net of any related expenses.
3. Capital gains allocable to corpus (i.e., principal) are not included; similarly excluded are capital gains that are not paid, credited, or required to be currently distributed to any beneficiary or charity.
4. Capital losses are not included except to the extent of capital gains that are paid, credited, or required to be distributed.

Here, DNI is equal to the amount of income currently required to be distributed by the will, or $15,000. However, the distribution deduction and the amount of the distribution that was taxable to the beneficiary is limited to $6,000 (i.e., the taxable interest ($40,000) less the expenses attributable to taxable interest ($34,000)).

Answer choice "A" is incorrect because it fails to reflect the deduction for the expenses attributable to taxable interest.

Answer choice "B" is incorrect because it represents the amount of income currently required to be distributed, and not the amount of income taxed to the beneficiary.

Answer choice "D" is incorrect because there is taxable income.

#36 (answer "C")

To be taxable, gifts have to exceed an annual exclusion of $10,000 ($20,000 in the case of joint gifts) per recipient.

All gifts between spouses are tax-free with no limitation.

Gifts are also unlimited if they are made for educational or medical purposes. The payment, however, must be made directly to the educational institution or the provider of the medical services.

In view of the above, the amount of the 1994 gift taxable to the Briars is $10,000 (i.e., the $30,000 gift reduced by a $20,000 joint gift tax exclusion).

Answer choice "A" is incorrect because it does not reflect any gift tax exclusion.

Answer choice "B" is incorrect because it reflects a $10,000 gift tax exclusion, rather than the $20,000 joint gift tax exclusion elected by the Briars.

Answer choice "D" is incorrect because it reflects a $30,000 gift tax exclusion, which does not exist under current tax law.

#37 (answer "A")

To be eligible as an exempt organization, and therefore not subject to income tax, the following conditions must be satisfied.

1. The entity must file a written application with the Internal Revenue Service, even when no official forms are provided, within 15 months after the end of the month in which the organization is formed.
2. Organization and operation of the entity must be exclusively for exempt purposes. (A "feeder organization," primarily conducting business for profit, but distributing

100% of its profits to tax-exempt organizations, cannot qualify for tax-exempt status.)
3. The operation of the entity must serve a public interest.
4. The organization may not be an "action organization," which is an organization that devotes a "substantial part" of its activities to propaganda or attempting to influence legislation. (An organization that participates in any political campaign is considered an "action organization.")
5. The entity's articles of organization must (a) state that the purpose of organization is limited to one or more exempt purposes, (b) specify the exempt purposes(s), and (c) state that all of the organization's assets will be utilized for the exempt purpose(s).
6. The organization may not participate in any prohibited transactions.
   Note: The IRS has the right to retroactively revoke the tax-exempt status of an organization.

In view of point #2 above, the organizational test to qualify a public service charitable entity as tax exempt requires the articles of organization to limit the purpose of the entity to the charitable (i.e., exempt) purpose.

The organizational test does not require that an information return be filed annually with the Internal Revenue Service. It should be noted, however, that in general, an annual information return must be filed by all exempt organizations. Two of the more common exceptions to the general rule are (1) churches and their internally supported auxiliaries, and (2) an entity, other than a private foundation, whose annual gross receipts do not exceed $25,000.

Answer choices other than "A" are based on incorrect assumptions and/or combinations.

#38 (answer "D")

Exempt organizations are liable for income tax on unrelated business income in excess of a $1,000 exemption and allowable deductions for ordinary and necessary expenses.

If the entity is a trust, the regular trust income tax rates will prevail. If an exempt organization is a corporation, the tax on unrelated business taxable income is computed at rates applicable to corporations.

Unrelated business income is any income derived from a trade or business regularly carried on by the exempt organization that is not substantially related to the purpose giving rise to the exempt status. Specifically excluded from the category of an unrelated trade or business are (1) any activities where substantially all work is performed for the organization without compensation (i.e., by volunteers), (2) any activities carried on for the convenience of its members, students, patients or employees, (3) any activities involving the selling of merchandise, substantially all of which have been received by the organization as gifts or contributions, and (4) any activity involving games of chance (e.g., bingo) if such games are (a) conducted in accordance with local laws, and (b) confined to nonprofit organizations (i.e., do not compete with profit-motivated business).

In view of the above, selling articles made by handicapped persons as part of their rehabilitation, when the organization is involved exclusively in their rehabilitation, will not result in unrelated business income. Similarly, operating a grocery store almost fully staffed by emotionally handicapped persons as part of a therapeutic program will not result in unrelated business income. Both situations represent activities related to the specific purpose of the related exempt organization.

Answer choices other than "D" are based on incorrect assumptions and/or combinations.

#39 (answer "C")

Total costs include both fixed costs and variable costs.

The following should be considered.

1. Within the relevant range, total fixed costs do not change in response to changes in volume; however, they will change on a per-unit basis.
2. Total variable costs change proportionately in response to changes in volume; however, they remain constant on a per-unit basis.

Based on the chart provided, the point where the total cost line intersects the Y-axis represents the cost incurred if no parcels are shipped; this is the fixed cost of $15,000.

Thus, the estimated cost for mailing 12,000 parcels is $51,000:

Total cost for mailing 20,000 parcels	$75,000
Less fixed cost	15,000
Variable cost of 20,000 parcels	$60,000
Variable cost per unit; $60,000/20,000	$3
Variable costs; 12,000 × $3	$36,000
Fixed costs	15,000
Total estimated cost for mailing 12,000 parcels	$51,000

Answer choice "A" is incorrect because it represents variable costs only (i.e., 12,000 parcels × $3 equals $36,000), and not total costs.

Answer choice "B" is incorrect because it represents 60% of total costs (i.e., [12,000/20,000] × $75,000 equals $45,000). As such, it treats all costs as variable and should not.

Answer choice "D" is incorrect because it represents the total variable costs for 20,000 parcels (i.e., 20,000 × $3 equals $60,000), and does not represent total costs for 12,000 parcels.

#40 (answer "C")

The number of units to be purchased must take into consideration the budgeted sales and the changes in the budgeted inventories (raw materials and finished goods).

The total budgeted kilo purchases for October 1995 is 186,000:

Budgeted unit sales	53,000
Add: Increase in finished goods inventory	6,000
Finished goods required for production	59,000
Required inventory for production; 59,000 × 4 kilos per unit	236,000
Less: Decrease in budgeted inventory of kilos	50,000
Total budgeted kilo purchases, October 1995	186,000

Answer choice "A" is incorrect because the increase in finished goods is subtracted, and should be added. As such, the total of (53,000 − 6,000) × 4 equals 188,000, which, when reduced by the budgeted decrease of 50,000 kilos, results in 138,000.

Answer choice "B" is incorrect because the purchase of kilos necessary for the increase in finished goods is not included, and should be (i.e., [53,000 × 4] − 50,000 equals 162,000).

Answer choice "D" is based on illogical application of the facts presented.

#41 (answer "C")

The master budget is prepared for a specific period and is static, rather than flexible. It is static in that it is based on a single, most probable level of output demand. Actual results are later compared with budgeted amounts.

Generally, master (static) budgeting is appropriate only if a company's operating volume can be estimated within close limits, and if the costs and expenses behave predictably.

Flexible budgets, as contrasted with fixed, static, or master budgets, require the separation of fixed and variable costs. Once this is accomplished under flexible budgeting, it becomes possible to compare actual and budgeted results at virtually any level of activity. This, of course, is bounded by the relevant range. The usefulness of a flexible budget is founded on adequate knowledge of both fixed and variable cost behavior patterns.

"Relevant range" refers to the level of production assumed in constructing a breakeven model. Within the assumed range of production activity, certain sales and expense relationships are considered to remain valid. Outside of the assumed range, the relationships are not valid and the particular model is irrelevant.

(While flexible budgets are generally associated with the control of overhead factors, they may also be used to control direct material and direct labor, as well as nonmanufacturing costs.)

In summary, the basic difference between a master budget and a flexible budget is that a master budget is based on one specific level of production and a flexible budget can be prepared for any production level within a relevant range.

Answer choice "A" is incorrect because both master and flexible budgets can be used before, during, and after the budget period.

Answer choice "B" is incorrect because flexible budgets can be applicable to single departments, several departments, or the entire production facility. In addition, flexible budgets can be used for nonmanufacturing activities as well.

Answer choice "D" is incorrect because a flexible budget allows for comparisons of actual and budgeted amounts at virtually any level of activity, which should not be inferred to mean that management has latitude in meeting its goals.

#42 (answer "D")

The net present value method of capital budgeting holds that at a desired rate of return, the discounted cash flow generated is equal to the original investment. Any excess of the discounted cash flow (i.e., after-tax present value) over the original investment is positive net present value, which indicates a rate of return higher than the desired rate; any excess of the original investment over the discounted cash flow indicates negative net present value and a lesser return. (The desired rate of return is built into the tables that are used.)

Discounted cash flow is determined by applying the desired rate of return to cash inflow for each period. When the inflows are uniform for each period, an annuity table is issued. When the cash inflows are not uniform, they must be discounted separately by using the present value of $1.

Where no tax rate is given, the cash effect of depreciation (i.e., amortization) is implied (and may be ignored in the computations) by language that reads "cash flow from operations, net of taxes," and so on.

By the same token, if the given cash inflow is before taxes and a tax rate is given, the cash inflow must be reduced by taxes.

Here, the cash inflow had to be reduced by taxes. The after-tax present value is $11,310:

Annual cash savings before taxes		$7,500
Less annual taxes:		
Increase in cash inflow	$7,500	
Less lease amortization for tax purposes	5,000	
Taxable income	$2,500	
Less taxes at 40%;		
$2,500 × 40%		1,000
Net (after-tax) cash inflow		$6,500
After-tax present value discounted at 10%;		
$1.74 × $6,500		$11,310

Note that the answer required only the calculation of the present value of the net cash inflow; in order to have calculated the net present value, the cash inflow would have been compared to the original investment (which was not provided).

Answer choice "A" is incorrect because it uses the increase in annual taxable income, rather than the increase in annual after-tax cash flows (i.e., [$7,500 − $5,000] .60 × $1.74) equals $2,610.

Answer choice "B" is incorrect because it ignores the effect of income taxes (i.e., [$7,500 − $5,000] × $1.74 equals $4,350), and should not.

Answer choice "C" is incorrect because it is based on an income tax of $2,000, which is presumably related to amortization (i.e., $5,000 × 40% equals $2,000), rather than taxable income. Thus, an incorrect answer results (i.e., [$7,500 − $2,000] × $1.74 equals $9,570).

#43 (answer "B")

In general, the breakeven point is the point at which there is neither profit nor loss. It represents the amount of fixed cost and expense that must be covered by contribution margin. Contribution margin equals sales minus variable costs.

By definition, the margin of safety is the excess of budgeted sales over breakeven sales.

Generally, the computations to determine the breakeven point are as follows:

1. Units to breakeven—Fixed costs and expenses are divided by the contribution margin (or "marginal income") per unit, which is the selling price per unit less the variable cost per unit.
2. Dollars to breakeven—Fixed costs and expenses are divided by the contribution margin percentage, which is contribution margin divided by sales.

Based on interpolation of the facts provided, Cott's fixed cost can be arrived at by multiplying the breakeven sales of $120,000 (i.e., budgeted sales of $200,000 less the margin of safety of $80,000) by the contribution margin of 20%. Thus, fixed cost is $24,000 (i.e., $120,000 × 20%).

Answer choice "A" is incorrect because it represents the margin of safety multiplied by contribution margin (i.e., $80,000 × 20% equals $16,000), which does not represent fixed cost.

Answer choice "C" is incorrect because it represents the margin of safety, which is not the fixed cost.

Answer choice "D" is incorrect because it represents the sum of the answers to choices "A" and "C" (i.e., $16,000 + $80,000 equals $96,000); these costs do not represent fixed cost.

#44 (answer "B")

A key assumption in breakeven analysis is that, within the relevant range, total costs and total revenues change at a linear rate.

With regard to costs, the assumption is that unit variable costs are unchanged; i.e., input costs are constant and production efficiency does not change.

With regard to revenues, the assumption is that unit selling prices remain unchanged.

Other significant assumptions in breakeven analysis are

1. All costs are either fixed or variable.
2. No distinction is made between product costs and period costs.
3. Fixed costs do not change within the relevant range.
4. There is only one product or mix of products.
5. All production is sold and there are no inventories.
6. The time value of money is irrelevant.

Clearly, breakeven analysis assumes that over the relevant range unit variable costs are unchanged.

Answer choice "A" is incorrect because unit revenues are linear within the relevant range; they will remain unchanged.

Answer choice "C" is incorrect because total costs change with an increase or decrease in production.

Answer choice "D" is incorrect because total fixed costs are linear within the relevant range; they will remain unchanged.

#45 (answer "A")

Direct costs are those costs directly involved with a manufacturing process; direct materials and direct labor would be examples of direct costs.

Indirect manufacturing costs are includible as part of factory overhead; these items are not directly or easily identified within the manufacturing process. Examples include indirect materials (i.e., glue, nails) and indirect labor (i.e., foreman, supervisors).

A value-adding activity increases the worth (i.e., value) of a product, while a nonvalue-adding activity increases the time spent on a product or service, but does not increase its worth (e.g., warehousing).

As such, payments to employees who develop computer programs are considered both direct costs and value-adding costs.

Answer choices other than "A" are based on incorrect assumptions and/or combinations.

#46 (answer "C")

Equivalent units of production in process cost accounting may be computed under either the first-in, first-out method, or the weighted-average method (as in this question).

To calculate the cost per equivalent unit, using the weighted-average method, divide the sum of the beginning inventory and current costs by the equivalent production for the period.

Under the weighted-average method, there are two components of equivalent production: units completed (transferred), and units in the ending inventory of work-in-process, multiplied by the percentage of completion (i.e., 80%) for each cost element (i.e., materials, labor, and overhead).

Generally, normal spoilage costs are charged to all production, whether completed or not. However, the facts specify that "the costs of spoiled units are assigned to units completed and transferred to the second department in the period spoilage is identified." As such, completed units would consist of both the normal spoilage of 500 units and the 7,000 units completed and transferred, or 7,500 units.

Accordingly, the conversion cost transferred to the second production department was $67,500:

Sum of beginning inventory and current costs; $10,000 + $75,500		$85,500
Equivalent production:		
Units completed; 500 spoiled units plus 7,000 units completed & transferred	7,500	
Ending work-in-process; 2,500 units × 80%	2,000	9,500

Cost per equivalent unit; $85,500/9,500 — $9

Conversion cost transferred to the second production department; 7,500 units × $9 — $67,500

Answer choices other than "C" are not logical based on the facts presented.

#47 (answer "B")

There are two variances to be computed for materials: the material price variance and the material quantity variance.

A material price variance represents the actual units purchased multiplied by the difference between the actual and standard unit prices.

A material quantity variance is the standard unit price multiplied by the difference between the actual and standard quantity allowed.

Actual units purchased	4,200
Difference in actual and standard price per unit; $2.50 − ($10,080/4,200)	.10
Material price variance (favorable)	$420

Clearly, since the actual price was less than the standard price, the variance is favorable.

Answer choice "A" is incorrect because it erroneously multiplies the $.10 savings by the standard quantity allowed of 4,000 units (i.e., 1,000 × 4 × $.10 equals $400 favorable).

Answer choice "C" is incorrect because it represents the total (net) variance (i.e., $10,080 − [1,000 × 4 × $2.50] equals $80 unfavorable), and not the material price variance.

Answer choice "D" is incorrect because it represents the multiplication of the actual rate of $2.40 (i.e, $10,080/4,200) by the difference between the actual quantity purchased of 4,200 units, and the standard quantity allowed of 4,000 units (i.e., 1,000 × 4). This results in the incorrect amount of $2.40 × 200, or $480 unfavorable.

#48 (answer "C")

Joint costs are those that arise from a common process yielding two or more goods or services having differing and significant economic unit values.

Under the relative sales value at split-off method, the established sales value at split-off is used as the basis for allocation of the joint costs. In establishing relative sales value at split-off, it is usually necessary to ascertain sales value at completion and to deduct therefrom any after-split-off costs to arrive at the net sales value at split-off.

(An underlying assumption is that the incremental revenue from further processing is equal to the incremental costs of further processing and selling.)

Answer choices other than "C" are incorrect conclusions. As indicated, the sales price at point of sale, reduced by cost to complete after split-off, is assumed to equal the net sales value at split-off.

#49 (answer "C")

The commonly used procedures for allocating support department costs to benefiting departments (i.e., schools) are the direct method, the step method, and the algebraic method.

The step method transfers service departments' costs in steps; that is, in a prescribed order by departments, primarily on the basis of producing, and other supporting departments' use of the respective services. Generally, the expenses of the support department with the largest total expense may be distributed first, followed by the department with the next highest expense, and so on. Once a service department's costs have been distributed, it is closed, and no further distributions are made to that department.

The support department costs allocated to the School of Education are $46,100:

		Schools		Support depts.	
	Total	Educa-tion	Tech-nology	Main-tenance	Power
Support departments' cost before distribution	$153,000	—	—	$99,000	$54,000
Distribution of Maintenance Dept.		$29,700	$49,500	(99,000)*	19,800
Power Dept.	—	16,400	57,400	-0-	($73,800)**
Total distribution of Support Dept. costs	$153,000	$46,100	$106,900		

*20/100 to Power; 30/100 to Education; 50/100 to Technology

**20/90 to Education; 70/90 to Technology

Answer choice "A" is incorrect because it uses the direct method rather than the step method (i.e., [$99,000 × 30%] + [$54,000 × 20%]) equals $40,500.

Answer choices "B" and "D" are not logical based on the information provided in the answer to "C."

#50 (answer "D")

The following relationships should be understood in order to arrive at an answer to this question.

1. Capital turnover is equal to net sales divided by average total assets.
2. Residual income is the excess of operating income (i.e., sales less the sum of variable costs and fixed costs) over the desired return (i.e., the imputed interest rate multiplied by average total assets).

Based on interpolation of the facts provided, the average total assets can be arrived at by dividing sales by the capital turnover; $400,000/4, or $100,000.

Operating income (given)	$40,000
Less: Desired return; $100,000 × 10%	10,000
Residual income, 1994	$30,000

Answer choice "A" is incorrect because it represents operating income less sales, multiplied by the imputed interest rate (i.e., $40,000 − [400,000 × 10%] equals $0); this is not residual income.

Answer choice "B" is incorrect because it represents operating income multiplied by the imputed interest rate (i.e., $40,000 × 10% equals $4,000); the desired return (i.e., average total assets multiplied by the imputed interest rate) should be subtracted from the operating income to arrive at residual income.

Answer choice "C" is incorrect because it represents the desired return (i.e., $100,000 × 10% equals $10,000); in turn, this should be subtracted from the operating income, and it is not.

#51 (answer "A")

The basic principle of a "just-in-time" production system is to receive raw materials as needed, rather than building up inventories. Fewer goods on hand requires less warehouse space and storage equipment, resulting in cost savings. It operates under the premise of "zero defects" in parts supplied by other companies, as well as products manufactured internally.

Variances should be negligible, but their occurrence should be recognized earlier in the process so that causes may be found and corrective action taken quickly. Because fewer raw materials would be stocked and work-in-process time should be short, traditional categories of direct labor and overhead may be combined and accounted for under the single category of conversion cost. Thus, a greater number of costs will be directly traceable to production under a JIT system.

Back-flush costing is a streamlined cost accounting system that speeds up, simplifies, and minimizes accounting effort in an environment that minimizes inventory balances, requires few allocations, uses standards costs, and has minimal variances from standard. During the period, this costing method records purchases of raw materials and accumulates actual conversion costs. Then, either at completion of production or upon sale of goods, an entry is made to allocate the total costs incurred to cost of goods sold and to finished goods inventory, using standard production costs. As such, back-flush accounting techniques basically eliminate the need for journal entries to trace production costs through the process.

Based on the facts in the preceding paragraphs, a just-in-time operation with a back-flush costing system would <u>decrease</u> <u>both</u> <u>inspections</u> <u>costs</u> <u>and</u> <u>detail</u> <u>of</u> <u>costs</u> <u>tracked</u> <u>to</u> <u>jobs</u>.

Answer choices other than "A" are based on incorrect assumptions and/or combinations.

#52 (answer "A")

The economic order quantity formula addresses the question of how much to order. It is equal to the square root of:

$$\frac{2 \times \text{Cost to place one order} \times \text{Demand per period}}{\text{Cost to hold one unit for one period}}$$

Clearly, the <u>periodic</u> <u>demand</u> <u>for</u> <u>the</u> <u>good</u> <u>is</u> <u>known</u> (i.e., it is included in the formula).

Answer choice "B" is incorrect because carrying costs per unit are assumed to remain constant and do not vary with quantity ordered.

Answer choice "C" is incorrect because costs of placing an order are assumed to be fixed and do not vary with the quantity ordered.

Answer choice "D" is incorrect because the purchase costs per unit are not used in the EOQ formula.

#53 (answer "B")

In probability theory, for a range of variables and occurrences, the "estimated probabilities" yield the "expected values" as weighted averages.

The following definitions are relevant.

1. Estimated <u>probabilities</u>—An estimated probability is the chance of an event happening. Further, the probably of an event is defined as the number of times an event will occur out of the total number of trials. Therefore, it would follow that the sum of several probabilities must equal one, or 100%.
2. <u>Random</u> <u>variables</u>—Those amounts of cost, revenue, and so on, in the estimated range that are multiplied by the estimated probability to arrive at an expected value (i.e., weighted amount).
3. <u>Expected</u> <u>value</u>—The random variable is multiplied by its probability of occurrence to become an "expected value," which in essence is a weighted average as to what may be expected from future events.

It should be noted that if an unprotected crop subject to frost has an expected market value of $40,000, and a protected crop subject to frost has an expected market value of $90,000, there is an increase of $50,000 if the crop subject to frost is protected.

However, the increase in expected market value would cost $10,000. Therefore, for Cal to be indifferent to spending $10,000 for frost protection, <u>the</u> <u>probability</u> <u>of</u> <u>a</u> <u>frost</u> <u>is</u> <u>.200</u> (i.e., $10,000/50,000).

Parenthetically, it may also be viewed that if the probability of a frost is .200, or 20%, then the probability of no frost is 80%; thus, the sum of the probabilities is 100%.

Answer choices other than "B" are not logical based on the facts provided.

#54 (answer "C")

The following should be considered:

Number of outages per month		Number of months		Total expected outages
0	×	3	=	0
1	×	2	=	2
2	×	4	=	8
3	×	3	=	9
		12		19

The estimated savings for 1995 would be $1,600.

Costs if no auxiliary generator is used;
$400 × 19 outages	$7,600
Less cost if auxiliary generator is leased;	
$500 × 12 months	6,000
Estimated savings, 1995	$1,600

Answer choice "A" is incorrect because it only considers the months in which outages occurred, and only the cost per outage. In addition, the savings that would result from leasing the generator were not considered. As such, there were additional expenditures of $3,600 (i.e., [2 + 4 + 3] × $400).

Answer choice "B" is incorrect because it only considers 12 (i.e., the number of months) rather than 19 power outages, which results in additional expenditures of $1,200 (i.e., [$500 × 12] − [$400 × 12].

Answer choice "D" is incorrect because it is based on 19 lease rentals (i.e., the number of outages) rather than the number of months (i.e. [$500 × 19] − [$400 × 19] equals a savings of $1,900).

#55 (answer "A")

Obviously, selling price would be expressed as 100%. Thus, if gross profit margin (i.e., selling price less variable cost) is to be 15%, then cost is 85%.

As such, the target price per unit equals ($990,000/500)/85%, or $2,329.

(Observe that the gross margin of 15% would be $349, and cost would be $1,980.)

Answer choice "B" is incorrect because a selling price of $2,277 less cost of $1,980 (i.e., $990,000/500) yields gross margin of $297, which

is 13% of sales (i.e., $297/$2,277), and not 15%.

Answer choice "C" is incorrect because a selling price of $1,980 less cost of $1,980 (i.e., $990,000/500) yields gross margin of $0, which is 0% of sales, and not 15%.

Answer choice "D" is incorrect because a selling price of $1,935 less cost of $1,980 (i.e., $990,000/500) yields a gross loss of $45, which is a negative 2.3% of sales (i.e., $45/$1,935), and not 15%.

#56 (answer "D")

This question requires an understanding of the difference between direct (variable) costing and absorption (conventional) costing; the essential difference lies in the treatment of fixed manufacturing overhead. The following should be noted.

1. Absorption costing
   a. Fixed manufacturing overhead costs are treated as product costs and are charged against income when sold; they are included in inventory.
   b. The cost of goods sold, inclusive of fixed manufacturing overhead costs, is subtracted from sales to arrive at gross margin (profit). Selling and general expenses, whether variable or fixed, are treated as period costs and are subtracted from gross margin to arrive at operating income.
   c. Because fixed manufacturing overhead costs are included in inventory, absorption costing is appropriate for external reporting.
2. Direct costing
   a. Fixed manufacturing overhead costs are treated as period costs and charged against income in the period incurred; they are not included in inventory.
   b. The variable cost of sales, as well as variable selling and general expenses, is subtracted from sales to arrive at "contribution margin." Fixed manufacturing overhead, along with fixed selling and general expenses, is subtracted from contribution margin to arrive at operating income.
   c. Since fixed manufacturing costs are not included in inventory, variable costing is appropriate for internal reporting, but not external reporting.

The following net income relationships should be noted:

1. Beginning <u>inventory equals ending inventory</u> (<u>production equals sales</u>)—Net income would be the same under either method because no increased fixed costs would be included in ending inventory. Under either method, all current fixed costs will have been charged against sales of the period.

2. Beginning <u>inventory exceeds ending inventory</u> (<u>sales exceed production</u>)—Net income would be higher under direct costing. This is so because under absorption costing, some previously deferred (i.e., inventoried) fixed costs would be included in the cost of goods sold along with current fixed costs; under direct costing, only the current fixed costs will be charged against sales.

3. Beginning <u>inventory is less than ending inventory</u> (<u>production exceeds sales</u>)—Net income would be higher under absorption costing. This is so because under absorption costing, some of the current fixed costs will be inventoried (i.e., deferred). Under direct costing, all current fixed costs will be charged against sales.

Furthermore, the current ratio is calculated by dividing current assets by current liabilities; whereas, the return on stockholders' equity is arrived at by dividing net income by the average stockholders' equity.

Based on the facts provided, in light of the fact that inventory levels remained the same for 1994, current year net income would be the same using absorption or variable costing. However, inventory would be higher using absorption costing because of the inclusion of fixed manufacturing overhead. Likewise, beginning stockholders' equity (i.e., retained earnings) would be higher with absorption costing because fixed overhead was included in inventory and not expensed in the period before 1994.

As a result, absorption costing as compared to variable costing would create a <u>greater current ratio</u>, because current assets (inclusive of inventory) would be greater under absorption costing, and a <u>smaller return on stockholders' equity</u>, because even though 1994 income was the same under both methods, stockholders' equity was higher under absorption costing.

Answer choices other than "D" are based on incorrect assumptions and/or combinations.

#57 (answer "C")

Background information with respect to the various funds and account groups in governmental accounting follows:

1. Fund—A fund is defined as a fiscal and accounting entity with a self-balancing set of accounts including cash and other financial resources, together with all related liabilities and residual equities or balances, and changes therein, which are segregated for the purpose of carrying on specific activities or attaining certain objectives in accordance with special regulations, restrictions, or limitations.

    There can be as many as seven different types of funds, and two account groups. Each fund has its own self-contained double-entry set of accounts. Some governmental units often need several funds of a single type, such as special revenue or capital projects funds. However, many governmental units do not need funds of all types at any given time. For example, many small governmental units do not require internal service funds.

2. Governmental <u>funds</u>
    a. General <u>fund</u>—used to account for all financial resources, except those required to be accounted for in another fund.
    b. Special <u>revenue fund</u>—similar to a general fund, except that it is used to account for the proceeds of specific revenue sources (other than expendable trusts or for major capital projects) that are legally restricted to expenditures for specified purposes. Examples of special revenue funds are those established for the purpose of financing schools, parks, or libraries.
    c. Capital <u>projects fund</u>—used to account for financial resources to be expended for the acquisition or construction of major capital facilities (other than those financed by proprietary funds and trust funds).
    d. Debt <u>service fund</u>—used to account for the accumulation of resources for, and the payment of, general long-term debt principal and interest.

3. <u>Proprietary</u> <u>funds</u>—Proprietary funds closely parallel for-profit accounting, inclusive of recognizing depreciation expense in the determination of net income.

There are two types of proprietary funds:

a. <u>Enterprise</u> <u>fund</u>—used to account for operations that are financed and conducted in a manner similar to private business enterprises, such as utilities.

Enterprise funds primarily deal with the general public, and may also service other funds within the governmental unit.

b. <u>Internal</u> <u>service</u> <u>fund</u> (also called "intragovernmental service fund" or "working capital fund")—used to account for goods or services performed by one department for another on a cost-reimbursement basis.

These funds usually do not deal with the general public.

4. <u>Fiduciary</u> <u>funds</u>

<u>Trust</u> <u>and</u> <u>agency</u> <u>fund</u>—used to account for assets held by a governmental unit as trustee or agent. These include expendable and nonexpendable trust funds, pension, and agency funds.

a. The distinction between "trust" and "agency" is that agency transactions wash out, while a trust implies custody over assets in a more permanent sense.

b. In general, a "nonexpendable" trust fund requires that principal be maintained while income may be available to support a specific activity. In the case of an "expendable" trust, principal need not be maintained.

Nonexpendable trust funds are accounted for in a manner similar to proprietary funds, while expendable trust funds are accounted for in a manner similar to a governmental fund.

c. A trust fund may be referred to as an "endowment" fund.

5. <u>Account</u> <u>groups</u>—These are self-balancing sets of accounts and not "funds" in the strict sense. The two types of account groups are:

a. <u>General</u> <u>fixed</u> <u>assets</u> <u>account</u> <u>group</u>—used to account for all fixed assets other than those specifically associated with and carried in a proprietary fund or certain trust funds. (This account group has no assets other than fixed assets.)

Depreciation is recognized for proprietary and/or nonexpendable trust funds, which have depreciable fixed assets, but not usually for general fixed assets. While there is no requirement to record depreciation on general fixed assets, it may be recorded as an optional procedure. Where this option is exercised, depreciation is recorded as a debit to the "investment in fixed assets" account, but not as an expenditure.

b. <u>General</u> <u>long-term</u> <u>debt</u> <u>account</u> <u>group</u>—used to account for the principal on all unmatured long-term debt (inclusive of lease-purchase agreements, etc.) except debt payable from a proprietary fund or trust fund.

All other unmatured general long-term liabilities of the governmental unit, which include special assessment debts for which the government is obligated in some manner, should be accounted for through this account group.

The long-term debt account group has only two assets. One is the "amount available in debt service funds," and the second is termed "amount to be provided for retirement of general long-term debt."

As assets available in debt service funds increase, the "amount to be provided" decreases, since fewer resources must be raised in the future.

Based on the background provided above, it should be clear that income determination is a measurement focus for proprietary funds and nonexpendable trust funds, but <u>not</u> <u>for</u> either <u>general</u> <u>funds</u> or <u>expendable</u> <u>trust</u> <u>funds</u>.

Answer choices other than "C" are based on incorrect assumptions and/or illogical combinations.

#58 (answer "B")

When a donation of property other than cash is made to a governmental unit, a new accounting basis begins, and the donation should be recorded <u>at</u> its <u>estimated</u> <u>fair</u> <u>value</u> <u>when</u> <u>received</u>.

Answer choices "A" and "C" are incorrect because neither represents the appropriate amount at which the assets should be recorded (i.e., their estimated fair values).

Answer choice "D" is incorrect because the assets should be recorded at their estimated fair values, and not as a memorandum entry only.

#59 (answer "A")

A summary of financial reporting objectives for governmental entities follows:

1. Accountability
   a. Should provide information to determine whether current-year revenues were sufficient to pay for current-year services.
   b. Should demonstrate whether resources were obtained and used in accordance with the entity's legally adopted budget. Should also demonstrate compliance with other finance-related legal or contractual requirements.
   c. Should provide information to assist users in assessing the service efforts, costs, and accomplishments of the governmental entity.
2. Evaluating the operating results
   a. Should provide information about sources and uses of financial resources.
   b. Should provide information about how the governmental entity financed its activities and met its cash requirements.
   c. Should provide information necessary to determine whether the entity's financial position improved or deteriorated as a result of the year's operations.
3. Assessing the level of governmental services and the entity's ability to meet its obligations as they become due
   a. Should provide information about the financial position and condition of a governmental entity.
   b. Should provide information about a governmental entity's physical and other nonfinancial resources having useful lives that extend beyond the current year.
   c. Should disclose legal or contractual restrictions on resources and risks of potential loss of resources.

As a component of accountability, "interperiod equity" is a concept that implies that a govern-

ment should operate within its budget, and not shift the burden of paying for current-year services to future taxpayers (i.e., a balanced budget is adopted).

Answer choice "B" is incorrect because the relationship of residual equity transfers in or out does not relate to interperiod equity. It should be noted that residual equity transfers relate to the establishment of and/or closing out of funds; they do not relate to operations of a period.

Answer choices "C" and "D" are based on incorrect assumptions and/or combinations.

#60 (answer "C")

In general, the nature of fund accounting lies in its nonprofit orientation. There is no profit motive; what is measured is accountability, rather than profitability. The main objective is stewardship of financial resources received and expended in compliance with legal requirements (i.e., flow of financial resources).

A fund is defined as a fiscal and accounting entity with a self-balancing set of accounts, including cash and other financial resources, together with all related liabilities and residual equities or balances, and changes therein, which are segregated for the purpose of carrying on specific activities or attaining certain objectives in accordance with special regulations, restrictions, or limitations.

Answer choice "A" is incorrect because a fund may be composed of assets other than cash or cash equivalents.

Answer choice "B" is incorrect because there is no requirement that resources must be incorporated into combined or combining financial statements.

Answer choice "D" is incorrect because resources need not be segregated physically; indeed, physical segregation may be impossible. Rather, segregation is for the purpose of carrying on specific activities or attaining certain objectives.

#61 (answer "A")

In general, governmental units will use either the accrual basis or the modified accrual basis of accounting. Use of the cash basis is generally not appropriate. However, the circumstances in this question represent an exception.

Under the accrual basis, revenue is recognized when it is earned and becomes measurable, and expenses are recognized in the period incurred. The accrual basis is recommended for use by proprietary funds (enterprise and internal service funds) and certain types of trust funds (including nonexpendable trust funds and pension trust funds).

Under the modified accrual basis, revenues are recognized in the accounting period in which they become available and measurable. Expenditures are generally recognized in the period in which the liability is incurred. Modified accrual is usually the basis for governmental funds, and includes general funds, special revenue funds, capital projects funds, and debt service funds.

The financial statement indicated is for a governmental-type fund. Proprietary funds would report on "revenues, expenses, and changes in retained earnings."

When a governmental entity legally adopts a cash-basis budget, as is the case in this question, the combined statement of revenues, expenditures, and changes in fund balances—budget and actual—should present comparisons of the legally adopted budget with actual data on the budgetary basis (i.e., the cash basis).

When this occurs, the actual data in the combined statement showing "budget and actual" would be different from the GAAP presentation in the combined statement for all fund types. The difference between the budgetary basis and GAAP should be explained in notes to the financial statements.

Answer choice "B" is incorrect because the modified accrual basis, although used for the combined statement for all fund types, should not be used for the combined statement showing budget and actual. In the case where the cash basis is legally used for budget purposes, that basis should be used and the differences between the cash basis and GAAP (i.e., modified accrual) should be disclosed in notes to the financial statements.

Answer choice "C" is incorrect because the accrual basis is appropriate for proprietary funds (and certain trust funds), but not for governmental funds. The financial statement indicated in the question relates to a governmental fund.

Answer choice "D" is incorrect because use of a "modified cash" basis is not appropriate in a governmental financial statement.

#62 (answer "D")

The basic financial statements of governmental units are prepared in accordance with generally accepted accounting principles as applied to governmental units.

The financial statements presented are those of the primary government; in effect, this is the governmental unit that "controls" subordinate governmental units.

The financial reporting entity consists of (1) the primary government, (2) organizations for which the primary government is financially accountable, and (3) other organizations for which the nature and significance of their relationship with the primary government are such that exclusion would cause the reporting entity's financial statements to be misleading or incomplete.

Clearly, <u>the basic criterion is therefore financial accountability</u>.

Answer choices other than "D" are incorrect because none represents the basic criterion used to determine the reporting entity for a governmental unit.

#63 (answer "B")

A statement of cash flows should be issued by proprietary funds but not by capital projects funds (which are governmental funds).

The presentation of cash flows requires that cash receipts and payments be classified into four categories.

1. <u>Operating activities</u>—Generally include the cash effects of transactions that enter into the determination of operating income.
2. <u>Noncapital financing activities</u>—Generally include grants, subsidies, and interfund transactions.
3. <u>Capital and related financing activities</u>—Generally include the acquisition, construction, and improvement of capital assets, as well as the related financing transactions, inclusive of debt service (both principal and interest).
4. <u>Investing activities</u>—Generally include the purchases and sales of investments, and

cash flows resulting from investment income.

Cash inflow from issuing bonds to finance city hall construction would be an activity of a capital projects fund; a statement of cash flows is not issued by such funds.

However, a city utility is a proprietary fund (i.e., an enterprise fund). As such, payments by the utility in lieu of property taxes would represent a cash outflow related to operating activities; such event should be included in the statement of cash flows.

Answer choices other than "B" are based on incorrect assumptions and/or illogical combinations.

#64 (answer "A")

A special assessment generically refers to services or capital improvements provided by local governments that are intended primarily to benefit a particular property owner, or group of property owners, rather than the general citizenry.

In general, there are two types of special assessment funds: service-type and capital improvements.

Service-type special assessments are reported in the fund type that best reflects the nature of the transactions: in a general fund, a special revenue fund, or an enterprise fund.

Capital improvement special assessments are generally reported in the same funds as any other capital improvement (i.e., capital project).

The treatment of a special assessment bond issue, and the related debt service transactions, depends on whether or not the government is obligated in some manner.

If the government is obligated in some manner to assume payments on special assessment debt, all transactions related to special assessments should be reported in the same funds and on the same basis as any other issue. In this connection, the bonds would be recorded in the long-term debt account group, and debt service would be handled in the appropriate manner.

However, if the government is not obligated in any manner, special assessment debt should not be presented in the financial statements. Rather, the notes should disclose the amount of the debt

and the fact that the government is in no way liable for repayment but is only acting as agent for the property owners in servicing the debt. Accordingly, the debt service (i.e., the collection and servicing activities phase of the special assessment) should be accounted for in the agency fund.

Answer choice "B" is incorrect because the debt service fund should be used only if Sea County was obligated on the debt; it is not.

Answer choice "C" is incorrect because a special assessment is not accounted for by a trust fund, either expendable or nonexpendable.

Answer choice "D" is incorrect because while the construction phase would be accounted for in the capital projects fund, the debt service would not be.

#65 (answer "C")

The revenues control account of a governmental unit is a nominal account, which reflects actual revenues. The account is increased when actual revenues, such as property taxes, are recorded. It should be noted that the revenues are recorded net of uncollectible accounts.

Answer choice "A" is incorrect because the encumbrance account is decreased when the items for which funds had been encumbered are received; it is not affected by revenues.

Answer choice "B" is incorrect because there is no relationship between the recording of appropriations and the recording of actual revenues.

Answer choice "D" is incorrect because estimated revenues, not actual revenues (i.e., revenues control), are increased when the budget is recorded.

#66 (answer "D")

In governmental accounting, there are three broad types of funds and two "account groups." The three broad types are governmental funds, proprietary funds, and fiduciary funds. The two account groups, which are self-balancing sets of accounts and not funds in the strict sense, are the general fixed assets account group and the general long-term debt account group.

Governmental-type funds include general funds, special revenue funds, capital projects funds, and debt service funds. Proprietary funds include enterprise funds and internal service funds. Fiduciary funds include trust funds and agency funds.

Long-term debt, inclusive of bonds and/or liabilities under a lease-purchase agreement, is accounted for in the general long-term debt account group, except debt payable by a proprietary fund, or a trust fund; the latter two fund types account for their own debt.

The bonds indicated in the question are both associated with proprietary funds, which maintain accountability for their own bonds. Therefore, $0 of the bonds indicated should be accounted for in the general long-term debt account group.

Answer choices other than "D" are incorrect because they include bonds from one or more proprietary funds; none should be included.

#67 (answer "A")

Fixed assets other than those accounted for in the proprietary funds or trust funds are general fixed assets. General fixed assets are accounted for in the general fixed assets account group, rather than in the governmental funds.

Long-term debt, other than debt accounted for in proprietary funds or certain trust funds, is general long-term debt, which is accounted for in the general long-term debt account group, rather than in a governmental fund itself.

In addition to bonds payable, the general long-term debt account group may include accountability for certain other long-term obligations, including capital leases.

General fixed assets acquired under lease agreements, along with the related liability, should be accounted for under the same criteria generally associated with capital leases; usually this is the present value of minimum lease payments.

As such, both the asset amount and the liability amount would increase.

The following should be noted parenthetically:

1. In addition to the recording of the asset and liability in the general fixed assets and general long-term debt account groups, the acquisition is accounted for in the general fund as an expenditure and "other financing source."
2. In future periods, as lease payments are made, in the general fund there will be a

debit to "other financing uses" and a credit to cash. Obviously, in the general long-term debt account group, the "amount to be provided in future years, etc.," and the lease liability would both decrease.

Answer choices other than "A" are based on incorrect assumptions and/or combinations.

#68 (answer "C")

Standards of accounting and financial reporting for municipal solid waste landfill (MSWLF) closure and postclosure care costs apply regardless of the reporting model or fund type used to report MSWLF closure and postclosure care costs.

The cost of equipment and facilities, as well as the cost of services, should be included in the estimated total current cost of MSWLF closure and postclosure care, regardless of their capital or operating nature.

Equipment and facilities included in the estimated total current cost of closure and postclosure care should not be reported as capital assets. Equipment, facilities, services, and final cover included in the estimated total current cost should be reported as a reduction of the accrued liability for MSWLF closure and postclosure care when they are acquired.

Thus, there is no effect on the asset amount, and a decrease in the liability amount.

Answer choices other than "C" are based on incorrect assumptions and/or combinations.

#69 (answer "B")

The following financial statements with columns for each fund type constitute the basic financial statements necessary for fair presentation in accordance with GAAP.

1. Combined balance sheet—All fund types, account groups, and discretely presented component units.
2. Combined statement of revenues, expenditures, and changes in fund balances—All governmental fund types and discretely presented component units.
3. Combined statement of revenues, expenditures, and changes in fund balances, budget and actual, general and special revenue fund types (for which annual budgets have been legally adopted by the primary government).

4. Combined statement of revenues, expenses, and changes in retained earnings, all proprietary fund types, and discretely presented component units.

5. Combined statement of cash flows, proprietary fund types (and nonexpendable trust funds), and discretely presented component units.

An enterprise fund is a proprietary fund; as such, it would include retained earnings in its balance sheet.

Answer choices other than "B" are incorrect because they do not represent proprietary funds; as such, they would not generally report retained earnings.

#70 (answer "C")

In general (i.e., "normally"), the compensated absences liability should be calculated based on the pay or salary rate in effect at the balance sheet date.

Answer choices "A" and "B" are incorrect because they do not represent appropriate rates for measuring the liability.

Answer choice "D" is incorrect because it does not represent the general rule, but rather an exception to the general rule. There were no facts in the question to assume anything other than the general rule.

#71 (answer "D")

Encumbrance accounting is peculiar to governmental accounting, particularly with respect to governmental-type funds. It is an integral part of budgetary accountability.

Encumbrances represent commitments related to unfilled contracts for goods and services. (It should also be noted that unpaid wages and salaries, a significant expenditure by governmental units, represent a known, incurred liability and, hence, are not encumbered.)

The purpose of encumbrance accounting is to prevent further expenditure of funds in light of commitments already made.

At year-end, encumbrances still open are not accounted for as expenditures and liabilities but, rather, as reservations of fund balance.

Journal entries for encumbrance accounting are as follows:

1. Recording of an encumbrance
When goods or services are ordered, the entry is as follows:
Dr. Encumbrances (control)   XXX
    Cr. Reserve for
      encumbrances   XXX
    Again, this is an estimated amount. It will be reversed when an actual invoice, etc., is received.

2. Actual expenditure for item previously encumbered
When the actual expenditure for an amount previously encumbered is made, there are two entries; one reverses the original encumbrance, the second records the expenditure.
  a. Dr. Reserve for
        encumbrances   XXX
      Cr. Encumbrances
        (control)   XXX
  b. Dr. Expenditures
        (control)   XXX
      Cr. Vouchers payable   XXX

Accordingly, when a purchase order is issued for supplies, the account credited is the reserve for encumbrances.

Answer choice "A" is incorrect because appropriations control is credited when the budget is recorded.

Answer choice "B" is incorrect because vouchers payable is credited when the expenditure is recorded upon receipt and acceptance of the supplies ordered.

Answer choice "C" is incorrect because encumbrance control is debited, not credited, when supplies are ordered.

#72 (answer "C")

Broadly, the journal entry to record the adoption of a general fund budget would appear as follows:

Dr. Estimated revenues control
Dr. Estimated other financing sources control
    Cr. Appropriations control
    Cr. Estimated other financing uses control
Dr. or Cr. Budgetary fund balance

The accounts indicated above for estimated revenues, appropriations, and estimated other financing sources and uses are budgetary (nominal) accounts that will be closed out at year-end along with actual transactions.

It should be noted that while "transfers in" and "transfers out" have the same impact as revenues and expenditures, they are classified separately in the financial statements under the captions "other financing sources" and "other financing uses," and not as revenues and/or expenditures per se.

Accordingly, the estimated revenues control account of a governmental unit is debited when the budget is recorded.

Answer choice "A" is incorrect because there generally would be a debit to a receivable account when actual revenues are recorded; "estimated revenues control" does not represent a receivable.

Answer choice "B" is incorrect because cash would generally be debited when actual revenues are collected.

Answer choice "D" is incorrect because the estimated revenues account would be credited, not debited, when the budget is closed at the end of the year.

#73 (answer "B")

An internal service fund is a proprietary fund, which typically performs services for other government agencies and departments; such services are recorded as operating revenues.

Answer choice "A" is incorrect because appropriations are provided through an authorization or legislative process rather than an earnings process.

Answer choice "C" is incorrect because the provision of services represents a permanent transfer of resources and not a temporary transfer, as might be suggested by the term "interfund exchanges."

Answer choice "D" is incorrect because services provided by internal service funds for other governmental units and/or departments, of a type that would be performed by external vendors in the absence of an internal service fund, are not intergovernmental transfers.

#74 (answer "A")

FASB Statement #117, "Financial Statements of Not-for-Profit Organizations," establishes standards for general-purpose external financial statements provided by a not-for-profit organization.

All such organizations are required to present a statement of financial position, a statement of activities, and a cash flow statement.

A statement of activities is required to report the amount of change in permanently restricted, temporarily restricted, and unrestricted net assets for the period.

Answer choices other than "A" are based on incorrect assumptions and/or combinations.

#75 (answer "B")

Following are the major statement of activity captions of a not-for-profit hospital:

1. Revenues—There are two main revenue captions.
   a. Patient service revenues—Patient service revenues are those directly related to patient care. They are presented net with disclosure of deductions from revenue optional. Bad debts are reported as an operating expense.
   b. Other operating revenues—This caption includes sources indirectly related to providing patient services (e.g., tuition from educational programs, cafeteria revenues, parking fees, the value of donated materials and supplies, gift shop revenues, and so on.
   Also included are transfers from specific purpose funds, which would be reported as net assets released from restrictions.
2. Operating expenses—Included in this caption are expenses directly related to operating items, including nursing services, administrative services, depreciation, and so on.
3. Nonoperating gains and losses—Includes gains and losses resulting from transactions that are peripheral or incidental to operations, and from events largely beyond management's control.
   Included are general contributions, the value of donated services, unrestricted bequests, unrestricted income from endowment funds, income from investments, rents, unrestricted income earmarked from specific purpose funds, and so on.

Therefore, as to a not-for-profit hospital, ongoing or central revenue transactions would generally be those directly related to patient care; both room and board fees from patients and recovery room fees would be so classified.

Answer choice "A" is incorrect because both items should appropriately be included.

Answer choices "C" and "D" are incorrect because in each case one item is not included, and both should be.

OTHER OBJECTIVE FORMATS/QUESTIONS

Answer 2

#76 (answer "6,140")

Lan should report net business income on its 1994 Form 1120S, U.S. Income Tax Return for an S corporation, Schedule K, in the amount of $6,140:

Gross receipts	$7,260
Less: Supplies	(1,120)
Net business income	$6,140

It should be noted that interest income on investments and charitable contributions are not considered in determining net business income; rather, they are accounted for separately as pass-through items because they are subject to special handling or limitation on the individual returns of the shareholders.

#77 (answer "2,700")

Since S corporations will essentially be treated as a partnership, each shareholder must report on his individual return, a pro-rata share of each item of income, deduction, and credit that would have been accounted for separately had the shareholder been a partner in a partnership. This reporting is required whether or not the shareholders actually receive distributions. A shareholder in an S corporation must be given a Form 1120S, Schedule K-1, which reflects the items to be reported on his tax return.

In view of the above, Pike should have reported net business income from Lan for the 334-day period (i.e., February 1, 1994–December 31, 1994) that Pike owned 40 shares of Lan stock. Accordingly, the amount of net business income that should have been reported on Pike's 1994 Schedule K-1 from Lan (rounded to the nearest hundred) is $2,700 (i.e., $14,520 × 40/200 × 334/363, or $2,672).

#78 (answer "3,150")

The basis of a shareholder's stock in an S corporation is increased by her ratable share of all taxable and nontaxable items of corporate income that are passed through to the shareholder, whether or not separately stated. The basis of the stock will be reduced by the shareholder's ratable share of: (1) all items of corporate loss and deduction, whether or not separately stated, (2) all nontaxable distributions, which represent return of capital, and (3) all expenses not deducted in computing taxable income and not properly chargeable to the capital account.

Accordingly, Pike's basis in his Lan stock at December 31, 1994, is $3,150, computed as follows:

Basis (i.e., cost), January 31, 1994	$4,000
Ordinary business loss	(1,000)
Municipal bond interest income	150
Basis, December 31, 1994	$3,150

#79 (answer "9,000")

Refer to #78 for background material pertaining to basis of a shareholder's stock in an S corporation.

Taylor's basis in Lan shares for determining gain or loss from the sale to Pike is $9,000:

Basis, January 3, 1994	$10,000
Ordinary income prior to sale	2,000
Cash distribution	(3,000)
Basis, January 31, 1994	$9,000

#80 (answer "F")

To be eligible for the S corporation election, a corporation may have only one class of stock. Differences in voting power attached to shares of stock will not be deemed to create more than one class of stock.

Consequently, Lan will not be eligible for S corporation status because it issued shares of both preferred and common stock to shareholders at inception on January 3, 1994.

#81 (answer "F")

An S corporation's election will be revoked if the corporation has passive investment income in excess of 25% of its gross receipts for three consecutive tax years and the corporation has accumulated earnings and profits (derived from its days as a corporation not under the provisions of Subchapter S) at the end of each of these three years. Passive investment income is generally defined as interest, rents, dividends, and so on.

In view of the fact that Lan has been an S corporation since inception, and therefore cannot possibly have accumulated earnings and profits (derived from days while not under the provisions of Subchapter S), Lan's S corporation election will not be terminated as of the first day of the fourth year.

Answer 3

#82 (answer "3,000")

The Moores realized a net long-term capital loss in the amount of $6,000, consisting of (1) a $10,000 (i.e., $15,000 − $25,000) long-term capital loss on the sale of the Revco stock, and (2) a $4,000 (i.e., $8,000 − $4,000) short-term gain on the sale of the Abbco stock.

The amount of the loss that should be included on page one of the Moores' 1994 Form 1040 is, however, limited to $3,000

(It should be noted that capital losses in excess of the $3,000 limitation may be carried forward indefinitely.)

#83 (answer "0")

The basis of property acquired by gift can generally be summarized as follows:

1. The basis for calculating a gain is the donor's adjusted basis at the time of the gift.
2. The basis for calculating a loss is the lower of the donor's adjusted basis or the fair market value of the property at the date of the gift.

In applying these rules, if, in determination of gain a loss results, and if, in determination of loss a gain results, there is no gain or loss recognized.

Accordingly, the Moores' gain or loss is computed as follows:

Gain	
Selling price	$56,000
Less: Basis (donor's basis)	60,000
Loss	$ 4,000

Loss	
Selling price	$56,000
Less: Basis (fair market value at date of gift)	50,000
Gain	$ 6,000

It should be observed that in determination of gain, a loss has resulted and in determination of loss, a gain has resulted. Accordingly, there is no gain or loss recognized.

#84 (answer "0")

A rent security deposit that is required to be returned to the tenant at the expiration of a lease does not represent taxable income; rather, it represents a liability on the part of the landlord. It should be noted, however, that all advance payments received for rent (including nonrefundable security deposits) will be taxed in the year of receipt, regardless of whether or not the income is actually earned.

The amount of the security deposit on the rental property that should be included on page one of the Moores' 1994 Form 1040 is $0 because they are required to return the security deposit to the tenant.

#85 (answer "55,000")

Premiums paid on a group-term life insurance policy where the corporation is not a beneficiary are excludible from gross income for coverage not in excess of $50,000. The value of excess coverage is included in the employee's gross income as wages.

The amount of employment income that should be included on page one of the Moores' 1994 Form 1040 is $55,000, inclusive of the regular wages ($53,000) and the value of the excess life insurance coverage ($2,000).

#86 (answer "1,250")

Under the tax benefit rule, a refund of state and local income tax is includible in gross income if the refund is for tax paid in a year for which the taxpayer itemized deductions, but only to the extent that the deduction resulted in a federal tax savings. The benefit amount to be included in income is the amount of the refund, limited to the lesser of excess itemized deductions over the standard deduction or the amount of the previous year's deduction for state and local taxes.

Based on the tax benefit rule, the amount of the state tax refund for 1993 overpayments that should be included on page one of the Moores' 1994 Form 1040 is $1,250.

#87 (answer "1,300")

The amount of the unemployment compensation benefits received by Joan that should be included on page one of the Moores' 1994 Form 1040 is $1,300 because all unemployment compensation benefits are includible in gross income.

#88 (answer "2,250")

The amount of net rental income that should be included on page one of the Moores' 1994 Form 1040 is $2,500:

Gross receipts		$8,400
Less:		
Bank mortgage interest	$1,200	
Real estate taxes	700	
Insurance	500	
MACRS depreciation	3,500	5,900
Net rental income		$2,500

(It should be noted that rental income is always considered to be passive income.)

#89 (answer "900")

In general, a stock dividend is not taxable. If, however, as in the question situation, a taxpayer has the option to receive cash or other property instead of the stock, the stock dividend is includible in gross income to the extent of the stock's fair market value.

In view of the above, the amount of the stock dividend that should be included on page one of the Moores' 1994 Form 1040 is $900 (i.e., the fair market value of the stock).

#90 (answer "0")

A deceased employee's beneficiary may receive and exclude from income a one-time death benefit of up to $5,000. (If the decedent had more than one beneficiary, the $5,000 exclusion must be apportioned among the beneficiaries.) In general, to be excludible, the decedent must not have had a nonforfeitable right to receive the income prior to death.

Therefore, the amount of the death benefit that should be included on page one of the Moores' 1994 Form 1040 is $0.

(The death benefit exclusion is repealed for decedents dying after August 20, 1996.)

#91 (answer "5,000")

Interest on U.S. obligations is generally not exempt from federal income tax, except for an available exclusion on Series EE U.S. saving bonds. To qualify for the exclusion: (1) the bonds must have been issued after 1989 in the name of the taxpayer (and/or his spouse), (2) the taxpayer must have attained the age of 24 at the time of the bond's issuance, and (3) the redemption proceeds must be used for the qualified higher education expenses of the taxpayer, the taxpayer's spouse, or the taxpayer's dependents.

The exclusion begins to be phased out when adjusted gross income exceeds certain amounts, which are subject to adjustment annually for inflation.

The amount of the proceeds from the redemption of the Series EE savings bond that should be included on page one of the Moores' 1994 Form 1040 is limited to the interest of $5,000. The Moores may not exclude the interest income because the bond was issued prior to 1989. It should be evident that principal received from the redemption of a bond is not taxable.

#92 (answer "8,000")

Alimony payments (but not child support payments) are deducted from gross income as an adjustment to arrive at adjusted gross income.

The amount of the adjustment to arrive at the Moores' 1994 adjusted gross income is therefore limited to the alimony payments of $8,000.

#93 (answer "A")

The loss sustained by Tom on the sale of the Zip stock on March 23, 1994, is not deductible on Form 1040 because Tom's repurchase of the stock on April 15, 1994, subjects the loss to the wash sale rules.

A wash sale results when a taxpayer realizes a loss on a sale or exchange of stock or securities and within a period of 30 days before and after the sale or exchange acquires (or enters into a contract or option to acquire) substantially identical stock or securities.

Losses resulting from wash sales are not deductible.

#94 (answer "B")

A personal property tax based on the value of the property is <u>deductible in full in Schedule A—Itemized Deductions</u>.

#95 (answer "D")

A donation of unappreciated property other than cash (e.g., used clothing) to a qualified charitable organization is <u>deductible in Schedule A—Itemized Deductions, subject to a limitation of 50% of adjusted gross income</u>, to the extent of its fair market value at the time of the gift.

Donations of appreciated ordinary income (and short-term capital gain) property are also subject to a limitation of 50% of adjusted gross income; the deduction, however, is generally limited to the property's basis.

Donations of long-term capital gain appreciated property, while deductible at the property's fair market value, are generally limited to 30% of adjusted gross income.

#96 (answer "A")

Premiums paid for insurance against loss of earnings are <u>not deductible on Form 1040</u>.

#97 (answer "F")

Subscriptions to professional journals used for business are <u>deductible in Schedule A—Itemized Deductions, subject to a threshold of 2% of adjusted gross income</u>.

If an individual is self-employed, the subscriptions to professional journals would be fully deductible in Schedule C—Profit or Loss from Business.

#98 (answer "B")

Interest on up to $100,000 of a home equity loan is <u>deductible in full in Schedule A—Itemized Deductions</u> as qualified mortgage interest, even if the loan proceeds are used for personal purposes.

It should be noted that qualified mortgage interest also includes interest on up to $1,000,000 of acquisition indebtedness (i.e., debt pertaining to acquiring, constructing, or substantially improving the taxpayer's principal and/or second residence, and that is secured by the residence).

#99 (answer "C")

Amounts paid in excess of insurance reimbursement for prescription drugs represent qualifying medical expenses and are <u>deductible in Schedule A—Itemized Deductions, subject to a threshold of 7.5% of adjusted gross income</u>.

Some other common qualifying medical expenses are medical insurance premiums, insulin, fees paid to doctors, dentists, hospitals and laboratories, and transportation expenses.

#100 (answer "A")

Federal expenses are <u>not deductible on Form 1040</u>.

A deduction for funeral expenses may only be claimed on Form 706—United States Estate Tax Return.

#101 (answer "E")

A personal theft or casualty loss in excess of insurance reimbursement is <u>deductible in Schedule A—Itemized Deductions, subject to a $100 floor and a threshold of 10% of adjusted gross income</u>.

It should be noted that losses of business or income-producing property are not subject to the limitations above.

#102 (answer "A")

Losses on personal property are generally not deductible unless resulting from casualities or thefts.

Accordingly, the loss on the sale of the family's sailboat is <u>not deductible on Form 1040</u>.

#103 (answer "B")

The interest paid on the $300,000 acquisition mortgage on the Moores' home is considered qualified mortgage interest and is <u>deductible in full in Schedule A—Itemized Deductions</u>.

Qualified mortgage interest includes interest on up to $1,000,000 of acquisition indebtedness (i.e., debt pertaining to acquiring, constructing, or substantially improving the taxpayer's principal and/or second residence, and that is secured by the residence) and interest on up to $100,000 of a home equity loan. The deduction for interest on a home equity loan is allowable even if the loan proceeds are used for personal purposes.

#104 (answer "A")

No deduction is allowed for the value of services performed for a charitable organization.

Accordingly, the estimated value of Joan's accounting services provided to the Red Cross is <u>not</u> <u>deductible</u> <u>on</u> <u>Form</u> <u>1040</u>.

#105 (answer "F")

Personal and dependency exemptions will be phased out and possibly eliminated for taxpayers whose adjusted gross income (AGI) is in excess of certain threshold amounts (to be indexed annually for inflation), which are dependent upon filing status. For 1994, the threshold for a married couple filing a joint return is $167,700.

The phaseout is 2% for each $2,500 (or part thereof) of AGI in excess of the applicable threshold amount.

<u>The</u> <u>Moores</u> <u>were</u> <u>not</u> <u>subject</u> <u>to</u> <u>the</u> <u>phaseout of</u> <u>their</u> <u>personal</u> <u>exemptions</u> because their $75,000 gross income was well below the applicable threshold amount.

#106 (answer "T")

<u>For</u> <u>alternative</u> <u>minimum</u> <u>tax</u> <u>(AMT)</u> <u>purposes,</u> <u>the</u> <u>deduction</u> <u>for</u> <u>medical</u> <u>expenses</u> <u>has</u> <u>to</u> <u>exceed</u> <u>10%</u> <u>of</u> <u>adjusted</u> <u>gross</u> <u>income</u>; this results from the adjustment to taxable income for medical expenses, which is generally equal to 2.5% of adjusted gross income.

#107 (answer "T")

<u>The</u> <u>Moores'</u> <u>personal</u> <u>exemption</u> <u>amount</u> <u>for</u> <u>regular</u> <u>tax</u> <u>purposes</u> <u>was</u> <u>not</u> <u>permitted</u> <u>for</u> <u>determining</u> <u>1994</u> <u>AMT</u>, because the starting point for determining alternative minimum taxable income is taxable income before exemptions (computed using regular income tax rules).

It should be noted, however, that an AMT exemption may be available to reduce alternative minimum taxable income (AMTI). The AMT exemption, which is based on filing status, starts to phase out when AMTI exceeds certain threshold amounts.

#108 (answer "T")

In general, an individual is required to make quarterly estimated tax payments if the individual expects her estimated income tax (including the alternative minimum tax) after credits to be $500 or more. The first three estimated tax payments are due by the 15th day of the 4th, 6th, and 9th months of the tax year. The last estimated tax payment is due on the 15th day of the first month of the following year.

If an individual does not pay estimated tax when due, an underpayment penalty may be charged for the period of underpayment, at a rate that is periodically determined by the Internal Revenue Service.

However, an individual generally will not be liable for the penalty if the individual's actual tax liability is $500 or more and she timely paid 90% of the tax liability for the year through withholding or estimated tax payments. Alternatively, an individual with adjusted gross income (AGI) in excess of $150,000 may avoid the underpayment penalty by paying 110% of the actual tax liability of the preceding year. If an individual's AGI does not exceed $150,000, the applicable percentage is 100%.

It should therefore be evident that <u>the</u> <u>Moores</u> <u>were</u> <u>not</u> <u>subject</u> <u>to</u> <u>the</u> <u>underpayment of</u> <u>tax</u> <u>penalty</u> because (1) their AGI (i.e., $75,000) was not in excess of $150,000, and (2) their 1994 federal tax withholding (i.e., estimated tax payments) equalled 100% of their 1993 tax liability.

#109 (answer "T")

In general, the part of an early distribution (i.e., a distribution received prior to reaching age 59½) from a qualified retirement plan (including an IRA) that is includible in gross income is subject to an additional 10% tax (i.e., penalty).

The penalty does not apply to certain distributions specifically excepted by the Internal Revenue Code. Some of the more common exceptions are (1) distributions due to death, (2) distributions due to total and permanent disability, and (3) distributions to the extent of deductible medical expenses (but only from qualified employee plans, which do not include IRAs, unless the IRA distributions are made after December 31, 1996).

In view of the above, <u>the</u> <u>Moores,</u> <u>both</u> <u>being</u> <u>under</u> <u>age</u> <u>59½,</u> <u>were</u> <u>subject</u> <u>to</u> <u>an</u> <u>early</u> <u>withdrawal</u> <u>penalty</u> <u>on</u> <u>their</u> <u>IRA</u> <u>withdrawals</u> <u>used</u> <u>for</u> <u>medical</u> <u>expenses</u>.

(The penalty also does not apply to distributions from IRAs made after December 31, 1996, that are used by certain unemployed individuals to pay health insurance premiums.)

#110 (answer "F")

The earned income credit is available to a low-income worker who maintains a household that is the principal place of abode of himself and a child of his who is under the age of 19, or who is a full-time student under the age of 24, or who is disabled. The credit is also available to a childless low-income earner who is at least 25 years old, but less than 65 years old, and is not a dependent of another individual.

The credit is zero when adjusted gross income or earned income reaches a certain level, which is adjusted annually for inflation.

It should be readily apparent from the facts presented in the question that the Moores are not low-income earners; accordingly, the Moores were not allowed an earned income credit against their 1994 tax liability.

Answer 4

#111 (answer "E")

The following background information from FASB Statement #117, "Financial Statements of Not-for-Profit Organizations," is helpful in answering questions #111 through #116.

1. Categories of net assets
   a. Permanently restricted—These are resources with a donor-imposed restriction, which stipulates that resources be maintained permanently, but permits the organization to use up or expend all or part of the income generated from the donated assets.
   b. Temporarily restricted—These are resources with a donor-imposed restriction that permits the organization to use up or expend the donated assets as specified, and is satisfied either by the passage of time or by actions of the organization.
   c. Unrestricted—These are resources that have no external restrictions as to use or purpose; they can be used for any purpose designated by the governing board,

as distinguished from funds restricted externally (i.e., by donors, for specific purposes or time periods). Board designated assets or funds are therefore internal restrictions.

2. Release from restrictions—Net assets are generally released from restrictions and/or reclassified when one of the following occurs:
   a. Program (i.e., purpose) restrictions are met.
   b. Time-based restrictions expire.
   c. Equipment-acquisition restrictions are satisfied.
3. Reclassification of net assets—Net asset reclassifications are reported separately in the statement of activities, generally as net assets released from restrictions.

In light of the explanation provided in the preceding background, it should be readily apparent that a board designation is an internal restriction, which does not fit into any of the categories indicated. Rather, there is no required reportable event.

#112 (answer "A")

Investment income, as well as unrealized and realized gains and losses, inclusive of those related to endowment assets, are generally recorded when earned as an increase in unrestricted revenues, gains, and other support, unless their use is temporarily or permanently restricted by explicit donor stipulations or by law. No such restriction exists.

#113 (answer "C")

Clearly, in light of the background provided, these funds represent an increase in temporarily restricted net assets.

The restriction will be released by a specified action (i.e., the building expansion).

#114 (answer "A")

Again, as indicated in the background provided, a release from restrictions is reported separately in the statement of activities as a net asset reclassification.

As such, use of the previously restricted funds to purchase the building results in an increase in unrestricted revenues, gains, and other support.

It should also be noted that while unrestricted net assets will increase, temporarily restricted net assets would decrease.

#115 (answer "A")

The fair value of donated or contributed services should be recorded only if they (1) create or enhance nonmonetary assets, or (2) require specialized skills (i.e., doctors, lawyers, CPAs, teachers, electricians, craftsmen, and so on). The services should be performed by qualified individuals and typically would need to be purchased if not donated.

Contributed services are an <u>increase</u> in <u>unrestricted</u> <u>revenues,</u> <u>gains,</u> <u>and</u> <u>other</u> <u>support</u>.

It should be noted that donated support that does not result in an asset is recorded with a corresponding entry to expense. That is, both the revenue and expense elements are recorded for reporting purposes.

#116 (answer "D")

The investments are subject to a donor-imposed restriction, which is permanent in nature. Thus, they represent an <u>increase</u> in <u>permanently</u> <u>restricted</u> <u>net</u> <u>assets</u>.

Answer 5

#117 (answer "104,500")

As noted in the third paragraph of information, the general fund transferred $104,500 to a debt service fund. This is an operating transfer out.

#118 (answer "17,000")

Only the current liability (i.e., the resources available at December 31, 1994), is reported as a general fund liability.

The balance in excess of available resources at the balance sheet date is reported in the general long-term debt group.

As such, the 1994 general fund liabilities, as noted in the fourth paragraph of information, are $17,000.

#119 (answer "125,000")

The treatment of inventories of materials and supplies in governmental accounting must be considered in arriving at the answer to this question.

Inventories of materials and supplies may be recognized under the "purchases" method or the "consumption" method.

Under the purchases method, inventories are reported as expenditures when they are acquired, regardless of when they are used.

Under the consumption method, inventories are recorded as expenditures when they are used, in the manner of a perpetual inventory.

Under the purchases method, inventory on hand is recorded with a corresponding entry to a fund balance reserve account: "reserve for inventories." Such reserves are a part of fund balance since expenditures reduced the fund balance when the books were closed.

The last item of information indicates that Dane uses the purchases method. Accordingly, there would be a "reserve for inventories" of $42,000 at December 31, 1994. This results in a "fund balance reserved" of $83,000 for outstanding general fund encumbrances plus $42,000 for inventories, or a total of $125,000.

#120 (answer "236,000")

Simply stated, the capital projects fund balance would be equal to the proceeds from general obligation bonds less construction expenditures during the period.

These amounts are set forth in the first paragraph of information; the answer is $236,000 (i.e., $600,000 − $364,000).

(The $364,000 expenditures for construction would also be recorded as "Construction in Progress" in the General Fixed Assets Account Group.)

#121 (answer "6,000")

Parenthetically, a special revenue fund is similar to a general fund, except that it is used to account for the proceeds of specific revenue sources (other than expendable trusts or for major capital projects) that are legally restricted to expenditure for specified purposes. Examples of special revenue funds are those established for the purpose of financing schools, parks, or libraries, and so on.

Facts related to the special revenue fund for tourist promotion are indicated in the second paragraph of information. As such, the special revenue fund balance would be equal to the $109,000 from hotel room taxes, less $103,000 of total expenditures (i.e., $81,000 + $22,000), or $6,000.

It should be noted that while the motor vehicle is an expenditure of the special revenue fund, it would also be recorded as a general fixed asset.

#122 (answer "104,500")

A debt service fund is used to account for the accumulation of resources for, and the payment of, general long-term debt principal and interest.

In accordance with the third paragraph of information, debt service fund expenditures totaled $104,500, the amounts used to repay debt and related interest.

#123 (answer "386,000")

The general fixed assets account group functions only to maintain double-entry control over fixed assets (other than those of a proprietary fund or certain trust funds). It has no assets other than such fixed assets, nor are there any liabilities. Fixed assets are recorded therein only after construction or acquisition.

Fixed assets are recorded by a debit to the fixed assets account, and a corresponding credit to "investment in general fixed assets."

As noted in the answer to Part #120 (i.e., construction expenditures of $364,000 in the capital projects fund), and Part #121 (i.e., an expenditure of $22,000 for a motor vehicle in the special revenue fund), $386,000 should be included in the general fixed assets account group for the cost of assets acquired in 1994.

#124 (answer "100,000")

The general long-term debt account group is used to account for the principal on all unmatured long-term debt (inclusive of lease-purchase agreements, etc.) except debt payable from a proprietary fund or trust fund. All other unmatured general long-term liabilities of the governmental unit, which includes special assessment debt for which the government is obligated in some manner, should be accounted for through this account group.

Payment of $100,000 through the debt service fund (as per Part #122) would also result in a decrease in the general long-term debt account group.

It should be noted that while the $100,000 represents an expenditure in the debt service fund, there would also be the following entry in the general long-term debt account group:

Dr. General obligation bonds payable	100,000	
Cr. Amount to be provided for the retirement of general long-term debt		100,000

#125 (answer "181,000")

As noted in the explanation to Part #119, under the purchases method, expenditures are recorded when the related item is acquired.

Consequently, the $181,000 credited to vouchers payable, as indicated in the last paragraph of additional information, would represent the 1994 supplies expenditures.

#126 (answer "190,000")

Clearly, supplies encumbrances would be equal to the $190,000 of purchase orders during 1994 (as noted in the last paragraph of information).

Remember: The placing of a purchase order results in an encumbrance; consequently, any other information presented in the question was not relevant.

Financial Accounting & Reporting—Business Enterprises (FARE)

FOUR-OPTION MULTIPLE-CHOICE QUESTIONS

Answer 1

#1 (answer "D")

The objective of financial reporting is to provide information that is useful in economic decision making. Specifically, the information should be useful in making investment and credit decisions and should be comprehensible to someone with a reasonable understanding of economic activities. Therefore, the objectives of financial reporting for business enterprises are based on <u>the needs of the users of the information</u>.

Answer choice "A" is incorrect because generally accepted accounting principles are those methodologies that are used to generate information that is useful in making economic decisions; they are not objectives of financial reporting in and of themselves.

Answer choice "B" is incorrect because reporting on management's stewardship is not a primary objective of financial reporting. Rather, it is information that should be presented in addition to information that is useful in making economic decisions.

Answer choice "C" is incorrect because the need for conservatism does not relate to an objective of financial reporting. Rather, conservatism is a modifying convention that is a prudent reaction to uncertainty.

#2 (answer "B")

The objective of financial reporting is to provide information that is useful in making economic decisions. The two primary user-specific qualities of accounting information are relevance and reliability; if either is missing, the information is not useful.

According to the conceptual framework, the ability to provide relevant and reliable information is subject to two quantitative constraints. The first is the <u>cost-benefit</u> constraint; the benefit from providing the information should exceed the cost of providing it. The second constraint is materiality; information may be relevant and reliable even though it contains immaterial errors.

Answer choice "A" is incorrect because consistency is a secondary and interactive quality; it is not a constraint.

Answer choice "C" is incorrect because reliability is a primary decision-specific quality; it is not a constraint.

Answer choice "D" is incorrect because representational faithfulness is an element of reliability; it is not a constraint.

#3 (answer "A")

According to FASB Concepts Statement #2, it may be prudent to immediately recognize a loss contingency as a means to ensure that uncertainties and risks inherent in business situations are adequately considered. However, a gain contingency is generally not recognized until it is realized. This is the underlying concept of <u>conservatism</u>.

Answer choice "B" is incorrect because relevance is a primary decision-specific quality, not an underlying concept. It is composed of three ingredients: predictive value, feedback value, and timeliness.

Answer choice "C" is incorrect because consistency (and comparability) suggests that the same accounting methods should be used over a period of time so that the differences in accounting representations reflect differences in underlying transactions.

Answer choice "D" is incorrect because reliability is a primary decision-specific quality, not an underlying concept. It is composed of three ingredients: verifiability, neutrality, and representational faithfulness.

#4 (answer "A")

This question is based on FASB Statement #7, "Accounting and Reporting by Development Stage Enterprises." A development stage enterprise is one that devotes substantially all of its efforts to establish a new business. The company has either not started its principal operations or no significant revenue has yet been derived from principal operations.

Generally accepted accounting principles applicable to established operating enterprises apply equally to a development stage enterprise, including both <u>revenue recognition</u> and <u>deferral of expenses</u>.

Answer choices other than "A" are based upon incorrect assumptions and/or combinations.

#5 (answer "D")

According to Statement of Financial Accounting Concepts #5, "Recognition and Measurement in Financial Statements of Business Enterprises," five different measurement attributes are used in practice: historical cost, current cost, current market value, net realizable value, and present value of future cash flows. Each of the above attributes is used to measure inventories except the <u>present value of future cash flows</u>, which is typically used to measure long-term receivables and payables.

Answer choice "A" is incorrect because historical cost, as approximated by LIFO, FIFO, or average, is used to measure inventories.

Answer choice "B" is incorrect because replacement cost is used to measure inventories when applying the lower-of-cost-or-market convention.

Answer choice "C" is incorrect because net realizable value is used to measure inventories when applying the lower-of-cost-or-market convention.

#6 (answer "A")

Certain provisions of APB Opinion #28, "Interim Financial Reporting," should be considered in connection with this question. These are

1. An interim period (i.e., month, quarter, or other interval of less than a full year) should be viewed as an integral part of the annual accounting period; the interim period is not a basic accounting period.
2. Generally, the same principles used to prepare the latest annual financial statements should be used to prepare the interim financial information. However, the Opinion affords several modifications to permit the interim information to be available in a timely manner:
   a. The gross profit method may be used to estimate inventory amounts and cost of sales.

   b. The cost of replacing temporarily liquidated LIFO layers may be included in cost of sales of the interim period.
   c. Standard cost variances that are expect to be absorbed by the end of the year may be deferred.
   d. Inventory losses from market declines should be not be deferred beyond the interim period in which the decline occurred. Recoveries in subsequent interim periods should be recognized in the period of the recovery.

Given the foregoing, interim financial statements can be described as emphasizing <u>timeliness over reliability</u>. That is, generally accepted accounting principles will forego some degree of reliability (i.e., verifiability) in order to achieve more relevance (i.e., timeliness) in interim financial reporting.

Answer choice "B" is incorrect because interim financial reporting emphasizes relevance (i.e., timeliness) over reliability (i.e., verifiability).

Answer choice "C" is incorrect because comparability is important in interim financial reporting. Disclosure is required of the seasonality of revenue and expense and of comparable information from prior interim periods.

Answer choice "D" is incorrect because according to the FASB conceptual framework, neutrality (an element of reliability) takes precedence over comparability for both annual and interim reports.

#7 (answer "D")

FASB Statement #57, "Related Party Disclosures," requires that material related party transactions that are not eliminated in consolidated or combined financial statements be disclosed in the financial statements of the reporting entity. Related party disclosure is required for <u>all those transactions other than compensation arrangements, expense allowances, and other similar items in the ordinary course of business</u>.

Disclosure should include the nature of the related party relationship; a description of the transaction; the dollar amount of the transaction for each period that an income statement is presented; and if not apparent in the financial statements, the terms of the transaction, the method of settlement, and amounts due to or from the related party.

Answer choice "A" is incorrect because disclosure is required for appropriate related party transactions, including those reported (i.e., recognized) in the body of the financial statement and those not so reported.

Answer choice "B" is incorrect because disclosure is required of appropriate related party transactions that receive accounting recognition, and those that do not receive accounting recognition (i.e., formally incorporated into the financial statements).

Answer choice "C" is incorrect because disclosure is required of all appropriate related party transactions without regard to their legality.

#8 (answer "D")

Under the provisions of FASB Statement #14, "Financial Reporting for Segments of a Business Enterprise," public entities are required to report specified information on a segmental basis.

The following is relevant:

1. In arriving at operating profit or loss, a segment should include traceable costs (those directly associated with production of segment revenue from sales, including expenses that relate to revenue from intersegment transfers), and common operating costs allocated on a reasonable basis. Such a basis might be sales, contribution margins, assets or investments, numbers of employees, or activity levels.
2. General corporate revenues and/or expenses, equity in income or loss from unconsolidated subsidiaries, income taxes, and interest expense are specifically excluded in determining the operating profit or loss of a segment.
3. The revenue of a segment will include intersegment sales of products or services similar to those sold to unaffiliated customers (even though such items are eliminated in consolidated financial statements).
4. A reportable segment is one that satisfies one or more of the following tests:
   a. Revenue is 10% or more of combined revenue.
   b. Operating profit/loss is 10% or more of the greater of:
      (1) Combined operating profit of all industry segments that didn't have a loss.
      (2) Combined operating loss of all industry segments that did have a loss.
   c. Identifiable assets are 10% or more of combined identifiable assets.

In light of the background provided, <u>Lion</u>, <u>Monk</u>, and <u>Nevi</u> are all deemed to be reportable segments because, in each case, their total revenues are 10% or more of combined revenues (i.e., $150,000).

Answer choices other than "D" are incorrect because, in each case, one or more of the business segments is not included, and each should be.

#9 (answer "C")

In general, FIFO is "balance-sheet oriented" to the extent that the most recent acquisition cost is included in inventory. By the same token, LIFO is "income-statement oriented" to the extent that the most recent cost is included in the cost of goods sold as a charge against income.

A higher beginning inventory decreases net income, and a higher ending inventory increases net income. Obviously, then, a lower beginning inventory increases net income, and a lower ending inventory decreases net income.

In a period of rising prices, a change from FIFO to LIFO will result in a <u>decrease in the ending inventory</u> valuation, because inventory under LIFO is valued at beginning-of-the-year costs rather than end-of-the-year costs as under FIFO. Further, a decrease in the ending inventory valuation will result in an increase in cost of sales and a <u>decrease in net income</u>.

Answer choices other than "C" are the result of incorrect assumptions and/or combinations.

#10 (answer "C")

Under the installment sales method, gross profit is realized only as cash is collected.

Revenue realized under the installment method is equal to the cash collected multiplied by the applicable gross profit percentage for the year in which the sale was made. Any gross profit not collected is "deferred" on the balance sheet pending collection. When collections are subsequently made, realized gross profit is increased via debit to the deferred gross profit account. At any point, the amount of the deferred gross profit on installment sales will be the installment receivable multiplied by the appropriate gross profit percentage.

Lang should report deferred gross profit in its December 31, 1994, balance sheet in the amount of $38,000:

Deferred gross profit at December 31, 1994, applicable to:

Installment receivables at 12/31/94 on 1993 sales	$30,000	
1993 gross profit rate; ($80,000 − $40,000)/ $80,000	× ½	$15,000
Installment receivables at 12/31/94 on 1994 sales	$69,000	
1994 gross profit rate; ($90,000 − $60,000)/ $90,000	× ⅓	23,000
Total deferred gross profit, December 31, 1994		$38,000

Answer choice "A" is incorrect because it represents the 12/31/94 deferred gross profit applicable to installment receivables on 1994 sales (i.e., $69,000 × 33⅓% equals $23,000), and ignores the 12/31/94 deferred gross profit applicable to installment receivables on 1993 sales.

Answer choice "B" is incorrect because it applies the 1994 gross profit percentage of 33⅓% to receivables applicable to both 1993 and 1994 installment sales (i.e., [$30,000 + $69,000] × ⅓ equals $33,000). The gross profit percentage for each year's sales is treated independently.

Answer choice "D" is incorrect because it is not a feasible combination of the information presented.

#11 (answer "B")

This question involves a sale-leaseback transaction. The following should be noted with respect to such transactions.

1. General rule—This general rule applies when the seller-lessee retains the right to substantially all of the remaining use of the property.

   If the lease meets one of the criteria for treatment as a capital lease, it shall be accounted for as such by the seller-lessee; otherwise as an operating lease.

   Since the sale-leaseback is considered a single transaction, any profit or loss on the

sale shall be deferred and amortized (as an increase or decrease in the related expense). Amortization is in proportion to the amortization of the leased asset, if a capital lease, or in proportion to the period of time the asset is expected to be used, if an operating lease.

2. Modification of the general rule—This modification applies when the seller-lessee has not retained the right to substantially all of the remaining use of the property.

   In either of the following circumstances, the seller in a sale-leaseback situation must recognize some profit or loss on the sale.

   a. If the present value of rentals for the leaseback represents 10% or less of the fair value of the asset sold, the seller is presumed to have retained the use of only a minor part of the property. The sale and leaseback are accounted for separately, and the profit or loss on the sale is recognized.

   b. If the present value of rentals exceeds 10%, the seller is presumed to have retained more than a minor part but less than "substantially all" of the use of the property. If, in such event, the profit on the sale exceeds the present value, such excess is recognized as profit at the sale date; the amount not recognized (i.e., the present value) is amortized in accordance with the general rule.

In situation I, the seller-lessee has transferred substantially all the risks of ownership to buyer-lessor; therefore, it must be assumed that the lease term is substantially less than the remaining useful life of the asset. Accordingly, the seller-lessee should not defer the gain on the sale.

In situation II, the seller-lessee retains the right to substantially all of the remaining use of the property. Thus, the general rule should be applied and the seller-lessee should defer the gain on the sale.

Answer choices other than "B" are the result of incorrect assumptions and/or combinations.

#12 (answer "C")

There are four criteria to determine if a lease is a capital lease. If one or more of the criteria are met, the lease is a capital lease; otherwise it is an operating lease. The criteria are

1. Property ownership transfers to the lessee by the end of the lease term.
2. The lease contains a bargain purchase option.
3. The lease term is at least 75% of the estimated life of the property.
4. The present value of minimum lease payments at the inception of the lease (excluding such executory costs as property taxes, maintenance, insurance, etc.) equals or exceeds 90% of the fair value of the property.

The following should be noted with respect to capital leases.

1. Recording of asset and obligation—Assets and liabilities are recorded at an amount equal to the present value (at the beginning of the lease term) of minimum lease payments during the lease term, excluding that portion of the payments representing executory costs such as insurance, maintenance, and taxes to be paid by the lessor, together with any profit thereon. (An annuity approach would be used to capitalize the minimum lease payments.)
   a. Any payment called for by a bargain purchase option or guarantee by the lessee of the residual value of the property is considered to be part of the minimum lease payments.
   b. If the present value of minimum lease payments exceeds the fair value of the leased property at the inception of the lease, the amount recorded shall be the fair value.
2. Discount rate for determining present value—The discount rate to be used by the lessee in determining the present value of the minimum lease payments shall be the lessee's incremental borrowing rate; that is, the rate at the inception of the lease that the lessee would have incurred to borrow over a similar term the funds necessary to purchase the leased asset. If, however, it is practicable for the lessee to learn the implicit rate computed by the lessor and such rate is less than the lessee's incremental borrowing rate, the lessor's rate should be used.
3. Allocation of minimum (gross) lease payments—During the lease term, each minimum lease payment shall be allocated between a reduction of the obligation (i.e.,

principal) and interest expense so as to produce a constant periodic rate of interest on the remaining balance of the obligation in accordance with the "interest method" described in APB Opinion #21. (The interest rate is applied to the present value of the obligation outstanding for the period.) It should be noted that if the first payment is made at the inception of the lease (i.e., an annuity-due situation), that entire lease payment is applied to principal.

In this case, the first lease payment was made on the date the lease was entered into; therefore, no interest expense would be recognized. Interest only accrues with the passage of time. The entire payment would consist of a reduction of the lease liability.

Answer choices other than "C" are based upon incorrect assumptions and/or combinations.

#13 (answer "D")

This question deals with the recognition of expenses and liabilities related to payroll. Amounts withheld from employees represent a liability of the employer but are not expenses of the employer; that is, the employer is simply acting as a collection agent for the government. However, FICA taxes are assessed on both the employee and the employer; thus, the employer's share does represent an expense.

Accordingly, Lime will report a payroll tax liability of $2,600 at January 31, 1995, and a payroll tax expense of $700 for the period then ended:

	Payroll tax	
	Liability	Expense
Employee's share FICA; $10,000 × 7%	$ 700	$ -0-
Employer's share FICA; $10,000 × 7%	700	700
Federal income tax withheld	1,200	-0-
Total	$2,600	$700

Answer choices other than "D" are based upon incorrect assumptions and/or combinations.

#14 (answer "C")

This question deals with FASB #87, "Employers' Accounting for Pensions." The minimum liability is a consideration in addition to the periodic pension cost and is intended to present a liability on the balance sheet when a pension plan is "significantly underfunded." No additional cost element results.

Immediate recognition of a minimum liability is required if the accumulated benefit obligation exceeds the fair value of plan assets. This is also known as the "unfunded accumulated benefit obligation."

The minimum liability is a combination of any existing pension asset or liability, and any additional liability required to reach the minimum amount, as follows:

1. Accrued pension liability—When an accrued pension liability (accrued amounts exceed funding) exists, the additional liability required is equal to the unfunded accumulated benefit obligation less the accrued pension liability.
2. Prepaid pension cost—When an asset exists (amounts funded exceed amounts accrued), the additional liability required is equal to the unfunded accumulated benefit obligation plus the prepaid asset.

No contributions had been made to the pension plan during 1994. Thus, at December 31, 1994, Hall reported an accrued pension cost of $8,000, which is the amount of unfunded net periodic pension cost of 1994. Therefore, the additional pension liability is $17,000:

Unfunded accumulated benefit obligation (minimum pension liability)	$25,000
Less: Accrued pension cost	(8,000)
Additional pension liability, December 31, 1994	$17,000

Answer choice "A" is incorrect because it is the difference between the unfunded accumulated benefit obligation and the sum of the unrecognized prior service cost and the accrued pension cost (i.e., $25,000 − [$8,000 + $12,000] equals $5,000). Unrecognized prior service cost is not considered in the determination of the additional pension liability.

Answer choice "B" is incorrect because it is the difference between the unfunded accumulated benefit obligation and the unrecognized prior service cost (i.e., $25,000 − $12,000 equals $13,000). Unrecognized prior service cost is not considered in the determination of the additional pension liability.

Answer choice "D" is incorrect because the $25,000 unfunded accumulated benefit obligation must be reduced by the accrued pension cost or increased by the prepaid pension cost to arrive at the additional pension liability.

#15 (answer "A")

This question essentially addresses the minimum liability under a defined benefit pension plan in accordance with FASB Statement #87, "Employers' Accounting for Pensions."

The minimum liability is a consideration in addition to the periodic pension cost and is intended to present a liability on the balance sheet when a pension plan is "significantly underfunded." No additional cost element results.

Immediate recognition of a minimum liability is required if the accumulated benefit obligation exceeds the fair value of plan assets. This is also known as the "unfunded accumulated benefit obligation."

The minimum liability is a combination of any existing pension asset or liability and any additional liability required to reach the minimum amount, as follows:

1. Accrued pension liability—When an accrued pension liability (accrued amounts exceed funding) exists, the additional liability required is equal to the unfunded accumulated benefit obligation less the accrued pension liability.
2. Prepaid pension cost—When an asset exists (amounts funded exceed amounts accrued), the additional liability required is equal to the unfunded accumulated benefit obligation plus the prepaid asset.

Further, when the additional pension liability is recognized, a corresponding intangible pension asset is generally recognized in order to maintain the integrity of the accounting equation. However, the amount of the intangible pension asset cannot exceed the amount of unrecognized prior service cost. Any excess of the additional pension liability over the unrecognized prior service cost is shown as a separate component of stockholders' equity.

Hall's statement of stockholders' equity should include the excess of additional pension liability over unrecognized prior service cost of $5,000:

Unfunded accumulated benefit obligation	$25,000
Less: Accrued pension cost	(8,000)
Additional pension liability	17,000
Less: Unrecognized prior service cost	(12,000)
Additional pension liability in excess of prior service cost	$ 5,000

Answer choice "B" is incorrect because it is the excess of the unfunded accumulated benefit obligation over the unrecognized prior service cost (i.e., $25,000 − $12,000 equals $13,000).

Answer choice "C" is incorrect because it is the amount of the additional pension liability, not the amount of the additional pension liability in excess of unrecognized prior service cost.

Answer choice "D" is incorrect because it is the amount of the unfunded accumulated benefit obligation, not the amount of the additional pension liability in excess of unrecognized prior service cost.

#16 (answer "D")

This question deals with the accrual of interest and the compounding of interest over more than one compounding period.

At December 31, 1994, Fine's note has been outstanding for 22 months (March 1, 1993, to December 31, 1994). Further, interest is to be paid at the maturity date of the note and is to be compounded annually.

Accordingly, liability for accrued interest at December 31, 1994, was $2,320:

Interest for period 3/1/93 through 2/28/94; $10,000 × 12%	$1,200
Interest for period 3/1/94 through 12/31/94; ($10,000 + $1,200) × 12% × 10/12	1,120
Accrued interest payable at December 31, 1994	$2,320

Answer choice "A" is incorrect because interest should be accrued as it is incurred, without regard to its scheduled payment date.

Answer choice "B" is incorrect because it is the amount of accrued interest payable at December 31, 1994, had the interest for the first year been paid on February 28, 1994 (i.e., $10,000 × 12% × 10/12 equals $1,000). The question states that interest is payable in full at maturity on February 28, 1995.

Answer choice "C" is incorrect because it is the amount of interest that accrued for the period March 1, 1993, through February 28, 1994 (i.e., $10,000 × 12% equals $1,200).

#17 (answer "A")

FASB Statement #5, "Accounting for Contingencies," provides two criteria for the accrual and disclosure of loss contingencies. These two criteria, both of which must be met before an estimated loss from a loss contingency is charged to income, are as follows:

1. The loss must be probable at the date of a company's financial statements.
2. The amount of the loss can be reasonably estimated.

Generally, disclosure is required for all loss contingencies unless management has determined that the likelihood of loss is remote. However, FASB #5 requires that all guarantees of the indebtedness of others be disclosed, even if the likelihood of default is remote.

In the facts given, the guarantee should be disclosed only in Eagle's financial statements because no loss is anticipated.

Answer choice "B" is incorrect because the loss is not probable and, as such, should not be accrued.

Answer choice "C" is incorrect because the loss is not probable and, as such, should not be accrued.

Answer choice "D" is incorrect because all guarantees of the indebtedness of others should be disclosed, even if the likelihood of loss is remote.

#18 (answer "A")

The following should be noted for background relative to this question.

1. By definition, the number of shares issued is the number sold by the corporation throughout its existence, less the number that have been reacquired and formally retired by an action of management. Outstanding shares are issued shares less the number reacquired but not formally retired (i.e., treasury shares).

2. In a stock split, the par or stated value is reduced in proportion to the split, and the number of shares issued is increased in proportion to the split. There is no effect on the financial statements other than a change in the number of shares issued and outstanding and the par or stated value of the shares; the total par or stated value of the shares issued remains unchanged.

　　When shares of stock are issued in connection with a stock split, there is retroactive adjustment as if the shares had been outstanding as of the beginning of the year.

3. When a corporation reacquires its own issued stock but does not formally retire them, it is termed treasury stock, and is accounted for as a contra-equity item. Also, treasury shares represent shares that are considered issued but not outstanding.

4. Protection of treasury stock against dilution simply means that when a stock split occurs, both outstanding shares and treasury shares are split.

This question concerns the number of shares of common stock issued and outstanding at December 31, 1994, which is determined as follows:

	Shares	
	Issued	Out-standing
Balance, December 31, 1993	100,000	95,000
Sold treasury shares	—	1,000
Sold unissued shares	10,000	10,000
Subtotal	110,000	106,000
2-for-1 stock split	110,000	106,000
Balance December 31, 1994	220,000	212,000

Answer choice "B" is incorrect because it considers only 4,000 shares of treasury stock as outstanding (i.e., 220,000 − 4,000 equals 216,000); after the split there were 8,000 treasury shares.

Answer choices "C" and "D" are based on illogical application of the facts presented.

#19 (answer "A")

When previously issued shares are reacquired by the issuing corporation, but not formally retired, they are classified as treasury shares and are no longer considered outstanding. Treasury stock may be accounted for by either the cost method or par value method.

Under the cost method, the cost of treasury shares held is shown as a reduction of total stockholders' equity on the balance sheet. Under the par value method, the treasury stock is recorded at par value (as a contra-account against common stock), and the excess of cost over par value first reduces additional paid-in capital up to the pro-rata amount associated with the same issue, and retained earnings is reduced by the remainder, if any.

When treasury shares are reissued, the following general rules should be considered under either the cost or par value methods.

1. An income statement gain or loss should never be recognized in a treasury stock transaction.
2. Retained earnings may be debited, but never credited, in a treasury stock transaction.
3. Additional paid-in capital may be debited or credited in a treasury stock transaction.

Accordingly, the acquisition of treasury shares under the cost method and their reissuance at more than acquisition cost will not affect retained earnings.

Therefore, Cyan should report retained earnings as $360,000 at December 31, 1994:

Balance, December 31, 1993	$300,000
Net income for 1994	60,000
Balance, December 31, 1994	$360,000

Answer choice "B" is incorrect because it increases retained earnings for the excess of the reissue price of the treasury shares over its acquisition cost (i.e., $300,000 + $60,000 + [$5 × 1,000] equals $365,000); this excess should be credited to additional paid-in capital.

Answer choice "C" is incorrect because it increases retained earnings for the excess of the $25 reissuance price of the treasury shares over its original issue price of $10 (i.e., $300,000 + $60,000 + [$15 × 1,000] equals $375,000). The amount partially involves additional paid-in capital, and should not be credited to retained earnings in any event.

Answer choice "D" is incorrect because it increases retained earnings for the excess of the $25 reissuance price of the treasury shares over its $5 par value (i.e., $300,000 + $60,000 + [$20 × 1,000] equals $380,000). This amount partially involves additional paid-in capital, and should not be credited to retained earnings in any event.

#20 (answer "B")

There are two methods of accounting for treasury stock (i.e., a corporation's own stock that has been reacquired and not canceled): the "cost" method and the "par value" method. Under either method, the total effect on stockholders' equity is the same.

Differences between the two methods are summarized below.

1. Cost method
   a. Acquisition—The cost is recorded as treasury stock and is deducted from total stockholders' equity.
   b. Resale—Upon resale, the treasury stock account is credited. Gains are credited to additional paid-in capital; losses are debited to additional paid-in capital to the extent available, otherwise to retained earnings.
   c. Retirement—The treasury stock account is closed out against capital stock. Any additional paid-in capital associated with the original issue is reduced; if there is an excess of the purchase price over the original issue price, retained earnings is debited. If the purchase price is less than the original issue price, there is a credit to additional paid-in capital.
2. Par value method
   a. Acquisition—The par value of the stock is recorded as treasury stock, which is a reduction of capital stock issued and outstanding. Any additional paid-in capital associated with the original issue is reduced. If there is an excess of the purchase price over the original issue price, retained earnings is debited. If the purchase price is less than the original issue price, there is a reclassification from additional paid-in capital to "paid-in capital from treasury stock."
   b. Resale—Upon resale, the treasury stock account is credited and the transaction is otherwise treated as an original issue of stock, except that if the resale price is less than par, retained earnings is debited.

c. Retirement—Simply, the treasury stock is offset against the capital stock account.

In the circumstances described, the treasury stock was carried at par value. Accordingly, Asp should report $125,000 as additional paid-in capital in excess of par in its December 31, 1994, balance sheet:

Issuance of stock;	
($15 − $10) × 20,000 shares	$100,000
Purchase of treasury shares;	
($15 − $10) × 5,000 shares	(25,000)
Reissue of treasury shares;	
($20 − $10) × 5,000 shares	50,000
Additional paid-in capital,	
December 31, 1994	$125,000

Answer choice "A" is incorrect because it is the excess of the original issue price over the par value of the shares issued on January 5 (i.e., 20,000 × [$15 − $10] equals $100,000). It does not consider the treasury stock transactions.

Answer choice "C" is incorrect because it reduces additional paid-in capital on July 14 for the excess of the purchase price of the treasury shares over its original issue price (i.e., $100,000 + $50,000 − [5,000 × $17 − $15] equals $140,000); this amount should reduce retained earnings, not additional paid-in capital.

Answer choice "D" is incorrect because it fails to consider the reduction of additional paid-in capital required by the purchase of treasury shares on July 14 (i.e., $100,000 + $50,000 equals $150,000).

#21 (answer "C")

Essentially, procedures involving stock rights are simple.

1. No entry is made upon issuance of the stock rights other than a memorandum notation.
2. When stock rights are exercised, common stock increases by the par value of the shares issued, and additional paid-in capital increases for the excess of the issue price over the par value of the shares issued.

As such, when stock rights are issued, neither common stock nor additional paid-in capital will be increased.

Answer choices other than "C" are based upon incorrect assumptions and/or combinations.

#22 (answer "C")

In general, no transaction is recorded with respect to stock rights until the rights are exercised. However, if the rights are redeemed, the effect is the same as if a cash dividend had been paid.

Hence, West's stockholders' equity was reduced by the amount of the dividend, which is $.10 per right for 120,000 shares, or $12,000.

Answer choice "A" is incorrect because it is based on 1/100 right per share (i.e., [120,000/100] × $.10 equals $120), and should be based on one right for each share.

Answer choice "B" is incorrect because it is the number of rights issued divided by the par value of the preferred stock (i.e., 120,000/$50 equals 2,400); this amount has no logical meaning in view of the background provided.

Answer choice "D" is incorrect because it is the amount of additional paid-in capital that would have been recognized had the preferred shares been issued (i.e., [$80 − $50] × 1,200 shares equals $36,000).

#23 (answer "A")

The division of partnership profits and/or losses is based on the partnership agreement. If the agreement is silent as to the manner of division, then all partners share equally.

In dividing profits, a partnership may consider bonuses, salary provisions, and interest on capital balances (which may be based on beginning balances, ending balances, or weighted-average balances). These are a manner of dividing profits based on unequal time devoted and/or capital invested. Any remainder not specifically allocated is divided in accordance with the profit and loss ratios.

Finally, a partnership cannot divide more or less than its total profit or loss. Therefore, if bonus, interest, and/or salary provisions are in excess of the total profit, a "loss" created by such division will be allocated in the profit and loss ratios.

Based on the preceding discussion, and as noted in the following table, Zinc's capital account would decrease by $1,000:

	Young	Zinc	Total
Interest	$16,000	$10,000	$26,000
Residual loss (allocated equally)	(11,000)	(11,000)	(22,000)
Change in partners' capital accounts for the year	$ 5,000	($1,000)	$ 4,000

It should be noted that the "residual loss" is equal to the $26,000 interest provision less the 1994 earnings of $4,000.

Answer choice "B" is incorrect because it does not consider the interest distributed to each partner based on average capital (i.e., $4,000 × 50% equals $2,000).

Answer choice "C" is incorrect because it is the residual loss that is allocated to each partner; it does not consider the interest distribution.

Answer choice "D" is not logical in view of the explanation provided in the answer to "A."

#24 (answer "C")

Under the cash basis of accounting, in contrast to the accrual basis of accounting, revenue is recognized as cash is received rather than when earned. Likewise, under the cash basis of accounting expenses are recognized when the cash is paid, rather than when the cost or expense is incurred.

Under the cash basis of accounting, capital at March 31, 1995, should be $6,000:

Initial cash investment	$2,000
Revenues	5,000
Withdrawals	(1,000)
Capital, March 31, 1995	$6,000

Answer choice "A" is incorrect because it is simply the original investment less the withdrawal (i.e., $2,000 − $1,000 equals $1,000); it ignores the net income for the period.

Answer choice "B" is incorrect because the $3,000 of expenses that were incurred in February but not paid until April are deducted, and should not be (i.e., [$2,000 + $5,000 − $1,000] − $3,000 equals $3,000). Under cash basis accounting, expenses are recognized when paid, not when incurred.

Answer choice "D" is incorrect because the $1,000 withdrawal taken in March is not subtracted, and should be; a withdrawal is recognized as a direct reduction of capital when taken.

#25 (answer "C")

A quasi-reorganization is a procedure for eliminating an accumulated retained earnings deficit by restating certain assets, liabilities, and capital accounts. It permits the company a fresh financial start when it appears that operations can be turned around. Such a procedure would be appropriate when it is considered that liquidation would not be in the best interests of all parties concerned. A quasi-reorganization is not a legal procedure under the federal bankruptcy statutes.

The following steps are taken to effect a quasi-reorganization.

1. Assets are written-down to fair value.
2. Shareholders and/or debtholders agree to reductions and/or restatement of their rights and claims. Capital stock generally decreases, creating additional paid-in capital by reducing par value.
3. The retained earnings deficit is absorbed by debiting additional paid-in capital, and crediting retained earnings. This brings retained earnings to a zero balance. Any capital in excess of this deficit remains in the paid-in capital account.

Note that the reorganized entity is required to date its reported retained earnings for a period of approximately ten years from the date of quasi-reorganization. This alerts readers to the fact that the corporation's retained earnings have undergone a readjustment and are not truly representative of its historic earnings and dividends situation.

Immediately after the quasi-reorganization, Brown should report additional paid-in capital as $190,000:

Balance, December 31, 1994	$150,000
Reduction of par value;	
($30 − $5) × 10,000 shares	250,000
Less retained earnings (deficit)	(210,000)
Additional paid-in capital	$190,000

Answer choice "A" is incorrect because it does not consider the impact on additional paid-in capital of reducing the par value of the common stock.

Answer choice "B" is incorrect because it does not consider any of the events described to effect the quasi-reorganization.

Answer choice "D" is incorrect because it does not consider the elimination of the deficit in retained earnings, which is a major objective of a quasi-reorganization.

#26 (answer "B")

The background for questions #26, 27, and 28 is APB Opinion #18, "The Equity Method of Accounting for Investments in Common Stock."

Generally, when an investor owns at least 20% of an investee company, there is the presumption that the investor is able to exercise significant influence over the investee, and that the equity method should be used. While it is clear that the equity method should be used since Grant owned 30%, this is further indicated by the language, wherein it is stated that Grant is able to exercise significant influence over South's operating and financial policies.

Under the equity method, the investor will recognize as income its proportional share of the income of the investee, with a corresponding increase in the carrying amount of the investment. Any dividend realized is considered a recovery of the investment, and is accounted for as a reduction of the carrying amount of the investment.

Accordingly, since Grant owned 30% of South throughout 1993, and South reported net income of $80,000 for 1993, Grant should record income as a result of its investment as $80,000 × 30%, or $24,000.

Answer choice "A" is incorrect because it represents the dividend that Grant realized from its investment in South (i.e., $50,000 × 30% equals $15,000). Under the equity method, Grant should report as income its proportional share of the income of South.

Answer choice "C" is incorrect because it is the total dividend paid by South. Under the equity method, dividends do not result in the recognition of earnings. Further, Grant did not own 100% in any event.

Answer choice "D" is incorrect because it is 100% of South's net income for 1993; Grant only owned 30% of South and, therefore, should recognize that proportion of South's income in its income statement.

#27 (answer "B")

See question #26 for background on APB Opinion #18, "The Equity Method of Accounting for Investments in Common Stock."

In Grant's December 31, 1993, balance sheet, the carrying amount of its investment in South should be reported as $209,000:

Cost of investment	$200,000
Add: Equity in earnings of South for 1993; $80,000 × 30%	24,000
Less: Dividends realized in 1993; $50,000 × 30%	(15,000)
Carrying amount of investment, December 31, 1993	$209,000

Answer choice "A" is incorrect because it is the cost of the investment, which does not represent the carrying amount at December 31, 1993, under the equity method.

Answer choice "C" is incorrect because it does not include the dividend received by Grant as a reduction of the carrying amount of the investment (i.e., $200,000 + $24,000 equals $224,000).

Answer choice "D" is incorrect because it includes 100% of South's net income for 1993, and 100% of South's dividends for 1993 as adjustments to the carrying amount of the investment (i.e., $200,000 + $80,000 − $50,000 equals $230,000). Grant only owned 30% of South; therefore, that proportion of income and dividends should affect the carrying amount of the investment.

#28 (answer "B")

See question #26 for background on APB Opinion #18, "The Equity Method of Accounting for Investments in Common Stock."

When an investment accounted for under the equity method is sold, gain or loss is based on the carrying amount of the investment on the date of sale.

In its 1994 income statement, Grant should report a gain from the sale of half of its investment as $30,500:

Selling price		$150,000
Less: 50% of carrying amount at July 1, 1994:		
Cost of investment	$200,000	
Equity in earnings for 1993; $80,000 × 30%	24,000	
Share of dividends, 1993; $50,000 × 30%	(15,000)	
Equity in earnings, 1/1/94–6/30/94; $100,000 × 30%	30,000	
Carrying amount, July 1, 1994	$239,000	
50% of carrying amount; $239,000 × 50%		119,500
Gain from sale of investment, 1994		$ 30,500

Answer choice "A" is incorrect because it includes South's earnings for the full year 1994, and the dividends paid in October 1994, in the determination of the carrying amount of the investment. Since the investment was sold on July 1, only income and dividends to that point should be factors in the carrying amount of the investment.

Answer choice "C" is an illogical application of the facts provided.

Answer choice "D" is incorrect because the gain is based upon the carrying amount of the investment on December 31, 1993; it should be based on the carrying amount on July 1, 1994.

#29 (answer "A")

This question relates to direct financing leases under FASB #13, "Accounting for Leases." In essence, a lease that is a capital lease to the lessee is either a direct financing or sales-type lease to the lessor.

The difference between a direct financing and a sales-type lease is that under a sales-type lease the lessor, who is a dealer or a manufacturer of the product, recognizes both a profit, or a loss, on the sale of the leased asset as well as interest revenue over the term of the lease. In a direct financing lease, only interest revenue is recognized over the term of the lease.

The difference between the lessor's gross investment in the lease (i.e., the total of the minimum lease payment plus the amount of any unguaranteed residual value) and the cost of the asset (or its fair value at the inception of the lease) is deferred and recognized as interest revenue over the term of the lease under the interest method.

The total amount of interest revenue that Glade will earn over the life of the lease is $51,600:

Fair value of equipment	$323,400
Divided by: Present value of an annuity due at 8% for 5 years	4.312
Annual minimum lease payments	75,000
Number of minimum lease payments	× 5
Total of minimum lease payments (gross investment in lease)	375,000
Less: Fair value of equipment	(323,400)
Interest revenue to be earned over life of lease	$ 51,600

Answer choice "B" is incorrect because it is the amount of the annual minimum lease payment, not the interest to be earned over the life of the lease.

Answer choice "C" is incorrect because it is the amount of interest that will be earned in the first year of the lease multiplied by the five-year term of the lease (i.e., $323,400 × 8% × 5 equals $129,360). Under the interest method, interest revenue will decline over the term of the lease as the amount of the unrecovered net investment declines.

Answer choice "D" is not a feasible combination of the information provided.

#30 (answer "C")

Accrual basis reporting must be assumed for financial statement purposes in the absence of information to the contrary. Therefore, the royalty revenue for 1994 must consider the cash collections applicable to 1994, as well as the appropriate accrual at December 31, 1994, for royalties earned in the last month of 1994 that will not be received until 1995.

Based on the facts given, all computations must consider that Rill's royalties are 20% of oil sales for 1994. Rill should report royalty revenue as $149,000:

Royalty received 7/31/94 for sales from 12/1/93 through 5/31/94; $400,000 × 20%	$ 80,000
Less royalties earned 12/1/93 through 12/31/93; $50,000 × 20%	(10,000)
Royalty received 1/31/95 for sales from 6/1/94 through 11/30/94; $325,000 × 20%	65,000
Royalties earned 12/1/94 through 12/31/94; $70,000 × 20%	14,000
Royalty revenue for 1994	$149,000

Answer choice "A" is incorrect because it is the total cash received from royalties in 1994 (i.e., [$300,000 + $400,000] × 20% equals $140,000), which does not represent the royalties earned in 1994.

Answer choice "B" is an illogical conclusion which is not consistent with the facts presented.

Answer choice "D" is incorrect because the $10,000 (i.e., $50,000 × 20%) received on July 31, 1994, that was earned in December 1993 is included (i.e., $149,000 + $10,000 equals $159,000), and should not be.

#31 (answer "D")

The installment sales and cost recovery methods of revenue recognition are appropriate in financial accounting only when there is reason to doubt collection of the full sales price. Under both methods, revenue is not recognized at the time of sale but, rather, after the sale, as cash is realized.

Under the installment sales method, the gross profit on an installment sale is recognized in proportion to the cash collections received.

Under the cost recovery method, no income is recognized until cash collections exceed cost, after which all cash collections are recognized in earnings.

Accordingly, no revenue is recognized prior to sale under either the installment method or the cost recovery method.

Answer choices other than "D" are based on incorrect assumptions and/or combinations.

#32 (answer "A")

This question is based on FASB Statement #52, "Foreign Currency Translation."

Gains and losses on transactions denominated in currencies other than the functional currency are generally included in determining net income for the period in which the exchange rates change.

When the exchange rate changes between the time goods are purchased and the time of payment, a gain or loss must be recognized as a <u>component</u> of <u>income</u> <u>from</u> <u>continuing</u> <u>operations</u>.

Answer choice "B" is incorrect because under APB Opinion #30, "Reporting the Results of Operations," gains or losses from foreign currency fluctuations, including major revaluations, are never considered extraordinary.

Answer choice "C" is incorrect because in general, a transaction gain or loss should not be deferred; it should be recognized in the period in which the exchange rate changed.

Answer choice "D" is incorrect because the cumulative adjustment that results from translating foreign currency financial statements is treated as a separate component of stockholders' equity; transaction gains and losses are a component of income from continuing operations.

#33 (answer "B")

The cost of a patent purchased from outsiders, along with legal costs incurred in connection with the successful defense of the patent, and the legal fees and other costs incurred in connection with securing or registering an internally developed patent, should be capitalized.

Such costs are amortized over the 17-year legal life of a patent, or its economic life, if less. When the economic life changes, the remaining unamortized cost is amortized over the remaining life.

Further, in accordance with FASB Statement #2, "Accounting for Research and Development Costs," all research and development costs must be expensed as incurred, unless such costs are contractually reimbursable; this includes both internal and external research and development costs.

Gray should capitalize the $45,000 of related costs incurred in 1991, and the $15,000 cost to successfully defend the attempted infringement in 1994.

Since Gray's policy is "to take no amortization in the year of disposal," amortization would be con-

sidered only with respect to the $45,000 initial cost, and only through 1993. Amortization would not be considered on the $15,000 of legal fees incurred during 1994.

Based on the facts provided, amortization would be over the 15-year useful life, and the gain would be <u>$24,000</u>:

Selling price		$75,000
Less carrying amount:		
Total costs;		
$45,000 + $15,000	$60,000	
Amortization on $45,000,		
1/2/91–12/31/93;		
($45,000/15) × 3	9,000	51,000
<u>Gain</u> <u>from</u> <u>sale</u> <u>of</u> <u>patent</u>		$24,000

Answer choice "A" is incorrect because it represents the legal fees incurred in 1994 to successfully defend the patent, not the gain from its sale.

Answer choice "C" is incorrect because it considers a fourth year of amortization on the original cost of the patent. The question states that Gray's policy is to take no amortization in the year of disposal.

Answer choice "D" is incorrect because it fails to consider the capitalization of the legal costs to successfully defend the patent.

#34 (answer "D")

Under an operating lease, rental revenue is recognized on a straight-line basis. In effect, therefore, the total expected rental revenue is recognized over the life of the lease. (If rentals are not received on a straight-line basis, that method nevertheless shall be used, unless another systematic and rational basis is more representative of the time pattern involved.)

In effect, the nonrefundable lease bonus paid by the lessee on signing an operating lease should be recognized as rental income <u>over</u> <u>the</u> <u>life</u> <u>of</u> <u>the</u> <u>lease</u>.

Answer choice "A" is incorrect because the nonrefundable lease bonus must be recognized over the life of the lease, without regard to when it was received.

Answer choice "B" is incorrect because the nonrefundable lease bonus should be recognized over the term of the lease, not at its inception.

Answer choice "C" is incorrect because the non-refundable lease bonus should be recognized over the term of the lease, not at its expiration.

#35 (answer "D")

When a corporation purchases life insurance on an officer or employee where the corporation is the beneficiary of the policy, the annual premium payments must be allocated between expense and an increase in the cash surrender value of the policy.

Cash surrender value is classified as an investment because it represents the amount of cash that can be realized if the policy is canceled. When the insured party dies, the corporation will recognize a gain equal to the difference between the face amount of the policy and its cash surrender value.

Jung should report no revenue in its income statements because the proceeds received less the cash surrender value of the insurance policy should be reported as a gain, not as revenue.

According to FASB Concepts Statement #6, "Elements of Financial Statements," revenues are inflows or other enhancements of the assets of an entity, or settlements of liabilities from delivering or producing goods or rendering services, or other activities that constitute the entity's ongoing major or central operations. Gains are increases in equity from peripheral or incidental transactions and events. Certainly, the death of an employee is not part of major or central operations but, rather, is an incidental event.

Answer choice "A" is incorrect because it does not consider the recovery of the cash surrender value of the policy, and because, in any event, the net insurance proceeds represent a gain, not revenue.

Answer choice "B" is incorrect because it is the amount of gain to be recognized, and not revenue, which should be recognized on the settlement of the life insurance policy.

Answer choice "C" is incorrect because the gain should be reduced by the cash surrender value, not increased by such amount, and because, in any event, the net proceeds represent a gain, not revenue.

#36 (answer "C")

In accordance with FASB Statement #109, "Accounting for Income Taxes," the total provision for income taxes is the sum of the amount of tax currently payable (i.e., current tax expense), and the net change in the deferred tax assets and deferred tax liabilities (i.e., deferred tax expense or benefit):

1. The amount of tax currently payable is the current year's taxable income multiplied by the current year's tax rate.
2. The net change in the deferred tax assets and liabilities is generally the result of changes in the amount of temporary differences.

Deferred tax assets must be reduced by a valuation allowance whenever it is more likely than not that some or all of the deferred tax assets will not be realized. Clearly, this is the case at December 31, 1994.

Accordingly, in its 1994 income statement, Shin should report total income tax expense as $10,000:

Current income tax expense		$13,000
Less deferred income tax benefit, 1994:		
Deferred tax asset, 12/31/94,		
net of allowance;		
$20,000 × 90%	$18,000	
Deferred tax asset, 12/31/93	15,000	3,000
Total income tax expense,		
1994		$10,000

It should be noted that an increase in the deferred tax asset decreases the total expense.

Answer choice "A" is incorrect because it does not consider the need for the valuation allowance equal to 10% of the deferred tax asset (i.e., $13,000 − [$20,000 − $15,000] equals $8,000).

Answer choice "B" is incorrect because it recognizes a valuation allowance equal to 10% of the change in the deferred tax asset, not 10% of the total deferred tax asset (i.e., $13,000 − 90% × [$20,000 − $15,000] equals $8,500).

Answer choice "D" is incorrect because it represents the current income tax expense only; it ignores deferred taxes.

#37 (answer "B")

This question can be answered in accordance with the provisions of FASB Statement #109, "Accounting for Income Taxes."

The current portion of the income tax provision is taxable income for the year multiplied by the effective tax rate enacted for the current year.

In order to arrive at taxable income, pretax financial income (i.e., book income) must be adjusted for the effect of temporary differences and permanent differences.

A temporary difference is the difference between the tax basis of an asset or liability that will reverse in the future, such as the use of different depreciation and/or revenue recognition methods for financial statements and tax purposes, or recognition of losses in excess of deductible amounts. In contrast, a permanent difference will never reverse because it is an event that will never be deductible or includible for tax purposes, such as the payment of premiums on officers' life insurance, and the receipt of tax-exempt interest.

Zeff reported taxable income of $140,000 for 1994; therefore, the income tax expense—current portion was $140,000 × 40%, or $56,000.

Answer choice "A" is incorrect because it inappropriately includes the long-term loss accrual in excess of deductible amount as an element of current taxable income (i.e., [$140,000 − $10,000] × 40% equals $52,000).

Answer choice "C" is incorrect because it is based upon pretax financial income less the nontaxable interest received on municipal securities. It ignores the excess long-term loss accrual and the depreciation temporary difference as elements of taxable income (i.e., [$160,000 − $5,000] × 40% equals $62,000).

Answer choice "D" is incorrect because it is based upon pretax financial income and does not consider any of the differences between financial income and taxable income (i.e., $160,000 × 40% equals $64,000).

#38 (answer "C")

In accordance with FASB Statement #109, "Accounting for Income Taxes," the deferred income tax liability is measured by multiplying the amount of the temporary difference by the tax rate scheduled to be in effect when the difference reverses.

A temporary difference is the difference between the tax basis and book basis of an asset or liability

that will reverse in the future. (By contrast, a difference that will not reverse in the future is generally not a temporary difference; it may be referred to as a "permanent" difference.)

Examples of temporary differences include the following.

1. Income included in taxable income after being included in accounting income (e.g., installment sales).
2. Expenses deducted for taxable income after being deducted for accounting income (e.g., loss accruals in excess of deductible amounts, such as bad debts).
3. Income included in taxable income before it is included in accounting income (e.g., rents received in advance).
4. Expenses deducted for taxable income before being recognized for accounting income (e.g., accelerated depreciation).

In this case, there are two temporary differences (i.e., the long-term loss accrual and depreciation), and one "permanent" difference (i.e., the nontaxable interest received on municipal securities). In its December 31, 1994, balance sheet, Zeff should report a deferred tax liability as $6,000:

Long-term loss accrual in excess of deductible amount	$10,000
Depreciation in excess of financial statement amount	(25,000)
Net taxable temporary difference	(15,000)
Income tax rate	× 40%
Deferred income tax liability, December 31, 1995	$ 6,000

Answer choice "A" is incorrect because it is based on the permanent difference (i.e., nontaxable municipal interest) only (i.e., $5,000 × 40% equals $2,000). Deferred taxes are only provided on temporary differences.

Answer choice "B" is incorrect because it is based upon the long-term loss accrual temporary difference only (i.e., $10,000 × 40% equals $4,000); deferred taxes must also be provided for on the depreciation temporary difference.

Answer choice "D" is incorrect because it is based upon all three differences, including the nontaxable municipal interest, which is not a temporary difference (i.e., [$160,000 − $140,000] × 40% equals $8,000). Deferred taxes are only provided for on temporary differences.

#39 (answer "B")

APB Opinion #30, "Reporting the Results of Operations," provides guidelines for the treatment of gains and losses that arise on the disposal of a segment of a business.

There are two elements of gain and loss with respect to a disposed segment, each of which is presented separately, net of tax:

1. Income or loss from operations—In the year that includes the measurement date (management's commitment to a formal plan of action), the results of discontinued operations are those from the beginning of the year up to and including the date prior to the measurement date. The results will include appropriate estimates.
2. Gain or loss on disposal—Presented in the year of disposal, except that if losses are anticipated, these must be provided for in the year that includes the measurement date, even if the disposal is not completed.

    Thus, an operating loss incurred subsequent to the measurement date is combined with the gain or loss on disposal. If a disposal loss is anticipated, it is recognized in the year that contains the measurement date; if a disposal gain is anticipated, it is recognized in the year of disposal.

    Included in the gain or loss on disposal are (a) costs directly associated with the decision to dispose of a segment, and (b) actual and/or expected net losses from operations between the measurement date and disposal date.

It should be observed that the 1993 operating losses of $600,000 are presumed to have occurred after the measurement date (i.e., the language "for 1993" is clearly subsequent to "January 1993"). As such, they are part of the gain or loss on disposal. Since the asset disposal occurred on January 15, 1994, and resulted in a gain of $900,000, which exceeded operating losses of $650,000 (i.e., $600,000 + $50,000), the estimated disposal gain would not be reported in 1993. An estimated disposal loss would have been reported in 1993, however.

In summary, the $600,000 operating loss incurred in 1993, and the $50,000 operating loss incurred in 1994 should be included with the $900,000 gain on disposal; the net gain of $250,000 (i.e.,

$900,000 − $600,000 − $50,000) should be recognized in 1994, the year of disposal. No amount of gain or loss should be recognized in 1993.

Answer choices other than "B" are inconsistent with the explanation provided.

#40 (answer "D")

See question #39 for background on APB Opinion #30, "Reporting the Results of Operations," which provides guidelines for the treatment of gains and losses that arise on the disposal of a segment of a business.

In its income statement for the year ended December 31, 1994, Deer should report the segment's operations for the period January 1 to April 30 (i.e., the measurement date) as a $300,000 loss from operations of a discontinued segment.

Answer choice "A" is incorrect because the operating loss of a discontinued segment, up to the measurement date, should be presented after income from continuing operations, not as part of continuing operations.

Answer choice "B" is incorrect because the operating loss of a discontinued segment, up to the measurement date, is presented separately from the loss on disposal of the segment.

Answer choice "C" is incorrect because the disposal of a segment does not result in an extraordinary item; it is presented above extraordinary items (on a net-of-tax basis).

#41 (answer "D")

In accordance with APB Opinion #30, "Reporting the Results of Operations," an extraordinary item must be both unusual and occur infrequently. Both circumstances must consider the environment in which the entity operates.

Extraordinary items are presented in the income statement net of tax effect, after discontinued operations and before any cumulative effects of changes in accounting principle.

The Opinion specifically provides that certain transactions are not extraordinary. These are:

1. The write-down or write-off of receivables, inventories, equipment leased to others, deferred research and development costs, or other intangible assets.

2. Gains and/or losses from exchange or translation of foreign currencies, including major revaluation.
3. Gains and/or losses on disposal of a business segment.
4. Gains and/or losses from sale or abandonment of fixed assets used in the business.
5. Effects of strikes.
6. Adjustments of accruals on long-term contracts.

A material transaction that is unusual but not infrequent should be reported separately as a component of income from continuing operations on a before-tax basis.

In addition to the specific treatment of certain gains and losses as set forth in Opinion #30, other promulgations of accounting standards provide for the treatment of certain transactions. Included in this latter category are gains and losses on the extinguishment of debt, which should be reported as extraordinary items (if material in the aggregate).

The question makes no mention as to whether Gold's purchase of its own bonds was material or not. For examination purposes, materiality should always be assumed in the absence of a statement to the contrary.

Based on the background provided, it should be concluded that while the sale of a long-term investment in bonds might be infrequent, it would be a normal consequence of business, not unlike the examples cited in points #1 through #6 above, and therefore is not an extraordinary item. However, Gold's gain on the purchase of its own bonds would per se be extraordinary.

Thus, Gold should report the effect of its own bond transaction as an extraordinary gain, and report the Iron bond transaction loss in income before extraordinary items (i.e., as a component of income from continuing items on a before-tax basis).

Answer choice "A" is incorrect because the loss on the Iron Corp. bonds is not an extraordinary item.

Answer choice "B" is incorrect because Gold's gain on the purchase of its own bonds is an extraordinary item, and should not be reported in income before extraordinary items.

Answer choice "C" is incorrect because the treatment is reversed; the effect of the Gold bond transaction gain should be an extraordinary item, and the Iron bond transaction loss should not.

#42 (answer "A")

In accordance with APB Opinion #30, "Reporting the Results of Operations," an extraordinary item must be both unusual and occur infrequently. Both circumstances must consider the environment in which the entity operates.

Extraordinary items are presented in the income statement net of tax effect, after discontinued operations (net of tax), and before any cumulative effects of changes in accounting principle (net of tax).

The Opinion specifically provides that certain transactions are not considered extraordinary. These are:

1. The write-down or write-off of receivables, inventories, equipment leased to others, deferred research and development costs, or other intangible assets.
2. Gains and/or losses from exchange or translation of foreign currencies, including major revaluation.
3. Gains and/or losses on disposal of a business segment.
4. Gains and/or losses from sale or abandonment of fixed assets used in the business.
5. Effects of strikes.
6. Adjustments of accruals on long-term contracts.

While a flood occurs as an act of nature, which generally is an extraordinary item, the fact that "Raim is located two miles from the river and sustains flood losses every two or three years" indicates that floods are not infrequent and are therefore not extraordinary items in Raim's environment. However, the fact that "Cane has been located fifty miles from the river for the past twenty years and has never before had flood losses," indicates that floods are infrequent and therefore are extraordinary in Cane's environment.

Therefore, Raim should report the loss as a component of income from continuing operations and Cane should report the loss as an extraordinary item.

Answer choice "B" is incorrect because Cane should report the loss as an extraordinary item.

Answer choice "C" is incorrect because the treatment is reversed; the Raim loss should be reported as a component of income from continuing operations, and the Cane loss as an extraordinary item.

Answer choice "D" is incorrect because the Raim loss should be reported as a component of income from continuing operations.

#43 (answer "A")

This question deals with the correction of an error, the treatment of which is prescribed in APB Opinion #20, "Accounting Changes," and FASB Statement #16, "Prior Period Adjustments."

For all practical exam purposes, the only prior period adjustments of which a candidate should be aware are corrections of errors. The correction of an error is appropriately reported on the retained earnings statement as an adjustment of the beginning balance, net of tax effect. This, of course, represents a retroactive adjustment.

Errors may be broadly classified into two categories.

1. Those resulting from mathematical mistakes, mistakes in the application of accounting principles, or oversight or misuse of facts that existed at the time the financial statements were prepared. (The last type of error should not be confused with an appropriate change in estimate, which is not a prior period adjustment.)
2. A change from an accounting principle that is not generally accepted to one that is generally accepted is a correction of an error.

Under APB Opinion #20, a change in accounting principle occurs when an entity changes from one generally accepted accounting principle to another generally accepted accounting principle. Usually, the cumulative effect of a change in accounting principle is presented as a separate component of income after income from continuing operations.

The change from the cash basis of accounting, which is not generally accepted, to the accrual basis of accounting, which is generally accepted, should be reported as a <u>prior period adjustment resulting from the correction of an error</u>.

Answer choice "B" is incorrect because prior period adjustments only result from error correc-

tions, not changes in principle, as explained in the answer to "A."

Answer choice "C" is incorrect because a correction of an error is presented as an adjustment to the opening balance of retained earnings, not as a component of income before extraordinary item.

Answer choice "D" is incorrect because presentation as a component of income after extraordinary item is appropriate for a cumulative effect type change (i.e., a change in accounting principle). A change from the cash basis, which is not generally accepted, to the accrual basis is treated as the correction of an error, not as a change in accounting principle.

#44 (answer "A")

APB Opinion #20, "Accounting Changes," prescribes reporting disclosures for several types of accounting changes, including cumulative effect type changes, and changes in accounting estimate.

The following should be noted.

1. <u>Cumulative effect type changes</u>—Such changes relate to changes in accounting principle (which are deemed to be inclusive of changes in method), and are equal to the difference between beginning retained earnings using the old principle and beginning retained earnings using the new principle. The cumulative effect of the change, net of income tax effect, is reported separately on the income statement, after extraordinary items. In addition, the new principle is used in current and future periods, and there is disclosure of the pro forma effects of retroactive application. Pro forma effects are disclosed in comparative financial statements, presenting the change as if it had been in effect in each year reported in such statements.
2. <u>Changes in accounting estimate</u>—Such changes usually result from new information becoming available (i.e., a change in the life of an asset, a change in recoverable reserves, a change in estimated warranty costs, or a change in the salvage value of an asset).

   Changes in accounting estimate require that the revisions be incorporated in the current period and future periods, if the change affects both. They are presented on a before-tax basis within income from continuing operations.

In its 1994 financial statements, <u>Oak</u> <u>should re</u>-<u>port</u> <u>warranty</u> <u>expense</u> <u>as</u> <u>$50,000</u> (i.e., sales for 1994 multiplied by the new warranty rate [$5,000,000 × 1%]). Since the change in estimate resulted from a technological advance at the beginning of 1994, the estimates of warranty costs for sales in prior years were not materially in error; thus, no catch-up adjustment is needed.

Answer choice "B" is incorrect because it is the average warranty expense for 1992 and 1993 (i.e., [$80,000 + $96,000]/2 equals $88,000), which does not represent warranty expense for 1994.

Answer choice "C" is incorrect because it is the current year's sales of $5,000,000 multiplied by the **old** warranty rate of 2% (i.e., $5,000,000 × 2% equals $100,000).

Answer choice "D" is incorrect because it represents an illogical combination of the current year's expense of $50,000 (i.e., $5,000,000 × 1%), plus the average expense of the prior two years ([$80,000 + $96,000]/2 equals $88,000), or a total of $138,000.

#45 (answer "B")

FASB Statement #128 requires that all publicly traded corporations disclose earnings per common share on the face of the income statement for each period in which an income statement is presented.

Presentation of both basic and diluted earnings per share is required. Basic earnings per share considers only the actual number of common shares outstanding during the period (and those contingently issuable in certain circumstances), while diluted earnings per share includes the impact of shares actually outstanding and the impact of convertible securities and stock options, stock warrants, and their equivalents.

Diluted earnings per share should not assume the conversion, exercise, or contingent issuance of securities that would have an antidilutive effect; that is, would increase earnings per share or decrease loss per share.

Basic earnings per share is determined as follows:

$$\frac{\text{Net Income Available to Common Stockholders}}{\text{Weighted Average Number of Common Shares Outstanding}} = \text{Basic EPS}$$

Net income available to common stockholders is net income less dividends declared on preferred stock plus dividends earned but not declared on cumulative preferred stock.

Basic earnings per share for 1994 is <u>$2.45</u>:

Earnings available to common stockholders:

Net income	$500,000
Less: Dividend on cumulative preferred stock; 25,000 shares × $.40	(10,000)
Earnings available to common stockholders	$490,000
<u>Earnings</u> <u>per</u> <u>share</u>;	
$490,000/200,000 shares	**$2.45**

Answer choice "A" is incorrect because the preferred dividends paid in 1994 are subtracted from net income (i.e., [$500,000 − $16,000]/200,000 equals $2.42). Since the preferred stock is cumulative, the required annual dividend should be subtracted from income, whether declared or not.

Answer choice "C" is incorrect because only the $4,000 of dividends in arrears for 1993 and 1994 (i.e., [25,000 × $10 × 4% × 2] − $16,000) is subtracted from net income (i.e., [$500,000 − $4,000]/200,000 shares equals $2.48). Since the preferred stock is cumulative, the required annual dividend should be subtracted from net income, whether declared or not.

Answer choice "D" is incorrect because it does not consider any of the preferred stock dividend in computing basic earnings per share (i.e., $500,000/200,000 equals $2.50).

#46 (answer "A")

FASB Statement #128 requires that all publicly traded corporations disclose earnings per common share on the face of the income statement for each period in which an income statement is presented.

Presentation of both basic and diluted earnings per share is required. Basic earnings per share considers only the actual number of common shares outstanding during the period (and those contingently issuable in certain circumstances), while diluted earnings per share includes the impact of shares actually outstanding and the impact of convertible securities and stock options, stock warrants, and their equivalents.

Diluted earnings per share should not assume the conversion, exercise, or contingent issuance of securities that would have an antidilutive effect; that is, would increase earnings per share or decrease loss per share.

Accordingly, the dilutive convertible bonds should be recognized in computing diluted earnings per share, but the antidilutive common stock options should be ignored. West should report diluted earnings for 1994 of $14.25 (i.e., $15.00 less $0.75).

Answer choice "B" is incorrect because it includes the effect of both the dilutive convertible bonds and the antidilutive common stock option (i.e., $15.00 less $0.75 plus $0.10). The antidilutive option should be ignored.

Answer choice "C" is incorrect because it ignores the effect of the dilutive convertible bonds that must be recognized in computing diluted earnings per share.

Answer choice "D" is incorrect because it ignores the effect of the dilutive convertible security and because it includes the effect of the antidilutive option. Dilutive items must be included, and antidilutive items must be ignored, in the computation of diluted earnings per share.

#47 (answer "D")

FASB Statement #95, "Statement of Cash Flows," classifies cash receipts and cash payments as cash inflows and cash outflows from investing activities, financing activities, and operating activities.

The focus of a statement of cash flows is to explain the change in cash and cash equivalents during the period. "Cash equivalents" are short-term, highly liquid investments that generally have original maturities of three months or less in the hands of the entity holding the investment.

Accordingly, the use of cash to purchase a cash equivalent is not reported in the statement of cash flows because it simply exchanges cash for its equivalent and does not affect the total amount of cash and cash equivalents.

Answer choice "A" is incorrect because the purchase of a cash equivalent does not relate to the operating activities of the entity.

Answer choice "B" is incorrect because the purchase of a cash equivalent does not relate to investing activities.

Answer choice "C" is incorrect because the purchase of a cash equivalent does not relate to financing activities.

#48 (answer "D")

This question is based on the provisions of FASB Statement #95, "Statement of Cash Flows."

The Statement classifies cash receipts and cash payments as cash inflows and cash outflows from investing activities, financing activities, and operating activities.

The following should be noted for background.

1. Cash flows from investing activities
   a. Making and collecting loans (but not related interest).
   b. Acquiring and disposing of debt or equity instruments of other entities, except for investments in "trading securities," as per FASB Statement #115, which are treated as operating cash flows (but not related interest or dividends).
   c. Acquiring and disposing of property, plant, and equipment and other productive assets.
2. Cash flows from financing activities
   a. Obtaining resources from owners and providing them with a return on, and a return of, their investment (but not related interest).
   b. Borrowing money and repaying amounts involved, or otherwise settling the obligation (but not related interest).
   c. Obtaining and paying for other resources obtained from creditors on long-term credit (but not related interest).
3. Cash flows from operating activities—Operating activities include the cash effects of all transactions and other events that are neither investing activities nor financing activities; essentially, operating activities relate to income statement items. They generally involve producing and delivering goods and providing services.

   It should be noted that receipts of interest and dividends from all sources, and interest paid to creditors, represent operating activities.

4. <u>Noncash activities</u>—Information about investing and financing activities not resulting in cash receipts or cash payments, such as issuing a mortgage note in exchange for a building, converting debt to equity, or exchanging common stock for plant and equipment, should be reported separately (as supplementary information) and not be included in the body of the statement.

5. <u>Direct and indirect methods</u>—Statement #95 encourages use of the direct method of presenting cash flow information, but also permits use of the indirect method.

Under the direct method, individual income statement items are presented as gross cash receipts and gross cash payments, including interest and income taxes paid. In addition, a reconciliation of net income and net cash flows from operating activities is presented as a separate schedule; this schedule has the same net result as gross cash receipts and cash payments from operating activities.

Under the indirect method, the reconciliation of net income and net cash flows from operating activities is the key element in the statement. It is presented either in the body of the statement, or in a separate schedule.

If presented in a separate schedule, the net cash flows from operating activities is presented as a single line item. There is no presentation of gross cash receipts and gross cash payments from operating activities. However, the amount paid for both interest and income taxes must be disclosed in a separate schedule under the indirect method.

Accordingly, each of the items indicated must be disclosed in a statement of cash flows presented under the direct method except <u>a reconciliation of ending retained earnings to net cash flow from operations</u>.

Answer choice "A" is incorrect because major classes of gross cash receipts and gross cash payments must be disclosed under the direct method.

Answer choice "B" is incorrect because the total amount of income taxes (and interest) paid must be disclosed under either the direct or indirect methods.

Answer choice "C" is incorrect because a separate reconciliation of net income to net cash flow from operations is required to be presented when the statement of cash flows is presented under the direct method.

#49 (answer "B")

In preparing consolidated financial statements, all intercompany transactions must be eliminated; this includes intercompany dividends.

When the business combination is accounted for under the purchase method, preacquisition dividends are not accounted for, since only those transactions of the subsidiary subsequent to the date of the purchase are presented in the consolidated financial statements.

Further, dividends paid by the subsidiary to the parent are eliminated in preparing the consolidated financial statements; dividends paid to minority shareholders of the subsidiary (i.e., the noncontrolling interest) are accounted for as a reduction of the minority interest in the subsidiary's net assets.

Accordingly, in its December 31, 1994, consolidated statement of retained earnings, <u>Pare should report dividends as $25,000</u>, the amount Pare paid to its shareholders.

Answer choice "A" is incorrect because it represents the amount that Kidd paid to Pare and the minority shareholders of Kidd; this amount is eliminated in consolidation.

Answer choice "C" is incorrect because it includes the dividends paid by Kidd to the minority shareholders of Kidd (i.e., $5,000 × 25%); this amount should be accounted for as a reduction in the minority interest in Kidd's net assets.

Answer choice "D" is incorrect because it includes the amount that Kidd paid to Pare and the minority shareholders of Kidd. The intercompany portion is eliminated in consolidation, and the minority interest's share reduces the minority interest in Kidd's net assets.

#50 (answer "B")

The minority interest represents the portion of total stockholders' equity owned by investors in a subsidiary who are not part of the controlling interest (i.e., the parent). It is determined by reference to the stockholders' equity accounts of the subsidiary standing alone (i.e., ignoring any adjustments made for the consolidated financial statements).

Examination of the facts indicates that the minority interest in Kidd's net assets is $30,000; total stockholders' equity of Kidd at December 31, 1994, multiplied by the portion of Kidd's stock not owned by Pare (i.e., $120,000 × 25%).

Answer choice "A" is incorrect because Kidd is not wholly-owned by Pare; thus, a minority interest must be recognized.

Answer choice "C" is incorrect it is 25% of Kidd's total assets (i.e., 25% × $180,000 equals $45,000), and the minority interest is based upon the subsidiary's stockholders' equity only.

Answer choice "D" is incorrect because it is 25% of Pare's (i.e., the parent's) total assets (i.e., 25% × $420,000 equals $105,000); this does not measure the minority interest in the subsidiary's (i.e., Kidd's) net assets.

#51 (answer "B")

In the preparation of the consolidated balance sheet, the entire stockholders' equity of the subsidiary must be eliminated.

Accordingly, in its December 31, 1994, consolidated balance sheet, Pare should report common stock as $100,000; this amount represents the par value of Pare's common stock issued at that date.

Answer choice "A" is incorrect because it is Kidd's common stock, which must be eliminated in consolidation.

Answer choice "C" is incorrect because it includes 75% of Kidd's common stock; 100% of Kidd's common stock must be eliminated in consolidation.

Answer choice "D" is incorrect because it is simply the sum of Pare's and Kidd's common stock; 100% of Kidd's common stock must be eliminated in consolidation.

#52 (answer "C")

The following should be noted for background relative to this question:

1. In a pooling of interests, assets and liabilities of the combined companies go forward based on the recorded (carrying) amounts.

2. In a purchase transaction, assets and liabilities are recognized at their fair values on the date of acquisition; new accounting bases result. Any excess of cost over net assets (i.e., book value) acquired is first allocated to identifiable assets and liabilities based on fair values. Any excess that remains after such allocation is recorded as goodwill, which is amortized over a period not to exceed forty (40) years.

Accordingly, if the business combination were accounted for as a pooling of interest, the long-term debt of the acquired company would be reported at carrying amount; under the purchase method, the long-term debt of the acquired company would be reported at fair value at the date of the combination.

Answer choices other than "C" are based upon incorrect assumptions and/or combinations.

#53 (answer "C")

Generally, in a purchase business combination, any excess of cost over the carrying amount of net assets acquired is first allocated to specific assets and/or liabilities based on fair values to the extent that identification is possible. If specific allocation is not possible, or if a further excess remains after such allocation, a blanket intangible, "goodwill," is recognized for the difference and amortized over a period not to exceed forty years.

In this question, the appraised values of the net identifiable assets exceeded the acquisition price. Given such circumstances, the excess is reported as a reduction of the values assigned to noncurrent assets and a deferred credit for any unallocated portion.

Note that the deferred credit is amortized in a manner similar to goodwill (i.e., written off over a period not to exceed forty years).

Answer choice "A" is incorrect because the excess must first be allocated to noncurrent assets before negative goodwill (i.e., deferred credit) is recognized.

Answer choice "B" is incorrect because the transaction described does not result in an increase in additional paid-in capital.

Answer choice "D" is incorrect because in the situation presented, the appraised value of the net identifiable assets acquired exceeded the acquisition price; therefore, positive goodwill did not result.

#54 (answer "D")

The underlying principle in personal financial statements is the presentation of assets and liabilities at estimated current (fair) values at the date of the financial statements. Where a business interest constitutes a large part of an individual's total assets, it should be presented in a personal statement of financial condition as <u>a single amount equal to the estimated current value of the business interest</u>.

Answer choice "A" is incorrect because the individual assets and liabilities should not be disclosed but, rather, the estimated current value of the entire business should be presented. Further, original cost is not appropriate in personal financial statements.

Answer choice "B" is incorrect because original cost is not an appropriate measurement base in personal financial statements. In addition, the interest should be presented as a single amount, and not as separate line items.

Answer choice "C" is incorrect because the proprietorship equity (i.e., book value) does not measure the current value of the business.

#55 (answer "D")

The underlying principle in personal financial statements is the presentation of assets and liabilities at estimated current (fair) values at the date of the financial statements.

Logically, Quinn should report both the stock investment and the jewelry at the best estimate of their current (fair) values. For the stock, that best estimate is the buyout value (i.e., $675,000) and for the jewelry, it is the fair value based on an independent appraisal (i.e., $70,000).

Accordingly, the stock and the jewelry should be reported in Quinn's April 30, 1995, personal statement of financial condition at <u>$745,000</u> (i.e., $675,000 + $70,000).

Answer choice "A" is incorrect because it represents the tax bases of the two assets (i.e., $430,000 + $40,000 equals $470,000). Tax basis is not an appropriate means of measuring assets in personal financial statements.

Answer choice "B" is incorrect because it is the sum of the tax bases of the stock, and the fair value of the jewelry (i.e., $430,000 + $70,000 equals $500,000). Tax basis is not an appropriate means of measuring assets in personal financial statements.

Answer choice "C" is incorrect because it is the sum of the buyout value of the stock and the tax basis of the jewelry (i.e., $675,000 + $40,000 equals $715,000). Tax basis is not an appropriate means of measuring assets in personal financial statements.

#56 (answer "A")

While financial statements are normally prepared in accordance with generally accepted accounting principles, financial statements are sometimes prepared in conformity with a comprehensive basis of accounting other than generally accepted accounting principles. According to Statement on Auditing Standards #62, "Special Reports," other comprehensive bases are restricted to the following:

1. A basis of accounting that the reporting entity uses to comply with requirements or financial reporting provisions of a governmental regulatory agency to whose jurisdiction the entity is subject.
2. A basis of accounting used by the entity to file its income tax return.
3. The cash receipts and disbursements basis of accounting, and modifications of the cash basis having substantial support, such as recording depreciation on fixed assets, or accruing income taxes.
4. A definite set of criteria having substantial support that is applied to all material items appearing in financial statements, such as the price-level basis of accounting.

The authoritative literature does not provide guidance with respect to captions to be used within financial statements prepared on another comprehensive basis of accounting. Therefore, there is no requirement to modify standard GAAP financial statement captions.

This suggests that the nondeductible portion of expenses such as meals and entertainment should be <u>included in the expense category in the determination of income</u> to arrive at the excess of revenue over expenses.

(Items in the tax-basis income statement, such as foreign taxes and disallowed meals and entertainment, are added back to the excess of revenue over expenses to arrive at taxable income.)

Answer choices other than "A" are inconsistent with the explanation provided.

#57 (answer "C")

This question is based upon FASB Statement #89, "Financial Reporting and Changing Prices," which encourages, but does not require, supplemental disclosure about the impact of inflation.

The following are possible measurement bases considered by the FASB:

1. Historical cost/nominal dollar—Financial statements are reported in terms of nominal (stated) dollars using historical costs; no consideration is given to changes in the general price level, or to current costs.
2. Current cost/nominal dollar—No consideration is given to general price level changes; however, the valuation basis changes from historical cost to current cost.
3. Current cost/constant dollar—Historical costs are first stated in terms of current costs. Current costs are then adjusted to constant purchasing power, using the average consumer price index for the current year.
4. Historical cost/constant dollar—Historical costs are adjusted to reflect constant purchasing power by using the average consumer price index for the current year.

Given the above, only current cost/constant dollar accounting includes adjustments for both specific price changes (i.e., historical cost to current cost) and general price-level changes (i.e., nominal dollars to constant dollars).

Answer choices other than "C" are inconsistent with the explanation provided.

#58 (answer "A")

The current ratio is equal to current assets divided by current liabilities, and the quick (i.e., acid-test) ratio is equal to the total of cash, receivables, and marketable securities divided by current liabilities.

The sale of trading securities (a current asset) at their carrying amounts would result in a decrease

in trading securities and an increase in cash of the same amount. Accordingly, this transaction would have no effect on either the current ratio or the quick ratio.

Answer choices other than "A" are based upon incorrect assumptions and/or combinations.

#59 (answer "B")

Quite simply, the debt-to-equity ratio is a ratio of total liabilities to total stockholders' equity.

Thus, $330,000 is the maximum additional amount that Barr will be able to borrow to achieve a debt-to-equity ratio of .75:

Stockholders' equity before additional stock issuance	$ 700,000
Additional stock issuance	300,000
Stockholders' equity after stock issuance	1,000,000
Desired debt-to-equity ratio	x .75
Desired total liabilities	750,000
Total liabilities before bank borrowing	(420,000)
Maximum additional borrowing	$ 330,000

Answer choice "A" is incorrect because it is 75% of present stockholders' equity less the amount of additional common stock to be issued (i.e., [$700,000 × 75%] − $300,000 equals $225,000). Here, the debt-to-equity ratio would not equal 75%.

Answer choice "C" is incorrect because it is simply 75% of present stockholders' equity (i.e., $700,000 × 75% equals $525,000), and does not represent the amount of additional borrowing that would be possible if additional common stock were issued.

Answer choice "D" is incorrect because it is the maximum amount of total debt that Barr could incur if the additional common stock were issued (i.e., [$700,000 + $300,000] × 75% equals $750,000); it is not the additional amount that Barr would be able to borrow.

#60 (answer "B")

Simply, return on assets is equal to net income divided by average total assets.

Accordingly, Cowl's rate of return on assets for the year ended December 31, 1994, was equal to net income of $150,000 divided by average total assets of $2,500,000 (i.e., [$3,000,000 + $2,000,000]/2), or 6%.

Answer choice "A" is incorrect because it is net income divided by ending (not average) total assets (i.e., $150,000/$3,000,000 equals 5%).

Answer choice "C" is incorrect because it is net sales (not net income) divided by ending (not average) total assets (i.e., $600,000/$3,000,000 equals 20%).

Answer choice "D" is incorrect because it is net sales (not net income) divided by average total assets (i.e., $600,000/$2,500,000 equals 24%).

OTHER OBJECTIVE FORMATS/ESSAY QUESTIONS

Answer 2

These questions are based on FASB Statement #115, "Accounting for Certain Investments in Debt and Equity Securities." The following selected background information should be considered.

1. Classification of securities

   At acquisition, an enterprise shall classify debt and equity securities into one of three categories.

   a. Trading securities—those that are bought and held principally for purposes of selling them in the near term. Trading generally reflects active and frequent buying and selling and is used to generate profits on short-term changes in prices.

   b. Held-to-maturity securities—debt securities that the enterprise has the positive intent and ability to hold to maturity.

      An enterprise should not classify a debt security as held-to-maturity if it has the intent to hold the security for only an indefinite period, nor should a debt security be classified as held-to-maturity if it would be available to be resold in response to changes in market conditions, such as prepayment risks and needs for liquidity, and so on.

   c. Available-for-sale securities—securities that are not classified as trading securities or held-to-maturity securities.

2. Financial statement presentation

   a. Trading securities—presented at fair value on the statement date, with unre-

alized gains and losses included in earnings.

   b. Held-to-maturity securities—presented at amortized cost on the statement date; unrealized gains and losses are not recognized.

   c. Available-for-sale securities—presented at fair value on the statement date, with unrealized gains and losses reported as a separate component of stockholders' equity.

   d. Realized gains and losses for securities classified as either available-for-sale or held-to-maturity are included in earnings.

   e. Declines in value that are other than temporary—when the decline in fair value of either an available-for-sale or held-to-maturity security is determined to be other than temporary, the decline is included in earnings as a realized loss. When the security is written-down, fair value at that date becomes its new cost basis.

#61 (answer "T")

A debt security bought and held for purposes of selling in the near term is classified as a trading security.

#62 (answer "H")

A U.S. Treasury bond, or any debt security, that the holder has the positive intent and the ability to hold to maturity is classified as a held-to-maturity security.

#63 (answer "A")

A debt security that is intended to be sold in three years (i.e., not in the near term) should be classified as an available-for-sale security.

#64 (answer "A")

A debt or equity security (preferred stock) that is not intended to be sold in the near term is classified as an available-for-sale security.

#65 (answer "G")

Since security ABC is classified as held-to-maturity, it should be reported in Dayle's December 31, 1994, balance sheet at amortized cost, which is $100,000.

#66 (answer "I")

Since security DEF is classified as a trading security, it should be reported in Dayle's December 31, 1994, balance sheet at fair value, or $155,000.

#67 (answer "J")

Since security JKL is classified as available-for-sale, it should be reported in Dayle's December 31, 1994, balance sheet at fair value, or $160,000.

#68 (answer "D,L")

Since security GHI is classified as an available-for-sale security, realized gains or losses on sale are recognized in earnings. The difference between the proceeds from the sale of the security (i.e., $175,000) and its cost (i.e., $190,000) results in a $15,000 loss.

#69 (answer "B,L")

Unrealized gains and losses on trading securities are reported in the income statement. Accordingly, the decline in value of security DEF (the only trading security) from $160,000 to $155,000, results in a $5,000 loss in Dayle's 1994 income statement.

#70 (answer "C,L")

Cumulative unrealized gains and losses on available-for-sale securities are reported as a separate component of stockholders' equity. Accordingly, the difference between the $170,000 cost of security JKL, the only available-for-sale security owned at December 31, 1994, and its $160,000 fair value results in a $10,000 unrealized loss being reported in a separate component of Dayle's stockholders' equity at December 31, 1994.

Answer 3

#71 (answer "Q")

This part of the question relates to the amount of (unamortized) discount at 6/30/94.

It should be noted that the carrying amount of bonds is equal to face value plus unamortized premium, or minus unamortized discount.

Clearly, then, if the face value of the bonds was $480,000, and the carrying amount at 6/30/94

was $363,600, the (unamortized) discount was $480,000 − $363,600, or $116,400.

#72 (answer "K")

Cash interest is equal to the face value of the bonds at the stated interest rate for the period of time covered.

Since the bonds pay interest semiannually, it is safe to assume (since no interest rate was given in the facts) that cash interest at 6/30/94, would be equal to cash interest given for 12/31/94, or $14,400.

Parenthetically, this conclusion may be viewed in another light. Given total interest expense of $18,000, and periodic amortization of $3,600, cash paid would again be $14,400; total interest is inclusive of cash paid and periodic discount amortization.

#73 (answer "T")

The carrying amount at 1/2/94 (upon issuance), would be equal to the carrying amount at 6/30/94 (i.e, given as $363,600) less discount amortization for the period ended 6/30/94 (i.e, given as $3,600), or $360,000.

(Note that discount amortization increases the carrying amounts. Thus, it must be subtracted to work back to an earlier date.)

#74 (answer "D")

The stated annual rate is equal to the total annual cash paid (i.e., $14,400 × 2, or $28,800), divided by the face amount of the bonds (i.e., $480,000). As such, the rate is $28,800/$480,000, or 6%.

#75 (answer "F")

The effective annual interest rate is used to determine interest expense for each period. Interest expense for the semiannual period ended 6/30/94 was $18,000, and the carrying amount of the bonds at 1/2/94 (as noted in #73) was $360,000; therefore, the semiannual effective interest rate was 5% (i.e., $18,000/$360,000), and the annual effective interest rate was 10% (i.e., 5% × 2).

#76 (answer "N")

Under the "interest" (or "effective interest," or "yield") method, an effective yield rate is applied to the net book (carrying) value of the bonds (face value plus unamortized premium or less unamortized discount) as of the beginning of each period to determine the total interest for the period, inclusive of both interest and amortization of premium or discount. The periodic interest at the nominal (face) rate is subtracted from the total amount computed to arrive at the amortization.

Thus, given a carrying amount of $363,600 at 6/30/94, and an effective interest rate of 10% (per #75), the total interest expense for the six months 6/30/94 through 12/31/94 <u>would</u> <u>be</u> $18,180 (i.e., $363,600 × 10% × 6/12).

#77 (answer "I")

As noted in #76, amortization of the discount for a period is the difference between (total) interest expense, and cash interest paid.

The <u>amortization</u> of the discount for the semiannual period ended 12/31/94 <u>was</u> therefore $3,780 (i.e., $18,180 − $14,400).

#78 (answer "B")

Generally, a gain contingency should not be recognized until realized or realizable. Here, the gain was, in fact, realized soon after the date of the financial statements but prior to their issuance; therefore, it was realizable at December 31, 1994. Accordingly, the gain should be <u>both</u> <u>accrued</u> <u>and</u> <u>disclosed</u> in the December 31, 1994, financial statements.

#79 (answer "N")

The following should be considered with respect to FASB Statement #5, "Accounting for Contingencies."

1. In order for a contingent loss to be accrued as a charge against income, the loss must be both probable at the date of the financial statements, and able to be reasonably estimated.
2. Where a range of estimates is involved, the best estimate within the range should be used. When no amount within the range is a better estimate than any other amount, the minimum amount should be accrued.
3. When a loss contingency is reasonably possible but not probable, footnote disclosure is required. Likewise, loss contingencies

that are probable but cannot be reasonably estimated are disclosed. The disclosure shall indicate the nature of the contingency and give an estimate of the possible loss, or range of loss, or state that an estimate cannot be made.
4. When the possibility of the loss contingency becoming real is remote, disclosure is usually not required. However, all guarantees of the indebtedness of others must be disclosed even if the chances of loss are remote.

Since Town's lawyer believes the suit is without merit, the chances of loss are remote. Accordingly, Town should <u>neither</u> <u>accrue</u> <u>nor</u> <u>disclose</u> the wrongful-dismissal suit.

#80 (answer "N")

Purchase orders in the ordinary course of business are <u>neither</u> <u>accrued</u> <u>nor</u> <u>disclosed</u> unless there is a reasonable possibility of loss in the future.

There is nothing in these circumstances to indicate a reasonable possibility of future loss.

#81 (answer "D")

Town's government contract is "reasonably possible," but not probable; thus <u>disclosure</u> <u>only</u> is required.

#82 (answer "B")

A loss contingency must be accrued by a charge against income whenever it is probable that a loss has been incurred, and where the amount can be reasonably estimated. Here, Town estimates that it is probable that its share of the remedial action will be approximately $500,000; therefore, <u>both</u> <u>accrual and disclosure</u> <u>is</u> <u>required</u>.

#83 (answer "D")

The refinancing of debt subsequent to the date of the financial statements does not represent a contingency as of the date of the financial statements. However, it does represent an important post-balance sheet event that could influence an investment or credit decision; thus, <u>disclosure</u> <u>only</u> is required in order for the financial statement not to be misleading.

Answer 4

Part 4(a)

Village Flowers

WORKSHEET TO CONVERT TRIAL BALANCE TO ACCRUAL BASIS
December 31, 1994

ACCOUNT TITLE	Cash basis DR.	Cash basis CR.	Adjustments DR.	Adjustments CR.	Accrual Basis DR.	Accrual Basis CR.
Cash	25,600				25,600	
Accounts receivable	16,200		(1) 15,800		32,000	
Inventory	62,000		(4) 72,800	(4) 62,000	72,800	
Furniture & fixtures	118,200				118,200	
Land improvements	45,000				45,000	
Accumulated depreciation & amortization		32,400		(6) 14,250		46,650
Accounts payable		17,000		(3) 13,500		30,500
Village, drawings			(9) 61,000		61,000	
Village, capital		124,600	(7) 2,000	(5) 2,600		125,200
All. for uncollectibles				(2) 3,800		3,800
Prepaid insurance			(5) 2,900		2,900	
Accrued expenses				(7) 3,100		3,100
Est. liability on lawsuit				(8) 50,000		50,000
Sales		653,000		(1) 15,800		668,800
Purchases	305,100		(3) 13,500		318,600	
Salaries	174,000			(9) 48,000	126,000	
Payroll taxes	12,400		(7) 1,600	(7) 1,100	12,900	
Insurance	8,700		(5) 2,600	(5) 2,900	8,400	
Rent	34,200				34,200	
Utilities	12,600		(7) 1,500	(7) 900	13,200	
Living expenses	13,000			(9) 13,000		
Provision for doubtful accounts			(2) 3,800		3,800	
Income summary-inventory			(4) 62,000	(4) 72,800		10,800
Depreciation & amortization			(6) 14,250		14,250	
Est. loss on lawsuit			(8) 50,000		50,000	
	827,000	827,000	303,750	303,750	938,850	938,850

JE #5—Insurance Expense/Prepaid Insurance

Prepaid insurance should be;
$8,700 × ⅓	$2,900
Expense adjustment re 1993—1994 payment; $7,800 × ⅓*	2,600
Net expense reduction	$ 300

*Increase beginning capital balance.

JE #6—Depreciation & Amortization

Amortization—land improvements; ($45,000/15) × 9/12	$ 2,250
Depreciation on furniture and fixtures	12,000
Total	$14,250

Part 4(b)

To: Mr. Baron, Village Flowers

From: Muir, CPA

Re: Requirement for accrual basis financial statements

Date: November 2, 1995

As you are aware, we are assisting you in the process of negotiating a bank loan to finance your company's expansion into the wholesale flower market. The bank has asked that you supply your 1994 financial statement prepared on the accrual basis of accounting.

The accrual basis of accounting recognizes revenue as it is earned and expenses as they are incurred, rather than when the cash is received or paid. The accrual basis of accounting is superior to the cash basis of accounting because it more accurately measures the results of operations of your business by matching revenues with the costs of generating those revenues. Further, it more accurately portrays the economic resources and obligations of your business at one point in time.

The bank, as a creditor, is primarily concerned about your ability to generate future cash flows that will be sufficient to service the loan they are extending to you. Accrual basis accounting provides information that is more useful in assessing the amount, timing, and uncertainty of future cash flows than does the cash basis of accounting. The bank also is concerned with the resources that would be available to them in the event of a default on the loan and with other obligations that could impact collectibility of the loan.

In conclusion, banks are better able to evaluate the creditworthiness of a business when its financial statements are prepared under the accrual basis of accounting than under the cash basis of accounting. Accrual basis information allows the financial community to more efficiently allocate financial resources to those entities that are the most creditworthy.

Please feel free to contact me if you have any further questions on this matter.

Answer 5

Part 5(a)

1. In general, intangible assets lack physical existence. Additionally, they are subject to a high degree of uncertainty concerning future benefits. Intangible assets may convey to the holder identifiable rights and/or privileges, such as those related to patents or copyrights, or the rights may be unidentifiable, as in the case of goodwill.

   Generally, it is easier to account for purchased intangible assets than internally developed intangibles because of the presence of a market transaction that establishes the value and the existence of the asset. It is assumed that a bargained arm's-length transaction between two independent parties establishes that future benefit exists for the intangible and its fair value.

   Typically, intangibles purchased from others are capitalized on the basis of cost. However, intangibles developed internally are generally not capitalized, except for the legal costs associated with securing the right, such as a patent or copyright, and/or the cost of a successful legal defense of a patent. In general, the costs of internally developed intangibles such as goodwill are expensed as incurred rather than capitalized because they cannot be distinguished from operations.

2. Intangible assets should be amortized (generally using the straight-line basis) over the expected period of benefit, which is the shortest of legal life, economic (i.e., useful) life, or forty years.

   The amortization period for an intangible asset is determined by the exercise of management judgment considering such factors as legal provisions (e.g., 17 years for a patent), changing economic and/or technological developments in the entity's environment, obsolescence, contractual provisions, and so on.

Because of the uncertainty of estimating the period of benefit, generally accepted accounting principles provide that the amortization period for intangibles, including those with indeterminable lives, may not exceed forty years. Amortization of intangibles with indeterminate lives is justified on the theory that most intangibles do not last forever.

3. On the income statement, amortization changes should be shown as expenses (related credits are to accumulated amortization accounts). Expenses related to intangible assets such as franchise fees should likewise be presented on the income statement.

On the balance sheet, Broca should disclose the existence and carrying amount (i.e., cost less accumulated amortization) of all major categories of intangible assets. Broca must disclose its policy for amortizing each major class of intangible asset, including the amortization method and the amortization period. Further, major revisions in prior estimates must be disclosed.

Part 5(b)

Broca Co.
Intangibles Section
Balance Sheet
as at December 31, 1994

Goodwill, net of accumulated amortization of $4,700	$183,300
Franchise, net of accumulated amortization of $12,000	48,000
Patent, net of accumulated amortization of $13,600	122,400
Total intangible assets	$353,700

Broca Co.
Intangibles—Related Expenses
Income Statement
1994

Amortization of goodwill; ($360,000 − $172,000)/40	$ 4,700
Amortization of franchise; $60,000/5	12,000
Annual franchise fee; $20,000 × 1%	200
Amortization of patent; ($51,000 + $85,000)/10	13,600
Total related expenses	$30,500

10.   At the Exam—General Suggestions

The attributes of successful candidates were identified in Chapter 3. They consist of being highly motivated, well-prepared, and confident. By examination day the first two have been accomplished. Confidence remains and must be sustained through the two days of the examination. As we have noted previously, the CPA exam is as much a test of a candidate's ability to cope with pressure as it is of his academic preparation.

Approaching the exam with confidence comes from knowing that you have done your homework and are ready to compete. You know what is likely to be covered on the exam and you know how to handle the pressures of time and concentration. Like any successful competitor, you have studied the situation, rehearsed your strategy, and have developed the mental discipline that separates winners from losers.

Discipline is essential. You must not only have a plan but must have the self-discipline to stick with it, both before and during the CPA exam. Ideally, you approach examination day at the peak of your readiness. If your review program has been sound, and if your belief in yourself is strong, you will have every reason to expect success on the CPA exam.

Since the 15½ hours of test-taking represent the culmination of many weeks of hard work and mounting hope, the concern of the candidate during the days of the exam is to not lose the readiness achieved because of factors peculiar to the exam environment. That possibility can be minimized by becoming as familiar as possible with the situations likely to be faced at the exam site.

THE EXAM SITE ENVIRONMENT

In many parts of the country, contending with the physical limitations of the site selected for administration of the test is one of the chief obstacles to be overcome by the candidate. Because of the large number of candidates sitting for the exam, a site is selected more on the basis of its ability to hold a large number of people than its suitability for concentrated intellectual effort.

There are no permanent examination centers because the CPA exam is administered only twice annually. Consequently, each administrative body must scramble to line up a facility in time for the dates scheduled by the AICPA. In large states with thousands of candidates, this means the use of such places as exposition centers, athletic arenas, and national guard armories. Many veterans of the CPA exam are fond of recalling the distractions endured while taking the examination, such as poor lighting, rickety tables, strange aromas, or jarring noises. Frequently, they sat for the exam amid the paraphernalia of circuses, trade shows, or military units.

Of course, you have no choice about where you will be sitting for the exam. The best you can do is expect the distractions or inconveniences that are likely to occur and regard them as minor impediments to achieving your objective of becoming a CPA. Like those before you, you will one day view those peculiarities of the exam site as amusing nostalgia.

If possible, you should reconnoiter the exam site some time in advance of arrival for LPR on Wednesday morning. The locations of eating facilities, restrooms, and parking places should be noted. Lighting and room temperature should also be noted so as to try to ensure sitting in a desirable area and dressing comfortably while taking the examination. Because the exam poses an arduous physical, as well as intellectual, challenge—sitting for long periods of time, bent in concentration—it is wise to avoid sitting in areas where there are drafts, glares, temperature changes, or distracting activity. Do not sit near doorways, drinking fountains, windows, or proctors' tables.

Determine what rules exist for bringing snacks into the examination room. Use common sense and select foods that are easily digestible and that will not distract neighboring candidates with noisy wrappers. Liquids should be drunk in moderate amounts so as to minimize trips to the restroom. Snacks should be light and energizing, not a hindrance to working efficiently.

ACCOMMODATIONS

One of the concerns of candidates who live more than a half-hour's drive from the exam site is the advisability of securing overnight accommodations near the site. Nightmares of transportation breakdowns or delays causing one to arrive late can cause anxiety. The last thing you need as you travel forth is a blown radiator hose or snarled train system. For those who live more than three hours away, the solution is obvious: stay near the exam site. For others, it is a question of willingness to assume some risk that travel will be uneventful.

The primary concern should be to preserve the concentration that presumably has peaked just at the right time. Continuity and stability are important. You need to approach the competition of the CPA exam poised and confident. There will be enough anxiety over the content of the exam itself without the added anxiety over the logistics of room, board, and travel.

Whether you stay at home or in a motel, your final hours before the exam should be relaxed. Your preparation program should have been concluded by the weekend preceding the exam so that all you need to do is give a quick once-over to subjects most likely to appear. By Monday of exam week, you should be able to say, with optimism and confidence, "If I don't know it now, I'll never know it." Any last-minute cramming will probably succumb to the law of diminishing returns. Whatever accommodations are arranged, they should ensure that nothing will dissipate the readiness you have worked so hard to achieve.

ARRIVAL AT THE EXAMINATION

Finally the day of expectation dawns! You arrive at the end of your arduous preparation journey, ready to contend with the only remaining obstacle between you and professional stature.

You should arrive early and be adequately supplied. Plan to arrive an hour before the designated starting time. Filing into the testing room will usually begin about a half-hour before starting time. This will give you an additional half-hour to stretch your legs, breathe some fresh air, and relax your mind. Make sure that all the necessary implements of test taking are on hand: *pencils, erasers, watches—bring two of everything!* Fine-lead mechanical pencils are excellent for essay writing and computational problems, but bring two! You wouldn't want the day to be lost because of a broken spring. The standard No. 2 pencil is necessary for entering answers to objective questions on machine-scored answer sheets. Bring three or four. Bring one rectangular eraser and one pencil-style eraser. Rulers are usually prohibited (too easy to write useful information on them), so plan on constructing a straight-edge at the exam by carefully folding a sheet of scrap paper. Items that should not be brought are any study materials you have been using during your review program. They will not be permitted inside the testing room, and you risk losing them by having to pile them along with everybody else's outside the door.

Once seated at your designated spot, arrange yourself comfortably and prepare to begin answering questions. There usually will be fifteen or twenty minutes of idle time while you wait for the rest of the candidates to get seated and for the proctors to get things organized. This time can be used constructively by doing two things: (1) unburdening your mind by jotting down on the scrap paper provided all of the key concepts and memory aids that you have been studying over the previous weeks, and (2) heading up the blank essay and computational answer sheets provided. Make sure, of course, that such activity is permitted by the proctors at your test site. Generally it is, but in some places there may be rules against writing anything other than headings before the examinations are distributed. Even if you are not permitted activity (1), it is still advisable to make such notations as soon as you are able. Very likely they will prove to be time-saving notes later on during the exam.

All answer sheets are intended to be anonymous as far as the grader is concerned. The only identifying information is (1) candidate number, (2) date, (3) state, (4) subject, (5) question number, and (6) page number. Do not write your name anywhere on the pages you turn in. While having your name replaced by a number may seem impersonal, that very impersonality will ensure that the grader will not be influenced by any of the factors of sex, race, religion, or nationality that can often be suggested by a surname. Once you have completed the exam, arrange your answer sheets in their proper sequence. Paper clips or staples, if permitted, are useful for grouping papers by individual questions.

READING DIRECTIONS

As was noted in our discussion of how to answer CPA exam questions (Chapter 5), the examination is a test of reading comprehension as much as any other skill. The need for reading directions carefully, therefore, should be obvious. Nevertheless, many candidates, in their haste to get started, neglect to read the set of directions printed on the cover page of each exam section and on the computer-graded answer sheet for the objective questions. The AICPA attempts to minimize the hazards of careless attention to directions by including the following instructions for the exam in its publication "Information for Uniform CPA Examination Candidates" (thirteenth edition):

Instructions for the Uniform Certified Public Accountant Examination

1. Prior to the start of the examination, you will be required to sign a *Statement of Confidentiality*, which states:

   I hereby attest that I will not divulge the nature or content of any question or answer to any individual or entity, and I will report to the board of accountancy any solicitations and disclosures of which I become aware. I will not remove, or attempt to remove, any Uniform CPA Examination materials, notes, or other unauthorized materials from the examination room. I understand that failure to comply with this attestation may result in invalidation of my grades, disqualification from future examinations, and possible civil and criminal penalties.

2. The only aids you are allowed to take to the examination tables are pens, pencils, and erasers.
3. You will be furnished a Prenumbered Identification Card (or Admission Notice) with your 7-digit candidate number on it. The Prenumbered Identification Card must be available for inspection by the proctors throughout the examination.
4. Any reference during the examination to books or other materials or the exchange of information with other persons shall be considered misconduct sufficient to bar you from further participation in the examination.

   Penalties will be imposed on any candidate who is caught cheating before or during the examination. These penalties may include expulsion from the examination and denial of applications for future examinations.
5. You must observe the fixed time for each session. It is your responsibility to be ready at the start of the session and to stop writing when told to do so.
6. The following is an example of point values for each question in the Business Law & Professional Responsibilities section as it might appear in the *Examination Questions* portion of the *Examination Question and Answer Booklet (Booklet)*. For each question, the point values are as follows:

	Point Value
No. 1	60
No. 2	10
No. 3	10
No. 4	10
No. 5	10
Total	100

When answering each question, you should allocate the total examination time in proportion to the question's point value.

7. The *Booklet* will be distributed shortly before each session begins. Do not break the seal around the *Examinations Questions* portion of the *Booklet* until you are told to do so.

   Prior to the start of the examination, you are permitted to complete page 1 of the *Booklet* by recording your 7-digit candidate number in the boxes provided in the upper right-hand corner of the page and by filling out and signing the *Attendance Record*. You are also permitted to turn the *Booklet* over and record your 7-digit candidate number and State on the *Objective Answer Sheet* portion of the *Booklet*.

You must also check the booklet numbers on the *Attendance Record, Examination Questions, Objective Answer Sheet,* and *Essay Ruled Paper*. Notify the proctor if any of these numbers are not identical.

You must also review the *Examination Questions* (after you are told to break the seal), *Objective Answer Sheet*, and *Essay Ruled Paper* for any possible defects, such as missing pages, blurred printing, or stray marks (*Objective Answer Sheet* only). If any defects are found, request an entirely new *Examination Question and Answer Booklet* from a proctor before you answer any questions.

8. For the Business Law & Professional Responsibilities (LPR), Auditing (AUDIT), and Financial Accounting & Reporting (FARE) sections, your answers to the essay/problem-type questions must be written on the paper provided in the *Essay Ruled Paper* portion of the *Booklet*.

After the start of the examination, you should record your 7-digit candidate number, State, and question number on the first page of the *Essay Ruled Paper* portion of the *Booklet* and on the other pages where indicated.

9. For the ARE and FARE examination sections, you will be provided with a calculator. You should test the calculator in accordance with the instructions on the cover page of the *Booklet*. Inform your proctor if your calculator is defective. Calculators will not be provided for the LPR and AUDIT examination sections because the number of questions requiring calculations are minimal and the calculations are simple.

10. All amounts given in objective items or essay/problem-type questions are to be considered material unless otherwise stated.

11. Answer all objective items on the *Objective Answer Sheet* provided. Use a No. 2 pencil only. You should attempt to answer all objective items as there is no penalty for incorrect responses. Since the objective items are computer-graded, your comments and calculations associated with them are not considered. You should blacken the ovals as darkly as possible and erase clearly any marks you wish to change. You should make no stray marks.

Approximately 10% of the multiple-choice items are included for pretesting only and are not included in your final grade.

12. The *Objective Answer Sheet* may vary for each section of the examination. It is important to pay strict attention to the manner in which your *Objective Answer Sheet* is structured. As you proceed with the examination, be certain that you blacken the oval that corresponds exactly with the item number in the *Examination Questions* portion of your *Booklet*. If you mark your answers in the *Examination Questions* portion of your *Booklet*, be certain that you transfer them to the *Objective Answer Sheet* before the session ends. Your examination paper will not be graded if you fail to record your answers on the *Objective Answer Sheet*. You will not be given additional time to record your answers.

13. If an objective item requires you to record a numerical answer, blacken the ovals on the *Objective Answer Sheet*. If zeros precede your numerical answer, blacken the zeros in the ovals preceding your answer. You cannot receive credit for your answers if you fail to blacken an oval in each column. You may write the numbers in the boxes provided to facilitate blackening the ovals; however, the numbers written in the boxes will not be graded.

14. Answer all essay/problem-type questions on the *Essay Ruled Paper* provided. Always begin the start of an answer to a question on the top of a new page (which may be the reverse side of a sheet of paper). Cross out anything that you do not want to be graded.

15. Selected essay responses will be graded for writing skills.

16. Include all computations to the problem-type questions in the FARE section. This

may assist the examiners in understanding your answers.

17. You may not leave the examination room with any examination materials, nor may you take notes about the examination with you from the examination room. You are required to turn in by the end of each session:
    a. *Attendance Record* and *Statement of Confidentiality.*
    b. *Examination Questions.*
    c. *Essay Ruled Paper* (for LPR, AUDIT, and FARE). Do not remove unused pages.
    d. *Objective Answer Sheet.*
    e. Calculator (for ARE and FARE).
    f. All unused examination materials.
    g. Prenumbered Identification Card (or Admission Notice) at the last examination section for which you sit (if required by your examining jurisdiction).

    Your examination will not be graded unless the above-listed items are handed in before you leave the examination room.

18. If you believe one or more questions contain errors and want your concerns evaluated, you must fax to the AICPA your comments, including the precise nature of any defect; your rationale; and, if possible, references. The fax should include your 7-digit candidate number and must be received by the AICPA within four days of the completion of the examination administration. Comments should be faxed to (201) 938-3443. This will ensure that all comments are reviewed before the grading bases for the Uniform CPA Examination are confirmed. Although the AICPA cannot respond directly to each fax, it will investigate all comments received within the four-day period.

19. Examination question booklets will be destroyed by the AICPA 30 days after the examination section is administered.

20. Contact your board of accountancy for information regarding any other applicable rules.

SCANNING AND PLANNING

Once the examination booklets have been distributed and the directions noted, you must progress with all due speed through the exam questions. But before you forge ahead, take time to plan your attack. Answering the questions in straight numerical sequence is not always the best approach. First, all of the questions should be scanned, and then an order for answering them decided upon.

Usually, working from easiest to most difficult is the best way to handle questions. This is because the question or two that at the start seemed most intimidating seem less so after the candidate has been answering questions effectively for the past two or three hours. In the course of answering perhaps sixty (or ninety) four-option multiple-choice questions and two to four essay, computational, and other objective formats questions, a great deal of knowledge has been brought to the forefront of the mind. You know more by the end of the exam than you did at the beginning.

One of the decisions to make regarding question sequence is whether to do the four-option multiple-choice questions first. Most candidates do. There are several reasons for this. One is that all of the four-option multiple-choice questions taken together represent the largest block of credit available and also the longest questions in terms of budgeted time. Second is that, as individual items, they represent a series of brief, manageable tasks that provide a warm-up for the more extended problems and/or essays to follow. Third is that, in the course of handling all of the four-option multiple-choice questions, most of the relevant body of information for that exam section will have been reviewed, thus preparing the way for the in-depth questions that follow. Fourth is that four-option multiple-choice questions are usually answerable in less time than the candidate allocates to these questions. Accordingly, the candidate often has a time surplus that can be allocated among the remaining other objective formats, essay or computational questions.

Another approach to dealing with exam sections having essay questions is the following:

Step 1: Analyze essay questions one by one and sketch, in outline form, a tentative answer to each.

Step 2: Answer objective questions, adding information to essay outlines as it occurs while answering objective questions.

Step 3: Write essay answers based on outlines generated.

Such an approach is systematic and logical, but the candidate must be careful about controlling her use of time. It will be more difficult to keep a time budget under control for a particular essay if it is handled in two separate stages as suggested above. The great danger in not using time efficiently is that the candidate will find herself out of time, but with answers still to be written. If *that* occurs, chances for passing the examination are not good.

GOING THE DISTANCE

If you are taking all four sections, the two days of examinations will be especially arduous. You will experience unparalleled physical, emotional, and mental strain. At 6:00 p.m. Wednesday afternoon, after completing three hours of LPR and/or four and one-half hours of AUDIT, your emotional state will run from grim pessimism to ebullient optimism, depending upon how you feel you performed earlier in the day. No matter how you feel, you should *not* give up at this point because you have no real way of determining how your test will be graded.

Further, your ability to shift smoothly from one subject to another is important to your success. Confidence and concentration—question by question, section by section—must be maintained throughout the two days. This is particularly true when Thursday afternoon rolls around and you are relieved to face your final obstacle, FARE. The tendency for many people—whether because of assumptions about past performance on other sections, fatigue, or overconfidence—is to let up on FARE. Discipline yourself to be no less conscientious on Thursday afternoon than you were on Wednesday.

One thing that should be avoided is rehashing an exam section with other candidates before the entire exam is over. While it is difficult not to discuss and compare answers, the end result of such conversations usually is to make everyone less confident about how he did. Wednesday evening should be spent in quiet relaxation, far from the pressures and concerns of the CPA exam.

The CPA exam should be a once-in-a-lifetime experience. Unfortunately, for many candidates it is experienced more than once. As we have seen elsewhere in this book, success on the CPA exam stems from preparation and commitment. Preparation must be thorough, both in terms of topical review and examsmanship skills. Nothing that can be prepared for should be ignored. Every situation should be anticipated so far as possible. The CPA exam is a crucible—a test of what a candidate is made of.

There are few satisfactions in life that can match knowing you have achieved a goal through your own hard work. For many candidates the two days of the CPA exam, and the months of preparation preceding it, represent the most demanding test they will ever experience. It is a measure of their abilities and their character. The satisfaction that comes from passing the CPA exam is all the more sweet because it has been earned.